**An Introduction to
the Law and Institutions
of the European Communities**

# An Introduction to the Law and Institutions of the European Communities

Third Edition

*by* **D. Lasok**

Q.C., Len Dr, LLM, PhD, Dr Juris, LLD,
*of the Middle Temple, Barrister;*
*Professor of European Law and*
*Director of the Centre of European*
*Legal Studies in the University of Exeter*

*and*

**J. W. Bridge**

LLB, LLM, PhD,
*Professor of Public Law*
*in the University of Exeter*

*Scire leges non hoc est verba earum tenere,*
*sed vim ac potestatem,* Celsus, 1.3.17

London
Butterworths
1982

| England | Butterworth & Co (Publishers) Ltd<br>88 Kingsway, London WC2B 6AB |
|---|---|
| Australia | Butterworths Pty Ltd<br>271–273 Lane Cove Road, North Ryde, NSW 2113<br>Also at Melbourne, Brisbane, Adelaide and Perth |
| Canada | Butterworth & Co (Canada) Ltd<br>2265 Midland Avenue, Scarborough, Ont M1P 451 |
| | Butterworth & Co (Western Canada) Ltd<br>409 Granville Street, Ste 856, Vancouver, BC V6C 1T2 |
| New Zealand | Butterworths of New Zealand Ltd<br>33–35 Cumberland Place, Wellington |
| South Africa | Butterworth & Co (South Africa) (Pty) Ltd<br>152–154 Gale Street, Durban 4001 |
| United States<br>of America | Mason Publishing Company<br>Finch Bldg, 366 Wacouta Street, St Paul, Minn 55101 |
| | Butterworth (Legal Publishers) Inc<br>160 Roy Street, Ste 300, Seattle, Wash 98109 |
| | Butterworth (Legal Publishers) Inc<br>381 Elliot Street, Newton, Upper Falls, Mass 02164 |

© Butterworth & Co (Publishers) Ltd 1982

ISBN Hardcover 0 406 26894 0
Softcover 0 406 26895 9

*Front cover illustration:* The European Court of Justice in Luxembourg. Adapted from a drawing by R. Downer.

Printed in Great Britain by Butler & Tanner Ltd, Frome and London

# Preface to the third edition

*Ubi Societias Ibi Jus*

This revised and enlarged edition takes into account the developments within the Community and the state of the literature on the subject. Thus Chapter 4 has been enlarged to reflect the expansion of General Principles of Community Law whilst Chapters 13 and 14 have been reduced in view of the publication of the *Law of the Economy in the European Communities* by the Authors in 1980. These two volumes should be regarded as both independent and complementary since each volume treats comprehensively a separate branch of the law and the two cover the whole area of the Communities and their law.

The present volume is devoted to the structure of the Institutions and the Principles of Community law with the necessary emphasis on the constitutional aspects and the relationship between Community, international and national law of the Member States. In this respect it follows the pattern of the previous editions.

It is intended for students of law and politics as well as practitioners interested in the fundamentals of the Community law as a system separate from, yet interwoven into the fabric of national law.

D.L.
J.W.B.
Exeter
May 1982

# Preface to the first edition

*Ubi Societi as Ibi Jus*


To understand the nature of the law one must understand the nature of the society from which it emanates and which it purports to govern.

We are used to the concepts of national and international law. The former is the law of a sovereign state and as such it governs the society comprised in a state that is a group of people living within a defined area under a government which has executive, legislative, judicial and administrative powers. International law, on the other hand, is the body of rules which governs relations between states and such international organisations as are set up and recognised by states as bearers of rights and duties. In exceptional situations individuals may be regarded as subjects of international law. As a body of rules international law is derived partly from custom and state practice, partly from the will of states expressed in treaties and partly generated by institutions (e.g. the United Nations Organisation) set up by states and based on a treaty.

The object of this book is to define and analyse a nascent body of law which can be described as the law of the European Community. It is neither a national nor an international system of law in the accepted sense of these terms but a *sui generis* system emanating from the will to create a European Community. It reflects, of course, the nature of this design. At this stage we can speak of the European Community only in general political terms as an organisation with limited, mainly economic objectives and a potential for development towards a federal organisation. In strictly juristic, institutional terms we have to speak of the European Communities, that is the European Coal and Steel Community, the European Atomic Energy Community and the European Economic Community and, therefore, a distinction between 'Community' and 'Communities' has to be borne in mind. The law of the European Community, as we understand it, comprises consequently elements of international and national law as well as the rules generated by the Communities, of which the European Economic Community may be regarded as a cornerstone of future developments. This we shall endeavour to emphasise.

The genesis of this book lies in the authors' experience of teaching European Community Law in the University of Exeter. They wish to express their thanks to their students, both undergraduate and post-graduate, for the patience and forbearance with which they endured the authors' experimental first steps in this field. The authors claim to have written no more than an introduction to the complex system of Community law. In order to explain its working to the reader it was thought necessary to stress the institutional aspects of the Community and matters of principle at the expense of the details of the law of the economy which is still at a formative stage. It is hoped, however, that it is informative and provocative in that by setting out the rudiments it will make the reader aware of the unprecedented challenge facing Europe, the United Kingdom and the citizen, be he lawyer or layman. The aim throughout has been to approach the subject from the standpoint of the United Kingdom joining a continental Community which is already a going concern and this explains the emphasis placed on the political background of the Community and the civil law framework within which it functions. The authors owe a considerable debt to the numerous pioneer writers on the Communities and their law and pay them generous tribute.

This is a joint work. Chapters 1, 3, 4, 10, 11, 13 and 14 were drafted by D. Lasok; Chapters 5, 6, 7, 8, 9 and 12 were drafted by J. W. Bridge; Chapter 2 was drafted jointly. The work of each author has been subject to the comments and criticisms of the other and both authors are in agreement on and each accepts responsibility for the form and content of the whole book.

The authors' gratitude is due to all the members of the secretarial staff of the Faculty of Law of the University of Exeter who, with their accustomed cheerfulness and efficiency, undertook the typing of the manuscript; to the Publishers; and to their wives and families to whom this book is dedicated.

D.L.
J.W.B.
Exeter,
Michaelmas, 1972

# Contents

# PART II   THE LAW OF THE INSTITUTIONS

Chapter 5
## The Commission of the European Communities 161

Chapter 6
## The Council of the European Communities   173

Chapter 7
## The Assembly of the European Communities (The European Parliament)   190

# Table of Statutes

References in this Table to *Statutes* are to Halsbury's Statutes of England (Third Edition) showing the volume and page at which the annotated text of the Act will be found.

# Table of European Communities Legislation

## Treaties

# Secondary Legislation

## DECISIONS

## DIRECTIVES

# Table of Conventions

# Table of other Enactments

# List of Cases

## A

## G

R

S

W

*Decisions of the European Court of Justice are listed below numerically.
These decisions are also included in the preceding alphabetical table.*

# 1 List of cases

lii  *List of cases*

# List of Principal Abbreviations

AJCL  American Journal of Comparative Law

AJIL  American Journal of International Law

Art  Article

Benelux  Belgium, The Netherlands and Luxembourg

BGB  Bürgeliches Gesetzbuch (Germany)

BYBIL  British Year Book of International Law

CECA  Communauté du Charbon et de l'Acier (see ECSC)

CEE  Communauté Economique Européenne (see EEC)

CEEA  Communauté Européenne de l'Energie Atomique (see EAEC/Euratom)

CMLR  Common Market Law Reports

CMLRev  Common Market Law Review

Comecon  Council for Mutual Economic Co-operation

EAEC/Euratom  European Atomic Energy Community

ECSC  European Coal and Steel Community

EEC  European Economic Community

EFTA  European Free Trade Association

ERTA  European Road Transport Agreement

GATT  General Agreement on Tariffs and Trade

Gaz Uff  Gazetta Ufficiale (Italy)

ICJ Reports  International Court of Justice Reports

ICLQ  International and Comparative Law Quarterly

ILO  International Labour Organisation

IMF  International Monetary Fund

JO  Journal Officiel des Communautés Européennes

JORF  Journal Officiel de la République Française

LQR  Law Quarterly Review

MB  Moniteur Belge

MLR  Modern Law Review

NATO  North Atlantic Treaty Organisation

OECD  Organisation for Economic Co-operation and Development

OEEC  Organisation for European Economic Co-operation

PCIJ Rep  Permanent Court of International Justice Reports

Recueil  Recueil de la Jurisprudence de la Cour de Justice des Communautés Européennes

Reg  Regulation

RP  Rule of Procedure of the Community Court

UNTS  United Nations Treaty Series

Part I

# The nature of the European Communities and of Community law

Chapter 1

# The European Community and its law

The recurrent dream of a unified Europe is part of our cultural heritage. Students of history are familiar with the attempts to create a united Europe mainly by force, for conquest and universalism go often hand in hand. Only within living memory have two powerful ideologies, Communism and Nazism, endeavoured to unify Europe in their own fashion. In August 1920 the advance of the Red Army 'through the heart of Poland to the conquest of Europe and world conflagration'[1] was brought to a halt at the gates of Warsaw in what was described[2] as the eighteenth decisive battle of world history. In 1945 ended the Second World War, unleashed by one Adolf Hitler who dreamed of a millennium of German domination over Europe. After six years of struggle most of Europe was reduced to smouldering heaps of rubble, physically and politically. The old Europe became just a phase in the Continent's saga and history began to work towards a different concept of unification.

Students of political thought are familiar with the rivalries for excellence between the concept of the sovereign state and federal ideas. From the middle ages right up to our time the state was regarded as the ideal self-sufficient unit, capable of securing protection and self-fulfilment of individuals. The 19th and the first half of the 20th centuries witnessed the apotheosis of the sovereign state as the supreme and sublime goal of human organisation. Everything was to be subordinated to the state. This Hegelian ideal, no doubt rooted in Plato's philosophy, being an element of the explanation of the universe and of historical determinism, was eagerly adopted by modern dictatorships both of the fascist and communist type and soon brought into disrepute. The Second World War did not solve Europe's problems but resulted in a new

1 General Tukhachevski in an order to his armies quoted by Umiastowski, R., *Russia and the Polish Republic* 1918-1941 (1944), p. 84.
2 By Lord D'Abernon; Fuller, J. F. C., *The Decisive Battles of the Western World*, 1792-1944, Vol. 2 (1970), p. 411.

division based on the conquest of its eastern half and a status of satellite states. In a sense it contributed to the creation of two European Communities; of the West (which is the subject of the present study) and of the East (which marks a political and ideological dependency on the Soviet Union). The Second World War, however, demonstrated the futility of conquests and the vulnerability of the sovereign state concept. The sovereign state could no longer guarantee the protection of the citizen and so the traditional concept of allegiance based on a *sui generis* contract broke down. Interdependence of states rather than independence became the key to post-war international relations, and was reflected in current trends of international law, especially in the ideology and structure of the United Nations. The slogan *si vis pacem para bellum* had to give way to the quest for justice among men and nations and *si vis pacem para pacem* had to become the order of the day. An admirable example of co-operation and a practical application of the call for peace is the European Coal and Steel Community built on the premise that, if the basic raw materials for war (coal and steel) are removed from national control, wars between the traditional enemies, France and Germany, will become virtually impossible as long as both are prevented from developing a substantial war industry. A corollary benefit of the international control of these resources, accruing not only to France and Germany but also to the other members of the Community, was brought about by the rationalisation of the coal and steel industries and the economic stimulus created by an enlarged market.

With the demise of the state ideology, federalism found a new lease of life. Federal doctrines have, in the past, set their face against the idolatry of the state, but physical, territorial federalism in Western Europe proved politically impossible. Federalism had to search for other, more realistic forms. Harold Laski, in an introduction to his book, *Liberty in the Modern State*[3], argued that the Second World War and its antecedents had shown that 'the principle of national sovereignty has exhausted its usefulness'. He wrote further: 'it is through supranational planning in fields like electric power, or transport, an integrated economy of coal and steel, that we can best hope to attain this end [i.e. to make liberty possible]. It is, of course, impossible to leave such planning in private hands'. Laski dubbed his idea 'functional federalism' because he was opposed to the concept of territorial federation, that is to say a

3 Re-published in 1948.

United States of Europe or a Federal Western Europe, an enlarged version of Switzerland, which he regarded as both obsolete and impractical.

Whilst 'functional federalism' has been accepted by the architects of the West European Community, Laski's pessimism about territorial federalism may yet prove unfounded. It is clear that economic co-operation and integration will tighten the political and organisational bonds between states and from this reality new political forms will emerge. Territorial federalism is not just round the corner but is not as remote as it may seem. It may well be that it will not be heralded by political theory but will grow up as a child of evolution. In the Community institutions, which we shall examine in detail, the stage seems to have been set for such a development.

The post-war practical exercise in international co-operation in Western Europe has proved that nations can live together and work together, that they can solve their differences amicably and, where need be, through appropriate legal and judicial process. It has demonstrated that the concept of a Community is not only viable but also capable of growth and development. The Community institutions have already been working for a generation and their very existence and practical usefulness will inevitably lead to their refinement. In due course the child will become man.

If we cast our minds back to the early post-war days we will realise that a Community approach was the practical answer to many problems. Europe was in ruins politically and economically; the European colonial empires faced liquidation; the importance of the single European states which dominated the League of Nations was diminished; the 'dollar-gap' resulted in great influence of the United States of America not only as a benovolent saviour but also as a potential master; an 'iron curtain' was drawn across Europe and the world cowered in the shadows of great powers: the United States of America and Soviet Russia facing each other menacingly across Europe. Only rapid recovery in concert could restore Europe's self respect. What is more it became only too obvious that economic reconstruction had to match political aspirations. Thus the idea of a European Community was forced upon Europeans as an economic and political necessity. As for grand designs, the architects of the Community soon realised that great ideologies and elaborate blueprints were of little practical use and that nothing could be achieved at one stroke. Robert Schuman[4], the great French European, said: 'L'Europe ne se fera pas d'un coup dans une construction d'ensemble, elle se fera par des réalisations concrètes créant d'abord une solidarité de fait . . .'

This factual solidarity can be traced to events of great importance to Europe and the world at large, as the work of world recovery and reconstruction began to create a fabric of international economic co-operation. We should mention, if only briefly, these events and forms of co-operation because they too contributed to European solidarity and in a sense paved the way for the institutional framework of the European Community.

### THE INTERNATIONAL MONETARY FUND AND THE WORLD BANK

The IMF was created at a conference at Bretton Woods in 1946, with the object of maintaining the stability of national currencies, reducing restrictions on the currency exchange and helping countries to maintain a balance of payments. The subscribing countries participate on a share basis: USA 28%, USSR 12·5% and Europe only 16%. The size of the share determines the voting power of the subscribers. Countries (including the United Kingdom) often borrow money to maintain their solvency. The World Bank was also created at Bretton Woods. Here again states participate on a share basis. The USA alone provides 38% of the capital. The Bank offers not only financial assistance but also provides experts in various fields. It has been useful to finance projects incapable of being financed otherwise, especially in the developing countries.

### THE HAVANA CHARTER AND GATT

Fifty-five countries, assembled at Havana on the initiative of the USA in 1947-48, drafted a Charter of International Commerce which envisaged a gradual reduction of customs tariffs; proposed suppression of import quotas (except in the case of agricultural produce) and imbalance of payments; prohibited discrimination in commerce (except in the case of former colonies, customs unions and free exchange areas); encouraged investments in the developing countries and suggested an International Trade Organisation. Liberia was the only country which ratified the Charter.

The idea of this Charter was nevertheless accepted by 23 coun-

---

4 Quoted by Lorette, L. de Sainte, *Le Marché Commun* (1961), p. 17.; Patijn, S., (Ed.), Landmarks in European Units (1970), p. 46.

tries which in October 1947 signed the General Agreement on Tariffs and Trade (GATT). It is concerned with customs and commercial policy. The Agreement has been in operation without being ratified between 83 countries which subscribe to its principles and a further 28 countries which apply its principles without having formally signed it. Under the auspices of GATT frequent meetings of experts are held and many customs laws have been modified.

The members of GATT have set up a permanent commission with a secretariat in Geneva. Moreover, member countries adhere, as a rule, to the principles propounded by GATT in the matter of customs, import quotas and preferences and enter into bi-lateral agreements in these fields. It is significant that the so called Schuman Plan and the European Economic Community Treaty were submitted to GATT to ensure conformity with its principles. As from 4 May 1964 the EEC, representing the Member States, has been taking part in negotiations within GATT.

## THE UN ECONOMIC COMMISSION FOR EUROPE

This Commission was established in 1947 in Geneva for the purpose of exchanging information and statistical data on coal, electricity and transport in Western and Eastern Europe. Twenty-eight countries, including the USA, are involved. The Commission has published analytical studies of the economic situations of several European countries, but as the division between the Western and Eastern blocs deepened, it failed as an instrument of co-operation.

## THE MARSHALL PLAN AND THE ORGANISATION FOR EUROPEAN ECONOMIC CO-OPERATION

In a speech at Harvard on 5 July 1947 General George Marshall, the US Foreign Secretary, announced a plan for European relief. Instead of loans to individual countries the US offered economic aid on the sole condition that the Europeans work out a common programme for the relief of poverty and economic reconstruction. His appeal was addressed to Europe as a whole stating that '... our policy is not directed against any country or against any doctrine but against hunger, poverty, despair and chaos; its aim is the renewal of active economy throughout the world'[5]. The plan was

5 Lorette, op. cit., p. 22.

welcomed in Western Europe and the Foreign Secretaries of France and the United Kingdom invited Soviet Russia to join them. Ten days later Molotov scorned the invitation and enjoined Czechoslovakia, Poland and Finland, who expressed interest, to have nothing to do with the Plan.

Sixteen West European countries participated in the conference and the ensuing Committee of Economic Co-operation which led to the creation of the Organisation for the European Economic Co-operation in April 1948. More than 13 milliard dollars were poured into Europe out of the American bounty. This was undoubtedly the first substantial move towards economic co-operation in Europe and the Americans quite rightly take pride in their contribution. Indeed European economic cohesion and strength was in the political interest of the USA even if Europe was to become a competitive force to be reckoned with. Thus American willingness to protect Western Europe from communist expansion contributed towards European unity[6].

At first the OEEC examined the various national plans of economic reconstruction and then worked out a programme of distribution of the American aid. From a legal point of view the important feature of the OEEC was its inter-governmental structure. The sovereignty of each country was safeguarded and no political strings were attached, so much so that even Switzerland, sworn to perpetual neutrality, could participate. The Organisation, which consisted of a Council of Ministers, an Executive Committee and a Secretariat, survived the completion of the Marshall Plan. It embraced 18 countries, including West Germany since 1949 and Spain since 1959 and Yugoslavia represented by an observer. The OEEC could take decisions which were binding on members. It endeavoured to co-ordinate national economic policies and provide experts who serve in an advisory capacity in special fields, i.e. transport, electricity, textiles, etc. It even tried to bring together rival groups like the EEC and the EFTA.

From its inception the OEEC endeavoured to liberalise European trade. It brought about a reduction of import quotas without tampering with the customs laws, which resulted in a short-lived trade boom. In 1952 the United Kingdom and France, contrary to the OEEC's advice, lapsed into import quotas and so exposed the weakness of the Organisation. As new forms of economic co-

---

6 Grosser, A., *Les occidentaux, le pays d'Europe et les Etats-Unis depuis la guerre* (1978), p. 224.

operation began to take shape, the OEEC exhausted its usefulness. In 1961 it was transformed into an Organisation for Economic Co-operation and Development (OECD) for the purpose of assisting the developing countries. The European countries were joined by the USA and Canada as well as the EEC in its corporate capacity, i.e. independently of its members.

## THE COUNCIL OF EUROPE

Parallel to this economic co-operation there was a movement towards political and military integration. The various European movements joined forces in a Congress of Europe held in May 1948 in the Hague under the presidency of Winston Churchill. This resulted in the Council of Europe inaugurated in 1949 at Strasbourg. It started with the five countries of the Brussels Military Alliance (now the Western European Union), viz. the UK, France, Belgium, Holland and Luxembourg, and now embraces 18 countries of Western Europe. Spain and Portugal are excluded and Greece was suspended from membership in 1967 and re-admitted in 1974.

The Council of Europe consists of a Consultative Assembly composed of parliamentary delegates of the member states, a Committee of Ministers and a Secretariat. It has a permanent seat at Strasbourg. As a political design it has proved a failure since it has not developed beyond the nuclear stage of a federal organisation. Its main achievements lie in the field of Human Rights, having established a Commission and a Court of Human Rights. But, above all, it has kept the idea of a United Europe alive.

In the economic field the Consultative Assembly in 1951 formulated proposals to turn Europe into a 'low tariff club' through the lowering of customs barriers. It also put forward, under the name of the 'Strasbourg Plan', ideas for the economic development of the former colonies of the European powers and for the adoption of preferential tariffs between these territories; the British Commonwealth on the one hand and the European countries on the other. Further initiatives aimed at the organisation of European agriculture (the so called green pool) and transport.

Whilst the economic initiatives of the Council of Europe have been superseded by the EEC and the political initiatives remain in an embryonic stage, the Council provides a forum for cultural and political contacts extending beyond the EEC and so preserves the concept of European unity.

### THE NORTH ATLANTIC TREATY ORGANISATION AND TRANSPORT

NATO developed from the North Atlantic Treaty of 1949 which was an extension of the Brussels Treaty of 1948. It now embraces all the West European countries (except Eire, Sweden and Switzerland) as well as the USA, Canada, Greece, Turkey and West Germany. France has withdrawn from NATO but remains party to the North Atlantic Treaty. It is important to note that, without a surrender of sovereignty, decisions[7] within NATO are taken collectively and that this co-operation, though confined to military matters, contributes to the cohesion of Western Europe.

In another technical field, that of transport, the Conference of European Ministers of Transport has for some years now achieved rationalisation of railway transport and, incidentally, enabled the 17 countries involved to make substantial economies. This means that railway carriages marked EUROP can be used and repaired anywhere within the organisation and need not be returned empty to their countries of origin. Complementing EUROP is EURO-FIMA (*Société de financement de matériel ferroviaire*) which by international agreement is entitled to exemption from customs and taxes in respect of railway equipment no matter where it is ultimately used within the organisation. The more complex problem of the rationalisation of transport by road is currently under consideration within the EEC Transport Policy.

### THE BENELUX COUNTRIES

For the purpose of customs, the three countries (Belgium, Netherlands, Luxembourg) have become one. This has been achieved by stages in spite of the disparity of their economic systems and policies. As from 1 January 1948 they removed customs barriers between themselves and agreed upon common customs tariffs vis-à-vis the outside world. In 1951 they adopted a common scheme of customs and excise duties, with the exception of excise on alcohol, sugar and petrol. In 1954 they authorised a free flow of capital which meant a freedom of investment and unrestricted transfer of currency within the three countries. Since 1956 they have entered

7 NATO Handbook (1978), p. 39.

into common commercial treaties with other countries and accepted a free movement of labour. In 1958 they signed a treaty of economic union which came into force on 17 November 1960. As from that date the economy of the Benelux countries was geared to the basic assumptions of an internal market, that is the removal of customs barriers, resulting in a free movement of goods and the free movement of capital and manpower. These three elements were adopted later on for the formation of the EEC by the Treaty of Rome.

The Benelux union did not destroy the national sovereignty of the three countries or affect their identity as subjects of International Law. Though economic integration led inevitably to a greater cohesion in a political and military sense, each country has preserved its political and legal system. The economic integration of the Benelux countries was not a painless operation for there were rival interests of industries across the border. However, as a result, the internal trade of these countries increased by 50% whereas their external trade jumped to fifth place after the USA, the UK, West Germany and Canada, thus surpassing France even though the population of France was twice that of the Benelux countries.

From 1948 to 1956 the national revenue of Belgium and the Netherlands increased considerably and so did their trade with the outside world. This minute Common Market proved to be profitable, not only to the three countries but also to others. Its unqualified success whetted the appetites of neighbouring states and the question arose whether the Benelux experiment could be projected on a larger scale.

THE SCHUMAN PLAN

Robert Schuman and Count Sforza thought that a customs union between France and Italy would be beneficial to both countries. A customs treaty was signed in 1949 but France and Italy lacked the will to see it through. This failure indicated that a less ambitious approach, limited perhaps to one basic industry, should be attempted. Thus coal and steel was selected as the industry basic to many other industries and one especially relevant to the business of war. If war were to be eliminated coal and steel must be put under international control and if economic progress were to breach the national frontiers this basic industry must be made to serve a community of nations.

This was not a novel philosophy, for back in 1948 the European

Movement proclaimed at the Hague the need for an industrial programme especially for the production and distribution of coal. A year later, at Westminster, the European Movement proposed a scheme for several basic industries, i.e. coal, steel, electricity and transport, envisaging a European Institution responsible for a general policy in respect of each of these four industries especially in the field of investments, the volume of production and prices and a consultative body consisting of employers and employees as well as representatives of the public interest.

This, in turn, led to the so called Schuman Plan. In May 1950 France, through her Minister of Foreign Affairs, Robert Schuman, proposed to place all the Franco-German production of coal and steel under a common authority and invited other countries to do the same. Schuman declared: '... Par la mise en commun de productions de base et par l'institution d'une Haute Autorité nouvelle, dont les décisions lieront la France, l'Allemagne et les pays qui adhéreront, cette proposition réalisera les premières assises concrètes d'une Fédération Européenne indispensable à la préservation de la paix ...'[8]

THE EUROPEAN COAL AND STEEL COMMUNITY

On 18 April 1951 the Ministers representing France, Germany, Italy, Belgium, Holland and Luxembourg signed in Paris a treaty which established the European Coal and Steel Community (*Communauté Européenne du Charbon et de l'Acier*). The Treaty was ratified, not without national opposition, e.g. it was ratified by the French Chamber of Deputies by 377 votes against 235 and by the Senate by 182 votes against 32. The industries concerned were unhappy as the Treaty was imposed upon them without prior consultation but it was, no doubt, a wise scheme.

The Treaty of Paris, this first instrument of European integration, consists of 100 articles, three annexes, three protocols and a convention of transitory provisions. The most important feature of the Coal and Steel Community is its supra-national character. It is no longer an inter-governmental but a truly supra-national organisation. It was aptly described[9] as 'a quasi federation in an important economic sector, the member-states retaining their sovereignty in all other sectors'.

8 Lorette, op. cit., p. 38.
9 By Guy de Carmay, *Fortune d'Europe* (1953).

Apart from supra-national organs the Community enjoys a faculty of self-administration manifested in the choice and recruitment of officials, a financial autonomy marked by the power of levying taxes and a measure of self-control vested in a parliamentary assembly.

The Community was endowed with five organs:

(1) an executive, called the High Authority,
(2) a Consultative Committee attached to the High Authority,
(3) a Special Council of Ministers,
(4) an Assembly, and
(5) a Court of Justice.

The High Authority was the permanent executive of the Community. It consisted of nine members, eight chosen unanimously by the six governments and the ninth co-opted by the eight members to emphasise the supra-national character of the Community. A third of the High Authority retired every second year and was replaced by new members irrespective of nationality. The functions of the High Authority included the launching and management of a common market in coal and steel, development and control of investments and scientific research, action to curb unemployment, discrimination and restrictive practices, the imposition of common taxes upon the production of coal and steel; all this without reference to the governments of the member states, subject only to responsibility to the Court and the Assembly. It is true that the field of independent action of the High Authority was restricted, but where it could act it took decisions which were binding upon the member states.

The High Authority was assisted by a Consultative Committee consisting of representatives of employers, trade unions and consumers designated by the Special Council of Ministers on the advice of the trade unions and the producer and consumer organisation.

The Special Council of Ministers represented the sovereign power. Its function was to harmonise the national economies on the recommendation of the High Authority in the fields of coal and steel. Political control was in the hands of the Assembly of the Coal and Steel Community, which consisted of 68 members, of which France, Germany and Italy provided 18 each and the remaining 24 represented the Benelux countries. Members were elected by their national Parliaments though they could have been elected directly.

By a two-thirds majority the Assembly could dismiss the High Authority and together with the member states propose amendments to the Treaty.

The Court consisted of seven members. Its function was to act as a watch-dog over the application of the Treaty, examine the decisions of the High Authority in the light of the Treaty provisions and adjudicate upon the alleged breaches of the Treaty. During the seven years of its existence the Court gave 137 decisions which were of a considerable importance to the Community. These decisions had a binding force in the member states. They are still relevant to Community law.

Several lessons could be drawn from this experiment. It proved that supra-national institutions could function in spite of diverse national interests; that far from being an economic disaster this first European common market greatly contributed to the economic progress of the member states. The enlarged market activated industries far beyond those directly connected with coal and steel. The greatest benefit accrued to Italy, the economically weakest member. However, all was not well all the time. In 1959 there was a crisis in the coal industry caused mainly by over-production and an increase in the use of oil which rendered coal mines, especially in Belgium and Germany, redundant. The High Authority endeavoured to finance stock-piling, to reduce production and even to lower wages, but the Council of Ministers refused to sanction these measures clearly because national interests were at stake. The High Authority was, therefore, forced to provide a special aid to Belgium, which was hit very badly, for the rehabilitation and re-training of miners and to restrict imports from outside the Community. The very existence of the Community enabled it to relieve at least one country but it also became clear that there must be a common European policy in the field of energy. Whilst the Community was successful in its field it was not able to cope with other economic problems and its success certainly did not satisfy those who worked for a United Europe in their lifetime.

## TOWARDS THE TREATIES OF ROME

The greater integration of Europe owes a great deal to military considerations for it is evident that military alliances have political and economic consequences.

The problem of the defence of Western Europe, especially the

American insistence on the participation of Germany in the defence of the Continent, raised delicate political and economic questions. The Germans were doing well without having to spend vast sums on defence, yet there was an aversion to their having a finger on the common trigger and some fear of the revival of German military might. These fears were assuaged partly by the international control of coal and steel, partly by the pacific stance of the German people. Moreover, in view of the cost of defence, it was quite inequitable that Germany should be shielded by her neighbours at their expense. A German contribution had to be sought within an international framework. France, especially, insisted on a supranational control of the armed forces and so in 1952 the European Defence Treaty was signed.

The Treaty envisaged a European Defence Community as a kind of federation without a central federal government. The organisation was to consist of a Commissariat, an Assembly, a Council of Ministers and a Court of Justice, all modelled upon the Coal and Steel Community. It is interesting to note that whilst internationalist France actively promoted the idea it was nationalist France which wrecked the edifice, as on 30 August 1954 the French National Assembly refused to ratify the treaty already ratified by other countries.

The failure to create a European Army led to the London Conference in September 1954 which resulted in turn in the admission of Italy and West Germany to the alliance by virtue of the Protocols to the Brussels Treaty signed in Paris in October 1954. The Final Act of the London Conference gave birth to yet another organisation, i.e. the Council of Western European Union embracing the United Kingdom, Belgium, Holland, Luxembourg, France, Germany and Italy. It has subsequently passed through certain mutations but achieved no prominence apart from defence in the NATO setting though logically it set the United Kingdom into the picture of West European integration.

For a while the unionist movement lay dormant, though on the Continent there were encouraging stirrings among the various industries, especially agriculture and the trade unions. The idea was resurrected at the meeting of the Foreign Ministers of the six members of the Coal and Steel Community in June 1955 at Messina. They were unanimous in their resolve to pursue the concept of an economic union and they were encouraged to do so by the governments of the Benelux countries.

At the beginning of the Conference the Ministers proclaimed their intention to 'pursue the establishment of a United Europe through the development of common institutions, a progressive fusion of national economies, the creation of a Common Market and harmonisation of social policies'[10]. During the Conference the Ministers became more precise as they considered that a 'constitution of a European Common Market must be their objective' though they realised that this could only be achieved by stages. To do this, again on the advice of the Benelux countries, the Ministers set up an Inter-Governmental Committee to study the various problems. The United Kingdom was invited to attend and indeed a minor official from the Board of Trade took part in the preliminary discussions.

In July 1955 the Committee met in Brussels with the object of co-ordinating the work of the various sub-committees set up to study the problems of investment, social policy, fuel and power, atomic energy and transport. The work continued during the summer and autumn of 1955 and among the sixty or so experts there were representatives of the Coal and Steel Community, the Organisation for European Co-operation, the Council of Europe and, for a while, of the United Kingdom. Then followed a period of considerable activity and several meetings of the Foreign Ministers of the six countries. Reports of experts were considered, until finally a treaty was drafted and signed in Rome on 25 March 1957. This was the first Treaty of Rome which established the European Economic Community (the EEC) commonly known as the Common Market. The Treaty consists of 248 articles, 4 appendices, 9 protocols and a convention relating to the association with the Community of the Overseas Countries and Territories which have special relations with Belgium, France, Italy and the Netherlands.

The second Treaty of Rome, setting up the European Community of Atomic Energy (Euratom) was signed on the same day. It consists of 225 articles, 5 appendices and 1 protocol.

Both treaties had to be ratified by the parliaments of the signatory states. The reaction of these parliaments is worthy of a comparison. In Germany both Houses of Parliament ratified the Treaties unanimously. In Belgium in the Chamber of Deputies 174 voted for and 4 against ratification; in the Senate 134 and 2 against. In France in the Chamber of Deputies 342 voted for and 239 against the

10 Quoted by Lorette, op. cit., p. 60.

ratification; in the Senate 222 for and 70 against. In Italy in the Chamber of Deputies 311 voted for and 144 against the ratification; the Senate voted unanimously for ratification. In Luxembourg 46 votes were cast for and 3 against ratification. In the Netherlands in the Chamber of Deputies 114 votes were cast for and 12 against ratification; in the Senate 44 for and 5 against. The numerical opposition in France and Italy is significant but can easily be explained by the existence of large Communist parties in those countries and the attitude of the mother-country of communism to European Unity[11].

The Treaties became operative on 1 January 1958.

THE THREE COMMUNITIES

The two Treaties of Rome added two new Communities to the Coal and Steel Community.

The European Atomic Energy Community (Euratom) was created as a specialist market for atomic energy. Atomic energy is a relatively new source of power with a virtually unlimited potential. It is hoped therefore, that it will satisfy the demands of our technological era. In the sixties the Six imported about a quarter of their energy from countries outside the Community. By 1975, it was considered, they will have to import 40% of their needs unless atomic energy takes over from the traditional sources of power. However this target was not realised as in 1973 the Community was importing some 63% of its energy and the oil crisis aggravated the situation. A common energy policy embracing the Euratom for which the Community has been striving, albeit without success, has become not only a matter of economic urgency but also a factor in European integration.

The object of Euratom is to develop nuclear energy, distribute it within the Community and sell the surplus to the outside world. In view of the development costs involved the Community must collectively engage in the necessary research and disseminate the accumulated knowledge. It must develop industry in a rational way ensuring a fair distribution within the Community and, finally, it must, as a body, consider the international implications of the pacific use of nuclear energy. In many respects Euratom corresponds to the Coal and Steel Community.

The objectives of the European Economic Community (EEC)

11 'Soviet unease over UK entry', *European Community* (February 1972), p. 16.

are wider than the objectives of the remaining two Communities, for the EEC is not a mere specialist organisation but an instrument of economic integration with a considerable political potential. Therefore whilst bearing in mind the three separate juristic entities the EEC is by far the most important and may be regarded as a prototype of an integrated European Community.

### THE MERGER OF THE COMMUNITIES

The main institutions of the ECSC as we have seen were five in number: an executive body known as the High Authority; a Consultative Committee; a Special Council made up of the representatives of the governments of the member states; a Parliamentary Assembly made up of representative parliamentarians of the national parliaments of the member states; and a Court of Justice. When the EEC and Euratom were established, their institutions were modelled upon those of the ECSC and this naturally suggested the merger of the separate institutions so as to avoid a multiplicity of institutions responsible for the achievement of similar tasks. This merger has taken place in two stages.

A Convention relating to certain Institutions common to the European Communities was concluded simultaneously with the Rome Treaties and provided for the establishment of a single Court of Justice and a single Parliamentary Assembly to serve all three Communities. The completion of this process of institutional merger was not immediately realised with the result that for some years each of the Communities retained its own executive body (High Authority in the case of the ECSC and Commissions in the case of the EEC and Euratom) and Council. This institutional separatism resulted from the adoption of a functional approach to European integration; three Communities were established by separate treaties and charged with the achievement of specific objectives. Further, the role of the Commissions and Councils in relation to the EEC and Euratom differed significantly from that of the High Authority and Special Council in relation to the ECSC, and so in 1957 separate institutions seemed appropriate. In practice this separation was found to be unsatisfactory. Whilst the objectives of each Community are distinct they also overlap and form part of a larger economic whole. In several fields, such as coal and steel and atomic energy, it was desirable for the Communities to co-ordinate their policy; the existence of separate institutions each with its own personnel with different views and ideas militated against this. Eventually a treaty was signed in May 1965 and took effect on 1 July 1967, providing for further fusion of the Communities[12]. This treaty instituted a single Commission to replace the High Authority of the ECSC and the Commissions of the EEC and Euratom, and a single Council to replace the separate Councils of the three Communities.

This 'Merger Treaty', which completed the institutional merger of the Communities, represents a further step towards the eventual merger of the three Communities to form a single European Community; but this will require the negotiation of a new treaty to replace the Treaty of Paris and the Treaties of Rome. For the time being 'the three Communities can be regarded as facets of one basic experiment, stages in an unfinished process, the future development of which cannot yet be foreseen'[13].

## THE UNITED KINGDOM AND EUROPEAN SOLIDARITY

The United Kingdom has contributed to European solidarity (particularly in the field of military co-operation) but has tended to remain aloof. It is true that in 1946 in his famous Zurich speech Winston Churchill urged the establishment of a United States of Europe based on a partnership between France and Germany. But the role which he assigned to the United Kingdom was that of a friend and sponsor of the new Europe, clearly a role which fell far short of full participation[14].

Successive British post-war governments adopted a lukewarm and sceptical attitude towards developments on the Continent. There were, perhaps, two main reasons for this. In the first place, unlike her continental allies, Britain had not endured defeat and enemy occupation. Although she had suffered economically as a result of the war, British institutions and the British way of life were not only preserved intact but could in a sense be said to be triumphant. From such a standpoint the prospect of compromising British independence in favour of union with continental Europe

---

12 The entry into force of this treaty was delayed by the crisis resulting from a clash between France and her five partners over the agricultural policy of the EEC.

13 Palmer, M., Lambert, J. et al., *European Unity* (1968), p. 169. On the background to and effects of the Merger Treaty, see Houben, P. H. J. M., 'The Merger of the Executives of the European Communities' (1965–66) 3 CML Rev 37 and Weil, G. L., 'The Merger of the Institutions of the European Communities' (1967) 61 AJIL 57.

14 Kitzinger, U., *The European Common Market and Community* (1967), p. 37.

was not very attractive. In addition, at that time Britain was still in possession of a considerable colonial empire to which, as well as to the independent members of the Commonwealth, she looked rather than to the Continent. There was also the special relationship which had been forged between Britain and the United States. The British attitude to European integration in the years immediately following the Second World War is, perhaps, summed up by the reaction of Ernest Bevin, when Foreign Secretary, to the proposal that Britain should participate in a European Assembly as part of the Council of Europe: 'I don't like it. I don't like it. If you open that Pandora's Box you will find it full of Trojan horses[15]'.

By the late 1950s British exclusion from the advantages which became apparent within the Community and the fear that she might lose political influence made her realise that the idea of the European Community, far from being a failure, was a force to be reckoned with. The United Kingdom never joined the Coal and Steel Community (although she did establish a form of association with it) and cold-shouldered the Common Market negotiations. In 1957 Britain proposed a 'free trade area' (the so called Maudling Plan) and, when this failed, created a rival organisation, the European Free Trade Association (EFTA) in 1959. However, in some respects EFTA, which embraced Austria, Denmark, Norway, Portugal, Sweden, Switzerland and the United Kingdom, proved less successful than the European Economic Community and a positive policy towards the European Community emerged.

In 1961 the Macmillan Government applied for membership of the EEC. The negotiations (the British team was headed by the Lord Privy Seal, Mr Edward Heath) dragged on, but when the British side, leaving some problems to further negotiations, was ready to sign in 1963 the French President, General de Gaulle, vetoed the British entry. In 1967 the Wilson Government renewed the application but it was vetoed again by France before negotiations could take place. The third attempt was made by the Heath Government in 1970 and the negotiations for entry were successfully concluded in January 1972.

Grand debates were held in Parliament and elsewhere during the summer and autumn of 1971 and the Government mounted a massive information service. Opinion polls revealed a considerable opposition to British entry into Europe and party politics obscured the discussion on the merits of the entry. It transpired that the

15 Robertson, A. H., *The Council of Europe* (2nd edn, 1961), p. 6, n. 23.

Labour Party, who would have been happy to accept the terms of the British accession when in power, was opposed to the terms when in opposition. The declared reasons that the situation had changed and that the country's economy did not warrant accession at this time, though hardly convincing, were vigorously advanced by the Labour Party opposition. Opponents in principle argued that there was anything but advantage in accession to the Community, whilst the surrender of sovereignty was an unforgivable folly. On 28 October 1971 the Government secured a reasonable majority[16] with the support of the Liberals and Labour dissenters from the official party policy who voted for the entry in principle but pledged themselves to oppose the consequential legislation. The historic decision, which merited a national unity, was soured by the antics of party politics. On 20 January 1972 the eleventh hour attempt to prevent the signing of the Treaty of Accession until the full text 'has been published and its contents laid before the House' failed, but the vote on the motion produced a majority of only 21 for the Government,[17] the Conservative opponents abstaining and the Labour members voting under a three line whip.

Because of the lack of bi-partisan policy the British participation in the Community depends much upon the party political game. Indeed the Labour Party opposition announced, in its electoral manifesto of 1974, that when returned to power it would embark upon 'fundamental re-negotiations' of the condition of entry[18]. Such negotiations did take place though it was difficult to see the real purpose other than to keep faith with the electorate and to placate the opposition within the Party. The Government advice that, on balance, Britain should remain in the Community was endorsed by a two-thirds majority of the electorate in what became a novel constitutional experiment: a 'consultative referendum' of 1975. However the Party never adopted any constructive attitude whilst the Labour Government failed to play a positive role or to demonstrate a European conviction. Moreover, when, again in opposition, the Party at its annual conferences at Blackpool (October 1980) and Brighton (October 1981) voted for withdrawal from the Community this, according to Mr Shore (the Shadow Foreign Secretary), was to be done without a referendum.

16 *Hansard, House of Commons* 1970–71, Vol. 823, col. 2212.
17 Ibid., 1971–72, Vol. 829, col. 800.
18 Lasok, D., 'Some Legal Aspects of Fundamental Re-negotiations' (1976) 5 EL Rev 375.

The Conservative Government of Mrs Thatcher, following the inconclusive meetings of the European Council in Dublin (November 1979) and Luxembourg (April 1980), wrenched out of the Community substantial budgetary concessions at the Brussels meeting of Foreign Ministers (May 1980) and the Council meeting in Venice (June 1980). Although the British burden was eased through the application of the 'corrective mechanism' a permanent solution of the problem remains yet to be found. The Government also hopes for a reform of the Common Agricultural Policy, especially its financial implications for Britain. Some cosmetic adjustments, (i.e. a market organisation for sheepmeat and a declaration on fishery policy), have been made but these hardly affect the principles of the CAP.

The United Kingdom has proved a difficult and somewhat unstable partner. Both major political parties are much to blame primarily for the lack of a national policy for Europe and the lack of a clear vision of the Community as well as the role this country ought to play in the European integration.

### THE TREATIES OF ACCESSION AND BEYOND

In simple legal terms the first Treaty of Accession, signed on 22 January 1972 on behalf of the six member states, the Communities (represented by Mr Gaston Thorn, Foreign Minister of Luxembourg and Chairman of the Council of Ministers) and the four prospective members Denmark, Eire, Norway and the United Kingdom, is a Treaty signifying admission of new members to the three Communities. However, only three joined since Norway, in view of the adverse result of the national referendum, was unable to accede. The Treaty consists of three articles stating that the new members accede to the existing Communities and accept all their rules. A lengthy Act, signed at the same time, confirmed the results of the negotiations and gave details of what membership entailed. Full membership as from 1 January 1973 was conditional upon the incorporation of the Community Law into the municipal laws of the new members. The period of transition was completed on 1 July 1977 which meant that as from that date the Community of Nine was fully established.

We shall discuss elsewhere the effects of the Treaty for the United Kingdom and the Community. It will suffice to say, at this stage, that neither the texts of the foundation Treaties nor the institutions established under these Treaties were radically changed, though they were adjusted to give effect to the enlarged membership.

The second Treaty of Accession[19] heralded the admission of Greece as the tenth member as from 1 January 1981, the period of transition to be completed in the main by 1 January 1986.

Long term adjustments postulate a new treaty. Such a treaty would provide an opportunity for a revision of the three foundation treaties, elimination of what has become obsolete and incorporation of the multifarious experience of the Communities as well as new ideas. The merger of the Communities could be brought to its logical conclusion, that is a complete fusion of the three Communities into a single legal entity. The present vague political idea of a Community of West European nations could be transformed into a more meaningful juristic concept.

An evolutionary approach to the problem of integration was advocated in the Tindemans Report published in January 1976. In his cautious Report the Belgian Prime Minister postulated a gradual development towards European Union building on the existing institutions and the practices which have evolved outside the Treaty framework. The Report envisaged a closer co-operation between the member states, notably a co-ordination of their foreign policy and regular meetings of heads of government acting as the 'European Council'[20]. It proposed 'to put an end to the distinction which still exists to-day between ministerial meetings which deal with political co-operation and those which deal with the subjects covered by the Treaty'. It proposed to strengthen the role of the European Council by making the Council of Ministers of Foreign Affairs responsible for the preparation of its meetings and by the European Council indicating the institution or organisation responsible for the execution of its decisions.

The Report emphasised further the need to develop a common foreign policy along with extended external economic relations and a common defence policy, converting policy commitments into 'legal obligations'. It advocated recourse to majority voting in the Council as a 'normal practice of the Community'. Avoiding any rigid timetable or development by stages the Report suggested a

19 Act of Accession of the Hellenic Republic OJ 1979, L2 91/17.
20 Based on the recommendations of the Heads of Government meeting in Paris in December 1974; EC Bull Supp 1/76; Mitchell, J. D. B., 'The Tindemans Report—Retrospect and Prospect' (1976) 13 CML Rev 455.

'two-speed plan of economic integration' in which the weaker members, i.e. Eire, Italy and the United Kingdom, should proceed at a slower pace than the others.

The lack of progress subsequent to the Tindemans Report prompted the Brussels European Council of 1978 to ask 'Three Wise Men[1]' to prepare a report on the political reform of the European Community[2]. Their Report[3], presented to the European Council in October 1979, listed the failures of the Community in carrying out its original and new policies. 'The reasons', it held[4], 'lie rather in political circumstances and attitudes that sometimes produced conflicting conceptions of the right way forward, and sometimes produced no clear conceptions at all' . . . Only the European Council had made a significant contribution towards an improvement of the Community decision-making procedure in so far as it became 'an escape from the bureaucracy weighing down the other institutions in order to provide leadership and guidance[5]'. The Three Wise Men thought that 'the principle needs to be affirmed yet again that the Commission is the natural executive organ of the Community[6]'. They rejected the idea of a 'two speed integration' advocated by Tindemans and appealed for solidarity in face of the economic recession[7].

Despite the gloomy outlook for institutional development the prospects of democratic control of the Community have improved. The decision of the Council of Ministers of 20 September 1976[8] to carry out the Treaty promise of direct elections to European Parliament resulted in 1979 in a fundamental change of that institution. Instead of being a body of delegates from national legislatures the Parliament is now truly representative of 'Euro-constituencies' and the national political parties. This has contributed towards the legitimacy of that Institution and, having raised its prestige, opened up the way to a more active and influential participation in the life of the Community.

The evolution from the stage of the 'Common Market' to that of the 'Economic Union' has proved slow and disappointing. Even

1 Borend Biesheuvel, Edmund Dell, Robert Marjolin.
2 EC Bull 12/1978, p. 97.
3 Duff, A. N., 'The Report of the Three Wise Men,' JO Common Market Studies, vol. XIX (1981), 237 et seq.
4 P. 19.
5 Report, p. 9.
6 P. 72.
7 Pp. 89-91.
8 JO 1976, L 278/1.

the Monetary Policy, mooted as early as 1964[9] and proposed in earnest in 1971 and 1972[10] to be completed by 31 December 1980, failed to produce a European Monetary System indispensable to a coherent economic policy and closer economic integration.

Squabbles regarding the national contribution towards the Community budget continue whilst the much discussed reform of the Common Agricultural Policy remains yet to be formulated. The oil crisis of the seventies, which has done so much damage to Western economy, failed to produce a united front whilst the continuing world economic recession preys upon the idea of unity within the Community. Yet unity seems the only hope for peace, security and prosperity in Europe and elsewhere. That unity, urged the Tindemans Report, is a 'self-evident good'.

It is evident that if, and when, such unity comes about, the form of the new Community will have to be considered. The Community may continue as an association of sovereign states (*l'Europe d'Etats*) or develop into a federal structure heralded by the EEC. Political developments will, no doubt, influence the institutions and the law of the Community. At present we have the world's largest trading unit with a total population of over 260 million consisting of states of different size, cultural heritage, wealth and aspirations.

9 Council Decision 64/301.
10 Council Resolutions, Compendium of Community Monetary Texts, 1979, pp. 25, 30, 33.

Chapter 2

# The concept and status of the European Communities

## 1 The legal status of the European Community

The European Community is a result of international solidarity which we have considered in the light of post-war developments in international relations, and of the conscious effort to create a kind of unity in Western Europe. When political unification proved premature the architects of the Community seized upon the economic elements of inter-state relations and built these into the three 'Communities' (Coal and Steel, Euratom and EEC), so much so that today within the vague notion of a political Community we have three legally definable treaty-based 'Communities'. It follows that in spite of the machinery for defence (NATO) and the economic co-ordination (the three Communities), and a friendly understanding in matters of foreign policy (which should not be overrated) the political structure remains still in the sphere of speculation. Political scientists[1] offer a variety of ideas but a blueprint which can become the basis of discussion at a Government level is yet to emerge. No doubt statesmen have their ideas too but at an official level less adventurous schemes can be expected. General de Gaulle spoke of a Europe of States and M Pompidou[2], speaking on the challenge of the enlarged EEC spoke guardedly about a confederation. Occasionally the EEC is described as a federation but, as we shall see later, neither the federal nor the confederal label fits the organisation.

### (A) FEDERATION OR CONFEDERATION?

In the long history of mankind only a few confederations can be recorded: Switzerland 1291–1848; The Netherlands 1581–1795;

1 For a summary see: Pentland, C. C., 'Political Theories of European Integration: Between Science and Ideology' in Lasok, D. and Soldatos, P. (Ed.), Les Communautés Européennes en Fonctionnement (1981), p. 546 et seq.
2 Times, 12 May 1972.

the USA 1776–1788; Germany 1815–1866. Since these confederations developed either into unitary states or federations it is worthwhile contrasting the confederal with the federal type of constitution. In a federal state the sovereign power is apportioned between a central government and a number of member states. There are two versions of federal states which can be best illustrated by a comparison between the USA and Canada. The US constitution is so arranged that power flows from the state to the federal government which has no powers, apart from those delegated to it by the states. The exact oppositite obtains in Canada where the power flows from the Dominion Government to the Provinces, which have no powers apart from those delegated to them by the Dominion Government. For the purpose of international relations a federal state is represented by a central government. Internally, the legislature, the judiciary, the administration and indeed the law can be divided into federal and state.

In a confederation the sovereignty enjoyed by the individual member states is said to be complete. It can be defined as a relationship of sovereign states, each member state retaining its status as a subject of international law. In a federation, on the other hand, the sovereignty of the individual member states merges into the one sovereignty of the federation. In a confederation the central government acts directly on the member states but only through the member states upon individuals. It follows that outwardly each member of a confederation can enter into separate relations with foreign states and, of course, may of its own right be a member of UNO, whereas members of a federation, as a rule[3], cannot enter into separate relations with foreign states. Inwardly members of a confederation maintain their independent and separate form of government, legislature, judiciary, administration and system of law, their relation to the central government being contractual rather than organic. A confederation has no distinct legal order for it is a political association of states rather than a composite state.

On balance the emerging European Community fits, in the light of the EEC Treaty, better into a federal than confederal form.

Since, of the three Communities, the EEC is the prototype of the legal structure of the European Community it is essential to examine its legal status, for it is a *pointer* to the relationship between

3 Cf. the anomalous position of two member republics of the USSR: Ukraine and Byelo-Russia; Dolan, E., 'The Member-Republics of the USSR as Subjects of the Law of Nations,' [1955] ICLQ 629–36.

the member states inter se, the member states to the Community and the Community to the outside world. The status of the EEC rests upon its constitution, i.e. the Treaty of Rome, and the appropriate rules of International Law, as well as the constitutional laws of the member states.

It is clear that the EEC is not a state[4] for it has no territory of its own, no population which is not a citizenry of the member states, whilst its 'government' has no powers except those defined by Treaty. However, it would be quite inadequate to define the EEC as the association of states which subscribe to the Treaty of Rome, since the Treaty lays down a foundation for something more than a loose partnership of states involved in a joint economic enterprise. The Treaty is not a mere contractual compact, it is an institutional stage of European unity.

The EEC though consisting of sovereign states, is a separate, albeit supra-national, entity, and in this respect it is governed by the law of international institutions in general and its own constitution in particular. In this context the law of international institutions, an offshoot of public international law, applies to the EEC as a regional arrangement.

It is perfectly legitimate for sovereign states in their capacity as the makers of international law to act in concert in setting up institutions and organisations furthering the interests of mankind. Of these the most impelling precedent is the UN which, though universal in character and purpose, does not exclude regional organisations. Indeed it has been pointed out[5] that the difficulty of developing global institutions raised the hope of a greater success in the field of regional organisations. Unlike its predecessor, the League of Nations, which was conceived merely to be an association[6], the United Nations Organisation[7] has the status of a legal person, i.e. it is a bearer of rights and duties pertinent to legal

---

4 According to art. 1 of the Montevideo Convention of 1933 on the Rights and Duties of States, 'the state as a person of international law should possess the following qualifications: (*a*) a permanent population, (*b*) a defined territory, (*c*) a government and (*d*) a capacity to enter into relations with other states'.

5 Jenks, C. W., 'World Organisation and European Integration', *European Yearbook*, Vol. I, p. 173; see also Scheuner, U., 'Europe and the United Nations', *European Yearbook*, Vol. VIII, pp. 67–90.

6 Although the Covenant did not confer juristic personality upon the League of Nations it was often argued that such personality was necessary for the League to fulfil its functions; cf. Jenks, C. W. [1945] BYIL 267.

7 United Nations Charter, art. 104; Advisory Opinion on Reparation for Injuries suffered in the Service of the United Nations, ICJ Reports (1949), p. 174.

personality because it was so willed by the founder states. The same is the position of the EEC. In their terse statement that 'the Community shall have legal personality'[8] the founder states unequivocally created a new international entity independent of its component parts and endowed it with the status and attributes of a legal person.

By virtue of customary international law two attributes, viz. the treaty-making power and the capacity of sending and receiving envoys, mark out an entity as a sovereign body and a subject of international law. The Holy See[9] was a classic example of this doctrine from 1870 when it lost territorial sovereignty until 1929 when it re-gained a symbolic territory by the Lateran Treaty. The EEC need not resort to custom to support its claim for the Treaty provides for both the legal personality (art. 210) and the treaty-making power[10]. The capacity to enter into diplomatic[11] relations derives generally from the legal personality of the EEC and specifically from art. 17 of the Protocol on the Privileges and Immunities of the European Communities of 1965. By the end of 1981 the EEC as a legal person distinct from its members has established diplomatic relations with more than 100 countries including the Holy See and China and maintains a delegation at the UNO. However, whilst there is no doubt about the international status and personality of the EEC vis-à-vis the member states and countries which treat with it as a corporate body, the question of a universally recognised personality must still remain open.

The EEC was set up by a treaty of unlimited duration (art. 240), and so was the EAEC (art. 208), but the ECSC only for fifty years (art. 97). By its design the Community is committed to a continuous progress, by its nature it appears irreversible. Theoretically it is possible for a member state to withdraw as long as it remains sovereign, that is as long as the political integration or transformation of the economic community into a more homegenous body politic has not materialised. However, in reality the economic structure of the member states and their national interests may become so intertwined in the course of time that a break-away may prove

---

8 EEC, art. 210; ECSC, art. 6 (1); EAEC, art. 184.

9 Kunz, J. L., 'The Status of the Holy See in International Law' (1952) 46 AJIL 308 et seq.

10 EEC, arts. 113, 114, 131, 228, 237, 238; ECSC, arts. 6, 71; EAEC arts. 101 and 206. The treaty making power of the ECSC was implicitly recognised by the UK in the agreement of 1954 between the UK and the ECSC, 258 UNTS 322.

11 Cf. UN Charter, art. 75.

well-nigh impracticable. On the other hand it is always possible to maintain the status quo and so reduce the Community to political stagnation. The Community itself has a built-in system which may either advance it towards political and institutional integration or preserve the self-contained units of sovereign states whilst developing the economy and creating wealth within the existing institutions. This depends on whether the Community institutions are strengthened at the expense of sovereignty or whether the sovereign element keeps the Community institutions in the servile role of functional bureaucracy[12].

Article 236 provides for revision of the EEC Treaty. The initiative rests with the government of any member state or the Commission who may submit to the Council of Ministers proposals for the amendments of the Treaty. The scope seems unlimited including, presumably, the winding-up of the Community. However, amendments must be passed by a unanimous conference of representatives of the governments of the member states, convened by the President of the Council on the recommendation of the Council, having previously obtained an approval of such conference by the Assembly and, in unspecified appropriate cases, by the Commission. However, any amendment must be ratified by all the member states in accordance with their respective constitutions[13]. In this way sovereignty of the member states has been safeguarded but also changes in the structure of the Community have been made dependent upon the common will of the member states. It follows that the position of the member states inter se and vis-à-vis the Community, as stated in the Treaty, will remain static unless there is a unanimous desire for change.

Enlargement of the Community is also subject to a unanimous decision of the member states followed by amendment of the Treaty duly ratified by all contracting states in accordance with their respective constitutions[14]. This means that the composition of the Community and the conditions of admission of new members are subject to negotiations between the member states and may be vetoed by a single vote of a mighty or not so mighty state.

It follows that the organisation as well as the relations between the Community and its members, on the one hand, and the member

12 ECSC, art. 95; EAEC, art. 204.
13 EEC, art. 236 (3); ECSC, art. 95; EAEC, art. 204.
14 EEC, art. 237; ECSC, art. 98; EAEC, art. 205.

states, inter se on the other, are fixed by the Treaty. In a sense this resembles the constitutional position within a composite state.

## (B) INSTITUTIONAL FRAMEWORK

The constitution of the EEC has clearly been devised upon a federal pattern. As in a state, the direction of the Community is in the hands of political organs which comprise the Assembly, the Council of Ministers and the Commission.

The Assembly consists of 'representatives of the peoples of the States brought together in the Community'[15] but the strength of this representation is weighted in accordance with the size of the population of the member states. The Assembly exercises a political control and acts as a deliberative and consultative body. In a sense it is the Parliament, albeit a weak one, of the Community.

The Council of Ministers is the supreme organ of the Community for it represents the sovereignty of the member states. It consists of the representatives of the governments[16], each government sending one delegate to their meetings. The responsibility for the execution of the objectives laid down by the treaty falls upon this body. It is the Council which takes the most important decisions and co-ordinates the economic policies of the member states[17]. However, these powers are exercised in conjunction with the Commission.

The Commission is a truly Community institution. Its members are chosen on account of their general competence and independence by member states, unanimously. Only the citizens of the member states are eligible but there may be no more than two from one particular state. The powers of the Commission[18] can be described as the powers of initiative, preparation and decision. The Commission formulates recommendations and opinions on matters with which the Treaty is concerned and participates in the work of the Council and the Assembly. It also has certain executive and quasi judicial powers.

The judicial power of the Community is in the hands of the Court of Justice, whose main function is to 'ensure that in the interpretation and application of this Treaty the law is observed[19]. Composed of eleven Judges and assisted by five Advocates-General

15 EEC, art. 137; ECSC art. 20; EAEC, art. 107.
16 EEC, art. 148; ECSC, art. 28; EAEC, art. 118.
17 EEC, art. 145; ECSC, art. 26; EAEC, art. 115.
18 EEC, art. 155; ECSC, art. 8, EAEC, art. 124; Treaty of Merger, art. 9.
19 EEC, art. 164; ECSC, art. 31; EAEC, art. 136.

chosen from persons of proven independence and qualified to hold
the highest judicial offices in their countries the Court is really not
an international court. If anything it resembles more a federal court
than the International Court of Justice at The Hague. It is in fact
an internal court of the Community. Its jurisdiction, as defined by
the Treaty, is not a substitute for the jurisdictions of the national
courts of the member states since it is confined to the administration
of Community law. It is, however, a fully-fledged judicial body
with the power of arbitration, adjudication, repression and advice.
The power of interpretation of the Treaty, of the acts of the Community institutions and of the bodies established by the Council,
which is sometimes exclusive, enables the Court to exercise a
quasi-legislative function and thus build up a body of case law
which, like the continental administrative tribunals, especially the
French Conseil d'Etat, contribute to the development of the law.
The power of annulment, which is an instrument of the control of
the acts of the Council and the Commission, puts the Court into
the unique position of authority. The Court is the custodian of the
Treaty, the watchdog of legality within the Community and the
executor of the supremacy of the Community law over the national
laws of the member states in case of conflict between the two
systems. Indeed the principle of supremacy of Community law is
perhaps the most important aspect of the status of the Community
vis-à-vis the member states.

The powers of the Community organs, which we have briefly
outlined above, would be quite meaningless if it were not for the
corresponding surrender of sovereignty by the member states. The
surrender of sovereignty is only partial and circumscribed by the
Treaty obligations, but it is sufficient to mark a relationship
between the member states and the Community. The relationship
is based not only on treaty obligations of a contractual type but also
on obligations which result in supra-national institutions and a
separate body of law. The relationship resembles more a federation
than a confederation and the Treaty is the Constitution, as it were,
of the Community.[20] The law of the Community, on the other
hand, is a distinct order from the municipal laws of the member
states but it is administered by both the national authorities and
the Community Institutions. The relationship of Community law
to the laws of the member states resembles that of a federal to

20 Wagner, H., *Grundbegriffe des Beschlussrechts der Europäischen Gemeinschaften*
(1965).

national law in so far as it is directly binding within the territory of the member states though it is not administered exclusively by a Community judiciary. The acceptance of the Treaty, the law enacted by the Community organs, and the obligation to enact municipal legislation in accordance with the Treaty and the directives of the Community organs emphasise still further the federal concept of the Community. All power of the Community flows from the member states but the Community has in the territory of the member states no more than the 'most extensive legal capacity accorded to legal persons under their Laws'[1]. This is insufficient as a criterion of a federal state, for federal states are based on constitutions which define the apportionment of power in terms of sovereignty. In the terms of the EEC Treaty the states endeavour to build Community institutions and to create a body of law to regulate the economic activities of the members. Although surrender of a certain portion of sovereignty is necessary in order to achieve these objectives the pooling of sovereignty is not explicit enough to create a federal state or a federal government of the Community. Therefore, at this stage of its development, the Community is merely is an association of sovereign states with a federal potential.

## 2 The status of the Communities in the law of the the Member States

### (A) CORPORATE CAPACITY

The three Treaties constituting the Communities are identical and quite explicit on the legal status of the Communities in the member states. Thus art. 211 of the EEC Treaty provides that 'in each of the Member States, the Community shall enjoy the most extensive legal capacity accorded to legal persons under their laws; it may, in particular, acquire or dispose of movable and immovable property and may be party to legal proceedings'.

It is clear from the Treaties that it is only the Communities themselves and not their separate institutions which have legal personality. In a case arising under the ECSC Treaty, *Algera v Common Assembly of the ECSC*[2], the Court of Justice laid it down

1 EEC, art. 211; ECSC, art. 6 (3); EAEC, art. 185.
2 Cases 7/56 and 3–7/57: [1957–58] ECR 39; Valentine, D. G., The Court of Justice of the European Communities (1965), Vol. 2, p. 748; cf. Case 63–69/72: *Wilhelm Werhahn Hansamühle v EC Council* [1973] ECR 1229 at 1246.

in as many words: 'only the Community and not its institutions possess legal capacity'. Although the Court in that case was referring to the institutions of the ECSC, it is equally applicable to the merged institutions which serve the three Communities. It is clear that the legal personality and capacity of the Communities, following the classic theory of the personality of corporations, is quite distinct from those of the member states. In a case before an Italian court in 1963 it was argued that the acts of the ECSC should be regarded by Italian law as the acts of the Italian state so that the ECSC could enjoy the preferential status in the Italian law of bankruptcy which is enjoyed by the Italian state. But the Court rejected that argument and held 'that the Community, while it is composed of the member states is ... a distinct and autonomous corporation which cannot be identified with them ... [It is] a free and autonomous private corporation, under no control from the State institutions'[3].

Whilst the Communities are 'private' corporations in the sense that they are autonomous and quite distinct from the member states because they regard themselves to be in a similar position towards the Communities as the promoters of a joint stock company towards the company itself, the Court of Justice of the Communities has held that the legal personality of the Communities is governed by public law. Thus in *Von Lachmüller v EEC Commission*[4] the Court stated that the legal personality of the Community is a personality which 'exists in public law by virtue of the powers and functions which belong to the Community'. This statement was made in accordance with the continental practice of classifying corporate bodies. Thus in French law, for example, the category *personnes morales de droit public* includes the state itself, administrative subdivisions of the state and state enterprises such as universities, hospitals and nationalised industries. The competence of such corporate bodies is governed by public law and not by the civil law which would govern the competence of *personnes morales de droit privé*, such as commercial companies[5]. In the *Von Lachmüller* case the Court held that contracts of employment between the EEC and its employees were governed by public law and as such were subject to the procedures of administrative law.

This is a distinction quite unknown to English law which has a

---

3 *High Authority v C O Elettromeccaniche Merlini* [1964] CMLR 184 at 194.
4 Cases 43, 45 and 48/59 [1960]: ECR 463; Valentine, op. cit., Vol. 2, p. 777.
5 See Amos and Walton, *Introduction to French Law* (3rd edn 1967), pp. 47 et seq.

single concept of contract. Thus in English law whether a contract is between John Brown and Bill Smith or between John Brown and the Department of the Environment or between John Brown and the National Coal Board all will be subject to the jurisdiction of the High Court. But in French law, which makes a distinction between the public sphere and the private, contracts to which at least one of the parties is a *personne morale de droit public* tend to be subject to the jurisdiction of the administrative courts, whereas contracts between private individuals or *personnes morales de droit privé* are subject to the jurisdiction of the ordinary civil courts. This jurisdictional distinction is thus reflected in Community law.

Since 1 January 1973, and by virtue of s. 2 (1) of the European Communities Act 1972, the Communities have enjoyed corporate status under the laws of the United Kingdom. But this was no innovation, for such a status is already enjoyed by other international organisations of which the United Kingdom is a member under the terms of the International Organisations Act 1968. That Act makes it possible for a special statutory status of a body corporate to be conferred upon such organisations[6].

Given that it is the Communities themselves which possess legal personality and not the individual institutions, this raises the practical question of how the Communities are represented in law. The Treaties answer this question. In the case of the ECSC art. 6 of the Treaty provides that 'the Community shall be represented by its institutions, each within the limits of its powers'. This has been interpreted in the sense that the ECSC may be represented by its institutions each within the limits of the field of competence given it by the Treaty. The Court of Justice has also held that the term 'institutions' means the institutions named in the Treaty and does not include the departments into which those institutions may be divided for administrative purposes[7]. In the cases of the EEC and Euratom the position is much simpler since, at art. 211 and art. 185 of their Treaties respectively, it is stated that 'the Community shall be represented by the Commission'. This is a role which the Commission, with its expert Legal Service, is particularly well equipped to fill.

While the Communities enjoy an extensive legal capacity in the

6 Cf. Bridge, J. W., 'The United Nations and English Law' (1969) 18 I & CLQ at 694 and 702.
7 Case 66/63: *Netherlands Government v High Authority of the European Coal and Steel Co* [1964] ECR 533, [1964] CMLR 522.

territories of the member states, they also enjoy privileges and immunities of the type usually accorded to the premises and officers of the international organisations. Article 28 of the Merger Treaty provides that that the European Communities shall enjoy in the territories of the member states 'such privileges and immunities as are necessary for the performance of their tasks'. The terms and conditions of those privileges and immunities are set out in a Protocol annexed to the Merger Treaty. The Protocol provides that the premises, buildings and archives of the Communities shall be inviolable[8]. The assets and revenues of the Communities shall be exempt from taxation[9]. Customs duties and restrictions shall not apply to either goods intended for official use or to Community publications[10]. The official communications of the Communities shall enjoy the treatment accorded to diplomatic missions and shall not be subject to censorship[11]. The members and servants of Community institutions shall be issued with *laissez-passer* for the purposes of travel[12]. The members of the Assembly shall enjoy freedom of movement to and from the meetings of the Assembly and their opinions expressed or votes cast in the course of Assembly proceedings shall not be the subject of inquiry or legal proceedings[13]. Both representatives of the member states taking part in the work of Community institutions and the officials and servants of such institutions shall enjoy the customary privileges and immunities. The Community Court, distinguishing between private and official business, held in *Sayag v Leduc*[14] that a Euratom official, not being employed as chauffeur by the Commission, was not entitled to immunity in respect of liability arising from a road traffic accident caused whilst carrying guests of the Commission in his own car.

The diplomatic missions of non-member states to the Communities shall equally enjoy such privileges and immunities[15]. Finally, the Protocol stresses that all these privileges, immunities and facilities are accorded solely in the interests of the Communities and that immunity should be waived whenever waiver is not contrary to Community interests[16].

8 Protocol on Privileges and Immunities, arts. 1 and 2.
9 Ibid., art. 3.     10 Ibid., art. 4.
11 Ibid., art. 6.     12 Ibid., art. 7.
13 Ibid., arts. 8–10.
14 Ibid., arts. 11–16; see Case 5/68: *Sayag v Leduc* [1968] ECR 395; [1969] CMLR 12. Case 9/69: *Sayag v Leduc* [1969] ECR 329.
15 Ibid., art. 17.
16 Ibid., art. 18. Cf. Bridge, op. cit., at 694 et seq.

(B) INVOLVEMENT OF NATIONAL LAW

The laws of the member states also impinge on the life of the Communities in connection with contractual and non-contractual liability[17]. As far as the contractual liability of the Communities is concerned it is governed by the law applicable to the contract in question. Thus contracts of employment with the Community are subject to the Staff Regulations[18] (formerly Statute of Service) whilst other contracts to which one of the Communities is a party are subject to the proper law of the contract, i.e. the relevant national law[19]. In practice clauses are inserted in the latter type of contract with the object of conferring upon the Community Court jurisdiction to hear disputes arising from such cases. The Community may be sued but it also may sue for breach of contract[20].

In the case of non-contractual liability the Treaties[1] provide that 'the Community shall, in accordance with the general principles common to the laws of the member states, make good any damage[2] caused by its institutions or by its servants in the performance of their duties'. Thus the Court of Justice is required to apply these general principles as an additional source of law in much the same way that the International Court of Justice can resort to 'the general principles of law recognised by civilised nations' as a source of international law[3].

A fundamental question which arises here is whether in order to be recognised and applied by the Court of Justice such general

17 EEC, art. 215 (1); EAEC, art. 188 (2), ECSC, art. 40 (3).
18 Council Regulation 259/68 (JO L56 of 4 March 1968, as subsequently amended; consolidated text JO C12 of 24 March 1973; cf. Case 31/72: *Angelini v European Parliament* [1973] ECR 403; Case 18/74: *Syndicat Général du Personnel des Organismes Européens v EC Commission* [1974] ECR 933, [1975] 1 CMLR 144.
19 Case 23/76: *Luigi Pellegrini and CSAS v Commission and Flexon-Italia SpA* [1976] ECR 1807, [1977] 2 CMLR 77.
20 See *EC Commission v CO DE MI Costruzioni SpA (Milan)* now before the CCJ; Europe 1/2 February 1982, No. 3300 p. 14.
1 EEC art. 215 (2); ECSC art. 40 (2); EAEC art. 188 (2) Lord Mackenzie Stuart, 'The Non-Contractual Liability of the European Economic Community' (1975).
2 Cf. Cases 5, 7 and 13-24/66 *Kampffmeyer v EC Commission* [1967] ECR 262, (1967-68) 5 CML Rev 208; Case 153/73: *Holtz and Willemsen GmbH v EC Council and Commission* [1974] ECR 692, [1975] 1 CMLR 91; Case 169/73: *Compagnie Continentale France v EC Council*, [1975] ECR 117, [1975] CMLR 578; Case 74/74: *Comptoir National Technique Agricole (CNTA) SA v EC Commission* [1975] ECR 533. Case 83/76: *Bayerische HNL Vermehrungsbetriebe GmbH & Co KG v EC Council and Commission* [1978] ECR 1209, [1978] 3 CMLR 566.
3 See art. 38 (1) (c) of the Statute of the International Court of Justice.

principles must be known to the municipal laws of all the member states. Certainly in connection with the International Court of Justice such an exacting condition has not been applied. Sir Hersch Lauterpracht has defined general principles of law as 'those principles of law, private and public, which in contemplation of the legal experience of civilised nations lead one to regard as obvious maxims of jurisprudence of a general and fundamental character'[4]. Thus the International Court of Justice must enquire of 'the way in which the law of States representing the main systems of jurisprudence regulates the problem in the situations in question[5]'. The Court of Justice of the Communities has adopted a similar approach. As one commentator has put it, 'whilst it is not necessary ... that *all* states concerned agree on a certain principle of law, it is equally true that such a principle must not merely exist in the law of one country or only in a minority of legal systems ... [It] is not desirable to have a *brouillard* consisting of diverse national legal systems, but rather an adequate solution which is germane to the legal order of the Communities. This result will be reached only after thorough comparative analysis of the legal systems. To the extent that such research reveals a common core, it is not unlikely that the solutions adopted will readily be approved by the member states in their national laws as well'[6]. Thus in the words of Advocate-General Lagrange the spirit which has guided the Court has been 'not simply [to] take a more or less arithmetical average of the different municipal solutions, but [to] choose those solutions from among the various legal systems prevailing in the different member states as, having regard to the objectives of the Treaty, appeared to it the best or, if one may use the word, the most progressive[7]'.

In recent years the ECJ has made a similar use of general principles of law for the interpretation of Community law and the recognition of human rights[8]. The Court has interpreted its duty to

4 *International Law, being the Collected Papers of Hersch Lauterpacht* (1970), Vol. I, p. 69.
5 Ibid., p. 71. For an account of the practice of the International Court also, see ibid., pp. 68–77.
6 Lorenz, K., 'General Principles of Law: Their Elaboration in the Court of Justice of the European Communities' (1964) 13 AJCL at 9, 10, 11.
7 Case 14/61: *Hoogovens v High Authority* [1963] CMLR 73 at 85, 86, [1963] ECR 231.
8 See generally Pescatore, P., 'Fundamental Rights and Freedoms in the System of the European Communities' (1970) 18 AJCL 343; Zuleeg, M., 'Fundamental Rights and the Law of the European Communities,' (1971) 8 CML Rev 446; Bridge, J. W., et al, *Fundamental Rights* (1973), Chapter 20.

ensure that the law is observed as permitting it to apply as part of Community law a body of unwritten, fundamental legal principles which are common to the national legal and political systems of the member states. The function of these fundamental principles in the Community legal order is, in the words of Advocate-General Duth-eillet de Lamothe, 'to contribute to forming that philosophical, political and legal substratum common to the member states from which emerges through the case law an unwritten Community law, one of the essential aims of which is precisely to ensure respect for the fundamental rights of the individual[9].' The Court has demonstrated its willingness to test the validity of Community acts against such criteria[10].

## 3 The external relations of the Communities

(A) THE INTERNATIONAL PERSONALITY AND CAPACITY OF
THE COMMUNITIES

It has already been pointed out that the Communities have person-ality and capacity under international law. Their personality and capacity may be classified as of the functional sort referred to by the International Court of Justice in its advisory opinion in the *Reparation for Injuries* Case[11]. That is to say that the Communities at international law have the degree of personality and capacity which is necessary to enable them to carry out their functions on the international plane. This general view is substantiated by the terms of the Treaties themselves.

Article 6 of the ECSC Treaty states clearly that 'in international relations the Community shall enjoy the legal capacity it requires to perform its functions and attain its objectives'. The EEC and Euratom Treaties, on the other hand, merely state that the Com-munities have legal personality but do not refer to any specific attribution of capacity in international law[12]. Nevertheless such

9 Case 11/70: *Internationale Handelsgesellschaft GmbH v Einfuhr-und Vorratsstelle für Getreide und Futtermittel* [1970] 2 ECR 1125 at 1146, [1972] CMLR 255 at 271.
10 See p. 133, post.
11 ICJ Reports 1949, 174. See generally Henig, S., *External Relations of the European Community* (1971) and Costonis, J. J., 'Treaty Making Powers of the EEC' (1967) European Yearbook 31; Coffey, P., *The External Relations of the EEC*, (1976); Soldatos, P., 'La politique extérieure' in Lasok, D. and Soldatos, P., *Les Communautés Européennes en Fonctionnement.* (1981) p. 477 et seq.
12 EEC Treaty, art. 210 and Euratom Treaty, art. 184.

latter capacity may not only be inferred from the nature of the Communities as the creatures of treaties but it has also been expressly confirmed by the Court of Justice in its judgment in the *Re ERTA, EC Commission v EC Council*[13]. There the Court observed that art. 210 of the EEC Treaty, by stating that the Community has legal personality, 'means that in its external relations the Community enjoys the capacity to establish contractual links with non-member States over the whole field of the objectives defined in Part One of the Treaty[14]'.

An examination of the EEC Treaty reveals numerous provisions concerned in one way or another with external relations. Article 3 (*k*) provides that the purposes of the Community are to be achieved in part through 'the association of the overseas countries and territories in order to increase trade and to promote jointly economic and social development'. This theme is taken up by article 131, whereby the member states agree to associate with the Community their former colonial possession with whom they have maintained a special relationship subsequent to independence. A similar agreement has been reached on the association of the non-European territories maintaining special relations with the United Kingdom and the Anglo-French Condominium of the New Hebrides[15]. Articles 111–116 contain provisions concerned with trading relations between member and non-member states. Articles 228–231 and 238 provide for the conclusion of agreements and maintenance of relations between the Community and both non-member states and international organisations. It is clear from article 238 that any such agreements must be compatible with the Treaty, and if not the Treaty must first be amended in accordance with the terms of article 236 in order to accommodate such an agreement. This has also been confirmed by the Court which has held that in order 'to determine in a particular case the Community's authority to enter into international agreements, one must have regard to the whole scheme of the Treaty no less than to its specific provisions[16]'. Article 228 (1) is equally clear on this point and enables the Council, the Commission or a member state to obtain a prior opinion from the Court of Justice on the compatibility of a proposed agreement with the terms of the Treaty. Where the opinion of the Court is

---

**13** Case 22/70 [1971] 1 ECR 263, [1971] CMLR 335.
**14** [1971] CMLR 335 at 354.
**15** See Act annexed to Treaty of Accession, art. 117.
**16** [1971] CMLR 335 at 354.

adverse the Treaty must be amended before the agreement in question may enter into force[17].

## (B) THE CONDUCT OF THE EXTERNAL RELATIONS OF THE COMMUNITIES

The authority to conclude agreements between the Communities and non-member states or international organisations is, in all cases, vested in the Council, although the other institutions do have a role to play. Under the terms of article 238 of the EEC Treaty agreements establishing an association, involving reciprocal rights and obligations, between the Community and a third state, a union of states or an international organisation shall be concluded by the Council, acting unanimously after consulting the Assembly. Somewhat similarly applications by Europeans states for full membership of the Community under the terms of article 237 shall be addressed to the Council which shall act unanimously after obtaining the opinion of the Commission. In connection with the negotiations for the admission of the United Kingdom, Ireland, Denmark and Norway the Commission suggested in its Opinion of 1 October 1969 that the negotiations should be divided into two phases: the first to be conducted by the Commission on behalf of the Community and subject to the directives of the Council; the second to be conducted by the Council in the light of the results of the first phase. The Council rejected the Commission's suggestion and decided that the conduct of the negotiations with the candidate states should be in the hands of the Council, after the Council, acting upon a proposal from the Commission, had settled the joint position of the Communities on the problems raised by the negotiations. The business of the Council in connection with the negotiations was prepared by the Committee of Permanent Representatives[18]. In these negotiations the role of the Commission upon the instructions of the Council was (i) to submit possible compromise solutions to particular problems; (ii) to explain the scope of Community law to the delegations of the candidate countries; (iii) to act as a go-between between the Council and

---

**17** See Opinion 1/75: *Re the OECD Understanding on a Local Cost Standard*
[1976] 1 CMLR 85; Opinion 1/76: *Re the Draft Agreement on European Laying-up Fund for Inland Waterway Vessels* [1977] ECR 741, [1977] 2 CMLR 279; Opinion 1/78: *Re Draft Convention of the International Atomic Energy Agency on the Physical Protection of Nuclear Materials, Facilities and Transport* [1978] ECR 2151, [1979] 1 CMLR 131; Opinion 1/78: *Re Draft International Agreement on Natural Rubber* [1979] ECR 2871, [1979] 3 CMLR 639.
**18** See *Bulletin of European Communities* (1970) Part 8 at 115-16.

candidate countries in the resolution of key political issues; and (iv) to study and report on the technical and linguistic problems facing Community law as a consequence of the enlargement of the Communities[19].

Although the role of the Commission in the procedure for the admission of new member states is only a subsidiary one it is given a leading role in those cases where the EEC Treaty provides for the conclusion of agreements between the Community and one or more states or an international organisation. Article 228 (1) provides that while such agreements shall be concluded by the Council, after consulting the Assembly where the Treaty so requires, the negotiations shall be conducted by the Commission. The respective roles of the Commission and Council under the terms of article 228 (1) have been settled in Court[20] in the ERTA case.

In January 1962, under the auspices of the UN Economic Commission for Europe, a European Road Transport Agreement (ERTA) was signed by a number of European States including five of the members of the Community. That Agreement has not yet come into force because of an insufficient number of ratifications. In 1967 negotiations were resumed to revise the ERTA. In 1969 the Council of the Communities made a regulation dealing with the harmonisation of certain social provisions in the field of road transport. In March 1970 at a meeting of the Council the attitude to be taken by the member states of the Communities in the final stage of the ERTA negotiations to be held in April 1970 was discussed. Those negotiations were then undertaken and concluded by the member states in the light of that discussion and the Economic Commission for Europe declared that the ERTA would be open for signature from July 1970. In May 1970 the Commission of the Communities instituted proceedings seeking an annulment of the Council's discussion of March 1970 on the grounds that the Council had acted in breach of article 228 of the EEC Treaty. This challenge raised the whole issue of the relative roles of Council and Commission in the conduct of the Community's external relations.

The Court stated that under article 228 the right to conclude an agreement with non-member states lay with the Council, with the Commission cast in the role of negotiator. But those institutions could only play those roles under the authority of either an express

---

**19** See the Commission's Report, *The Enlarged Community* (1972) at 22–24.
**20** Case 22/70: *Re ERTA* op. cit.

Treaty provision or a decision taken under the Treaty[1]. The bulk of the negotiations for the ERTA had been concluded before the Community had a developed transport policy, therefore the Community as such had no authority to negotiate and ratify the ERTA. At the time of the Council discussions which were in issue, the ERTA negotiations had already reached such an advanced stage that it would have jeopardised the whole Agreement to have attempted to re-open them. Thus the Court held that the procedures specified in article 228 were clearly inapplicable. The only obligation on the member states was to ensure that nothing was done to prejudice the interests of the Community and so that the Council in co-ordinating the attitudes of members states to the ERTA in the light of Community interests had acted quite properly[2]. Thus even where the provisions of the Treaties are not directly applicable to the external relations of the member states they are nevertheless under a continuing obligation, under the terms of article 5 of the EEC Treaty, to 'abstain from any measure which could jeopardise the attainment of the objectives of the Treaty'.

(C) THE ESTABLISHED EXTERNAL RELATIONS OF THE COMMUNITIES

This capacity to enter into external relations which has been described above has been frequently exercised by the Communities, particularly in the case of the EEC. Firstly, in connection with individual states, the Communities have entered into both association and external trade agreements. The purpose of an association agreement is to create a customs union as between Community members and the associated state with, in some cases, the provision of financial loans to the associated state and in others the extension of other Community benefits such as rights of establishment. Such association agreements have been entered into with Greece, Turkey, Malta, Cyprus, Morocco and Tunisia, which, in the former two cases, by progressive stages were intended to lead to full membership of the Communities. In fact Greece has become the tenth member of the Community as from 1 January 1981. Spain and

---

1 The Court also pointed out that where the Council and Commission are acting by virtue of such authority the member states have no right to act individually in such a matter: [1971] CMLR 335 at 355.
2 It was also pointed out that the Commission had not exercised its right under arts. 75 and 116 to make proposals concerning the ERTA negotiations: [1971] CMLR 335 at 361, 362.

Portugal are currently engaged in negotiations with a view to full membership.

External trade agreements have been concluded with a number of states. These usually provide for preferential reductions in Community tariffs in relation to such states. Some of these agreements, such as those with India, Pakistan and Switzerland are limited to certain sorts of goods; other, such as those with Israel, Spain and Yugoslavia, are more general in scope.

By virtue of the terms of Article 108 of the Act of Accession, from the date of accession the new member states must apply the terms of the agreements with Greece, Turkey, Tunisia, Morocco, Israel, Spain and Malta. This obligation is subject to the transitional measures and any specially negotiated adjustments which may prove to be necessary.

In addition to these bilateral agreements, multilateral association agreements have been entered with those non-European states which have a special relationship with the member states. These agreements have been designed to promote the economic and social development of those countries and to establish economic links between them and the Community as a whole, such as giving their exports preferential treatment by bringing them within the European customs union. On a provisional basis a form of association was set up by a convention annexed to the EEC Treaty. That was replaced in 1964 by a new Association Convention signed by 18 independent Associated African States and Madagascar. The Convention was signed at Yaoundé, the capital of Cameroon. The original Yaoundé Convention lasted five years and was replaced in 1969 by the Second Yaoundé Convention which remained in force until January 1975. The precedent of the Yaoundé Convention was applied to three Anglophonic countries of East Africa, Kenya, Uganda and Tanzania, in what was known as the Arusha Convention which was signed at Arusha in Tanzania in 1968 and renewed in 1969. The terms of the Arusha Convention were broadly similar to the Yaoundé Convention subject to the important difference that there was no provision for financial aid.

In February 1975 a new agreement was concluded at Lomé, the capital of Togo[3]. This agreement, known as the Lomé Convention replaces both the Second Yaoundé and Arusha Conventions and establishes an association between the Community and 46 African,

---

3 For the text of the Convention see *Encyclopedia of European Community Law*, Vol. BII, p. B 12475.

Caribbean and Pacific States including 21 members of the British Commonwealth. The Convention remained in force until March 1980 and was subject to renegotiation. It established three institutions, a Council of Ministers, a Committee of Ambassadors and a Consultative Assembly to direct the relations between the Community and the Associated States. Any disputes arising under the Convention were initially referred to the Council of Ministers and, as a last resort, to a specified arbitration procedure. The terms of the Convention gave free entry to the Community, without reciprocity, to goods from the Associated States; financial aid principally in the form of grants to develop small and medium sized industries; and stabilise the export earnings of the Associated States by protecting them against fluctuations in commodity prices.

In 1979 a new Lomé Convention[4] came into force. It now embraces 63 countries. It is an improved version of Lomé I in so far as the existing structural framework has been consolidated, the machinery for consultations and commercial and industrial co-operation made more efficient and trade and financial arrangements further expanded.

In addition to having relations with non-member states the Communities have established relations with a number of international organisations. Relations are maintained with the United Nations and particularly those of its specialised agencies concerned with economic affairs. An agreement for the exchange of information and for technical assistance has been made with the ILO. Through the Commission the Communities engage in tariff negotiations within GATT. The Commission is represented at inter-governmental meetings of the Council of Europe and there is an annual joint session of the Assembly of the Communities and the Consultative Assembly of the Council of Europe. The Commission also participates in the work of the OECD. The Community has also negotiated free trade area agreements with the remaining EFTA countries (Austria, Switzerland, Finland, Sweden, Portugal, Norway and Iceland)[5]. For some time contact has also been maintained with the East European Council for Mutual Economic Co-operation (Comecon) with a view to finding a common platform for trade between the two European economic organisations. Thus in these

---

4 For full text and comments see The Courrier No. 58, Special Issue November 1979; see also Kirkpatrick, C. H., 'Lomé II' (1980) Jo of World Trade, p. 352 et seq.
5 See EFTA *EFTA Bulletin*, No 8 (1972) and Nos 5 and 8 (1973).

various ways mutually advantageous links are established with other international and European organisations.

## (D) EFFECT UPON MEMBER STATES

In the ERTA case the ECJ held that whenever the Community has acted within its jurisdiction the member states no longer enjoy a 'concurrent right'[6]. This has a double effect: on the one hand the member states lose their freedom of independent action and on the other acquire rights and obligations by proxy as if they themselves have concluded the given transactions. Since treaties are a source of law in the Community[7] they may impinge upon the member states' legal order. However that legal order remains in force until the obligation to bring it in line with the Community Law has been imposed[8].

A Community Treaty may also, under the principle of direct applicability, affect the rights of individuals even vis à vis their own country. Thus it was held that a Belgian wine importer could invoke the Association Agreement with Greece in order to protect himself against a countervailing charge levied upon his imports[9]; a French fruit importer could rely on the Yaoundé Convention not only to have his case referred to the ECJ under article 177 of the EEC Treaty but also to defeat the preference of his government for suppliers of bananas from former French colonies[10]; and an Italian importer of hide was afforded protection from the imposition of a charge equivalent to a customs duty under the same Convention[11].

In the British jurisdiction judicial notice was taken of the EEC-Portugal Free Trade Agreement of 1972 as the Court of Appeal[12] held that it was enforceable under section 2 (1) of the European Communities Act 1972. However the Court referred to the ECJ the question whether article 14 of the EEC-Portugal Agreement

---

6 Op. cit. at 355, reiterated in the Advisory Opinion 1/75: *Re OECD Understanding on a Local Cost Standard* [1976] 1 CMLR 85.

7 See p. 87 et seq post.

8 Case 3/76: *Officier Van Justitie v Kramer* [1976] ECR 1279, [1976] 2 CMLR 440.

9 Case 181/73: *Haegeman v Belgian State* [1974] ECR 449, [1975] 1 CMLR 515.

10 Case 48/74: *Charmasson v Minister for Economic Affairs and Finance* [1974] ECR 1383, [1975] 2 CMLR 208.

11 Case 87/75: *Bresciani v Amministrazione delle Finanze* [1976] ECR 129, [1976] 2 CMLR 62.

12 *Polydor Ltd and RSO Records v Harlequin Record Shops Ltd* [1980] 2 CMLR 413.

prohibiting quantitative restrictions on imports and exports had a direct effect so as to prevail over section 16 (2) of the UK Copyright Act 1956. The ECJ,[13] citing its own judgment in the *Terrapin*[14] case, held that the enforcement by the proprietor of the copyright protected by national law was justified within the terms of article 23 of the EEC—Portugal Agreement which provided that ... 'The Agreement shall not preclude prohibitions or restrictions on imports, exports or goods in transit justified on grounds of ... the protection of industrial and commercial property....' Therefore the enforcement did not constitute any restriction on trade envisaged in article 14 (2) of the said Agreement. Clearly the relationship between the EEC and Portugal did not create a 'common market' or a complete customs union and the case had to be distinguished from the cases cited in the preceding paragraph. Two points must be borne in mind in this context, i.e. that a Community Treaty must be read in its entirety and that its effects upon the rights of individuals depend upon its nature and scope.

Article 234 of the EEC Treaty guarantees respect for the rights and obligations arising from the member states's agreements concluded with third parties before their entry into the Community but imposes upon them a duty to eliminate from such agreements any incompatabilities with their membership of the Community. This spells out a duty to revise such obligations as soon as the opportunity arises but at the same time guarantees the protection of vested rights. Thus the ECJ[15] conceded that article 234 did not alter the nature of private rights or duties, derived from pre-membership or pre-accession Treaties between the EEC countries and non-member states. It held, accordingly, that the London Fisheries Convention of 1964 which governs maritime relations between Eire and Spain prevailed over Community Law under article 234. Since, however, national law was held to be applicable in the circumstances the penalties for illegal fishing prescribed by it were not incompatible with the interim regime imposed by Council Regulation 1376/78 designed to provide a framework of the relations between Spain and the Community.

---

13 Case 270/80: [1982] 1CMLR 677.
14 Case 119/75: *Terrapin (Overseas) Ltd v Terranova Industrie CA Kapferer & Co* [1976] ECR 1039 at 1061, [1976] 2CMLR 482 at 506.
15 Case 812/79: *Attorney General A-G v Burgoa* [1980] ECR 2787, [1981] 2 CMLR 193.

Chapter 3

# The nature and challenge of Community law

## 1 The meaning of Community law

It is axiomatic that a body which itself is a distinct legal entity will have its own law either infused into its forms by a superior legislator or generated by its organs or both. In the Community legal order both elements are present: the law of the Treaty and the law generated by the Community organs. Moreover, a certain area of the law will be enacted by the member states themselves in accordance with the Treaty and, although this law is, strictly speaking, a product of the sovereign legislatures of the member states it should be included in the wider concept of Community law[1]. These are the dimensions of Community law in the light of its sources. However, before analysing the sources of Community law it seems necessary to consider its nature and scope. This is particularly important from a British point of view, bearing in mind that at accession there was a wholesale reception of Community law and that since accession we have participated in a legislative process which differs consider-. ably from our own.

Community law defies the accepted classifications of law; it is both international and municipal, public and private, enacted and formulated in precedents. It is a *sui generis* law and must be treated as such. Therefore it has to be studied in its international setting with due attention to its impact upon the laws of the member states and the quasi-autonomous law-making capacity of the Community organs.

The three Communities, being a result of Treaties, are subject to public international law but constitute their own legal order. The treaty obligations are defined in terms of duties of states vis-à-vis

1 The Second European conference of Law Faculties held in April 1971 in Strasbourg under the aegis of the Council of Europe recommended that the authorities in member states be urged to introduce or reinforce the teaching of (1) the law of European Organisations, (2) the substantive law created by or within European Organisations, and (3) the law of European States.

the contracting parties and the Community itself whilst the rights and obligations of individuals derive directly from the Treaties. Therefore Community Law is to the member states both 'external' (i.e. derived from outside) and 'internal' (i.e. in force in their territories).

The execution of the Treaties is in the hands of the Community organs and the Community Court has the exclusive power of authoritative interpretation of the Treaties (art. 177 (1)).[2] Disputes between states (art. 182) and complaints against states (arts. 169 and 170) are resolved judicially in a manner appropriate to inter-state relations rather than relations between private parties where the court exercises a sovereign authority. In other words, unlike individuals who have no choice, states submit to the jurisdiction of the Court either by agreement (art. 182) or by virtue of treaty obligations. Indeed article 219 expressly provides that disputes between the member states arising from the interpretation and application of the Treaty must be resolved according to the methods provided in the Treaty. In adjudicating upon disputes in which states are involved the Court, like the International Court of Justice, determines the legal position of the parties and recommends, rather than orders, the state in default to take the necessary measures to comply with the judgment (art. 171). The sanctions are also limited (arts. 169 and 171) and appropriate to the status of states at international law. The cardinal rule of public international law that states, large and small, are equal applies in principle within the Community though in the government of the Community consideration is given to the size of the member states.

However, the Community, as stated by the Community Court,[3] 'constitutes a new legal order in International law for whose benefit the states have limited their sovereign rights, albeit within limited fields, and the subjects of which comprise not only the member states but also their nationals'. It corresponds to the territorial law of a state.

By incorporation of the Treaties into the municipal law of the member states Community law becomes part of the internal legal structure of the member states. Moreover, under the doctrine of the approximation of laws a wide area of economic law will, in due

---

2 Unless otherwise stated references are to articles of the EEC Treaty.
3 In Case 26/62: *Van Gend en Loos v Nederlandse Administratie der Belastingen* [1963] ECR I at 29, [1963] CMLR 105 at 129.

course, become uniform throughout the Community. This in a sense will become both Community and municipal law of the member states. It is apposite to mention in this context the conflict of laws or private international law. It is a system of rules designed to facilitate enforcement of foreign judgment and to solve problems which involve a foreign element and, therefore, in justice and convenience cannot be left to the exclusive power of domestic law. Each country has its own conflict rules. However, the primary object of the Community is cohesion. This is achieved partly by incorporation of Community law into the municipal systems and partly by approximation of laws in the areas of a specific Community interest. In this way it is expected conflicts will be eliminated. Outside the scope of Community law the member states are left to their own devices as to how to solve the problems arising from the co-existence of several systems of law, though the Community promotes a rational approach to jurisdiction and the enforcement of foreign judgments in the territory of the member states (art. 220)[4]. A process of approximation of substantive rules of the Conflict of Laws has begun with a Draft Convention on the Law applicable to Contractual and Non-Contractual Obligations[5] but so far progressed towards a Draft Convention on the Law applicable to Contractual Obligations[6]. Approximation in other fields has been slow and haphazard[7].

The once (so it seemed)[8] clear-cut distinction between public and private law has been blurred in the course of time. If we consider that public law is concerned with the organisation of the state and the relations between the citizen and the state whilst private law governs relations between individuals and/or corporations we shall observe that Community law contains both elements. It has an impact upon the constitutions and public powers of the member states, it is concerned with the creation of a supra-national organisation out of the pooled sovereignty of the member states and brings the citizen politically and in his economic activities face

---

4 Cf. Convention on Jurisdiction and the Enforcement of Judgments in Civil and Commercial Matters 1968.

5 Lando, O., et al. *European Private International Law of Obligations* (1975).

6 For text, see [1979] 2 CMLR 776.

7 See p. 407 et seq post; see also Lasok, D. *The Law of the Economy in the European Communities* (1980), pp. 393 et seq.

8 Publicum jus est, quod ad statum rei Romanae spectat, privatum quod ad singulorum utilitatem: sunt enim quaedam publice utilia, quoadem privatim, *Digesta* 1, 1, 1, 2; cf. Llewellyn, K., *The Bramble Bush* (1960), p. 18.

to face with a supra-national authority and a new 'European' allegiance. Private law relations (and here we can safely discard the controversy whether 'commercial law' is 'private law' or a separate branch of the law) are affected too but only to a degree, that is to say in so far as the economic policies enforced by Community law impinge upon such relations. As legal machinery is used for the execution of the economic policies enshrined in the Treaty some aspects of Community law can be described for the want of a better term as 'economic law' or the law of the economy. This phenomenon, characteristic of the Community, will be considered in detail[9]. The bulk of private law relations comprised in the law of contract, tort, property, family relations and succession remains outside the scope of Community law. So does criminal law, though criminal sanctions will have to be developed in order to check abuses of the Community system[10].

True to the civil law tradition the corpus of Community law has been laid down in treaties and derivative legislation but it would be a mistake to assume that precedent plays no active role in the Community law-making process. We shall discuss the sources of Community law in detail and it may suffice to say that the Community Court, like the French Counseil d'Etat upon which it has been modelled, often has an opportunity of explaining the law and laying down rules in precedents and it has not refrained from using this power. As practice develops the Community Court tends to follow its own decisions in the spirit of *jurisprudence constante*[11] but will not hesitate to deviate for good reason[12]. And so the Court considers itself free to decide in a different way the same legal point if it arises between different parties and in a different context[13].

Without attempting a definition of Community law (which, incidentally, cannot be found in the Treaties) we should reiterate that Community law consists of that portion of public international law which governs treaties and international institutions, of the Treaties and their Annexes, of the rules generated by the

9 See Part IV, below.
10 See Bridge, J. W., 'The European Communities and the Criminal Law', *Criminal Law Review*, February 1976, p. 88.
11 E.g. Case 32/58: *Aciéries du Temple v High Authority of the European Coal and Steel Community* [1959] ECR 127.
12 E.g. Case 48/72: *Brasserie de Haecht v Wilkin-Janssen* [1973] ECR 77, [1973] CMLR 287.
13 E.g. Cases 28–30/62: *Da Costa en Schaake NV v Nederlandse Administratie der Belastingen* [1963] ECR 31, [1963] CMLR 224.

Community organs and those portions of the municipal laws of the member states which they are bound to enact in the execution of their obligations. These are not distinct branches but merely the dimensions of Community law.

## 2 Legal styles

Community law is a new legal order but to a British lawyer it is also an alien order because it has emanated from the civil law systems and, despite the British participation in the legislative process, remains under the civil law influence. This does not necessarily mean that it is inferior or oppressive, as has been suggested from time to time in the passion of debate, but that it is simply different from ours. It should be borne in mind that in its background lies the philosophy of sophisticated, long-established legal systems and the will to create a Community through legal integration of which the enacted law is the preferred instrument. Being intertwined with the legal systems of the founder states Community law cannot be isolated from these but historically and philosophically has to be seen as a child of civil law.

In order to make a valid comparison between civil law and common law and thus elicit some general features of the Community legal system it will first be necessary to debunk some popular myths. There is in England some, albeit unfounded, aversion to codes of law and even the Code Napoléon, of which the French are justly proud, does not escape criticism as if no branch of English law had been codified or codification had not been the long-term aim of the Law Commission. Critics believe that codes of law stultify the growth of the law and turn it into a pool of stagnant water whilst common law for ever remains a stream of fresh water. Forgetting that codes are essentially a work of compromise they assume that they are the tools of autocracy. Moreover, it is readily assumed that, whilst in this country we are governed by the wisdom of judges contained in precedents, the continentals are denied this privilege and, because of their rejection of *stare decisis*, suffer from the uncertainty of the law. It would be futile to recite the various misconceptions and try to rebut them. What has to be recognised is the fact that the origins and the evolution of the civil law and common law systems happen to differ and that as a result two different legal styles have developed. Comparative studies help one to understand these differences but not being engaged in a comparative study we have to content ourselves with few generalities. Because we have joined the Community as a going concern, with a legal system well on its way, the British lawyer has to face the unprecedented challenge of the continental legal style[14].

Codes of law are not mere comprehensive, systematically arranged statutes. In a sense they are also codes of morals for in their legal institutions, especially general principles of the law, they offer guidelines to a way of life. The law tends to proceed from general principles to particular rules of conduct and so the administration of justice tends to be deductive rather than inductive. Contrast the British fragmentary legislation and tightly drafted statutes which, according to Lord Scarman[15], 'are elaborate to the point of complexity; detailed to the point of unintelligibility; yet strangely uninformative on matters of principle'. The English administration of justice tends, therefore, to be inductive, so much so that one can say that we have a system of remedies established by precedent and statute rather than a plain statement of rights and duties from which remedies can be deduced. Community law follows this latter style as it tends to prescribe the right conduct for governments and individuals and grants remedies in the event of deviation.

The codes of law, being systems of generalities provide but a façade for case law, because decided cases are the real witness of the living law. However, in view of the supremacy of legislation and the constitutionally limited power of judges to adjudicate not *legislate*, precedents have only a persuasive authority and cannot be cited as the source of law or superior authority. The theory that codes have no gaps enables the courts to legislate by way of extensive interpretation from analogy or simply through *equitas*. The European Court of Justice is in a similar position though its scope for legislative activities is wider than that of the civil courts of the member states.

In England the judge comes, as a rule, from the Bar and remains a member of his Inn of Court even when elevated to the Bench. On the Continent the judge is a product of special training and a judicial career, he stands aloof from the Bar and resembles more an

14 See Lord Denning MR in *H P Bulmer Ltd v J Bollinger SA* [1974] 2 All ER 1226 at 1231–1232, [1974] 2 CMLR 91 at 119 and 120; Scarman, Sir Leslie, *English Law: The New Dimension*, Hamlyn Lectures, Twenty-sixth Series, 1974, p. 21 et seq.
15 BBC Third Programme, *The Listener*, 9 January 1969, pp. 44–46.

academic lawyer than an advocate. The English administration of justice has a strong personal flavour because as a rule the judge sits alone and delivers a personal judgment of 'his court'. In the Court of Appeal or the House of Lords, though no longer alone, he still delivers his personal, concurring or dissenting, judgment which often conceals an advocate in judicial robes. The continental judge as a rule, sits as a member of a team, does not deliver his individual judgment whether or not he agrees with the judgment of his brethren and so preserves a kind of judicial anonymity. The European Court of Justice is a 'continental' court in all respects, sits as a team and delivers a single judgment. It is assisted by advocates-general (an office unknown in this country), whose functions shall be considered elsewhere[16].

The style of the administration of justice is greatly influenced by the scope and rules of judicial interpretation. As compared with their continental brethren and the European Court, English judges seem to have a narrower scope in the field of interpretation. The *Bosch*[17] case is a good illustration. Whilst our judges are not allowed to study the '*travaux préparatoires*', that is the materials and debates in Parliament leading to the passing of legislation, in order to find out the mind of the legislature, the continental judges are allowed to do so and base their judgment on their study. The *Bosch* case involved cartel agreements under article 85 of the EEC Treaty and Regulation 17 which implemented articles 85 and 86 of the Treaty. More precisely the question was whether or not article 85 came into effect before Regulation 17. The Dutch court of the first instance ruled that article 85 was not operative before Regulation 17 was made; the Court of Appeal referred the case to the Community Court under EEC article 177 and the plaintiff appealed to the Dutch Supreme Court. The final ruling was that it was the intention of the EEC that article 85 shall not be operative until the appropriate machinery has been created and so Bosch, though involved in a restrictive practice, had not at that time contravened Community law. An English Court would have accepted article 85 without considering the purpose of the delegated legislation embodied in Regulation 17 and probably decided against Bosch.

**16** See chapter 9.

**17** Case 13/61: *Robert Bosch GmbH v Kledingverhoopbedrijf de Geus en Uitdenbogerd* [1962] ECR 95, [1962] CMLR 1; D. Thompson, 'The Bosch Case' (1962) 11 ICLQ 721; Case 14/70: *Deutsche Bakels GmbH v Oberfinanzdirektion München* [1970] 2 ECR 1001, [1971] CMLR 188; Case 42/72: *Alfons Lütticke GmbH v Hauptzollamt Passau* [1973] ECR 57 at 74-75, [1973] CMLR 309 at 316-317.

Another attribute of the continental courts is the power to resort to teleological interpretation of codes and statutes which enables them to apply old law in the context of social change or give the rules of law a dynamic and functional effect[18]. In this country (perhaps with the exception of the House of Lords) courts have no such power and, indeed, should an iconoclast judge venture into such practices he would soon find his judgments overruled by higher courts. The Community Court, it seems, enjoys this attribute of judicial power in the best traditions of continental courts and, having established in authority, does occasionally resort to this kind of interpretation. Unlike literal interpretations the Court puts into the mouth of the legislator the meaning of words he should have used rather than words he has actually used to express his intention[19].

The Courts' role is much coloured by the rules of procedure. The predominant feature of continental procedural law is the inquisitorial system. This system places a heavy duty on the court to enquire into the facts of the case in order to ascertain the objective truth. Unlike the English judge the continental judge is not an impartial umpire watching the contest of the parties and seeing merely that the rules of the game are observed. The inquisitorial system requires a greater involvement of the court which, among others, manifests itself in the examination of witnesses and parties by the judge. Although the inquisitorial powers have not been expressly spelt out in the foundation Treaties they can be found in the Protocol on the Statute of the Court of Justice[20] and the Rules of Procedure. It is clear that the European Community Court functions like any continental court and this involves a tight control of the proceedings, powers to require parties to produce documents

18 Cf. Pescatore, P., Interpretation of Community Law and the Doctrine of Acte Clair, in Bathurst, M., et al. (editors) *Legal Problems of an Enlarged European Community*, 1972, 27 at pp. 32–34.

19 E.g. Case 14/63: *Forges de Clabecq v High Authority* [1963] ECR 357, [1964] CMLR 167; Case 9/73: *Schlüter v Hauptzollamt Lorrach* [1973] ECR 1135 at 1153; Case 6/72: *Europemballage Corpn and Continental Can Inc v EC Commission* [1973] ECR 215, [1973] CMLR 199; Case 8/73: *Hauptzollamt-Bremerhaven v Massey-Ferguson* [1973] ECR 897; Case 37–38/73: *Sociaal Fonds voor de Diamant Arbeiders v N V Indiamex and Association defait De Belder*, [1973] ECR 1609; Case 151/73: *Government of Ireland v EC Council* [1974] ECR 285 at 296 and 297; [1974] 1 CMLR 429 at 446–447. Most prominent examples of teleological interpretation include Van Gend, op. cit; Case 93/71: *Leonesio v Italian Ministry of Agriculture and Forestry* [1972] ECR 287, [1973] CMLR 343; Case 43/75: *Defrenne v SABENA* [1976] ECR 455, [1976] 2 CMLR 98.

20 EEC Statute, arts. 21, 22, 26, 28; ECSC Statute, arts. 24, 25, 28 (3), EAEC Statute, arts. 22, 23, 27, 29; Rules of Procedure, present codified version OJ 1982, C39. arts. 47 (1), 77, 94.

and supply the information the court deems necessary as well as the examination of witnesses and parties by the court.

Other salient features of continental procedure are the predominance of written pleadings which contain mainly legal arguments, hence the art of written advocacy somewhat similar to our Chancery proceedings; the absence of drama in court engineered in this country by the public examination and cross-examination of witnesses. Oral procedure consists of the hearing of any witnesses or experts followed by succinct summary of the main points submitted by the advocates of each party to the proceedings. Then follows a collective judgment of the court, after due deliberations in private, usually read in open court on the appointed day together with other judgments. The report of the court is brief and concise based on the draft prepared by the Reporting judge. All the features of a civil law court are attributable to the European Community Court and offer a challenge our lawyers have to meet in Community practice.

## 3 The challenge of Community law

Because of its wide dimensions, Community law offers a challenge to three types of lawyers: lawyers in government service, lawyers in commerce and industry, and lawyers in private practice.

The three Communities fashioned and worked their institutions through civil servants drawn from the member countries. Since policies enshrined in the foundation Treaties had to be carried out through the instrumentality of legal machinery and since legal studies are regarded, on the Continent, as the most appropriate background for the civil service, it is not surprising that lawyers form a considerable proportion of the European bureaucrats. These lawyers have managed to overcome the language barriers and have acquired a community spirit. Through working together with those who initiate and carry into effect the various policies they have developed their own style. They have also perfected the skill of working with non-lawyers and as a supra-national bureaucracy they have become a force to be reckoned with. After all, they draft the various rules and regulations which by virtue of the Treaty obligations become the municipal law of the member states. The enlarged Community provides an opportunity for the newcomers to contribute to the growing body of Community law. The national impact will always depend on the quality of the civil servants detailed to the Community service.

The task of the lawyer in commerce and industry is different from that of the Community lawyer and those who are engaged as managers, administrators and legal advisors need little adaptation. Large corporations, already straddling several countries, have perforce become international and Community-minded. They are most likely to draw on local talent and gear their activities to their respective fields of operation. Their lawyers would by now have acquired the essential skills and will keep abreast of the developments of Community law and the relevant areas of the domestic law of the member states. Their main interest lies in the economic directions of the Community and the impact of these directions in the member states in addition to the fiscal and business laws of the member states. More particularly they are likely to encounter problems arising from the law of corporations, restrictive practices, establishment, movement of persons, social security and labour relations, taxation, trade marks and patents, movement of goods and capital, agriculture, bankruptcy, sale of goods and agency in addition to the mass of the Community rules and regulations which affect investments and commercial operations in their various ramifications. Whilst the importance of Community law for commercial operations must not be underrated, it has to be borne in mind that the role of the corporation lawyer is somewhat limited. In more complex cases, especially litigation, his employers will rely on the services of lawyers in private practice with whom, no doubt, he will co-operate in the initial stages.

The most formidable is the challenge of Community law in the field of practice of the law in a strictly professional sense. Broadly speaking the lawyer's work consists of consultancy, litigation and all sorts of paper work where drafting skills take precedence over counselling and advocacy. Two aspects can be distinguished here: the conduct of legal business from a home base or agency abroad, and practice before the Community Court and the national courts of the member states.

The greater proportion of legal business is conducted on home ground and in this respect no difficulty should arise given a knowledge of Community law and its effect in this country. In the context of Community law the solicitor may have to advise his British clients on matters affecting their position here or abroad or foreigners on matters of English law and Community law applicable to foreigners in this country. In most cases he will be on familiar ground at home, but far more challenging is the prospect of advising clients on Community matters abroad because these matters have to be considered in the light of the Community and the municipal law of the country concerned. Specialisation is needed and firms of solicitors practising in this field will establish close relations with foreign practioners or open branches abroad. Undoubtedly skilled people are needed to man the branch or do the liaison work. An agency system, on the basis of reciprocity, may develop as the cheaper and more effective method. In the initial stage the most essential is the classification of the business into domestic and Community matters and, where necessary, the engagement of a specialist.

Turning now to a more daunting, though not impossible proposition: article 52 of the Treaty of Rome gives lawyers the 'right of establishment' on the basis of free movement within the Community. So far this right has not resulted in a migration of lawyers within the Community simply because the practice of law is essentially national. However, difficulties have come to light because admission to practise is, in most countries, governed by law and restrictive practices of the profession. In accordance with article 52 (2) the Community Court held, in *Reyners v The Belgian State*[1], that a Dutch national living in Belgium and having appropriate Belgian professional qualifications was unlawfully excluded from the exercise of the profession of *avocat* on the ground that according to Belgian law only Belgian nationals were admitted to practice. The principle was applied to remove a disqualification on the ground of the lack of habitual residence of a Dutch lawyer who lived in Belgium but wished to practise in the Netherlands[2]. The same ruling was made with regard to a Belgian who acquired French professional qualification and wished to practise in Paris[3]. However a Madagascan national with French legal qualification could not rely on the Lomé Convention in order to practise at the French Bar[4].

Assuming that we continue with the divided profession, there is at present no rule to prevent an alien, as an alien, becoming a

---

1 Case 2/74: [1974] ECR 631, [1974] 2 CMLR 305.
2 Case 33/74: *J H M Van Binsbergen v Bestuur van de Bedrijfsvereniging voor de Metaalnijverheid* [1974] ECR 1299, [1975] 1 CMLR 298.
3 Case 71/76: *Thieffry v Conseil de l'Ordre des Avocats à la Cour de Paris* [1977] ECR 765, [1977] 2 CMLR 373.
4 Case 65/77: *Re Jean Razanatsimba* [1977] ECR 2229 [1978] 1 CMLR 246.

member of the Bar. Solicitors, allegedly on the basis of s. 3 of the Act of Settlement 1701 (which declared aliens incapable of enjoying certain offices or places of trust) and a counsel's opinion of some vintage and doubtful weight, had to be British subjects but this discrimination has now been removed[5]. As far as practice is concerned solicitors must observe the general code of their profession whether they handle 'domestic' or 'foreign' business. A foreign lawyer wishing to practise in England and Wales must, subject to professional qualifications, elect to practise either as a barrister or a solicitor. He cannot do both. A British solicitor cannot enter into a partnership with a foreign lawyer in England and Wales but may do so abroad subject to local rules. He may however allow his foreign associate to have a seat in his office[6].

Under the freedom of establishment British lawyers are entitled to set up in practice abroad on an equal footing, their success depending, of course, on their proficiency in foreign and Community law. There is a theoretical and practical side to it. In theory the right of establishment and the principle of non-discrimination apply. By article 52 of the EEC Treaty the freedom of establishment included the right to engage in and carry on self-employed occupation under the conditions laid down by the law of the country of establishment for its own nationals. The treaty is clear—free movement of persons—but how does it affect lawyers? Article 60 (1) (*d*), defining the term 'service', refers to 'liberal professions' and this, traditionally, includes the legal profession. But lawyers are, in some respect, involved in the administration of justice which is a public process and an excercise of the authority of the state, not just commercial enterprise or service with which the Common Market is concerned. English solicitors are designated as 'Officers of the Supreme Court' and barristers are supposed to be helping the court in its work. German *Rechtsanwälte*, who combine the work of the English barrister and solicitor and are engaged more in litigation than conveyancing, are too 'officers of the court'. The French have a diversified profession but those who are involved in court work are regarded as 'auxiliaries of justice' or of 'tribunals'. The *avocats*, who are the aristocracy of the French legal profession may be called to the Bench or replace public prosecutors, so there is too a considerable involvement in the administration of justice.

5 Solicitors' Amendment Act 1974, s. 1; Solicitors' Act 1974, s. 29.
6 Further details, *Law Society's Gazette*, Vol. 70 (1973), p. 1568.

One can, of course, envisage difficulties[7], e.g. in France and Germany only specially appointed lawyers may appear before the Supreme Court; in England the position is rather complicated because of the relations between the two branches of the profession and the existence of Queen's Counsel and Juniors. To face these problems the Bar Council[8] has relaxed the rules by allowing a barrister to accept a brief from a foreign lawyer directly without the intermediary of an English solicitor and a Queen's Counsel to act without a Junior in Community matters. However these rules apply only to 'foreign work' and are not meant to change the nature of the practice at the Bar in England and Wales or allow the barrister to do the solicitor's work. A barrister may enter into any association including partnership with any lawyer (except solicitors practising in the UK) for the purpose of sharing any office or services abroad but in the UK cannot undertake work not normally performed by a practising barrister in England and Wales, receive or handle client's money or accept the status of an employee or of a commercial agent or business agent.

In December 1975 an agreement[9] between the Paris Bar and the English Bar was made to the effect that members of one may appear and plead before the Courts of the other provided they are led by members of the local Bar. In England and Wales this rule applies to all courts where only barristers may plead. This arrangement may well lead to similar bi-lateral agreements between the English Bar and the corresponding branches of the profession of the remaining member states of the Community.

Discrimination and restrictive practice apart the stumbling block to the harmonisation of the legal profession is the lack of recognition of professional qualifications obtained abroad. Pending the solution of this problem Council Directive 77/249[10] was passed to 'facilitate the effective exercise by lawyers of freedom to provide services'. Since there is as yet no mutual recognition of diplomas and profes-

---

7 See Case 138/80: *Re Jules Borker* [1980] ECR 1975, [1980] 3 CMLR 638 and *Public Prosecutor of Cologne v Lischka et al.* (Cologne Court of Appeal) [1981] 2 CMLR 189.

8 *Law Society's Gazette*, Vol. 68 (1971), pp. 187, 193, 194; Vol. 70, p. 1568; Vol. 71, p. 378; *Guardian Gazette*, 27 April 1974, p. 114.

9 *Times*, December 1975; the relationship between the Paris Bar and the Law Society of England and Wales is governed by an agreement signed on 12 April 1976. In *R v Tymen* [1981] 2 CMLR 544, the British judge expressed his appreciation of the skill with which the French advocate pleaded his client's case in English.

10 J 1977, L 78/17, see European Communities (Service of Lawyers) Order 1978.

sional qualifications the persons to whom the Directive applies must qualify and obtain the professional title used in the member state in which they intend to become established. In the spirit of the Directive the Consultative Committee of the Bars and Law Societies of the European Community (CCBE) has introduced as from October 1978, lawyers' 'Euro-Cards' to enable their holders to identify themselves before the national authorities as the persons qualified to practise the law. This is a general rule which does not exclude bilateral arrangements across the frontiers.

In view of the difficulties experienced with the present arrangements the Consultative Committee agreed in October 1980 upon a draft directive to provide for the reciprocal recognition of diplomas and relevant professional qualifications and to clarify the practice rules. Accordingly a distinction between 'enrolled' and 'established' lawyers is to be made. The former will include lawyers in practice enrolled with the Bar or Law Society of the state in which they have qualified; the latter will comprise lawyers qualified in one state who seek to practise in another state. The 'established' lawyers are to have the basic right to practise in the Community but the member states may exclude them from certain functions which reflect the peculiarities of national systems, e.g. the preparation of documents relating to the transfer of interests in land or obtaining title to administer estates. They may also exclude them from practising in or giving advice on their national law generally or provide that an 'established' lawyer representing a client in court must act in conjunction with an 'enrolled' lawyer but these restrictions may be imposed only to the extent to which they are 'objectively' justified in the public interest[11].

Practice before the Community Court presents its own problems. The Court was set up largely on the pattern of the French Conseil d'Etat. Its jurisdiction includes supervision over the execution of the Treaties, adjudication of disputes between member states, control of legality of the acts of the Community Institutions and the interpretation of the Treaty and Community legislation. Its procedure is French with some German admixtures. In the main the proceedings are conducted in writing and this emphasises the importance of the art of 'written advocacy' as a feature of the continental legal style. Since the existing practice was not changed to accommodate British lawyers, new skills have to be learned and unusual difficulties overcome. The case law approach of the Court

---

11 Leach, P., *Law Society's Gazette*, 28 January 1981, p. 103.

in developing the Community law is a hopeful sign but should not lull us into a sense of false security.

As for the right of audience before the Community Court—some rules have been laid down in article 17 of the Protocol on the Statute of the Court of Justice. This provides that parties must be represented by a lawyer entitled to practise before a court of one of the member states and this includes also university teachers if, as in Germany, they have the right of audience before the national courts. The operative words are not very clear: the French version refers to 'avocat inscrit à un barreau de l'un des Etats membres'; the German to 'ein Anwalt, der in einem Mitgliedstaat zugelassen ist'. This would mean that English solicitors could appear before the Court during the whole process, written and oral, provided they have the right of audience before the courts in this country. Since their audience is limited at present, the question appears still open.

# 4 The language of Community law

Language is the main tool in the legal workshop and it is common ground that each legal system has its own technical language. So it is with Community law. Within the Community of the Six the problem of the legal language was magnified sixfold as lawyers from the six countries tried first to frame the Treaty and then establish a common interpretation of the texts of Community law. In the enlarged Community the problem has been further magnified and has been complicated through the accession of two common law countries and Greece.

The problem of language has a special bearing upon the legislative process, the interpretation and administration of the law and harmonisation of national laws. It will be considered in relation to these three areas.

### (A) THE TREATY AND COMMUNITY LEGISLATION

The Treaty of Rome was drawn up in a single document in the German, French, Italian and Dutch languages, all four texts being equally authentic[12]. By contrast the ECSC Treaty is in one authentic version in the French language.

---

**12** Art. 248; the languages are listed in alphabetical order in accordance with the French nomenclature of the four countries.

The Treaty of Brussels concerning the accession of Denmark, Ireland, Norway and the United Kingdom was also drawn up in a single document in the Danish, Dutch, English, French, German, Irish, Italian and Norwegian languages, all eight texts being equally authentic[13]. The same principle was adopted on the accession of Greece, Greek being the ninth authentic Treaty language.

This is an accepted form of a multi-lateral, multi-lingual treaty for which the United Nations Charter is one of the outstanding precedents. The effect of the formula 'equally authentic' is that all texts, having an equal status, can be cited as the authoritative statement of the law and that no one text takes precedence over the others. This does not solve the problem of the discrepancies in the various texts which inter se are nothing but translations. With the greatest care and skill expended on the formulation of treaties discrepancies are inevitable because the translation of a legal text is not merely a matter of language. The question of interpretation of authentic texts which reveal a discrepancy in the meaning of words attributable to legal concepts and institutions resolves itself into the question of the intention of the parties. The rule of international law, which has evolved to deal with this problem, is that there is a presumption against an interpretation which is contrary to any one of the equally authentic texts. It follows that it is necessary to find a meaning which is compatible with all the texts. In order to achieve this object it is necessary first to establish the meanings of each text and then select the meaning which is not contrary to any particular text. A practical illustration of the application of this rule is the *Mavrommatis* case[14], in which the Permanent Court of International Justice explained that 'when considering two equally authentic texts, one of which appears to have a wider meaning than the other it is the duty of the Court to apply the narrower text since such an interpretation is compatible with both texts and, no doubt, corresponds to the common intention of the parties'.

In *Fédération Charbonnière de Belgique* v *High Authority*[15] the Community Court considered the argument that the ECSC Treaty being an international treaty was subject to restrictive interpretation and broadly agreed with the principle, though it

---

13 Art. 3; the languages are listed in alphabetical order according to Cmnd. 4862, but since Norway failed to ratify the Treaty there are in the Community six official languages; see Adaptation Decision, art. 2. and seven since the admission of Greece.
14 [1927] PCIJ Rep Ser A, No. 2, p. 12.
15 Case 9/55: [1954-1956] ECR 311.

considered that rules of interpretation used in both international law and national laws were perfectly acceptable. However, in later cases a broader formula has evolved. In *Milchwerke Heinz Wöhrmann & Sohn KG v EC Commission*[16] Advocate-General Roemer submitted that where three texts revealed a clear meaning but the fourth was inconsistent with them the latter should follow suit. In *de Geus v Bosch*[17] Advocate-General Lagrange submitted that where all four texts conveyed different meanings the Court should decide the issue according to the spirit of the text. In *Mij PPW Internationaal NV v Hoofdproduktschap voor Akkerbouw-produkten*[18], concerning the issue of certificates for export refunds, the Court held that no argument could be drawn either from any linguistic discrepancies between the various texts or from the number of the verbs used in one or other version because the meaning of the relevant provisions had to be determined in the light of their objectives.

Moreover in a case[19] concerning the application of rules governing the grant of aid for skimmed milk the ECJ held that ... 'the elimination of linguistic discrepancies by way of interpretation may in certain circumstances run counter to the concern for legal certainty in as much as one or more of the texts involved may have to be interpreted in a manner at variance with the natural and usual meaning of the words. Consequently it is preferable to explore the possibilities of solving the point at issue without giving preference to any one of the texts involved.' However where the word 'spouse' used in all other languages was rendered into Dutch as 'wife'[20] the ECJ preferred a 'sexually neutral construction' meaning either 'wife' or 'husband', as the case may be, thus giving weight to legislative policy rather than language and ensuring at the same time uniformity throughout the Community.

Since the Treaties of Paris, Rome and Brussels are 'self-executing' there is no need of their being 'transformed' by statute into the domestic law of the member states. Consequently, as far as the authentic texts are concerned, the Treaties have to be taken as they stand. The danger of producing a different text for the purpose of

16 Case 31 and 33/62: [1962] ECR 501, [1963] CMLR 152.
17 Case 13/61: [1962] ECR 45, [1962] CMLR 1 at 23.
18 Case 61/72: [1973] ECR 301; see also (re family allowances) Case 6/74: *Moulijn v EC Commission* [1974] ECR 1287.
19 Case 80/76: *North Kerry Milk Products Ltd v Minister for Agriculture and Fisheries* [1977] 2 CMLR 769 at 781.
20 Case 9/79: *Wörsdörfer (née Koschniske) v Raad van Arbeid* [1979] ECR 2717, [1980] 1 CMLR 87.

legislation, not uncommon in the process of translation of inter-national conventions, has been excluded. This does not solve the problem of Community law in the countries whose language has not been included in the authentic texts or, as in the case of the United Kingdom, countries which have subsequently adhered to the Treaties. The general rule of international law may be too narrow and so the spirit rather than the letter of the Treaty should prevail.

In their endeavour to give effect to the common intention of the parties comprised in a multi-lingual treaty the draftsmen try to exclude discrepancies and potential conflicts of interpretation but this is quite an impossible task. The end product must be a com-promise if not a synthesis of the systems involved. Where this is impossible they have to choose consciously the technical language which seems most appropriate or most commonly used or the language of the legal system which has the greatest influence in the deliberations. The Treaties unmistakably bear the imprint of French Law for the French have the uncanny knack of assisting the international law making process with their texts as the starting point of deliberations and, hopefully, the wording to be adopted. However the ECJ needs not to be perturbed by textual discrepan-cies for, in the best traditions of continental jurisprudence, it can rely on teleological interpretation. In other words, when in doubt, the spirit rather than the letter of the law should prevail thus giving weight to the legislative policy aimed at by the law maker. Or, as put by Judge Kutscher[1] ... 'the difficulties of interpretation arising from the multi-lingual nature of Community law are frequently resolved not through a grammatical interpretation but by resorting to an examination of the objects of the provision and its place in the system of the Treaty' ... Indeed committed to a dynamic and evolutionary interpretation of Community law[2] the Court on its own admission 'cannot ... be content with a literal interpretation ...'[3] Moreover the objective envisaged may prompt a liberal inter-pretation as was, e.g. the case of 'identification' of persons on social security to their entitlement of butter at reduced price without injury to their pride[4].

1 Kutscher, H., *Methods of Interpretation as seen by a Judge at the Court of Justice*, Judicial and Academic Conference 27-28 September 1976, p. 20.
2 Ibid., p. 39.
3 Case 6/60: *Jean E Humblet v Belgian State* [1960] ECR 559.
4 Case 29/69: *Stauder v City of Ulm* [1969] ECR 419, (paras 4 and 5), [1970] CMLR 112.

This attitude appears to be reflected in certain dicta of Lord Denning MR[5] who, in his iconoclastic way, may have given the impression that teleological interpretation should be adopted generally, not merely in respect of Community law. When referring to an English statute which incorporated the International Convention on the Carriage of Goods by Road 1956, he said that 'by interpreting the Treaty of Rome ... we must certainly adopt the new approach'[6]. For that he was duly rebuked since ... 'membership of the EEC does not involve abandonment of national construction of multi-lateral conventions ...'[7] No doubt this is correct as regards international treaties other than the Community Treaties. However, taken out of context, the dictum that ... 'no assistance from methods said to be used in interpreting the Treaty of Rome by the European Court of Justice ...'[8] may become a source of mischief. There is no way of denying that Community law, whether comprised in Treaties or derivative legislation, is a *sui generis* law and has to be interpreted by national courts in the light of the jurisprudence of the Community Court. Should there be a difficulty in this respect the matter ought to be referred to the Community Court for a preliminary ruling under article 177 of the EEC Treaty.

Whilst the Treaty is a 'once and for all' exercise the Community legislation is a continuous process. The techniques have already been perfected through common effort of the Community lawyers and here, perhaps, the lawyer no longer feels a champion of his own system (which, as every lawyer knows, is the best system in the world!) or suffers under the limitations of his national training and the inhibitions acquired from his legal language becoming his second nature. The newcomers to this task are at a certain disadvantage and their contribution initially must perforce be rather limited. This is a special practical challenge to the British civil servant joining the legal service of the Community.

Article 191 (1), (2) of the EEC Treaty provides that 'regulations shall be published in the Official Journal of the Community' and that 'directives and decisions shall be notified to those to whom they are addressed'. At first the *Official Journal* was published in Dutch, French, German and Italian but article 155 of the first Act

5 *H P Bulmer Ltd v J Bollinger SA* [1974] Ch 401 at 419–425.
6 *James Buchanan Co Ltd v Babco Forwarding and Shipping (UK) Ltd* [1977] 2 CMLR 455 at 459, CA.
7 Ibid., [1978] 1 CMLR 156 at 161, HL.
8 Ibid.

of Accession, as amended by the Adaptation Decision, provided that 'the texts of the Acts of the Institution of the Community adopted before the accession and drawn up by the Council or the Commission in the Danish and English languages shall, from the date of accession, be authentic under the same conditions as the texts drawn up in the four original languages'[9]. The same principle was adopted in article 147 of the second Act of Accession regarding Greece.

Since directives and decisions have to be 'notified' but, apparently, need not be 'published' difficulties arose in the past[10] and these prompted the Community Court to suggest that publication be improved. As a result directives and decisions are now, as a rule, published in the *Official Journal*.

Let us turn now to some specific pitfalls of the technical language of Community law, problems known only too well to British translators of the Community texts who soon discovered that 'corresponding' legal terms in two languages seldom correspond *exactly*[11].

In the drafting of conventions the generalisations about the civil law system are brought to the test and, usually, to grief. Illusions of the oneness of the system based on Roman Law and codes are quickly exposed and we are left with a vague notion of a common core of the law, a common historical heritage, and a similarity of styles. As in a large family there are traces of common genes but also manifestations of mutations and acquired differences. As in a family the stronger members prevail and so one can trace in multi-lingual texts the influence of a particular system. It is not surprising that the French legal language provides a starting point for the consideration of the problems of language in the Community texts.

The student of Community law must from the start familiarise himself with the problem of language known only too well to the student of comparative law. Examples from the EEC Treaty, given below, have already tested translators and commentators of the texts and in some cases exercised the minds of judges because they present linguistic as well as conceptual teasers.

9 Reg. 857/72 of 24 April 1972 establishing special editions of the Official Journal; JO L 101, 1972.
10 Joined Cases 73 and 74/63: *Internationale Crediet-en Handelsvereniging 'Rotterdam' NV v Minister van Landouw en Visserij* [1964] ECR 1 at 13–14 [1964] CMLR 198; Case 69/69: *Alcan v EC Commission* [1970] 1 ECR 385 at 396, [1970] CMLR 337 at 340.
11 Hall, D. F., 'Translating the Treaties', *European Review*, Spring Issue 1972; Héraud, G., 'La Communauté Européenne et La Question Linguistique' (1981) 5 *Rev d'Integration Européenne*, 5 et seq.

Parallel French and English Official Texts (Figures in brackets refer to articles of the Treaty)

| | |
|---|---|
| mission (2) | task[12] |
| action (3) | activities |
| tâches (4) | tasks |
| buts (5) | objectives[13] |
| règlementation (7) | rules |
| a le droit (8) | shall be entitled |
| instance d'arbitrage (8) | arbitration board |
| marchandises (9) | goods[14] |
| produits (9) | products[15] |
| en provenance (9) | coming from[16] |
| ristourne (10) | drawback |
| arrêtant (10) | adopting |
| droits de douane (11) | customs duties |
| perception (15) | collection |
| perception douanière (17) | customs receipts |
| faculté (17) | right |
| réduction des entraves aux échanges (18) | lowering of barriers to trade[17] |
| mise en place (23) | introduction |
| contingents (25) | quotas |
| concurrence (29) | competition |
| moralité publique (36) | public morality[18] |
| ordre public (36) | public policy[19] |
| sécurité publique (36) | public security |
| monopoles nationaux (37) | state monopolies[20] |

---

12 Case 6/72: *Europemballage Corpn and Continental Can Co Inc v EC Commission* [1973] ECR 215 at 244; Case 36/74: *Walrave and Koch v Association Union Cycliste Internationale* [1974] ECR 1405, [1975] 1 CMLR 320.

13 Case 2/73: *Riseria Luigi Geddo v Ente Nazionale Risi* [1973] ECR 865 at 878; Case 34/73: *Variola SpA v Amministrazione Italiana delle Finanze* [1973] ECR 981 at 991; Case 31/74: *Filippo Galli* [1975] ECR 47, [1975] 1 CMLR 211.

14 Case 8/73: *Hauptzollamt Bremerhaven v Massey-Ferguson GmbH* [1973] ECR 897 at 907; Case 155/73: *Guiseppe Sacchi* [1974] ECR 409.

15 *Geddo etc.*, op. cit.; *Variola etc.*, op. cit.

16 Case 39/73: *Rewe-Zentralfinanz GmbH v Direktor der Landwirtschaftskammer Westfalen-Lippe* [1973] ECR 1039 at 1043-1044; Case 179/78: *Procureur de la République v Rivoira* [1979] ECR 1147, [1979] 3 CMLR 456.

17 Cases 37-38/73: *Sociaal Fonds voor de Diamantarbeiders v NV Indiamex and Association de fait de Belder* [1973] ECR 1609 at 1622-1623.

18 Case 34/79: *R v Henn and Darby*, [1979] ECR 3795, [1980] 1 CMLR 246.

19 Case 7/78: *R v Thompson* [1980] QB 229, [1978] ECR 2247.

20 Case 6/64: *Costa (Flaminio) v ENEL* [1964] ECR 585; Case 83/78: *Pigs Marketing Board v Redmond* [1978] ECR 2347, [1979] 1 CMLR 177.

| | |
|---|---|
| formation professionnelle (41) | vocational training[1] |
| vulgarisation agronomique (41) | dissemination of agricultural knowledge |
| règlements (43) | regulations[2] |
| directives (43) | directives[3] |
| décisions (43) | decisions[4] |
| marché national (43) | national market[5] |
| restrictions quantitatives (44) | quantitative restrictions |
| prix minima (44) | minimum prices |
| échanges (44) | trade |
| marché commun (44) | common market |
| majorité qualifiée (44) | qualified majority |
| régime (44) | system |
| accords ou contrats (45) | agreements or contracts |
| marché intérieur (45) | domestic market[6] |
| marché mondial (45) | world market |
| organisation nationale du marché (46) | national market organisation[7] |
| règlementation interne (46) | internal rules |
| taxe compensatoire (46) | countervailing charge |
| sortie (46) | export |
| rétablir l'équilibre (46) | redress the balance |
| recours (46) | measures |
| travailleurs (48) | workers[8] |
| libre circulation (48) | freedom of movement[9] |
| discrimination (48) | discrimination[10] |

1 Case 2/74: *Reyners v Belgian State* [1974] ECR 631 at 648; Case 33/74: *J H M van Binsbergen v Bestuur van der Bedrijfsvereniging voor de Metaalnijverheid* [1974] ECR 1299, [1975] 1 CMLR 298; Case 39/75: *Coenen et al v Sociaal Economische Raad* [1975] ECR 1547, [1976] 1 CMLR 30.
2 Cases 16–17/62: *Confédération Nationale des Producteurs de Fruits et Légumes v EEC Council* [1962] ECR 471 at 476–479; Case 10/73: *Rewe-Zentral AG v Hauptzollamt Kehl* [1973] ECR 1175 at 1190.
3 Case 28/67: *Molkerei-Zentrale Westfalen/Lippe GmbH v Hauptzollamt Paderborn* [1968] ECR 143.
4 Case 25/62: *Plaumann & Co v EEC Commission* [1963] ECR 95 at 106–108.
5 Case 48/74: *Charmasson v Minister for Economic Affairs and Finance (Paris)* [1974] ECR 1383, [1975] 2 CMLR 208.
6 Ibid.    7 Ibid.
8 Case 61/65: *Vaasen-Göbbels v Beambtenfonds voor het Mijnbedrijf* [1966] ECR 261, [1966] CMLR 508; Case 152/73: *Sotgiu v Deutsche Bundespost* [1974] ECR 153 at 162–165.
9 Case 41/74: *Van Duyn v Home Office* [1975] Ch 358, [1974] ECR 1337.
10 Case 36/74: *Walrave and Koch v Association Union Cycliste Internationale* [1974] ECR 1405.

| | |
|---|---|
| santé publique (48) | public health |
| dispositions législatives (48) | law |
| dispositions règlementaires (48) | regulations |
| dispositions administratives (48) | administrative action |
| administration publique (48) | public service[10a] |
| administrations ... du travail (49) | employment ... services |
| niveau de vie (49) | standard of living |
| sécurité sociale (51) | social security[11] |
| leurs ayants droit (51) | dependants[12] |
| totalisation (51) | aggregation[13] |
| droit aux prestations (51) | right to benefit |
| liberté d'établissement (52) | freedom of establishment[14] |
| agences (52) | agencies |
| succursales ... filiales (52) | branches ... subsidiaries |
| ressortissants (52) | nationals[15] |
| activités non salariées (52) | activities as self-employed |
| gestion d'entreprises (52) | manage undertakings |
| sociétés (52) | companies |
| travailleurs salariés (54) | [wage-paid] workers |
| travailleurs non salariés (54) | self-employed persons |
| propriétés foncières (54) | land and buildings |
| organes de gestion ou de surveillance (54) | managerial or supervisory posts |
| à titre occasionnel (55) | occasionally |
| autorité publique (55) | official authority |
| prescriptions (56) | provisions |
| régime spécial (56) | special treatment |
| siège statutaire (58) | registered office |
| but lucratif (58) | profit-making [object] |

10a Case 149/79: *Re Public Employees, EC Commission v Belgium* [1981] 2 CMLR 413.
11 Case 75/63: *Hoekstra-Unger v Bestuur der Bedrijfsvereniging voor Detailhandel en Ambachten* [1964] ECR 177 at 184–186.
12 *Vaasen-Göbbels*, op. cit.
13 Case 92/63: *Nonnenmacher (Moebs) v Bestuur der Sociale Verzekeringsbank* [1964] ECR 281 at 287–289; Case 191/73: *Niemann v Bundesversicherungsanstalt für Angestellte* [1974] ECR 571.
14 *Reyners*, op. cit.; Case 136/78: *Ministére Public v Vincent Auer* [1979] ECR 437, [1979] CMLR 373.
15 Case 19/74: *Donato Casagrande v Landeshauptstadt Münich* [1974] ECR 773 at 778–779; Case 68/74: *Angelo Alaimo v Préfet du Rhône* [1975] ECR 109.

| | |
|---|---|
| prestaire (60) | person providing a service |
| libre circulation des services (61) | freedom to provide services[16] |
| localisation du placement (67) | place where capital is invested |
| emprunts (68) | loans |
| investissement (68) | investment |
| restriction de change (71) | exchange restriction |
| marché des capitaux (73) | capital market |
| domaine des prix (78) | [transport] rates |
| taxes ou redevances (81) | charges or dues |
| frais réels (81) | costs actually incurred |
| navigation maritime et aérienne (84) | sea and air transport[17] |
| entreprises (85) | undertakings[18] |
| prix d'achat ou de vente (85) | purchase or selling prices[19] |
| répartir les marchés (85) | share markets[20] |
| partenaires commerciaux (85) | trading parties[1] |
| usages commerciaux (85) | commercial usages |
| nul de plein droit (85) | automatically void[2] |
| position dominante (86) | dominant position[3] |
| pratiques abusives (86) | abuse[4] |
| non équitable (86) | unfair |
| conditions de transactions (86) | trading conditions[5] |

---

**16** Case 36/74: *Walrave and Koch v Association Union Cycliste International* [1974] ECR 1405.
**17** Case 167/73: *EC Commission v French Republic* [1974] ECR 359, [1974] 2 CMLR 216.
**18** Case 23/58: *Mannesmann AG Hoesch -Werke AG v High Authority* [1959] ECR 117; Case 15/74: *Centrafarm BV v Sterling Drug Inc* [1974] ECR 1147, [1974] 2 CMLR 480.
**19** Case 73/74: *Groupement des Fabricants de Papiers Peints de Belgique v EC Commission* [1975] ECR 1491, [1976] 1 CMLR 589.
**20** Case 56/65: *Société Technique Minière v Machinenbau Ulm GmbH* [1966] ECR 235 at 249; Case 8/72: *Vereeniging van Cementhandelaren v EC Commission* [1972] ECR 977, [1973] CMLR 7; Case 19/77: *Miller International Schallplatten GmbH v EC Commission* [1978] ECR 131, [1978] 2 CMLR 334.
**1** Case 48/69: *Imperial Chemical Industries Ltd v EC Commission* [1972] ECR 619, [1972] CMLR.
**2** *Technique Minière*, op. cit.
**3** Cases 6–7/73: *Instituto Chemioterapico Italiano SpA and Commercial Solvents Corpn v EC Commission* [1974] ECR 223 at 247–255; Cases 40–48, 50, 54–56, 111, 113–14/73: *Suiker Unie UA v EC Commission* [1975] ECR 1663.
**4** Case 127/73: *BRT v NV Fonior: SABAM v NV Fonior; BRT v SABAM and NV Fonior* [1974] ECR 313 at pp. 315–319.
**5** Case 1/70: *Parfums Marcel Rochas Vertriebs GmbH v Bitsch* [1970] ECR 515, [1971] CMLR 104.

| | |
|---|---|
| règlements ou directives utiles (87) | appropriate regulations or directives |
| contrôle administratif (87) | administration |
| ententes (88) | agreements[6] |
| exploitation abusive (88) | abuse |
| infraction présumée (89) | suspected infringement |
| décision motivée (89) | reasoned dicision |
| monopole fiscal (90) | revenue-producing monopoly |
| pratiques de dumping (91) | dumping[7] |
| état membre lésé (91) | injured member state |
| libre pratique (91) | free circulation |
| aides accordées (92) | aid granted[8] |
| régimes d'aides (93) | systems of aid |
| saisir … la Cour (93) | refer … to the Court |
| impositions intérieures (95) | internal taxation[9] |
| taxe sur le chiffre d'affaires (97) | turnover tax[10] |
| taxe cumulative à cascade (97) | cumulative multistage tax system |
| droits d'accise (98) | excise duties |
| exonérations et remboursements (98) | remissions and repayments |
| rapprochement (100) | approximation[11] |
| politique de conjoncture (103) | conjunctural policies[12] |
| matière monétaire (105) | monetary field |
| balance des paiements (106) | balance of payments |
| transactions invisibles (106) | invisible transactions |
| déséquilibre global (108) | overall disequilibrium[13] |
| devises (108) | currency |
| moyens (108) | means |

---

**6** *Ibid.*

**7** Case 13/63: *Italy v EEC Commission* [1963] ECR 165 at 177.

**8** Cases 6–11/69: *EC Commission v France* [1969] ECR 523 at 538–543; Case 78/76: *Steinike und Weinlig v Federal Republic of Germany* [1977] ECR 595, [1977] 2 CMLR 688.

**9** Case 57/65: *Alfons Lütticke GmbH v Hauptzollamt Sarrelouis* [1966] ECR 19 at 26–27; Case 10/65: *Deutschmann v Federal Republic of Germany* [1965] ECR 469; Case 74/76: *Iannelli and Volpi SpA v Meroni* [1977] ECR 557, [1977] 2 CMLR 688.

**10** *Molkerei-Zentralle*, op. cit., p. 69 note 3, ante.

**11** Case 32/74: *Firma Friedrich Haaga GmbH* [1974] ECR 1201, [1975] 1 CMLR 32.

**12** Case 5/73: *Balkan Import-Export GmbH v Hauptzollamt Berlin-Packhof* [1973] ECR 1091; Cases 88–90/75: *Societa SADAM v Comitato Interministeriale dei Prezzi* [1976] ECR 323, [1977] 2 CMLR 183.

**13** *Commission v France*, op. cit., note 8, ante.

| | |
|---|---|
| concours mutuel (108) | mutual assistance |
| détournement de trafic (108) | deflection of trade |
| politique commerciale (110) | commercial policy |
| commerce extérieur (111) | external trade |
| droit syndical (118) | right of association |
| négociations collectives (118) | collective bargaining |
| unité de mesure (119) | unit of measurement |
| congés payés (120) | paid holidays |
| travailleurs migrants (121) | migrant workers |
| situation sociale (122) | social conditions |
| Fonds social européen (123) | European Social Fund |
| organisations syndicales de travailleurs (124) | trade unions |
| rééducation professionnelle (125) | vocational retraining |
| indemnités de réinstallation (125) | resettlement allowances |
| domicile (125) | home |
| résidence (125) | residence |
| Banque européenne d'investissement (129) | European Investment Bank |
| échanges commerciaux (132) | trade |
| Assemblée (137) | Assembly [Parliament] |
| pouvoirs de délibération et de contrôle (137) | advisory and supervisory powers[14] |
| suffrage universel direct (138) | direct universal suffrage |
| règles constitutionnelles (138) | constitutional requirements |
| réunit de plein droit (139) | [shall] meet without requiring to be convened |
| règlement intérieur (140) | rules of procedure |
| suffrages exprimés (141) | votes cast |
| motion de censure (144) | motion of censure |
| gestion (144) | activities |
| abandonner collectivement leurs fonctions (144) | resign as a body |
| dispose d'un pouvoir de décision (145) | have power to take decisions[15] |
| recevoir délégation (150) | act on behalf of |

14 Cases 138–139/79: *Roquette Frères SA v EC Council* [1980] ECR 3333.
15 Case 81/72: *EC Commission v EC Council* [1973] ECR 575; Case 70/74: *EC Commission v EC Council* [1975] ECR 795.

| | |
|---|---|
| statut des comités (153) | rules governing committees |
| formation des actes (155) | shaping of measures |
| exerce les compétences (155) | exercise the powers |
| assure le respect du droit (164) | ensure that . . . the law is observed |
| séance plénière (165) | plenary session[16] |
| chambres (165) | chambers |
| mesures d'instruction (165) | preparatory enquiries |
| saisie par un Etat membre (165) | brought by a Member State |
| questions préjudicielles (165) | preliminary rulings |
| avocats généraux (166) | Advocates-General |
| conclusions motivées (166) | reasoned submissions |
| jurisconsultes (167) | jurisconsults |
| compétences notoires (167) | recognised competence |
| Son mandat est renouvelable (167) | He may be re-elected |
| greffier (168) | Registrar |
| avis motivé (169) | reasoned opinion[17] |
| pleine juridiction (172) | unlimited jurisdiction |
| sanctions(172) | penalties |
| contrôle la légalité (173) | review the legality |
| incompétence (173) | lack of competence |
| violation du . . . traité (173) | infringement of . . . treaty |
| violation des formes substantielles (173) | infringement of an essential procedural requirement |
| détournement de pouvoir (173) | misuse of powers[18] |
| nul et non avenu (174) | void |
| acte contesté (174) | act concerned |
| s'abstient de statuer (175) | fail to act |
| personne morale (175) | legal person |
| faire grief (175) | complain |
| titre préjudiciel (177) | preliminary ruling[19] |
| recours juridictionnel (177) | judicial remedy |
| est tenue (177) | shall bring |
| est compétente (178) | shall have jurisdiction |

16 Cases 28–30/62: *Da Costa en Schaake NV v Nederlandse Belastingadministratie* [1963] ECR 31 at 37–39.
17 Case 45/64: *EEC Commission v Italy* [1965] ECR 857; Case 70/72: *EC Commission v Federal Republic of Germany* [1973] ECR 813.
18 See p. 80, post.
19 See Chapter 10.

| | |
|---|---|
| litige (179) | dispute[20] |
| agents (179) | servants |
| connaître des litiges (180) | shall ... have jurisdiction in disputes |
| délibérations (180) | measures |
| violation des formes (180) | non-compliance with the procedure |
| clause compromissoire (181) | arbitration clause |
| différend (182) | dispute |
| compromis (182) | special agreement |
| soustraits à la compétence (183) | excluded from the jurisdiction |
| moyens (184) | grounds |
| effet suspensif (185) | suspensory effect |
| acte attaqué (185) | contested act |
| mesures provisoires (186) | interim measures[1] |
| ont force exécutoire (187) | shall be enforceable |
| forment titre exécutoire (192) | shall be enforceable |
| exécution forcée (192) | enforcement |
| formule exécutoire (192) | order for ... enforcement |
| vérification de l'authenticité du titre (192) | vertification of the authenticity of the decision |
| caractère consultatif (193) | advisory status |
| règlements financiers (209) | financial regulations |
| ordonnateurs et comptables (209) | authorising officers and accounting officers |
| personnalité juridique (210) | legal personality |
| capacité juridique (211) | legal capacity[2] |
| ester en justice (211) | [be] a party to legal proceedings |
| fonctionnaires et agents (214) | officials and ... servants |
| responsabilité contractuelle (215) | contractual liability |
| dans l'exercice de leurs fonctions (215) | in the performance of their duties |
| régime linguistique (217) | rules governing the languages |
| double imposition (200) | double taxation |
| sociétés (220) | companies or firms |
| décisions judiciaires (220) | judgments |

---

20 Case 18/74: *Syndicat Général du Personnel des Organismes Européens v EC Commission* [1974] ECR 933.
1 Case 31/77R: *EC Commission v United Kingdom* [1977] ECR 921.
2 Case 22/70: *Commission v EC Council* [1971] ECR 263.

| | |
|---|---|
| sentences arbitrales (220) | arbitration awards |
| régime de la propriété (222) | system of property ownership |
| troubles intérieurs (224) | internal disturbances |
| à huis clos (225) | in camera |
| procédure d'urgence (226) | emergency procedure |
| mesures de sauvegarde (226) | protective measures |
| exemplaire unique (248) | single original |
| les quatre textes faisant également foi (248) | all four texts being equally authentic |
| en foi de quoi (248) | in witness whereof |

To appreciate the difficulty inherent in the translation of legal texts the student is advised to study the above selection of phrases in their proper context, especially in the light of decided cases and to consider the accuracy of their English version from a literal and contextual point of view.

(B) LANGUAGE IN THE COMMUNITY COURT

The Community Court, the single court of the three Communities[3], is a multi-lingual court not only in a linguistic but also a juristic sense.

The requirement that judges must be fit to occupy the highest judicial offices in their respective countries is both an advantage and a handicap. The advantage is obvious in the quality of the judicial body and the potential of having the best legal traditions of the member states in the service of the Community Court. The handicap is that judges, perhaps more than any other lawyers, are conditioned by their own system. However, until truly Community judges emerge the national judges will continue to enrich and shape the Community judiciary with their native skills and characters. Judge Donner thus summarised the position of the national judge: 'I remember one of my colleagues saying at the end of a long debate in which he had tried to win us over to his national solution on a particular point, "Well, gentlemen, if you do not want to adopt my approach, you will at least have to admit that it is the only reasonable one".[4]'

3 Convention relating to Certain Institutions common to the European Communities of 27 March 1957 annexed to the EEC and EAEC Treaties and amending the ECSC Treaty.
4 Donner, A. M., *The Role of the Lawyer in the European Communities* (1968) p. 43.

In order to assist the Court with the linguistic problems the Rules of Procedure[5] enabled the Court to set up a language department consisting of experts, combining the knowledge of several of the official languages of the Court and law (RP 22). Originally the official languages of the Court were French, German, Italian and Netherlands (RP 29 (1))[6] but with the enlargement of the Community the rules of procedure[7] had to be adapted to include the new official languages. At present the official languages of the Court are: Danish, English, French, German, Italian, Netherlands and, since 1 January 1981, Greek; but Irish (though not official) may also be used. These changes resulting in an increased number of the official languages will no doubt further multiply the problems involved.

The present position is that only one of the official languages may be used as the procedural language (RP 29(2)). The choice is, in principle, left to the applicant. However, if the defendant is a member state or a person or corporation subject to a member state the procedural language will be the official language of that state. Should there be more than one official language involved the applicant would be able to choose one from these. If the parties to the case so desire, the Court, upon their joint application, may designate the use of another official language as the procedural language. In exceptional circumstances the Court may authorise the total or partial use of another official language as the procedural language if so requested by one of the parties. Such a request has to be considered in the light of the comments by the other party and the advocate-general but is not open to any of the organs of the Community. In the proceedings involving a preliminary ruling under EEC, article 177[8] on matters of the interpretation of the Treaty, the validity and interpretation of the act of the Community organs and the interpretation of the statutes of bodies established by the Council, the procedural language shall be that of the Court or tribunal which requests the preliminary ruling in question.

The procedural language is used to procure written evidence and

5 These Rules were adopted by the Court on 3 March 1959, in succession to the Treaties of the three Communities and the Statutes of the Courts of Justice envisaged by the Treaties; present codified version OJ 1982, C 39.
6 Dutch, as the language of Holland, is not synonymous with the 'Netherlands language' which is also spoken in certain parts of Belgium. Such Belgians enjoy two 'official languages': French and Netherlands.
7 Act of Accession, art. 142 (4); see p. 63, note 13 and p. 66.
8 EEC Statute, art. 20; EAEC Statute, art. 21; ECSC Treaty, art. 41.

pleas before the Court. Documents produced in another language must be accompanied by a translation in the procedural language. These documents are regarded as 'authentic' which means in practical terms that they cannot be challenged merely on linguistic grounds (RP 31).

Witnesses and experts ought to use the procedural language or one of the official languages but, if unable to do so the Court will allow them to use another language. The witness or expert is allowed to speak through an interpreter or address himself to a judge of his native language[9] but at the end a record will be made under the direction of the Court's Registrar in the procedural language.

The President of the Court, the Presidents of Chambers when directing the proceedings, the Judge-Rapporteur when making his preliminary report and judges and advocates-general when asking questions and the advocates-general when making their submissions may use an official language in preference to the procedural language. However, their utterings will be translated into the procedural language under the direction of the Registrar.

The Registrar will also, on the application of a judge, advocate-general or one of the parties, ensure that a translation into the official languages of his choice is made of what has been said or recorded during the proceedings before the Court or Chamber (RP 30), is delivered in the procedural language (RP 29 (2)) and then published by the Registrar in all the official languages (RP 68). Since the final version of the judgment will generally be in French the authentic text is usually a translation into the language of the case and it is vetted by a judge whose mother tongue is the same[10]. This may occasionally produce difficulties as e.g. the inaccurate translation of the German *Gefährdungen der öffentlichen Ordnung* into its French *equivalent des menaces à l'ordre public* into English *breaches of the peace*[11].

In spite of the tremendous language problem only few cases have so far involved the technical question of the use of language. In *De Gezamenlijke Steenkolenmijnen in Limburg v High Authority*[12] the Court had to rule on the use of the procedural language by an

9  Case 18/63, where the witness and the President of the Court were Italians but the counsel was French, and the President acted virtually as an interpreter.

10  Lasok, K.P.E., 'Practice and Procedure before the ECJ' (1981) ECLR, 89.

11  Case 67/74: *Bonsignore v Oberstadtdirektor der Stadt Köln* [1975] ECR 297, [1975] 1 CMLR 472 and Case 30/77: *R v Bouchéreau* [1977] ECR 1999, [1977] 2 CMLR 800, respectively.

12  Case 30/59: [1961] ECR 1 at 48.

intervener. The Court held that 'it is only as from the moment that he is admitted to intervene that the intervener is obliged to use the language required for the procedure in the main action, without prejudice to the application of RP 29 (2) (*c*)'.

In *Acciaieria di Roma v High Authority of the European Coal and Steel Community*[13] the admissibility of documents drawn up in languages other than the procedural language was challenged. The Court held that: '... The documents in question were deposited with the Registry before the close of the oral procedure and consequently were within the cognisance of the Court before it rendered judgment. By a production of a document drawn up in one of the official languages of the Community it is not only its physical existence but also its content which is brought to the cognisance of the Court. Indeed, like all the institutions of the three Communities, the Court is quadri-lingual by virtue of a presumption *juris et de jure*. The provisions concerning the language of procedure cannot be regarded as being of public policy (*ordre public; zwingendes Recht; openbare orde; ordine pubblico*)—

(*a*) because the language of procedure is that of the applicant, unless the defendant is one of the member states of the three Communities or a legal person subject to the jurisdiction of one of the member states;

(*b*) because, both on the joint application of the parties and on the application of a single party and without the consent of the other party being necessary, the Court can authorise the use of an official language other than the language of the procedure.

That, therefore, the first fundamental condition required by ECSC article 38 (the discovery of a fact unknown not only to the party that applies for re-consideration, but also to the Court) is not met in the present case....'

The challenge failed.

The rules governing the language of procedure are fairly clear but they do not explain what actually happens when the multilingual Court retires for deliberations in private before proceeding to judgment. Judge Donner[14] explained the problems the judges have to face and stressed how difficult it is for a lawyer to shed his second nature acquired in the practice of his national law and to sublimate his experience to a Community concept of law which

13 Case 1/60: [1960] ECR 165 at 169.
14 Donner, op. cit., p. 44.

must perforce savour of a synthesis of the laws of the member states. No doubt the personality of the individual judge and the authority of his national law play a part in the deliberations.

The deliberations are entirely private and in the absence of translators. Practice established French to be *the lingua franca* with the consequent disadvantage to judges whose fluency in French is not as good as might be desired. To get round this difficulty former Judge Riese[15] used to state his position in his native German and then restate it in French. In this way he endeavoured to have his say as best he could first in the legal jargon of his own country, and then give his brethren the benefit of an authentic translation into the 'working' language. It is clear that the Court must live with the problem (further aggravated by the enlargement of the Community) until the relevant portion of the law has become uniform and a new generation of truly Community lawyers has replaced the judges schooled in their native lands.

Still more complex is the jurisprudence of the language of the law. On more than one occasion the Community Court had to turn its mind to the interpretation of technical terms only to confirm that similarities conceal divergencies and nuances in the legal systems. The following examples illustrate the point.

1. *Détournement de pouvoir*[16]—A notion of French administrative law to cover a variety of cases of misuse of power has been before the Court on several occasions. In *Associazione Industrie Siderurgiche Italiane (Assider) v High Authority of the European Coal and Steel Community*[17] Advocate-General Lagrange reviewed painstakingly the concept of the misuse of power in each of the six member states. In that case an association of Italian steel enterprises complained of being adversely affected by certain decisions[18] of the High Authority of the Coal and Steel Community which concerned the publication of price lists and conditions of sale by the steel industry. The plaintiffs contended that the general decisions of the High Authority in these matters constituted a threat to Italian steel enterprises, and that they were vitiated by the *détournement de pouvoir*. Moreover, since those enterprises which had infringed the previous regulations were not subjected to any sanction, the plaintiffs considered this to be a manifest injustice, and thus a misuse of

15 Riese, O., 'Erfahrungen aus der Praxis des Gerichtshofes der Europäischen Gemeinschaft für Kohle und Stahl', *Deutsche Richterzeitung* (1958), 270–272.
16 Ermessemissbrauch, sviamento de potere, misbruik van beveogdheid; further discussion p. 244 et seq post.
17 Case 3/54: [1954–56] ECR 63.
18 Case 1/54: JO, 13 January 1953, 217; Case 2/54; ibid., 218; Case 3/54, ibid., 219.

power in respect of those enterprises which had observed the Treaty. The Court held that since decision 2/54 was annulled by the judgment in the case of *French Government v High Authority of the European Coal and Steel Community*[19] and decision 3/54 repealed by the High Authority it was unnecessary for the Court to define *détournement de pouvoir*. Decision 1/54, having been upheld by the Court in the case of *Italian Government v High Authority of the European Coal and Steel Community*[20] could not be regarded as misuse of power in the absence of new arguments. In the circumstances the Court was able to fall back on the classical dodge of not having to define an awkward concept. The plaintiffs fared no better in their request for an interpretation of the judgment[1] as the Court held that the judgment, being free from obscurities, presented no occasion for interpretation.

The saga of the *détournement de pouvoir* is likely to continue in spite of the attempts by the Court to offer an objective definition of *détournement* as 'the use made by a public authority of its powers for an object other than that for which a power was conferred upon it'[2] simply because of the variations of the use and abuse of public power. The procession of cases will continue.

2. *Faute de service*—In several cases the Community Court considered grievances arising from alleged 'default of the administration' (*faute de service*). On one occasion a Belgian corporation[3] complained that it was unable to sell coal in France because of the refusal of a licence by French authorities which, in effect, impeded the free flow of coal within the Community. Repeated requests to the Coal and Steel Community were of no avail and the corporation suffered damage as a result of inaction of the Community. The Court held that the plaintiff was entitled to redress for *faute de service* without insisting that the act complained of had to be annulled first. However, in *Plaumann & Co v EEC Commission*[4] damages were refused in the absence of a declaration of nullity but the decision turned upon different considerations. In subsequent cases[5] the Court recognised the independent nature of the action in

---

19 Case 1/54: [1954–56] ECR 1.
20 Case 2/54: [1954–56] ECR 37.
1 Case 5/55: [1954–56] ECR 135.
2 Case 8/55: *Fédération Charbonnière de Belgique v High Authority* [1954–56] ECR 245 at 272–273.
3 Cases 9–10/60: *Société Commerciale Antoine Vloeberghs SA v High Authority of the European Coal and Steel Community* [1961] ECR 197.
4 Case 25/62: [1963] ECR 95, [1964] CMLR 29.
5 Case 5/71: *Aktien-Zuckerfabrik Schöppenstedt v EEC Council* [1971] 2 ECR 975; Cases 63–69/72: *Werhahn v EEC Council* [1973] ECR 1229.

accordance with article 215 (2) and 178, but considered that where a claim is made in respect of injury attributable to a legislative act of the Community involving choices of economic policy the claimant can succeed only if there is a 'sufficiently flagrant infringement of a superior rule of law protecting the individual'[6].

Several other cases[7] threw light on the concept of *faute de service* but perhaps the most instructive are the cases involving grievances of Community employees. It was held[8] that failure to renew a contract of employment in an irregular fashion constituted *faute de service* and so did an unlawful activity of an organ of the Community preventing a person from carrying on his normal occupation and causing him material and moral damage[9].

The many aspects of *faute de service* were considered from a comparative point of view in *Algera v Common Assembly*[10], a case of disputed validity of the re-grading of employees. The Court stated[11]:

'... A study of comparative law reveals that in the six Member States an administrative act creating substantive rights in a particular party cannot in principle be revoked, provided that it amounted to a legal act. In such a case, the substantive right having been acquired, the necessity of ensuring confidence in the stability of the situation thus created outweighs the interest of the administration which might wish to revoke its decision. This applies particularly in the appointment of an official.

If, on the contrary, the administrative act is illegal, the law of all the Member States recognises the possibility of revocation. The lack of an objective legal basis for the act affects the substantive right of the party concerned and justifies the revocation of the said act. It is appropriate to emphasise that this principle is generally recognised and that it is only the conditions for its exercise which vary.

French law requires that the revocation of the illegal act must occur before the expiration of the time limit for bringing an appeal, or if an appeal is brought, before judgement. Belgian, Luxembourg and Dutch law, with certain differences, appear to follow analogous rules.

6 *Werhahn*, op. cit.
7 E.g. Cases 19/60, 21/60, 2-3/61: *Société Fives Lille Cail v High Authority of the European Coal and Steel Community* [1961] ECR 281 at 295–296, [1962] CMLR 251 at 281–282; Cases 5-7/66, 13-24/66, 30/66: *Firma E Kampffmeyer v EEC Commission* [1967] ECR 245; Case 36/62: *Société des Aciéries du Temple v High Authority of the European Coal and Steel Community* [1963] ECR 289, [1964] CMLR 49 at 56; Case 3/65: *Société Anonyme Métallurgique d'Espérance Langdoz v High Authority of the European Coal and Steel Community* [1965] 2 ECR 1065, [1966] CMLR 146 at 167; 11 Rec. 1321.
8 In Case 1/55: *Kergall v Common Assembly* [1954–56] ECR 151.
9 Case 18/60: *Worms v High Authority of the European Coal and Steel Community* [1962] ECR 195, [1963] CMLR 1.
10 Cases 7/56, 3 and 757 [1957–58] ECR 39.
11 Valentine, D. G., *The Court of Justice of the European Communities*, Vol. 2 (1965), p. 757–758.

On the other hand, German law does not recognise a time limit for the exercise of the right of revocation unless such a limit is provided by a special provision. Thus, the Federal law concerning public officials, by article 13 thereof, allows the withdrawal of an appointment only within a period of six months. However, it is generally recognised that the principle of good faith (*Treu und Glauben*) is opposed to an unduly delayed withdrawal ...

... Italian law is particularly precise upon this question. Any administrative act is vitiated by incompetence, violation of the law or ultra vires (*eccesso di potere*) can be annulled *ex tunc* by the administration which enacted it, independently of the substantive rights to which it might have given rise ...

The revocability of an administrative act tainted with illegality is, therefore, recognised in all the Member States ...'

*Faute de service* was proved and the earlier decision in *Kergall v Common Assembly* was cited with approval.

3. *Exception d'illégalité*—The defence of illegality, which is often resorted to in order to contest the legality of an administrative act, is well known in the six member states of the Community. It can also be pleaded before the Community Court. In a leading case[12] Advocate-General Lagrange thus summarised the contribution of the six legal systems to the concept of *exception d'illégalité*:

'... In three of the member states, France, Belgium and Italy, this *exception* is freely admitted, being considered as forming part of the normal sphere of application of the claim for annulment. This is due to the fact that in these three countries, rules made by the executive power are considered, as far as the right to appeal against them is concerned, from the formal point of view, that is to say being administrative acts they are liable to be annulled if they are contrary to the law. Given that the direct claim for annulment is possible with regard to them, there is no objection in principle to the [judicial] control of their legality being also exercised when individual claims are made of which they are the object. The advantage is that the *exception* may be set up at any time, even when the time limit for a claim against the regulation or the general decision has expired. On the other hand, if the claim is successful only the individual decision is annulled, which avoids the grave consequences of the annulment of the regulation itself, declared with retrospective effect *erga omnes*.

As far as France is concerned we will cite, among many, two judgments of the Conseil d'État: *Abbé Barthélémy*, 9 July 1926, Recueil 713; *Marcin-Kowsky*, 28 November 1957, Recueil 548. These decisions are

12 Case 15/57: *Compagnie des Hauts Fourneaux de Chasse v High Authority of the European Coal and Steel Community* [1957–58] ECR 199. See also Case 9/56: *Meroni & Co Industriche Metallurgiche SpA v High Authority of the European Coal and Steel Community* [1957–58] ECR 133; Cases 31, 33/62: *Milchwerke Heinz Wöhrmann & Sohn KG v EC Commission* [1962] ECR 501, [1963] CMLR 152.

interesting because they begin by rejecting as presented out of time the submissions that the rule should be annulled, and, immediately following, pass judgment on the legality of the very same rule in respect of submissions directed against an individual decision applying the rule. Case law shows, however, that the legality of the rule can only be contested in respect of those of its provisions which provided the basis for the individual decision taken in application of the rule (*Dame Denayer*, 18 February 1949, Recueil 80).

In the three other countries of the Community, Germany, Holland and Luxembourg, there is a strong tendency to remain attached to the material criterion, by virtue of which a regulation is a piece of secondary legislation no different in its legal nature from the law itself. Nevertheless the subordination of the rule to the (general) law remains an established legal principle and, if the former conception causes some hesitation with regard to direct claims for annulment of regulations, the second conception, on the other hand, more readily permits the setting up of the *exception d'illégalité*. In criminal law this *exception* is very freely admitted. The principal difficulties in the latter field lie mainly in determining which judge is competent to rule on the question of legality: that happens, particularly, in France, a country in which the principle of the separation of powers is very strictly applied and where, in consequence, a reference to the administrative court for a preliminary ruling on legality is often made in defiance of the principle according to which the judge in the action is also judge in respect of the *exception*, but such considerations do not arise where, as in the instant case, the same judge has competence.

Are there any special reasons for adopting a different solution for the application of the Treaty? We do not think so. On the contrary, article 41, which confers jurisdiction on the Court—without any restriction as to the nature of the grounds which may be put forward, nor as to the nature of the decision against which the claim is made—to give a preliminary ruling as to the validity of resolutions of the High Authority when the question arises in a dispute the subject of litigation before a national court is an added argument in favour of there being no restrictions, for there is no reason which could justify a more restrictive solution in respect of undertakings having direct access to the Court, than in respect of third parties who may on occasion need the Court's judgment with regard to a decision of the High Authority.'

Since the study of cases is the best method of studying law the student will, no doubt, find in many cases decided by the Community Court the problems of legal concepts of which the three mentioned above are only examples.

(C) LANGUAGE AND THE APPROXIMATION OF LAWS

Under the directions of the Council the member states are committed to a process of approximation of their laws in the fields directly affecting the establishment and functioning of the Common Market. In fulfilling these obligations they are free to resort to their own methods and, what goes with it, their own legal language. However, two points must be borne in mind in this connection: that the direction comes from the Community and must, therefore, be a blueprint of uniformity; and that the member states, being committed to the ideal of the Common Market, should comply as best as they can with the spirit of the direction, compromising, if necessary, their legal language. Since approximation is not easy to achieve it requires at the Community level special skills of draughtsmanship and persuasion and, at the member states' level, a resolute Community orientation.

# Chapter 4

# Sources of Community law

The phrase 'source of law' can be used in several senses. It can mean the causes of law that is to say the creative elements which contribute to the making of the law and this can be the law itself. These may be historical facts devoid of any authority or political, social and economic conditions of the society which may, or may not, be regarded by the law as authoritative. The European Community owes its existence to international solidarity and the will to create a better Europe through economic cohesion. As 'causes', or sources of Community law they are rather remote and only of a passing interest to lawyers though lawyers ought to make themselves aware of 'the "grand design" underlying the European construction'[1]. In their work lawyers are concerned more with formal sources that is authorities which maybe cited in court and which are thus judicially cognisable. When analysing these we look to their authors and places where they can be found.

## PART ONE
## The origins of Community law

Unlike the International Court of Justice at the Hague, which is directed to apply international conventions, international custom, the general principles of law recognised by civilised nations and judicial decisions and the teachings of the most highly qualified publicists of the various nations[2], the Community Court is left without specific guidance. Each of the relevant Treaties is content with the direction that 'the Court of Justice shall ensure that in the interpretation and application of this Treaty the law is observed[3]',

1 Pescatore in Bathurst et al. op. cit. at pp. 32–34.
2 Statute of the International Court of Justice, art. 38.
3 EEC, art. 164; Euratom, art. 136; ECSC, art. 31—words 'and justice' omitted but words 'and of the regulations for its execution' added.

without actually defining the *law* or its sources. In spite of this the Court has functioned vigorously applying Community law from a variety of sources[4].

In the sense of the author or authority from which Community law is derived we can distinguish between *primary* and *secondary* sources.

# Primary sources

(A) CONSTITUTIONAL TREATIES

They are the *Constitutional Treaties* because together they form the organisational law of the Community. They constitute the basis of the Community legal order and the *fons et origo* of all Community law; they are its primary sources.

The primary sources of Community law consist of the three foundation Treaties (ECSC, EAEC and EEC) with their Annexes, and Protocols, which supplement the Treaties; the Convention on Certain Institutions Common to the European Communities (1957); the Merger Treaty (1965); the Luxembourg Treaty on Budgetary Matters (1970); the first Treaty of Accession and its Annexes (1972); the Second Budgetary Treaty (1975) and the second Treaty of Accession and its Annexes (1979).

The foundation Treaties are 'self-executing'[5] treaties which means that, when ratified, they become law automatically within the member states. In contrast with 'non-self-executing' treaties (which constitute international obligations but require implementing legislation before they become applicable in internal law), 'self-executing' treaties must be applied directly by the municipal courts as the law of the land. A treaty is, by its nature, a contract between two or more states; it is not a legislative act. However, it may be regarded as a legislative act whenever it is designed by the signatory states as a declaration of their understanding of what a particular rule of law is, or an expressly formulated norm of future behaviour, or a constitution of an international organisation. The legislative nature of the EEC Treaty is indicated by its purpose and specific provisions (articles 227 and 247 (2)) and confirmed by the 'Act concerning the Conditions of Accession and the Adjustment of

---

4 See Bebr, G., *Judicial Control of the European Communities* (1962), p. 26.
5 On self-executing treaties see the judgment of Chief Justice Marshall in *Foster and Elam v Neilson* 2 Pet 253 (US 1829).

the Treaties' (article 2)[6]. The status of the Protocols is the same as by virtue of article 239 they 'form an integral part' of the EEC Treaty.

The content of the EEC Treaty is complex not only because it creates institutions and defines the objectives of the Community, but also because it provides the basis and authority for Community legislation. It provides for an Executive, a Bureaucracy, a Parliament and a Court and charges these institutions with the execution of the Treaty. The Treaty remains a treaty, that is an agreement between the signatory states, but it differs from a typical treaty not only because it creates supra-national institutions but, more importantly, because, unlike a typical treaty, its execution has been taken out of the hands of the parties. The institutions it creates, notwithstanding their imperfections and limitations, can be likened to the corresponding institutions of the internal law. Their strength lies in the fact that certain important powers have been transferred or delegated by the states to these institutions making them quasi-autonomous. Their weakness lies in the fact that their functioning is contingent upon the continuous discharge of the Treaty obligations by the member states. If a country withdraws from the Community havoc could be caused but the Community would not come to an end and the institutions would not cease to function. But if a number of states withdrew the Community would cease to be a practical possibility. If we apply a juristic construction to the Treaty modelled upon internal law it can be argued that the Treaty is the Constitution of the Community[7] or, to use Judge Donner's phrase, that the member states have undertaken obligations 'not simply on a reciprocal basis but primarily towards the new collectivity they set up'[8]. The authors of this book subscribe to the constitutional theory in spite of arguments advancing an opposite opinion, namely that the Treaty is merely a bundle of contractual obligations.

In addition to the Constitution of the Community the Treaty contains what continental lawyers would term 'ordinary legislation' implying thereby a hierarchy of legal norms[9]. The Treaty 'legisla-

---

6 Attached to both Treaties of Accession.

7 E.g. Wagner, H., op. cit., p. 24 and Pescatore, P., *L'Ordre Juridique des Communautés Européenes* (1971), pp. 36 et seq.; for same opinion see German Federal Constitutional Court (First Chamber), Decision of 18 October 1967, [1967] AWD 477-8 (1980) Europarecht, 134-7.

8 The Constitutional Powers of the Court of Justice of the European Communities', 11 CML Review, 1974, p. 128.

9 I.e. the Constitution, Acts of Parliament, legislative acts of the Executive and delegated legislation.

tion' is quite detailed in some areas, e.g. the customs union, and only in a general outline in others, e.g. taxation. The relationship between 'constitutional' provisions and the 'ordinary legislation' of the Treaty, obvious to continental lawyers but rather obscure to British lawyers, who are not familiar with the theory of hierarchy of legal norms, is of some practical importance as far as the legislative function of the Community organs is concerned. The point is whether the Treaty alone can provide sufficient authority for legislation by these organs or whether the growth of Community law must depend on its original source, i.e. the power delegated by the member states. The answer seems to be in the affirmative, assuming, of course, that the Community organs do not act ultra vires. The Treaty could not have envisaged all the eventualities but provided[10] a wide scope for Community initiatives, safeguarding at the same time the principle of legality through the instrumentality of the Court and the vital interests of the member states through the instrumentality of the Council. Thus, in order to attain the Community objectives the Council by a unanimous decision may take the appropriate measures (which, presumably, include appropriate legal measures) on the recommendation of the Commission and in consultation with the Assembly. These powers are wide but circumscribed by the Treaty and so, it was argued[11] that the provisions of article 235 constitute no blanket authority for 'implied powers'. The problem, did arise under the ECSC Treaty and the Community Court considered ultra vires the delegation of powers vested in the High Authority to an agency in Brussels set up for the purpose of operating a system of subsidies to equalise the cost of scrap iron[12].

In order to supplement the powers of the Community organs (and thus, presumably, curtail the temptation to rely on 'implied powers') a practice under the ECSC Treaty was established whereby a certain amount of law-making power was exercised by assembled representatives of the member states[13]. The practice spread to

10 EEC, art. 235; EAAC, art. 203; ECSC, art. 95.
11 Wohlfarth, E., Everling, H., Glässner, H. J., Sprung, R., 'Die Europäische Wirtschaftsgemeinschaft', *Kommentar zum Vertrage* (1960), comment (7) on art. 235.
12 Case 9/56: *Meroni & Co Industrie Metallurgiche SpA v High Authority of the ECSC* [1957-1958] ECR 133 at 149-154.
13 ECSC, art. 69, concerning free movement of skilled labour (JO 586/55 and 1647/63); ECSC, art. 70, concerning international railroad tariffs (JO 607/55, 701/55, 130/56 and 431/59); see Kaiser, 'Die im Rat vereinigten Vertreter der Regierungen der Mitgliedstaaten', *Festschrift Ophüls* (1965), pp. 107-24.

the EEC, the most interesting example of this being the decisions which resulted in the acceleration of the setting up of the customs union[14]. The legal nature of these devices (described as 'acts of representatives'[15]) is obscure. They are regarded as 'international agreements in simplified form'[16] and 'borderline of international law and Community law'[17]. These 'acts of representatives' no doubt contribute to the development of Community policy and law and in a sense provide a substitute for the revision of the Treaty. A further dynamic application of article 235 can be seen in the implementation of the Dublin agreement of 1975 on the adoption of the correcting mechanism in respect of the budgetary obligations of the member states[18].

The view that the Treaty provides the Constitution of the Community is fortified by the fact that so far recourse has been taken to the Community Court and Community law rather than international law sources for the purpose of the interpretation of the Treaties and legislative acts made under the Treaties. The Court itself, through the Advocate-General Lagrange[19], considered the role of general international law as a source of Community law rather limited because:

'... our Court is not an international tribunal, but is concerned with a community which has been created by six states and which resembles more a federation than an international organisation ... The Treaty ... although concluded in the form of international treaties and undoubtedly being one, nevertheless also constitutes, from a substantive point of view, the character of the Community and as a consequence the legal provisions derived from the Treaty must be viewed as the internal law of the Community....'

An international treaty creating rights and obligations of states may be regarded as special law within the general compass of international law. The point which concerns the EEC Treaty as a

14 JO 1217/60 and 1284/62.
15 Brinkhorst, L. J., 'Implementation of (non-self-executing) Legislation of the European Economic Community, including Directives', *Legal Problems of an Enlarged European Community*, edited by Bathurst, M. E., et Al. (1972), p. 72.
16 Pescatore, P., 'La personalité internationale de la Communauté', *Les relations extérieures de la Communauté unifiée* (Liège 1969), p. 585.
17 Resolution following the parliamentary report by Burger (E.P. doc. 215/1968–69) concerning collective acts of the member states of the Community, JO 1969, C.
18 *Bulletin of the European Communities* 1975, No. 3, p. 6.
19 In Case 8/55: *Fédération Charbonnière de Belgique v High Authority* [1954–56] ECR 245 at 277.

source of law is whether the obligations contained therein can be derogated from by reference to general principles of international law. One of such general rules (albeit discredited through abuse) is the doctrine of necessity[20], which suggests that states in cases of extreme emergency may resort to breaches of international law. As states are rather prone to resort to legal subterfuge under the guise of real or imagined emergency[1] article 226 of the EEC Treaty provides a specific procedure to deal with such situations within the complexity of the Common Market. Accordingly, as decreed by the Community Court[2], the plea of necessity cannot succeed in face of article 226. Furthermore, having safeguarded certain state interests (e.g. articles 36, 56 (1), 108, 223) the Treaty has reduced[3] the scope of arbitrary 'emergency' action states may be tempted to take in protection of their 'sovereign rights'. Although article 226 was designed to correct matters arising during the transitional period there is no reason why its general principle and mechanism should not be applied in a wider sense.

There is, however, no reason why a rule of international law recognised by the member states as a general rule of law should not be applied in the interpretation of the Treaties or Community legislation. Thus, e.g., in *Van Duyn v Home Office*[4] the Community Court upheld the principle of international law that, whilst a state has a duty of receiving its own nationals, it has no such duty in respect of the nationals of another state though Community nationals may claim a right of entry by virtue of a directly applicable provision of the EEC Treaty. In *Nold v EC Commission* 'the Court considered that 'international agreements in which the member states have participated or to which they have adhered contain indications which have to be taken into account within the framework of Community law'[5] but in an earlier case[6] the Court held that 'the validity of acts of the institutions within the meaning of article 177 of the Treaty cannot be tested against a rule of International

20 Oppenheim, L., *International Law*, Vol. 1 (8th edn 1955), pp. 297 et seq., and Brownlie, I., *International Law and the Use of Force by States* (1963), pp. 40–44.
1 Cf. the measures taken by the Labour Government in the UK when coming to power in 1967 which resulted in breaches of several treaties.
2 Case 7/61: *EEC Commission v Government of Italy* [1961] ECR 317 at 000, [1962] CMLR 39 at 52, 56.
3 Commission decision of 23 July 1968, No. 68/301/EEC, authorising the French Government to take certain measures under art. 108 (3).
4 Op. cit., p. 69 note 9.
5 Case 4/73: [1974] ECR 491 at 507, [1974] 2 CMLR 338 at 354.
6 Case 9/73: *Schlüter v Hauptzollamt Lörrach* [1973] ECR 1135 at 1157.

Law unless that rule is binding on the Community and capable of creating rights of which interested parties may avail themselves in a court of law'.

In the light of the above it seems that the Community, being an autonomous organisation created within the framework of international law, is governed by its own law and its Court will apply the rules of international law only if such rules are relevant to the definition of Community rights[7].

As far as the pre-membership treaty obligations are concerned the Community respects these (article 37 (5)) but expects the members states to eliminate any incompatibilities (article 234) so that each member state is in line with the others and its Community obligations. As regards future treaty obligations, membership of the Community entails a certain limitation of their treaty-making power (article 113) whilst the treaties made by the Community in its autonomous capacity shall be binding upon the Community and the member states as well (article 228 (2)). It follows that whilst the member states are free to enter into treaties with third parties they must bear in mind their Community obligations when doing so (article 234)[8].

## (B)  CONVENTIONS BETWEEN MEMBER STATES

As each country remains sovereign and retains its own legal system it has become necessary to enter into separate conventions between the member states. All this is but a stage in the harmonisation of municipal laws and the elimination of conflicts in the field of commercial laws with which the Common Market is particularly concerned. According to article 220 member states ought to negotiate conventions to secure for the benefit of their nationals the protection of rights, abolition of double taxation, mutual recognition of companies and reciprocal recognition and enforcement of judgments of municipal courts and arbitration awards. It goes without saying that such conventions shall have the force of treaties and be binding accordingly. By these conventions the member states can create new laws and, in view of the sovereign power of states, these

---

7 *Van Duyn*, op. cit.; Cases 21–24/72: *International Fruit Co v Produktschap voor Groenten en Fruit* [1972] 2 ECR 1219 at 1226; Case 36/75: *Rutili v Ministère de l'Interieur* [1975] ECR 1219, [1976] 1 CMLR 140.

8 Cf. Case 22/70: *EC Commission v EC Council* [1971] ECR 263, [1971] CMLR 335. Opinion 1/75: *Re OECD Understanding on a Local Cost Standard* [1976] 1 CMLR 85.

laws can go far beyond the scope of the foundation Treaties. Should this be the case the Community Court might have to rule whether such laws, being in excess of the foundation Treaties, are cognisable by the Court as a source of Community law. Rules seem to be devolving both by the Community Court and the national courts of the member states. Thus it was held by the Paris Court of Appeal that Community law superseded rights and obligations arising from previous bilateral social security conventions between member states inconsistent with the foundation Treaty[9], though the Community Court[10] held that Community law would not prevent additional social benefits arising under municipal law.

Conventions between member states subsequent to the foundation Treaty were held by the Community Court unable to alter the existing Community law[11] though doubts were cast on the position in the submission of Advocate-General Roemer in *Federal Republic of Germany v EEC Commission.*[12]

Since the position is somewhat uncertain, a cautious approach should be adopted to the problem of conventions between member states as a source of Community law. If they are within the scope of article 220 no question will arise for the conventions should be regarded as an instrument of harmonisation or approximation of national laws. They will be negotiated and concluded within the Community spectrum, the Commission taking an active part in the process. The scope of the conventions envisaged in article 220 is wider than the scope of the harmonisation of laws under articles 100-102 of the EEC Treaty. However little progress has been achieved to date. In fact only two such conventions have been signed: the 1968 Convention on Jurisdiction and the Enforcement of Judgments in Civil and Commercial Matters, signed in 1969[13], in force between the original six member states as from 1 February 1973[14] and the 1968 Convention on the Mutual Recognition of Companies and Bodies Corporate signed in 1969 but not yet in force.

In accordance with the first and the second Act of Accession[15]

9 *Nani v Caisse d'Assurance Vieillesse des Travailleurs Salariés de Paris* [1964] CMLR 334; 4 CMLRev. 70-71.
10 Case 92/63: *Nonnenmacher Moebs v Bestuur der Sociale Verzekeringsbank* [1964] ECR 281, at 288, [1964] CMLR 338 at 347.
11 Case 33/64: *Betriebskrankenkasse der Heseper Torfwerk GmbH v Koster (née van Dijk)* [1965] ECR 97, at 104, [1966] CMLR 191 at 208.
12 Case 24/62: [1963] ECR 63, [1963] CMLR 347 at 361-362.
13 OJ 1972, L299/32.
14 Denmark, Eire and the United Kingdom signed the convention on 9 October 1978 (OJ 1978, L304).
15 Articles 3 (2) and 3 (2) respectively.

the new member states are bound to acceede to the conventions subject to adjustments which may be necessary in individual cases. Further conventions, i.e. on Know-How (1967), Bankruptcy (1970), Mergers of Companies (1973) and the Law applicable to Contractual Obligations (1979), are in a draft form. As a result of this process a new body of law will come into being, a law broadly founded upon the founding Treaties but in fact emanating from direct legislation of sovereign states within the Community. It will be subject to the jurisdiction of the ECJ as far as reference for preliminary rulings are concerned[16].

If the subject matter of a convention is outside the scope of article 220 but nevertheless within the scope of the Community as laid down in the founding Treaties such a convention may well be regarded as a source of Community law. An example to the point is the Luxembourg Convention for the European Patent for the Common Market of 1975[17]. It has been entered into by the member states with the object of creating one patent territory and establishing a uniform legal regime applicable to patents in the whole of the Common Market. It has been actively encouraged by a resolution of the Council of Ministers[18] and the Commission had a hand in it. The convention in its preamble, claims to have accomplished one of the Community objectives and, in article 73, enables the national courts to refer matters of its interpretation to the ECJ for a preliminary ruling in accordance with article 177 of the EEC Treaty. Finally it states expressly, in article 93, that none of its provisions 'may be invoked against the application of any provision' of the EEC Treaty. Clearly this sets the pattern for future conventions and ensures their compatibility with Community law.

Outside the power delegated to the Community the member states have retained their treaty-making capacity and may conclude conventions between themselves as they please. However, any such convention incompatible with their duties to the Community or any other member state not a party to it would entail a breach of the relevant founding Treaty though it may well be enforceable under international law. Should this occur the Community would face a serious crisis if not a prospect of its own disintegration.

16 Protocol to the Judgments Convention, OJ 1975 L204/28.
17 OJ 1976, L17/1; see Lasok, op. cit. p. 269 et seq.
18 OJ 1976, L17/43.

(C) COMMUNITY AGREEMENTS

We have observed earlier that the Community, as a legal person, enjoys treaty-making powers. The question which has to be considered is whether, and if so in what circumstances, agreements between the Community and the outside world are binding upon the member states and thus become a source of Community law. The treaty-making powers of the Community, unlike that of a state, is not unlimited for by virtue of article 228 the Community can enter into agreements with the states and international organisations where so provided by the Treaty. It provides further that such agreements shall be binding upon the member states if concluded in accordance with the procedure laid down in article 228.

Accordingly such agreements shall be negotiated by the Commission and concluded by the Council after consulting the Assembly. In order to ensure that the agreement is consistent with the Treaty the Council, the Commission and any member state may seek the opinion of the Community Court[19]. It follows that by submitting to the Treaty the member states delegate to the Community an important portion of their sovereign power to create international obligations and new laws in as far as the agreement may be a source of law[20]. The delegation is not absolute for it is exercised subject to the participation of each member state in Council and the recourse to the Court. However, the Court acts as the watchdog of the Community legality but not of the interests of the member states.

So far a number of agreements have come into being resulting in a network of relations between the Community and the outside world[1]. These bind the Community with states which have a special interest in West European co-operation as well as states which, being the former dependencies of the member states of the Community, retained their economic ties with them.

All these agreements, in so far as they shape the trade pattern between the Community and the outside world and thereby affect both the internal arrangement of the Community and the legal obligations of the member states, can be regarded as a source of Community law from which individual rights may be derived[2].

**19** See Opinion 1/75: *Re the OECD Understanding on a Local Cost Standard* [1976] 1 CMLR 85, and other Opinions, p. 41 note 17, ante.
**20** Cf. Sir Gerald Fitzmaurice, 'Some Problems Regarding the Formal Sources of International Law', *Symbolae Verzijl*, p. 160, quot. by Morand, C. A., *La législation dans les Communautés Européennes* (1968) p. 16.
**1** See p. 41 et seq., ante.
**2** See p. 46 ante.

# Secondary sources

By the secondary sources of Community law we understand the law-making acts of the Community organs which result in a body of law generated by the Community itself in its quasi-autonomous capacity. We regard these sources as secondary because their authority is derived from the provisions of the founding Treaties. Moreover in hierarchy of legal norms they rank second to Treaty provisions. Their scope is circumscribed and their validity can be tested against the criteria laid down in the Treaties. To all intents and purposes they resemble delegated legislation. The importance of the law-making power of the Community cannot be overemphasised because, as stated by a distinguished jurist, 'the first and most essential means by which a supra-national organisation endeavours to carry out its objectives ... resides in the law-making power'[3]. In brief we are concerned with Community legislation.

Legislation denotes rules of law made deliberately in the prescribed form by some competent authority. The founding Treaties carefully avoid the term *legislation* and refer instead to *regulations*[4], apparently, as has been suggested[5], to ward off the wrath of the national parliaments likely to be provoked by the suggestion that an outside body shall usurp their legislative function. The Community Court also preferred to refer to *pouvoirs réglementaires*[6], although on another occasion[7] references were made to *compétence réglementaire* (p. 687), *normative* (p. 688) and *légiférante* (p. 692). Without going into semantic niceties[8] the law-making power of the Community organs can be identified as one corresponding to a generally accepted notion of legislation. This means that it results in rules of conduct addressed to subjects of Community Law which emanate from a definite organ, are made in a set form and by virtue of the authority vested in the organ have an obligatory character.

3 Guggenheim, P., 'Organisations économiques supranationales, independance et neutralité de la Suisse', *Rev. de droit suisse*, Vol. 82 (1963) II, p. 247.
4 EEC, art. 189 (2), EAEC, art. 161 (2), ECSC, arts. 31 and 35 (1) and (2).
5 Pescatore, P., 'Les aspects fonctionnels de la Communauté économique européenne', *Les aspects juridiques du marché commun* (1958), p. 67; cf. Catalano, N., 'La fusion des voies de droit', *Colloquium at Liège* (1965), p. 284.
6 Case 15/57: *Compagnie des Hauts Fourneaux de Chasse v High Authority of the ECSC* [1958] ECR 211.
7 Case 20/59: *Italy v High Authority of the ECSC* [1960] ECR 325 terms taken from Rec. (1960) 662 at 687, 688, 692.
8 Morand, C. A., *La législation dans les Communautés Européennes* (1968), pp. 7-17.

(A) OBLIGATORY ACTS

These consist of regulations, directives and decisions made by the Council or the Commission in order to carry out their task in accordance with the Treaty (EEC, article 189).

The nomenclature adopted in the EEC and EAEC Treaties is identical but it differs in the ECSC Treaty. Thus under article 14 of the ECSC Treaty we have decisions, recommendations and opinions. 'Decisions' under the ECSC Treaty correspond to regulations under the remaining two Treaties because they are said to be 'binding in their entirety'. However the ECJ, depending on the scope of the given act, distinguished between 'general decisions'[9] which are equivalent to regulations and 'individual decisions'[10] which are equivalent to decisions under the EEC and EAEC Treaties. 'Recommendations' under the ECSC Treaty correspond to directives under the other two Treaties. 'Opinions' correspond to opinions and, as under the EEC and EAEC Treaties, they have no binding force. Bearing in mind these nuances we shall examine the position in terms of the EEC Treaty.

(a) *Regulations*

Regulations have a general scope, are 'binding in their entirety' and are 'directly applicable' in all member states (article 189 (2). It follows that, apart from their applicability without the intermediary of the state, regulations are meant to be an instrument of uniformity within the Community. Uniformity is the desired aim but cannot always be achieved and so it may be necessary to leave implementation to the member states. The agricultural regulations illustrate the point and the problem, for they leave it to each state to execute in its own fashion the system of levies and restitutions, to establish the necessary procedures and impose sanctions. In some cases, e.g. the free movement of workers[11] and social security of migrant workers[12], the regulations are too general to be applied directly without the necessary detailed rules which have to be worked out nationally. The regulation authorising Germany to accept the import of cattle from Denmark is a further variation on the theme as

---

9 Case 18/57: *Nold KG v High Authority of the ECSC* [1957] ECR 121; Case 18/62: *Barge v High Authority of the ECSC* [1963] ECR 259, [1965] CMLR 330.

10 Case 20/58: *Phoenix-Rheinrohr AG v High Authority of the ECSC* [1959] ECR 75; Cases 22 and 23/60: *Raymond Elz v High Authority of the ECSC* [1961] ECR 181; Cases 23, 24, 52/63: *Société Anonyme Usines Émile Henricot v High Authority of the ECSC* [1963] ECR 217, [1964] CMLR 119.

11 Reg. 1612/68, JO 1968, L 257/2, art. 4 (12) (13) (15).

12 Reg. 1408/71, OJ 1971, L 149/1. Codified OJ 1980, C138/1.

it concerns one country only and simply gives leave to take measures appropriate to the situation in hand[13].

In order to constitute a regulation the act of the Community organ must comply with certain conditions. In the first place regulations must rest upon the authority of the Treaty which means that they are made where so provided by the Treaty; if not so provided by the Treaty that act cannot have the character of a regulation[14]. Regulations have to be reasoned (*motivés*) or 'substantiated' in the terms of the Treaty[15] which, in the submission of Advocate-General Lagrange[16] means that they indicate in general terms the aims pursued by the regulations, the reasons which justify the regulations and the outlines of the system adopted.

However, as stated by the ECJ[17], 'the extent of the requirement laid down by article 190 . . . to state the reasons on which measures are based depends on the nature of the measure in question' . . .

The justification for substantiation is clear for it is a safeguard against arbitrary exercise of authority. It is also essential for the parties concerned to know their legal position and to be able to defend their rights. In other words, as explained the ECJ[18] '. . . In imposing upon the Commission the obligation to state reasons for its decisions, article 190 is not taking mere formal considerations into account but seeks to give an opportunity to the parties of defending their rights, to the Court of exercising its supervisory functions and to Member States and to all interested nationals of ascertaining the circumstances in which the Commission has applied the Treaty' . . . What the Court said about the Commission can equally be said about the Council and what can be said about a decision can equally be said about a regulation. Therefore, where the reasons turn out to be insufficient in the circumstances of the case, the sanction of nullity may be applied on the ground of the infringement of an essential procedural requirement[19]. Perhaps the

13 Reg. 15/64, JO 573/64.
14 This can be inferred from the judgment of the ECJ Cases 1 and 57, 14/57: *Société des Usines à Tubes de la Sarre v High Authority of the ECSC* [1957–58] ECR 105, referring to 'decision' under the ECSC Treaty.
15 EEC, art. 190; ECSC, art. 15; EAEC, art. 162.
16 Case 18/62: *Barge v High Authority of the ECSC* [1963] ECR 259, [1965] CMLR 330.
17 Case 5/67: *W Beus GmbH & Co v Hauptzollamt München* [1968] ECR 83 at 95, [1968] CMLR 131.
18 Case 26/62: *Germany v EEC Commission* [1963] ECR 63 at 69.
19 EEC art. 173: Case 18/57: *Nold K G v High Authority of the ECSC* [1959] ECR 41 at 52; Case 6/72: *Europemballage Corpn and Continental Can Co Inc v EC Commission* [1973] ECR 215, [1973] CMLR 199; Case 73/74: *Groupement des Fabricants de Papiers Peints de Belgique v EC Commission* [1975] ECR 149, [1976] 1 CMLR 589.

most instructive examples of the annulment on that ground are the Isoglucose cases[20] which have incidentally raised important questions concerning the Parliament's (albeit very limited) participation in Community legislation and the right of intervention before the ECJ. At issue was the validity of Council Regulation 1293/79 (OJ 1979, L 162/10) fixing quotas for the production of isoglucose and imposing a tax on this product. The Regulation was successfully challenged by isoglucose producers since it discriminated in favour of sugar producers. However the Regulation was also bad because in the circumstances the essential requirement, i.e. consultation with Parliament in accordance with article 43 (2) of the EE Treaty, was not observed.

Defective[1] regulations are presumed valid and effective as long as they have not been declared invalid by the Community Court.

Regulations have to be published in the Official Journal of the Community. They become binding on the date specified or, in the absence of a commencing date, on the twentieth day following their publication[2]. However, neither the publicity nor the form of the act will be decisive in determining the nature of the act, that is whether or not it is a regulation. The Community Court took the view that it was necessary to consider the contents rather than the form of the act to determine its legal nature[3]. Should this be otherwise, improper acts dressed up as regulations would enable the Community organs to exercise their powers arbitrarily and so would erode the legal protection under the Treaty.

As we have observed earlier, regulations have a mandatory effect. They bind the states and have the force of law in their territories without the need of transformation or confirmation by their legislatures. Thus it was held by the Community Court[4] that Council

20 Joint Cases 103/77 and 145/77: *Royal Scholten-Honig (Holdings) Ltd v Intervention Board for Agricultural Produce and Tunnel Refineries Ltd v Intervention Board for Agricultural Produce* [1978] ECR 2037, [1979] 1 CMLR 675; Case 138/79: S A *Roquette Frères v EC Council* [1980] ECR 3333; and Case 139/79: *Maizena GmbH v EC Council* [1980] ECR 3393; Jacobs, F., *Isoglucose Resurgent Two Powers of the European Parliament upheld by the Court*, 18 CML Rev (1981), p. 219.
1 Case 101/78: *Granaria BV v Hoofdproduktschap voor Akkerbouwprodukten* [1979] ECR 623, [1979] 3 CMLR 124.
2 EEC, art. 191 (1); EAEC, art. 163 (1).
3 Cf. Cases 16 and 17/62: *Confédération Nationale des Producteurs des Fruits et Légumes v EEC Council* [1962] ECR 471 at 478–479, [1963] CMLR 160 at 173–174.
4 Case 93/71: *Orsolina Leonesio v Italian Ministry of Agriculture* [1972] ECR 287 at 295, [1973] CMLR 343.

Regulation 1975/69 and Commission Regulation 2195/69, which provided for the payment of a premium in respect of slaughtered dairy cows, were 'directly applicable' and required no domestic provisions to make them effective in Italy so as to create rights vested in the individuals concerned. They left no discretion to member states. Therefore Italy was in default because she failed to meet her obligation, the inefficiency of the national apparatus affording no defence[5]. In the literature the power to legislate in this way reflects the 'institutional autonomy'[6] of the Community and the concept of 'delegated legislation'[7]. The member states are at the receiving end and it is their duty to see that the regulation is carried out. 'Consequently', held the ECJ[8], 'all methods of implementation are contrary to the Treaty which would have the result of creating an obstacle to the direct effect of Community Regulation and jeopardising their simultaneous and uniform application in the whole of the Community' . . .

The obligatory nature of the regulation and the duty to implement it are well illustrated in the Tachograph[9] case where the British Government unsuccessfully contended that it was free to enact a permissive measure when Council regulation 1463/70 insisted that the installation of recording equipment in certain vehicles was compulsory and subject to sanction for non-compliance. Holding the United Kingdom liable for a breach of the Treaty the ECJ ruled that it would be inconceivable to allow a member state to implement a regulation . . . 'in an incomplete or selective manner' . . . 'So as to render abortive certain aspects of Community legislation which it has opposed or which it considered contrary to its national interest[10] . . .'

Earlier the ECJ[11] defended the integrity of Community law by pointing out that a member state, when passing a regulation into the national law, must not disguise its Community character by altering, for example, the date on which the regulation came into force. However for practical reasons, a regulation may have to be

5 Case 39/72: *EC Commission v Italy* [1973] ECR 101, [1973] CMLR 439.

6 Rideau, J. *Le rôle des états membres dans l'application du droit communautaire,* AFDI, 1972, p. 864 (884-5).

7 Pescatore, P. *L'ordre juridiques des Communautées européennes,* 2nd edn 1975, pp. 192-3.          8 Note 5, op. cit. at 114.

9 Case 128/78: *EC Commission v United Kingdom* [1979] ECR 419, [1979] 2 CMLR 45; see also Case 39/72: *EC Commission v Italy* [1973] ECR 101, [1973] CMLR 439.

10 At 46.

11 Case 34/73: *Variola SpA v Amministrazione Italiane delle Finanze* [1973] ECR 981.

converted into the terms of domestic law (as was, for example, the case of the EEC Egg Marketing Regulations 2772/75 and 95/69 on labelling and quality control) in which case a national measure would be permitted if not incompatible with the terms of the regulation[12]. In other words, in the absence of any provision in the Regulations regarding the purchase of bands and labels to be affixed to egg packs, the member states are free to make arrangements for the issue of bands and labels and charge for the supervision of the marketing system. The position of regulations *vis-à-vis* the municipal law has been firmly established by the ECJ ruling that a regulation cannot be overriden by subsequent national legislation inconsistent with it[13].

Since both the Council and the Commission are empowered to make regulations, a theoretical and practical question of precedence between these two organs may arise. Indeed Advocate-General Roemer argued in a case[14] concerning regulations issued by the Council that they should override regulations issued by the Commission. Theoretically there should be no conflict, practically a conflict can arise if powers are delegated as seems possible under article 87. The problem resolves itself into a question of interpretation. Thus it was held[15] that under article 155 (4) (exercise of powers conferred on the Commission for the implementation of the rules laid down by the Council) there can be no delegation of powers by the Council and that, consequently, article 235 could not be relied on in order to justify delegation of discretionary power to the Commission in respect of export security.

Over the years regulations have been mounting steadily indicating that this is a measure favoured by the Community organs[16].

12 Case 31/78: *Bussone v Italian Ministry for Agriculture and Forestry* [1978] ECR 2429 at 2444, [1979] 3 CMLR 18 at 30.
13 Case 6/64: *Costa Flaminio v ENEL* [1964] ECR 585 at 586–587, [1964] CMLR 425 at 456; Case 43/71: *Politi SAS v Italian Ministry of Finance* [1971] 2 ECR 1039 at 1048–1049, [1973] CLMR 60, *Simmenthal Cases* 35/76; [1976] ECR 1871, [1977] 2 CMLR 1; 106–77 (No 2) [1978] ECR 629, [1978] 3 CMLR 263; 70/77 (No 3) [1978] ECR 1453, [1978] 3 CMLR 670.
14 Case 32/65: *Italian Government v EEC Council and EEC Commission* [1966] ECR 389 at 415, [1969] CMLR 39 at 46.
15 In cases 11/2–79/67: *Re Export of Oat Flakes* [1969] CMLR 85.
16 Brinkhorst, L. J., 'Implementation of (non-self-executing) Legislation of the European Economic Community, including Directives', *Legal Problems of an Enlarged European Community*, edited by Bathurst, M. E., and Others (1972), p. 74.

## (b) *Directives*

As compared with regulations which are, in principle, 'binding in their entirety', directives issued by the Council and the Commission are 'binding as to the result to be achieved, upon each member state to which it is addressed' and the choice of the method is left to the state concerned (article 189 (3), but under ECSC, article 14 recommendations correspond to directives). We can see that, unlike regulations, directives are not meant to be an instrument of uniformity even if the same objective is aimed at when a directive is addressed to several states simultaneously. In practice, therefore, directives are used to effect approximation of national laws as testified by the Community activity in this field[17].

Directives must be addressed to states, they cannot be addressed to individuals[18]. This does not preclude creation of rights for individuals or pleading the directive before the municipal courts[19].

Whilst the choice of the method is left to the adressee the Community usually sets a time limit upon the implementation of the directives which, like regulations, emanate either from the Council or the Commission. The reason for this is that time is needed in order to adapt the municipal law accordingly. Even so states are not always able to comply promptly. The speed with which the Value Added Tax was introduced in Italy is a good example of this, showing, incidentally, that a directive is probably less effective than a regulation.

Like regulations directives have to be reasoned or 'motivated' and based on the Treaty. They have to be notified to the addressees and will take effect upon such notification[20]. They may be addressed in the language of the addressee state[1].

As a source of Community law directives appear less prominent than regulations but their potential should not be underestimated. Their direct effect in the member states, i.e. whether they create rights which the citizen can vindicate in his national courts, has

17 See *Third General Report of the Communities* (1970), para. 63.
18 Cases 56–58/64: *Consten and Grundig v EEC Commission* [1966] ECR 299 at 337, [1966] CMLR 418 at 468.
19 E.g. directive 64/221/EEC, JO 850/64, art. 4 (3): 'The member states cannot introduce new measures or acts which are of a more restrictive nature than those in force at the time of notification of this directive'; Case 41/74: *Van Duyn v Home Office (No 2)* [1975] Ch 358, [1975] ECR 1337; cf. Case 28/67: *Molkerei-Zentrale v Hauptzollamt Paderborn* [1968] ECR 143, [1968] CMLR 187; see also, Case 9/70: *Grad v Finanzamt Traunstein* [1970] 2 ECR 825, [1971] CMLR 1. (decision and directives on turnover tax).
20 EEC, art. 191 (2); EAEC, art. 163 (2).
 1 Council Regulation 1/58, art. 3, JO, 6 October 1958, p. 385/58 (5th edn 1952–1958, p. 59).

been subject to controversy. The Belgian Counseil d'Etat held[2] that directive 64/221 purporting to co-ordinate the rules of deportation of foreign nationals had such effect in Belgium, but several years later, despite the judgment of the ECJ in the *Van Duyn* case (which shall be considered later) the French Conseil d'Etat denied the direct effect of the same directive[3].

Being addressed to the states and having to be implemented by the states in whatever manner they deem appropriate, directives, by their designation appear to have an indirect effect. However, in substance they may well be sufficiently explicit and detailed to make transformation a mere formality. In such a case, if inconsistent with municipal law, they should have an overriding effect. This seems to be the tenor of the decision of the Belgian Conseil d'Etat cited above. The Community Court was more definite in this respect. In *Grad v Finanzamt Traunstein*[4] the Court stated that 'if, in accordance with article 189, regulations are directly applicable and consequently are, by their very nature, capable of producing direct legal effects, it does not follow that the other acts mentioned in this article can never have similar effects' and concluded that 'the provisions of the decision and of the directives, taken together, produce direct effects in the relations between the member states and their citizens and create for the latter the right to enforce them before the courts'. Grad, a haulage contractor, was caught in a tax law confusion. By Council decision 65/271[5] a uniform turnover tax system to promote competition in transport was introduced. Later two Council directives[6] provided for the introduction of the Value Added Tax as from 1 January 1972. Germany brought the VAT into operation ahead of the Community schedule and as from 1 January 1968 applied it to transport in lieu of the previous tax system. However it imposed a new tax on road transport as from 1 January 1969 providing that it would cease to apply by 31 December 1970. Grad objected to this new tax which, in turn, raised the question of the effect of the decision in Germany.

2 *Corvelyn v Belgium*, 7 October 1968, [1969] *Cahiers de droit européen* 343, at 345-46.

3 In *Minister of the Interior v Cohn-Bendit* [1979] Dalloz 155; [1980] I CMLR 543; see also Bundesfinanzhof in *Re Value Added Tax Directives* (Case VB 51/80), [1982] I CMLR 527.

4 Op. cit., 9/70: [1970] 2 ECR 825 at 837, see also on turnover tax Case 20/70, *Transports Lesage & Cie v Hauptzollamt Freiburg* [1970] ECR 861, [1971] CMLR 1; Case 23/70: *Haselhorst v Finanzamt Düsseldorf-Altstadt* [1970] ECR 881, [1971] CMLR 1.        5 OJ Sp. edn 1965, p. 67.

6 Directive 67/227, OJ Sp edn, 1967, p. 14 amended by Directive 69/463, OJ Sp. edn, 1969, p. 551.

The ECJ held that the decision was directly applicable and so were the two directives. At the end there was no consolation for Grad because the relevant provision of the decision applied only from 1 January 1972, i.e. the date of the introduction of the VAT in the Community and, therefore, the internal tax system prevailed in the interim. However the case broke new ground as regards the effectiveness of measures other than regulations.

The second important case in this respect was SACE[7]. In order to accelerate the process of the removal of customs duties ahead of the Treaty schedule directive 68/31[8] required Italy to abolish certain administrative charges imposed on imports by 1 July 1968. The directive was prompted by the Decision 66/532[9]. The point was whether in order to benefit SACE, the combined effect of the decision and the directive overruled the Italian law which authorised the charges imposed after the date fixed by the directive but before the expiry of the transitional period envisaged by the Treaty. The ECJ held that Italy was under obligation to accelerate the process in accordance with the directive and, therefore, SACE had a directly enforceable right in this respect.

In *Re Forestry Reproductive Material*[10] case the Court reaffirmed its position saying that ... 'if in respect of member states to which it is addressed, the provisions of a directive have no less binding an effect than that of any other rule of Community law, such an effect applies all the more to provisions relating to the time limits for implementing the measures provided for' ...

Further decisions along the same lines followed. In *Van Duyn v Home Office*[11] the ECJ held directive 64/221 together with article 48 (3) as having a direct effect as far as the right of entry of a worker and the derogation on the ground of public policy on the part of a member state were concerned. Thus the directive explained and complemented the relevant provision of the Treaty. In the second *Defrenne* case[12] the combined effect of article 119 of the EEC Treaty and directive 75/117[13] to implement the principle of equal pay for equal work (laid down in the above-mentioned article) vindicated the right of a Belgian Air hostess to an equal treatment with her

7 Case 33/70: *SACE SpA v Italian Ministry for Finance* [1970] ECR 1213, [1971] CMLR 123.
8 JO 1968, 12/8.                              9 JO 1966, 2971.
10 Case 79/72: *EC Commission v Italian Republic* [1973] ECR 667 at 672, [1973] CMLR 773 at 781.
11 Case 41/74: [1974] ECR 1337, [1975] 1 CMLR 1.
12 Case 43/75: *Defrenne v SABENA* [1976] ECR 455, [1976] 2 CMLR 98.
13 OJ 1976, L 39.

male colleagues but only as far as their pay was concerned. The decision was much criticised[14] as one stretching the teleological interpretation too far and virtually usurping a legislative function which the Court does not possess but, it seems, it cannot be faulted on that ground. However in subsequent proceedings[15] the Court felt unable to stretch the point to cover all conditions at work. The *Defrenne* case stands out not only as an example of extensive interpretation of a directive made in aid of a Treaty provision but also of direct effect of a directive on the rights of individuals.

An individual may rely on a directive not only to claim a right rooted in Community law but also to bring a valid defence to prosecution under national law which is at variance with it. The point is well illustrated in the *Ratti* case[16]. Ratti was prosecuted for offences against Italian law in respect of packaging and labelling of certain products. His defence was that he complied with directive 73/173[17] and directive 77/728[18] on the packaging and labelling of solvents and varnishes respectively, neither directive having been implemented in Italy. He both succeeded and failed. The former was to be implemented by 8 December 1974, the latter by 9 November 1979 but Ratti anticipated both and in doing so was in collision with Italian law which remained unamended. On reference for a preliminary ruling the ECJ held that a directive can become directly effective when the time limit put for its implementation has been reached. Thus Ratti was protected under the former but not under the latter directive and, therefore, had a defence to charges in respect of solvents but none in respect of varnishes. The fact that he imported some of the varnishes from Germany where the relevant directive had been implemented afforded him no defence under Italian law. It follows that the date of the entry into force of the directive according to Community law is decisive[19].

The ghost of Grad appeared recently in a case[20] where a German taxpayer claimed exemption from VAT in respect of credit negotiation transactions based on directive 77/388 concerning the har-

---

14 Hamson, C. J., Methods of Interpretation – A Critical Assessment of the Results; *Judicial and Academic Conference*, 27–28 September 1976.
15 Case 149/77: *Defrenne v SABENA* [1978] ECR 1365; [1978] 1 CMLR 312.
16 Case 148/78: *Pubblico Ministero v Ratti* [1979] ECR 1629, [1980] 1 CMLR 96; see also Case 79/72: *EC Commission v Italian Republic* [1973] ECR 667 at 672, [1973] CMLR 773 at 781.
17 OJ 1973, L 189/7.  18 OJ 1977, L 303/23.
19 See also concerning a regulation: Case 244/78: *Union Laitière Normande v French Dairy Farmers Ltd* [1979] ECR 2663, [1980] 1 CMLR 314.
20 Case 8/81: *Becker v Finanzamt Münster – Innenstadt* [1982] 1 CMLR 499 at 512.

monization of turnover taxes which at that time had not been implemented in Germany. The ECJ, repeating virtually verbatim its dictum on the nature of directives expressed in Grad, concluded that, especially in the light of the Ratti case, the taxpayer may rely on the provisions of a directive if they are unconditional and sufficiently precise. In such a case a state cannot take advantage of its failure to implement the directive. However the German Federal Fiscal Court, relying expressly upon the decision of the French Conseil d'Etat in the *Cohn – Bendit* case denied the direct effect of directive 77/388 on the ground that it had not been enacted into a national statute. It thought that whilst the directive was binding upon member states it could not create 'directly applicable law in those states'[1].

As mentioned earlier directives, according to article 189, are meant to be different from regulations. In a sense they are because they allow a defined objective to be achieved by diverse methods. However some directives are drafted in considerable detail leaving little discretion for the member states and, where they provide a blue print for an entirely novel legislation, they are indistinguishable from regulations. However qualitatively they are distinguishable from regulations in so far as they are addressed to the member states and not to the whole world generally; they do not rule *erga omnes* but the states; and where they affect individuals they do it by perfecting otherwise imperfect Community rights[2] or affording Community defences against prosecutions by the states in default[3]. In that sense directives are 'indirectly applicable'[4]. However their efficacy depends upon whether they are intended to create a 'direct effect' e.g. by perfecting the right of establishment of the medical profession through common requirements for medical training and the recognition of professional qualifications, or whether they merely impose an obligation upon the member states, e.g. by ordering them to introduce a humane method of animal slaughter[5]. In both cases the directives impose obligations upon the member states but in the former case the directive differs from a regulation only in form and nomenclature.

1 *Re Value Added Tax Directives* (Case VB 51/80), [1982] 1 CMLR 527 at 529.
2 E.g. *Defrenne*, op. cit.          3 E.g. *Ratti*, op. cit.
4 Cf. Opinion of A. G. Reischl in *Ratti*, op. cit. ECR at 1650; Warner, J.-P., The Relationship between European Community Law and the National Law of the Member States [1979] 93 LQR 349 at 359; but see Leitao, A. R., L'effet direct des directives: une mystification? [1981] RTDE 425.
5 Directive 75/577, OJ 1974, L 316/10.

Failure to enact a directive into national law will, as in the case of a regulation, expose the member states to enforcement proceedings[6]. In both cases the state concerned would be guilty of a breach of article 5 of the EEC Treaty and the relevant regulation or directive. Once the obligation has been perfected there is no defence, not even on the ground that the failure to implement the measure has had no adverse effect on the functioning of the Common Market[7].

Since directives have become the main instrument of harmonization or approximation of national laws their potential as a source of Community Law is quite considerable. However in practice the clear cut distinction between regulations and directives implied in the Treaty has been blurred.

## (c) *Decisions*

A decision[8] of the Council or the Commission is binding in its entirety upon those to whom it is addressed. It may be addressed either to member states or to individuals or corporations. It differs from a regulation which is formulated in an abstract manner. However a regulation does not become a decision merely because the addressees can be identified or, in other words, because its scope can be individualised[9]. It must be reasoned and notified to whom it is addressed though no particular form of notification is needed[10]. It takes effect upon notification[11].

Unlike a regulation a decision is binding upon the addressee only, but, unlike a directive, it is 'binding in its entirety' leaving no discretion in the manner in which it is to be carried out. However, a decision may be the result of an obligation imposed on the Commission by a regulation[12]. The term 'decision' has of course a special meaning to denote one of the sources of Community law. It is not, therefore, a mere conclusion of a process of reasoning or settlement or solution of a problem. Furthermore it is not a mere repetition of

---

**6** E.g. *Re Tachograph*, op cit (regulation); Case 147/77: *Re Animal Slaughter Directive EC Commission v Italy* [1978] 3 CMLR 428.

**7** Case 95/77: *EC Commission v Netherlands* [1978] ECR 863.

**8** EEC, art. 189 (4); EAEC, art. 161 (4); ECSC, art. 14 (2).

**9** Case 789/79: *Calpak SpA v EC Commission* [1981] 1 CMLR 26.

**10** Case 6/72: *Europemballage Corpn Continental Can Co Inc v EC Commission* [1973] ECR 215 at 221, [1972] CMLR 690 at 691.

**11** Cases 98/78: *Racke v Hauptzollamt Mainz* [1979] ECR 69 and 99/78: *Decker KG v Hauptzollamt Landau* [1979] ECR 101.

**12** Case 16/65: *Schwarze v Einfuhr- und Vorratsstelle für Getreide und Füttermittel* [1965] ECR 877, [1966] CMLR 172.

an established rule[13] or a stage in internal procedure[14], or an instruction to an agency set up by the Community[15]. The many cases under article 14 of the ECSC Treaty provided an opportunity for the Community Court to define the meaning of 'decision' and the definition in one of such cases seems apposite to the position under the EEC Treaty. The Court held that 'a decision must appear as an act originating from the competent organisation intended to produce judicial effects, constituting the ultimate end of the internal procedure of this organisation and according to which such organisation makes its final ruling in a form allowing its nature to be identified[16].

Whether an administrative act of the organs of the Community is a regulation, directive or decision is determined not by its form but by its content and object[17], or, as put by the Advocate-General Roemer[18], it is the function of the act rather than the process of its formation which should be primarily examined.

Under article 33 of the ECSC Treaty a distinction is made between general and individual decisions depending on the manner in which the addressees are affected[19]. General decisions are 'quasi legislative acts made by a public authority and having a rule-making effect *erga omnes*'[20]. Individual decisions were held to be decisions in which the competent authority had to 'determine such concrete cases as are submitted to it'[1]. In the cited case the High Authority had to determine the principles concerning the calculation of contribution towards compensation due from certain undertakings.

The problem under the EEC Treaty is one of 'mixed acts' that is

---

**13** Case 9/56: *Meroni & Co, Industrie Metallurgiche SpA v High Authority of the ECSC* [1957–58] ECR 133.
**14** Cases 53–54/63: *Lemmerz-Werke GmbH v High Authority of the ECSC* [1963] ECR 239 at 247, 248 [1964] CMLR 384 at 399.
**15** Case 21/58: *Felten und Guilleaume Carlswerke Eisen- und Stahl AG v High Authority of the ECSC* [1959] ECR 99.
**16** Case 54/65: *Compagnie des Forges de Châtillon, Commentry et Neuves-Maisons v High Authority of the ECSC* [1966] ECR 185 at 195, [1966] CMLR 525 at 538.
**17** Cases 16–17/62: *Confédération Nationale des Producteurs de Fruits et Légumes v EEC Council* [1962] ECR 171 at 477–479, [1963] CMLR 160 at 173–174.
**18** Case 40/64: In *Sgarlata v EEC Commission* [1965] 1 ECR 215 at 231, [1966] CMLR 314 at 318.
**19** Case 18/57: *Nold KG v High Authority of the ECSC* [1959] ECR 41 at 49–50; Cases 55–59/63, 61–63/63: *Modena v High Authority of the ECSC* [1964] ECR 211 at 227, 228 [1964] CMLR 401 at 413.
**20** *Nold*, op. cit. at 50.
 **1** Case 20/58: *Phoenix-Rheinrohr AG v High Authority of the ECSC* [1959] ECR 75 at 88–89.

to say acts with the character of regulations[2] and decisions or directives[3] and decisions. Such mixed measures seem impossible under the ECSC Treaty[4] but they came to light under the EEC Treaty. Assuming that such measures are valid per se the practical question of the scope of their application arises or, more precisely, whether they affect individuals apart from states and whether they can give recourse to individuals under article 173 (2). It was held[5] that a measure which could be classified as a regulation could contain provisions applicable to individuals and thus enable them to take action under article 173 (2). On the other hand, a Commission decision merely to reject a claim for amendment of a regulation will be treated as analogous to a regulation[6] with the result that an individual may not have the necessary locus standi under article 173 (2) which provides that 'any natural or legal person may ... institute proceedings against a decision addressed to that person or against a decision which, although in the form of a regulation or a decision addressed to another person, is of direct and individual concern to the former'.

The problem[7] of a directive and decision was raised by the *Finanzgerichte* (Finance Courts) of Munich (Case 9/70), Baden-Würtemberg (Case 20/70) and Düsseldorf (Case 23/70) which moved the Community Court to rule whether article 4 of *Decision* 65/271/ EEC, JO 1500/65, read together with article 1 of the first *Directive* on Turnover Tax, JO 1301/67 'are directly binding in the relations between Member States and private persons and create individual rights which can be invoked before municipal courts'. The Community Court ruled that article 189 does not prevent private individuals from founding their actions before municipal courts upon *Directives* and *Decisions* addressed to member states. Concluding that these measures can have, in appropriate cases, an internal effect, a learned jurist remarked that, as a result, an important

---

2 E.g. *Plaumann*, op. cit., p. 81 where the ECJ held that to be a decision an act ought to be addressed to a particular person and have a binding effect upon that person.

3 E.g. *Consten v Grundig*, op. cit., p. 102, note 18. See also Grad, op. cit.

4 *Nold*, above, and Case 9/55: *Fédération Charbonnière de Belgique v High Authority of the ECSC* [1954–56] ECR 245 at 247, also Advocate-General Lagrange in Case 30/59: *De Gezamenlijke Steenkolenmijnen in Limburg v High Authority of the ECSC* [1961] ECR 1.

5 In Case 30/67: *Industria Molitoria Imolese v EEC Council* [1968] ECR 115, 5 CML Rev 480 see also Case 123/77: *UNICME v EC Council* [1978] ECR 845 at 851.

6 Case 42/71: *Firma Nordgetreide GmbH & Co KG v EC Commission* [1973] CMLR 177.

7 Brinkhorst, L. J., op. cit., p. 75; and Mitchell, J. D. B., 'Community Legislation', ibid., p. 100.

barrier against the legal protection of private parties against these Community measures has been removed[8].

In the course of time certain categories of 'decision' having diverse effects have emerged. These include:

*Executive decisions,* e.g. to engage the Community in external relations whether strictly within the Treaty framework (i.e. trade agreements and association agreements) or peripheral to it (e.g. to take diplomatic initiatives in regard to the Middle East problems taken during the British Presidency of the Community in the latter half of 1981). The former, as we have seen, create rights and obligations vested in the member states and individuals, the latter do not. In the area of organisational law, e.g. the Commission by Decision 73/351[9] set up an Advisory Committee on Customs Matters. By a series of Council decisions the monetary policy such as it is has been put into operation[10]. These acts of the Institutions do not resemble exactly the definitions of decisions so far elicited from the judgments of the ECJ mentioned above.

*Administrative decisions* comprise the internal acts of the Community such as the appointment, promotion and dismissal of officials or the distribution of functions within the Community bureaucracy. They also comprise Commission decisions in the field of dumping, state aids and allocation of funds in the execution of certain policies e.g. regional, social.

*Quasi-judicial decisions* in their classical forms comprise the decisions of the Commission in a process of adjudication of the behaviour of member states (i.e. preliminary to enforcement proceedings) or enterprises in the field of competition (i.e. negative clearance, exemptions, determination of infringements).

The variety of 'decisions' is confusing for some are, some are not, legally binding. However a distinction can be made between binding and non-binding decisions. The former are made within the legal framework of the Treaty in the sense of EEC article 189. They are formal acts complying with procedural requirements; they impose rights or obligations upon the Institutions, or the member states or individuals and are subject to judicial control by the ECJ. The latter do not constitute formal acts of the Institutions, do not comply with strictly legal and formal Treaty requirements and, therefore, are not subject to judicial control. They are taken within

---

**8** Brinkhorst, L. J., op. cit., p. 76.
**9** OJ 1973, L 321/37 amended by decision 76/921, OJ 1976, L 362/55.
**10** Lasok, op. cit., p. 152 et seq.

the political framework of the Community to conduct or settle Community affairs and, consequently, do not impose rights or obligations upon the Institutions, or the member states or individuals.

## (B) NON-OBLIGATORY ACTS

It is debatable whether recommendations[11] and opinions[12] can be regarded as sources of Community law. These are listed in article 189 of the EEC Treaty as attributes of the power of the Council and Commission necessary for the execution of their task but, unlike regulations, directives and decisions, are said to have 'no binding force'. Unfortunately there is a certain terminological confusion resulting from the interaction of the three foundation treaties as the basic sources of Community law. The law-making acts of the ECSC (article 14) differ from those of the EEC (article 189) and EAEC (article 161). The High Authority of the ECSC can make *decisions* which are mandatory in all their aspects and *recommendations* within the scope defined by the Treaty, the choice of the methods of executing recommendations being left to those to whom they are addressed. In this way *decisions* of the ECSC correspond to both *regulations* and *decisions* of the EEC whilst *recommendations* of the ECSC correspond to *directives* of the EEC and EAEC. The High Authority of the ECSC can promulgate opinions which are not binding.

Taking the binding force as a criterion of the authority of the acts of the Community organs *opinions* cannot be regarded as a source of Community law but *recommendations* can only in so far as they are made under the ECSC Treaty. *Recommendations* under the EEC Treaty have no force of law. The existence of 'non-binding' acts is not exclusive to the European Community. Such acts are typical of international organisations of sovereign states[13], which in theory cannot take orders from outside. The European Community, in spite of some measure of cohesion, still remains a community

---

11 E.g. *Re Luxembourg Agricultural Policy* 65/300/EEC 26 May 1965, (1965) CMLR 355.

12 E.g. Case 7/61: *EEC Commission v Italian Republic* [1961] ECR 317 at 326, [1962] CMLR 39 at 50.

13 Cf. Sloan, B., 'The Building Force of a "Recommendation" of the General Assembly of the United Nations', (1948), 25 BYBIL 1; Johnson, D. H., 'The Effect of Resolutions of the General Assembly of the United Nations', (1955-56) 32 BYBIL 97.

of sovereign states and so it has to be recognised that the Community organs have to carry out a variety of functions, some of which call for legislation, others for guidance[14]. Therefore, neither recommendations nor opinions of the Council and Commission should be disregarded. Their role is persuasive and constructive in the formulation and execution of the policies of the Community. Though they cannot be formally cited as sources of Community law they ought to be regarded, in the light of their potential, as auxiliary elements of the law making process of the Community.

In addition to the listed non-binding acts, various other instruments, such as memoranda[15], communications[16], deliberations[17], programmes[18], guidelines[19] and resolutions[20] came to light. These are non-Treaty acts descriptive of the various actions or procedures undertaken or carried out in the life of the Community. They have no binding legal effect unless, despite their nomenclature, they meet the criteria laid down in the Treaty for binding Community acts. Thus 'deliberations' were held to be capable of annulment because in the particular circumstances they were intended to bind the member states[1]. In *EC Commission v Luxembourg and Belgium*[2] the ECJ held that a resolution of the Council had no binding effect because it was merely an expression of intention. Probably in the

14 Cf. ECJ judgment in joint Cases 1/57 and 14/57; *Société des Usines à Tubes de la Sarre v High Authority of the ECSC* [1957–58] ECR 105 at 115.
15 E.g. Commission's Memorandum to Council of 18 March 1970 on the establishment of Industrial Policy, Fourth Ge. Report 1970 item 205 et seq; Commission to Council on action in the cultural sector EC Bull Supp 6/77, p. 5.
16 Communication by an official: Case 48/69: *Imperial Chemical Industries Ltd v EC Commission* [1972] 2 ECR 619, [1972] CMLR 557; Case 56/72: *Goeth-Van der Schuress v EC Commission* [1973] ECR 181; Commission's Communication to the Council on Admission to Institutions of Higher Education (Com) (78) 468 and 469, both of 22 September 1978.
17 Case 81/72: *EC Commission v EC Council* [1973] ECR 575, [1973] CMLR 639.
18 E.g. Council Decision 77/294, OJ 1977, L 101/1 adopting the Fourth Medium-term Programme. Council action programme to implement the Environmental Policy, JO, 1977, C 139/1.
19 E.g. Council Resolution laying down guidelines for the Regional Policy, OJ, 1979, C 36/10.
20 E.g. Resolution of the Council and of the Representatives of the Governments of 22 March 1972 concerning the implementation of the Resolution of 21 March 1972 concerning the setting up of an Economic and Monetary Union, OJ, 1972, C 38/3. In case 9/73: *Schlüter v Hauptzollamt Lörrach* [1973] ECR 1135 at 1162 a resolution was referred for interpretation to the ECJ.
1 ERTA case op. cit. p. 92, note 8, ante.
2 Case 90, 91/63 [1964] ECR 625, [1965] CMLR 58.

same category would be the joint resolution of the Parliament, the Commission and the Council[3] which proclaims that:

'1. The European Parliament, the Council and the Commission stress the prime importance they attach to the protection of fundamental rights, as derived in part from the constitutions of the Member States and the European Convention for the Protection of Human Rights and Fundamental Freedoms.'

'2. In the exercise of their powers and in pursuance of the aims of the European Communities they respect and will continue to respect these rights.'

A resolution may not be binding or creative of rights but, it seems, can be pleaded in support of a Treaty. It is doubtful though, whether like a directive, it can convert a programmatic provision of the Treaty into one having a direct effect. Such was the position in the Manghera case[4]. Manghera, in defiance of a state monopoly for the manufacture, import and sale of tobacco, imported a quantity of the product directly from another member state without paying the duties due under Italian law. This occurred after a resolution[5] of the Council of Ministers which endorsed the undertaking of two states in default (i.e. France and Italy) to abolish the existing commercial state monopolies by a certain date. On reference, the ECJ considered that Manghera had a good defence not by virtue of the resolution which the Court found incapable of engendering private rights but by virtue of the direct effect of article 37 (1) of the Treaty as from the end of the period of transition.

Under certain provisions of the EEC Treaty[6] the Commission has been authorised to issue recommendations to member states. In the terms of article 189 these instruments have no binding effect but form an important step in the process of the harmonisation of laws. Therefore, it has been suggested[7], that recommendations might be used as instruments of harmonisation alongside the binding acts, viz. regulations and directives. Whilst recognising the potential of recommendations as a starting point in the process of Community legislation it is difficult to concede to their promotion

---

3 OJ, 1977, C 103/1.
4 Case 59/75: *Pubblico Ministero v Flavia Manghera* [1976] ECR 91, [1976] 1 CMLR 557.
5 JO 1970, C 50.
6 Arts. 27, 64, 81, 102.
7 Soldatos, P. and Vandersanden, G. 'La recommandation, source indirecte du rapprochement', in De Ripainsel-Landy, D., et al *Les instruments du Rapprochement des Legislations dans la Communauté Economique Européene*, (1976) p. 95 et seq.

from non-binding to binding acts without an amendment to the Treaty.

### (C) CONTROL OF THE COMMUNITY LEGISLATION

All the acts of the Community organs are subject to the principle of legality as is the case with the executive and administrative acts of a law-abiding state. This principle imposes a certain limit upon the Community organs as they have to operate within the scope of their organic powers (*infra legem*) or within the scope of their delegated powers. The Treaties are quite explicit in this respect. Article 4 of the EEC Treaty provides that the functions of the Community shall be carried out by the Assembly, the Council, the Commission and the Court of Justice and that 'each institution shall act within limits of the powers conferred upon it by the Treaty'.

If we accept the analogy of the EEC Treaty to a state constitution we can construe a system of control of the acts of the Community organs parallel to that of the acts of state organs. In most systems we can note a triple form of control: constitutional, political (or parliamentary) and judicial, to which we can add for good measure the control by what passes for 'public opinion'.

Thus the constitution (Treaty) sets up the system and defines the functions and powers of the state (Community) organs. The constitutional control is a strictly legal control in so far as it rests upon the assumption that the state itself is governed by law (*Rechtsstaat*, see Bracton on the Rule of Law) and that the machinery of the state operates according to law. Since all the member states of the Community subscribe to the notion of the *Rechtsstaat* there is no reason to suppose that the Community would be different.

Political or parliamentary control of the executive takes various forms: debate, questions, censure. The legislative acts of the executive are subject to parliamentary scrutiny and where breaches of the constitution are alleged the matter may be considered by a constitutional tribunal or (as in the case of the United Kingdom) parliament itself. This does not preclude a judicial review. The Assembly of the European Community can hardly be regarded as a parliament in the accepted sense of the word. It is a deliberative body and in a limited sense a controlling body. Its control is confined to the control of the Commission as the chief bureaucratic body but, not being a fully-fledged parliament, it neither legislates nor controls the legislative acts of the Community organs[8].

In the Community the control of legality is in the hands of the Community Court[9]. Thus, apart from the duty of ensuring that the law is observed in the interpretation and application of the Treaty, the Court has the power of judicial review of the legality of acts of the Council and the Commission. These include regulations, directions and decisions which are 'binding' but exclude recommendations and opinions which are 'not binding'. The legal status of the Community acts determines the scope of judicial control. It follows that only the 'binding acts' may, in accordance with the Treaties[10], be subject to judicial control.

The making, the notification and the publication of the binding acts are subject to the Court's scrutiny from the point of view of legality, form and publicity of these acts. The Court has jurisdiction in actions brought by a member state, the Council or the Commission and may pronounce nullity of the act concerned on grounds of 'lack of competence, infringement of an essential procedural requirement, infringement of the Treaty or of any rule of law relating to its application, or misuse of powers'[11].

A natural or legal person can also institute proceedings for the annulment of a decision addressed to that person or a decision which, 'although in the form of a regulation or a decision addressed to another person, is of direct and individual concern to [the complainant'[12]. Therefore, held the ECJ[13], an application for annulment of a decision was unfounded if the applicant had no longer any legally recognised interest in the matter. Indeed it would constitute an abuse of the judicial process to pursue the action when a judgment of the ECJ concerning the same parties and a similar question was already given in another case. Thus the application for annulment of a Commission decision fixing the minimum price of frozen beef put up for sale by the intervention agency had to be dismissed when the applicant having offered a lower price (which was rejected), brought an action for annulment of the decision rejecting his offer.

8 However see the *Isoglucose* cases, op. cit. p. 99 ante.
9 EEC, art. 164, 173, 177.
10 EEC, art. 173; EAEC, art. 146; ECSC, art. 33.
11 EEC, art. 173 (1).
12 EEC, art. 173 (2).
13 Case 243/78: *Simmenthal SpA v EC Commission* [1980] ECR 593.

(D) JUDICIAL LEGISLATION

## (a) *The powers of ECJ*

The Court has the duty of ensuring observance of the law and whilst doing so may explain and complement the Treaties and subordinate Community legislation. This gives the Court an opportunity of laying down or defining Community law. The powers and functions of the Court will be analysed elsewhere[14] and it will suffice here to investigate the ways in which the Court may contribute to the sources of Community law.

The Court, as a fully-fledged judicial body, has the power necessary to carry out its duties as specified in the Treaties. Its jurisdiction is exceptional in the sense that it is not a substitute for the national courts of the member states, and that its jurisdiction is circumscribed by the Treaties. In all respects it is the internal Court of the Community and as far as legal style is concerned it is a continental court modelled upon the French Conseil d'Etat.

The powers of the Court include:

(*a*) the power of annulment which is the instrument of legality of the acts of the Community organs[15];

(*b*) the power of adjudication (*contentieux de pleine jurisdiction*)[16], which enables the Court to put pressure upon the member states in order to make them carry out their obligations;

(*c*) the power of repression[17], which enables the Court to enforce Community law;

(*d*) the power of arbitration[18];

(*e*) the power to decide disputes between the member states[19]; and

(*f*) the power of interpretation of the Treaties, the acts of the Community organs and of the constitutions of bodies established by the Council[20].

In so far as the Court has to ensure observance of the law it acts as an instrument of sovereignty; in so far as it has to ensure the

---

14 See Chapter 9, post.
15 EEC, arts. 173, 174, 175, 184.
16 EEC, arts. 169, 170, 171.
17 EEC, art. 170.
18 EEC, art. 181.
19 EEC, art. 182.
20 EEC, art. 177.

correct interpretation and application of the law as regards both the functioning of the Community and the development of the Community law, it exercises a law-making function appropriate to a judicial body. We shall address ourselves to the latter.

It is axiomatic that, given the requisite power, the lesser the precision of the law the greater the scope for judicial legislation. The Community Treaties are far from being precise and tightly drafted. In so far as they represent the Community framework it is the task of the Court to complete the system and fill the gaps.

### (b) Judicial interpretation

Interpretation is the principal method, and since the Court is a continental court it has adopted what might be termed the 'continental style'[1]. In the civil law systems the court has no law-making power and precedent is not regarded as a source of law. However, through the instrumentality of interpretation judges are in the position of filling the gaps in the legal system and through the definition of rights and duties in judgments they create a body of rules which, without any statutory authority, has a persuasive force. The Community Court is in a unique position: it is a court of first and only instance, it has the power to review the legality of the acts of the Community organs, has no parliament to look up to as a sovereign source of law and, above all, has to interpret Treaties which comprise general policies alongside precise rules of law[2]. In the circumstances the Community Court cannot help contributing to the growth of Community law.

In the absence of any canons of interpretation the Court is free to draw on rules evolved in the member states and will do so not only in the spirit of the Community but also for practical reasons, because Community law, in order to command general respect and acceptance has to be a synthesis of the laws of the member states and, at every stage of its growth, has to draw strength from the practices and principles already well established.

Literal, or grammatical, interpretation is always the basic method and where the meaning of the text is clear there is no need of interpretation for *clara non sunt interpretanda*. However, in the Community set-up Community legislation must conform to the

1 See p. 52 et seq., ante.
2 Cf. submissions of Advocate-General Roemer in Case 13/60: *Ruhrkohlen Verkaufs-GmbH v High Authority of the ECSC* [1962] ECR 83, [1962] CMLR 113 at 125, 128.

relevant Treaty so much so that the clear language of an act of a Community organ must not be allowed to prevail if, in the light of the Treaty, it leads to absurdity[3].

On the question of linguistic differences and inconsistencies between the different provisions of the Treaty, Advocate-General Roemer submitted in *Internationale Crediet- en Handelsvereniging 'Rotterdam' v Ministry of Agriculture and Fisheries*[4] that the same standard of draftsmanship as that in the national legislation cannot be expected in Treaties[5]. Literal interpretation must take this into account.

Next to literal interpretation comes the logical interpretation which requires the Court to consider the text within the context of the system. In *Simon v Court of Justice of the European Communities*[6] the Court held that where the text is ambiguous the most reasonable solution must be sought, and in *Société Technique Minière v Maschinenbau Ulm GmbH*[7] the Court restricted prohibitions in the Treaty to matters which it considered detrimental to the aims of the Community. In *Federal Republic of Germany v EEC Commission*[8] Advocate-General Roemer submitted that the Court should be guided by considerations which make good sense both politically and administratively, and in *Costa Flaminio v ENEL*[9] Advocate-General Lagrange stated that excessive formalism should give way to the Community spirit in relations between the Community and the member states. In a more technical sense Advocate-General Lagrange put in a nutshell the purpose of logical interpretation when he stressed in *Bosch v de Geus*[10] that the Court must not be defeated by obscurities or contradictions in the wording of the text for the real meaning can be deduced from the context or spirit of the text. In this vein several cases have been decided illustrating both the technique and law-making potential of logical interpretation[11].

---

3 Case 14/63: *Forges de Clabecq v High Authority of the ECSC* [1963] ECR 357 at 372, 373 [1964] CMLR 167 at 176; Case 2/67: *De Moor v Caisse de Pension des Enployés Privés* [1967] ECR 197, [1967] CMLR 223 at 230-31, 235.

4 Cases 73-74/63: [1964] ECR 1, [1964] CMLR 198 at 206.

5 Cf. Lord Denning in *H.P. Bulmer Ltd v J. Bollinger SA* [1974] 2 All ER 1226 at 1231-1232.

6 Case 15/60: [1961] ECR 115 at 125.

7 Case 56/65: [1966] ECR 235 at 248, 249, [1966] CMLR 357 at 371, 376.

8 Case 34/62: [1963] ECR 131 at 156, [1963] CMLR 369 at 380.

9 Case 6/64: [1964] ECR 585 at 609, [1964] CMLR 425 at 448.

10 Case 13/61: [1962] ECR 45 at 70, [1962] CMLR 1 at 23.

11 E.g. Case 10/61: *Re Italian Customs Duty on Radio Valves* [1962] CMLR 187 at 201-202; ref. to arts. 12, 14 (1) and 19 (2) (III); Case 75/63: *Unger v Bestuur der Bedrijfsvereniging voor Detailhandel en Ambachten* [1964] CMLR 319, ref. to art. 51; Case 24/62: *Re Tariff Quota on Wine* [1963] CMLR 347 at 336-367, ref.

Courts are notoriously reticent about the use of teleological in-terpretation which, though basically literal, brings out the intention of the legislature in the light of the conditions prevailing at the time of the judgment. The Treaties have not existed long enough to have, in the absence of revision, their lives extended by interpre-tation, but references to the spirit or the aims of the Treaties[12] enable the Court to fill the gaps in the system and so 'up-date' the text.

The Court does not act arbitrarily but judicially, which means that it has to see that its interpretation reflects the intention of the parties to the Treaties and the *ratio legis* of the text[13]. In tracing the intention the Court is free to consult materials extraneous to the Treaty. These consist of the *travaux préparatoires* leading to the conclusion of Treaties and statements on behalf of the Community. The former are the various publications which reflect the substance of the negotiations and the attitudes of the negotiating parties from the inception to the conclusion of the Treaties. One could single out in this context official communiques and minutes of meetings, should these be available, and the official views of the negotiating governments. In view of the nature of the negotiations and the way governments work in their international relations the materials available are not abundant. They have, according to a learned jurist[14], 'a certain value, though their precise juristic meaning is

to arts. 25 (3) and 29; Case 10/65: *Deutschmann v Federal Republic of Germany* [1965] CMLR 259, ref. to arts. 13 and 95; Case 27/67: *Fink-Frucht GmbH v Hauptzollamt München* [1968] CMLR 228 at 299, ref. to arts. 30 and 95; Case 29/68: *Milch- Fett- und Eierkontor GmbH v Hauptzollamt Saarbrücken* [1969] CMLR 390, ref. to arts. 9, 12, 13; Case 13/72: *Re Food Aids: Netherlands v EC Commission* [1973] ECR 27 at 40-42; see also the opinion of A. G. Roemer in Case 5/71: *Aktien-Zuckerfabrik Schoppenstedt v EEC Council* [1971] 2 ECR 975 and A. G. Warner in Case 81/72: *Re Civil Service Salaries EC Commission v EC Council* [1973] ECR 575 at 595-596, [1973] CMLR 639 at 652-653.

12 E.g. Case 56/65: *Société Technique Minière v Maschinenbau Ulm GmbH* [1966] ECR 235, [1966] CMLR 357; Case 24/62: *Federal Republic of Germany v EEC Commission* [1963] ECR 131, [1963] CMLR 369; Case 6/64: *Costa Flaminio v ENEL* [1964] CMLR 425; Case 13/61: *Bosch v de Geus* [1962] ECR 45, [1962] CMLR 1; Case 6/54: *Netherlands Government v High Authority* [1954-56] ECR 103; Case 6/60: *Jean E Humblet v Belgian State* [1960] ECR 559; Case 8-11/66: *Re Noordwijks Cement Accoord* [1967] CMLR 77 at 104-105; Case 9/55: *Fédération Charbonnière de Belgique v High Authority of the ECSC* [1954-56] ECR 245; Case 16/61: *Modena v High Authority of the ECSC* [1962] CMLR 221 at 241; *Continental Can*, op. cit. [1973] ECR at 243-245; [1973] CMLR at 223-225, 233-235; Case 151/73: *Ireland v EC Council* [1974] 1 CMLR 424 at 446-447.

13 Case 6/60: *Jean-E. Humblet v Belgian State* [1960] ECR 559, op. cit. at p. 1154.

14 Reuter, P., *La CECA* (1953), p. 30.

arguable'. So far the Court does not seem to have taken much notice of the *travaux préparatoires* though the advocates-general have referred to these in their submissions[15].

Statements on behalf of the Community may[16] elucidate the Community legislation but the views of the Community officials on the interpretation of the Treaties are hardly relevant[17]. They are equally ineffective as far as the interpretation of the Community legislation is concerned[18].

It follows that *travaux préparatoires*, as explained by Advocate-General Lagrange[19] have no compulsory place in the interpretation of Treaties, but it is universally accepted that judges may turn to them for information in order to clarify the thoughts of the legislator. The judges are entirely free in their evaluation of these materials.

In addition to interpretation in a technical sense further elements play an auxiliary part in the development of Community law. Of these we shall mention briefly references to the municipal laws of the member states, references to general principles of law and references to learned writings.

The Treaties, like the rules of public international law, are influenced by the rules of municipal law. More than that they are derived from the laws of the six founding states. It is natural, therefore, that the Community Court should turn for guidance to the laws of the member states. As submitted by Advocate-General Roemer[20] the Court has to 'call upon the law of the the different Member States in order to arrive at a meaningful interpretation of our Community

---

15 Cf. Lagrange in Case 9/55: *Fédération Charbonnière de Belgique v High Authority of the ECSC* [1954–56] ECR 245; Roemer in Case 6/54: *Netherlands Government v High Authority of the ECSC* [1954–56] ECR 103; Cases 90–91/63: *Re Import of Milk Products* [1965] CMLR 58 at 65; Case 13/60: *Ruhrkohlen-Verkaufs-GmbH v High Authority of the ECSC* [1962] CMLR 113 at 146; Cases 73–74/63: *Internationale Crediet- en Handelsvereniging 'Rotterdam' v Minister von Landbowwen Visseri* [1964] CMLR 198 at 207; Case 26/68: *Caisse Régionale de Securité Sociale du Nord v Torrekens* [1969] CMLR 377 at 382–383; and in Case 38/69: *Re Customs Duties on Lead and Zinc* [1970] CMLR 77 at 85; Case 42/72: A. G. Roemer in Alfons *Lütticke GmbH v Hauptzollamt Passau* [1973] ECR 57 at 74–75, [1973] CMLR 309 at 316–317.
16 Cases 2–10/62: *Societa Industriale Acciaierie San Michele v High Authority of the ECSC*, [1964] CMLR 146 at 165.
17 Roemer in Cases 90–91/63: *Re Import of Milk Products* [1965] CMLR 58 at 65; Cases 8–11/66: *Re Noordwijks Cement Accoord* [1967] CMLR 77 at 87.
18 Cases 53–54/63: *Lemmerz-Werke GmbH v High Authority of the ECSC* [1964] CMLR 384 at 398.
19 Case 9/55: *Fédération Charbonnière de Belgique v High Authority of the ECSC* [1954–56] ECR 245.
20 Case 6/54: in *Netherlands Government v High Authority of the ECSC* [1954–56] ECR 103.

law'. As a result some cases comprise a detailed comparative study. Perhaps the best examples are the cases involving misuse of power and withdrawal, with retrospective effect, of an illegal administrative act[1].

In the latter case the Court came to the conclusion that 'a study of comparative law shows that whenever an administrative act is wrong in law, the laws of the Member States admit the possibility of revocation', and in accordance with this finding decreed that such an act was revokable with a retrospective effect. It does not follow, however, that the laws of all the member states must be consulted. If the problem is peculiar to two countries a consideration of the two systems will be sufficient[2], and on occasions reference to one country only may suffice[3]. The other extreme, which the Court is free to adopt, is that sometimes a national system cannot be regarded as apposite[4]. More intriguing is the possibility of reference to the law of a non-member state, but this must be regarded as a special case. Indeed the Community law of monopolies and restrictive practices, being modelled upon American law, invites such a reference[5]. Before the British accession the English law of estoppel[6] was considered whilst recently Advocate-General Warner made a significant British contribution to the discussion of natural justice[7]. With the progress of time a body of general principles of law will emerge.

Echoing article 38 of the Statute of the International Court of Justice the Community Court also refers to 'general principles

1 See also Cases 7/56 and 3-7/57: *Alegra v Common Assembly* [1957-58] ECR 39; Case 14/61: *Hoogovens v High Authority of the ECSC* [1963] CMLR 73 at 90-91, 96; further examples: Campbell, A., *Common Market Law* (1969), Vol. I, 7.258, pp. 531-532.
2 A.G. Lagrange in Case 5/55: *Associazione Industrie Siderurgiche Italiane v High Authority of the ECSC* [1954-55] ECR 135.
3 French law: Cases 7 and 9/54: *Groupement des Industries Siderurgiques Luxembourgoises v High Authority of the ECSC* [1954-55] ECR 175; Case 12/74: *EC Commission v Federal Republic of Germany* [1975] ECR 18 at 209; German law: Case 18/57: *Nold KG v High Authority of the ECSC* [1959] ECR 41 pp. 110-111; Cases 17 and 20/61: *Kloeckner Werke und Hoesch v High Authority of the ECSC* [1962] ECR 325 at 351-353.
4 E.g. Case 1/64: *Glucosiéries Réunies v EEC Commission* [1964] CMLR 596 at 599.
5 Case 13/60: A.G. Roemer in *Ruhrkohlen-Verkaufs-GmbH v High Authority of the ECSC* [1962] CMLR 113 at 141; Case 16/61: *Modena v High Authority* [1962] CMLR 221 at 229-230, 232.
6 A.G. Roemer in Cases 41 and 50/59: *Hamborner Bergbau AG v High Authority of the ECSC* [1960] ECR 493. Cf. Case 48/72: *Brasserie de Haecht v Wilkin-Janssen*) [1973] ECR 77 at 87, [1973] CMLR 287 at 302.
7 Case 17/74: *Transocean Marine Paint Association v EC Commission* [1974] ECR 1063, [1974] 2 CMLR 459.

of law'. These can be traced to doctrines developed within the context of public international law[8] or the municipal law of the member states, but others remain untraceable[9]. No doubt the reference to 'general principles of law' has a certain scope as such principles may mean general doctrines of the law, e.g. justice, the right to be heard, etc., or rules of law expressed in general terms, e.g. contractual freedom, liability for wrongful act, non-discrimination, etc. Learned commentators[10] recognise the competence of the Court to take recourse to 'general principles of law'. Their views have been summarised as follows: 'il semble que lorsqu'une notion juridique existe, identique, dans le droit interne de tous les Etats membres, celle-ci s'impose aux organes de la Communauté comme un principe général qui doit être appliqué sous peine de la violation d'une règle de droit relative à l'application du traité'[11].

Finally we should note the contribution of learned writers (the so called *doctrine*) to the *Jurisprudence* of the Community Court. Here again an analogy to article 38 of the Statute of the International Court of Justice comes to mind where reference is made to 'the teachings of the most highly qualified publicists'. Continental courts are familiar with the contribution of learned writers to the development of the law and these, to command authority, need not necessarily be dead. Community law is still a relatively undeveloped system, a law in books rather than fully entrenched in life and, therefore, offers a challenge and scope for creative comments. *Doctrine* represents, of course, well founded opinions on what the law should be, not any piece of 'creative writing', by those who have established a reputation in their field. Its influence should not be exaggerated but viewed from the perspective of the standing of the academic lawyer in the civil law countries and the closer affinity of continental judges to the academic world rather than the Bar. The fact that, in spite of the abundance of academic writings on Community law, the Court only in few cases, albeit through the

---

8 E.g. on equality and discrimination, A.G. Lagrange in Case 13/63 *Re Electric Refrigerators* [1963] CMLR 289 at 303, on the status of international administrative tribunals; A.G. Roemer in Case 1/56: *Bourgaux v ECSC Common Assembly* [1954-56] ECR 361.

9 E.g. on the meaning of 'discrimination' and 'comparable price conditions to consumers in comparable circumstances' in Cases 3-18 and 25-6/58: *Barbara Erzbergbau v High Authority* [1960] ECR 173.

10 Reuter, P., 'Le recours de la Cour de justice des Communautés européennes à des principes généraux de droit', in *Mélanges Henri Rolin* (1964), p. 263.

11 Mathijsen, P., *Le droit de la CECA* (1958), p. 142.

advocates-general[12], referred to juristic writings indicates both the scope and limitations of their contribution.

### (c) Community precedents

Since *Jurisprudence* represents the body of case law evolved through interpretation of the texts a few comments on the role of precedents in the Community system seem necessary. The judgment of the Court can be divided into two parts: the *motifs* (reasons) and the *dispositif* (the ruling). From the parties' point of view the ruling is of a primary interest because, after all, it decides the issue. Indeed, under the doctrine of *res judicata* the judgment is binding upon the Court where there is an identity of parties, cause and object[13]. Apart from *res judicata* the Court is not bound by its previous decisions but this does not mean that precedents are ignored.

In the eyes of the continental lawyer precedents have only a persuasive force in the sense that they reflect the application of the law in practice. However they must be taken into account when assessing the likely success of arguments in court or prognosticating the outcome of litigation. Assuming that courts do not administer justice in an erratic manner the concept of *jurisprudence constante* suggests that their decisions provide a reliable guide. Under the doctrine of separation of powers the judges have no law-making function and indeed by article 5 of the French Civil Code they are prohibited from deciding cases in a general or stereotyped manner. Their decisions must be based on the law, not on previously decided cases. Should the latter be the case the decision in France would probably be quashed by the Cour de Cassation because of *défaut de base légale*[14]. However, there is no harm in considering cases and citing precedents in the *motifs* of the judgment. Judges who study

---

12 A.G. Roemer in Case 13/60: *Ruhrkohlen-Verkaufs-GmbH v High Authority of the ECSC* [1962] CMLR 113 at 159, on oligopoly by a 'noted author'; in Cases 106-107/63: *Toepfer KG v EEC Commission* [1966] CMLR 111 at 118, on the power of intervention of the Council of Ministers by Wohlfart, E., Everling, U., Glaesner, H. J., and Sprung, R., 'Die Europäische Wirtschaftsgemeinschaft', *Kommentar zum Vertrag* (1969); A.G. Lagrange in Case 67/63: *Sorema v High Authority of the ECSC* [1964] CMLR 350 at 352, on the definition of an association of undertakings by Reuter, P., *La Communauté Européenne du Charbon et de l'Acier* (1953); A.G. Warner in Case 31/74: *Filippo Galli, Preliminary Ruling* [1975] ECR at 70 on the direct applicability of regulations by J. A. Winter in 9 CML Rev, 1972 p. 425 at 435-436; A.G. Reischl. in Case 72/74: *Union Syndicale, Service Public Européen v ECC Council* [1975] ECR 401 at 416 cites several writers on Administrative Law.

13 Cases 28-30/62: *Da Costa en Schaake NV v Nederlandse Administratre der Belastingen* [1963] CMLR 224 at 229, 237.

14 David, R., *Le Droit Français* (1960), p. 161.

reports of cases cannot fail to notice the interpretation adopted by the Courts. They have the benefit of learned comments and opinions expressed in the *doctrine*, and during oral arguments counsel do not neglect the opportunity of impressing upon the Court the fact that a certain decision was reached on similar facts in previous cases. However, by tradition, when deciding a case judges must arrive at the particular interpretation by themselves just in case the Court which decided the previous case made a mistake. Therefore, judgments are substantiated by reference to the law comprised in codes and statutes. In the absence of a code or statute the case will be decided according to custom and in the absence of custom according to 'equity, reason, justice, tradition', but never according to 'precedent'[15].

The scope for the persuasive influence of precedent is very great indeed in the uncodified areas of the law, notably Administrative law. Here in addition to statutes the 'general principles of the law' play a considerable part and these, in turn, can often be found applied in precedents. The French Conseil d'Etat not only administers a body of law derived from precedents but also endeavours to relate its decisions to the pattern of case law.

The Community Court, modelled upon the Conseil d'Etat, fulfils a similar function and relies on its own decisions in a similar manner. On several occasions it either followed or referred to its previous decisions[16] in the *motifs*, which correspond to the *ratio decidendi* of the Common Law doctrine of precedent. There is a growing tendency of citing precedents not only by the Court but also, and to a greater extent, by the Advocates-General[17].

---

**15** Ibid., p. 162.

**16** Cases 28–30/62: *Da Costa en Schaake NV v Netherlands Revenue Department* [1963] ECR 31, [1963] CMLR 224; Case 44/65: *Hessische Knappschaft v Maison Singer* [1965] ECR 965, [1966] CMLR 82; Case 28/67: *Mölkerei-Zentrale Westfalen-Lippe GmbH v Hauptzollamt Paderborn* [1968] CMLR 187 at 216–219; *Filippo Galli* op. cit. 123; Case 68/74: *Angelo Alaimo v Préfet du Rhône* [1975] ECR 109, [1975], 1 CMLR 262; Case 12/74: *EC Commission v Federal Republic of Germany* [1975] ECR 181, [1975] 1 CMLR 340; Case 67/74: *Bonsignore v Oberstadtdirektor der Stadt Köln* [1975] ECR 297, [1975] 1 CMLR 472; *Union Syndicale* op. cit 123; Case 94/74: *IGAV-Industria Gomma etc v Ente Nazionale etc* [1975] ECR 699 at 701, 705, 708; Case 7/75: *Mr & Mrs F v Belgian State* [1975] ECR 679 at 684; Case 21/75: *Schroeder KG-Hamburg v Oberstadtsdirektor der Stadt Köln* [1975] ECR 905 at 910 to name some older cases.

**17** *Fillipo Galli* at 68; *Angelo Alaimo* at 113; *EEC Commission* at 206 et seq.; *Bonsignore* at 310; *Union Syndicale* at 708; Case 7 9/74: *Berthold Küster v European Parliament* [1975] ECR 725 at 734; *IGAV-Industria Gomma etc v ENCC-Ente Nazionale etc* at 715; *Mr & Mrs F* op. cit. at 692; Case 8/75: op. cit.*Caisse Primaire d' Assurance Maladaise Sélestat (Bas-Rhin) France v*

Advocate-General Roemer thus stated the position in the Community Court[18]: 'it is in the nature of the development of the Common Market that facts appear, which, by reason of their novelty and the impossibility of foreseeing them, may bring about a revision of well established legal opinions' and concluded that previous decisions cannot have the binding force of precedents. In another case[19] involving the interpretation of EEC article 85 in which the parties abundantly cited previous decisions, he said: 'It is, therefore, appropriate ... to resort to these decisions with discretion, even where the general terms of propositions suggest their application to problems not arising in the case before the Court when they were formulated.'

Whilst the judgments of the ECJ are precedents in their own right because they have settled important points of law and in many cases broken a new ground the question arises whether they are *precedents* in the accepted sense of the word or, more precisely, within the Common Law doctrine of *stare decisis*.

The doctrine of *stare decisis* rests upon the hierarchy of courts and the style of judgments and reports. The ECJ is a unique court of a first and last instance. Although it is the internal court of the Community it is not an exact replica of a supreme federal court; still less it resembles the Court of International Justice. However it functions like a supreme court of a federation as well as the only judicial organ of an inter-state organisation. In that capacity it has to decide matters of principle and policy. In the latter context the ECJ has been using its Olympian position in furtherance of a legal integration of the Community[1].

Like a supreme court it is not and cannot be bound by its own decisions. Indeed in the Community context it is doubtful whether it has the power, let alone the wish, to declare itself bound by its own decisions[2]. However it may wish to cite its own decisions either

---

*Association du Football Club Andlau (Bes-Rhin) France* [1975] ECR 739 at 757; *Schroeder KG* op. cit. at 915; Case 112/76 *Manzoni v Fonds National de Retraite des Ouvriers Mineurs* [1977] ECR 1647; [1978] 2 CMLR 416 to name some older cases.

18 In Case 1/64: *SA Glucosiéries Réunies v EEC Commission* [1964] CMLR 596 at 598.

19 Case 23/67: *Brasserie de Haecht v Wilkins* [1967] ECR 407, [1968] CMLR 26.

1 Lasok, D., *La Cour de Justice, instrument de l'intégration communautaire*, (1979) *Rev. d'intégration européenne*, p. 391 et seq.

2 Cf the British House of Lords ruled to be so bound in *London Street Tramways Co Ltd v LCC* [1898] AC 375 but discarded the rule per Lord Gardiner L.C., reported at [1966] 3 All ER 77, [1966] 1 WLR 1234

to indicate a continuing line of reasoning or, simply, to cut corners. This is a matter of the style of citation.

There is a rather haphazard approach to citation in the ECJ decisions. Originally, in the few cases in which a previous ruling was adopted there was no trace of the pedigree of the new ruling. Whole sentences or paragraphs were incorporated in the judgment without reference or acknowledgement of the source. The famous dictum that 'the Community is a new legal order etc' taken from the *Van Gend* case appeared often in the report[3]. As of late the formula 'As the Court has already stated in' ... with reference to the cited case[4] or words to that effect has been adopted. No doubt this is an improvement but we still have to wait for the Court's express acknowledgement of the persuasive authority of its own decisions and for the Court distinguishing rulings inconsistent with the previous ones and giving the reasons for the distinction. So far the Court has tended to ignore previous decisions from which it has deviated.

The doctrine of precedent is supported by a comprehensive system of law reporting. The decisions of the ECJ are reported systematically whether in the private collections (e.g. CMLR) or the Court's own Reports (ECR). However not all cases are so reported and the ECR, though an official publication of the Court, does not carry the seal of authenticity. Probably no such guarantee can be given in view of the linguistic problems of translations but, in view of the quality of the reports, there is no reason to suppose that they are not a faithful reproduction of the Court's records.

There is no hierarchical relationship between the national judiciary and the ECJ. Even in the field of reference for preliminary rulings the ECJ does not operate as a court of appeal or review but simply as a court of reference, albeit with the unique and supreme power of interpretation. Therefore the essential condition upon

---

3 E.g. see p. 49 note 3 ante.
4 E.g. Case 70/77: *Simmenthal SpA v Amministrazione delle Finanze dello Stato* [1978] ECR 1453 at 1469, [1978] 3 CMLR 670 at 684; Case 50/76: *Amsterdam Bulb BV v Produktschap voor Siergewassen* [1977] ECR 137 at 146, [1977] 2 CMLR 218 at 240; Case 128/78: *EC Commission v United Kingdom, Re Tachograph* [1979] ECR 419 at 428, [1979] 2 CMLR 45 at 55; Case 153/78: *Re Health Control on Imported Meat: EC Commission v Germany* [1980] 1 CMR 198 at 207; Cases 66/79, 127–128/79: *Amministrazione delle Finanze v Meridionale Industria Salumi SRL* [1980] ECR 1237 at 1261 [1981] 1 CMLR 1 at 17; Case 811/79: *Amministrazione delle Finanze dello Stato v Ariete SpA* [1980] ECR 2545 at 2553, 2555, [1981] 1 CMLR 316.

which the doctrine of *stare decisis* rests is not present. The judgments of the ECJ are not subject to appeal or *exequatur* within national jurisdictions and their executive authority, except in the case of judgments against the member states, is assured by Treaty provisions[5]. However since their status ranks no higher than a *res judicata* it depends upon the given national system whether they are treated as precedents or otherwise. Thus the curious result of section 3 (2) of the European Communities Act 1972 is that their status in the United Kingdom appears to be higher than that in the Civil Law countries[6].

Despite the arguments against the *'government of judges'*[7] the status of preliminary rulings appears to be different from the judgment in contentious proceedings. Here the Court makes a ruling on an abstract point of law which, in a sense, becomes the property of the whole Community in view of the procedure in which the Commission and all the member states may participate and the general interest the point should have for the entire Community legal system. Therefore, as argued Advocate-General Warner[8], these rulings should have effect *erga omnes*. In reality they can be so regarded despite the fact that national courts are free to raise similar if not identical questions repeatedly and that the ECJ too is free to change its mind.

In conclusion the creative role of the ECJ in the interpretation and formulation of the principles of Community law has to be recognised without necessarily ascribing to its case law the status of a formal source of law.

(d) *Basic doctrines*

In furthering ... 'the intention of the contracting states ... to create a Community designed for progressive integration[9]' ... the Court developed certain doctrines which characterise the Community legal order as an original system and determine its relationship to the municipal law of the member states:

(i) *Unity.* From an early stage the Court advanced the idea of a

5 EEC, arts. 187 and 192 (2); ECSC, arts. 44 and 92; EAEC, arts. 159 and 164.
6 Wall, E. A., European Communities Act 1972, (1973) p. 28.
7 *Lecourt, R., Le juge devant le marché commun*, (1970), p. 57; *L'Europe des Juges*, (1976).
8 Case 112/76: *Manzoni v Fonds National de Retraite des Ouvriers Mineurs* [1977] ECR 1647 at 1661–1663, [1978] 2 CMLR 416 at 429–430.
9 Kutscher, op. cit. p. 32.

functional unity of the three Communities[10] which, in the jurisprudence of the Court, meant that one foundation Treaty should
be interpreted with the aid of the others[11]. Of these cases one
involving a Community official merits a special attention[12]. Sr.
Campolongo, who was employed by the High Authority of the Coal
and Steel Community was discharged and took up an appointment
with the European Investment Bank instituted under the EEC
Treaty. He claimed various benefits including a re-installation
allowance, but the Court decreed that he was not entitled to it
because the 'functional unity' of the Communities does not permit
accumulation of payments due on the termination of employment
with one and commencement of employment with another institution of the Communities. The Court recognised the separate legal
personalities of the Communities according to articles 6, 210 and
184 of the Treaties which founded the ECSC, EEC and EAEC,
respectively, but emphasised that through the Treaty of Merger a
strong legal bond between the Communities has been established.
Advocate-General Roemer, whose submissions in this respect were
followed by the Court, stated that 'the European Treaties are nothing by a partial implementation of a grand general programme,
dominated by the idea of a complete integration of the European
States'.

The idea of unity in the uniform interpretation and application
of the Community and the equal acceptance of Treaty obligations
by the member states was emphasised by the Court on several
occasions. In the *Gingerbread*[13] cases the Court underlined the
unitary and mandatory nature of Community law without which it
would be impossible to establish the Common Market. This theme
was followed in the *Costa*[14] case where, inter alia, the compatibility
of the nationalisation of Italian electricity industry with the EEC
Treaty was raised and cases in which the Court insisted that certain
key terms of Community law such as, *scrap equalisation charge*[15];

10 Colin, J.-P., *Le gouvernement des juges dans les Communautés Européennes* (1966)
   74 et seq.
11 Case 6/60: *Humblet v Belgian State* [1960] ECR 559; Case 30/59:Gezamenlijke
   Steen Kolenmijnen in *Limburg v High Authority of the ECSC* [1961] ECR 1;
   Case 9/59: (1959), 6 Rec. 27.
12 Cases 27/59 and 39/59: *Alberto Campolongo v High Authority of the ECSC*
   [1960] ECR 391
13 Cases 2-3/62: *EC Commission v Luxembourg and Belgium ( Imported licences for
   ginger bread)* [1962] ECR 425, CMLR 199.
14 Case 6/64: *Costa v ENEL* [1964] ECR 585, [1964] CMLR 425.
15 Case 26/66: *Koninklijke Nederlandsche Hoogovens v High Authority of the
   ECSC* [1967] ECR 115.

*rediscount rate*[16]; *public policy*[17]; to give just a few examples, have a 'Community meaning' and must be interpreted and applied as such. In respect of the member states' duties the Court stressed that a state ... 'cannot ... unilaterally opt out of ... its obligations' and that ... 'non-compliance ... strikes at the very root of the Community legal order ...' and ... 'brings into question the equality of member states before Community law ...'[18].

(ii) *Autonomy*. The doctrine of the autonomy of Community law rests on the one hand on the concept of unity and on the principle of the separation of powers or functions, on the other. The constitutional principle of separation means, in the Community context, a division of functions between the Community Institutions and the Member States[19] and, in the administration of justice, between the Community Court and national courts[20].

The autonomy of Community law means that it is 'quite independent of the legislation passed by the member states'[1]. It is derived from an extraneous source albeit an organisation created by the member states themselves, it extends equally and uniformly over their territories, and has to be applied by their courts in its original form. The uniformity of its interpretation is assured by the obligation to seek preliminary rulings from the Community Court.

The practical application of the doctrine of autonomy has manifested itself in areas where the integrity and efficacy of Community law has to be safeguarded[2] or where it has to be distinguished from national law as, for example, in the field of competition where the two systems overlap[3]. Thus held the ECJ: the efficacy of the Treaty would be impaired if, in the context of partial integration with national law, the specific tasks entrusted to the Community were not interpreted as totally independent[4]. It follows that the member

---

**16** Cases 6 -11/69: *EC Commission v French Republic* [1969] ECR 523, [1970] CMLR 43.
**17** *Van Duyn*, op. cit. p. 104, note 11; Case 30/77: *R v Bouchereau* [1977] ECR 1999, [1977] 2 CMLR 800.
**18** Case 128/78: *EC Commission v United Kingdom, Re Tachographs* [1979] ECR 419, [1979] 2 CMLR 45.
**19** ERTA Case, op. cit; Case 30/59: *De Gezamen lijke Steenkolenmijnen in Limberg v High Authority of the ECSC* [1961] ECR 1 at 3.
**20** A. G. Roemer in Case 6/54: *Government of the Netherlands v High Authority of the ECSC* [1954-56] ECR 103.
**1** Case 28/67: *Mölkerei-Zentrale Westfalen/Lippe GmbH v Hauptzollamt Paderborn* [1968] CMLR 187 at 217.
**2** *Variola*, op. cit. p. 100, note 11.
**3** Case 14/68: *Wilhelm v Bundeskartellamt* [1969] ECR 1, [1969] CMLR 100.
**4** Case 30/59: op. cit.

states are in no position of taking unilateral measures to carry out the mandatory provisions of Community law[5]. The concept of the autonomy of Community law, first mentioned by the ECJ in *San Michele v High Authority*[6] *of the ECSC*, sets it apart from national law as a separate and independent legal order yet ruling directly over the territories of the member states. It reflects a federal legal system.

(iii) *Supremacy of Community law.* The supremacy of Community law when in conflict with national law is the logical consequence of the federal concept of the Community[7]. The doctrine itself is nowhere mentioned in the Treaties but can be deduced from the member states' constitutional law[8] and their readiness to make the Community function. In other words, since the creation of the Community and the endowment of its Institutions with executive, legislative and judicial functions implies a delegation of sovereignty the Community could not function as a supranational organisation if the delegated powers were insufficient or capable of being withdrawn. Therefore supremacy does not reflect any inherent superiority of Community Law but merely a working relationship.

Supremacy was first mentioned by the ECJ in a case involving the effect of the ECSC Treaty on previously enacted Belgian tax law[9]. On that occasion the Court saw the relationship between the two systems in the light of the monist theory of International Law. In *Van Gend*, that most important constitutional case, the Court saw the 'new legal order' in the light of a federalist concept[10]. Thus the base of the doctrine was shifted but firmly established in *Costa v ENEL*[11] in which, inter alia, the question of compatibility of the Italian decree nationalising the electricity industry with the Community legal order was raised. The Court held that ... '(The Treaty) ... has created its own legal system which, on the entry into force of the Treaty, became an integral part of the legal systems of the member states and which their courts are bound

---

5 E.g. Case 13/68: *Salgoil Spa v Italian Ministry of Foreign Trade (Re Import quotas)*[1968] ECR 453, [1969] CMLR 181; Cases 90–91/63: *EEC Commission v Luxembourg and Belgium (Re special import on milk products)* [1964] ECR 625, [1965] CMLR 58; Case 52/77: *Cayrol v Rivoira and Figli (Re import licence)* [1977] ECR 2261, [1978 2 CMLR 253; Case 128/78: *EC Commission v United Kingdom, Re Tachographs* [1979] ECR 419; [1979] 2 CMLR 45.

6 Case 9/65: [1967] ECR 1 at 30.

7 Ipsen, H. P., 'Rapport du droit des Communautés Européennes avec le droit national', *Le Droit des Affaires* (1964), No. 47.

8 Cf. European Communities Act 1972, s. 2 (1).

9 Case 6/60: *Humblet v Belgian State* [1960] ECR 559 at 569.

10 [1963] ECR 1 at 12, [1963] CMLR 105.

11 Case 6/64; [1964] ECR 585 at 593 and 594, [1954] CMLR 425 at 455, 456.

to apply ... because of its special and original nature ... (it) could not be overriden by domestic legal provisions, however framed, without being deprived of its character as Community law and without the legal basis of the Community itself being called into question'.

Commenting specifically on the impact of the Community upon national legislation the Court thought that ... 'The transfer by the States from their domestic legal system to the Community legal system of the rights and obligations arising under the Treaty carries with it a permanent limitation of their sovereign rights, against which a subsequent unilateral act incompatible with the concept of the Community cannot prevail'[12] ...

In the same vein, in the *Second Art Treasures*[13] case, the Court, condemning Italy's attempt to introduce a tax on the export of art treasures, held that ... 'the Member States' assignment of rights and powers to the Community in accordance with the provisions of the Treaty entails a definitive limitation of their sovereign rights against which no provisions of municipal law, whatever their nature, can be legally invoked' ...

More recently the Court held that, where the lowest minimum export price of flower bulbs has been fixed by the Community, the exporting country ... 'may neither adopt nor allow national organisations having legislative power to adopt any measure which would conceal the Community nature and effects' of such provisions, even if the minimum price would render the transaction unprofitable[14]. Implying that a national provision inconsistent with a binding Community role must be void the Court held that such a Community rule would ... 'preclude the valid adoption of new legislative measures to the extent to which they would be incompatible with Community provisions'[15] ... Addressing itself to the national judicature the ECJ ruled that ... 'A national court which is called upon ... to apply provisions of Community law is under a duty to give full effects to those provisions, if necessary refusing of its own motion to apply any conflicting provisions of national legislation, even if adopted subsequently, and it is not necessary for the court to request or await a prior setting aside of such provision by

12 Ibid ECR at 594.
13 Case 48/71: *EC Commission v Italy* [1972] CMLR 699 at 708.
14 Case 106/76: *Amsterdam Bulb BV v Produktschap voor Siergewassen* [1977] ECR 137 at 151, [1977] 2 CMLR 218 at 243.
15 Case 106/77: *Amministrazione delle Finanze delle Stato v Simmenthal SpA* 1978 ECR 629 at 643, [1978] 3 CMLR 263 at 283.

legislative or other constitutional means'[16] ... The ECJ has no express power to declare void national legislation but can achieve the same effect through the doctrine of supremacy.

However the most dramatic assertion of supremacy occurred in the case of an alleged violation of the German Basic Law by a Community regulation[17]. The Court ruled that ... 'no provision of municipal law, of whatever nature they may be, may prevail over Community law ... lest it be deprived of its character as Community law and its very legal foundation be endangered. The validity of a Community act or its application in a Member State remains, therefore, unimpaired even if it is alleged that the basic rights ... of the national constitution were violated' ...

(iv) *Direct applicability and direct effect.* Like the doctrines of autonomy and supremacy the doctrine of direct applicability of Community law has been enunciated in the *Van Gend* case. On that occasion the ECJ held that article 12 of the EEC Treaty was applicable to the member state and the citizen alike and that it created rights which the citizen could rely on and which his national courts were bound to uphold even against national legislation. The doctrine holds the key to the relationship between Community law and national law and unmistakenly points to a federal character of the former because in a federal system federal law bears directly upon the citizen of the component states. We shall discuss it when assessing the impact of Community law upon the national systems[17]. At this stage it will suffice to consider its theoretical implications. In the literature a distinction is made between 'direct applicability' and 'direct effect' of Community law[18]. This is a valid distinction but not exclusive to Community law. As pointed out by Advocate-General Warner[19] the distinction is known to national statutes 'some provisions of which impose obligations on the State or public authorities without conferring rights on citizens'. Indeed one has to distinguish not only between the contents of legal rules but also between the addressees of these rules. In the *Van Gend* case the argument on behalf of the state concerned (incidentally

---

16 Ibid ECR at 647, CMLR at 283.
17 Case 11/70: *Internationale Handelsgesellschaft mbH v Einfuhr-und-Vorratsstelle für Getreide und Futtermittel* [1970] 2 ECR 1125 at 1127, [1972] CMLR 255 at 283.
18 Winter, J., 'Direct Applicability and Direct Effect: Two Distinct and Different Concepts in Community law' (1972) CML Rev p. 425; Wyatt, D., 'Directly applicable Provisions of EEC law' (1975) 125 NLJ, pp. 458, 575, 669, 793.
19 In case 31/74: *Filippo Galli* [1975] ECR 47 at 70, [1975] 1 CMLR 211.

accepted by the Advocate-General) was that the obligation contained in the relevant Treaty provision concerned the state involved and did not give rise to any claim on behalf of the importer. However the Court, in its famous dictum, enclosed both the state and the importer and concluded that the provision was applicable in litigation before national courts and that, because of its content and purpose, it generated remedies available to the importer. In other words, a directly applicable provision had, as its effect, an enforceable Community right.

The doctrine, as we shall see later, is of an immense practical importance as far as individuals are concerned. It also strengthens the federal concept of the Community.

(v) *General principles of law.* Next to the basic doctrines the Court has to be credited with the development of general principles of Community law. To these we have already alluded in the context of interpretation[20]. It remains now to discuss these in the context of the legal integration through the Court's jurisprudence.

By a doctrine, as distinguished from a principle or a rule of law, we understand a general proposition or guidance relating to a fundamental issue such as e.g. the nature of Community law or the conflict between the Community and national law. A principle, or a rule of law, on the other hand, can be construed more narrowly as a rule of conduct prescribed in the given circumstances and carrying a sanction for non-compliance. Thus a principle or rule of law consists of a hypothesis, a disposition and a sanction. The hypothesis postulates a factual situation which ought to be responded to in accordance with the disposition or prescribed conduct. The law as a normative system is vindicated by the appropriate sanction which is, on the one hand, civil i.e. nullity of the act in question, damages or both and, punitive, on the other. A punitive sanction often serves to vindicate a civil obligation.

Codified systems consist of general and particular rules. The former come close to doctrines in the sense the term has been used above. However, though they can be vindicated like any particular rule, they serve a dual purpose: as pointers to interpretation by the courts and as indications of policy to legislators. Thus such general rules as e.g. public policy or equality indicate the limits of interpretation in particular cases and also enable the courts to fill the gaps which are not supposed to exist in codes of law but, in reality, do become exposed because life is more imaginative than the most

**20** See p. 122 ante.

astute legislator. With reference to the same examples a particular application of public policy or equality may be subject to separate legislation, e.g. to restrict the sale of firearms or combat racial or sex discrimination, or simply a general principle may be further developed in the code.

The above mentioned legislative techniques are well exemplified in the text of the EEC Treaty. There we find general principles such as the principle of solidarity (article 5) which governs the relationship between the member states and the Community and the principle of non-discrimination on the ground of nationality (article 7) applicable to matters governed by the Treaty. In these two articles the Court found a powerful support in the interpretation of the Treaty provisions as well as a formal source to complement inadequately expressed intentions of the makers of the Treaty.

The principle of the freedom of movement of persons (article 48) within the Community has been not only partly elaborated in the Treaty but also carried into effect in considerable detail by derivative legislation comprising rules on migration and social security. The right of establishment of liberal professions (article 52) too has been developed partly in the text, partly outside the text of the Treaty by derivative legislation. The same technique has been adopted to all Treaty policies, some of which remaining still in their embryonic stage.

Faced with this kind of enacted law the Court, in the absence of interpretation clauses, has to resort to every method of interpretation known to national judiciaries. It also has to dip into the treasury of national tradition in order to adopt for the Community some well established and universally recognised principles of national law. In the EEC Treaty there is only one reference to 'general principles common to the laws of the member states' in article 215 (2) according to which the non-contractual liability of the Community should be judged. However in practice the Court may take recourse to article 173 (1) which enables it to annul Community acts which 'infringe the Treaty or any rule of law relating to its application'. These other 'rules of law' begin to emerge as follows:

(a) *Due process and natural justice.* In civilised societies the existence and observance of procedural rules provide a safeguard and protection of substantive rights. The making and enforcement of rules of conduct have to conform to a notion of 'due process' where the authorities do not act arbitrarily and the accused is informed of his charges, has a right to be heard and represented by an independent advocate.

Thus the sanction of nullity applies to Community acts made in contravention of 'an essential procedural requirement'[1]. The Court, following the Advocate-General's strong plea for the recognition of the principle *audi alteram partim* even in the absence of express legislation to that effect, held in a competition case[2] that 'a person whose interests are perceptibly affected by a decision taken by a public authority must be given the opportunity to make his point of view known'[3]. This implies that the party concerned must be informed of the conditions under which the Treaty has been applied[4].

(b) *Equality*. Equality before the law is, next to due process, an essential ingredient of justice. In the EEC Treaty equality is to be achieved through supression of discrimination on the ground of nationality (article 7); as between consumers and producers of agricultural produce (article 40 (3)) and as between employees on account of their sex (article 119). The Court, however, deduced from these scanty provisions a general principle of Community law[5].

In developing the theme the Court made a start under the Coal and Steel Treaty by combating discriminatory practices expressly prohibited by articles 4 (b) and 60[6]. More significant is the development under the EEC Treaty where the Court applied the principle of non-discrimination to goods, persons and states. However it made it plain in the case of a discriminatory reception of Italian refrigerators in France[7] that 'the different treatment of non-comparable situations does not lead automatically to the conclusion that there is discrimination'.

Thus the principle of equality in comparable situations forms the basis of the Common Market. Indeed the free movement of

1 EEC, art. 173 (1).
2 Case 17/74: *Transocean Marine Paint Association v EC Commission* [1974] ECR 1063, [1974] 2 CMLR 459.
3 See also Case 75/77: *Mollet v EC Commission* [1978] ECR 897.
4 Case 24/62: *Germany v EEC Commission* [1963] ECR 63 at 69, [1963] CMLR 347; see also Case 34/77: *Oslizlok v EC Commission* [1978] ECR 1099; Case 85/76: *Hoffmann-La Roche v EC Commission* [1979] ECR 461, [1979] 3 CMLR 211.
5 See Case 1/72: *Frilli v Belgian State* [1972] ECR 457, [1973] CMLR 386; Case 152/73: *Sotgiu v Deutsche Bundespost* [1974] ECR 153.
6 E.g. Case 8/57: *Haute Fourneaux et Aciéries Belges v High Authority of the ECSC* [1958] ECR 245 at 256.
7 Case 13/63: *Italy v EEC Commission* [1963] ECR 165, [1963] CMLR 289.

goods is assured by enforcing the prohibition of discriminatory measures whether they are equivalent to customs duties[8] or quantitative restrictions[9] or whether they are fiscal measures designed to protect a national produce at the expense of a similar imported one[10].

Equality of treatment was also vindicated in cases involving subsidies to producers in the context of the Common Agricultural Policy. Thus the Court declared invalid Commission regulation 563/76 which, in order to reduce the stocks of skimmed milk powder, obliged animal feed producers to purchase skimmed milk powder instead of soya used as protein ingredient with the consequent result that the cost of animal feed had increased and upset farmers. The Court held the regulation contrary to the principle of equality in so far as it made the producers purchase skimmed milk powder 'at such a disproportionate price that it was equivalent to a discriminatory distribution of the burden of costs between the various agricultural sectors'[11] ...

A similar attitude was adopted in the *quellmehl and gritz*[12] cases. Quellmehl is a product of maize or wheat used in the production of bread, gritz is a product of maize used in brewing. A Community subsidy was provided in order to enable starch to compete with

8 See p. 358, post.
9 See p. 359, post.
10 E.g. Cases 52 and 55/65: *Germany v EEC Commission (tax on imported meat)* [1966] ECR 159, [1967] CMLR 22; Case 28/67: *Mölkerei-Zentrale Westfalen-Lippe GmbH v Hauptzollamt Paderborn (powdered milk)* [1968] ECR 143, [1968] CMLR 187; Case 232/78: *EC Commission v France (Sheepmeat)* [1979] ECR 2729, [1980] 1 CMLR 418; Case 168/78: *EC Commission v France (tax on alcoholic drinks)* [1980] ECR 347, [1981] 2 CMLR 631; Case 169/78: *EC Commission v Italy (tax on alcoholic drinks)* ECR ibid. 385, CMLR ibid 673; Case 171/78: *EC Commission v Denmark (tax on alcoholic drinks)* ECR ibid 447, CMLR ibid. 688 but see also Case 140/79: *Chemical Farmaceutici SpA v DAF SpA* [1981] ECR 1, [1981] 3 CMLR 350; Case 46/80: *Vinal SpA v Orbat SpA* [1981] ECR 77, [1981] 3 CMLR 524.
11 Cases 83, 94/76: *Bayerische HNL Vermehrungsbetriebe GmbH & Co KG v EC Council and EC Commission* [1978] ECR 1209, [1978] 3 CMLR 566; see also Case 114/76: *Bela-Mühle KG v Grows-Farm GmbH* [1977] ECR 1211, [1979] 2 CMLR 83; Case 116/76: *Granaria BV v Hoofdproduktschap voor Akkerbouw-Produkten* [1977] ECR 1247, [1979]; Cases 119, 120/76: *Olmühle Hamburg AG v Hauptzollamt Hamburg Waltershof (first skimmed milk powder cases)* [1979] ECR 1269, [1979] 2 CMLR 83.
12 Cases 64, 113/76, 167, 239/78, 27, 28, 45/79: *Dumortier Frères SA v EC Council* [1979] ECR 3091; Case 238/78: *Ireks-Arkady v EC Council and Commission* [1979] ECR 2955; Cases 241, 242, 245-250/78: *DGV v EC Council and Commission* [1979] ECR 3017; Cases 261, 262/78: *Interquell Stärke-Chemie GmbH & Co KG and Diamalt AG v EC Council and Commission* [1979] ECR 3045.

synthetic products. However the unexpected result was that subsidised starch (because it is up to a point interchangeable with quellmehl and gritz) had obtained an unfair advantage over these products and began to replace quellmehl in bakeries and gritz in breweries. To even up the competitive position subsidies were extended to quellmehl and gritz. However subsequently by a resolution the Council withdrew the subsidies from quellmehl and gritz but not from starch. The quellmehl and gritz producers obtained a judgment against the Council on the ground of discrimination[13] but subsidies were reinstated only as from the date of the judgment. The claim for compensation under EEC Treaty article 215 (2) covering the period during which subsidies were withdrawn was recognised by the Court on the ground that the producers of quellmehl and gritz were a small, clearly definable, group and that the loss they suffered exceeded the normal risk pertinent to their business. Therefore they were entitled to compensation based on the subsidy they would have received had they been treated equally with the producers of starch. The quantum (left to be determined in later proceedings) was to be reduced by the proportion of the loss they were able to pass to their customers.

The third instance of equal treatment of products is exemplified by the *Isoglucose*[14] Cases which, as noted elsewhere[15], have released potential powers of the European Parliament. Again, to reduce the surplus of sugar, a substantial levy was imposed by regulation on isoglucose, a recently produced sweetener in heavy competition with sugar. According to the complainants this levy was of such a deterrent proportion that it would have made the production of isoglucose uneconomical. The Court restored the balance between the competing products on the ground that discriminatory regulation offended the principle of equality. The levy was eliminated with retrospective effect. However the claim for compensation failed, the Court in an almost perfunctory manner concentrating

---

13 Cases 117/76, 16/77: *Firma Albert Ruckdeschel & Co v Hauptzollamt Hamburg-St Annen* [1977] ECR 1753; [1979] 2 CMLR 445; Cases 124/76, 20/77: *Moulins et Huileries de Pont-a-Mousson SA v Office National Interprofessionnel des Céréales* [1977] ECR 1795, [1979] 2 CMLR 445.

14 Cases 103, 145/77: *Royal Scholten-Honig (Holdings) Ltd and Tunnel Refineries Ltd v Intervention Board for Agricultural Produce (first Isoglucose cases)* [1978] ECR 2037; [1979] 1 CMLR 675; and *Second Isoglucose Cases* 116, 124/77: *Amylum NV and Tunnel Refineries Ltd v EC Council and Commission* [1979] ECR 3497; Case 143/77: *Koninklijke Scholten Honig NV v Council and Commission* [1979] ECR 3583.

15 See p. 99, ante. See also Jacobs, F., Isoglucose Resurgent: 'Two Powers of the European Parliament,', 18 CMLRev (1981), 219.

on the nature of the offending legislation rather than the conse-quential loss suffered by the producers of isoglucose[16].

There is as yet no equality between Community citizens in a general sense but only in the context of the freedom of movement of workers[17] and the right of establishment and in the context of enforceable Community rights. As held in the *Van Duyn*[18] case a member state cannot, in accordance with the rules of international law, refuse entry to its own citizens but may do so according to the EEC Treaty to the citizens of the fellow member states if the Community right of entry falls within the exception of public policy. However once admitted a Community citizen must not be discriminated against whether it concerns his freedom of move-ment[19]; employment[20]; or the whole variety of social rights[1]. A mere threat of discrimination contained in national law is incompatible with Community rules[2].

The hard-won Community right to equal pay within the national systems[3] has provided an opportunity for broadening up national rules in the name of equality between the sexes[4]. Some problems involving sex equality arose in connection with employees of the Community but these cases had to be decided in the light of the interpretation of contractual rights. Thus an Italian official of the European Parliament who married a Luxembourg national was to be deprived of an expatriation allowance unless she was the head of the family. The Court refused to accept the principle that the entitlement should depend on sex and annulled the decision de-priving her of the allowance[5]. Similarly an expatriation allowance

16 *Second Cases*, op. cit., note 14.
17 See p. 99 and 137, ante.
18 Case 41/74: *Van Duyn v Home Office* [1974] ECR 1337, [1975] 1 CMLR 1.
19 E.g. Case 36/75: *Rutili v Minister for the Interior* [1975] ECR 1219; [1976] 1 CMLR 140.
20 E.g. Cases 44/72: *Marsman v Rosskamp* [1972] ECR 1243, [1973] CMLR 501; 152/73: *Sotgiu v Deutsche Bundespost* [1974] ECR 153; 15/69: *Württembergische Milchverwertung-Südmilch AG v Ugliola* [1969] ECR 363, [1970] CMLR 194; 36/74: *Walrave and Koch v Association Union Cycliste Internationale* [1974] ECR 1405, [1975] 1 CMLR 320; 13/76: *Dona v Mantero* [1976] ECR 1333; [1976] 2 CMLR 578.
1 See p. 365, et seq post.
2 Case 167/73: *EC Commission v French Republic* [1974] ECR 359; [1974] 2 CMLR 216.
3 Case 43/75: *Defrenne v SABENA* [1976] ECR 455; [1976] 2 CMLR 98.
4 E.g. Cases 129/79: *Macarthys Ltd v Smith* [1980] ECR 1275, [1980] 2 CMLR 205; 69/80: *Worringham and Humphreys v Lloyds Bank Ltd* [1981] ECR 767, [1981] 2 CMLR 1; 96/80 *Jenkins v Kingsgate (Clothing Productions) Ltd* [1981] ECR 911, [1981] 2 CMLR 24; *Garland v British Rail Engineering Ltd* (reference to ECJ) [1981] 2 CMLR 542; Case 12/81: (ECJ) [1982] 1 CMLR 696; *Burton v British Railways Board* (reference to ECJ) [1981] 3 CMLR 100.

of a Belgian employee at a Euratom centre in Italy, who married an Italian and thereby automatically acquired Italian citizenship without relinquishing her Belgian citizenship, was preserved since citizenship acquired involuntarily should not be the determining factor[6]. However in a slightly different situation, where a French Community official working in Belgium married a Belgian citizen and would not have acquired Belgian citizenship if she had made a declaration that she wished to retain her old one, the inaction on her part was interpreted as her acquiescence. Therefore she had to take the consequences the Court saying that ... 'there are no reasons associated with equal treatment why her Belgian nationality should not be taken into account in applying the provision concerned'[7] ...

Even computers are not allowed to discriminate since access to the computerised procedure for the prosecution of debts expressed in foreign currency cannot be denied to a creditor resident in another member state if such claims can be pursued in ordinary legal proceedings[7a]

In matters involving the conduct of the member states the Court has often emphasised their duties vis-à-vis each other and the Community they have created, such duties being a reflection of equality and reciprocity. A breach ... 'strikes at the very root of the Community legal order' ... and ... 'brings into question the equality of member states before Community law and creates discrimination at the expense of their nationals'[8] ...

(c) *Fundamental human rights.* Fundamental human rights whether expressed in a solemn declaration (French system), a constitutional guarantee (German system) or case law (British system), whether extensive or fragmentary, form part of West European heritage. This heritage was enriched by the European Convention on Human Rights of 1950 to which all the Member States of the Community adhere in principle though not in every detail. The Community itself, through a joint declaration of the Commission, Council and Parliament[9] of 5 April 1977, echoed by the European Council[10] on 7/8 April 1978 proclaimed its respect for fundamental human rights and postulated their observance in the work of its Institutions. Human rights and representative democracy, stressed the European Council, are the essential conditions of the member-

5 Case 20/71: *Sabbatini v European Parliament* [1972] ECR 345, [1972] CMLR 945.

6 Case 21/74: *Airola v Commission* [1975] ECR 221.

7 Case 37/74: *Van den Broeck v Commission* [1975] ECR 235.

7a Case 22/80: *Boussac Saint-Frères SA v Gerstenmeier* [1982] 1 CMLR 202.

8 ECJ Court in the *Tachograph* case, op. cit., at para 12.

9 OJ 1977, C 103/1; EC Bull 3/1977, p. 5.

10 EC Bull 3/1978, p. 5.

ship of the Community. In 1979[11] the Commission urged the Community to adhere to the Convention in its corporate capacity. Irrespective of the formal position the Court held that . . . 'In fact, respect for fundamental rights forms an integral part of the general principles of law protected by the Court of Justice. The protection of such rights, whilst inspired by the constitutional traditions common to the Member States, must be ensured within the framework of the structure and objectives of the Community'[12] . . . However, despite the emotive sound of 'fundamental human rights' the Court, probably because of the nature of its business, had so far few genuine cases involving such rights and putting its sincerity to the test.

In *Stauder v Stadt Ulm*[13] the ECJ rejected as unfounded the claim of a German citizen that the Community scheme to provide butter at a reduced price to certain persons was invalid because, having required him to reveal his identity, it hurt his dignity and this constituted an infringement of his fundamental human rights. The Court held that the Community scheme did not insist that his identity must be revealed and suggested that the clumsy method of proving the entitlement, for which the national authorities were responsible, could have been replaced by a more sophisticated code.

In *Nold v EC Commission*[14] the Court was at pains to show its faith in fundamental human rights but refused to annul a Commission decision on the marketing of coal which, in effect, denied direct access to source of supply to wholesale dealers whose turnover fell below the minimum laid down by the Commission. The plea of discrimination and of the denial of economic opportunities made no impact upon the Court when measured against market rationalisation pursued under the Coal and Steel Treaty.

In *National Panasonic (UK) Ltd v EC Commission*[15] the Court, citing Nold, held that there was no violation of the right to privacy guaranteed by the Convention in the Community procedures governing search and seizure for the purpose of enforcing the Community competition law. It is clear that a human rights argu-

---

11  EC Bull 4/1978, p. 16 and Commission Memorandum on the Accession to the European Convention on Human Rights, EC Bull Suppt. 2/1978.

12  Case 11/70: *Internationale Handelsgesellschaft* op. cit. [1970] ECR 1125 at 1134, [1972] CMLR 255 at 271; see also Cases 25, 26, 30/70; *Einfur-und Vorratsstelle etc v Köster, Berodt & Co; Henck und Scheer* [1970] ECR 1161, [1972] CMLR 255 (para 22).

13  Case 29/69: [1969] ECR 419, [1970] CMLR 112.

14  Case 4/74: [1973] ECR 491, [1974] 2 CMLR 338.

15  Case 136/79: [1980] ECR 2033, [1980] 3 CMLR 169.

ment cannot be allowed to frustrate the legal process necessary for the enforcement of Community obligations.

In *Prais v EC Council*[16] the Court, whilst acknowledging the freedom of religion guaranteed by the European Convention, refused to annul a process of selecting Community employees in favour of a person who complained of unfair treatment because the selection process, held simultaneously in the Community capital cities, happened to coincide with a holyday in the calendar of her religious persuasion.

In *Hauer v Land Rheinland-Pfalz*[17] the Court, following Nold, drew a distinction between rights to property guaranteed by the Convention and the EEC Treaty and the exercise of such rights which can be interfered with by virtue of the Protocol to the Convention, the Community law as well as the Constitutions of the Member States. In the circumstances it refused to annul a Council regulation concerned with agricultural planning the effect of which was a restriction on the planting of vines.

The Court has heard so far not only actions against the Community alleging breaches of fundamental human rights including trade union rights[18] and the protection from expropriation without compensation[19] but also actions against the member states alleging breaches of Community rights through non-observance of fundamental human rights[20]. However no Community measure has been struck down to date. No doubt this reflects the weakness of the claims but also, some may fear, the readiness of the Court to assert the supremacy of Community law. Indeed, dismissing as unfounded the argument that regulations which imposed a forfeitable deposit for the grant of export and import licences had violated fundamental rights (i.e. the right of economic freedom and proportionality) guaranteed by the German Constitution, the Court held that ... 'no provisions of municipal law, of whatever nature they may be, may prevail over Community law ... lest it be deprived of its character as Community law and its very legal

---

**16** Case 130/75: [1976] ECR 1589, [1976] 2 CMLR 708.
**17** Case 44/79: [1979] ECR 3727, [1980] 3 CMLR 42.
**18** Cases 175/73: *Union Syndicale etc, Massa and Kortner v EC Council* [1974] ECR 917, [1975] 1 CMLR 131; 18/74: *Syndicat Général du Personnel des Organismes Européens v EC Commission* [1974] ECR 933, [1975] 1 CMLR 144.
**19** Cases 56–60/74: *Kampffmeyer v EC Commission and Council* [1976] ECR 711.
**20** Rutili, op. cit.; Case 149/77: *Defrenne v SABENA* [1978] ECR 1365, [1978] 3 CMLR 312—sex discrimination contrary to EEC art. 119, the ILO Convention No 111 of 1958 and the European Social Charter of 1961; Case 98/79: *Pecastaing v Belgian State* [1980] ECR 691, [1980] 3 CMLR 685 (fair hearing in deportation proceedings).

foundations be endangered. The validity of a Community act or its application in a Member State remains, therefore, unimpaired even if it is alleged that the basic rights ... of the national constitution were violated'[1] ...

This dictum has to be seen in the context of a weak case in which the Court, nevertheless, like in Stauder and later in *Nold* and *Hauer* repeatedly asserted its adherence to fundamental human rights as 'the general principles of law ... which should be followed within the framework of Community law'[2] ... The ECJ is not a court of human rights as such but the Court of the Community whose law has been fashioned according to the laws of the Member States. Since the Community legal order, albeit limited in its scope, is derived from a delegation of sovereignty, it is, as pointed out by Advocate-General Warner[3], unthinkable that the delegation would exceed the powers contained in their Constitutions. It follows that fundamental right so guaranteed must be respected in the Community. However for the time being they cannot rank higher than 'general principles of law'.

(d) *Protection of vested Rights.* The protection of 'vested rights' has a long tradition in Western Europe. It is based on certain premises such as the impartiality and independence of the judiciary, the running of the affairs of the state according to law and non-retrospective legislation. In exercising its general function the ECJ has endeavoured to incorporate these postulates into the Community legal order and in doing so protect vested rights by recourse to certain general principles of law.

Vested rights, that is rights acquired within the society's legal framework and according to legal process, need a climate of legal certainty. This means, on the one hand, stability of the legal system and predictability, on the other. One ought to know one's legal position and, when a change occurs in the law, one should not be affected adversely as far as one's existing rights are concerned. In more technical terms one's rights should not be taken away or forfeited by retrospective legislation and one's legitimate expectations, built upon the existing legal system, should not be frustrated.

Thus, in principle, Community law is not retrospective. Where it is retrospective it has to be expressly stated to be so and justified

---

1 *Handelsgesellschaft*, op. cit. [1970] ECR at 1127, [1972] CMLR at 283.
2 See *Nold* op. cit. at ECR 507.
3 Case 7/76: *IRCA v Amministrazione delle Finanze dello Stato* [1976] ECR 1213 at 1237.

on the ground that the legitimate objective could not be attained otherwise[4]. It is not quite clear what the legitimate objective means in abstract. It seems to mean an objective of the Treaty as a superior rule of law which has to be carried into effect by subordinate legislation. Such legislation may, therefore, have to be enacted with a retrospective effect. The position remains yet to be clarified by the ECJ since the judicial authority on the subject is still rather scanty and ambiguous[5]. It seems that the need for a retrospective measure has to be substantiated by the legislator and, where questioned, approved by the Court within its power of review of the legality of Community acts.

There appear to be two safeguards of the non-retrospective principle: interpretation and the protection of legitimate expectations. Thus, in the absence of a clear provision to the contrary, legislation is presumed to regulate future relations, that is, not to be retrospective[6]. The principle is well illustrated in a case involving the operative date of a regulation[7]. On 30 June 1976 the Commission passed a regulation curtailing the right of exporters of sugar to have their export licences cancelled. The regulation was to enter into force on 1 July 1976. However the publication of the measure in the Official Journal was delayed until 2 July. On 1 July the applicant applied for cancellation of licences he held at that time but this was refused by virtue of the regulation. Therefore he moved for the annulment of the regulation. This the Court found unnecessary holding that the regulation must be construed to have come into force on the date of its publication, i.e. 2 July, and thus protecting the rights vested in the applicant. The Court inferred that the Commission did not intend the regulation to have a retrospective effect[8].

A prudent person's reliance on the certainty of the law ought to be rewarded by the protection of his confidence in the system[9].

---

4 Case 98/78: *Racke v Hauptzollamt Mainz* [1979] ECR 69; 99/78: *Decker KG v Hauptzollamt Landau* [1979] ECR 101.

5 See Case 37/70: *Rewe-Zentrale des Lebensmittel-Grosshandels GmbH v Hauptzollamt Emmerich* [1971] ECR 23, [1971] CMLR 238.

6 See case 100/63: *Kalsbeek v Sociale Verzekeringsbank* [1964] ECR 565 at 575; see also A. G. Mayras in case 70/72: *EC Commission v Germany* [1973] ECR 813 at 844 and A. G. Warner in case 7/76 op. cit.; see also *Rewe-Zentrale*, op. cit., *Racke*, op. cit., *Decker*, op. cit.

7 Case 88/76: *Exportation des Sucres v EC Commission* [1977] ECR 709.

8 See also Case 112/77: *Töpfer & Co GmbH v EC Commission* [1978] ECR 1019 (facts on p. 246 post).

9 Vertrauensschutz, protéction de la confiance légitime.

Hence the principle of 'legitimate expectations'[10] derived from German law.

The principle was first applied in the *Staff Salaries*[11] case where the Commission sought an annulment of a Council decision which reversed a previous decision fixing criteria for the remuneration of Community civil servants and substituting a new formula. The previous decision was a result of negotiations and was to remain in force for three years. It created a legitimate expectation that the Community would pay its employees according to the agreed scales. The Court upheld this contention and annulled the offending measure but ruled, in accordance with EEC article 174 (2), that it should remain in force until a new one has been enacted, thus safeguarding the interim pay regime.

The most illuminating examples of the application of the principle can be found in the jungle of the Common Agricultural Policy. To begin with the *Deuka*[12] case: in order to reduce the surplus of produce and yet maintain the market prices the Commission adopted a system of premiums to encourage the process of denaturing, i.e. rendering the produce in question unfit for human consumption. The amount of the premium was fixed for each crop on an annual basis subject to adjustments in response to market fluctuations. To qualify for a premium the processor had to obtain a prior authorisation from the relevant authority, carry out the process and prove its completion. By a new regulation coming into force on 1 June 1970 the Commission abolished the relevant regulation, which provided for an increased premium for the denaturing of wheat of a certain grade.

During June and July 1970 Deuka had denatured a quantity of wheat which the company had purchased before 1 June 1970. It then claimed the increased premium in accordance with the now abolished regulation arguing that the new regulation was invalid. On reference from a German court the ECJ did not annul the regulation but, in the name of legal certainty, held that it ought to be so interpreted as to make the increased premium payable even if the denaturing process occurred after 1 June, provided that the wheat was purchased and the authorisation to process it was obtained before 1 June. Deuka had embarked on a venture

---

10 Usher, J. A., The Influence of National Concepts on Decisions of the European Court, [1976] 1 ELRev. 359 at 363, note 28.

11 Case 81/72: *EC Commission v EC Council* [1973] ECR 575, [1973] CMLR 639.

12 Case 78/74: *Deuka etc v Einfur-und Vorratsstelle für Getreide und Futtermittel* [1975] ECR 421, [1975] 2 CMLR 28.

which had the backing of the law and its expectations had to be protected.

The stress is, therefore, on the requirement that the expectation is 'legitimate'[13], that is, conceived in the mind of a prudent person who acts according to the letter and the spirit of the law in confidence that his fidelity to the law will be reciprocated. Mere speculation will not do. This is illustrated by the *Mackprang*[14] case. In the Spring of 1969 the fall in the forward rate of the French franc opened up a prospect of a profit on the exchange rate to dealers in cereals who purchased the produce in France and sold it to the German Agricultural Intervention Agency (EVGF). Under the CAP such national agencies are bound to purchase agricultural produce[15]. The intensified market activities posed a threat to the German intervention system as well as the storage capacity of the Agency. In the circumstances the Commission by Decision 69/138[16] authorised the German Government to restrict intervention purchases to wheat and barley grown in Germany. Identical decisions were adopted for Belgium and the Netherlands. The Decision was issued on 8 May 1969, took effect on the same day but exempted offers made before that date. On 6 May Mackprang, a German dealer in cereals, offered to the EVGF eight lots of wheat purchased in France stating that the produce was situated in various parts of Germany whilst in actual fact it was still in transit from France to Germany. On 8 May the EVGF accepted the offer but subsequently declined to accept deliveries to its warehouses. Mackprang's claim to compensation on the ground of a legitimate expectation failed. The ECJ, on reference, conceded that the Decision being a derogation from the relevant Regulations had to be interpreted in the light of the objectives pursued by those Regulations but held it was . . . 'a justified precaution against purely speculative

---

13 E.g. Cases 95–98/74, 15, 100/75: *Union Nationale des Coopératives Agricoles de Céréales v EC Commission* [1975] ECR 1615; 44–51/77: *Union Malt v EC Commission* [1978] ECR 57, [1978] 3 CMLR 702; 78/77: *Lührs v Hauptzollamt Hamburg-Jonas* [1978] ECR 169, [1979] 1 CMLR 657; 130/78: *Salumificio di Cornuda SpA v Amministrazione delle Finanze dello Stato* [1979] ECR 867, [1979] 3 CMLR 561; Case 12/78: *Italian Republic v EC Commission* [1979] ECR 1731, [1980] 2 CMLR 573 (*Re Monetary Compensatory Amounts for Durum Wheat*); and Case 84/78: *Tomadini SNC v Amministrazione delle Finanze* [1979] ECR 1801, [1980] 2 CMLR 573; 49/79: *Pool v EC Council* [1980] ECR 569, [1980] 3 CMLR 279.
14 Case 2/75: *Einfur-und Vorratsstelle für Getreide und Futtermittel v Mackprang* [1975] ECR 607, [1977] 1 CMLR 198.
15 See p. 377 post.
16 OJ 1969, L 112.

activities'[17]. Therefore it did not constitute an infringement of the principle of protection of legitimate expectation. Advocate-General Warner, holding that the transaction was 'subversive to the intervention system', thus disposed of the argument: . . . 'No trader who was exploiting that situation in order to make out of the system profits that the system was never designed to bestow on him could legitimately rely on the persistence of the situation. On the contrary, the only reasonable expectation that such a trader could have was that the competent authorities would act as swiftly as possible to bring the situation to an end. Nor . . . could he expect particular tenderness at their hands' . . .

If a loss occurs as a result of frustrated legitimate expectations an action for damages may be brought under EEC article 215 (2). In such a case the claimant must prove not only that he had such an expectation on which he had acted reasonably but also a causal link between his loss and the relevant Community act. The case of *CNTA v EC Commission*[18] provides an interesting example. By Regulation 974/71 the Council had established a system of monetary compensatory amounts in order to make good losses arising from fluctuations in exchange rates. The system was extended to colza seed by Commission Regulation 1471/71, further extended to France by Commission Regulations 17/72 and 144/72. By Regulation 189/72 made on 26 January 1972 the Commission abolished the system as from 1 February 1972. The CNTA (a French company) was in the colza business which was covered by both Regulations. Before the second Regulation was enacted the CNTA made a number of export contracts which were to be performed after the scheme had been abolished. It claimed that it had suffered loss as a result of the sudden and unexpected abolition of the scheme without there being any provision in respect of transactions entered into during the lifetime of the scheme. CNTA's claim was further strengthened by reference to a scheme of export refunds whose rates fluctuated but could be fixed in advance in respect of any particular transaction. To that end the exporter had to lodge a deposit which would be forfeited if he failed to export as arranged. CNTA having obtained advance fixing of the refunds in respect of certain transactions before 26 January, claimed that it entered these on the assumption that monetary compensatory amounts would be payable and calculated its profits accordingly.

17 Ibid. para. 4.
18 Case 74/74: [1975] ECR 533, [1977] 1 CMLR 171 and [1976] ECR 797.

In order to establish liability under article 215 (2) CNTA had to prove that 'in accordance with general principles common to the laws of the Member States', the Commission had acted wrongly. CNTA argued, accordingly, that Regulation 189/72 constituted an act envisaged by the said article because it infringed the principle of legal certainty and frustrated its legitimate expectations. The Court conceded the force of this argument and held that: ... 'In these circumstances, a trader may legitimately expect that for transactions irrevocably undertaken by him because he has obtained, subject to a deposit, export licences fixing the amount of the refund in advance, no unforeseeable alteration will occur which could have the effect of causing him inevitable loss, by re-exposing him to the exchange risk' ...

... 'The Community is therefore liable if, in the absence of an overriding matter of public interest, the Commission abolished with immediate effect and without warning the application of compensatory amounts in a specific sector without adopting transitional measures which would at least permit traders either to avoid the loss which would have been suffered in the performance of export contracts, the existence and irrevocability of which are established by the advance fixing of the refunds, or to be compensation for such loss' ...

... In the absence of an overriding matter of public interest, the Commission has violated a superior rule of law, thus rendering the Community liable, by failing to include in Regulation 189/72 transitional measures for the protection of the confidence which a trader might legitimately have in the Community rules'[19] ...

Having said that the Court did not declare Regulation 189/72 invalid. Thus the wrongful act was not the Regulation itself but the omission to issue a warning to traders and to institute a transitional regime to protect transactions already in progress. This omission constituted a violation of a 'superior rule of law', i.e. the protection of legitimate expectations.

Turning to the question of damages the Court held that, in the circumstances, the Community was not liable to compensate the claimant for all the losses incurred. It held that ... 'it is necessary to take into consideration the fact that the maintenance of the compensatory amounts was in no way guaranteed ... and that it could not therefore legitimately expect under all circumstances to

**19** Ibid. paras 42–44; see also *Re Monetary Compensatory Amounts for Durum Wheat*, op. cit. p. 145, note 13 ante.

make the profits which would have accrued to it from the contract under the system of compensatory amounts' ... 'The protection which it may claim by reason of its legitimate expectation is merely that of not suffering loss by reason of the withdrawal of those amounts'[20] ...

In subsequent proceedings to determine the actual damages the claimant was unable to prove any loss arising from the withdrawal of the scheme within the limits stated above because payments for the shipments were made in French currency. Any loss of anticipated profits was covered by the commercial risk involved[1]. However the principle of the protection of legitimate expectations has been established.

(e) *Equity*. It seems convenient to group under a general title of Equity several principles which have been applied or put forward in order to mitigate hardship arising from a strict application of the law. Apart from this common feature these principles can be traced to the municipal law of one or several member states.

*Good faith* was pleaded in *Meganck v EC Commission*[2] where a temporary official drew certain family allowances to which strictly he was not entitled. When faced with the demand for repayment he claimed, successfully, that he received these in good faith not knowing from his salary slips that he was in fact overpaid.

*Fairness or equity* appeared in several cases. Mr Casacurta's[3] application for admission to internal competition for a position in the Community service was rejected without sufficient reasons being given by the relevant selection board. The ECJ annulled the decision of the board on the ground that in the circumstances, it was *unfair* to the official.

In the *Reich*[4] case the claimant failed to observe the time limit provided for in a licence for the importation of maize from a member state. He argued that this was due to *force majeure*, i.e. the delay in importation due to a fault of the railway authority and not his own. The ECJ held that, since *force majeure* was a valid excuse under the regulation governing imports from non-Community countries, there was no reason why *in equity* this principle should not apply to imports from a member state of the Community.

20 Ibid., paras 45–46.
 1 [1976] ECR 797.
 2 Case 36/72: [1973] ECR 527 at 534.
 3 Case 31/75: *Costacurta v EC Commission* [1975] ECR 1563 at 1570.
 4 Case 64/74: *Reich v Hauptzollamt Landau* [1975] ECR 261, at 268, [1975] 1 CMLR 396.

Lührs[5], an exporter of potatoes to Sweden, who in the circumstances, could not rely on the plea of legitimate expectations,
claimed that he was nevertheless unfairly treated because of the
uncertainty inherent in the regulations governing the exchange of
the tax on exports into national currency. The ECJ held that *natural
justice* required that of the two rates of exchange which could have
been applied in his case the one, which at the material time was less
onerous to the taxpayer, should be applied.

*Force majeure* was pleaded both in the *Handelsgesellschaft*[6] and
the third *Kampffmeyer* case[7]. Both were concerned with the operation of the system of export/import licences and advance fixing
certificates for agricultural produce. The issue of licences was subject to a forfeitable deposit in the event of the authorisation to
export/import not being exhausted within the stated period. If as
a result of *force majeure* the transaction was not completed the
national authority operating the system could either refund the
deposit or extend the period for completion. The system was challenged in the *Handelsgesellschaft* case on several grounds including
*force majeure* in so far as the referring court enquired whether, on
the proper construction of the regulation in question, the forfeiture
of the deposit was excluded only in cases of *force majeure*. Should
this be the case the ground would be too narrow to do justice to the
appellant. The ECJ answered in the negative but gave a broad
definition of *force majeure*. It held ... 'The concept of *force majeure*
is not limited to absolute impossibility but must be understood in
the sense of unusual circumstances outside the control of the importer or exporter, the consequences of which, in spite of the
exercise of all due care, could not have been avoided except at the
cost of excessive sacrifice. The concept implies a sufficient flexibility regarding not only the nature of the occurrence relied upon
but also the care which the exporter should have exercised in order
to meet it and the extent of the sacrifice which he should have
accepted to that end' ... (at para 23).

In the *Kampffmeyer* case the issue was whether the loss of an
import licence following despatch by non-registered letter constituted *force majeure* so as to absolve the trader from the forfeiture of
his deposit. It was basically a matter of fact, that is, whether a

5 Case 78/77: *Lührs v Hauptzollamt Hamburg-Jonas* [1978] ECR 169 at 180,
   [1979] 1 CMLR 657.
6 Op. cit. p. 132, note 17 and p. 142 note 1 ante.
7 Case 158/73: *Kampffmeyer v Einfur-und Vorratsstelle für Getreide und
   Futtermittel* [1974] ECR 101.

diligent trader fulfils his duty of care in the context of his business and the Community licensing system if he sends his licence by ordinary post. Holding that ... 'in the absence of any express provision of Community law, it is for the national court to say whether such a trader has or has not exercised all reasonable care' ... the ECJ ruled that the matter was one of application, not of interpretation and left the decision to the referring court. In German law the responsibility lay with the trader.

Another abortive attempt to take advantage of *force majeure* occurred in *IFG v Commission*[8] where a trader sought from the Community compensation in respect of a transaction which, due to floods in Rumania, was not completed within the period of his import licence. His claim was supported by the argument that due to a change in the Community law his legitimate expectations were frustrated. The ECJ, whilst recognising *force majeure* to be a cause ... 'of derogation from the strict requirements of the law,' ... could not find any reason why the Community should be liable under EEC article 215 (2) in the present case. Indeed, held the Court, remedy should be sought from the other contracting party.

However a French exporter of wheat to the United Kingdom was successful[9]. His cargo perished in the North Sea but his claim for 'accession compensatory amounts' due under Regulation 269/73 was refused on the ground that he was unable to prove that the goods had reached their destination. The Regulation, unlike Regulation 192/75 governing export refunds for agricultural produce, did not contain the *force majeure* formula. Therefore, on reference, the ECJ rectified the position by applying by analogy Regulation 192/75. It held that ... 'Regulation 269/73 is to be interpreted as meaning that where goods exported from an old Member State to a new Member State have perished in transit as a result of *force majeure*, the exporter is entitled to the same compensatory amounts as would have been due to him if the goods had reached their destination and if import formalities had been completed there' ...[10]. Thus the Court not only applied an equitable general principle to mitigate hardship but also in doing so filled a lacuna in the Community system.

The principle of *proportionality*, which is an aspect of the Aris-

8 Case 68/77: *Intercontinentale Fleischhandelsgesellschaft mbH & Co KG v EC Commission* [1978] ECR 353, [1978] 2 CMLR 733.
9 Case 6/78: *Union Française de Céréales v Hauptzollamt Hamburg-Jonas* [1978] ECR 1675.
10 Ibid., para 6.

totelian distributive justice, embodied in the German Constitution, made an early debut[11] before the Community Court but was most dramatically, though unsuccessfully, pleaded in the *Handelsgesellschaft* case. In simple terms the principle means that social burdens should be distributed fairly according to the capacity of the members of the society. According to Advocate General Dutheillet de Lamothe[12] it means that such burdens may be imposed only for the purposes of the public interest to the extent that is strictly necessary for the attainment of such purposes.

Dealing with the argument that forfeitable deposits instituted under Regulation 120/67 infringed the principle of proportionality (as persistently claimed by the trader and maintained by the Verwaltungsgericht at Frankfurt) the ECJ held that it was a matter of Community law which could not be overridden by principles of national law even of a constitutional character. The system itself was justified as it served the purposes of the Treaty in supporting the common organisation of agricultural markets.

The system was more positively defended by the ECJ in another case[13], since the burdens it imposed were not 'manifestly out of proportion to the object in view'[14] whilst 'the competent authorities must be in a position constantly to follow trade movements in order to assess market trends and apply the measures laid down in the Regulation'.[15] However whilst the forfeiture of a deposit for not complying with the licensing system is fully justified[16] it is not so justified on the ground of failing to comply with purely bureaucratic requirements such, for example, as the delay in submitting a proof of imports of tomato concentrates[17]. The principle of proportionality has been applied with diverse results in several other cases dealing with such problems as: the movement of goods[15] and

11 Case 9/55: *Federation Charbonnière de Belgique v High Authority of the ECSC* [1954–56] ECR 292 at 299.
12 Case 11/70: *Internationale Handelsgesellschaft*, op. cit. [1970] ECR 1125 at 1146.
13 Case 5/73: *Balkan-Import-Export GmbH v Hauptzollamt Berlin-Packhof* [1973] ECR 1091 at 1112.
14 See also Cases 119 and 120/76: *Ölmühle Hamburg AG v Hauptzollamt Hamburg Waltershof and Becher v HZA Bremen-Nord* [1977] ECR 1269, [1979] 2 CMLR 83.
15 ECJ reciting a preamble to Regulation 120/67 in the third *Kampffmeyer* case, op. cit. p. 149, note 7 ante.
16 Case 85/78: *Bundesanstalt für Landwirtschaftliche Marktordnung v Jacob Hirsch & Sohne GmbH* [1978] ECR 2517, [1979] 2 CMLR 631.
17 Case 122/78: *Buitoni SA v Fonds d'Orientation et de Regularisation des Marches Agricoles* [1979] ECR 677, [1979] 2 CMLR 665.
15 Case 62/70: *Bock KG v EC Commission* [1971] ECR 897 at 909, [1972] CMLR 160; Case 52/77: *Cayrol v Rivolira and Figli* [1977] 2 ECR 2261 at 2281, [1978] 2 CMLR 253.

persons[16] and state responsibility for the implementation of the CAP[17].

Finally, the derogation clauses: *public policy*[18]; *public morality*[19]; *public security*[20]; and *public health*[1] which enable the Member States to limit the freedom of movement of persons and goods. All these principles, taken from national laws, form part of the Community system. However in view of their nature and function they have to be interpreted restrictively so as not to become the tools of legal subterfuge. The ECJ, whilst insisting on a uniform interpretation of these principles, has not as yet offered an authoritative definition of any of them. Speaking of public policy it conceded that it is necessary 'to allow the . . . national authorities an area of discretion within the limits imposed by the Treaty'[2] . . .

Reflecting on the use and development of general principles of law at the hands of the Community Court one should not underestimate their potential for the interpretation of Community law and for the closing of gaps which the system reveals in practice. However one should not overestimate this potential or attribute to it the character of a Community 'common law' system[3] implying thereby a new body of rules superimposed upon the law derived from the Community Treaties.

(vi) *Opinions of the Advocates-General*. The Advocate-General participates in every case before the ECJ and his opinion forms an obligatory part of the adjudicating process though not of the judgment itself. In the light of his function and the nature of the Community Court the Advocate-General can be likened to a judge of a first instance court within the Community administration of justice. Therefore, if he is followed by the Court his opinion may

---

**16** Case 36/75: *Rutili v Minister of the Interior* [1975] ECR 1219, [1976] 1 CMLR 140; Case 8/77: *Re Sagulo, Brenca and Bakhouche* [1977] 2 ECR 1495 at 1506, [1977] 2 CMLR 585. Case 30/77: *R v Bouchereau* [1977] ECR 1999.

**17** Case 166/78: *Italy v EC Council* [1979] ECR 2575 at 2601.

**18** Cases *Van Duyn*, op. cit. 30/77: *R v Bouchereau* [1978] QB 732, [1977] ECR 1999; 7/78: *R v Thompson* [1978] ECR 2247, [1979] 1 CMLR 47.

**19** 34/79: *R v Darby, R v Henn* [1979] ECR 3795, [1980] 1 CMLR 246.

**20** See Irish case *McAfee v Smyth and Quigley* [1981] 1 CMLR 410.

**1** E.g. Cases 35/76: *Simmenthal SpA v Italian Ministry of Finance* [1976] ECR 1871 at 1876, [1977] 2 CMLR 1; 153/78: *EC Commission v Federal Republic of Germany* [1979] ECR 2555, [1980] 1 CMLR 198.

**2** *Van Duyn* op. cit. para 18; see also *Boucherau*, para 34, *Rutili* para 26; *R v Henn, R v Darby*, para 15.

**3** As suggested by Hartley, T. C., *The Foundations of European Community Law*, 1981, p. 144, and Wyatt, D., and Dashwood, A., *The Substantive Law of the EEC*, 1980, p. 47; see also A. G. Dutheillet de Lamothe in the *Handelsgesellschaft* case, op. cit. at 1141.

be regarded as a concurring judgment by analogy to individual judgments of a collegiate common law court. If he is not followed, by the same analogy, his opinion may be regarded as a dissenting judgment.

In the common law system dissenting and concurring judgments are studied with equal interest since at the ultimate instance a dissent in a court below may become the final ruling. Even without that change of fortune a dissenting judgment may be used in argument on another occasion in the hope that a fresh approach may sharpen its force. In the Community system, on the other hand, the opinion of the Advocate-General has to be seen as a personal judgment and an invitation to the Court to follow suit. It is fully reasoned and it tends to relate the proposed solution to the pattern of case law established by the Court. One can therefore discern a greater appreciation of Community precedents in the opinions of Advocates-General than in the judgments of the Court.

The Advocates-General have made a significant contribution to the development of Community law. Their opinions, in view of their personal style, appear by and large to be more readable than the judgments of the Court. However, no matter their weight as a persuasive force or part of dynamic jurisprudence, they lack the authority of the *res judicata*.

## PART TWO
## Where to find Community law

## I   Treaties and related instruments

The authentic and official English texts of the Community Treaties are available in a variety of forms:

1. Editions published by the Community:

(i) *Treaties establishing the European Communities: Treaties amending these Treaties: Documents concerning the Accession* (European Communities Office for Official Publications, 1978). This volume contains all the Treaties and their annexes in force on 1 July 1978.

(ii) *Documents concerning the accession of the Hellenic Republic to the European Communities* (*Official Journal of the European Communities, 1979*, L. 291).

(iii) *Collected agreements concluded by the European Communities* (8 volumes published to date). These volumes contain the texts of agreements with non-member states and international organisations during the years 1958–1978.

2. HM Stationery Office Editions of the Treaties are also available as follows:

(i) *Treaty establishing the European Coal and Steel Community, Paris 18 April 1951* (Amended text: Cmnd. 7461). The sole authentic text of this Treaty is in French which is printed together with an English translation; the latter has no official standing.

(ii) *Treaty establishing the European Economic Community, Rome 25 March 1957; Treaty establishing the European Atomic Energy Community, Rome 25 March 1957* (Amended text: Cmnd. 7460).

(iii) *Treaty concerning the Accession of the Kingdom of Denmark, Ireland, the Kingdom of Norway and the United Kingdom of Great Britain and Northern Ireland to the European Economic Community and the European Atomic Energy Community and Decision of the Council of the European Communities concerning the Accession of the said States to the European Coal and Steel Community, Brussels 22 January 1972* (Amended text: Cmnd. 7463).

3. The texts of the principal Treaties and of some other Community instruments are also available in Sweet & Maxwell's *European Community Treaties* (4th edn, 1980). Rudden and Wyatt's *Basic Community Laws* (1980) is an excellent compilation for students which contains the major Treaties and the texts of basic secondary legislation.

4. Annotated texts of the Treaties and of related Community instruments are to be found in *Halsbury's Statutes of England* (3rd edn), Volume 42A, European Continuation Volume 1, 1952–72 and in Sweet and Maxwell's *Encyclopedia of European Community Law*, Volumes BI, II and III. Both of these works are kept up to date by Supplements.

## II Secondary legislation

The secondary legislation of the Communities, i.e. decisions and recommendations in the case of the ECSC and regulations, directives and decisions in the cases of the EEC and Euratom, are published in the *Official Journal of the European Communities*. This appears, almost daily, in each of the official languages of the Communities. An English edition has been published since 9 October 1972. Since 1968 the *Official Journal* has appeared in two series: one devoted to secondary legislation (the 'L' series), the other containing non-normative communications and information (the 'C' series).

Authentic English texts of pre-accession secondary legislation have been published in *Special Editions of the Official Journal of the European Communities* covering the period 1952–72. The same texts have also been published by HM Stationery Office in 42 volumes arranged under subject headings under the title *Secondary Legislation of the European Communities: Subject Edition*. Annotated texts of Community secondary legislation are to be found in *Halsbury's Statutes of England* (3rd edn), Volume 42A and Supplements and in the *Encyclopedia of European Community Law*, Volumes CI to VI. Community and national legislation relating to economic activites is summarised in *European Law Digest* (1973 and continued). The T.M.C. Asser Institute's *Guide to EEC Legislation* (1979), in two volumes with an annual cumulative supplement, provides an invaluable subject index to past and current Community legislation.

## III  Case law

The texts of its judgments and opinions with the submissions of the advocates-general are published in periodical parts by the Court of Justice in each of the official languages of the Communities. The version in the procedural language in respect of a particular case is the only authentic version. The French version, which was commonly used in the United Kingdom before accession is entitled *Recueil da la Jurisprudence de la Cour*. An English version entitled *European Court Reports* has been published in periodical parts since 1973. English translations of the pre-accession volumes of reports of cases before the Court from 1953 to 1972 have been published.

Since 1962 English translations of the judgments of both the Court of Justice and of some of the courts of the member states on points of Community law and decisions of the Commission on restrictive practices have been published under the name *Common Market Law Reports*. Since 1970 these Reports have also included the texts of the judgments in the procedural language. English translations of the judgments of the Court of Justice prior to the commencement of the *Common Market Law Reports* are to be found in Volume 2 of Valentine's *Court of Justice of the European Communities* (1965).

English translations of the judgments of the Court of Justice are also to be found in *Common Market Reports* published by the Commerce Clearing House Inc. of Chicago. Since May 1972 leading cases have been published in the *Times* newspaper. Community and national case-law relating to economic activities is summarised in *European Law Digest* (1973 and continued). Eversen, Sperl and Usher's *Compendium of Case Law relating to the European Communities* covers the years 1973–1976 and is to be replaced by a *Digest of Case Law* which is being prepared under the auspices of the Court of Justice.

# IV  Subsidiary sources

(i) *Official papers of Community institutions.* There is a vast amount of such material covering all the activities of the Communities. It ranges from general reports and journalism to highly specialised monographs on detailed aspects of Community activity. Most of this material appears in all the official languages and some of the pre-accession papers are also available in unofficial English versions. From the lawyer's point of view the most significant and informative include the following:

Reports and opinions of the Commission and the consultative committees published in the *Official Journal*. Discussion documents and draft legislative proposals are available in mimeographed form with the prefixes COM (for Commission) and SEC (for Secretary General).

The Debates and Working Documents (*Documents de Séance*) of the European Parliament. The Debates are published as an annexe to the Official Journal and the Working Documents are published individually by the Parliament itself.

*The Bulletin of the European Communities* published in periodical parts by the Secretariat of the Commission. In addition to giving a monthly account of current activities and developments the Supplements to the *Bulletin* are convenient sources of the texts of important reports and proposals for legislation.

The annual *General Report on the Activities of the Communities* submitted by the Commission to the Assembly. The General Secretariat of the Council also publishes an annual *Review of the Council's Work.*

(ii) *Journals.* There are four English language journals devoted to Community matters. The *Common Market Law Review* (1963/1964 and continued), the *European Law Review* (1975/1976 and continued) and *Legal Issues of European Integration* (1974 and continued) are all concerned with the law. *The Journal of Common Market Studies* (1962 and continued) is not exclusively legal and also covers economic and political aspects of Community activities. Articles on Community legal topics are also to be found in the *International and Comparative Law Quarterly*, the *British Yearbook of International Law* and the *Journal of Business Law.*

(iii) *Treatises.* The companion volume to this work, Lasok's *The Law of the Economy in the European Communities* (1980) is a comprehensive study of the substantive law of the Community. A full and scholarly treatment of Community law will also be found in both Lipstein's *Law of the European Economic Community* (1974) and Kapteyn and Verloren Van Themaat's *Introduction to the Law of the European Communities* (1973). Collins' *European Community Law in the United Kingdom* (2nd edn, 1980) is a valuable study of structural and procedural aspects of Community law in the context of the law of the United Kingdom. The role of the Court of Justice is comprehensively treated in Schermers' *Judicial Protection in the European Communities* (2nd edn, 1979) and Toth's *Legal Protection of Individuals in the European Communities*, 2 volumes (1978).

Among the large quantity of continental literature Gide, Loyrette and Nouel's *Dictionnaire du Marché Commun* in four large loose-leaf volumes and Megret's *Le Droit de la Communauté Economique Européenne* (10 of 14 projected volumes published to date) are particularly valuable.

Part II

# The law of the Institutions

Chapter 5

# The Commission of the European Communities

## I Introduction

It has already been pointed out that the European Communities were brought into existence by means of multilateral treaties between sovereign states signed and ratified in accordance with their customary constitutional procedures. These original treaties, subject to subsequent amendments[1], are the source of the constitutional law of the Communities. They set out the objectives and purposes of the Communities, create the institutions of the Communities, define the powers of those institutions and regulate their relations both inter se and with the member states. In superficial form the Communities are cast in the classic mould of international organisations which has been so frequently used in modern times: the creation, by means of a multilateral treaty, of an organisation which possesses a distinct legal personality and which acts through the agency of institutions set up and regulated under the terms of the constituent treaty. In possessing these characteristics the European Communities fall within a recognisable and well-defined pattern. But despite this superficial identity which the European Communities have with other international organisations both universal and regional, the Communities may also be said to be unique; this uniqueness lies in their institutions. Not, it is true, in the existence of those institutions as bodies independent and autonomous of the member states for such institutions are commonly and necessarily found in international organisations. Nor does this uniqueness lie in the capacity of the institutions to impose obligations on the member states for that is a power possessed, for example, by the Security Council of the United Nations. The uniqueness of the

---

1 Notably by the Merger Treaty 1965, the Budgetary Provisions Treaty 1970, the Treaty of Accession 1972 concerning the accession of Denmark, Ireland and the United Kingdom, the Financial Provisions Treaty 1975, the Direct Election Decision 1976 and the Treaty of Accession 1979 concerning the accession of Greece.

Communities stems from the deep involvement of their institutions in matters traditionally within the exclusive control of each individual state and their capacity to make rules directly and automatically binding not only on the member states themselves but also on individuals and corporate bodies within those states. Thus the unique character of the Communities lies in the degree of their penetration into the internal legal relations of the member states, whereas classical international organisations tend to be involved merely with the external legal relations of their members.

The institutions of the European Communities fall into two main categories. In the first place there are institutions vested with a variety of political, legislative, executive and administrative functions and powers. These are the Commission, the Council and the Assembly (European Parliament), assisted by a number of ancillary organs. Institutions in this category defy more precise classification for two main reasons. One is that these institutions cannot be said to be exclusively executive, administrative, legislative or political but each possesses more than one of these attributes. The other is that in functional terms the Treaties conceive of these institutions not only co-operating but indeed working as a team so that the role and significance of any one of them cannot fully be appreciated in isolation. In the second place there is the Court of Justice, the judicial organ of the Communities.

The institutions will be treated in the above order.

# II  The Commission of the European Communities

## (A)  COMPOSITION AND APPOINTMENT

The Commission of the European Communities is composed of fourteen members chosen on the grounds of their general competence[2]. The Treaties provide that the Commissioners must be persons whose independence can be fully guaranteed. They are required to act with complete independence in the performance of their duties solely in the interests of the Communities and they must neither seek nor take instructions from any national government or other body. Each member state, for its part, pledges to respect the independence of the Commissioners and not to seek to

---

2 Merger Treaty, art. 10 (1), as amended by the Council Decision of 1 January 1973 and the Act concerning Greek Accession 1979, art. 15.

influence them in the performance of their duties. During their term of office Commissioners may not engage in any other occupation, paid or unpaid[3]. When entering upon their duties they give a solemn undertaking before the Court of Justice of the Communities that they accept the obligations of their office.

The Commissioners must be nationals of the member states. Each member state must have at least one but may not have more than two of its nationals on the Commission[4]. The present practice is for each of the larger member states, viz. France, Germany, Italy and the United Kingdom to have two Commissioners and for the Benelux countries, Denmark, Greece and Ireland to have one each. In the case of the United Kingdom the Commissioners have always been nominated so as to reflect the two dominant political parties[5]. The Commissioners are appointed by mutual agreement between the member states. They hold office for renewable periods of four years[6]. The President and the five Vice-Presidents of the Commission are appointed by the same process and hold office for renewable periods of two years[7].

A Commissioner's term of office may be terminated by death in office or by resignation. A Commissioner may resign voluntarily; but if he no longer fulfils the conditions required for the performance of his duties or if he has been guilty of serious misconduct he may be compulsorily retired by the Court of Justice upon the application of either the Commission itself or the Council[8]. The whole Commission may be compelled to resign if the European Parliament passes a motion of censure upon it by a two-thirds majority of the votes cast, representing a majority of the European Parliament's members[9]. These powers of compulsory retirement and parliamentary censure have yet to be invoked.

Prior to the accession of Denmark, Ireland and the United Kingdom the Commission was composed of nine members. The enlargement of the Communities raised the question of the representation of the new member states on the Commission by persons of their nationality. In strict law, since the Commissioners are not national representatives but independent individuals, there was no necessity

3 Ibid., art. 10 (2).
4 Ibid., art. 10 (1).
5 See Times, 15 October 1980.
6 Merger Treaty, art. 11.
7 Ibid., art. 14, as amended by the First Act of Accession, art. 16.
8 Ibid., art. 13.
9 E.g. EEC Treaty, art. 144.

to increase the membership of the Commission to accommodate
new member states. In reality it would have been impractical to
adopt such a legalistic approach. The negotiations over the membership of Denmark, Ireland, Norway and the United Kingdom
and latterly of Greece appear to have proceeded on the basis that if
new members were admitted the membership of the Commission
would be increased so as to accommodate the new members and
maintain the existing level of representation of the original members[10]. This was in fact done by the Council exercising its power
under article 10 (1) of the Merger Treaty to increase the number of
members of the Commission[11].

(B) ORGANISATION

The Commission functions as a collegiate body in the sense that
the Commission collectively and not the Commissioners individually bears responsibility for the acts of the Commission[12]. The
Commission acts by a majority vote[13]. Its rules of procedure provide that the quorum of members is eight and that the conclusions
of the Commission shall be final when they receive at least eight
votes in support[14]. There is, nevertheless, an inevitable degree of
subject specialisation as far as individual Commissioners are concerned. It is now an established practice for special responsibilities
to be allocated to each Commissioner[15]. There is a temptation to
compare these responsibilities, by analogy, with the portfolios
given to members of a national government. However, the analogy
is imperfect since unlike a member of a national government a
Commissioner bears no personal responsibility for his portfolio.

Although the Commission is collectively responsible for its acts,
it may authorise its members to take agreed action on its behalf.

---

10 See the Commission's report *The Enlarged Community* (1972), para. 36, the
White Paper, *The United Kingdom and the European Communities* (Cmnd 4175),
para. 71 and *The Second Enlargement of the European Community* (European
Documentation 5/79, p. 31.
11 By a decision of 1 January 1973 and the Act concerning Greek Accession 1979,
art. 15.
12 See *Règlement Intérieur de la Commission*, 63/41/CEE, art. 1, JO, 31 January
1963, and the Commission's Provisional Rules of Procedure, 67/426/EEC, art.
1, OJ 1967, L147.
13 Merger Treaty, art. 17 (1).
14 Provisional Rules of Procedure, 67/426/EEC, art. 2, as amended by Decision
73/1, OJ 1973, L7 and Decision 81/2, OJ 1981, L8. Many decisions of the
Commission are in fact unanimous.
15 See Vacher's *European Companion*, No. 37, p. 14.

This practice is provided by article 27 of the *Règlement Intérieure de la Commission*[16] and was approved by the Court of Justice in *Re Noordwijks Cement Accoord* (1967)[17]. Further, to prevent the principle of collective responsibility from imposing unnecessary delays on the Commission's work, considerable use is made of the so-called written procedure in accordance with the terms of article 11 of the *Règlement Intérieure*. By this procedure draft decisions are circulated among the Commissioners and if no amendments or objections are made within a fixed period (usually one week) the draft is deemed to have been adopted by the Commission as a whole. Where amendments or objections are made or where a Commissioner specifically requests further discussion drafts will be considered at a full meeting of the Commission. This written procedure was not questioned by the Court in *Re Noordwijks Cement Accoord* and so its legality appears to have been accepted[18].

Each Commissioner is assisted by a *cabinet* in the French sense of a private office or departmental staff whose members tend to be of the same nationality of the Commissioner they serve. A *chef de cabinet* or principal private secretary may deputise for his Commissioner at Commission meetings. In addition to the *cabinets* of the Commissioners the Commission has a staff of some 8,400 divided between the various departments and auxiliary services of the Commission. Each department is presided over by a Director-General who is responsible to the Commissioner whose 'portfolio' includes that department[19]. The Directors-General are always of different nationality from the Commissioners they serve. On the lower levels of the administrative hierarchy the aim is to have an equitable representation of all the nationalities of the Communities. In view of the multilingual nature of the Communities with seven official languages, viz. Dutch, French, German, Greek, Italian, Danish and English, linguists play a vital role in the activities of the Communities; there are over 1,200 translators and interpreters on the

16 *Loc. cit.* in note 13 above. Also see Decision 72/2, OJ 1972, L7 on delegation of signature, Decision 74/55, OJ 1974, L34, on the exercise of certain powers in respect of Community revenue and expenditure and Decision 75/461, OJ 1975, L199 on the taking of measures of management and administration.

17 Cases 8-11/66: [1967] ECR 75, [1967] CMLR 77.

18 In 1978 the written procedure was used on 1,782 occasions. See Noel, E., *The European Community: How it works* (1979) p. 66.

19 There are 19 Directorates-General in addition to the Secretariat-General, the Legal Service, the Spokesman's Group, the Statistical Office and some other general services: see Vacher's *European Companion*, No. 37, pp. 15-30.

Commission's staff[20]. In recruiting its staff the Commission relies heavily on secondment from the national civil services of the member states.

## (c) FUNCTIONS AND POWERS

The Merger Treaty provides in article 9 that the Commission shall exercise the powers and competences bestowed by the Community Treaties upon the High Authority of the ECSC and the Commissions of the EEC and Euratom. The functions and powers of the Merged Commission thus vary from Treaty to Treaty. But despite these differences it is possible to categorise the functions and powers of the Commission into three broad groups: it is an initiator and co-ordinator of Community policy; it is the executive agency of the Communities; it is the guardian of the Community Treaties.

As an initiator of policy the scope of the Commission differs in relation to the ECSC and Euratom on the one hand and the EEC on the other. The ECSC and Euratom Treaties are *traités-lois* in that they lay down codes of specific rules relating to the relatively limited fields of concern of those Communities. In such a context the opportunities for formulating policy are limited since the policy decisions and the rules implementing them were largely taken at the time those Treaties were negotiated and were incorporated into the Treaties themselves. But the EEC Treaty with its more wide ranging concern with the entire economies of the member states is a *traité cadre* and sketches in bolder strokes the main lines which are to be followed in achieving an economic union. Thus the EEC Treaty leaves the details of the policies to be followed in the attainment of that goal to be worked out by the institutions of the Community and in this task the Commission plays a major and perhaps its most significant role.

In assisting in the formulation of policy the Commission first engages in consultations with interested parties at the political, civil service and trade union levels. Then, with the assistance of its own specialist departments and advised by its Legal Service[1], it proceeds

---

20 The official languages of the Communities are determined by Regulation 1 of 15 April 1958, OJ 17, 6 October 1958, p. 385/58 (S. edn. 1952-1958, p. 59) as amended by Act of Accession, 1972, art. 29 and Annex I, point XIV, para. 1; the Adaptation Decision of 1 January 1973, OJ 1972, L2 and the Act concerning Greek Accession 1979, art. 147.

1 See Ehlermann, C.-D., *The Role of the Legal Service of the Commission in the Creation of Community Law* (University of Exeter, 1981), pp. 6-10.

to the consideration, often prolonged, of policy proposals until it reaches its final position which is submitted to the Council. It was in this way, for example, that the Commission prepared its opinion on United Kingdom membership of the Communities and its proposals on the agricultural policy of the Communities. After the main lines of policy have been finally agreed the Commission embarks on a consideration of the practical details of the implementation of that policy. The departments of the Commission concerned with a particular policy convene meetings with experts from the member states for the purpose of working out the practical implications of the policy. The experts are invited from the national civil services of the member states and although they have no brief to commit their respective governments they will be aware of their wishes and so will be in a position to advise the Commission on the acceptability of the Commission's proposals to the governments of the member states[2]. By this process the Commission formulates its proposals for submission to the Council. As an indication of the scale of this aspect of the Commission's work, during 1980 it sent 542 proposals to the Council plus 208 memoranda, recommendations and communications[3].

The merged Commission is also the co-ordinator of policy as between the three Communities. Prior to the merger such co-ordination was virtually impossible because the Communities were institutionally separate. Since the merger the Commission has been able to take steps towards the formulation of common policies in such fields as industry, energy, research and technology which cut across the boundaries of the individual Communities. This co-ordination of policy may be regarded as a further stage in the process leading to a complete merger of the three Communities.

The Commission as the initiator and co-ordinator of policy also gives expression to the interests of the Communities; in this role we see the Commission as the conscience of the Communities. The member states despite their acceptance of the obligations of membership are apt to be deflected by national interests. Thus it is for the independent Commission constantly to remind both the Communities and the member states of the fundamental objectives of the Communities and to seek the achievement of those objectives

2 The Commission is indeed under an obligation not to seek or take instructions from any Government; see Merger Treaty, art. 10 (2).
3 *Fourteenth General Report on the Activities of the European Communities* (1981) p. 30.

to the fullest extent[4]. This was clearly expressed by Signor Malfatti when President of the Commission, in a statement to the European Parliament in September 1970: 'The Commission is, at one and the same time, the guardian of the Treaties and the motive force of integration, capable of accepting with courage the dialectic consequences which go with its twofold task—exercising the vigilance that is needed to preserve us from risks run by the venturesome and acting to correct any excess of vigilance which would inevitably lead to stagnation[5].' In this role the Commission's views of the Communities have not infrequently differed from those of the governments of the member states. Over the enlargement of the Communities, for example, the Commission produced a reasoned opinion in 1967 in favour of the admission of the United Kingdom, Ireland, Denmark and Norway to the Communities subject to certain conditions and recommended the opening of negotiations with those countries. That recommendation was not adopted because of the opposition of the French Government to British entry in particular and to the enlargement of the Communities in general.

Secondly, the three Treaties confer upon the Commission a wide range of legislative and executive powers and functions.

Under article 8 of the ECSC Treaty the Commission has the duty of ensuring 'the attainment of the objectives set out in this Treaty, under the conditions laid down herein'. This and many other articles of the Treaty gives the Commission wide rule-making powers. For example, article 60 of the ECSC Treaty gives the Commission the power to define practices which come within the prohibition on unfair competitive prices which might tend towards the creation of a monopoly. Similarly article 155 and article 125 of the EEC and Euratom Treaties respectively confer upon the Commission the authority to see 'that the provisions of [the] Treaty and the measures pursuant to it taken by the institutions are carried out'. Thus, for example, article 48 (3) (*d*) of the EEC Treaty enables the Commission to make regulations laying down the conditions under which workers have a right to live in a member state in which they have been employed. During 1980 the Commission adopted no less than 5,901 acts (Regulations, Decisions, Directives, Recommendations and Opinions)[6].

---

4 See *Premier Rapport Général sur l'activité de la CEE* (September 1958), para. 8.
5 *Statement to the European Parliament* (15 September 1970), p. 22.
6 *Fourteenth General Report on the Activities of the European Communities* (1981), p. 30.

In addition to such powers specifically conferred upon the Commission by the Treaties the Commission may also be invested with powers to ensure the enforcement of decisions made by the Council. This is of particular significance in the EEC where, in connection with the common agricultural policy, the Council has delegated wide rule-making powers to the Commission. In June 1974 the Council declared its intention of making wider use of these powers in future[7]. As a measure of the degree of importance which these powers occupy in the Commission's work, of the more than 2,700 regulations made by the Commission during 1978 the vast majority related to the common agricultural policy[8].

The executive authority vested in the Commission is that of ensuring that the rules of the Treaties are applied to particular cases, whether concerning the government of a member state or a commercial undertaking. Under the ECSC Treaty the Commission deals directly with coal and steel enterprises. Article 54 of that Treaty, for example, enables the Commission to promote and co-ordinate the capital spending of coal and steel enterprises and it has the power to prohibit the financing of any programme put forward by an enterprise which conflicts with the rules of the Treaty. Under the Euratom Treaty the Commission has responsibilities of a supervisory nature in relation to the protection of the health of workers in the nuclear industry and the supply and use of fissile material[9]. In the EEC Treaty similar powers are conferred upon the Commission particularly in relation to the prohibition of restrictive practices and the control of state subsidies[10].

The Commission is also given a number of representative, financial and administrative functions. The Commission represents the legal persona of the Communities[11]. It represents the Communities in negotiations with non-member states and international organisations[12]. The Commission is responsible for the administration of Community funds. In the ECSC a levy on coal and steel production is paid to the Commission direct[13]. In the EEC and Euratom the Commission is charged with giving effect to the budgets of the Communities as adopted by the European Parliament[14].

7 See *Bulletin of the European Communities* (1974), Part 6, p. 122.
8 Noel, E., *The European Community: How it works* (1979), pp. 18, 19.
9 See Euratom Treaty, Title Two, Chapters 3 and 6.
10 See EEC Treaty, Part Three, Title 1.
11 E.g. EEC Treaty, art. 211.
12 E.g. EEC Treaty, arts. 228 et seq.
13 ECSC Treaty, art. 49.
14 EEC Treaty, art. 205; Euratom Treaty, art. 179.

The EEC and Euratom were originally financed out of contributions from the member states. But under the terms of a Council Decision of 1970[15], since 1 January 1975 the Communities have been very largely financed out of their own resources, the main sources of which are customs duties and agricultural levies. The Commission also administers four special funds which form part of the Communities' budget: the European Social Fund which is used to redeploy and retrain workers and to promote social welfare[16]; the European Development Fund which makes grants and loans to overseas territories and countries associated with the Communities[17]; the European Agricultural Guidance and Guarantee Fund which is used to cover agricultural market support costs and to assist farm modernisation schemes[18]; and the European Regional Development Fund which has been set up to correct regional imbalances within the Community[19]. Under the terms of article 18 of the Merger Treaty the Commission is also required to publish an annual general report on the activities of the Communities.

Lastly, the Commission as the guardian of the Treaties acts as a watchdog to ensure that treaty obligations are observed. If an allegation is made that there has been an infringement of Treaty obligations it is for the Commission, as an impartial body, to investigate that allegation, reach a conclusion and notify the action necessary to correct the error. In the case of such an error in respect of the ECSC Treaty, article 88 authorises the Commission to take steps to ensure that member states fulfil their obligations under the Treaty. Where a member state will not voluntarily carry out its obligations the Commission may, with the concurring vote of a two-thirds majority of the Council withhold from the defaulting member state sums of money which the Commission may owe that state under the Treaty and authorise the other member states to withhold certain benefits under the Treaty from the defaulting state as a sanction for its wrong doing. If these measures prove ineffec-

---

**15** Decision 70/243, OJ L94, 28 April 1970, p. 19 (S. edn 1970 (I) p. 224). Also see Council Regulation 2/71 applying that Decision, OJ L3, 5 January 1971, p. 1 (S. edn 1971 (I), p. 3).

**16** EEC Treaty, Part Three, Title 3, Chapter 2.

**17** See Implementing Convention of the Association of the Overseas Countries and Territories with the Community 1957, annexed to the EEC Treaty and the Second Lomé Convention, Title VII, Chapter 2, *Encyclopedia of European Community Law*, Vol. BIII, p. B12931.

**18** This fund was established by Council Regulation No. 25 of 4 April 1962, OJ 1962, p. 991/62 (S. edn 1959–1962, p. 126).

**19** See Regulation (EEC) 724/75, OJ 1975, L73.

tive the Commission shall bring the matter before the Council. This procedure may be subject to review by the Court of Justice of the Communities[20]. Also under the ECSC Treaty the Commission has the power to impose a monetary penalty on any coal and steel undertaking which acts contrary to its obligations under the Treaty.[1]

The provisions of the ECSC Treaty authorising action to be taken against a member state were found to be complex and cumbersome and have been seldom used in practice. Partly because of this experience the equivalent provisions of the EEC and Euratom Treaties are simpler and more effective. Article 169 of the EEC Treaty lays down a general procedure for dealing with breaches of treaty obligations by member states. It provides that where 'the Commission considers that a member state has failed to fulfil an obligation under the Treaty, it shall deliver a reasoned opinion on the matter after giving the state concerned the opportunity to submit its observations. If the state concerned does not comply with the terms of the opinion within the period laid down by the Commission, the latter may bring the matter before the Court of Justice[2].' In 1980, for example, 115 actions were brought by the Commission under this procedure[3]. In earlier years most of the infringements concerned customs duties and quotas but latterly the cases have involved a wider range of Treaty provisions, notably in the field of the common agricultural policy. With the advent of further common policies this is likely to remain an important part of the Commission's activities. In addition to this general procedure the Treaties also confer authority on the Commission to deal with special infringements. For example article 89 of the EEC Treaty authorises the Commission to investigate suspected infringements of the Community's rules of competition. If the suspicion is well founded and if the infringements are not brought to an end the Commission may direct the member states to take the steps necessary to remedy the situation.

(D) PROPOSED REFORMS

Suggestions have been made from time to time concerning the

---

20 See Chapter 9, below.
 1 E.g. arts. 64–66.
 2 Also see Euratom Treaty, art. 141 and Chapter 9, below.
 3 *Fourteenth General Report on the Activities of the European Communities* (1981), p. 354, Table 2.

composition, structure and working methods of the Commission. At the time of the First Accession, for example, there was criticism of the increase in the size of the Commission on the grounds that a larger body would be unwieldy and less effective[4]. In 1976, in his Report on European Union, Mr Tindemans proposed that the European Parliament should be given a role in the appointment of the President and Members of the Commission[5]. More recently attention has again been focussed on the size of the Commission and its method of working.

Two independent studies authorised by the Commission[6] and the Council[7] in 1979 both agreed that in recent years the Commission has tended to become less effective institution. The increase in the size of the Commission together with the difficulty of giving equally meaningful portfolios to each Commissioner have been identified as contributing to the loss of collegiality in the Commission. The desirability of the four larger member states having two Commissioners of their nationality was also questioned. It was said that such an arrangement runs counter to the independent nature of the Commission and that national interests are properly and adequately protected by the system of weighted voting in the Council[8] and the distribution of seats in the European Parliament[9].

Both of these studies recommend a smaller Commission of one member for each member state, and that the departments and services of the Commission should be reorganised so that each Commissioner has a portfolio of equal weight[10]. This, it is suggested, would not only strengthen the Commission and make it more efficient but would also help it to re-establish its image as a team. Some fairly modest steps have been taken to make better use of the Commission's staff[11]. But there is, as yet, no indication that the more fundamental proposals for reform are likely to be implemented. It seems unlikely that these matters will be taken much further until decisions have been reached on the accession of Portugal and Spain.

4 See *Problems of British Entry into the EEC* (P.E.P. European Series, No. 11, 1969) p. 101.
5 See *Bulletin of the European Communities*, Supp. 1/76, pp. 31, 32.
6 *Proposals for Reform of the Commission of the European Communities and its Services (Spierenburg Report)* (1979).
7 *Report on European Institutions (Three Wise Men's Report)* (1979).
8 See Chapter 6, infra.
9 See Chapter 7, infra.
10 *Spierenburg Report*, para. 43 and Table I; *Three Wise Men's Report, pp. 67, 68.*
11 See *Fourteenth General Report on the Activities of the European Communities* (1981) pp. 30, 31.

Chapter 6

# The Council of the European Communities

The Council is made up of one representative of the government of each of the member states[1]. The composition of the Council varies depending upon the subject matter to be discussed. A basic distinction is drawn between so-called General Council meetings and Specialised Council meetings. The former are attended by Foreign Ministers and the agenda may include not only matters relating to external affairs but also matters of general Community concern such as those relating to the institutions. The latter are attended by those ministers whose portfolios relate to the specific subject on the agenda, for example agriculture, finance, industry or transport[2]. In practical terms the Merger Treaty had very little effect on the working of the Council. Because of the common identity of membership there had been virtually a de facto merger of the separate Councils since 1958. The Merger Treaty formalised this arrangement and provided for unified rules of procedure[3]. The office of President of the Council rotates among the members for terms of six months in strict alphabetical sequence: Belgium, Denmark, Germany, Greece, France, Ireland, Italy, Luxembourg, Netherlands and the United Kingdom[4]. The Council meets in private and its meetings are convened upon the initiative of the President or at the request of either a member or of the Commission[5].

1 Merger Treaty, art. 2.
2 On some occasions joint Council meetings are held attended by ministers with different responsibilities in order to deal with problems extending over a range of sectors of the economy. See *Tenth General Report on the Activities of the European Communities* (1977), p. 33. Also see *Twenty-seventh Review of the Council's Work* (1980), pp. 9, 10.
3 Merger Treaty, art. 5. For the text of the Rules of Procedure see OJ 1979, L268.
4 Ibid., art. 2 as amended by the adjusted First Act of Accession 1972, art. 11 and the Second Act of Accession 1979, art. 11.
5 Merger Treaty, art. 3 and Council's Rules of Procedure, arts. 1 and 3, loc. cit., in n. 3 supra.

(B) THE POWERS OF THE COUNCIL AND ITS RELATIONSHIP WITH THE COMMISSION

As in the case of the Commission, the Council exercises the powers conferred by the Community Treaties upon the former separate Councils[6]. One of the most interesting features of the constitution of the Communities is the relationship between the Council and the Commission. This has already been adumbrated in an earlier reference to the role of the Commission in the formulation of policy and as the exponent of the interests of the Communities. There is, however, a noticeable difference in this relationship between the ECSC and Euratom on the one hand and the EEC on the other. The ECSC and Euratom Treaties, at articles 26 and 115 respectively, stress the Council's harmonising and co-ordinating role in relation to the policies of the member states; the EEC Treaty at article 145 specifies in addition a power to take decisions. In general terms, under the ECSC Treaty it is the Commission which has the power to take decisions subject to consultation with the Council; under the EEC Treaty the power of decision largely lies with the Council usually acting upon a proposal from the Commission. These differences appear to indicate that the Commission has more power under the ECSC Treaty than it has under the EEC Treaty and that the supra-national character of the Commission in the ECSC is not enjoyed in relation to the EEC. In fact, the importance of these formal differences is more apparent than real. We have already seen that in the ECSC the opportunities for the Commission to initiate policy are limited because of the essential character of the treaty as a *traité-loi*. This gives the Commission powers of a largely executive character to give effect to the rules already laid down in the Treaty. The Commission has similar but less extensive powers under the EEC Treaty itself. But that Treaty's essential character is that of a *traité cadre* which, as we have seen, gives the Commission an important role in initiating and formulating policy, subject to the final decision of the Council. Once such a policy decision has been taken, as in the case of agriculture for example, the Council confers upon the Commission the necessary executive powers to implement such policy. Further, whilst the Commission under the ECSC Treaty has in law wide powers of independent decision, in practice it has made a point of seeking the opinion and approval of the Council even in cases in which this was not strictly

6 Merger Treaty, art. 1.

necessary[7]. Bearing in mind the different character of the ECSC and EEC Treaties, the powers of the Commission are broadly of the same order in each with the important addition that under the EEC Treaty the Commission has a vital role in the formulation of policy.

The Commission's initiative in policy-making is enhanced by the fact that in exercising its power of decision under the EEC Treaty the Council can in general act only upon a proposal from the Commission. The Council may amend a Commission proposal only by unanimous vote[8]. Failing that it can accept it, reject it or return it to the Commission for reconsideration. Thus the text of a Commission proposal tends to go through many drafts passing between the Council and the Commission until a final version is agreed. The Commission's position in this process is further strengthened by the rules of voting in the Council. Whilst the normal rule of voting in the Council is by a simple majority[9], in fact most of the law-making powers of the Council have to be exercised by a qualified majority. For this purpose a system of weighted voting is employed: France, Germany, Italy and the United Kingdom have ten votes each, Belgium, Greece and the Netherlands have five, Denmark and Ireland have three and Luxembourg has two[10]. Where a Council decision is required to be taken upon a proposal from the Commission, for example under article 94 of the EEC Treaty for the application of the rules concerning aids granted by states, a qualified majority of any 45 of the available 63 votes will suffice. In such a case France, Germany, Italy and the United Kingdom who together command a total of 40 votes could not impose their will on the other six members. In other cases in which the Council can act on its own initiative the qualified majority of 45 must be cast by at least six member states, for example under article 6 of the Merger Treaty where the Council may determine the salaries of the Commissioners and the Judges and officers of the Court of Justice. Here again the four larger members cannot dictate to the other members and a clear majority of members is required. Thus the Treaty introduces a system of checks and balances into the decision-making powers of the Council.

7 See von Lindeiner-Wildau, K., *La Supranationalité en tant que Principe de Droit* (1970), pp. 104, 105.
8 EEC Treaty, art. 149; also Euratom Treaty, art. 119.
9 EEC Treaty, art. 148 (1); also Euratom Treaty, art. 118 (1).
10 EEC Treaty, art. 148 (2) and Euratom Treaty, art. 118 (2) as amended by the adjusted First Act of Accession 1972, art. 14 and the Second Act of Accession, 1979, art. 14.

(C) THE COMMITTEE OF PERMANENT REPRESENTATIVES

The common experience of European organisations set up since 1945 has been that where they have institutions made up of ministerial representatives of governments which, because of other demands on their time and attention, can only meet infrequently, a permanent representative body of ambassadorial rank is necessary not only to carry out routine matters of administration but also to undertake preparatory work for meetings of the ministers and supply an element of continuity in their work. This has been the experience of the OEEC, the Council of Europe, the Western European Union and NATO[11]. In view of this experience it is somewhat surprising to find that the ECSC Treaty made no provision for the Special Council of Ministers to be assisted by a committee of permanent representatives. But by 1953 the need for such assistance had become apparent and the Special Council used its general power to establish committees to set up the so-called Co-ordinating Committee made up of senior officials of the national administrations of the members to prepare material for Council meetings and to undertake ad hoc tasks at the Council's request[12].

This practice prompted the incorporation in the EEC and Euratom Treaties of provisions to the effect that the Council's Rules of Procedure 'may provide for the setting up of a committee consisting of representatives of Member States' the tasks and powers of which shall be determined by the Council[13]. This power was used to establish a Committee of Permanent Representatives, who were in practice the ambassadors of the member states accredited to the Communities, to carry out work preparatory to Council meetings and any other specific tasks[14]. The Merger Treaty institutionalised this arrangement providing, in article 4, that 'a committee consisting of the Permanent Representatives of the Member States shall be responsible for preparing the work of the Council and for carrying out the tasks assigned to it by the Council'[15]. Thus in effect the ECSC's Co-ordinating Committee was abolished and the EEC/Euratom Committee of Ambassadors extended to the ECSC. This

11 See the account of these organisations in Palmer, M., et al, *European Unity* (1968).
12 See *Les Novelles: Droit des Communautés européennes* (1969), pp. 241 et seq.
13 EEC Treaty, art. 151; Euratom Treaty, art. 121.
14 See Noel, E., 'The Committee of Permanent Representatives', 5 *Journal of Common Market Studies* (1967), pp. 219, 220.
15 Also see Council's Rules of Procedure, art. 16, OJ 1979, L268.

Committee is commonly known as COREPER, an acronym derived from its French title: *Comité des Représentants Permanents*.

The Permanent Representatives were originally regarded as merely the servants, the eyes and the ears of their governments[16]. But in the course of time the Committee has acquired a Community character and has come to play a distinctive and important role in the affairs of the Communities. At first the establishment and institutionalisation of this Committee was treated with suspicion. Its German title *Ständige Vertreter* (Permanent Representatives) was for a time parodied as *Ständige Verräter* (Permanent Traitors) because it was feared that they might endanger the Community's institutional balance[17]. The specific fear was that the Commission/Council dialogue might become gradually replaced requiring the Commission to deal with a group of subordinate Permanent Representatives rather than with the ministers themselves. This would erode the supra-national role of the Commission and would effectively place more power in the hands of the Council. In 1958 when the EEC/Euratom Committee of Permanent Representatives was set up the Commission asked the Council for an assurance that there was no intention of delegating the Council's powers of decision to the Permanent Representatives. This assurance was unanimously given by the Council[18]. The Committee of Permanent Representatives is not a Committee of Minister's Deputies. The power of decision and responsibility for decisions remains where the Treaties put it with the Council and the institutional balance resulting from the dialogue between Commission and Council appears to have been preserved[19].

This assurance paved the way for the establishment of a fruitful relationship between the Permanent Representatives and the Commission. This has resulted in the settlement of problems which would otherwise waste the time of Ministers and the joining of support for Commission proposals in the face of initial hesitation on the part of the governments of the member states. In practice the functions and services of the Committee of Permanent Representatives fall into three main categories:

16 See Noel, E., op. cit. in note 14, above, at p. 223.
17 See Mayne, R., *The Institutions of the European Community* (1968), p. 37.
18 See Noel, E., op cit. in note 14, above, at pp. 228, 229.
19 The limited role of the Committee is confirmed by the Council's Rules of Procedure, art. 16, OJ 1979, L268. But cf. Salmon, J. J. A., 'Le rôle des representations permanentes', *La Décision dans les Communautés Européennes* (1969), pp. 57 et seq.

(*a*) liaison between national administrations and Community institutions and the mutual supply of information;

(*b*) participation in the working out and co-ordinating of national attitudes; and

(*c*) direct involvement in work of the Community institutions[20].

In addition to the Committee of Permanent Representatives, the Council is also assisted by a General Secretariat[1]. This has its own Legal Service and six Directorates-General each covering a homogeneous group of Community activities[2]. While the General Secretariat reflects the civil service structure of the Commission, it only has a staff of 1,600 because of the heavy reliance which the Council places on civil servants in the national administrations of the member states.

### (D) THE COUNCIL'S WORKING METHODS

When the Council receives a proposal from the Commission the invariable procedure is to refer it, in the first instance, to an appropriate committee or working party made up of civil service experts. Each of the fields of activity of the Communities is covered by such committees and working parties who advise the Council and whose work is co-ordinated by the Committee of Permanent Representatives. The Commission is represented at these preparatory meetings and may amend its proposals in the light of the discussion, although it is under no obligation to do so.

When the Council meets to consider Commission proposals its agenda is divided into so-called 'A' items and 'B' items[3], a procedure based on the practice of the French Council of Ministers. 'A' items are those upon which provisional agreement has been reached in the course of the preparatory meetings and 'B' items are those on which there is still disagreement. 'A' items have of course to be formally approved by the Council but they are usually settled quickly. 'B' items occupy most of the business of Council meet-

---

20 See Noel, E., op. cit. in n. 14, above, at pp. 223 et seq. and Noel, E. and
   Etienne, H., 'The Permanent Representatives Committee and the
   "Deepening" of the Communities', 6 *Government and Opposition* (1971),
   p. 447.
1 Council's Rules of Procedure, art. 17, OJ 1979, L268.
2 See Vacher's *European Companion*, No. 37, pp. 11–14.
3 Council's Rules of Procedure, art. 2 (6), OJ 1979, L268.

ings[4]. Members of the Commission take part by invitation in Council meetings[5]. The role of the Commissioners at these meetings is that of mediator and honest broker. Whilst the Commission is anxious for an agreement which is in tune with Community interests it can also amend its proposals at any time and may thus be able to suggest a compromise which may be acceptable to all sides.

At the Paris Summit Meeting in October 1972 the Heads of State or Government of the enlarged Community pledged themselves to improve the Council's decision-making procedures and the cohesion of Community action[6]. As a result, during 1973 and 1974 the Council adopted a number of measures designed to achieve those objectives[7]. These measures are largely of a practical nature and do not introduce any new matters of principle. They include: advance planning of the timetable for Council meetings; co-ordination of national cabinet meetings so as to make ministers available for Council meetings; the circulation of papers at least a week before a meeting; more careful planning of the agenda in consultation with the President of the Commission; an agreement that the instructions of the Permanent Representatives should give them wider scope for negotiation so that whenever possible agreement may be reached at the level of the Committee of Permanent Representatives.

The *Three Wise Men's Report* has, however, shown that the internal problems of the Council which detract from its efficiency and effectiveness as a Community institution remain unsolved. The principal issues are the burden of business and the way in which it is handled[8]. As the *Report* notes, the key to these matters lies in the Presidency of the Council which has failed to provide a coherent pattern of work[9]. While the six-month rotating term of office is accepted as having advantages over any other system, the *Report* recommends that the authority and organisational support of the Council be strengthened and that more matters be delegated to the Commission and devolved on the Committee of Permanent Representatives.[10]

---

4 See Torrelli, M., *L'Individu et le droit de la CEE* (1970), p. 60; Noel, E. and Etienne, H., 'Quelques aspects des rapports et de la collaboration entre le Conseil et al Commission' and Salmon, J. J. A., op. cit., both in *La Décision dans les Communautés Européennes* (1969), at pp. 43 and 67 respectively.
5 Council's Rules of Procedure, art. 3 (2), OJ 1979, L268.
6 See *Sixth General Report of the Activities of the Communities* (1973), pp. 15, 16.
7 See *Bulletin of the European Communities* (1973), Part 7/8, p. 76, (1974), Part 2, pp. 103, 104 and Part 6, p. 122.
8 *Report on European Institutions* (1979), pp. 32–34.
9 Ibid., p. 35 et seq.　　　　　　　　　10 Ibid., p. 45 et seq.

The solution of particularly difficult problems has been achieved as a result of the famous marathon sessions of the Council[11]. The longest of these concerned the making of regulations to implement the agricultural policy; it took place during December 1961/January 1962 and lasted almost three weeks. During the course of these marathons the Council may attempt to reach the unanimity necessary to amend the Commission's proposal. The Commission will suggest its own counter amendments. Adjournments may be granted in an attempt to enable the Commission to work out a package-deal which may be acceptable to the Council, and so on.

Although most decisions of the Council are reached by the process described above and are based on an initiative of the Commission, in some the Council has sought to exercise a power of initiative of its own. In so doing it has claimed that it is acting in accordance with article 152 of the EEC Treaty which provides that 'the Council may request the Commission to undertake any studies which the Council considers desirable for the attainment of the common objectives and to submit any appropriate proposals'. On the face of it this is an innocuous provision which was probably intended to provide a safeguard in two senses. First, to enable the Council to spur the Commission to action should it appear to be neglecting its duty in any respect and, secondly, to enable the Council to suggest possible lines of enquiry to the Commission. In either case provided the actual terms of any proposal inspired by article 152 emanate from the Commission itself the basic relationship between Commission and Council will be preserved. But when the Council purports to act under article 152 it tends to go far beyond making a general request to the Commission to consider a particular matter, but it has indicated to the Commission the precise terms its proposal should take[12]. This is quite clearly a distortion of the relationship between Commission and Council as established by the Treaties and an abuse of article 152.

In practice the Commission has co-operated with the Council in such cases and has supplied proposals in the terms suggested. It has probably done this for the reason that when the Council has resorted to article 152 it has presented a united front to the Com-

---

11  See Alting von Geusau, F. A. M., 'Les sessions marathons du Conseil des ministres', *Le Décision dans les Communautés Européennes* (1969), pp. 99 et seq.

12  On this use of art. 152 see Torrelli, op. cit., pp. 42, 43, and Louis, J. V., *Les Règlements de la Communauté Economique Européenne* (1969), pp. 6–8 and notes. Also see Megret, J., *Le Droit de le Communauté Economique Européenne*, Vol. 9 (1979), pp. 149–151.

mission and so the matter is cut-and-dried and the Commission has little, if any, room to negotiate[13].

## (E) THE CONSTITUTIONAL CRISIS OF 1965

In some cases the problems facing the Communities have proved insoluble, even after recourse to a marathon session. Intransigence on the part of one or more of the member states may provoke a constitutional crisis in the Communities as in 1963 resulting from the French veto on British membership[14] and again in 1965. The latter crisis has had a significant effect on working relations between the Council and the Commission and on the Council's voting procedure.

The 1965 crisis arose in the following way[15]. After the 1963 crisis, relations between France and the other members remained strained and instead of all members working harmoniously to solve problems in the light of the interests of the Communities each side was only prepared to reach agreement if its own interests were safeguarded. In 1965 the Commission, in an attempt to solve a number of outstanding problems at one blow suggested a package-deal embracing three unconnected items: (i) the completion of the farm price regulations, which was sought by France in particular; (ii) a Commission proposal for the independent financing of the Communities out of their own resources instead of relying on contributions from the member states; and (iii) the granting of greater budgetary powers to the European Parliament which was being demanded by the Parliament itself with the support of the Netherlands. This package-deal was opposed by France ostensibly on the ground that the Commission had made the details of its proposals known to the European Parliament before the French Government had had an opportunity to consider them.

The other member states were willing to consider the package deal as a whole, but France insisted that only the farm finance question should be settled. A deadline of 30 June 1965 had been fixed by the Council for the settlement of this issue and when no agreement had been reached by midnight on that date the French

13 Clearly if the Council is unanimous it would be able to amend any counter proposal from the Commission.
14 See *Sixth General Report on the Activities of the EEC* (1963), introduction.
15 See *Ninth General Report on the Activities of the EEC* (1966), Chapter 1.

Foreign Minister, who happened to be the current President of the Council, refused to over-run the time-limit and, despite protests, brought the meeting to an end. Thereafter for seven months France refused to take part in any meeting of the Council designed to advance the purposes of the Communities whilst continuing to observe existing Community policies and regulations. The Council continued to meet in the absence of the French representative and called upon France to resume her place. The French Government urged the *révision* of the institutional structure of the Communities. Both sides in the dispute maintained their positions and eventually France was induced to attend a special private meeting of the Council held in Luxembourg partly, no doubt, because of the possibility that the five might use their power of decision in the absence of France.

The formula worked out at the Luxembourg meeting and known as the *Accords de Luxembourg* was really little more than an agreement to disagree[16]. On the one hand the five whilst refusing to permit any restriction on the Commission's powers under the Treaties accepted a number of relatively minor points concerning Council/Commission relations designed to facilitate their co-operation without compromising their respective competences and powers. It was agreed that before adopting any particularly important proposal the Commission should establish appropriate contacts with the Permanent Representatives without compromising the Commission's right of initiative. And that proposals and any other official acts which the Commission submits to the Council and to member states should not be made public until the recipients have had formal notice of them and are in possession of the texts[17]. On the question of voting in the Council it was agreed that, where a decision may be reached by the qualified majority vote on a proposal of the Commission, the Council should endeavour to reach such a decision unanimously in all cases where very important interests of one or more of the member states are involved. France further insisted that where very important interests are involved the discussion should be continued until unanimous agreement is reached; but the Council failed to produce any agreed policy on what should be done in the event of a failure to reach a unanimous agreement.

**16** *Ninth General Report on the Activities of the EEC* (1966), pp. 31–33.
**17** This met the French complaint that the European Parliament was informed of Commission proposals before the Council and member states.

This crisis brought to the surface the latent conflict between opposed views on the form which economic union should take: the advocates of integration and ultimate political union on the one hand (represented by the five) and the advocates of national sovereignty and looser political links on the other (represented by France). The 1965 crisis and its resolution illustrates the interdependence of the member states within the Communities. This is an example of what has been called the process of *engrenage*. Literally this term means 'gearing' or 'meshing' but in this usage it refers to the process whereby as soon as a state becomes involved in the machinery of economic integration it is progressively drawn further into the machine so that matters which in the past were within the sole competence of national governments gradually and irrevocably became part of the Community's decision-making process[18]. This is perhaps the beginning of the replacement of traditional international diplomacy by European constitutional law.

In constitutional terms the legal validity of the *Accords de Luxembourg* is highly suspect. They cannot be regarded as an amendment of the EEC Treaty. Article 236 lays down the procedure for such amendment; that procedure, which was followed in the cases of the Merger Treaty and the Treaty of Luxembourg 1970, was not followed in this case, nor have the *Accords* been ratified in accordance with the constitutional processes of the member states. Equally, the *Accords* cannot be regarded as resolving disputed questions of treaty interpretation, for under article 219 of the EEC Treaty the member states undertake not to submit a dispute concerning the interpretation or application of the Treaty to any method of settlement other than those provided for therein, in other words such disputes must be referred to the Court of Justice of the Communities. Thus, in so far as the *Accords de Luxembourg* require the Council to be unanimous in cases in which the Treaty, in accordance with the terms of article 148, merely requires a majority, the *Accords* are constitutionally invalid. They are in direct conflict with the obligation imposed by article 4 (1) of the EEC Treaty that 'each institution shall act within the limits of the powers conferred upon it by [the] Treaty'. Although the *Accords* have not been formally considered by the Court of Justice, the above stated conclusion is supported by its case law on the extent of the authority of the institutions of the Community. The Court has, for example, stressed that the institutional balance established by the Treaties

18 Mayne, R., *The Institutions of the European Community* (1968), p. 50.

must not be disturbed[19]. Similarly, it has held that attempts by the Council to act in derogation from the express provisions of the Treaties can have no legal effect[20].

The Commission, for its part, whilst it has never expressly approved of the *Accords*, has nevertheless acquiesced and co-operated in their implementation. It would be open to the Commission to challenge before the Court acts of the Council taken under the terms of the *Accords* but it has not done so[1]. This is no doubt largely due to the acceptance of the view that in the light of the attitudes of the Governments of some of the member states further achievement of the aims of the EEC is only possible within the terms laid down by the *Accords*. Treaty amendment is also impracticable because of the lack of unanimity in the Council on this issue.

Although the *Accords* have not affected the legal relations and powers of the Commission and Council, in practice they have had a limiting effect on the life of the Communities. This has been expressed by the Commission in no uncertain terms[2]. In 1969 the Commission expressed its concern in its revised *Opinion concerning the Applications for membership from the United Kingdom, Ireland, Denmark and Norway*[3]. It referred to the efficacy of the Council's decision-making methods as being a major problem in the institutional life of the Community largely as a result of the application of the unanimity rule in cases where the Treaties do not require it. This has had the result of slowing down and sometimes completely blocking the progress of integration.

The Commission has frequently stressed that its own right of initiative, independence and authority are of absolutely basic importance for the efficient functioning of the Community. The conviction was expressed that 'it is only by returning to respect for both the letter and the spirit of the institutional arrangements laid down in the Treaty, by ensuring that they operate efficiently and

---

19 See Cases 25/70: *Einfuhr-und Vorratsstelle für Getreide und Füttermittel v Köster* [1970] ECR 1161 and Opinion 1/78: *International Agreement on Natural Rubber* [1979] ECR 2871.
20 See Case 59/75: *Pubblico Ministero v Manghera* [1976] ECR 91, [1976] 1 CMLR 557 and Case 43/75: *Defrenne v SABENA* [1976] ECR 455, [1976] 1 CMLR 98.
1 Under the terms of EEC Treaty, art. 173.
2 Cf. *Second General Report on the Activities of the Communities* (1969), pp. 14 et seq. Some obstacles have since been overcome as a result of the Hague Conference of December, 1969; see *Fourth General Report on the Activities of the Communities* (1971), pp. x et seq.
3 Reproduced in *Bulletin of the European Communities* (1969), No. 9/10, Supplement, pp. 33, 34.

by strengthening them in the light of developments and the requirements of Community life, that the Community will be able to
accept in security the risks involved in enlargement'[4]. The Commission has drawn attention in particular to the dangers of insisting
on unanimity in the Council, with the consequent power of veto, in
an enlarged Community. It has urged that these dangers should be
obviated by the acceptance and implementation of two principles:
(i) that decisions by majority vote should again be the normal
practice of the Council except where the Treaties provide otherwise; and (ii) that where unanimity in the Council is required it
should only apply to outline policy decisions and majority voting
should then be the rule in connection with the decisions necessary
to implement such policies[5].

In 1974 the Heads of Government of the member states declared
publicly that 'it is necessary to renounce the practice which consists
of making agreements on all questions conditional on the unanimous consent of the Member States'[6]. There is, indeed, evidence
that that was more than a mere declaration of intent. It is now
standard practice for the *tour de table* procedure[7] and majority
voting to be used in Council decision making[8]. Member states have
clearly become more willing to abstain rather than to insist on
exercising a power of veto[9]. But while progress has been made,
the *Accords* have not yet been abandoned completely. In recent
years British Governments have claimed the right to obstruct acts
which affect vital national interests[10]. *The Three Wise Men's Report*
also regards an insistence on unanimity as available to a member
state when, in its judgment, its very important interests are at
stake[11].

4  See *Bulletin of the European Communities*, Vol. 2 (1969), No. 9/10, Supplement,
   p. 34. Similar recommendations are contained in the *Vedel Report*, Chapters 3
   and 7.
5  Also see *Bulletin of the European Communities* (1974) Part 1, p. 5 and *Eighth
   General Report on the Activities of the European Communities* (1975), p. 9.
6  See *Eighth General Report on the Activities of the European Communities* (1975),
   p. 298.
7  Council members vote in alphabetical order of the member states starting with
   the member who, in that order, follows the member holding the Presidency.
   See Council's Rules of Procedure, art. 5 (1), OJ 1979, L268.
8  See *Eleventh General Report on the Activities of the European Communities*,
   (1978), p. 23.
9  See Noel, E., *The European Community: How it works* (1979), p. 29.
10 See *The United Kingdom and the Communities* (Cmnd 4715), paras. 29, 70 and
   *Britain's New Deal in Europe* (HMSO 1975), p. 12.
11 *Report on European Institutions* (1979), p. 51. Also see the recent rejection of a
   British veto on the question of farm prices, *The Times*, 19 May 1982, pp. 1, 5
   and 30.

(F) THE COUNCIL AND THE POLITICAL FUTURE OF THE COMMUNITY

It is clear that whilst the immediate aims of the Communities are economic, their long term aims are political. The preamble to the EEC Treaty expresses the determination 'to lay the foundations of an ever closer union among the peoples of Europe' and article 2 of the Treaty itself refers to the establishment of closer relations between the member states. During recent years the questions of political co-operation and political union of the member states have been the subject of active consideration.

When, in 1969, it was announced that a Summit Conference of the Heads of State or Government was to be held at The Hague in December both the European Parliament and the Commission took the opportunity of expressing the hope that the Conference would take steps to ensure that progress will be made towards political union[12]. In their Final Communique the Heads of State or Government reaffirmed their belief in the political objectives of the Community and took the modest step of instructing their Foreign Ministers to study and make proposals for the achievement of progress in the matter of political unification in the context of an enlarged Community[13]. The Foreign Ministers requested a Committee made up of senior officials of their Ministries and presided over by M Davignon, Director of Political Affairs in the Belgian Foreign Ministry, to prepare a draft report on this matter. The resulting document, the Davignon Report, was approved by the Foreign Ministers on 20 July 1970[14].

In the Davignon Report the desire is expressed to make progress towards political unification through co-operation on foreign policy. The object of this co-operation is to achieve a better mutual understanding on major problems of international policy and to strengthen the sense of common purpose by harmonising ideas, concerting attitudes and taking common action whenever this is possible and desirable[15]. To those ends it was proposed that the Foreign Ministers of the member states should meet regularly at

---

12 See the European Parliament's Resolution and the Commission's Memorandum reproduced in an annexe to the *Third General Report on the Activities of the Communities* (190), at pp. 482 and 484 respectively.

13 Reproduced ibid., see paras. 4 and 15, at pp. 487 and 489 respectively.

14 The Report is reproduced in the *Bulletin of the European Communities*, Vol. 3 (1970), No. 11, at pp. 9 et seq. Also see the *Report of the Political Affairs Committee on the Political Future of the European Community* (European Parliament Working Document 118/70).

15 *Davignon Report*, Part Two, sections I and IV.

least at six-monthly intervals[16]. Preparations for these meetings should be undertaken by a Political Committee made up of the Heads of the Political Departments of the respective Foreign Ministries, the Committee itself should meet at least four times a year and may set up working groups responsible for specific tasks[17]. The Report also proposed that if the circumstances are sufficiently grave or the subject matter sufficiently important a ministerial meeting may be replaced by a conference of Heads of State or Government[18]. These proposals were implemented and a regular pattern of ministerial meetings in May and November of each year was established[19]. At these meetings such matters as East-West relations, the European security conference and the Middle East were discussed.

At the Paris Summit Meeting in October 1972, in the context of their declared aim to achieve European Union by 1980, the Heads of State or Government agreed to intensify the level of political consultation and asked their Foreign Ministers to prepare a further report on methods to improve political co-operation[20]. That report was completed in July 1973 and subsequently approved by the Heads of State or Government[1]. As a result the Foreign Ministers of the nine now meet at least four times a year. The report also confirmed the role of the Political Committee and established the so-called 'Group of Correspondents' to assist it in its work[2]. The machinery for political consultation between the member states of the Community has been given a further dimension by a decision of the Heads of Government at their meeting in Paris in December 1974 to meet regularly three times a year accompanied by their Foreign Ministers[3]. These institutionalised summit meetings are known as meetings of the European Council and they have become a regular feature of Community life.

16 Ibid., section II.
17 Ibid. 3 sections II (3) and III. In practice the Political Committee meets much more frequently; see Annex to the Second Report on European political co-operation, *Seventh General Report on the Activities of the European Communities* at p. 509.
18 Ibid., section II (1) (b).
19 Meetings were held in May and November commencing in November 1970.
20 See the Declaration issued at the end of the Summit Meeting, paras. 14 and 15, *Sixth General Report of the Activities of the European Communities* (1973) pp. 15, 16.
1 The Report is printed in *Seventh General Report of the Activities of the European Communities* (1974) at p. 502.
2 See Part II of the Report, ibid. at p. 504.
3 See the Communiqué issued at the end of the Meeting, para. 3, *Eighth General Report on the Activities of the European Communities* (1975) at p. 297.

The European Council has been hailed as an example of 'the Community's capacity for self-renewal in difficult circumstances'[4]. By the early 1970s a new political impetus was needed as the Community moved from the shelter of the Treaties into largely uncharted waters. It is the European Council's role to supply that impetus. As the *Three Wise Men's Report* has observed[5], the European Council (i) provides a forum for free and informal exchange of views between the Heads of Government; (ii) it can range over matters of Treaty competence, of political co-operation and of common concern to the member states; and (iii) it can generate an impetus for the progressive development of the Community.

The status and significance of these developments in the context of the institutional framework of the Communities calls for some comment. By the creation of machinery for political consultation distinct from yet parallel to the institutions of the Communities the Governments of the member states are attempting to distinguish between matters of international politics on the inter-governmental level on the one hand and the activities of the Communities based on legal obligations contained in the Treaties on the other[6]. Matters of mutual political concern to the member states which do not directly relate to the Treaties are discussed by the Foreign Ministers outside the Community structure and assisted by the Political Committee; matters which do directly relate to the Treaties are discussed within the Council of the Communities assisted by the Committee of Permanent Representatives. The newly created European Council is a hybrid which if discussing non-Community matters is no more than a Summit Conference and if discussing Community matters may be regarded as a manifestation of the Council of the Communities[7]. The level and range of matters considered by the European Council are illustrated by its activities in 1980[8]. Its first meeting in that year was devoted to problems of convergence and the United Kingdom contribution to the Community's budget. The second meeting was dominated by matters

4 *Report on European Institutions* (1979), p. 15.
5 Ibid., pp. 16, 17.
6 See Second Report on European Political Co-operation, *Seventh General Report on the Activities of the European Communities* (1974) at p. 507.
7 There is no reason why the Council should not be made up of Heads of Government; see Merger Treaty, art. 11. For recent confirmation of this analysis of the European Council as a hybrid see *Report on European Institutions* (1979), pp. 17, 18.
8 See *Fourteenth General Report on the Activities of the European Communities* (1981), pp. 28, 29.

of international relations in the context of the Middle East, the Euro-Arab dialogue, the Lebanon and Afghanistan. The third meeting was devoted to aid for the Italian earthquake victims, East-West relations, the Middle East and aid to Poland.

This separation of powers in relation to the European Council clearly has implications for the institutional life of the Communities[9]. Matters of mutual political concern to the member states are almost always on the periphery of Community affairs. Regular extra-Community meetings of Foreign Ministers together with the institutionalisation of Summit Meetings will tend to enhance the ascendancy of the Governments of the member states within the constitutional framework of the Communities and further undermine the Commission's role as an initiator. Both the Davignon Report and the Second Report on European Political Co-operation are to some extent conscious of such dangers[10]. Where 'the work of the Ministers is liable to affect the activities of the Commission' the Commission has been invited to express its views and to participate in meetings of the Foreign Ministers and of the Political Committee and of the European Council. The Commission has in fact been invited to play an increasing role in these activities and is fully involved in most aspects of political co-operation[11]. Equally, steps are taken to keep the European Parliament informed of developments in political co-operation. Every six months joint meetings are held by the Foreign Ministers and the European Parliament's Political Affairs Committee and an annual report on progress towards political union is given by the President-in-Office of the Council to the European Parliament[12]. It is in the interests of the Community that the practical significance of the legalistic distinction between political co-operation and Community activities be minimised. The European Council can play a unifying role in this connection by giving encouragement, coherence and an overall direction to the work of the other institutions of the Community[13].

9 E.g. the Commission's threat of collective resignation in May 1972; see Berthoud, R., Times, 27 May 1972.
10 See *Davignon Report*, Part Two, Sections II and V and the Annex to the Second Report, loc. cit., supra.
11 See *Eighth General Report on the Activities of the European Communities* (1975) at pp. 7, 8.
12 See *Davignon Report*, Part Two, Section VI and the Annex to the Second Report, loc. cit., supra.
13 Cf. *Report on European Institutions* (1979), p. 19.

Chapter 7

# The Assembly of the European Communities

## (The European Parliament)

(A) COMPOSITION AND ORGANISATION

Article 137 of the EEC Treaty provides that the European Parliament 'shall consist of representatives of the peoples of the States brought together in the Community'. The European Parliament, which since 1958 has served the three Communities in common[1], is designed to introduce a democratic element into the workings of the Communities[2]. Through the intermediary of the European Parliament the citizens of the Member States are called upon to co-operate in the functioning of the Communities[3]. At present the European Parliament has 434 members made up in the following way: France, Germany, Italy and the United Kingdom have 81 members each; the Netherlands has 25 members; Belgium and Greece have 24 members each; Denmark has 16 members; Ireland has 15 members; and Luxembourg has 6 members[4].

In very general terms the allocation of the numbers of seats to particular member states reflects the size of their population. A strictly mathematical proportional representation is not aimed at and would not indeed be practicable because of the vast difference between the population of the smallest member Luxembourg with 350,000 inhabitants and France with some 50 millions. A strictly mathematical exercise would give a derisory number of delegates to the small states and an overwhelmingly large number to the big states[5]. The figures actually employed represent a compromise so as on the one hand to recognise the relative size of population of the member states, but on the other to ensure that even the smallest

---

1 Common Institutions Convention 1957, section 1.
2 See Case 138/79: *SA Roquette Frères v EC Council* [1980] ECR 3333 at 3360.
3 See Case 26/62: *Van Gend en Loos v Nederlandse Administratie der Belastingen* [1963] ECR 1 at 12.
4 Decision and Act of the Council concerning Direct Elections, art. 2, OJ 1976, L278, as amended by Second Act of Accession, 1979, art. 10.
5 On the basis of the figures quoted if Luxembourg had five delegates France would be entitled to some 700.

member is given a number large enough to enable it to have a reasonably representative delegation. And, at the same time not to produce an overlarge unwieldy body.

From the commencement of the European Community in 1952 down to June 1979 the members of the European Parliament were not directly elected. During that period its members were nominated by the national parliaments of the member states from among their own members[6]. Under the terms of article 138 (3) of the EEC Treaty the European Parliament is directed to 'draw up proposals for elections by direct universal suffrage in accordance with a uniform procedure in all Member States'. It is then for the Council, acting unanimously, to lay down the appropriate provisions for adoption by the member states in accordance with their respective constitutional requirements[7].

In 1960 the European Parliament acting in pursuance of the mandate given it by the Treaties, submitted detailed proposals for election by direct universal suffrage for the consideration of the Council[8]. The Council studiously ignored the proposals[9]. It was not until after the first enlargement that the governments of the member states generally made a positive response to the issue of direct elections. During the 1960s (with the exception of the Netherlands) the original member states, from their entrenched position in the Council, were not favourably disposed towards the matter. This was largely because they were opposed to the possibility of giving more power to the European Parliament, the claims for which would be likely to be strengthened as a consequence of direct elections. However, this hostility gradually disappeared. The Heads of Government of the member states at their meeting in Paris in December 1974, not only acknowledged the Treaty objective of direct elections but also urged that it should be achieved as soon as possible[10].

In January 1975 the European Parliament submitted a new set of

6 See ECSC Treaty, art. 21; EEC Treaty, art. 138 (1) and (2); Euratom Treaty, art. 108 (1) and (2); First Act of Accession 1972, art. 139 (1).

7 Euratom Treaty, art. 108 (3) is to the same effect.

8 For the text of the 1960 proposals see *The Case for Elections to the European Parliament by Direct Universal Suffrage* (European Parliament, 1969), pp. 238 et seq.

9 In March 1969 the European Parliament adopted a resolution of protest, ibid., p. 277.

10 See *Eighth General Report on the Activities of the European Communities* (1975), p. 299. Also see the Green Paper: *Direct Elections to the European Assembly*, Cmnd 6399 (1976), para. 1.

proposals for direct elections to the Council[11]. After a prolonged period of consideration the governments of the member states in September 1976 finally agreed on the Decision and Act concerning Direct Elections[12] in accordance with which the first direct elections were held in June 1979. Adjustments have been made to that instrument in order to accommodate the accession of Greece. Pending the holding of a special election, the 24 Greek members have been nominated by the Greek Parliament from among its own members in accordance with the old procedure[13].

The Decision and Act concerning Direct Elections not only specifies the number of representatives to be elected in each member state, it also lays down basic rules concerning candidature and the conduct of the elections. Members of the European Parliament are elected for a term of five years[14]. In principle, anyone may stand for election. But that principle is subject to a provision that the holding of certain offices is incompatible with membership of the European Parliament. Those offices include membership of the government of a member state, of the Commission and of the Court of Justice and employment by an institution of the Community[15]. Such offices are incompatible in the sense that they would tend to prejudice either the terms on which they are held or the individual and non-mandated role of the Members of the European Parliament[16]. Under the superseded rules governing the composition of the European Parliament[17], members had to be members of their national parliament. Under the rules governing direct elections, such a dual mandate is simply permissive[18].

Members of the European Parliament enjoy certain privileges and immunities[19]. These include freedom of movement when travelling to and from meetings of the Parliament[20] and freedom from legal process in respect of the opinions expressed or votes cast in the performance of their duties[1]. During sessions of the European

---

11 For the text of these proposals see *Bulletin of the European Communities* (1975), Part I, p. 95.
12 OJ 1976, L278.
13 Second Act of Accession 1979, art. 23.
14 Decision and Act, art. 1.
15 Ibid., art. 6 (1).
16 Ibid., art. 4 (1).
17 E.g., EEC Treaty, art. 138 (1).
18 Decision and Act, art. 5.
19 Ibid., art. 4 (2).
20 Protocol on Privileges and Immunities annexed to the Merger Treaty 1965, art. 8.
1 Ibid., art. 9.

Parliament they are also entitled to enjoy in their own state the privileges and immunities accorded to the members of parliament of that state, and in other member states immunity from detention and from legal proceedings[2].

It did not prove possible for the governments of the member states to agree on a uniform electoral procedure for the first direct election. That election was held in accordance with the national electoral procedures in each member state[3]. The European Parliament has been charged with the task of drawing up proposals for a uniform procedure[4]. Any casual vacancies are filled in accordance with procedures to be laid down by each member state[5].

In the United Kingdom, effect is given to the Decision and Act concerning Direct Elections by the European Assembly Elections Act 1978[6]. In addition to providing that United Kingdom representatives to the European Parliament shall be elected[7], the Act also establishes constituencies, allocates seats and, pending a decision on a uniform procedure, specifies the methods of voting. For the purpose of direct elections to the European Parliament, the United Kingdom is divided into 79 constituencies: 66 in England; 8 in Scotland; 4 in Wales; and 1 in Northern Ireland[8]. The 81 United Kingdom representatives are allocated so that the English, Scots and Welsh constituencies each return one member and the Northern Irish constituency returns three members[9]. In England, Scotland and Wales, the simple majority system of voting is to be used, and in Northern Ireland the single transferable vote system[10]. By virtue of authority conferred by the Decision and Act concerning Direct Elections[11], the Act generally disqualifies from membership of the European Parliament persons who are disqualified from membership of the British House of Commons[12]. But that disqualification is subject to an exception in the case of peers, ordained clergy and ministers of religion. Provision is also made for the holding of bye-elections[13]. At August 1981 the distribution of

---

2 Ibid., art. 10.                         3 Decision and Act, art. 7 (2).

4 Ibid., art. 7 (1). A major obstacle is the commitment of both major British political parties to the simple majority system, whereas in many other member states forms of proportional representation are favoured. Cf. *Direct Elections to the European Assembly*, Cmnd 6399 (1976), para. 28.

5 Decision and Act, art. 12.

6 1978, c10 (amended by the European Assembly Elections Act 1981).

7 S. 1.                                    8 Sch. 1, para. 1., and Sch. 2.

9 S. 2.                                    10 S. 3. and Sch. 1, para. 2.

11 Art. 6 (2).                             12 Sch. 1, para. 5.

13 Sch. 1, para. 3.

United Kingdom representatives in terms of national political affiliation was as follows: Conservative Party 66; Labour Party 17; Scottish National Party, Social Democratic and Labour Party, Democratic Unionist Party, and Ulster Unionist Party 1 each[14].

Although, as we shall shortly see, the European Parliament is more of a deliberative and consultative body than a parliament in the true sense, it has nevertheless parliamentary pretensions. In the first place although the Treaties still refer to it as the Assembly, since 1962 it has formally adopted the title European Parliament[15] and it is invariably referred to by this name in Community circles and Community documents. Secondly, it has organised itself as if it were a legislative and not a consultative body. The members are not seated in national groups but sit in multinational political groups. The Rules of Procedure of the European Parliament provide a procedure for the recognition of political groups. In particular minimum numbers are laid down: 21 if the members come from one member state; 15 if they come from two member states; 10 if they come from three or more member states[16]. Thus in the European Parliament we find the nucleus of European political parties made up of individuals of differing nationality linked by common political beliefs. At present there are seven political groups in the European Parliament: the Socialists with 120 members; the European People's Party (Christian Democrats) with 109; the European Democrats (Conservatives) with 63; the Communists and Allies with 45; the Liberals and Democrats with 39; the European Progressive Democrats with 22; and the Group for the Technical Co-ordination and Defence of Independent Groups and Members[17] with 11. In addition there are 9 non-attached members, plus 16 Greeks who have yet to make up their minds. Of the United Kingdom representatives, the Conservatives have formed their own group (the European Democrats) which the Ulster Unionist has also joined, the Labour and Social Democratic and Labour members have joined the Socialist Group, the Scottish Nationalist has joined the European Progressive Democrats, and the Democratic Unionist remains non-attached[18].

14 Vacher's *European Companion*, No. 37, pp. 45–49.
15 See Resolution of 30 March 1962, JO 1962, 1045.
16 Rule 36. The current Rules of Procedure are set out conveniently in the *Official Handbook of the European Parliament* (1980).
17 This is not so much a political group as a device in order to benefit from the advantages of belongings to a group.
18 This information is taken from Vacher's *European Companion*, No. 37.

The European Parliament is organised in 15 standing committees each specialising in an aspect of the Communities' activities, e.g. Economic and Monetary Affairs, Budgets, External Economic Relations, Legal Affairs, etc[19]. These committees were originally set up to draft reports upon the basis of which the general debate in a plenary session of the European Parliament could take place. This is a procedure based on continental parliamentary practice whereby a debate before the whole house is invariably preceded by an examination of the subject of the debate by a committee of the house. The debate then proceeds on the basis of that committee's report[20]. In practice the committees of the European Parliament have come to play an independent Community role largely because an international body like the European Parliament cannot meet as frequently as a national parliament. Therefore, the committees have not only prepared reports for debates in the European Parliament, but have also maintained contact with the Commission and Council in the interim between parliamentary sessions. Thus the Committees act as a safeguard for the continuity and effectiveness of parliamentary control. As standing committees they can meet at any time at the request of their chairman or the President of the European Parliament[1] and so by this means the European Parliament is kept abreast of developments within the Communities as they occur and not after the event.

One final point concerning the organisation of the European Parliament, in which it differs from a national parliament, is that it is not of course divided into government and opposition parties. The European Parliament is not organised or run by any particular political group represented within it. Its officers and the composition of its committees reflect both political and national representation[2].

Practical questions concerning the organisation of the European Parliament are in the hands of the Bureau of Parliament which is elected for a term of two and a half years and consists of the President and twelve Vice-Presidents[3] advised by five Quaestors. The latter have particular responsibility for administrative and

---

**19** See Rules of Procedure Chapter X and OJ 1979, C203/35.
**20** See Rule 26 (1).
 **1** See Rule 39 (1). In 1980 the Committees held 364 days of meetings; see *Fourteenth General Report on the Activities of the European Communities* (1981), p. 28.
 **2** Rules 7 (1) and 37 (2).
 **3** See Rules 5 (1), 7A, 7B.

financial matters directly concerning members. The details of sessions of the European Parliament and its agenda are worked out by the so-called Enlarged Bureau which consists of the Bureau and the chairman of the political groups[4]. In these administrative and organisational chores the European Parliament is assisted by a Secretary-General and a Secretariat of over 2,000 persons[5] divided into five Directorates-General. The role of the Secretary-General is similar to that of the Clerk of the British House of Commons[6].

The European Parliament holds a number of part sessions each year. During 1980 it was in session for a total of 64 days[7]. It may also meet in extraordinary session at the request of a majority of its members or of the Council or Commission[8]. Between sessions each Committee will meet at least once. Commissioners and members of the Council may be invited to appear before it to give an account of decisions taken and of proposals referred to the Council[9]. The Committees follow the working of the Council and Commission closely and they are able to keep the European Parliament as a whole well informed of activities and developments within the Communities.

(B) THE FUNCTIONS AND POWERS OF THE EUROPEAN PARLIAMENT AND ITS RELATIONS WITH THE COMMISSION AND THE COUNCIL

As has already been mentioned the European Parliament is in no sense a legislative body; its functions are of a supervisory and advisory nature. As a supervisory body it possesses a power of censure over the Commission. If a motion of censure is passed by a two-thirds majority of the votes cast, which also represents a majority of the total membership of the European Parliament, the entire Commission must resign and be replaced[10]. Although motions of censure have occasionally been tabled, none has ever been carried[11]. On the face of it this is a far reaching power; a power

---

4 Rule 5 (2).
5 See *Fourteenth General Report on the Activities of the European Communities* (1981), p. 28.
6 Rules 17 (4) and 49.
7 See *Fourteenth General Report on the Activities of the European Communities* (1981), p. 28.
8 See EEC Treaty, art. 139 and Rule 14.
9 See Rule 40 (2).
10 E.g. EEC Treaty, art. 144.
11 For an analysis of the use of the motion of censure see Herman, V. and Lodge, J., *The European Parliament and the European Community* (1978), p. 48 et seq.

which is found in no other international organisation. The power of censure does have its limitations however. In the first place the European Parliament has no direct voice in the nomination of Commissioners to replace a censured Commission. But, more important than that, the power of censure over the Commission is somewhat inappropriate since in general both the European Parliament and the Commission share a common European attitude to Community matters and tend to be both ranged against the Council as the exponent of national interests. That is not to say of course that the views of the European Parliament and the Commission are naturally identical. They can and do differ particularly in terms of tactics: the Commission may be prepared to make concessions in the face of the views of the Council in an attempt to reach a workable compromise and the European Parliament may be inclined to take a harder line. But in any event the mere existence of the power of censure does enhance the authority and influence of the European Parliament in that it is a force to be reckoned with and not to be ignored[12].

Secondly, the European Parliament has the means of exercising a degree of supervision over the day-to-day activities of the Communities through its power to ask questions[13]. This is a procedure reminiscent of the British member of parliament's right to question ministers. Written questions can be put to the Commission and to the Council and ample use is made of this procedure: during 1980 1,995 written questions were put to the Commission and 271 to the Council[14]. Written questions and the replies to them are published in the Communities' *Official Journal*. Oral questions may also be put to Council or Commission during a plenary session of the European Parliament and these may be followed by debate. In addition, at each part-session of the European Parliament a period is set aside for Question Time during which oral questions may be put. This provides an opportunity for short, pointed questions to be put followed by supplementary questions thus enabling a dialogue to take place between the members of the Assembly and the members of the Commission and the Council. During 1980 the Commission replied to a total of 57 questions and the Council to 23[15].

12 Cf. the *Vedel Report*, Chapter 3, section II (4); see *Bulletin of the European Communities*, Vol. 5 (1972), Supplement to No. 4.
13 E.g. EEC Treaty, art. 140. Also see Rules of Procedure, Chapter XI.
14 *Fourteenth General Report on the Activities of the European Communities* (1981) at p. 28.
15 Ibid.

This right to ask questions enables an eye to be kept on developments in Community policy both generally and in relation to particular topics, including matters of political co-operation discussed by the Foreign Ministers of the member states[16]. Thus the European Parliament is able to comment on issues more or less as they arise, rather than becoming involved in the more protracted procedure of the Parliament's Committees investigating a certain matter and then reporting back. A further example of the supervisory powers of the European Parliament lies in the debates which are held on the Commission's Annual Report on Activities in the Communities. This enables the European Parliament to discuss and comment upon the whole field of Community activity[17].

As an advisory body the most important of the European Parliament's powers lie in its right to be consulted over major policy proposals in the EEC and Euratom[18]. This process of consultation may take place at either or both of two stages in the decision-making process: the Council may consult the European Parliament after it has received a proposal from the Commission; the Commission itself may consult the European Parliament when it is in the process of drafting its proposals. The Commission has frequently sent its proposals to the European Parliament at the same time as it has sent them to the Council. It will be recalled that one of the contributing factors to the 1965 crisis was the French accusation that the Commission had made its views known to the European Parliament before it communicated them to the governments of the member states. At the Luxembourg meeting in 1966 it was therefore agreed that proposals and other official acts which the Commission submits to the Council and to the member states are not to be made public until the recipients have had formal notice of them and are in possession of the texts.

In this consultative role the European Parliament acts largely through its committees. A given proposal will be submitted to the appropriate committee which will produce a report containing a draft opinion. That draft will then be debated by the full Parliament and the final agreed version will be communicated to the Council or Commission as the case may be. This right of consultation is not a power of decision: the Council is not in any way bound by nor is

16 *Fourteenth General Report on the Activities of the European Communities* (1981) at p. 28.
17 E.g. EEC Treaty, art. 143.
18 E.g. EEC Treaty, arts. 43, 54, 56, 87 and Euratom Treaty, arts. 31, 76, 85, 90.

the Commission obliged to pay heed to, a Parliamentary opinion. But, as the European Court has pointed out, where the Treaties require the Council to consult the European Parliament before an act is adopted, the opinion of the European Parliament must be sought and obtained before an act can be lawfully adopted. If, in such a case, the Council purports to adopt an act without consultation, such an omission would supply grounds for seeking the annulment of the act because an essential procedural requirement had been infringed[19].

In practice the influence of the European Parliament has tended to vary depending on the subject matter. The explanation of these variations appears to be that the European Parliament's influence is greater where matters can be decided relatively quickly and its influence decreases as negotiations between Council and Commission become more prolonged. In the context of a marathon session on agricultural policy, for example, where there is a sharp difference of view between Council and Commission, the object of the marathon is to find a solution which both sides can accept and in such a context it is more likely that the European Parliament's opinion will be disregarded.

In the interests of promoting co-operation between the Council and the European Parliament in matters of decision-making, a conciliation procedure has been established. In 1975 in a Joint Declaration[20], the Parliament, the Council and the Commission agreed on a procedure which may be invoked in certain cases in which the Council intends to depart from the opinion of the European Parliament. The procedure applies to Community acts of general application which have appreciable financial implications. The Council, together with representative parliamentarians[1], acts as a Conciliation Committee. The Commission also participates in this process. The aim is to seek to reach agreement, normally within a three month period. The conciliation procedure was first invoked in 1978[2] and extensive use has been made of it[3]. While, in the Council's view, it has 'brought a new dimension to the role of the Parliament in the Community legislative process'[4], in practice it is

---

**19** See Case 138/79: *SA Roquette Frères v EC Council* [1980] ECR 3333.
**20** OJ 1975, C89.
 **1** Rules of Procedure of the European Parliament, rule 22A (3).
 **2** See *Twenty Sixth Review of the Council's Work* (1979) at p. 12.
 **3** *Twelfth General Report on the Activities of the European Communities* (1979), at p. 26.
 **4** *Twenty Sixth Review of the Council's Work* (1979) at pp. 12, 13.

a device of limited scope which cannot resolve deeply seated differences[5]. In the last resort the will of the Council prevails[6].

## (C) INCREASED BUDGETARY POWERS FOR THE EUROPEAN PARLIAMENT

The European Parliament has long had pretensions towards becoming a truly parliamentary body and it has kept up steady pressure for increasing its powers. The European Parliament has been particularly insistent that its control not only over its own budget but also over the budget of the Communities as a whole should be increased[7]. In the first place it has always had the power to draft its own estimates and to debate the Community budgets. But apart from that the budgetary powers of the European Parliament differed as between the ECSC on the one hand and the EEC/Euratom on the other. In the case of the former, where funds were paid direct to the Community in the form of levies, the Parliament had virtually full power over its budget and had in practice (although not by virtue of any Treaty provision) acquired advisory rights over the whole of the ECSC budget. In the case of the EEC/Euratom, where finances derived from contributions from member states, the European Parliament had no power at all and it was the Council which had a decisive voice over both the Parliament's budget and the Communities' budgets generally. Since the European Parliament received one-third of its budget from each Community this meant that it had no direct control over the allocation of two-thirds of its budget.

The question of enlarging the European Parliament's powers was discussed in 1964 in connection with the Merger Treaty but no action was taken. The matter was revived in the following year in connection with the agricultural policy. The Commission urged that the Parliament should be given an effective voice in approving the Community budget on the grounds that the direct revenues which it was proposed to raise as a result of implementing the agricultural policy should be subject to parliamentary approval. It will be recalled that this proposal that the Communities be financed independently out of their own resources instead of out of contri-

---

5 See *Report on European Institutions* (1979), Annex 3.
6 For example, see the case of Regulation 214/79, OJ 1979, L35, concerning the European Regional Development Fund reported in the *Fourth Annual Report of the European Regional Development Fund* (1979), at p. 7.
7 On this topic see *Les ressources propres aux Communautés européennes et les pouvoirs budgétaires du Parlement européen* (European Parliament, 1970).

butions from the member states was part of the proposed package-deal which was the focus of the constitutional crisis of 1965. When the matter was considered by the Council prior to the crisis there was a general consensus in favour of postponing the establishment of direct revenues until 1970 and all members except France were in favour of firmly linking the question of direct revenues with that of increasing the European Parliament's powers. After the crisis it was agreed to postpone these matters until the end of the Communities' transitional period.

These matters were resumed at the Summit Meeting of the Six held at The Hague in December 1969. At that meeting it was agreed that with effect from 1 January 1971 the Communities would progressively draw a greater proportion of finance directly from the revenue of customs duties and levies on agricultural imports. From 1 January 1975 all such duties and levies would be paid direct to the Communities subject to 10% rebate to cover collection costs. The balance of the revenue necessary for the Communities would be made up out of not more than 1% of a Value Added Tax which would then be in force in the member states plus some contributions from the member states[8]. The member states at The Hague Summit also drew up the Budgetary Treaty which amended certain budgetary provisions of the Treaties. These included the conferment upon the European Parliament of increased budgetary powers over part of the Communities' budget, the so-called non-compulsory part, which deals with the functioning of the Communities' institutions. During the period 1971-74 the European Parliament's budgetary powers were strengthened by making it more difficult for the Council to reject amendments proposed by the Parliament. Since 1 January 1975 the European Parliament has had complete control over that part of the budget including the power to amend it[9]. The non-compulsory part of the budget amounts, in practice, to some 25%[10]. The political importance of this control may outreach the amount of money actually involved. Control over the non-compulsory part of the budget gives the European Parliament important powers in relation to the activities of the other institutions of the Communities because he who holds the purse strings can effectively control the means whereby the independent

8 Council Decision of 21 April 1970, 70/243/ECSC/EEC Euratom, JO No. L94, 28 April 1970, and annexed to the Budgetary Treaty of 1970, Cmnd 4867.
9 Budgetary Treaty 1970, arts. 1-9.
10 See Noel, E., *The European Community: How it works* (1979), p. 44.

functioning of the other institutions of the Communities is guaranteed.

As far as the remaining part of the budget is concerned the European Parliament has not been given the last word in this field. This is called the compulsory part of the budget in that it is the automatic consequence of Community rules, most notably the cost of implementing the agricultural policy. In respect of this part of the budget the European Parliament may only propose modifications to the Council which has undertaken to give its reasons to the Parliament if it does not accept such modifications[11].

At the time the Budgetary Treaty was signed in 1970 the Commission undertook to draft proposals to increase further the budgetary powers of the European Parliament[12]. After some delay, occasioned by the membership negotiations and the enlargement of the Community, the Commission eventually submitted its proposals in June 1973 in the form of a draft Treaty to amend further the budgetary provisions of the Community Treaties[13]. On the basis of those proposals, the governments of the member states eventually agreed and accepted the Financial Provisions Treaty of 1975[14], which came into force on 1 June 1977. The principal changes brought about by that Treaty are (i) to give the European Parliament the exclusive authority to adopt the annual budget and to give a discharge to the Commission in respect of its implementation; (ii) the creation of an independent Court of Auditors as a new Community institution to replace the Audit Board; and (iii) that the so-called 'inverted majority rule' be applied to some proposed modifications to the compulsory part of the budget, i.e. that those proposals should be deemed to have been adopted unless expressly rejected by the Council. In order to promote co-operation on budgetary matters between the Council and the European Parliament a special conciliation procedure has been established under the terms of a Council Resolution of 22 April 1970[15].

The role of the European Parliament in the budgetary procedure as amended by the Budgetary and Financial Provisions Treaties,

---

11 E.g. Budgetary Treaty 1970, art. 4.
12 *Sixth General Report on the Activities of the European Communities* (1973), pp. 5, 6.
13 See *Bulletin of the European Communities* (1973), Supplement 9/73.
14 OJ 1977, L359.
15 For the text of the Resolution see *Treaties Establishing the European Communities* (1978 edn), at p. 885. This conciliation procedure is quite distinct from that which was created in 1975 in connection with decision-making: see p. 199, ante.

may be described as follows[16]. The financial year of the Community is the calendar year. Each year, as a preliminary step, the Commission establishes by reference to such factors as gross natural products and inflation the maximum rates by which expenditure in the coming year may be increased. Within that framework, each institution draws up estimates of its expenditure and sends them to the Commission by 1 July. The Commission collates these estimates and forwards them to the Council by 1 September as a preliminary draft budget. This will be the subject of the so-called 'first reading' by the Council. On the basis of the preliminary draft and acting by a qualified majority[17] the Council will establish the draft budget. By 5 October the draft budget must be placed before the European Parliament for its 'first reading'. This gives the Parliament the opportunity, during the ensuing forty-five days, to adopt the budget or to make amendments by majority vote to non-compulsory items and to propose modifications by an absolute majority to compulsory items.

If such amendments are made and/or modifications proposed, the draft budget thus revised is sent back to the Council for a 'second reading'. At this stage the Council, acting by a qualified majority, can in its turn modify any of the European Parliament's amendments to non-compulsory items. As far as the Parliament's proposed modifications to compulsory items are concerned, the Council can accept or reject them by a qualified majority. But that basic rule is subject to important qualifications, depending whether the effect of the European Parliament's proposed modifications is simply to reallocate sums of expenditure within the total sum established in the draft budget, or whether it is to increase the size of that total sum. In the former case, the European Parliament's modifications will stand as accepted in the absence of a Council decision to reject them; in the latter case, the European Parliament's modifications will stand as rejected in the absence of a Council decision to accept them. If, at this stage, the Council should accept the modifications proposed and amendments made by the European Parliament, the draft budget is deemed to be adopted. If not, the draft budget will be returned for a 'second reading' by the European Parliament. At this final stage the Parliament has no further specific powers in respect of items of compulsory expenditure. The European Parliament does however have the last word

**16** See EEC Treaty, art. 203, as amended.
**17** In accordance with EEC Treaty, art. 148 (2), as amended.

on items of non-compulsory expenditure. The European Parliament can further amend these; for example it may reinstate its own 'first reading' amendments which may have been changed by the Council at its 'second reading'. For this purpose the Parliament must act by a majority of its members and 3/5 of the votes cast. A period of 15 days is allocated for this.

When this complex procedure has run its course, it is for the European Parliament formally to adopt the budget, i.e. to transform it from a draft to an operational budget for the coming year. But if there are, in the opinion of a majority of the members of the European Parliament and 2/3 of the votes cast, 'important reasons'[18] why the budget should not be adopted as it stands, the Parliament may reject it and ask for a new draft budget to be submitted to it. If, as a result of such a rejection, no budget has been adopted at the beginning of the next financial year, the Community is financed on the 'provisional twelfths' basis. Until a budget is adopted, an amount not exceeding one twelfth of the previous year's budget may be spent during each month[19].

The European Parliament has shown that it is prepared to reject a draft budget if it is not satisfied with it. During the consideration of the draft budget for 1980 the European Parliament made it clear that its adoption of the budget would depend, inter alia, on the Council's acceptance of increases in non-compulsory items and the implementation of measures to curb agricultural expenditure[20]. A lengthy use of the conciliation procedure[1] failed to secure the Council's agreement, particularly in relation to the latter point. The European Parliament therefore rejected the budget on 13 December 1979 because the conditions which it had set had not been satisfied[2]. The budget for 1980 was not finally agreed and adopted until 9 July 1980[3], the date on which the Commission completed its preparation of the preliminary draft budget for 1981[4]! Thus the European Parliament 'demonstrated its determination to exercise its budgetary powers to the full'[5].

18 See EEC Treaty, art. 203 (8).
19 See EEC Treaty, art. 204.
20 See *Bulletin of the European Communities*, 1979 – 11, pp. 86, 108.
 1 See *Thirteenth General Report on the Activities of the European Communities* (1980), pp. 46, 48.
 2 See *Bulletin of the European Communities*, 1979 – 12, p. 120.
 3 See *Fourteenth General Report on the Activities of the European Communities* (1981), p. 47.
 4 Ibid., pp. 47, 48.
 5 See *Thirteenth General Report on the Activities of the European Communities* (1980), p. 24. Also see Sopwith, Sir C., 'Legal Aspects of the Community

## (D) A LEGISLATIVE ROLE FOR THE EUROPEAN PARLIAMENT?

The general question of the future role of the European Parliament was taken up by the Commission in July 1971. It set up an ad hoc Working Party of 14 independent experts to examine the whole corpus of problems connected with the enlargement of the Parliament's powers. The Working Party was under the chairmanship of Professor Vedel, a distinguished French constitutional lawyer, and included experts not only from the existing member states but also from the then candidate countries. In its wide ranging report the Working Party proposed that the powers of the European Parliament should be increased by means of a two-stage plan[6].

During the first, transitional, stage it was proposed that the European Parliament should have a power of co-decision with the Council in four matters referred to as list A, viz. the revision of the Treaties; decisions to give the Communities any necessary new powers; the admission of new members; and the ratification of international agreements concluded by the Communities. In such cases it was proposed that decisions of the Council would take effect only after receiving the approval of the Parliament. Also during this first stage the consultative powers of the Parliament would be extended to cover additional matters, referred to as list B, which would include the common agricultural policy, harmonisation of laws and taxes, the common transport policy and the mutual recognition of diplomas. In connection with these and other matters it was proposed that the European Parliament should be given a suspensive veto. In the event of a difference of opinion between the Council and the European Parliament on any of these matters it would enable the Parliament to suspend the decision for one month and require the Council to reconsider the matter. The Council's second decision, whether amended or not, would be final. During the second stage, the Parliament's power of co-decision would be extended to all matters in list B. The matters in list A were chosen because they cover questions which materially involve either the constitutive powers of the Communities or their relations with other international persons. The matters in list B are largely those

---

Budget' (1980), 17 CML Rev 315 and Pipkorn, J. 'Legal Implications of the Absence of the Community Budget at the Beginning of a Financial Year', (1981) 18 CML Rev 141.
**6** *Vedel Report*, Chapter 4, sections I and II.

which involve harmonisation measures of one sort or another. Because of the importance of these matters to the life of the Communities and the obligations which they will impose on member states it was thought appropriate to involve the European Parliament in their determination initially in the form of consultation supported by the suspensive veto and eventually by co-decision with the Council.

The Working Party also made a number of other recommendations designed to increase the democratic control exercised by the European Parliament. The report commented that as European integration extends to include new sectors national parliaments will gradually become less able to exercise their traditional democratic control over legislation affecting their countries. It was suggested that this should be corrected by increasing the powers of the European Parliament.

This general theme has been taken up subsequently by the Commission and the European Parliament itself. Following the Vedel Report, the Commission made a strong recommendation to the governments of the member states that the European Parliament should participate in the legislative process of the Community and should have the last word on such matters as the approximation of legislation[7]. Later, during the debate on European Union, the Commission advanced the view that in the longer term the legislative power of the Community should be exercised by a bicameral Parliament composed of a 'Chamber of Peoples' and a 'Chamber of States'[8]. The European Parliament in its own contribution to that debate resolved that it should 'participate on at least an equal footing in the legislation process, as is its right as the representative of the peoples of the Union'[9]. Indeed, now that the European Parliament is directly elected its claims for an increased legislative role are clearly strengthened. As President Ortoli observed: 'If the elected Parliament is to be true to its calling, it must be given legislative power[10].'

Little progress has, however, been made in this direction. At the Paris Summit in December 1974, the governments of the member

7 *Sixth General Report on the Activities of the European Communities* (1973), p. 5.
8 *Report on European Union, Bulletin of the European Communities*, Supp. 5/75, pp. 30–34.
9 *Reports on European Union, Bulletin of the European Communities*, Supp. 9/75, p. 11.
10 *Ninth General Report on the Activities of the European Communities* (1976), p. xx.

states agreed that the European Parliament's competence 'will be extended, in particular by granting it certain powers in the Communities' legislative process'[11]. The only product of that undertaking has been the conciliation procedure which was mentioned earlier[12]. If, however, the European Parliament's powers are ever increased along the lines described above, it will then be well on the way to becoming a Parliament in a real sense[13].

11 *Eighth General Report on the Activities of the European Communities* (1975), p. 299.
12 See p. 199, ante.
13 It is disappointing, but perhaps significant, that the 'Three Wise Men' had very little to say on this subject; see *Report on European Institutions* (1979) p. 76 et seq.

Chapter 8

# Ancillary Community Institutions

In addition to the subsidiary bodies already mentioned there are a number of ancillary institutions which either advise on or otherwise participate in the activities of the Communities. Some of these owe their origin to the Treaties themselves; others have been established in the light of experience.

## (A) CONSULTATIVE BODIES

Of all the ancillary institutions, pride of place should perhaps be given to the Consultative Committee of the ECSC and the Economic and Social Committee which serves both the EEC and Euratom. Both of these advisory bodies consist of representatives of the various sections of economic and social life in the Communities. Thus the Consultative Committee, appointed under the terms of article 18 of the ECSC Treaty[1], consists of not less than 60 and not more than 84 members (84 members at present) including an equal number of producers, workers, consumers and dealers in the coal and steel industries. The Economic and Social Committee, appointed under the terms of articles 193 and 198 of the EEC Treaty, articles 165 and 169 of the Euratom Treaty[2] and article 5 of the Common Institutions Convention, consists of 156 persons representing producers, farmers, carriers, workers, dealers, craftsmen, professional occupations and the general public. The 156 members are allocated on a national basis as follows: France, Germany, Italy and the United Kingdom have 24 each, Belgium, Greece and the Netherlands have 12 each, Denmark and Ireland have 9 each and Luxembourg has 6.

In the case of both Committees although the members are ap-

1 As amended by the First Act of Accession 1972, art. 22 and the Scond Act of Accession 1979, art. 138.
2 As amended by the First Act of Accession, art. 21 and the Second Act of Accession, art. 17.

pointed by the Council they are appointed in their private capacity and are expressly forbidden to act on any mandate or instructions from the bodies nominating them. There is also an obligation on the Council to consult the Commission on appointments to the Economic and Social Committee and it may also obtain the opinion of European organisations representing particular economic and social sectors of interest. The role of these Committees is an advisory one. They may be consulted by the Commission or Council whenever it is thought appropriate and in some cases consultation is obligatory. Under article 60 (1) of the ECSC Treaty, for example, the Commission may define unfair competitive pricing practices after consulting the Consultative Committee and the Council and similarly under article 75 of the EEC Treaty the Council, on a proposal from the Commission, may lay down common rules applicable to international transport between or across the territories of member states after consultation with the Economic and Social Committee. Thus these Committees provide a sounding board for informed and general opinion on matters relating to the policies of the Communities, roughly on a parallel with the practice in the United Kingdom of consulting interested parties prior to the making of legislation whether parliamentary or subordinate.

Although the opinions of these consultative committees are in no way binding they are not without their influence. The suggestion has been made that they may be more influential than the opinions of the European Parliament since they are the informed views of those involved in activities likely to be affected by the policies of the Communities[3]. The Commission appears to treat their views with respect and the Economic and Social Committee has certainly tended to support the Commission's proposals. The Council in the past adopted a more restrictive attitude[4]. But at the Paris Summit in 1972 the Heads of State or Government invited the Community institutions 'to recognise the right of the Economic and Social Committee in future to advise on its own initiative on all matters affecting the Community'[5]. The Committee's Rules of Procedure have been amended to recognise this new right of initiative[6] and

3 See Torelli, M., *L'Individu et le Droit de la CEE* (1970), at p. 58, and Zellentin, G., 'The Economic and Social Committee' (1962), 1 *Journal of Common Market Studies* 22.
4 See Palmer, M., et al., *European Unity* (1968), at p. 186.
5 *Sixth General Report on the Activities of the European Communities* (1973) at p. 16.
6 See Decision 74/428/EEC, Euratom, OJ L228, 19 August 1974, p. 1.

use has been made of it[7]. The Rules of Procedure have also been amended to give formal recognition of the Committee's de facto division into three groups each representing particular interests: the Employers' Group, the Workers' Group and the General Interests Group[8]. It has been the experience of the Committee, rather like that of the Assembly and its political groups, that its members tend to vote by group and not by nationality.

(B) TECHNICAL COMMITTEES

There are numerous agencies and committees of experts relating to specific areas of Community activity; some of the more important of these are as follows. A Monetary Committee set up under the terms of article 105 of the EEC Treaty to keep the monetary and financial position in the member states under review. The Committee appointed by the Council under the terms of article 111 of the EEC Treaty to assist the Commission in tariff negotiations with non-member states. The Scientific and Technical Committee set up under the terms of article 134 of the Euratom Treaty. The Administrative Commission for the Social Security of Migrant Workers which supervises the social security arrangements for citizens of community members working in a country other than their own. The Short Term and Medium Term Economic Policy Committees: the former assists in the co-ordination of day-to-day economic policies; the latter studies the likely development of the Community's economy over a five-year period. The membership of these Committees is commonly drawn from the national administrations of the member states and their role is purely advisory.

(C) EUROPEAN INVESTMENT BANK

The European Investment Bank is an independent institution, established by article 129 of the EEC Treaty and endowed with legal personality. The members of the Bank are the member states of the Community. The task of the Bank, as set out in article 130, is to contribute, by means of its own resources and access to the

---

**7** See Economic and Social Committee, *The Right of Initiative of the Economic and Social Committee* (1977).
**8** See *Seventh General Report of the Activities of the European Communities* (1974), pp. 71, 72.

capital market, to the balanced and steady development of the Common Market. To that end the Bank, operating on a non-profit-making basis, is empowered to grant loans and to give guarantees to facilitate the financing of three types of project in all sectors of the economy: (i) projects for developing the less developed regions of the Community; (ii) projects for modernising or converting undertakings or for developing fresh activities called for by the progressive establishment of the Common Market; and (iii) projects of common interest to several member states. In the cases of the latter two types of project, the Bank's assistance is limited to projects which are of such a size or nature that they cannot be entirely financed by the various means available in the individual member states.

The organisation, function and powers of the Bank are set out in detail in a separate Statute annexed to the EEC Treaty. The Bank was originally set up with a capital of 1,000 million units of account subscribed by the member states[9]. Over the years the total capital of the Bank has been increased. At the accession of Greece it was set at 7,200 million units of account; the largest contributions are those from France, Germany and the United Kingdom at 1,575 million each ranging down to Luxembourg at 10.5 million[10].

The seat of the Bank is in Luxembourg. The Bank is directed and managed by a Board of Governors, a Board of Directors and a Management Committee[11]. The Board of Governors consists of the Ministers of Finance of the member states. The essential role of the Board of Governors is to lay down directives for the credit policy of the Bank and to ensure that those directives are implemented[12]. The system of voting which is provided for the Council by article 148 of the EEC Treaty also applies to the Board of Governors[13]. The Board of Directors consists of 19 directors with 11 alternates. They serve five-year renewable terms and are appointed by the Board of Governors. Three directors are nominated by each of France, Germany, Italy and the United Kingdom; one

---

**9** Statute of the Bank, art. 4 (1). For the method of calculating the value of the European Currency Unit see Regulation 3308/80, OJ 1980, L345 and Financial Regulation 80/1176, ibid.

**10** See Second Act of Accession 1979, Protocol 1, art. 2.

**11** Statute of the Bank, art. 8. Privileges and immunities are enjoyed by the members of the organs, the staff of the Bank and the national representatives on the Bank under the terms of the Protocol on Privileges and Immunities 1965, art. 22.

**12** Statute of the Bank, art. 9.

**13** Ibid., art. 10.

director is nominated by each of Belgium, Denmark, Greece, Ireland, Luxembourg, the Netherlands and the Commission. Germany, France, Italy and the United Kingdom nominate two alternates each; the Benelux countries by common accord and Denmark, Greece and Ireland by common accord nominate one alternate each, as does the Commission[14]. It is the task of the Board of Directors to manage the Bank in accordance with the Treaty and Statute and the general directives laid down by the Board of Governors. It has the sole power to grant loans and guarantees and to raise loans and it fixes the interest rates and commission payable on loans and guarantees respectively[15]. The current business of the Bank is in the hands of the Management Committee consisting of a President and five Vice-Presidents. These are appointed for six-year renewable terms by the Board of Governors upon a proposal from the Board of Directors. The Management Committee acts under the authority of the President and the supervision of the Board of Directors. Its functions are to prepare the decisions of the Board of Directors on both the raising of loans and the granting of loans and guarantees and to ensure the implementation of those decisions[16]. The President, or in his absence one of the Vice-Presidents, acts as non-voting Chairman of the Board of Directors[17].

The Bank obtains its funds primarily from loans floated on the capital markets of the world. Between its foundation and the end of 1980 the Bank had signed loan and guarantee contracts totalling 17,000 million units of account. During 1980 the Bank signed over 190 loan contracts the combined value being over 3,000 million units of account[18]. This included 44 loans for projects in the United Kingdom totalling 688 million units of account (£417.3 million)[19]. Although most loans and guarantees are in connection with projects within the territories of the member states, it has also been empowered to assist overseas territories and states associated with the Community[20].

Under the terms of article 180 of the EEC Treaty the Court of Justice of the Communities has jurisdiction over certain types of dispute concerning the Bank. In particular the Board of Directors

---

**14** See Second Act of Accession 1979, Protocol 1, art. 4.
**15** Statute of the Bank, arts. 11 and 12.
**16** Ibid., art. 13.
**17** Ibid., art. 11 (2).
**18** See the *European Investment Bank's Annual Report for 1980*, at p. 21.
**19** For further details see ibid. at pp. 49, 50.
**20** See Second Lomé Convention 1979, Title VII, Chapter 2, OJ 1980, L347.

enjoy the powers conferred on the Commission by article 169 of the EEC Treaty in connection with the non-fulfilment by member states of obligations under the Statute of the Bank; also under the terms of article 173 of the EEC Treaty any member state, the Commission or the Board of Directors may challenge measures adopted by the Board of Governors and similarly any member state or the Commission may challenge measures adopted by the Board of Directors. No proceedings appear to have been brought under any of these heads. Article 29 of the Statute of the Bank provides that disputes between the Bank and its creditors and debtors shall be decided by the competent national courts unless jurisdiction has been conferred on the Court of the Justice of the Communities.

(D) MANAGEMENT AND RULE-MAKING COMMITTEES

We have already seen that with the development of the common policies of the Communities into new areas, particularly agriculture, the Council has delegated to the Commission considerable law-making powers. Under the terms of the Treaties the Commission is not in a subordinate position to the Council, and so if this delegation took the form of empowering the Commission to act independently it would remove such matters entirely from the control of the Council. Further, since these powers would have been transferred to the Commission by the Council upon the Commission's proposal, it is believed that the Commission could only be deprived of such powers by the same process, namely on the Commission's initiative. The member governments wished to avoid these consequences of delegation which might prove disadvantageous to themselves. In addition, particularly in the field of agriculture, it was practically desirable that the process of implementing the common policies should be carried out in close consultation with the governments of the member states. The system of Management Committees or *Comités de Gestion* was devised to achieve those objectives.

The management committee procedure was introduced by Regulation 19 of 1962[1]. Article 25 of that Regulation established a Management Committee for Cereal Products made up of representatives of the member states and presided over by a representative of the Commission. Similar management committees have since

---

1 JO No. 30 of 4 April 1962, p. 933/62, since replaced by Regulation 2727/75, OJ 1975, L281.

been set up for each of the main categories of agricultural products. The chairman of a management committee is a member of the staff of the Commission, usually the head of the Department which covers the products dealt with by the Committee. The chairman has no vote. The procedure is for the Commission to submit a draft implementing measure to the appropriate management committee for its opinion. The management committee employs the system of weighted voting used in the Council itself. The management committee's opinion is not binding on the Commission. The Commission may modify its draft in the light of the opinion or adhere to its original proposal. In either event the Commission's decision, after submission of its proposal to the management committee, will have the immediate force of law. But if there is a conflict between the views of the Commission and the opinion of the Committee and if that opinion has received the qualified majority of 45 votes, the matter must be referred to the Council which may within a period of one month reverse the Commission's decision. If, on the other hand, the Commission's draft is acceptable to the Committee or if the Committee is opposed to it but cannot muster the qualified majority or if the Committee fails to respond to the request for an opinion[2], the Commission's decision is not subject to an appeal to the Council.

It is generally agreed that the management committee procedure works well in practice. In 1980 as a result of 696 meetings of management committees over 1,800 regulations and decisions were adopted and only one negative opinion on a Commission draft was expressed[3]. A considerable degree of co-operation and mutual confidence between the Commission and the member states has been engendered by this procedure. When the Commission differs from a committee opinion given by a qualified majority, which happens infrequently, the procedure operates as an alarm mechanism and gives a clear indication of a serious problem which can be effectively resolved only by the member states acting through the Council. The original intention was that this procedure should only be resorted to during the transitional period of the Community's development but because of its success it has been expressly continued in existence for an indefinite period[4].

2 See Case 35/78: *N G J Schouten B V v Hoofdproduktschap Voor Akkerbouwprodukten* [1978] ECR 2543 at 2558.
3 See *Fourteenth General Report on the Activities of the European Communities* (1981) at pp. 175, 176.
4 See Regulation 2602/69, JO 1969, L324.

Another development has been the application of a similar procedure to areas of community activity other than the agricultural, with a result that committees of government representatives have been set up to assist in the implementation of the common customs tariff and in connection with the control of standards in relation to food and animal health[5]. These latter committees, whilst they are manifestations of the management committee procedure, are usually distinguished from the management committees properly-so-called and are referred to as rule-making committees. In connection with these committees the powers delegated by the Council to the Commission are more circumscribed. The Commission's proposal only has immediate binding effect if it is approved by the committee. If the Committee disapproves of a proposal by an opinion reached by the qualified majority, or if no opinion is forthcoming because of the committee's inability to reach the qualified majority, then the Commission must refer its proposal to the Council for acceptance by a qualified majority vote. There is a final rider to this procedure, however, and that is if the Council in such a case has failed to take a decision within three months then the Commission itself may adopt the proposed measure and it will thereby acquire the force of law. The management committee procedure has also been incorporated into the machinery for administering the European Regional Development Fund[6].

The constitutional validity of the management and rule-making committee procedures has been questioned in some quarters[7]. The crux of the question is the vagueness of the Treaty provisions relating to the delegation of powers by the Council to the Commission. Article 155 of the EEC Treaty in its final provision states that the Commission shall 'exercise the powers conferred on it by the Council for the implementation of the rules laid down by the latter'. It has been argued that the force of that provision is to enable the Council to confer upon the Commission powers which are materially identical with the powers possessed by the Council itself. Thus, where under article 43 (2) of the EEC Treaty the Council has the power to adopt regulations for the implementation of the

---

5 E.g. the Committee on Origin, established by Regulation 802/68, JO 1968. L148; the Standing Veterinary Committee established by Council Decision 68/361, JO 1968, L255; and the Common Customs Tariff Nomenclature Committee established by Regulation 97/69, JO 1969, L14.

6 Regulation 724/75, arts. 11-13, OJ 1975, L73.

7 E.g. Schindler, P., 'The Problems of Decision-Making by way of Management Committee Procedure in the EEC' (1971) 8 CMLRev 184.

common agricultural policy, if the Council purports to delegate that power to the Commission it may only do so absolutely and not conditionally. By imposing the management committee procedure upon the powers delegated it has been suggested that the Council is making an unlawful change in the decision-making powers of the Commission. In other words the suggestion is that the management committee procedure depends on political expediency within the Communities rather than on constitutional authority under the terms of the Treaty.

The view taken by both the Commission and Council in support of the management committee procedures is that they are perfectly compatible with the Treaties. The view of these institutions was clearly put by the Commission in its *Second General Report on the Activities of the Communities* (1968)[8]. There it is pointed out that whilst article 155 of the EEC Treaty does not prevent the Council from exercising its implementing powers itself, it is clear that any implementing powers not retained by the Council may only be delegated to the Commission. Further the Council is, in any event, bound to observe the institutional balance of the Communities.

As early as 1958 in the case of *Meroni & Co v High Authority*[9] the Court of Justice commented on the general concept of delegated powers in the Communities. In its judgment in that case the Court stressed the necessity of preserving the balance of powers which is a characteristic of the institutional structure of the Communities and concluded that any delegation of a discretionary power upon institutions different from those established by the Treaties would be invalid[10]. These principles laid down in the *Meroni* case underlie the judgment of the Court in three cases decided in December 1970 in which the validity of the management committee procedures was directly challenged[11].

Part of the Community's agricultural policy takes the form of regulations to forestall unexpected movements of agricultural products which, if permitted, would threaten the common organisation of markets in those products. To that end the Commission has made regulations providing for compulsory import and export

8 Paras. 639–42. Also see *Rapport sur les procédures communautaires d'exécution du droit communautaire dérivé* (European Parliament, Document de Séance, No. 115/68).
9 Case 9/56; [1957–58] ECR 133.
10 Ibid at 150. Also see Case 23/75: *Rey Soda v Cassa Conguaglio Zucchero* [1975] ECR 1279 at 1300.
11 Cases 25, 26 and 30/70: *Einfuhr-und Vorratsstelle für Getreide und Füttermittel v Köster, Berodt & Co,* [1970] ECR 1161, [1972] CMLR 255.

certificates to be obtained by those who wish to make imports or exports of particular agricultural products. It is further required that such certificates should be supported by the payment of a security which will be forfeit if the imports or exports were not made during the period of the certificate's validity. In these cases the legality of this system of certificates was challenged on the ground, inter alia, that the management committee procedure which had been employed in the making of the regulations was contrary to the EEC Treaty.

The arguments against the legality of the management committee procedure were that it permitted the management committees to interfere in the legislative activities of the Commission, that it gives to the member states a right of appeal to the Council against a Commission regulation, thus derogating from the role of the Court, and that consequently it disturbs the institutional balance of the Community. The Council expressed the contrary view in terms which have already been outlined above. The Court supported the Council's view. It held that article 155 which authorises the Council to delegate rule-implementing powers to the Commission must be understood as permitting the Council to lay down provisions and procedures whereby its own policy decisions may be implemented. The management committee procedure was held to come within the modalities upon which the Council is allowed to make such an authorisation of the Commission dependent. Further, the allegation that the management committees interfere in the legislative activities of the Commission was not substantiated since the role of a management committee is merely to give opinions and it has no power to make decisions. Its views may influence the Commission but, subject to one proviso, the power of decision remains with the Commission. As far as the proviso is concerned, which involves the allegation that the management committee procedure gives a right of appeal to the Council from a decision of the Commission, this the Court also held to be unsubstantiated. The management committee procedure merely enables the Council to take action instead of the Commission where the committee hands down a negative opinion. Practice has shown these cases to be exceptional and in any event whether the final decision is made by the Commission or Council the powers of the Court to review such decisions are left unimpaired.

Finally, the Court said that there is no question of this procedure disturbing the institutional equilibrium of the Communities. The

Council has in effect delegated powers to the Commission subject to the condition that the opinion of the appropriate management committee is sought. Regardless of the contents of that opinion the Commission has the power to make binding decisions. In the event of an adverse opinion the Commission is obliged to refer its decision to the Council which may then choose to substitute its own decision for that of the Commission. Thus the Council is merely reserving to itself the freedom to use its own rule-making power in circumstances in which there is a substantial difference of opinion between its delegate, the Commission, and the representatives of the member states. Since the role of the management committees is essentially consultative and since, subject to the power to delegate, the rule-making powers are conferred by the Treaty upon the Council, the institutional order was held to be unaffected. It is submitted that these conclusions apply equally to rule-making committees.

There is general agreement that the management committee procedure works well. Not only has it been decided to retain it indefinitely but more use is likely to be made of it in future in view of the Council's decision to make wider use of its powers under the last paragraph of article 155 of the EEC Treaty[12]. In delicate areas of Community policy which impinge on individual national interests the management committee procedure has made it possible for considerable progress to be made in the implementation of that policy. But for the introduction of management committee procedures which provide a means for close consultation between the Commission and the governments of the member states, the Council would probably have been reluctant to transfer wide-ranging legislative powers to the Commission. As a result the Commission's authority within the EEC has tended to be strengthened. Thus the political significance of the management committee procedures must not be overlooked. As one commentator has observed, it has enabled the wills of the member states to be joined in common activity thus achieving one of the basic aims of the Communities[13]. It is also noteworthy that these procedures appear to be crisis-proof; during the 1965-66 constitutional crisis, whilst Community legislation by the Council came to a virtual standstill as a result of

12 See *Bulletin of the European Communities* (1974), Part 6, p. 122. Also see comments on the role of management committees in *Report on European Institutions* (1979) at pp. 47, 48.
13 Bertram, C., 'Decision-making in the EEC: the Management Committee Procedure' (1967-68), 5 CML Rev 264.

the absence of the French representative, the French continued to participate in management committee activities throughout the crisis[14].

(E) THE COURT OF AUDITORS

The Court of Auditors was established in 1977 under the terms of the Financial Provisions Treaty 1975[15]. The Court of Auditors replaced the two former audit bodies of the Communities: the ECSC Auditor and the Audit Board which served the EEC and Euratom. The decision to set up this new body was linked with the decision to grant to the European Parliament the sole responsibility of discharging the Commission of its responsibility concerning the accounts of the Community. The European Parliament for several years had been urging the reform of the Community's auditing arrangements[16]. It was therefore felt that the new financial arrangements introduced by the 1975 Treaty 'should be accompanied by an intensification of control and audit and this could best be achieved by the creation of a new instrument, the Court of Auditors'[17].

In some respects the rules governing the membership of the Court of Auditors are similar to those governing the Court of Justice[18]. The Court of Auditors is composed of ten members appointed by the Council in consultation with the European Parliament for renewable terms of six years. The Court elects a President from amongst its members for a renewable term of three years. Members of the Court are chosen from persons who have had relevant auditing experience. They must not only be independent, but must also act at all times in the interest of the Community. They may be removed from office, but only if the Court of Justice is satisfied that the conditions and obligations of office are no longer being met. They enjoy the same privileges and immunities as members of the Court of Justice.

While the Court of Auditors is charged with the responsibility of examining the legality and regularity of the accounts of the

14 Ibid.
15 Financial Provisions Treaty, 1975 art. 15, replacing EEC Treaty, art. 206. Also see Financial Regulation of 21 December 1977, Title VI, OJ 1977, L356.
16 See European Parliament, *The Case for a European Audit Office* (1973).
17 Report of the Court of Auditors for the Financial Year 1977, OJ 1978, C313, at p. 5, para. 1.3.
18 Financial Provisions Treaty 1975, art. 15.

Community and presenting an annual report[19], that is not its only responsibility. It is also part of its task to assess financial management within the Community. In other words, it not only assesses the financial soundness of operations actually carried out, but also judges whether the means employed are the most economic and efficient. The extent of its authority is perhaps best conveyed in the terms of its own first Annual Report[20]:

> 'The principal distinctions between the Court and its predecessors are that the Court enjoys a quasi-institutional status, its members are full-time, it has enhanced powers especially as regards the auditing of all Community income and expenditure (whether budgetized or not), it may start its work immediately expenditure has been committed, i.e. it need not wait until the accounts are closed, it is entitled to carry out on-the-spot audits in the Member States on its own initiative, it can make observations at any time on specific questions of its own choosing, it gives opinions on financial legislation and it publishes its reports in the Official Journal.'

The institutions of the Community have the right to seek the opinion of the Court of Auditors on specific questions[1]. The European Parliament, in particular, regards this as a means of reinforcing its own authority over Community resources and expenditure. In a resolution on parliamentary control of Community finances which it adopted in 1976, it declared its intention 'to make use of the close and permanent assistance of the Court of Auditors'[2].

---

19 Ibid., art. 16, adding art. 206a to the EEC Treaty.
20 OJ 1978, C313, p. 6, para. 1.5.
 1 Financial Provisions Treaty, 1975, art. 16. (art. 206a (3)).
 2 OJ 1976, C159, at p. 16. In 1980 the Court of Auditors produced a special report on Community food aid at the request of the European Parliament; see *Bulletin of the European Communities*, 1980–11, at p. 93.

# Chapter 9

# The Court of Justice of the Communities

## I Composition and procedure

(A) COMPOSITION AND ORGANISATION[1]

The Court of Justice of the Communities, as we have seen, has its origins in the Court which was originally set up under the ECSC Treaty. In the words of the EEC Treaty the role of the Court is to 'ensure that in the interpretation and implementation of [the] Treaty the law is observed'[2].

The Court is composed of eleven judges unanimously elected by the Governments of the member states. In practice each member state has a judge of its nationality on the Court[3]. It has been agreed that the eleventh judgeship will be held in rotation by nationals of the four larger member states, in alphabetical order of those member states commencing with France[4]. They hold office for six-year renewable terms. The Treaties provide that the judges must be chosen 'from persons whose independence can be fully relied upon and who fulfil the conditions required for the exercise of the highest judicial office in their respective countries or are legal experts of universally recognised ability'[5]. In practice the Bench has been made up of a mixture of professors of law, judges, lawyers in private practice and government legal advisers.

The judges enjoy the usual guarantees of independence and impartiality. They enjoy immunity from suit and legal process during their tenure of office and they retain that status after ceasing

---

1 See EEC Treaty, arts. 165-168 (as amended by the adjusted First Act of Accession 1972, arts. 17-19, Council Decision of 1 January 1973 increasing the number of advocates-general, Second Act of Accession 1979, arts. 16 and 135 and Decisions 81/208 and 81/209, OJ 1981, L 100) and Protocol on the Statute of the Court of Justice, Titles I and II.
2 Article 164; see also ECSC Treaty, art. 31 and Euratom Treaty, art. 136.
3 Since accession the United Kingdom judge has been Lord Mackenzie Stuart, a former judge of the Scottish Court of Session.
4 See *Bulletin of the European Communities*, 1981-3, p. 63.
5 EEC Treaty, art. 167.

to hold office in respect of acts done in the performance of their duties. This immunity may, however, be suspended by the Court itself in plenary session[6]. The judges also enjoy privileges and immunities in respect of taxation, currency and exchange regulations. They may not hold any office of an administrative or political nature nor engage in any occupation or profession paid or unpaid, although in the case of the latter in an exceptional case permission may be given by the Council[7].

Judges may resign or be removed from office. To resign, a judge must inform the President of the Court who in turn notifies the President of the Council which latter act creates the vacancy. A judge may be removed from office if, in the unanimous opinion of his brethren, he no longer fulfils the conditions required or meets the obligations resulting from his office. The Court's decision to remove a judge must be communicated to the President of the European Parliament and the President of the Commission and must be notified to the President of the Council. The latter notification produces a vacancy[8].

The President of the Court is appointed by the judges from among their own number by an absolute majority vote in a secret ballot. A President holds office for a three-year term which may be renewed. The Court may sit for certain purposes in chambers and so there are three Presidents of Chambers who each preside over a chamber. They are elected for one-year renewable periods by the same process used to elect the President[9]. The number of judges may, at the request of the Court, be increased by a unanimous decision of the Council[10].

The judges of the Court are assisted by five advocates-general who must possess the same professional qualifications as the judges and are also appointed for a six-year renewable term by a unanimous decision of the Council[11]. Each of the four larger Member States has an advocate-general of its nationality. The fifth office of advocate-general is to be held in rotation by nationals of the six smaller member states, in alphabetical order of those member

6 Protocol on the Statute of the Court, art. 3.
7 Ibid., art. 4.
8 ibid., arts. 5 to 7.
9 Rules of Procedure of the Court, art. 10.
10 EEC Treaty, art. 165.
11 EEC Treaty, arts. 166, 167; as amended by the Council Decision of 1 January 1973 increasing the number of advocates-general, OJ 1973, L2 and Decision 81/209, OJ 1981, L100.

states commencing with the Netherlands[12]. One of their number is designated annually by the Court as First Advocate-General[13]. The office of advocate-general is one which has no precise parallel in the English legal system. The institution of advocate-general, like much of the procedure of the Court itself, is largely derived from French law. The function of the advocate-general is similar to that of the *Commissaire du Gouvernement* at the French *Conseil d'Etat*. It is the role of the *Commissaire du Gouvernement* to act as what Professor Hamson has called 'the embodied conscience of the Court'[14]. He is required to consider the issues in a case impartially and individually and to reach his own personal conclusion as to what in law and justice should be done. Before the *Conseil d'Etat* considers its judgment the *Commissaire*, orally and in public, states the facts and the law as he sees them and suggests the principles in accordance with which he thinks the case should be decided. The *Commissaire* does not participate in the giving of judgment still less is he the representative of or subordinate to the government. His purpose is to act as an entirely uncommitted and fearless defender of the law and justice. Similarly, in the case of the advocates-general of the Court of Justice of the Communities, the Treaties require them to 'make reasoned submissions in open court, with complete impartiality and independence', on cases before the Court[15]. Their task is a threefold one: to propose a solution to the case before the Court; to relate that proposed solution to the general pattern of existing case law; and, if possible, to outline the probable future development of the case law. The advocates-general therefore represent neither the institutions of the Communities nor the public; they function only as the spokesmen of the law and justice in the context of the Treaties.

As in the case of the submissions of the French *Commissaires du Gouvernement* so the submissions of the advocates-general are in no way binding on the Court. But their submissions are invariably published with the judgment of the Court and where, as often happens, the Court agrees with the advocate-general, the advocate-general's full consideration of the wider aspects of the case not only throws valuable light on the Court's comparatively

12 See *Bulletin of the European Communities*, 1981-3, p. 63. The present British advocate-general is Sir Gordon Slynn, formerly a judge of the Queen's Bench Division of the High Court and President of the Employment Appeal Tribunal.
13 Rules of Procedure of the Court, art. 10.
14 *Executive Discretion and Judicial Control* (1954), p. 80.
15 E.g. EEC Treaty, art. 166.

brief judgments, but also act as an indicator of the direction the jurisprudence of the Court is likely to take in the future. In this way the advocates-general are in a position to influence the development of Community law[16].

As has been said there is no precise parallel in the English legal system to the office of advocate-general. The Attorney-General does have a role as guardian of the public interest or protector of public rights, e.g. as a party in civil proceedings for an injunction or declaration in cases of public nuisance and his appearance before public tribunals of inquiry as a spokesman for the public interest. Similarly, in matrimonial proceedings, the Queen's Proctor has a right of intervention to prevent a decree nisi being made absolute on the ground, for example, that material facts have not been put to the court. A court may also ask the Official Solicitor to instruct counsel to ensure that all points of view on matters of law are fully before the court. But in these cases the roles of the Attorney-General, the Queen's Proctor and the Official Solicitor are limited and special whereas that of the advocates-general is unlimited and general[17]. The role of the advocate-general is a hybrid in that it has both advocatory and judicial characteristics. As an independent advocate of the legal interests of the Community, he may be regarded as a sort of institutionalised *amicus curiae*. As a person appointed with the same qualifications and on the same conditions as the judges and whose views have a formative influence on the law, he may be regarded almost as a first instance judge whose opinions are never decisive but are always subject to review by the Court[18]. Advocates-general may retire and be removed by the same procedure as in the case of judges and they enjoy similar privileges and immunities. The Treaties are silent on the nationality of the judges and advocates-general but in practice of course they are always of the nationality of one of the member states.

The seat of the Court is in Luxembourg and, subject to public holidays and the usual vacations, it is in permanent session. In case of urgency the President may convene the Court during vacations.

The day-to-day administration of the Court is in the hands of

**16** See Brown, L. N. and Jacobs, F. G., *The Court of Justice of the European Communities* (1977), chapter 4.
**17** See Edwards, J. Ll.J., *Law Officers of the Crown* (1964), Chapter 14; *Rayden on Divorce* (13th edn, 1979), pp. 477–479; *Halsbury's Laws of England* (4th edn), Vol. 10, para. 950.
**18** Cf. Warner, J.-P., 'Some Aspects of the European Court of Justice' (1976), 14 JSPTL (NS) 15, pp. 17–19.

Registrar (*Greffier*) and his staff. The Registrar is elected by the judges by majority vote after consultation with the advocates-general. The Registrar's term of office is six years and he is eligible for re-election. The Court may dismiss him if he no longer complies with the obligations of his office[19].

Each judge and advocate-general is assisted by *attachés* or legal secretaries. *Attachés* are of the same nationality as their masters and are required to have legal training. Their main tasks are to prepare pre-trial studies on the legal questions involved in a case before the Court and to assist in the drafting of opinions and judgments. They thus provide a service similar to that of the Law Clerks to the Judges of the United States Supreme Court[20].

In principle the Court sits in plenary session with a quorum of seven, but it is enabled to set up separate chambers and has established three chambers of three judges each presided over by a President of Chamber. It is the function of these chambers, at the request of the Court, to undertake preliminary examinations of evidence in particular cases. They can also hear and decide cases brought by one of the officials of a Community institution against that institution, references for preliminary rulings and any actions brought by natural or legal persons the nature or circumstances of which do not necessitate a hearing by the full Court. If a member state or a Community institution is party to the latter type of action it can insist on a hearing by the full Court[1]. Each chamber is assisted by an advocate-general[2].

## (B) PRACTICE AND PROCEDURE

The practice and procedure of the Court are based on a code of Rules of Procedure drawn up by the Court[3]. The procedure of the Court is divided into three stages: a written stage; an *instruction* (preparatory enquiry) stage; and an oral stage. As soon as a complaint (a *requête*) is filed with the Registrar, the President appoints one of the judges as *juge-rapporteur* (reporting-judge). The task of the *juge-rapporteur* is to prepare a preliminary report on the case

---

**19** See Rules of Procedure of the Court, Part 1, Chapter 3.
**20** For comment on the *attachés* see Feld, W., *Court of the European Communities* (1964), p. 27 and Brown and Jacobs, op cit., pp. 19–20.
**1** See Rules of Procedure, art. 95, as amended in 1979. See OJ 1979, L238, p. 3.
**2** See Rules of Procedure of the Court, art. 10.
**3** The Rules require the unanimous approval of the Council; EEC Treaty, art. 188. The present Rules were approved on 26 November 1974; see OJ 1974, L350. For subsequent amendments see OJ 1979, L238.

for the consideration of the Court. This is followed by the First Advocate-General assigning one of his colleagues to the case[4].

The written stage takes the form of pleadings. The plaintiff in his *requête* will set out his claim against the defendant and the grounds upon which it is made. The defendant will then be notified of the *requête* and will be given the period of one month within which to prepare and submit to the Court a statement of defence. The plaintiff may make a written reply to the defence and the defendant may then also make a final rejoinder. This exchange of submissions comprises the written stage in the proceedings. It should be pointed out that these written submissions go far beyond the scope and purpose of English pleadings. The arguments of the parties are set out fully together with the nature of the evidence upon which reliance is placed. This form of documentary advocacy has the effect of stressing the written stage at the expense of the other two stages[5].

The *juge-rapporteur* then examines the pleadings and considers whether the case requires an *instruction*, i.e. an enquiry or proof-taking stage which is a familiar part of continental legal procedure. The *juge-rapporteur* reports to the Court on whether an *instruction* is necessary and after the Court has also heard the advocate-general on this point it will decide whether to proceed to an *instruction*. If the Court decides that an *instruction* is necessary it can be held before the full court, before one of the chambers of the court or it may be entrusted to the *juge-rapporteur* himself. In any event, the *instruction* will take the form of a personal appearance of the parties and their witnesses for oral examination and the production and inspection of documentary evidence. This procedure of *instruction* is principally conducted not by the lawyers representing the parties, but, following continental practice, by the Court, chamber or *juge-rapporteur* as the case may be. The advocate-general may also participate in the *instruction*. The representatives of the parties may only question witnesses 'subject to the control of the President[6].' In addition to witnesses who are called at the request of the parties, the Court and the advocate-general also have the power to summon witnesses. Evidence is given on oath sworn either in accordance with the laws of the state of the witness's nationality, or alternatively in the form set out in the Rules of Procedure. The Court has the

---

4 See Rules of Procedure of the Court, arts. 9 and 10 and Title 2.
5 For example, in 1971 the Court gave judgment in 60 cases in which the written procedure totalled 18,000 pages; Campbell, op cit., Vol. 3, para. 7.23.
6 Rules of Procedure, art. 47 (4).

power to exempt a witness from taking the oath[7]. At the end of the *instruction* the Court may allow the parties to submit written observations on matters which have arisen in the course of the *instruction*.

After the conclusion of the *instruction*, or, if there has been no *instruction*[8], at the end of the written proceedings, the oral stage takes place before the court. Immediately prior to the oral stage the *juge-rapporteur* will present his report which will outline the case, summarise the arguments of the parties and make a statement on the facts of the case on the basis of the evidence presented during the written and *instruction* stages. This will be followed by oral argument on behalf of the parties. There is no hearing of witnesses or oral examination at this stage. The parties must be legally represented during the oral stage[9].

Members of the Court and the advocate-general may put questions to agents and counsel during the oral proceedings. The Court may also at this stage order further *instruction* to be held either by a chamber or by the *juge-rapporteur*. At the conclusion of the case the parties' representatives make closing speeches to the Court: plaintiff first, followed by defendant. The advocate-general then makes his submissions which bring the oral proceedings to a close. There is usually an adjournment between the speeches by counsel and the advocate-general's delivery of his submissions.

The judges withdraw to deliberate in private without the participation of advocates-general, legal secretaries or interpreters. In the course of their deliberations they may re-open the oral proceedings if they so wish. These deliberations finally result in the Court's judgment which is drafted by the *juge-rapporteur*. Judgment is delivered in open court. Again, following continental practice, the court renders a single collegiate judgment; separate or dissenting opinions are not permitted. Even if the judgment is based on a majority decision that fact, let alone the nature of the majority, is not disclosed[10]. It has already been pointed out that in the vast

7 Rules of Procedure, arts. 47 (5) and 110.
8 As is usually the case. See Brown and Jacobs, op cit., p. 166.
9 Member states and Community institutions must be represented by an agent who may be assisted by a lawyer entitled to practise before a court of a member state. Corporate bodies and individuals may also have an agent but they must be represented by a lawyer entitled to practise before a court of a member state. See Protocol on the Statute of the Court, art. 20. Cf. Jacobs F. G. and Durand, A., *References to the European Court* (1975), pp. 177, 178.
10 For comment on the practice of single collegiate judgments see Bebr. op cit., p. 24 and Feld, op cit., p. 99.

majority of cases the Court accepts the conclusions of the advocate-general. But in those cases where the Court has not followed the advocate-general, his submissions can in a sense be regarded as a dissenting opinion[11].

The languages of the Court are the official languages of the Communities, viz. Danish, Dutch, English, French, German, Greek and Italian; Irish may also be used although it is not an official language[12]. All documents submitted to the Court must be translated into these languages. French has become the working language of the Court and it is the language in which the Court's deliberations are conducted. Only one of the Community languages may be used as the procedural language in a given case. The basic rule is that the choice of procedural language is made by the plaintiff where one of the Communities' institutions is the defendant, on the basis that the representatives of the Communities are well versed in all the official languages. But where the defendant is one of the member states or the court of a member state is seeking a preliminary ruling then the procedural language must be the language of that state. The Court's judgments, together with the submission of the advocates-general, are published in each of the official languages; the copy in the procedural language of a given case being regarded as the authentic and definitive version[13].

The Court's judgments have binding force from the date of their delivery[14]. As far as the enforcement of the Court's judgments is concerned the position varies depending on the outcome of the case and the identity of the defendant. If the Court upholds or declares invalid an act of a Community institution then either that act may be implemented or not depending upon the decision of the Court; in such cases there is no question of enforcing the judgment in the strict sense. If the Court gives judgment against a member state under the ECSC Treaty enforcement is achieved by enabling the Commission, acting jointly with the Council, to impose sanctions on the defaulting member. This procedure is not reproduced in the Treaties of Rome which contain no enforcement measures for use against member states. The Rome Treaties merely provide that the

---

11 A list of cases in which the Court has disagreed with the advocate-general is given in Campbell, A., *Common Market Law*, Vols. 1 and 3, para. 6.33.
12 Rules of Procedure, art. 29 (1).
13 See Rules of Procedure arts. 29, 30 and 31. On the problems of multilingual judicial deliberations see Feld, op cit., pp. 100, 101 and Hartley, T. C., *The Foundations of European Community Law* (1981), p. 53.
14 Rules of the Court, art. 65.

member state in question is required to take the measures necessary to execute the Court's judgment. Lastly, if the Court gives judgment against a corporate body or individual in the form of a fine, such judgment debts are enforceable without further formality by the national courts of the member states[15].

## (C) REVISION AND INTERPRETATION OF JUDGMENTS

The Court of Justice of the Communities is a court of first and only instance. Thus the decisions of the Court are final and are not subject to appeal; it is not open to a national court when called upon to enforce a judgment of the Community Court to challenge that judgment in any way. The only possible course of action open to an unsuccessful litigant is to request a revision of the Court's judgment[16]. Such a request may be made on the ground of the discovery of a fact likely to prove of decisive importance which, before judgment, was unknown both to the Court and to the party requesting revision. Two periods of limitation apply to requests for revision: the request must be made within ten years of the date of the judgment and within three months of the date on which the new fact became known to the applicant. If these conditions are satisfied, and without prejudice to the merits, the Courts hears the advocate-general and considers the parties' written submissions before deciding whether the alleged new fact does exist and whether it justifies revision. If the Court decides that the request is admissible then it proceeds to consider the merits of the case and this can, if necessary, involve a completely new trial. In *Feram v High Authority of the ECSC* (1960) the Court made it clear that the newly discovered fact must have been unknown both to the Court and to the party, and that knowledge of it prior to judgment by either Court or a party will make the request inadmissible[17]. In *Fonderie Acciaierie Giovanni Mandelli v EC Commission* (1971), the Court refused an application for revision in a similar case in which a relevant document could have been obtained by the applicant either at the time of the commencement of the original action or at the enquiry stage[18]. The Court regards the procedure for revision as an exception to the doctrine of res judicata. As such it interprets the

15 EEC Treaty, arts. 187, 192.
16 See Protocol on the Statute of the Court, art. 41 and Rules of Procedure of the Court, art. 98 to 100.
17 Case 1/60: [1960] ECR 165.
18 Case 56/70: [1971] ECR 1.

conditions for revision strictly and will not allow the procedure to be used for the purpose of bringing an appeal[19].

A final point concerning the practice of the court relates to the possibility in case of difficulty as to the meaning or scope of a judgment of asking the Court to interpret its judgment[20]. Such a request may be made by any of the parties to the case or by a Community institution which can show that it has an interest in the decision. The only part of a judgment which may be the subject of a request for interpretation is the operative part or what we would call the ratio decidendi. As the Court itself put it in *Assider v High Authority of the ECSC* (1955)[1] 'the only parts of a judgment which can be interpreted are those which express the judgment of the Court in the dispute which has been submitted for its final decision and those parts of the reasoning upon which this decision is based and which are, therefore, essential to it ... the Court does not have to interpret those passages which are incidental and which complete or explain that basic reasoning'.

In the later case of *High Authority v of the ECSC Collotti* (1965)[2] the Court considered the nature of the 'difficulty' necessary to justify a request for an interpretation. In the *Assider* case the court had said that it was sufficient for the parties to give different meanings to the judgment. In the *Collotti* case the Court defined the nature of the difficulty more precisely. The Court held: 'In order to be admissible, an application for interpretation ... must not raise the possible consequences of the judgment in question on cases other than the one decided, but only the obscurity and ambiguity of the meaning and scope of the judgment itself in relation to the case decided by the judgment in question.'

## II  The contentious jurisdiction of the Court[3]

The Court is the creature of the Community Treaties and so its jurisdiction derives exclusively from those Treaties. Any attempt to attribute other jurisdiction to the Court will fail.

**19** Case 116/78 Rev: *Bellintani v EC Commission* [1980] ECR 23.
**20** See Protocol on the Statute of the Court, art. 40 and Rules of Procedure of the Court, art. 102.
 **1** Case 5/55: [1954-56] ECR 135.
 **2** Case 70/63 bis: [1965] ECR 275.
 **3** The Court's jurisdiction to give preliminary rulings at the request of the courts of the member states will be discussed later in connection with the relationship between Community law and municipal law; see Chapter 11.

In the case of *Schlieker v High Authority of the ECSC* (1963)[4] the plaintiff alleged that through the inactivity of the High Authority she had suffered loss. It was argued on behalf of the the High Authority that the right to bring proceedings before the Court based on the inactivity of a Community institution was limited by the Treaty to member states, other Community institutions and undertakings and associations. Frau Schlieker argued in reply, upon analogy with German municipal law, that the Court had a residual jurisdiction to enable it to protect the interests of individuals where the Treaty texts are silent. This view was rejected both by the advocate-general and the Court. The advocate-general observed that 'the Treaty system ... does not in a general clause guarantee legal protection without any gaps. Reference to ... the Basic Law (*Grundgesetz*) of the Federal Republic of Germany cannot lead to any other solution, for the Court can define the limits of its supra-national legal protection only by using the text of the Treaty and not by following national law.'[5] The Court agreed with this submission and held that 'Whatever may be the consequence of a factual situation of which the Court may not take cognizance, the Court may not depart from the judicial system set out in the Treaty'. Thus in interpreting the Treaties the Court is bound to adhere strictly to the provisions of the text, and, being the creature of the Treaty, it has no power other than that conferred by the Treaty[6].

The jurisdictional provisions of the Treaties are somewhat complex; as one commentator has observed 'no international tribunal has ever been equipped with so varied a jurisdictional competence as has the Court of the European Communities.'[7] The contentious jurisdiction conferred upon the Court by the Treaties falls under two main heads which will be treated in the following order:

(a) Actions against member states; and

(b) Actions against Community institutions.

## (A) ACTIONS AGAINST MEMBER STATES

Actions against member states take two forms:

(i) Actions by member states against member states.

---

4 Case 12/63: [1963] ECR 85, [1963] CMLR 281.
5 Unwritten rules of Community law for the protection of fundamental rights may, however, be derived from national law; see Chapter 2, supra.
6 See Case 66/76: *CFDT v EC Council* [1977] ECR 305, [1977] 1 CMLR 589.
7 Bowett, D. W., *Law of International Institutions* (3rd edn 1975), p. 278.

(ii) Actions by Community institutions against member states.

(i) All the Treaties confer upon the Court a compulsory jurisdiction to decide disputes between member states concerning the application of the terms of the Treaties and a permissive jurisdiction, based on the consent of the parties, over disputes between states related to the object and purpose of the Communities in general. Thus the EEC Treaty provides first at article 170 that 'Any Member State which considers that another Member State has failed to fulfil any of its obligations under this Treaty may bring the matter before the Court of Justice[8].' Secondly, the EEC Treaty provides at article 182 that 'The Court of Justice shall be competent to decide any dispute between Member States connected with the subject of this Treaty, if that dispute is submitted to it under a special agreement between the parties[9].' The Court's jurisdiction over both of these types of dispute is exclusive; recourse by member states to other means of settlement is expressly forbidden by the Treaties. Article 219 of the EEC Treaty provides that 'Member States undertake not to submit a dispute concerning the interpretation or the carrying out of this Treaty to any method of settlement other than those provided therein'[10]. This insistence on referring inter-state disputes to the Court of Justice underlines one of the major purposes of the Court and that is to guarantee uniformity of interpretation and application of the law of the Communities.

Under the terms of article 170 of the EEC Treaty, before one member state brings another before the Court the matter must be referred to the Commission. This gives the Commission an opportunity to deliver a reasoned opinion on the alleged breach of Treaty in the light of observations made by the member states in dispute. This procedure seems to be designed for the purpose of promoting the resolution of the dispute without resort to litigation. But whether or not the Commission delivers such an opinion, the member state making the allegation can insist on proceeding with the action. In general, member states prefer to resolve their disputes outside the courtroom since only one article 170 action has so far been heard. In that case[11] France alleged that the United Kingdom's fishery conservation measures were contrary to Community law.

---

8 Cf. ECSC Treaty, art. 89, and Euratom Treaty, art. 141.
9 Cf. ECSC Treaty, art. 89, and Euratom Treaty, art. 154.
10 Cf. ECSC Treaty, art. 87, and Euratom Treaty, art. 193.
11 Case 141/78: *France v United Kingdom* [1979] ECR 2923; [1980] 1 CMLR 6.
  Also see p. 336 post.

The Commission delivered an opinion in support of the French view. The European Court agreed with that opinion and gave judgment against the United Kingdom[12].

(ii) By virtue of article 88 of the ECSC Treaty the Commission is given the power to decide whether a member state has failed to comply with its obligations under the Treaty. If it so decides in relation to a given member state the Commission must invite that state to express its views on the matter. The Commission may then record the state's wrongdoing in a reasoned opinion and give the state a limited time within which to take steps to fulfil its obligations. The purpose of this process is to enable both the Commission and the member state to exchange views in the hope that the issue may thereby be settled. If it is not, it is open to the member state in question to bring proceedings before the Court challenging the Commission's decision. Although such litigation takes the form of a member state bringing proceedings against the Commission, in substance the issue before the Courts is an alleged breach of Treaty obligations by a member state; the Treaty places the onus of challenging that allegation upon the member state. In the EEC Treaty by virtue of article 169 a somewhat different procedure is followed[13]. There if the Commission considers that a member state has failed to fulfil any of its obligations under the Treaties then it shall issue a reasoned opinion after giving the state concerned the opportunity to submit its comments. If the member state does not comply with the terms of such opinion within the period laid down by the Commission the Commission may bring the matter before the Court of Justice. Thus, whilst in the ECSC the Commission has the power to determine finally a member state's breach of obligations subject to the member state's right to appeal to the Court, in the EEC and Euratom the Commission can only provisionally determine the breach of obligation and it must apply to the Court for that determination to be confirmed. A similar right of action by the Commission against a member state is given by article 93 (2) of the EEC Treaty in the context of the rules concerning state aids. If the Commission finds that financial aid granted by a member state is incompatible with the Treaty it shall require that member

---

12 Disputes between member states may be at the root of litigation between the Commission and a member state. See Case 232/78: *EC Commission v France* [1979] ECR 2729 where the dispute had earlier been the subject of an art. 170 action brought by Ireland against France (Case 58/77: OJ 1977, C142) which was later withdrawn (OJ 1978, C76).

13 Also Euratom Treaty, art. 141.

state to abolish or alter such aid. If the member state does not comply within the prescribed period, the Commission may refer the matter to the Court direct.

The Commission has brought well over one hundred actions[14] against Member States under the terms of articles 169 and 93(2), the overwhelming majority of cases arising under article 169. Proceedings will lie against member states not only for any acts on the part of a member state but also for omissions, including administrative failures to implement Community law[15]. This reflects the dual duty which article 5 of the EEC Treaty imposes on member states: to take all appropriate measures to ensure the fulfilment of Treaty obligations and to abstain from any measure which could jeopardise the attainment of Treaty objectives. These actions not only serve the narrow purpose of enforcing the obligations of member states in specific cases, but they also provide the Court with a vehicle for elaborating more broadly the nature of the Treaty obligations of member states.

In one of the early cases, the Commission brought actions against Belgium and Luxembourg in which it alleged that a tax which those member states were imposing on import licences for dairy products was contrary to the EEC Treaty[16]. The defendant governments argued that a Council resolution of 1962 which had not yet been implemented would have justified the tax. They maintained that the Commission had no authority to require the abolition of a tax which but for the failure to implement the Council resolution would be part of Community policy. But the Court held that, except for cases expressly authorised by the Treaty, member states are prohibited from taking justice into their own hands. Therefore a failure by the Council to carry out its obligations could not excuse the defendant member states from carrying out theirs. Similarly, in a later case against Italy the Court rejected an attempted defence which was based on the fact that member states other than Italy had also failed to carry out the obligation in question by the required date[17].

In other cases in which a member state has failed to fulfil its Treaty obligations the Court has not been moved by pleas that such

14 See *Fourteenth General Report on the Activities of the European Communities* (1981), Table 2, p. 354.
15 See Case 31/69: *EEC Commission v Italy* [1970] ECR 24, [1970] CMLR 175.
16 Cases 90–91/63: *EEC Commission v Luxembourg and Belgium* [1964] ECR 625, [1965] CMLR 58.
17 Case 52/75: *EC Commission v Italy* [1976] ECR 277, [1976] 2 CMLR 320.

failure is attributable to the special characteristics of the legal and constitutional order of a member state or to prevailing political or economic conditions. Therefore, a political crisis in Italy which paralysed Italian legislative processes was not accepted as a defence to an article 169 action[18]. In the same way the Court rejected a plea by the United Kingdom that its refusal to comply with a Community obligation was justified for economic and practical reasons including opposition by Trade Unions[19]. As the Court said in that latter case, 'practical difficulties which appear at the stage when a Community measure is put into effect cannot permit a Member State unilaterally to opt out of fulfilling its obligations'[20]. Partial and idiosyncratic implementation of Community obligations will not satisfy the Court[1]. Nor can a member state avoid an article 169 action by delaying taking implementing measures until the particular obligation has been revoked[2]. Community law must apply in each member state independent of its unilateral will.

The case law on article 169 of the EEC Treaty also throws some light on the nature of the reasoned opinion which the Commission must make concerning the alleged breach of Treaty obligations. In *EEC Commission v Italy* (1961)[3] the Commission wrote a letter to the Italian Government, after giving the Government an opportunity to make its observations, stating that a particular Italian decree was contrary to the Treaty. The Government was asked to end the alleged infringement within one month. This letter did not contain a full review of the situation of the Italian market nor whether that situation justified the decree. Italy did not comply with the Commission's request within the stated period and so the Commission instituted proceedings under article 169. Italy challenged the admissibility of these proceedings on the ground, inter alia, that the Commission's letter was not a reasoned opinion within the meaning of article 169. The Court rejected that argument and said that an opinion is considered to be reasoned 'when it contains, as in the present case, a coherent statement of the reasons which convinced

**18** Case 30/72: *EC Commission v Italy* [1973] ECR 161.
**19** Case 128/78: *EC Commission v United Kingdom* [1979] ECR 419, [1979] 2 CMLR 45.
**20** Ibid at 429. Also see case 102/79: *EC Commission v Belgium* [1980] ECR 1473 at 1487.
**1** Case 39/72: *EC Commission v Italy* [1973] ECR 101, [1973] CMLR 439.
**2** Ibid. In the context of art. 169 and 93 (2) actions, interim measures may be taken against a member state in emergency situations; see cases 31, 53/77R: *EC Commission v United Kingdom* [1977] ECR 921.
**3** Case 7/61: [1961] ECR 317, [1962] CMLR 39.

the Commission that the state in question had failed to fulfil one of its obligations under the Treaty'. This was also the view expressed by the advocate-general in his submissions where he said that 'no formalism is required . . . because . . . the reasoned opinion is not an administrative act, checked by the Court as far as its legal character is concerned. There is no question here of 'insufficient reasons' giving rise to a formal defect. The only purpose of the reasoned opinion is to specify the point of view of the Commission in order to inform the Government and, possibly, the Court.' Thus, if a purported reasoned opinion did not coherently express the Commission's view point that would be a ground on which the Court might dismiss the Commission's case[4].

In the case of article 88 of the ECSC Treaty if the member state does not appeal to the Court or if it loses its appeal, the Commission may, subject to a concurring two-thirds majority of the Council, impose on the member state the sanctions mentioned earlier. In the cases of the EEC and Euratom Treaties no such sanctions are available. Both article 171 of the EEC Treaty and article 143 of the Euratom Treaty state that, if the Court of Justice finds that a member state has failed to fulfil any of its obligations under the Treaty, such state shall take the measures required for the implementation of the judgment of the Court[5]. Thus in such cases the Court's judgments are essentially declaratory in nature indicating that in the last analysis the success of the Communities depends upon the good faith of member states. A member state's failure to implement a judgment given against it would also be likely to have an unfavourable political effect on its relations with its fellow members[6].

## (B)  ACTIONS AGAINST COMMUNITY INSTITUTIONS

We have already seen that French law has exerted a strong influence on the procedure of the Court of Justice of the Communities. This is also true of the jurisdiction of the Court to exercise control over the acts of the institutions of the Communities. French administra-

---

4 Another essential part of the pre-litigation procedure under art. 169 is the giving of a member state an adequate and realistic opportunity to make observations on an alleged breach of treaty obligations; Case 31/69, *EC Commission v Italy* [1970] ECR 24, [1970] CMLR 175.
5 A failure by a member state to execute a previous judgment of the Court will constitute an infringement of EEC Treaty, art. 171; Case 48/71: *EC Commission v Italy* [1972] ECR 527, [1972] CMLR 699.
6 On the effectiveness of art. 169 proceedings see *Hartley*, op cit., p. 315 et seq.

tive law traditionally recognises two main categories of litigation the *recours de la légalité* and the *recours de pleine juridiction*. The former is a kind of judicial review of the legality of administrative acts in which the Court is merely asked to annul, i.e. declare void, an administrative act on one of a number of specified grounds. In such a case if the Court finds that a given act is unlawful on one of those grounds it can merely give judgment to that effect; it cannot substitute its own decision on the merits for that of the institution whose act has been challenged, nor can it award any other remedy such as damages. In addition to *recours de la légalité* French administrative courts may also hear *recours de pleine juridiction*. In such cases those courts are not limited to controlling the legality of acts on specific grounds but they are free to pronounce on the actual merits of the parties' case and to substitute their own decision for that of the administrative authority. Such jurisdiction is *pleine*, i.e. full or plenary, in the sense that when exercising it the court has the complete powers of a civil court to award compensation for damage. These two types of administrative jurisdiction are possessed by the Court of Justice of the Communities and the following discussion will be in terms of that classification:

(a) *Actions concerning legality (recours de la légalité)*

    (i) *Actions for annulment (recours en annulation)*—The acts of the institutions of the Communities take a variety of forms but not all of them are susceptible to challenge. Only those acts which are binding in law are susceptible to challenge. Under the ECSC Treaty the Commission may act in three forms: decisions, recommendations and opinions. Of these decisions and recommendations are legally binding whilst opinions have no binding force; thus article 33 gives the Court jurisdiction to hear actions for the annulment of such decisions and recommendations. Under the EEC and Euratom Treaties the acts of the Commission and the Council may take five forms: regulations, directives, decisions, recommendations and opinions; of these the first three are legally binding and are susceptible of an action for annulment. Thus the Court has declined to entertain an action for annulment in connection with any act which is not designed to produce binding legal effects. In *Sucrimex SA and Westzucker GmbH v EC Commission* (1980)[7] the Court rejected an action challenging the legality of a telex message from the Commission to the authorities of a member state. In

---

7 Case 133/79: [1980] ECR 1299, [1981] 2 CMLR 479.

accordance with Community rules Sucrimex had exported a quantity of sugar to Westzucker. When the appropriate national authority was asked to pay the export refunds in respect of that transaction, payment in full was refused in accordance with the terms of the Commission's telex message. In dismissing the action, the Court held that under Community law the application of provisions concerning export refunds was a matter for the appropriate authorities of the member states. In these matters the Commission had no power of decision, but it could express an opinion. This was confirmed by the contested telex message which did not disclose any intention to produce binding legal effects. The Court does, nevertheless, adopt a flexible approach to this issue. It will look to the substance of an act rather than to its form. Therefore, if an act is in the form normally used for non-binding acts, but in the view of the Court it does in fact create binding obligations, such an act would be actionable despite its apparent informality[8].

Actions may be brought not only by member states and by Community institutions but also by private parties. In the first place, article 173 (1) of the EEC Treaty states that the legality of measures taken by the Council or by the Commission may be challenged in proceedings instituted by a member state, the Council or the Commission[9]. In general terms only a party which can show sufficient legal interest in a case can institute proceedings before the Court, but such is the nature of the Communities that all member states are deemed to have an interest in the legality of all Community acts. Thus, for example, in the *Netherlands v High Authority of the ECSC* (1964)[10] the Netherlands was permitted to challenge a decision of the High Authority which was in fact addressed to some German coal enterprises on the ground that it conflicted with the terms of ECSC Treaty. The unfettered nature of the right of member states to challenge Community acts is illustrated by a case in which Italy sought the annulment of a regulation for which it had voted in the Council. The Court rejected the Council's plea that the action was inadmissible. It held that every member state has the right to challenge every Council regulation 'without the exercise of this right being conditional upon the position taken up

---

8 See Case 22/70: *EC Commission v EC Council* [1971] ECR 263, [1971] CMLR 335.

9 Cf. ECSC Treaty, arts. 33 and 38, and Euratom Treaty, art. 146.

10 Case 66/63: [1964] ECR 533, [1964] CMLR 522.

by the ... Member States ... when the regulation in question was adopted[11].'

It is clearly possible under the Treaties for one Community institution to challenge an act of another Community institution. To date this has not happened very often[12]. In his submissions in the first of those cases the advocate-general referred to the novelty of the proceedings and attributed this to the fundamental harmony which reigns between these two institutions. Be that as it may, in that action the Commission challenged certain activities of the Council in the field of the external relations of the Communities. In March 1970 the Council discussed the attitude to be taken by the members of the Communities at a meeting to be held in April of that year to conclude the negotiations for a European Road Transport Agreement (ERTA) under the auspices of the UN Economic Commission for Europe. At that April meeting the members of the Communities negotiated and concluded the Agreement in accordance with the terms of the Council's discussion. The Commission challenged the validity of that discussion on the ground that it involved violation of Treaty provisions, particularly since under article 228 the Commission is given the task of negotiating agreements between the Community and non-member states subject to the approval of the Council. The Council challenged this action on the grounds of its admissibility and its merits. On the question of admissibility the advocate-general submitted that, whilst in principle the action was admissible because the discussion in issue was an official discussion of the Council, upon analysis that discussion was not a legally binding act of the Council as defined by the Treaty and so was not susceptible to challenge. The Court disagreed with the advocate-general on this point and held that the action was admissible. The Court pointed out that article 173 of the EEC Treaty specifically excluded recommendations and opinions from review by the Court. Not only was this discussion neither a recommendation nor an opinion, it had definite legal effects on the member s States since during their negotiations on the ERTA they consistently acted in accordance with the conclusion of the Council discussion. But although the Court differed from the

11 Case 166/78: *Italy v EC Council* [1979] ECR 2575 at 2596.
12 See Case 22/70: *EC Commission v EC Council* [1971] ECR 263, [1971] CMLR 335; Case 81/72: *EC Commission v EC Council* [1973] ECR 575, [1973] CMLR 639 and Case 70/74: *EC Commission v EC Council* [1975] ECR 795, [1975] 2 CMLR 287.

advocate-general on the question of admissibility they both agreed that the action should be rejected on the merits[13].

Secondly, actions may be brought against acts of Community institutions by private parties, that is to say by individuals or corporate bodies[14]. The locus standi of private parties differs somewhat as between the ECSC on the one hand and the EEC on the other. In the ECSC undertakings or associations of undertakings may challenge acts of Community institutions where either those acts apply to them individually or, although acts of a general nature, nevertheless involve a misuse of powers affecting them[15]. *Groupement des Industries Sidérurgiques Luxembourgeoises v High Authority* (1956)[16] is a clear illustration of this. The plaintiffs were manufacturers of steel and the main industrial consumers of coal in Luxembourg. They challenged the refusal of the High Authority to declare illegal a Luxembourg levy on coal for industrial use. The Luxembourg government intervened in the proceedings and argued that the plaintiffs' action was inadmissible on the ground that they were steel producers and the action was solely concerned with coal. But the Court held that the Treaty did not limit actions relating to coal undertakings and, since prima facie this levy was detrimental to the plaintiffs, their right of action could not be denied. In the EEC, on the other hand, the right of action is not limited to undertakings but is available to any individual or corporate body against either a decision directed to him or it or a decision which, although in the form of a regulation or a decision addressed to someone else is of direct and individual concern to him or it[17].

Certain points of principle concerning the locus standi of private parties to challenge acts in the context of the EEC are clear. The Treaty does not recognise an *actio popularis* but requires the party bringing the action to have sufficient legal interest in the issue. This is comparable to the notion of the person aggrieved in English administrative law[18] and to the French maxim *pas d'intérêt, pas*

---

13 The merits of this case have already been discussed in connection with the external relations of the Communities; see pp. 42, 43, above.
14 The novelty of this right of audience is fully justified by the fact that Community law applies directly to private parties.
15 E.g. ECSC Treaty, arts. 33 (2) and 80.
16 Cases 7 and 9/54: [1954–56] ECR 175.
17 EEC Treaty, art. 173 (2); also see Euratom Treaty, art. 146 (2).
18 See de Smith, S. A., *Judicial Review of Administrative Action* (4th edn 1980), p. 409 et seq.

*d'action*[19]. A right of action is admitted against three types of act: decisions addressed to the party bringing the action; decisions in the form of regulations addressed to other persons; and decisions addressed to other persons. In the last two cases the party bringing the action must be able to satisfy the Court that the decisions affect him directly and individually. Despite dicta in some cases in which a generous interpretation of these provisions has been suggested[20], the Court has tended to interpret them restrictively and the resulting case law has not yet evolved an entirely consistent line of authority.

Least difficulty arises where the act challenged is a decision expressly addressed to the private party bringing the action, such as in connection with the Community's rules on competition. In such cases there appears to be a conclusive presumption that the plaintiff has locus standi[1]. On the question whether a given act is a decision, particularly in the context of decisions in the form of regulations, the Court looks to the object and content of the act rather than to its form[2]. A distinction is drawn between acts which apply to a limited, identifiable number of designees and acts of a normative character which apply to categories of persons envisaged in the abstract and as a whole; the former are decisions, the latter regulations[3]. Thus the Court has held that a regulation relating to the manufacture of a particular product by a limited number of producers is nevertheless a regulation because of its objective, normative character[4]. Whereas a regulation which was only concerned with import licences which had been sought before that regulation was made was, in fact, a bundle of individual decisions[5].

---

**19** See Brown, L. N. and Garner, J. F., *French Administrative Law* (2nd edn 1973), pp. 86, 87.
**20** See Case 25/62: *Plaumann & Co v EEC Commission* [1963] ECR 95 at 106, 107; and Case 69/69: *S A Alcan Aluminium Raeren v EC Commission* [1970] ECR 385 at 393.
**1** E.g. Case 48-57/69: *Imperial Chemical Industries Ltd v EC Commission* [1972] ECR 619, [1972] CMLR 557; Case 6/72: *Europemballage Corpn and Continental Can Co Inc v EC Commission* [1973] ECR 215, [1973] CMLR 199, and Cases 6 and 7/73: *Istituto Chemioterapico Italiano SpA and Commercial Solvents Corpn v EC Commission* [1974] ECR 223, [1974] 1 CMLR 309.
**2** Cases 16-17, 19-22/62: *Confédération Nationale des Producteurs de Fruits et Légumes v EEC Council* [1962] ECR 471 at 478.
**3** Ibid. at 478, 479.
**4** Case 6/68: *Zuckerfabrik Watenstedt GmbH v EC Council* [1968] ECR 409, [1969] CMLR 26. Also see Case 123/77: *UNICME v EC Council* [1978] ECR 845 and Case 101/76: *Koninklijke Scholten Honig NV v EC Council and EC Commission* [1977] ECR 797.
**5** Cases 41-44/70: *N V International Fruit Co v EC Commission* [1971] ECR 411,

This distinction between regulations and decisions also impinges on the requirement that decisions addressed to other persons[6] must be of both direct and individual concern to the party bringing the action. The Court has tended to reverse the order of these two conditions as they are set out in the Treaty on the ground that if the applicant is not individually concerned by the decision, it becomes unnecessary to enquire whether he is directly concerned[7]. In *Plaumann & Co v Commission* (1964) the Court defined individual concern in the following terms: 'Persons other than those to whom a decision is addressed may only claim to be individually concerned if that decision affects them by reason of certain attributes which are peculiar to them or by reason of circumstances in which they are differentiated from all other persons and by virtue of these factors distinguishes them individually just as in the case of the person addressed[8].' In applying that definition the Court has declined to find individual concern where a decision is addressed to an abstractly defined category of persons even where in reality the decision only affects an ascertainable number of such persons[9]. Such a decision potentially affects an indeterminate number of persons. But where, on the other hand, at the time a decision is made the number of persons affected by it is already finitely determined, e.g. if the decision is retroactive or if it refers to certain persons by name, then those persons are individually concerned[10].

The Court's approach to the question of direct concern appears to depend on whether the party to whom the decision was addressed

---

[1975] 2 CMLR 515. Also see Case 138/79: *SA Roquette Frères v EC Council* [1980] ECR 3333.

6  'Other persons' includes member states; see Case 25/62: *Plaumann & Co v EC Commission* [1963] ECR 95. It may also include other private parties; see Case 26/76: *Metro-SB-Grossmärkte GmbH & Co KG v EC Commission* [1977] ECR 1875, [1978] 2 CMLR 1.

7  Case 25/62: *Plaumann & Co v EEC Commission* [1963] ECR 95 at 107.

8  Ibid.

9  E.g. Case 1/64: *Glucoséries Réunis v EEC Commission* [1964] ECR 413; Case 38/64: *Getreide-Import Gesellschaft v EEC Commission* [1965] ECR 203, [1965] CMLR 276; and Case 63–65/69: *Compagnie Française Commerciale et Financière SA v EC Commission* [1970] ECR 205, [1970] CMLR 369.

10  See Cases 106–107/63: *Alfred Toepfer and Getreide-Import Gesellschaft v EEC Commission* [1965] ECR 405, [1966] CMLR 111; Case 62/70: *Bock v EC Commission* [1971] ECR 897, [1972] CMLR 160; and Cases 41–44/70: *NV International Fruit Co v EC Commission* [1971] ECR 411, [1975] 2 CMLR 515; Cases 113, 118–121: *NTN et al v EC Council and EC Commission* [1979] ECR 1185, [1979] 2 CMLR 257.

had a discretion to implement it. If there was no discretion then, subject to the other criteria, the decision is of direct concern; if there was a discretion then it is not. In *Alfred Toepfer v EEC Commission* (1966)[11] the plaintiff's application for a licence to import maize was rejected by the German authorities on 1 October 1963, because of protective measures which they were taking under the terms of the EEC. Regulation No. 19. On the same day the German authorities notified the Commission of those measures which were subject to confirmation, amendment or rejection by the Commission within four days of notification. On 3 October the Commission made a decision authorising the German authorities to maintain the protective measures in force between 1 to 4 October inclusive. The plaintiffs challenged that decision. The Court of Justice held that they had the necessary *locus standi*. The decision concerned them directly because it was immediately enforceable and left no discretion with the German authorities; it concerned them individually because the number and identity of the persons affected was determined before 3 October.

There is clearly a close relationship between the notion of a decision as an act which determines what is to happen in a limited number of particular cases and the notions of direct and individual concern. In one case the Court apparently assumed that if an act affects persons directly and individually then that act is a decision[12]. The Court adopted this approach expressly in *UNICME v EC Council* (1978)[13] in which the annulment of a regulation was sought. This is possible at the suit of a private party only if the act in question is a decision in the form of a regulation. But the Court observed: 'It is unnecessary to consider whether the contested measure may be regarded as a regulation and it is sufficient to establish whether it is in fact of direct and individual concern to the applicants[14].'

On the question of the grounds of action all three Community treaties mention the same four grounds which are derived from French Administrative law, viz.

(i) lack of competence, or

(ii) infringement of an essential procedural requirement, or

11 Loc. cit. in previous note.
12 Case 100/74: *Société CAM SA v EC Commission* [1975] ECR 1393 at 1402, 1403.
13 Case 123/77: [1978] ECR 845.
14 Ibid at 851.

(iii) infringement of the Treaties or of any rules of law relating to their application, or

(iv) misuse of powers[15].

(i) Lack of competence, which is an approximation of the French *excès de pouvoir* or *incompétence*, is broadly comparable to the English doctrine of substantive ultra vires. 'Each institution,' in the words of article 4 of the EEC Treaty, 'shall act within the limits of the powers conferred upon it ...' Therefore, if a Community institution acts without authority that act may be declared void on the ground of lack of powers. Lack of competence covers situations in which the Communities have no power, or in which the Communities have power but it has been exercised by the wrong body. Thus in *Meroni v High Authority* (1958)[16] the plaintiff challenged certain levies imposed by the High Authority on the basis of decisions taken by subordinate bodies to whom the High Authority had purported to delegate certain powers. The Court held that those subordinate bodies lacked the power to take such decisions since the Treaty did not authorise the High Authority to delegate its decision-making power. Other areas in which questions of lack of competence have arisen are where an institution has claimed implied powers or the authority to extend its jurisdiction beyond the territorial limits of the Community. While the Court has acknowledged the existence of implied powers in relation to the EEC[17], there are clearly limits to such powers. If those limits should not be respected, a plea of lack of competence could be raised[18]. In the context of the Community's rules on competition[19], on several occasions the Commission has imposed penalties for breach on corporations based outside the Community. Pleas by such corporations that the Commission lacked competence to impose those penalties have so far failed. The Court has been satisfied that the penalties related to activities carried on within the Community[20].

**15** ECSC Treaty, art. 33; EEC Treaty, art. 173; Euratom Treaty, art. 146.
**16** Case 9/56: [1957–58] ECR 133.
**17** See Case 22/70: *EC Commission v EC Council* [1971] ECR 263, [1971] CMLR 335.
**18** Cf. Case 8/55: *Fédération Charbonnière de Belgique v High Authority* [1954–56] ECR 245.
**19** EEC Treaty, arts. 85–90.
**20** E.g., Case 48/69: *Imperial Chemical Industries v EC Commission* [1972] ECR 619, [1972] CMLR 557 and Cases 6–7/73: *Istituto Chemisterapico Italiano SpA and Commercial Solvents Corpn v EC Commission* [1974] ECR 223, [1974] 1 CMLR 309.

But here again there is clearly a limit to the Commission's authority which if exceeded would justify a plea of lack of competence.

(ii) Infringement of essential procedural requirements (*vice de forme*) also has an equivalent in English law, viz. procedural ultra vires. But, as in the case of both English and French administrative law, the Court of the Communities will not annul an act merely because some minor and unimportant procedural rule has not been observed; an action for annulment on this ground will only be granted when the procedural rule which has been infringed is an essential rule in the sense that it is substantial or basic. Such procedural requirements can be imposed either by the Treaties or by secondary legislation. An example of the former is provided by the case of *Germany v EEC Commission* (1963)[1]. Prior to the establishment of the EEC Germany used to import cheap wines for the production of 'Brennwein'. In 1961 it asked the Commission for a tariff quota of 450,000 hectolitres of wine for this purpose. The Commission granted a quota of only 100,000 hectolitres. Article 190 of the EEC Treaty requires that the Commission's decisions shall 'state the reasons on which they are based.' Germany challenged the partial rejection of its request on the ground that that decision was insufficiently reasoned. The Commission had merely said that its decision was based on 'information that has been gathered' which indicated 'that the production of wines of this nature within the Community is amply sufficient'. The Court agreed with the advocate-general that the Commission's decision should be annulled on the ground that it gave inadequate reasons and thus infringed an important procedural rule. The Court said 'In imposing upon the Commission the obligation to state reasons for its decisions, article 190 is not taking mere formal considerations into account but seeks to give an opportunity to the parties of defending their rights, to the Court of exercising its supervisory functions and to Member States and to all interested nationals of ascertaining the circumstances in which the Commission has applied the Treaty. To attain these objectives, it is sufficient for the decision to set out, in a concise but clear and relevant manner, the principal issues of law and of fact upon which it is based and which are necessary in order that the reasoning which has led the Commission to its decision may be understood[2].' This the Court held,

---

1 Case 24/62: [1963] ECR 63, [1963] CMLR 347. Also see Case 73/74: *Groupement des Fabricants de Papiers Peints de Belgique v EEC Commission* [1975] ECR 1491, [1976] 1 CMLR 589.
2 [1963] ECR at 69.

the Commission's vague statements failed to do[3]. In *Transocean Marine Paint Association v EC Commission* (1974)[4] the procedural requirement arose under a Regulation. In 1967 the plaintiff had been granted an exemption from applicability of the Community's rules on competition under the terms of article 85 (3) of the EEC Treaty. In 1972 the exemption came up for renewal. The Commission refused to renew it on the original terms and imposed additional conditions because of changes which had occurred in the competitive situation. The plaintiff found one of the additional conditions particularly onerous and sought its revocation on the ground that no notice was given of it nor any opportunity to comment. The Court held that the Regulation under which the Commission had acted incorporated 'the general rule that a person whose interests are perceptibly affected by a decision of a public authority must be given the opportunity to make his point of view known[5].' That obligation had not been fulfilled in this case and so the Commission's Decision was, to that extent, annulled.

(iii) Infringement of the Treaty or of any rule of law relating to its application is a ground broad enough to embrace the other three more specific grounds of challenge. Indeed, cases brought on any of those grounds could equally be brought under this. In practice however this general ground has by no means been superfluous. Its broad formulation has provided the juridical basis upon which the Court has developed the Community concept of legality beyond the terms of the Community Treaties and secondary legislation to general principles of law recognised by the member states. An illustration is provided by *August Töpfer & Co GmbH v EC Commission* (1978)[6]. The plaintiff held a number of export licences for sugar. In accordance with Community rules the amount of export refund he would receive in respect of such transactions was fixed in advance. In principle, if the value of such refunds changes as a result of currency fluctuations before the transaction is carried out, the licence holder may apply to have the licence cancelled. In this instance this basic scheme was varied by a Commission Regulation which withdrew the plaintiff's right of cancellation and substituted the payment of compensation. This was financially disadvantageous to the plaintiff and so he sought the annulment of the Regu-

---

3 A failure to consult the European Parliament when required so to do by the Treaty is also a violation of an essential procedural requirement; see Case 138/79: *SA Roquette Frères v EC Council* [1980] ECR 3333.
4 Case 17/74: [1974] ECR 1063, [1974] 2 CMLR 459.
5 Ibid at 1080.                                    6 Case 112/77: [1978] ECR 1019.

lation. He alleged that the Regulation breached a general principle of law, namely the principle of legitimate expectation. The plaintiff maintained that by the terms under which his export licences had been granted, he could expect either to receive the export refunds or be able to exercise his right of cancellation. Because of the Commission's intervention that expectation had not been realised. Although the Court dismissed the plaintiff's action on the merits, it did acknowledge expressly that the plaintiff's argument was one which it would entertain. 'The submission that there has been a breach of [the] principle [of legitimate expectation] is admissible in the context of proceedings instituted under article 173, since the principle in question forms part of the Community legal order with the result that any failure to comply with it is an "infringement of this Treaty or of any rule of law relating to its application" within the meaning of the article quoted'. It follows from this that the breach of any principle accepted by the Court as a general principle of Community law may be invoked as a ground for the annulment of a Community act. Such principles are regarded by the Court as forming an integral part of the legal order of the Community established by the Treaties.

(iv) Misuse of powers (*détournement de pouvoir*) provides the basis of an action for annulment when it can be shewn that a discretionary power has been used to achieve some object other than that for which the power was conferred. Thus proceedings for an action on this ground involve the Court in determining the object which the act in question was intended to achieve and then to decide whether that object comes within the purpose for which the power was conferred. As the advocate-general put it in *Fédération Charbonnière de Belgique v High Authority*[8] 'it is a matter of discovering what was the object in fact pursued by the author of the act, when he took the decision, in order to be able to compare it with the subject he ought to have pursued and which, unless the contrary is proved, he is deemed to have pursued'. The question is, therefore, whether the author of the act really had an illegal or legal object in view at the time he took the act. It is not necessary for an illegal objective to have been actually achieved, it is sufficient that the motive behind the act was illegal. Further, if an act achieves a legal object but also incidentally achieves other illegal objects that will not be a misuse of power, provided that the legal object is the dominant object. In

7 Ibid at 1033.
8 Case 8/55: [1954–56] ECR 245.

*France v High Authority* (1954)[9], for example, the High Authority, purporting to act under article 60 of the ECSC Treaty, made a number of decisions authorising steel enterprises to deviate from their published prices provided that such deviations did not constitute discrimination which is forbidden by the Treaty. The French Government challenged those decisions alleging that the High Authority had no power to achieve those particular aims under article 60 but should have acted under articles 61 and 65 for the real object of those decisions was to lower steel prices generally and prevent price agreement and this could only be done under those latter articles. Therefore it was asserted that by issuing those decisions under article 60 it had misused its powers. But the Court held that in fact there had been no misuse of powers, for even if those decisions had in fact been made to achieve an unjustified object the decisions would not be vitiated provided the essential object of the power was achieved. The Court held that was so in this case. Misuse of powers has a particular significance under the ECSC Treaty since it is the ground upon which coal and steel undertakings may challenge Community acts which are general in character[10]. In the other two Communities this ground has had little significance[11].

An action for annulment must be brought within limited periods of one month under the ECSC Treaty and two months under the EEC and Euratom Treaties[12]. These periods are necessarily short since the economic regime set up by the Treaties is a dynamic thing which it would be impossible to alter long after the event by actions against decisions taken. In the case of regulations, which must be published in the Official Journal, time begins to run from the fifteenth day after publication. In the case of directives and decisions, which do not have to be published but must be notified to their addressees, time runs from the day after the date of notification[13] or if there has been no notification from the day after the date upon which the decisions or directives came to the knowledge of the addressees[14].

In general the effect of an annulment is quite simply to declare the Community act in question to be void and this is the basic rule

---

9 Case 1/54: [1954–56] ECR 1.    10 ECSC Treaty, art. 33 (2).

11 But see Cases 18, 35/65: *Gutmann v EAEC Commission* [1966] ECR 103 and Case 105/75: *Guiffrida v EC Council* [1976] ECR 1395 concerned with the terms of appointment of Community officials.

12 ECSC Treaty, art. 33; EEC Treaty, art. 176; Euratom Treaty, art. 146.

13 Rules of Procedure of the Court, art. 81 (1).

14 See Case 6/72: *Europemballage Corpn and Continental Can Co Inc v EC Commission* [1973] ECR 215 at 241.

to be found in all three treaties[15]. In the ECSC the Commission is required to take steps to give effect to the annulment and to compensate for any loss suffered as a result of the annulled act. The EEC and Euratom Treaties simply require the institution whose act has been annulled to take the necessary steps to comply with the Court's judgment. Thus, subject to compensation under the ECSC Treaty, which in any event is awarded by the Commission, annulment has a purely negative effect. But the annulment may not affect the whole of the act against which an action has been brought. Article 174 of the EEC Treaty enables the Court to confirm particular parts of a regulation which it has otherwise annulled. Thus in a case in which a regulation concerned with the price of fruit and vegetables was challenged, the Court declared void that part of the regulation which related to tomatoes[16]. The EEC Treaty itself does not expressly extend this possibility of partial annulment to acts other than regulations, but nevertheless we find the Court in *Consten and Grundig v EEC Commission* (1966)[17] annulling a decision in part. In that case Consten and Grundig entered into a contract whereby Consten became the sole agent for the distribution of Grundig products in France. Other firms selling Grundig products in France complained to the Commission that this contract was contrary to article 85 of the EEC Treaty, which controls restrictive practices. The Commission issued a decision which stated that the contract did violate article 85. Consten and Grundig then brought these proceedings challenging the decision and the Court held that certain elements in the contract infringed the Treaty and certain others did not therefore the decision was partially annulled and partially upheld. This is an example of the flexible approach which the Court adopts towards the question whether a particular administrative act is a regulation or a decision. Indeed there would seem to be no reason in principle why a process of partial annulment should not be applied in appropriate cases to acts other than regulations *stricto senso*[18].

(ii) *Actions against inactivity (recours en carence)*—The second

---

**15** ECSC Treaty, art. 33; EEC Treaty, art. 174; Euratom Treaty, art. 147.
**16** Case 151/73: *Ireland v EC Council* [1974] ECR 285, [1974] 1 CMLR 429. In Case 138/79: *SA Roquette Frères v EC Council* [1980] ECR 3333 the Court declared an entire regulation void despite the fact that the private plaintiffs sought only its partial annulment and that they only had locus standi in respect of those parts of the regulation which concerned them directly and individually.
**17** Cases 56 and 58/64: [1966] ECR 299, [1966] CMLR 418.
**18** Also see Case 17/74: *Transocean Marine Paint Association v EC Commission* [1974] ECR 1063, [1974] 2 CMLR 459.

main category of actions concerning legality is the action against inactivity. Where the Treaties impose a duty to act on the Council or Commission and they fail to act then an action may be based on a violation of the Treaty through inactivity. The inactivity must first be brought to the attention of the institution concerned and if it has not taken satisfactory steps to remedy or justify its inactivity an action may be instituted[19]. Under the ECSC Treaty such actions may be brought against the Commission either by member states, or by the Council or by undertakings or associations of undertakings. Under the EEC and Euratom Treaties while the member states and the other Community institutions (including the European Parliament) have a general competence to challenge the inactivity of either Commission or Council, individuals and corporate bodies may only do so if they can shew that one of those institutions has failed to address an act (other than a recommendation or opinion[20]) to him or it[1]. An example of such an action under the ECSC Treaty is *Groupement des Industries Sidérurgiques Luxembourgeoises v High Authority* (1956)[2]. The Luxembourg Government imposed a levy on coal intended for industrial use for the purpose of subsidising the price of household coal. The plaintiffs, who were the main users of industrial coal, alleged that this levy was contrary to the ECSC Treaty and requested the High Authority to use its powers to require the Luxembourg Government to abolish the levy. During the two months following this request the High Authority did nothing and the plaintiffs brought an action under article 35 of the ECSC Treaty and the Court held that the action was admissible. Cases brought by private parties under the EEC Treaty show that an article 175 action will fail if the act sought is one which cannot be properly addressed to the plaintiff. In one case a complaint that the Commission had failed to issue a decision amending the rules concerning intra-Community trade was dismissed since the proper addressees of such a decision would have been the member states[3]. Similarly, where a plaintiff's claim could only be met by making a regulation the action was dismissed since a regulation cannot be described 'by reason either of its form or of its nature' as an act

---

**19** ECSC Treaty, art. 35; EEC Treaty, art. 175; Euratom Treaty, art. 148.
**20** See Case 6/70: *Borromeo Arese v EC Commission* [1970] ECR 815, [1970] CMLR 436.
**1** See Case 103/63: *Société Rhenania Schiffahrts-und Speditions-Gesellschaft mbH v EEC Commission* [1964] ECR 425 per Advocate-General Roemer at 431, 432.
**2** Cases 7 and 9/54: [1954–56] ECR 175.
**3** Case 15/71: *Firma C Mackprang, Jr v EC Commission* [1971] ECR 797, [1972] CMLR 52.

which could be addressed to the plaintiff[4]. An article 175 action will also fail if the allegedly defaulting institution has 'defined its position' within two months of being called upon to act. Thus in *Alfons Lütticke GmbH v EEC Commission* (1966)[5] the action was held to be inadmissible since within that two-month period the Commission had declared its position and had made clear its attitude to the matter in question. This clearly falls far short of compelling the performance of a specific act. The Court also distinguishes between a failure to act and a refusal to act. While the former prima facie comes within the scope of article 175, the latter does not since it is regarded as constituting a negative decision. A refusal by the Commission to revoke an allegedly illegal act has been held not to be actionable under article 175[6]. In the same way, if, when called upon to act, the Commission adopts a measure other than that sought by the plaintiff the action will fail[7]. In such cases the appropriate remedy is to seek the annulment of the act in question under the terms of article 173.

(iii) *The defence of illegality (l'exception d'illégalité)*—We have seen that a restrictive period of limitation is applied to actions for annulment with the general result that if an act is not challenged within that period the act becomes unassailable. But a situation may arise in an action before the Court under some Treaty article other than that which provides for actions for annulment in which the illegality of an unchallenged act may be in issue. If the period of limitation were to be applied strictly such an issue could not be raised outside the period, but to overcome such a possible result all three Treaties make it possible for such a question of illegality to be raised in such proceedings[8]; this again is a form of procedure known to French law. Under the ECSC Treaty both types of binding act, namely decisions and recommendations, may be challenged by this procedure. But under the EEC and Euratom Treaties only regulations are open to challenge. This provision can only be relied upon as a defence; it does not of itself give rise to an independent cause of action[9]. If such a defence of illegality is successfully

---

4 Case 90/78: *Granaria BV v EC Council and Commission* [1979] ECR 1081 at 1093.
  5 Case 48/65: [1966] ECR 19, [1966] CMLR 378.
6 Cases 10 and 18/68: *Società 'Eridania' Zuccherifici Nazionali v EC Commission* [1969] ECR 459.
7 Case 8/71: *Deutscher Komponistenverband eV v EC Commission* [1971] ECR 705, [1973] CMLR 902.
8 ECSC Treaty, art. 36; EEC Treaty, art. 184; Euratom Treaty, art. 156.
9 Cases 31 and 33/62: *Milchwerke Heinz Wöhrmann and Sohn KG v EEC Commission* [1962] ECR 501, [1963] CMLR 152.

pleaded its technical effect will not be to declare the act in question illegal in terms of its general application but only in so far as it applies to the plaintiff. This is made clear by the case law. In *Meroni & Co v High Authority* (1958)[10] the High Authority requested Meroni to pay a levy on the authority of earlier decisions of a general nature which it had taken. Meroni declined to pay and challenged the High Authority's request on the ground that the general decisions on which it was based were illegal. The High Authority argued that such a plea was inadmissible since the time limit for the challenge of those decisions had expired. The question therefore arose whether Meroni could rely on the defence of illegality. The Court held that he could and in its judgment considered the nature of this defence: 'An applicant's right, after the expiration of the period prescribed [for actions for annulment] ..., to take advantage of the irregularity of general decisions or recommendations in support of proceedings against decisions or recommendations which are individual in character cannot lead to the annulment of the general decision, but only to the annulment of the individual decision which is based on it[11]'. In view of the limited right which individual and corporate bodies have to sue for the annulment of general decisions this defence of illegality is important since it widens the legal protection of such parties.

It does not immediately appear from the wording of article 184 of the EEC Treaty in what precise context the illegality of a regulation may be pleaded. When attempts were made to use this procedure to challenge regulations directly and in isolation, the Court elaborated on the view which it had earlier expressed in the *Meroni* case[12] and made it clear that a regulation may only be challenged by virtue of article 184 when it provides the legal basis of an act which is the primary objective of the action. For example, in *Italy v EEC Council and EEC Commission* (1966)[13] the primary objective of the action was to challenge a 1965 regulation. In addition the Italian Government invoked article 184 and asked that two 1962 regulations be declared inapplicable. The action was dismissed on the ground that the 1962 regulations did not provide the legal basis of the 1965 regulation, so that if the former were declared inapplicable they would in no way affect the authority of the latter. The Court

10 Case 9/56: [1957–58] ECR 133.
11 Ibid at 140.
12 Case 9/56: [1957–58] ECR 133.
13 Case 32/65: [1966] ECR 389.

said that the intention of article 184 'is not to allow a party to contest at will the applicability of any regulation in support of an application. The regulation of which the legality is called in question must be applicable, directly or indirectly, to the issue with which the application is concerned[14]'. Another uncertainty concerns the meaning of 'regulation' in relation to article 184; is the defence of illegality available in respect of a Community act which is not a regulation in form but is in substance a general act which determines rights and obligations objectively and in advance? Consistent with its approach to the distinction between general and individual acts, the Court has held that an act which is general in substance but not in form shall be treated as a regulation for the purposes of article 184[15].

Article 184 of the EEC Treaty refers to 'any party' being able to plead this defence and the question has been raised whether this expression includes Community institutions and member states as well as individuals and corporate bodies. As far as Community institutions are concerned it is generally agreed that the defence is not available on both legal and practical grounds. In the first place the defence is designed to protect the private interests of a party which may be affected by an illegal general act, but a Community institution has no private interests only a share in the general interests of the Communities. Further, Community institutions have no restrictions on their right to challenge a general act and so, unlike the case of individuals and corporate bodies, there is no reason to extend the period of limitation in this way. Secondly, it is difficult to envisage in practice a situation in which, say, the Council would direct an individual decision to the Commission requiring it to respect a Council regulation. As far as member states are concerned there are also reasons in principle why the defence should not be available. Member states, as in the case of institutions, have no restrictions on their competence to challenge acts provided they do so within the period of limitation and so in their case also there would appear to be no reason to make the defence of illegality available. Secondly, the member states wield political influence over Community acts through the Council and this influence plus the general right of challenge should give ample protection to their interests[16].

14 Ibid at 409.
15 See Case 92/78: *Simmenthal SpA v EC Commission* [1979] ECR 777 at 800.
16 See Bebr, op cit., pp. 141 et seq.

For some time it was believed that the Court supported the view that member states could plead the defence of illegality. In *Italy v EEC Council and EEC Commission* (1966)[17] the Italian Government had relied on article 184 and although, as we have seen, the plea was dismissed the Court did not question its admissibility. But in the light of a more recent case, the better view probably is that article 184 is only available to private parties. In an enforcement action brought by the Commission against Belgium under article 93 (2) of the EEC Treaty[18], Belgium maintained that the decision which had been addressed to it under that article had no legal basis. The legality of the decision had not been challenged under article 173, but on analogy with article 184 Belgium pleaded the illegality of that decision. The action could have been disposed of on the sole ground that the act in issue was an individual decision, but the Court considered the case on a broader basis. It referred to the right which Belgium had to challenge the decision under article 173 and to the period of limitation in that article being intended to safeguard legal certainty. It then observed: 'it is impossible for a Member State which has allowed the strict time limit laid down ... in article 173 to expire without contesting by the means available under that article the legality of the Commission decision addressed to it, to be able to call in question that decision by means of article 184 of the Treaty[19].' While the Court addressed itself expressly to the individual decision in issue, its reasoning is equally applicable to any act, including a regulation, which a Member State could have challenged under article 173. This would certainly be in keeping with the Court's own view that the purpose of article 184 is 'to provide those persons who are precluded ... from instituting proceedings directly in respect of general acts, with the benefit of a judicial review of them at the time when they are affected by implementing decisions which are of direct and individual concern to them[20].'

(b) *Plenary jurisdiction (pleine juridiction)*
In addition to its jurisdiction to declare actions of Community institutions to be null and void the Court has a plenary jurisdiction in certain cases. This enables the Court in those instances to go into the merits of the parties' cases and to substitute its own judgments

17 Case 32/65: [1966] ECR 389, [1969] CMLR 39.
18 Case 156/77: [1978] ECR 1881.
19 Ibid at 1896.
20 Case 92/78: *Simmenthal SpA v EC Commission* [1979] ECR 777 at 800.

for those of the Communities' institutions. We have in fact already dealt with one example of this plenary jurisdiction in connection with violations of the Treaties by member states. In addition there are three other instances of plenary jurisdiction.

In general the liability of the Communities in contract falls under the jurisdiction of municipal courts, unless in accordance with article 181 of the EEC Treaty the contracting parties agree to the contrary[1]. Article 183 of the EEC Treaty provides that, subject to the powers of the Court of Justice, there is nothing to prevent a case to which the Community is a party from being determined by the domestic courts of the member states[2]. But jurisdiction over non-contractual (tortious) liability on the other hand has been conferred upon the Court of the Communities. Under article 34 of the ECSC Treaty an action for damages will lie where the Commission fails to comply within a reasonable time with a judgment declaring a decision or recommendation to be void. Article 40 of the ECSC Treaty provides for liability for wrongful administrative acts in terms that an action will lie in respect of damage resulting from acts or omissions on the part of the Community or its servants. The EEC and Euratom Treaties do not expressly distinguish between legislative and administrative wrongdoing as grounds for seeking damages. Articles 178/215 and 151/188 respectively provide generally for non-contractual liability in the context of damage caused by the institutions or servants of the Communities in the performance of their duties in accordance with the general principles common to the laws of the member states.

Under all three Treaties the extent of this non-contractual liability is in practice in terms of the distinction known to French law as that between *faute de service* and *faute personnelle*[3]. *A faute de service* occurs where damage results from the malfunctioning of Community institutions or Community servants; there is said to be a *faute personnelle* when the damage results from some personal wrongdoing on the part of a Community official which is in no way linked with his official position. In the case of a *faute de service* the Communities are liable; in the case of a *faute personnelle* the individual wrongdoer alone is personally liable. This distinction is comparable, although not identical, with the distinction well known

1 Euratom Treaty, art. 153 is to the same effect; see Case 23/76: *Pellegrini and CSas v EC Commission* [1976] ECR 1807, [1977] 2 CMLR 77.
2 Also see ECSC Treaty, art. 40 (3) and Euratom Treaty, art. 155.
3 See Brown, L. N., and Garner, J. F., op. cit., p. 99 et seq.

to English law between a servant acting in the course of his employment and a servant on a frolic of his own. The non-contractual liability of the Community is that of a public authority. It is not liable for what may be termed ordinary torts committed in the course of Community activities, but only in respect of wrongs arising out of activities which form a necessary part of its official activities as defined in the treaties, i.e. the legislative and administrative acts of the Institutions and their officials. In accordance with this view, the Community was not held liable for injuries resulting from a road accident caused by a Euratom engineer who was driving his own car in the course of his work: 'the Community is only liable for those acts ... which ... are the necessary extension of the tasks entrusted to the institutions[4].' Within those limits actual liability under the EEC Treaty is in accordance with the general principles common to the laws of the member states. This involves the Court in a comparative study of the relevant national laws in order to pick out the decisive elements which may reflect a trend. National law is not analysed in order to produce a principle acknowledged by all the member states. Such an exercise would be unlikely to produce a workable legal principle. The aim is to identify trends generally, but not necessarily universally, recognised and to use them as the juridical basis for the development of particular rules of Community liability[5].

The relationship between the action for damages and the actions for annulment and inactivity has caused the Court some difficulty. When first confronted with this question the Court expressed the view that the action for damages was quite distinct both by reason of its object and the grounds upon which it can be brought[6]. But when, later, an action for damages arose out of an allegedly unlawful act which had not been annulled, the Court changed its mind and held that 'An administrative measure which has not been annulled cannot of itself constitute a wrongful act on the part of the administration inflicting damage upon those whom it affects. The latter cannot therefore claim damages by reason of that measure[7].' More recently, against the background of strong criticism[8], the Court has

4 Case 9/69: *Sayag v Leduc* [1969] ECR 329 at 336.
5 Ibid at 340, per Advocate-General Gand.
6 Cases 9 and 12/60: *Société Commerciale Antoine Vloeberghs SA v High Authority of the EEC* [1961] ECR 197.
7 Case 25/61: *Plaumann & Co v EEC Commission* [1963] ECR 95 at 108.
8 E.g. Advocate General Roemer's submissions in Case 5/71: *Aktien-Zuckerfabrik Schöppenstedt v EC Council* [1971] ECR 975 at 990 et seq.

reverted to its original view. In *Alfons Lütticke GmbH v EC Commission* (1971)[9] it observed that the action for damages is an independent action having its own special purpose and subject to conditions which were designed for that purpose. It would be contrary to the independence of this right of action if its exercise was made subject to other Treaty provisions designed for different purposes. This view has been reiterated in a series of subsequent cases which appears now to represent the *jurisprudence constante* of the Court[10]. Where an action for damages is brought in respect of an illegal legislative act the Community will only be liable if the individual plaintiff can prove that there has been a sufficiently serious breach of a superior rule of law protecting him[11]. Such a rule could be either a rule in the Treaty such as the prohibition on discrimination[12] or one of the unwritten rules of Community law, such as the principle of legitimate expectation, which the Court draws from the rules of the constitutions of the member states which are designed to protect individual rights[13]. The plaintiff in an action for damages must, of course, establish a causal connection between the injury and the act or omission on the part of the Community and the quantum of damages must be ascertainable and not speculative[14].

The Court's plenary jurisdiction also extends to the settlement of disputes between the Communities and their employees over contracts of employment. The terms of service are set out in the Communities' Staff Regulations, and article 179 of the EEC Treaty, for example, provides that the Court shall be competent to adjudicate in any dispute between the Community and its servants within the limits and under the conditions laid down by their service

---

9 Case 4/69: [1971] ECR 325.
10 See Case 5/71: *Aktien-Zuckerfabrik Schöppenstedt v EC Council* [1971] ECR 975; Cases 9 and 11/71: *Compagnie d'Approvisionnement de Transport et de Crédit SA and Grands Moulins de Paris SA v EC Commission* [1972] ECR 391, [1973] CMLR 529; Case 43/72: *Merkur Aussenhandels GmbH v EC Commission* [1973] ECR 1055.
11 E.g. Case 153/73: *Firma Holtz and Willemsen v EC Council and EC Commission* [1974] ECR 675 at 692 and Cases 83 and 94/76, 4, 15 and 40/77: *Bayerische HNL Vermehrungsbetriebe GmbH & Co KG v EC Council and Commission* [1978] ECR 1209 at 1224.
12 E.g. Cases 44–51/77: *Groupement d'Intérêt Economique 'Union Malt' v EC Commission* [1978] ECR 57, [1978] 3 CMLR 702.
13 See E.g. Case 74/74: *Comptoir National Technique Agricole SA v EC Commission* [1975] ECR 533.
14 See Cases 5, 7 and 13–24/66: *Firma E Kampffmeyer v EEC Commission* [1967] ECR 245 and Case 30/66: *Kurt A Becher v EC Commission* [1967] ECR 285, [1968] CMLR 169.

regulations or conditions of employment. Actions concerning contracts of service cannot be lodged directly with the Court of Justice. Claims must first be made to the appointing body via an hierarchial administrative process. If the dispute is not resolved by this process then a right of appeal lies to the Court of Justice which has the power to consider the dispute in its entirety and to settle it by its judgment. This is a fairly fertile source of litigation before the Court but it is somewhat specialist and it is neither appropriate nor practicable to discuss it in the present context[15].

Lastly the court has plenary jurisdiction to hear appeals against fines and other pecuniary penalties. The Court not only has jurisdiction to quash a penalty of this sort but it may also lower or increase this penalty when in the Court's view it is either unacceptable or inappropriate[16]. An example is provided by article 17 of Regulation 17 which authorises appeals against fines and periodic penalty payments imposed by the Commission for breaches of the Community's rules on competition[17].

**15** For further information, see Brown & Jacobs, op. cit., chapter 8.
**16** ECSC Treaty, art. 36 (2); EEC Treaty, art. 172; Euratom Treaty, art. 144.
**17** E.g. Case 45/69: *ACF Chemiefarma NV v EC Commission* [1970] ECR 661 and Case 7/72: *Boehringer Mannheim GmbH v EC Commission* [1972] ECR 1281, [1973] CMLR 864.

Part III

# The relationship between Community law and the Municipal law of the Member States

## Chapter 10

# Implementation of Community law in the legal systems of the Member States

## I INTRODUCTION

The most intricate and complex aspect of Community law is its relationship to the municipal law of the Member States. Conceptually Community law, like public international law, feeds upon the internal law of states but once emancipated and worked into a system Community law emerges as a different, quasi-autonomous body of law.

Volumes have been written on the subject from a theoretical and practical point of view not only because the growth of the Community law is symptomatic of the growth of the Community but also because of the theoretical and practical consequences of conflicts between Community law and the municipal law of the member states. To a British student of Community law the matter is of a particular interest as an empirical experience of the Six and as a pointer to the likely impact of Community law in the United Kingdom.

At a theoretical level the starting point of a discussion on the relationship between Community law and the municipal law of the member states, that is between an 'external' and an 'internal' system of law, is the doctrine of sovereignty; at a practical level it is the Treaty obligation and the resulting status of Community law in the territory of the member states.

Sovereignty is a conceptual chameleon: it can be seen in different colours and be described in different ways. In classic terms Jean Bodin (1530–96) wrote that 'it is the distinguishing mark of the sovereign that he cannot in any way be subject to the commands of another, for it is he who makes Law for the subject, abrogates Law already made, and amends obsolete Law. No one who is subject either to the Law or to some other person can do this. That is why it is laid down in the civil Law that the prince is above the Law, for the word *Law* in Latin implies command of him who is invested with sovereign power . . .¹' For the purpose of our discussion sovereignty may be described in positive terms as the oneness of the legal system within the territory of a state. Oneness does not exclude plurality of laws within the system (as is, e.g., the case in the United Kingdom or the USA) but implies one supreme source of law embodied in the constitution of the state; in other words the jurisdiction over the territory is in the hands of one authority (e.g. government in Parliament) which is supreme. In negative terms sovereignty means a system of law and administration of justice which is free from outside interference. Proceeding from the assumption of the oneness of the legal system the member states of the Community are not entirely sovereign for, by Treaty, they have delegated a portion of their law-making power to an external authority (the Community) and at the same time consented to abide by the law so made. In the field of the administration of justice they recognise the authority of the Community Court over matters and persons in their territory falling within the jurisdiction of that Court and also consent to their municipal courts taking judicial cognisance of Community law. In theory, therefore, as long as the state remains a member of the Community there should be no conflict between the municipal (internal) law of the member states and the Community (external) law because the latter becomes part of the former. In fact, however, conflicts do arise and this raises the question of the supremacy of the one over the other. Reduced to a practical level sovereignty means the ultimate authority in respect of a particular matter and raises the question whether the Community or the state law governs a particular situation.

Another digression into the theory of relations between external and internal law leads us to the consideration of two rival doctrines dualism (parallelism) and monism² which purport to explain the basis of legal obligation. According to the positivist philosophy of law, the relationship between the law of a sovereign state and the law of mankind, reflected in the law generated by agreements between states, has been expressed in the dualist (parallelist) doctrine. In simple terms this doctrine presupposes the existence of two separate systems of law: international and national, co-existing side by side as it were in watertight compartments. Though international law is the universal law of mankind it stops at the door of

---

1 *Six Books of the Commonwealth*, Book I, Chapter 8.
2 Starke, J. G., 'Monism and Dualism in the Theory of International Law' (1936) 17 BYBIL 66.

the sovereign state and remains outside unless admitted to the territory of the state. It means that international law binds states in their relations with each other but has, subject to few exceptions, no binding force in the territory of the state unless transformed or translated into rules of municipal law. This doctrine, favouring sovereignty, is still the reigning theory and the United Kingdom is among its adherents.

Monism is the rival doctrine propounding the existence of a single system of norms or legal rules binding states and individuals alike. States are, after all, nothing but forms of organisation or legal fictions whilst the individual is the ultimate subject of law. Both international and municipal law are only parts of the same structure and their rules are interrelated. Consequently monism cuts across sovereignty bringing the individual face to face with international law and relieving the state of the task of transforming it into rules of domestic law. The origins of monism can be traced to the medieval concept of the unity of law as Natural Law was considered to be a reflection of the wisdom of God through the reason of man. It ceased to be fashionable when the theory of Natural Law was superseded by the theory of Positive Law. The 20th century revival of the monist doctrine in its positivist rather than naturalist garb is a reaction against the 19th century apotheosis of the sovereign state degenerating into nationalism which saw international law solely as a product of the 'will' of states.

The legal concept of the European Community reflects a monist approach. Therefore, to understand the relationship between the Community law and the law of the member states it is unhelpful to think in terms of sovereignty (nationalism) versus internationalism. We have to formulate instead a functional approach which in practical terms reconciles the need of a Community law with the aspiration of states to be supreme within their territories. Once this is appreciated the question of the supremacy of one system or the other resolves itself into a division of labour or functions of the respective bodies of rules within a unitary concept of law. Within its respective sphere each system is supreme as stated by the Community Court[3]:

'... The Community is founded on a common market, common objectives, and common institutions ... Within the specific domain of the Community, i.e. for everything which relates to the pursuit of the

3 Case 30/59: *De Gezamenlijke Steenkolenmijnen in Limburg v High Authority of the ECSC* [1961] ECR 1.

common objectives within the common market the institutions [of the Community] are provided with exclusive authority ... Outside the domain of the Community, the governments of the Member States retain their responsibilities in all sectors of economic policy ... They remain masters of their social policy; the same undoubtedly holds true for large segments of their fiscal policy ...'

Ten years later, in the ERTA Case which was, inter alia, concerned with the treaty-making power of the Community and the member states the Court held that

'... By the terms of article 5, the member states are required on the one hand to take all appropriate steps to ensure the carrying out of the obligations arising out of the Treaty ... and on the other hand to abstain from any steps likely to jeopardise the attainment of the purposes of the Treaty. If these two provisions are read in conjunction, it follows that to the extent that Community rules are promulgated for the attainment of the purposes of the Treaty, the member states cannot, outside the framework of the Community institutions assume obligations likely to affect such rules or alter their scope ...'[4]

These two dicta delimit the respective spheres of the Community and the member states both in the 'internal' and 'external' aspect of sovereignty.

Let us turn now to the foundation Treaties, especially the EEC Treaty, which is a unique treaty. It cannot be compared with traditional international treaties which set out the obligations of the parties and, in most cases, leave the implementation and enforcement of the obligations to the forces which make international law effective. It is a self-executing treaty. The EEC is, by the will of the founding states, a separate legal entity, a new subject of law and, although it takes life from the agreement of states, it has a quasi-independent existence. Being a subject of law it enjoys the treaty-making power and the power of diplomatic representation but, above all, it has its own institutions and a law making power. Community law is therefore an autonomous legal order binding not only the member states but also their citizens directly and immediately.

The EEC Treaty itself has a legal framework—actually two such frameworks—the constitutional framework which we have already analysed and the economic framework which we shall consider later on. What we must discuss now is the impact of the Treaty and the

4 Case 22/70: *EC Commission v EC Council* [1971] ECR 263 at 275, [1971] CMLR 335 at 355; at paras. 21 and 22; see also Case 1/75: *Re the OECD Understanding on a Local Cost Standard* [1975] ECR 1355, [1976] CMLR 85.

Community legislation on the legal systems of the member states. In doing so we should bear in mind[5] that '... the Community constitutes a new legal order of international law, in favour of which the States within certain areas have limited their sovereign rights ...' because it reflects the difficulties inherent in the 'dualist' thinking which has so far dominated the European legal scene. Indeed some of the constitutions of the member states had to be amended in order to ease the process of assimilation of international obligations inherent in the Community Treaties into the law of the land. In this respect the United Kingdom is not in a unique position.

## II CONSTITUTIONS OF THE MEMBER STATES AND TREATY OBLIGATIONS

The admission of external law to the territory of a state raises a constitutional problem of transmission, on the one hand, and supremacy in the case of a conflict with municipal law, on the other. A further problem, as far as the civil law countries are concerned, arises from the internal relationship between the constitution and the ordinary law of the land. The constitution, as the basic law of the land, consists not only of the rules which organise the political framework of the state but also of the general principles on which rests the whole edifice of law and order. It follows that there is a hierarchy of legal norms or in Pound's rather inelegant phrase, 'authoritative starting points for legal reasoning[6]' which, in the event of a conflict with external law, raises the question whether external law is superior/subordinate to the law of the Constitution and the ordinary law of the land alike or whether the hierarchy of legal norms will affect the issue.

In view of the diversity of the legal systems involved it seems necessary to investigate the position in each member state.

### (a) *Ratification of the EEC Treaty*
According to the constitutions of the original six member states treaties are made and ratified by the Head of State[7]. However in

---

5 Case 26/62: *NV Algemene Transport- en Expeditie Onderneming van Gend en Loos v Nederlandse Tariefcommissie* [1963] ECR 1 at 12, [1963] CMLR 105 at 129; see also Case 6/64: *Costa v ENEL* [1964] ECR 585 at 594, [1964] CMLR 425 at 456.
6 Pound, R., 'Hierarchy of Sources and Forms in Different Systems of Law' [1933] *Tulane Law Review* 475 at 483.
7 Belgium, art. 68; France (Constitution of 1946 which was in force at that time), art. 31, Constitution of 1958, art. 52; Federal Republic of Germany, art. 59; Italy, art. 80; Luxembourg, art. 37; The Netherlands, art. 50.

the case of especially important treaties these Constitutions require a parliamentary approval in the form of either a resolution or a special law. In France, Italy, Germany and the Netherlands a special Act enabling the Head of State to ratify and thus commit the country internationally was necessary[8]. Accordingly these laws were passed during 1957[9]. The position in Belgium and Luxembourg is somewhat different. The effect of the law passed by reference to article 37 (1) of the Constitution of Luxembourg, which enables the Grand Duke to conclude treaties, is to exercise parliamentary control over the acts of the executive[10]. The interpretation of the Belgian Constitution is subject to controversy as to the role of Parliament in this matter[11] but Parliament approved the Treaty by the Law of 22 December 1957 and so according to custom the Treaty may 'sortir son plein et entier effet[12]'.

In the United Kingdom treaties are made and ratified by the Crown[13] so much so that the battle about the membership of the Community was fought in the political arena of the House of Commons rather than the courts of law. Formally the Treaty obligations were implemented by the European Communities Act 1972, which has the effect of both a 'constitutional' and an 'ordinary' law. In Eire treaties are made by the government and ratified by *Dail Eireann*[14]. However in order to enable the country to accede to the Communities a bill was passed by the *Oireachtas* in 1971 adding subsection 3 to article 29.4 of the Constitution and a Referendum was held in 1972. According to the Danish Constitution of 1953 (article 19) the Monarch acts in international affairs on behalf of the Kingdom but without the consent of the *Folketing* cannot commit the country to any obligations of importance or for which parliamentary approval is necessary. Therefore in practice treaties are negotiated and ratified by the Executive subject to parliamentary approval. Accession to the Communities was approved by the *Folketing* and a referendum held in 1972. Attempts to have the

---

8 France, art. 27; Italy, art. 80; Germany, art. 59 (2); the Netherlands, art. 60.

9 France, 8 August 1957, Germany, 27 July 1957, Italy, 14 October 1957, the Netherlands, 5 December 1957.

10 Law of 30 November 1957; Pescatore, P., *Introduction à la Science du Droit* (1960), pp. 170 and 175.

11 Constantinides-Mégret, C., *Le Droit de la Communauté Economique Européenne et l'Ordre Juridique des Etats Membres* (1967), pp. 14–15.

12 Constantinides-Mégret, op. cit., p. 15.

13 *Blackburn v A-G* [1971] 1 WLR 1037 (see Lord Denning MR at 1040). Also see Chapter 12 below.

14 Constitution of 1948, arts. 28 and 29.

procedures leading to the accession declared unconstitutional[15] and the 'signatures on the treasonable document declared void and unauthorised whereby our Queen may be saved from the biggest swindle in the history of Denmark[16]' were dismissed by the courts on the ground that the Head of State could not be held to account before her courts. In Greece too treaties are negotiated by the Executive subject to parliamentary approval[17].

## (b) *Incorporation of the Treaty into municipal law*

The method of incorporation depends on whether a country follows the monist or the dualist doctrine. Among the Six, France and Italy represent the two extremes: the former is monist the latter is dualist, whilst the remaining four occupy a middle position with a distinct dualist leaning. Denmark, Eire, Greece and the United Kingdom fall into the dualist category.

The French Republic started with a dualist posture but by article 26 of the Constitution of 1946 reversed the tradition and turned monist. Article 26 provided that Treaties duly ratified by the Head of State and published have the force of law even if they are inconsistent with French law 'without there being any need to resorting to any legislative measures other than those necessary to secure ratification'. The Constitution of 1958, now in force, not only adopted the position but article 55, as if to confirm the supremacy of Community law, provided that Treaties or Agreements ratified or approved 'have an authority superior to that of laws'. It follows that Treaties are not subject to transformation into the rules of French municipal law but take their place automatically by virtue of the Constitution in the internal legal order, subject to reciprocity and the sovereign will of the French people. However in the case of the EEC Treaty the condition of reciprocity is satisfied in the light of article 170 which contains Community remedies to enforce it[18].

The Italian Constitution of 1948 contains no reference to the incorporation of treaties into Italian law. Article 11 permits a delegation of sovereignty to international organisations but fails to

---

**15** *Tegen v Prime Minister of Denmark* [1973] CMLR 1.
**16** *Aggergren v The Queen and Prime Minister* [1973] CMLR 5.
**17** Act No. 945 (Official Gazette Part I. No. 170 of 27 July 1979, Roucounas, E., 'Pour le dialogue entre droit communautaire et droit grec' (1980) *Rev Hellenique de Droit International* 11 at 15.
**18** *Administration des Douanes v Société Cafés Jacques Vabre et J Weiget et Compagnie Sarl, Cour de Cassation* [1975] CMLR 336, 13 CMLR Rev 128–32.

deal with the problem of treaties. Accordingly a practice has been established in accordance with the hierarchy of legal rules: if the treaty affects a law the execution of the treaty takes the form of a law, if it affects merely administrative rules a decree of the Executive will take care of the situation. Reflecting this formula the law of ratification of the two Treaties of Rome passed on 14 October 1957 provided in article 2 that 'the agreements specified in article 1 will receive full and complete execution'. In this way the act of ratification became the act of execution or incorporation of the Treaties into Italian law. The consequences, as far as supremacy is concerned, are quite significant because, being equal to an internal legislative act, the Treaty, in principle, assumes no higher or lower rank than the corresponding piece of Italian legislation. Conflicts with domestic law are implicitly avoided in accordance with the principle that *lex posterior derogat priori*[19]. In practice, as we shall see later, difficulties arise.

In Germany, the general view is that the act of ratification signifies not only the approval of the Treaty but also incorporation[20]. Article 24 of the Federal Constitution provides for the transfer of sovereign powers to intergovernmental institutions. Article 25, on the other hand, provides that the 'general rules of international law shall form part of federal law; they shall take precedence over the laws and create rights and duties directly applicable to the inhabitants of the territory of the federation'. This has been interpreted restrictively to include the general customary rules of international law but to exclude the conventional rules[1]. It follows that international treaties have the force of a federal law, that is, ordinary *law*, not constitutional law. Being no more than *law* in the hierarchy of legal rules they can derogate from a preceding federal law or the law of the *Länder* but cannot override a constitutional rule of the Federation of (presumably) the *Länder*. This was at the heart of the controversy over the alleged breach of the German *Grundgesetz* by Commission Regulations instituting a system of forfeitable export/

---

19 Cf. the decision of the Italian Constitutional Court of 7 March 1964 in *Costa v ENEL* [1964] CMLR 425 at 456; *Frontini v Ministero delle Finanze* No. 183/1973 [1974] 2 CMLR 372, Const. Court.

20 Seidl-Hohenveldern, I., 'Transformation or Adoption of International into Municipal Law' (1963) 12 ICLQ, p. 101 et seq.

1 Bebr, G., 'Law of the European Communities and Municipal Law' (1971) 34 MLR 481 at 487 quoting Mangeldt-Klein, *Das Bonner Grundgesetz* (1957) 675–677; Carstens, 'Der Rang europäischer Verordnungen gegenüber deutschen Rechtsnormen', *Festschrift für Otto Riese* (1964) 65, 75.

import deposits. On that occasion[2] the Bundesverfassungsgericht held that: '. . . Article 24 does not actually give authority to transfer sovereign rights, but opens up the national legal system (within the limitations indicated) in such a way that the Federal Republic of Germany's exclusive claim to rule is taken back in the sphere of validity of the Constitution and room is given, within the State's sphere of rule, to the direct effect and applicability of law from another source.'

According to a recent amendment of the Constitution of Belgium[3] article 25 bis provides that 'the exercise of powers may be conferred by a Treaty or by Law on institutions of Public International Law'. This formula resembles the delegation of powers under the Italian Constitution and certainly confirms the dualist approach to treaties which are denied the authority of superior law. Amidst the discussions[4] on the relations between the constitution and Treaty law the Belgian Cour de Cassation struck a valiant blow for the recognition of the supremacy of the Treaty law in the judgment of 27 May 1971[5]. The Constitution of Luxembourg was amended in a similar way, article 49 bis providing for a delegation of legislative and administrative powers to international organisations[6].

The effect of the delegation of sovereignty in these three constitutions seems to provide room for the recognition of the binding force of the Community Law enshrined in treaties whilst retaining at the same time the sovereignty of parliament. It now remains to be seen whether the formula is sufficiently wide to read into it the supremacy of Community Law necessary for the functioning of the Community as a supranational organisation.

To meet this situation the amendment of the constitution of the Netherlands of 1956[7] provided that international treaties and agree-

---

2 Cases 166/73 and 146/73 *Internationale Handelsgesellschaft mbH v Einfuhr- und Vorratsstelle für Getreide und Futtermittel* [1974] CMLR 540. Majority decision of Federal Constitutional Court of 29 May, 1974.
3 Law of 18 August 1970; Louis, J. V., 'L'article 25 bis de la constitution belge' [1970] *Rev du Marché Commun* 136, 410–416.
4 Ganshof van der Meersch, W. J., 'Le juge belge à l'heure du droit international et du droit communautaire' (1969), 84 *Journal des Tribunaux* 4671, 537–551; Waelbroeck, M. in Donner, A. M., et al., *Le juge devant le droit national et le droit communautaire* (1966) at pp. 29 et seq.
5 *Etat Belge v SA Fromagerie Franco-Suisse le Ski* (1971) RTDE 494.
6 Pescatore, P., 'L'autorité en droit interne des traités internationaux selon jurisprudence luxembourgeoise' (1962) 18 *Pasicrisie Luxembourgeoise* 99–115.
7 Van Panhuys, H. F., 'The Netherlands Constitution and International Law' (1964), 58 AJIL 88–108; Van Dijk, P., 'The Implementation and Application of the law of the European Communities within the Legal Order of the Netherlands' (1969) 6 CML Rev 283–308.

ments shall be the supreme law of the land (article 68). However this authority is reserved only to self-executing treaties and the power to determine which treaties are self-executing is vested in the Dutch courts. So, subject to this qualification, international treaties override the constitution and the ordinary law irrespective of whether they are precedent or subsequent (article 63). Although the courts are not competent to decide the constitutionality of international treaties (article 60) they have the power to review legislation and determine whether or not it is compatible with self-executing provisions of treaties.

The three members admitted in 1973 proceed from a dualist position. In the United Kingdom it was necessary to pass the European Communities Act 1972[8] in order to transform the Treaty obligations into domestic law, to adopt the so-called 'enforceable Community rights' and to set up machinery for the implementation of the remaining rules of Community law. In Eire, too, this object was achieved by the European Communities Act 1972, which provided, inter alia, that 'from the first day of January 1973, the Treaties governing the European Communities and the existing and future acts adopted by the institutions of those Communities shall be binding on the state and shall be part of the domestic law thereof under the conditions laid down in those Treaties'. In Denmark the law of 11 October 1972 expressly adopted the Treaties enumerated therein and made provision for the delegation of sovereign powers to the Communities and for the adoption of Community acts directly applicable by virtue of Community law.

The Greek constitution of 1975 enacted in anticipation[9] of admission to the Community provides (article 28) for the limitation of the exercise of national sovereignty subject to safeguards of human rights, democratic government and the principle of equality and reciprocity with her partners. The same article (28) guarantees incorporation and supremacy of international law and international conventions duly ratified under the condition of reciprocity. However article 93 (4) which governs the review of the constitutionality of laws states that courts are not bound to apply laws which are contrary to the constitution. This is a potential source of conflict with Community law.

This brief survey of the constitutional scene of the member states shows not only a diverse approach to the status of the Treaties but

**8** See Chapter 12, below.
**9** Roucounas, op. cit. p. 13.

also indicates a cautious commitment of the majority of these states to the Community rather than a formal and irrevocable abdication of their national sovereignty.

## III INCORPORATION OF THE COMMUNITY LEGISLATION

(a) *Reception of Community law*

The logic of the acceptance of Treaty obligations demands an unconditional reception not only of the primary but also of the derivative rules of Community law. Article 5 of the EEC Treaty reminds the member states that they must 'take all appropriate measures, whether general or particular, to ensure fulfilment of the obligations arising out of this Treaty or resulting from action taken by the institutions of the Community. They shall facilitate the achievement of the Community tasks. They shall abstain from any measure which could jeopardise the attainment of the objectives of the Treaty'. Moreover, the member states must 'in close co-operation with the institutions of the Community, co-ordinate their respective economic policies to the extent necessary to attain the objectives of the Treaty' (article 6 (1)). Since policies are enforced through the instrumentality of the law, the member states must adapt and modify their laws in order to bring about harmony within the Community and, above all, remove the legal barriers to the creation and working of the Community. Since the EEC is concerned with customs duties, movement of goods, persons, services and capital, agriculture and fisheries, transport, competition and restrictive practices, state aid to industry, taxation, and social security, and whilst the ECSC and Euratom are concerned with coal, steel and nuclear energy industries, the member states undertake a considerable number of specific obligations. These obligations are in many respects regulated by Community legislation whose scope ranges from relatively trivial provisions like the calculation of the compensation for hatching eggs[10] to the most solemn historical provisions regarding the establishment of the Common Market.

In the case of the members admitted in 1978, the accumulated volume of Community law became the object of a wholesale recep-

---

10 Article 77 (2) of the Act of Accession provides that 'the compensatory amount per hatching egg shall be calculated on the basis of the compensatory amount applicable to the quantity of feed grain required for the production in the Community of one hatching egg'.

tion at the time of their accession. By article 2 of the Act of Accession they became subject to 'the provisions of the original Treaties and the acts adopted by the institutions of the Communities' whilst by article 149 they were considered 'as being addressees of and having notification of directives and decisions within the meaning of article 189 of the EEC Treaty and of article 161 of the EAEC Treaty, and of recommendations and decisions within the meaning of article 14 of the ECSC Treaty, provided that those directives, recommendations and decisions have been notified to all the original Member States'. The same principles govern the position of Greece.

The impact of Community law upon the laws of the Member States depends on two principles: the direct applicability and the supremacy of Community law. The former is relevant to the implementation, the latter to the enforcement of Community law. Apart from a reference to the direct applicability of regulations, the Treaties do not contain a detailed exposition of these principles, which are essential to the Community, therefore they had to be elaborated by the Court of Justice of the Community.

### (b)   *Directly applicable rules of Community law*

Depending on their nature and function the rules of Community law are either 'directly' or 'indirectly' applicable. In this context a distinction should be made between rules which are 'directly applicable'[11], that is rules becoming automatically upon their enactment part of the corpus juris of the member states and rules 'directly enforceable' that is rules having a 'direct effect' as far as rights and obligations of the citizen are concerned[12].

Despite the subtle distinction between 'direct applicability' and 'direct effect', which we have noted earlier[13], the ECJ has not been using these terms consistently. Thus, for example, it held that 'article 52 of the Treaty is a directly applicable provision[14]' and that 'in such a situation, at least, article 119 is directly applicable and may thus give rise to individual rights which the Courts must

---

11 'Enforceable Community rights' according to s. 2 (1) of the British European Communities Act 1972.
12 See Winter, J., 'Direct Applicability and Direct Effect—Two Distinct and Different Concepts in Community Law' [1972] CML Rev 425; Wyatt, D., 'Directly Applicable Provisions of EEC Law' [1975] 125 NLJ, pp. 458, 575, 669, 793.
13 See p. 132, ante.
14 Case 2/74: *Reyners v Belgium* [1974] ECR 631, [1974] 2 CMLR 305.

protect[15]'. In the *Van Gend* case[16], on the other hand, it decreed that 'article 12 must be interpreted as producing direct effects and creating individual rights which Courts must protect' and on another occasion[17] stated that in 'applying the principle of co-operation laid down in article 5 of the Treaty, it is the national courts which are entrusted with ensuring the legal protection which citizens derive from the direct effect of the provisions of Community law ...'[18] It seems accordingly that 'directly applicable' provisions take force in the territory of the member states without further enactment whilst provisions having a 'direct effect' are capable of creating enforceable Community rights. The latter follows from the former. These rights are created either by the Treaty directly or, as stated the ECJ[19] ... 'also by reason of obligations which the Treaty imposes in a clearly defined way upon individuals as well as upon the member states and upon the institutions of the Community' ...

The notion of 'direct applicability' is derived from the monist concept of international law and the self-executing nature of certain Treaties or Treaty provisions. It, therefore, enables the rules of Community law, despite their extraneous source, to become automatically part of the corpus juris of the member states. The notion of 'direct effect', on the other hand, is derived from the judicial interpretation of the will of the legislator who decides whether a provision is merely programmatic[20] or constitutes a command to its subject[1], or a right vested in an individual[2], or an obligation imposed upon him[3]. Thus, whilst the distinction between 'direct applicability' and 'direct effect' appears of little significance in the eyes of the Community Court, its jurisprudence, through

15 Case 43/75: *Defrenne v SABENA* [1976] ECR 455, [1976] 2 CMLR 98.
16 Op. cit. [1963] ECR 1 at 13, [1963] CMLR 105 at 130, 131.
17 Case 33/76: *Rewe-Zentralfinanz eG v Landwirtschaftskammer für das Saarland* [1976] ECR 1989, (1977) 1 CMLR 533.
18 Cf. Case 9/73: *Schlüter v Hauptzollamt Lörrach* [1973] ECR 1135 where art. 5 was held not having a direct effect.
19 *Van Gend*, op. cit. at p. 12.
20 E.g. EEC, art. 74: 'The objectives of this Treaty shall, in matters governed by this Title, be pursued by Member States within the framework of a common transport policy'.
1 E.g. EEC, art. 72: 'Member States shall keep the Commission informed of any movements of capital to and from third countries which come to their knowledge'.
2 E.g. EEC, art. 175 (3): 'Any natural or legal person may ... complain to the Court'.
3 E.g. EEC, art. 86: 'Any abuse ... of a dominant position within the common market ... shall be prohibited'.

the instrumentality of the doctrine expressed by both terms, has advanced the rights of individuals grounded in Community law.

The doctrine of direct effect can be traced to certain leading cases. In the *Van Gend* case[4] the ECJ held that there was an unconditional obligation on the part of the member state to refrain from introducing new customs duties which, in turn, created a corresponding right in favour of the citizen. The alternative to the direct effect, thought the Court, . . . 'would remove all direct judicial protection of the individual rights' . . . In *Alfons Lütticke v Haupt-zollamt Saarlouis*[5] the Court held that a member state must not impose on the product of another member state any internal tax in excess of that applicable to similar domestic products and this safeguarded the importer's interests. In *Salgoil SpA v Italian Ministry of Foreign Trade*[6] the ECJ confirmed that a member state had no discretion in the application of the Treaty provisions governing import quotas within the Community. In the *Van Duyn* case[7] the freedom of movement was recognised as an enforceable right though in the circumstances it was curtailed by the application of a derogation clause. Both the right and the exception were held to be 'directly applicable[8]'. The right of establishment of a lawyer who, though not a national was qualified according to the law of the host state, was deduced from article 52[9] and Italy was held to be in breach of the same article for having failed to remove a nationality qualification in respect of customs agents[10]. In the much criticised[11] *Defrenne* case[12] a Belgian air hostess was able to vindicate her right to equal pay by virtue of EEC article 119 which, coupled with a directive, was held to have a direct effect as from the end of the period of transition.

However the Community Court has stated the doctrine in a most

---

4 Op. cit., p. 265 note 5, ante.
5 Case 57/65: [1966] ECR 205, [1971] CMLR 674; see also Case 28/67: *Mölkerei-Zentrale Westfalen/Lippe GmbH v Hauptzollamt Paderborn* [1968] ECR 143, [1968] CMLR 187.
6 Case 13/68: [1968] ECR 453, [1969] CMLR 181.
7 Op. cit., p. 104 note 11, ante.
8 Cf. the opposite decision of the French Conseil d'Etat in the *Cohn-Bendit* case, Dalloz 1979, J155.
9 Case 2/74: *Reyners v Belgian State* [1974] ECR 631, [1974] 2 CMLR 305; see also Case 71/76: *Thieffry v Conseil de l'Ordre des Avocats à la Cour de Paris* [1977] ECR 765, [1977] 2 CMLR 373.
10 Case 159/78: *EC Commission v Italy* [1979] ECR 3247 at 3264, [1980] 3 CMLR 446 at 463.
11 Hamson, C., 'Methods of Interpretation—a Critical Assessment of the Results', *Reports of the Judicial and Academic Conference Luxembourg* (1976.)
12 Op. cit., p. 273 note, 15, ante.

forthright manner in the second *Simmenthal* case[13] emphasising that a directly applicable Community rule takes precedence over the national legislation whether antecedent or subsequent to the relevant Treaty provision. Irrespective of the constitutional implications the national courts are bound to give effect to it. The message of the Community Court is that certain provisions of the Treaty are by their very nature and purpose directly enforceable in national courts. As they affect private interests they create Community rights which, as a corollary, correspond to Community obligations imposed upon the member states. These, as confirmed by the Community Court, and national courts, include the following:

(1) Article 7 which prohibits discrimination on grounds of nationality[14];

(2) Articles 9 and 11 on the customs union as from the end of the transitional period[15];

(3) Article 12 which forbids new customs duties or similar charges[16];

(4) Article 13 (2) on the abolition of charges having an equivalent to customs duties on imports[17];

(5) Article 16 on the abolition of customs duties on exports[18];

(6) Articles 30 and 31 which forbid quantitative restrictions and measures having equivalent effect[19];

(7) Article 32 (1), (2) on the abolition of quotas in trade between member states[20];

**13** Case 106/77: *Amministrazione delle Finanze dello Stato Simmenthal SpA* [1978] ECR 629, [1978] 3 CMLR 263.

**14** Case 14/68: *Wilhelm v Bundeskartellamt* [1969] ECR 1, [1969] CMLR 100. Case 1/78: *Kenny v Insurance Officer* [1978] ECR 1489, [1978] 3 CMLR 651.

**15** Case 33/70: *SACE SpA v Italian Ministry of Finance* [1970] ECR 1213, [1971] CMLR 123. Case 18/71: *Eunomia di Porro & C v Italian Ministry of Education* [1971] ECR 811, [1972] CMLR 4.

**16** Case 26/62: *Van Gend*, op. cit.

**17** Case 77/72: *Capolongo v Azienda Agricolo Maya* [1973] ECR 611 at 622, [1974] CMLR 230. Case 63/74: *W Cadsky SpA v Instituto Nazionale per il Commercio Estero* [1975] ECR 281, [1975] 2 CMLR 246.

**18** Case 48/71: *EC Commission v Italy* [1972] ECR 527, [1972] CMLR 699. Case 45/76: *Comet BV v Produktschap voor Siergewassen* [1976] ECR 2043, [1977] 1 CMLR 533.

**19** Case 13/68: *Salgoil SpA v Italian Ministry of Foreign Trade* [1968] ECR 453, [1969] CMLR 181. Case 12/74: *EC Commission v Federal Republic of Germany* [1975] ECR 181, [1975] 1 CMLR 340. Case 74/76: *Iannelli and Volpi SpA v Meroni* [1977] ECR 557, [1977] 2 CMLR 688.

**20** Case 13/68: *Salgoil*, op. cit.

(8) Article 36 as far as 'disguised restrictions on trade' are concerned[1];

(9) Article 37 (1) and (2) which forbids measures likely to restrict the abolition of customs duties and quantitative restrictions between member states or adjustment of state monopolies[2];

(10) Article 48 (2) on discrimination between workers on the ground of nationality[3];

(11) Article 48 (3); Regulations 15 and 38/64; Directive 64/221 on the restrictions of the freedom of movement[4];

(12) Article 52 concerning the right of establishment[5];

(13) Article 53 which forbids new restrictions on the right of establishment[6];

(14) Articles 59 and 62 on the freedom to provide services[7];

(15) Articles 85 and 86 on competition[8];

(16) Article 90 (2) on revenue-producing monopolies[9];

(17) Article 93 (3) concerning aids by states[10];

1 Case 78/70: *Deutsche Grammophon GmbH v Metro-SB-Grössmärkte GmbH & Co KG* [1971] ECR 487, [1971] CMLR 631. Case 192/73: *Van Zuylen Frères v Hag AG* [1974] ECR 731, [1974] 2 CMLR 127. Case 29/72: *Marimex SpA v Italian Finance Administration* [1972] ECR 1309, [1973] CMLR 486. Case 21/75: *Firma I Schröeder KG v Oberstadt-direktor der Stadt Köln* [1975] ECR 905, [1975] 2 CMLR 312.

2 Case 6/64: *Costa v ENEL*, op. cit. Case 59/75: *Pubblico Ministero v Flavia Manghera* [1976] ECR 91, [1976] 1 CMLR 557.

3 Case 167/73: *EC Commission v French Republic* [1974] ECR 359, [1974] 2 CMLR 216. Case 41/74: *Van Duyn v Home Office* [1975] Ch 358, [1974] ECR 1337, [1975] 1 CMLR 1. Case 13/76: *Dona v Mantero* [1976] ECR 1333, [1976] 2 CMLR 578.

4 Case 67/74: *Bonsignore v Oberstadtdirektor der Stadt Köln*, [1975] ECR 297, [1975] CMLR 472. Case 41/74: *Van Duyn v Home Office*, op. cit.

5 Case 2/74: *Reyners v Belgian State* [1974] ECR 631, [1974] 2 CMLR 305. Case 33/74: *Van Binsbergen v Bestuur van de Bedrijfsvereniging voor de Metaalnijverheid* [1974] ECR 1299, [1975] 1 CMLR 298. Case 11/77: *Patrick v Ministre des Affaires Culturelles* [1977] ECR 1199, [1977] 2 CMLR 523.

6 Case 6/64: *Costa v ENEL*, op. cit.

7 Case 33/74: *Van Binsbergen*, op. cit.; Case 36/74: *Walrave and Koch v Union Cycliste Internationale* [1974] ECR 1405, [1975] 1 CMLR 320. Case 39/75: *Coenen v Sociaal Economische Raad* [1975] ECR 1547, [1976] 1 CMLR 30. Cases 110 and 111/78: *Ministère Public and Chambre Syndicale des Agents Artistiques et Impresarii de Belgique, ASBL v van Wesemael* [1979] ECR 35, [1979] 3 CMLR 87.

8 Case 13/61: *Kledingverkoopbedrijf de Geus en Uitdenbogerd v Robert Bosch GmbH* [1962] ECR 45, [1962] CMLR 1. Case 127/73: *BRT v SABAM* [1974] ECR 51 and 313, [1974] 2 CMLR 238.

9 Case 155/73: *Italy v Sacchi* [1974] ECR 409, [1974] 2 CMLR 177.

10 Case 120/73: *Lorenz v Federal Republic of Germany* [1973] ECR 1471.

(18) Article 95 which prohibits internal taxation of products of other member states[11].

(19) Article 119 on equal pay for men and women[12].

It goes without saying that the majority of articles 137–248 representing the 'organisational law' of the EEC are 'directly applicable' though by their nature and function they do not constitute rights enforceable by individuals[13].

The list is by no means complete as certain provisions of the Treaty remain yet to be considered judicially. As for the criterion of direct enforceability, the Community Court[14] held as follows:

'... The Treaty's objective of establishing a common market the functioning of which affects the subjects of Member States entails that the Treaty is something more than an agreement creating obligations between states parties alone. The Community is a new legal system, in support of which the Member States have limited their sovereign rights in certain fields, and the subjects of the new legal system are not only the member states but their inhabitants as well. Community Law, being independent of the legislation passed by member states, therefore, creates rights as well as duties for individual persons who are subject to the legal order of Member States. These rights and obligations arise not only when they are expressly provided for in the Treaty, but also as a result of the duties imposed by it in a clearly defined manner upon nationals of Member States, the States themselves and the institutions of the Community ...'

Advocate-General Mayras, quoting several precedents in the *Van Duyn* case[15], thought that ... 'the provisions must impose on the member state a clear and precise obligation; it must be unconditional, i.e. not accompanied by any reservation ..., and the application of the Community rule must not be conditional on any subsequent legislation whether of the Community institutions or of the member states; and must not lead to the latter having an effective power of discretionary judgment as to the application of the rule in question' ...

The test of direct effect is, therefore, primarily the capacity of the text to produce rights and obligations which individuals may seek to enforce against the state. The national law should not bar

---

11 Case 28/67: *Mölkerei-Zentrale Westfalen/Lippe GmbH v Hauptzollamt Paderborn* [1968] ECR 143, [1968] CMLR 187.

12 Case 43/75: *Defrenne v SA Sabena* [1976] ECR 455, [1976] 2 CMLR 98.

13 For exceptions, see EEC arts. 173, 184, 215.

14 Case 28/67: *Mölkerei-Zentrale Westfalen/Lippe GmbH v Hauptzollamt Paderborn* [1968] ECR 143 at 152, [1968] CMLR 187 at 217.

15 Op. cit. at p. 8.

the enforcement of such rights and obligations[16], even though the enforcement may in the context of national law present considerable technical difficulties. However, as indicated by decisions arising from the application of EEC article 85 and article 86, a text may, even indirectly, give rise to directly enforceable rights and obligations[17]. In this sense the nature of a specific provision may have to be inferred from its purpose and the intention of the authority which brought into being such a provision (i.e. whether the Treaty or Community legislation).

To what extent procedures prescribed by the Treaty may give rise to directly enforceable rights and obligations remains to be seen. Procedural law is, in many respects, the guarantor of substantive rights. Where the prescribed procedures are not observed, the individual may suffer and should, in justice, be entitled to relief. This, among other things, seems to have been in the mind of the Giudice Conciliatore Fabbri in *Flaminio Costa v ENEL*[18] when he considered a complaint that the Italian decree nationalising the electricity industry, passed in the absence of consultation with the Commission (articles 101 and 102), distorted the conditions of competition and infringed the rights of the individual. Although the Community Court held that article 102 created no directly enforceable rights, the general question seems to remain open.

To take another example Article 177 is surely directly applicable. It is also capable of creating an expectation in the minds of litigants that their case will be heard by the Community Court. However the procedure for the preliminary ruling is governed entirely by the national systems[19] which may, through cumbersome procedures or appeals on the point whether or not to refer, frustrate that expectation. In the opinion of the ECJ a state policy to restrict the reference would amount to a breach of the Treaty[20] and so would

---

16 *Salgoil SpA*, above.
17 E.g. Case 48/72: *Brasserie de Haécht v Wilkin-Janssen)* [1973] ECR 77, [1973] CMLR 287; Case 127/73: *BRT v SABAM* [1974] ECR 51, [1974] 2 CMLR 238.
18 Cf. World Court in *The Free Zones Case* [1932] PCIJ Rep Ser A/B, No 46; *Wimbledon Case* [1923] PCIJ Rep Ser A No 1; *German Settlers Case* [1923] PCIJ Rep Ser B No 6.
19 E.g. Case 36/80: *Irish Creamery Milk Suppliers Association v Ireland* [1981] ECR 735, [1981] 2 CMLR 455.
   Case 244/78: *Union Laitiere Normande v French Dairy Farmers* [1979] ECR 2663, [1980] 1 CMLR 314.
   Case 146/73: *Rheinmühlen-Düsseldorf v Einfuhr-und Verratsstelle für Getreide und Futtermittel* [1974] ECR 139, [1974] 1 CMLR 523.
20 Case 77/69: *EC Commission v Belgium* [1970] ECR 237.

procedural discrimination against a person endeavouring to assert a Community right[1]. Whilst the ECJ made it plain that ... 'in the absence of Community rules on this subject it is for the domestic legal system of each member state to designate the courts having jurisdiction and to determine the procedural conditions governing actions at law intended to ensure the protection of the rights which citizens have from the direct effect of Community law' ...[2] it would be a rather tenuous proposition that procedural safeguards implicit in the enforcement of Community rights do themselves constitute 'enforceable Community rights'.

The principle of direct applicability of Treaty provisions defined by the Community Court applies also to secondary legislation. Regulations[3] fall into that category unless they give the member states discretion in their implementation[4]. If they do not allow any discretion an action, as in the slaughtered cows case[5], may be brought against the state by the individual whose Community right has been impaired through the deficiency of the national system. Moreover, in such a case, the state in default will be exposed to enforcement proceedings.

Directives, as we have observed earlier[6], may gave a direct effect creating thereby enforceable Community rights. However they have also another potential since ... 'the individual invokes a provision of a directive before a national court in order that the competent national authorities, in exercising the choice which is left to them as to the form and the methods for implementing the directive, have kept within the limits as to their discretion set out in the directive[7] ...'

### (c) *Indirectly applicable rules of Community law*

In addition to provisions which contain rules of law directly applicable in the territory of the member states the foundation Treaties

---

1 Case 33/76: *Rewe Zentralfinanz eG and Rewe Zentral AG v Landwirtschaftskammer für das Saarland* [1976] ECR 1989, [1977] 1 CMLR 533 (limitation of actions).
2 Ibid.
3 See p. 97 et seq. See also Case 83/78: *Pigs Marketing Board v Redmond* [1978] ECR 2347, [1979] 1 CMLR 177.
4 E.g. Reg. 15/64/EEC (JO 573/64) concerning the import of cattle from Denmark to Germany; See also Galli, op. cit.
5 *Leonesio*, op. cit.
6 Case 51/76; *Verbond van Nederlandse Ondernemingen v Inspecteur der Invoerrechten en Accijnzen* [1977] ECR 113 at 127, [1977] 1 CMLR 413: See also Case 21/78: *Delkvist v Anklagemijndigheden* [1978] ECR 2327 at 2340.
7 Case 51/76: *Verbond van Nederlandse Ondernemingen v Inspecteur der Invoerrechter en Accijnzen* [1977] ECR 113 at 127, [1977] 1 CMLR 413.

comprise a number of policies or general provisions which have to be implemented by state legislation. The former are cognisable by the national courts and for all intents and purposes are regarded as having a direct and immediate effect with regard to persons and things in the territory of the member states. The latter consist of Treaty obligations which by virtue of the Treaty provisions have to be transformed into detailed rules of law. To these we can add the decisions and directives of the Community organs addressed to one or several states which are of a general or mixed character and have to be further elaborated. The rules of law indirectly applicable have this in common that they have to be enacted by the member states to become part of their municipal law and that the member states have a considerable discretion in the choice of the methods. In most cases the Member States have merely to adapt their existing laws to the overall strategy of the foundation Treaties, notably the Common Market in the EEC. However the intensity of the adaptation and the degree of discretion accorded to member states depend on the Treaty provisions. Thus according to the EEC Treaty three such degrees can be discerned[8].

Firstly, the states may enjoy complete discretion in the implementation of their obligations. Two examples, discussed by a learned writer[8a], illustrate the point. To implement Regulation No. 3 concerning the social security of migrant workers (reference to EEC article 51) Italy set up a special pension for miners[9]; the Netherlands, on the other hand, considered that their existing law was inadequate and took the opportunity of remodelling the system and adapting it to the problems of migrant workers[10]. To implement the EEC agricultural policy France passed a general statute (*loi d'orientation agricole*)[11], whilst Belgium decided to recast the whole system and so repealed the law of 1931 on import, export and transit of goods and substituted for it a new law on agriculture[12].

Secondly, the states may have a choice of either implementing or not implementing the Community law, but in the exercise of their

---

**8** Sohier, M., and Megret, C., 'Le rôle de l'exécutif national et du législateur national dans la mise en oeuvre du droit communautaire' *Semaine de Bruges* (1965), op cit., pp. 108 et seq; Constantinidès-Mégret, op cit., pp. 132 et seq.
**8a** Constantinidès-Mégret, op cit., p. 133.
**9** Law of No. 5, 3 January 1960, Gaz. Uff., No. 27, 1960.
**10** Law of 13 January 1965; reference to Regulations 15 and 38/64 on the free movement of workers, EEC, art. 48.
**11** Law of 8 August 1962, JORF, 10 August 1962.
**12** Law of 11 September 1962; MB 26 October 1962, p. 9491, and Law of 20 July 1962; MB 26 July 1962, p. 6218.

option they have to act within the scope of authority accorded to them. The following provisions of the EEC Treaty are relevant in this respect:

*Article 25*, which enables the Council to grant to the member states, on the recommendation of the Commission, tariff quotas at a reduced rate of duty or duty free[13];

*Article 115*, which enables the Commission to authorise the member states to take protective measures in derogation from the general principles of the commercial policy of the Community[14];

*Article 226*, which enables the Commission to authorise the member states to take protective measures during the transitional period in derogation from the rules of the Treaty[15].

Thirdly, there are measures which the member states have to take in order to discharge their obligations. In this respect they act merely as agents of the Community instrumental in the execution of the Community law. For example, to carry into effect the CAP member states have to set up Agricultural Intervention Boards. These are national institutions founded upon Community law. They administer the Community system and collect, inter alia, charges levied by the authority of Community legislation. Should such charges be declared illegal because based upon an invalid regulation the repayment of these charges falls upon national law[16].

### (d) *Techniques of Incorporation*

A study of the problem of state legislation turning the rules of Community law indirectly applicable into the municipal law of the member states reveals not only a diversity of approach, but, above all, a slow progress. Parliaments are far from being eager to act and their procedures are lengthy and cumbersome. As guardians of national sovereignty they seem to resent the intrusion of extraneous law-making authority although they have accepted the Community Treaties. As legislators parliaments, no doubt, do not relish their

---

13 E.g. decisions of the Commission of 9 November 1964 (JO 1964, p. 3259) and of 12 November 1964 (JO 1964, p. 3549) quoted by Constantinidès-Mégret, op cit., p. 134.

14 E.g. decision of 21 September 1964 (JO 1964, p. 2497, op cit., p. 134).

15 E.g. decisions of 20 December 1963 (JO 1964, p. 145) and of 16 April 1964 (JO 1964, p. 1162).

16 Case 130/79: *Express Dairy Foods Ltd v Intervention Board for Agricultural Produce* [1980] ECR 1887, [1981] 1 CMLR 451; See also Case 68/79: *Hans Just I/S v Danish Ministry of Fiscal Affairs* [1980] ECR 501, [1981] 2 CMLR 714; Cases 66, 127 and 128/79: *Amministrazione delle Finanze v SrL Meridionale Industria Salumi* [1980] ECR 1237, [1981] 1 CMLR 1.

subordinate position, or having their functions reduced to mere formality, in the matter of Community legislation. As parliament debates seem nugatory in view of clear Treaty obligations to execute Community law, the tendency is to leave the matter in the hands of the Executive[17].

Should parliament turn perverse and pass a law inconsistent with the Treaty obligations, precious little can be done. Evidently the state concerned could be in breach of the Treaty which in turn would enable the Commission to act under article 169. Should the state be recalcitrant in not heeding the 'reasoned opinion' of the Commission, the matter could be brought before the Community Court[18]. If the Community Court decides against the state, the state is bound to 'take the necessary measures to comply with the judgment' (article 171), which means the repeal of the offending legislation. However, in theory, the game could go on for ever if the government concerned were unable to influence its parliament. Although the Community would be in jeopardy, the Community Court could not strike down the municipal legislation it considers 'illegal' in the eyes of the Community law, simply because the Court has no direct authority in the territory of the member state. Rather than putting the Community at risk the member states have evolved a practical, though individualistic, approach to the implementation of Community law. Their solution of the problem depends on the Constitution.

The French Constitution of 1958 sharply distinguishes between legislation by statute (*loi*) and legislation by decree (*décret*). Whatever is not listed in article 34 as being subject to legislation by Parliament falls, by virtue of article 37, into the Government's lap and becomes subject to *pouvoir réglementaire*. In addition the Government may be authorised to make ordinances by statute which is usually of a limited duration but may be renewed. Consequently the French Government appears well equipped constitutionally to deal with Community legislation, assuming, of course, that politically this is acceptable to Parliament. However the government will, if necessary, refer to the *Conseil Constitutionnel* matters which may impinge upon the constitution. Thus when certain budgetary provisions of the EEC Treaty were modified in

17 Reports on Constitutional Laws in France (1964–65) by M de Grailly (The House of Deputies) and M Marcilhacy (Senate) quoted by Constantinidès-Mégret, op. cit., p. 145.

18 Cf. Case 45/64: *EEC Commission v Republic of Italy* [1965] ECR 857 at 864, 865, [1966] CMLR 97 at 107–108.

1970, the government asked the Conseil Constitutionnel to consider whether the new Treaty included any provisions contrary to the constitution or necessitating an amendment to the constitution. The answer was in the negative[19]. More recently the Conseil was asked to rule whether the direct universal suffrage to the European Parliament[20] by the French electorate did affect the sovereignty of the French parliament. Here too the answer was in the negative. In *Re Isoglucose*[1] (No 1 and No 2) the Conseil confirmed that Community taxation was directly enforceable in France though when included in the national Budget it had to be distinguished from the national revenue.

On 10 July 1966 the law 'relative to the application of certain treaties' authorised the government to issue ordinances to ensure the implementation of EEC directives. The government ordinances are made by the Council of Ministers after advice from the Conseil d'Etat. They come into force on publication but become void if the bill ratifying them is not submitted to Parliament before the date fixed by the enabling statute[2]. Parliament too makes statutes to harmonise French law with Community law[3]. The result[4] is a very complex and diverse system of implementation based in principle on parliamentary delegation authorised by article 38 of the Constitution and the government's own power of legislation.

Countries in which the executive cannot rely on a direct constitutional authority in this respect, have evolved a system of delegation of powers. This implies parliamentary approval of the acts of the government which, in practice, is often granted retrospectively so much so that parliament appears to exercise a merely formal control.

Examples of this practice can be taken from the Benelux countries, notably in the field of customs law and agriculture[5]. In France the Code of Customs Law enables the Government to take certain

**19** JCP 1970, II. 16510.
**20** [1977] 1 CMLR 121.
 **1** [1978] 2 CMLR 361 and 364.
 **2** E.g. 24 July 1966 on commercial companies; 3 July 1970 on monopoly over all explosives; 22 May 1971 on forestry reproductive materials; 8 July 1971 on customs bonded warehouses.
 **3** E.g. 15 April 1970 on the nationality of public service concessionaries; 11 February 1971 on transport; 22 February 1971 on investments in the Community.
 **4** For a complete and up-to-date account, see Bailleux A., *Techniques d'application du Droit Communautaire dans l'ordre juridique français*, unpublished doctoral thesis, Nice, 1975.
 **5** Constantinidès-Mégret, op. cit., pp. 150–154.

measures which have to be approved by Parliament. This method was used in order to carry out the Community customs regulations[6].

In Belgium the Customs and Excise Law of 2 May 1958, having authorised the King to take measures by decree subject to parliamentary approval, has adopted basically the French solution. A similar law was passed in the Netherlands on 25 June 1960 but it does not require parliamentary sanction for measures taken under the authority of the said law.

The execution of the agricultural policy of the Community in the Benelux countries reveals a more complex picture. Without going into details it may suffice to note that in Belgium under the law of 1962, which replaced the law of 1931 on import, export and transit of agricultural produce, powers were delegated to the King to make decrees relevant to the Community agricultural policy. A similar law was passed in Luxembourg.

In the Netherlands, where the agricultural system is quite unique, and complex because it is based on a network of 'professional' organisations endowed with a great deal of autonomous power, authority, under the Agricultural Law, is delegated to the Queen to carry out the Community agricultural policy by decree.

Summing up the position in the Benelux countries we can say that their governments put into effect Community law by virtue of a general delegation of power. A system of general delegation can be said to exist also in the new member states: in Denmark by virtue of the Constitution[7] (article 20) and in Eire and the United Kingdom by virtue of the European Communities Acts 1972, ss. 2 and 2 (2) respectively. In Eire, dissatisfaction with the operation of the 1972 Act led to the enactment of the European Communities (Amendment) Act 1973. Under this Act ministerial regulations have statutory effect but the control over the exercise of this power is in the hands of a watchdog committee drawn from the Dail and the Seanad. Its function is to monitor all drafts prepared by the Commission and all acts of the Communities as well as all regulations issued by the Irish ministers as a result of the membership of the Communities. It can also make recommendations to Irish Parliament.

An authority for general delegation can be found in article 78 (5)

---

6 E.g. the decision of the EEC Council of 4 April 1962 was incorporated in art. 19 of the French Customs Code by decree, JO 1962, p. 999.

7 Sørensen, M., 'Compétences supranationales et pouvoirs constitutionnels en droit danois', *Miscellanea W. J. Ganshof van der Meersch* (1972), Vol. 2, p. 481 et seq.

of the Greek Constitution which provides for delegated legislation to carry out 'economic measures within the framework of international relations with economic organisations'. Community legislation prior to accession is to be implemented by presidential decrees on the proposal of competent ministers. Similar instruments are to be used to implement post-accession legislation under parliamentary supervision since, according to article 3 of the Act of Accession, the government is obliged to submit annual reports on Community affairs. A parliamentary watchdog committee is likely to be established[8].

A system of specific delegation of legislative power operates in Italy and the German Federal Republic.

Article 76 of the Italian Constitution provides that the exercise of the legislative power may be delegated to the Government for a specific purpose and only for a limited period. On this principle article 4 of the act of ratification of 14 October 1957 authorises the Government to promulgate by decree having the force of ordinary law, in accordance with the 'general principles enshrined in the EEC Treaty', the necessary rules to:

(i)  ensure the execution of the obligations arising from article 11;

(ii)  carry out measures provided in articles 37, 46, 70, 89, 91, 107, 108, 109, 115 and 226;

(iii)  carry out dispositions and principles comprised in articles 95, 96, 97 and 98 of the EEC Treaty.

The original delegation expired in 1961 but has been extended quinquennially. By virtue of this delegation several decrees have been passed. However, before taking any measure the Government has to seek advice of a Parliamentary Commission consisting of 15 Members of the House of Deputies and 15 Members of the Senate.

Article 80 (1) of the Basic Law of the German Federal Republic of 1953 provides for the delegation of legislative power to the Executive by statute which has to determine the context, purpose and extent of the delegation. The law of ratification[9] granted to the Federal Government the power to carry into effect articles 14, 16, 17 (1), and 23 (2) of the EEC Treaty (Customs Provisions) as well

8 Evrigenis, D., 'Legal and Constitutional Implications of Greek Accession to the European Communities' (1980) 17 CML Rev, p. 157 at 168.
9 See p. 268, ante.

certain provisions of the protocols on mineral oils and bananas. Such decrees could be made without approval of the Federal Parliament (*Bundestag*) unless the Parliament objected within three weeks from the date when draft decrees were laid before it. No approval of the decrees by the Federal Council (*Bundesrat*) was required though the Council had fourteen days to make comments on the draft decrees.

The Customs Law of 1957[10] made under the above rules was amended by the Law of 1961[11] which enlarged the powers of the Federal Government. Article 77 of the Law of 1961 is particularly relevant to the implementation of Community law. It concerns measures under EEC article 103 (short-term economic policy) and, more generally, Community legislation. The former will be studied by the relevant parliamentary committee and submitted to the Bundestag which will accept or reject the decrees. The Bundestag cannot approve these by silence. They will also be submitted to the Bundesrat but merely for opinion. Drafts of decrees for the implementation of the Community legislation are laid before the Bundestag and the Bundesrat and the Bundestag is presumed to have approved the decrees if within three months from this submission they have not been formally abrogated by Parliament. The function of the Bundesrat is purely advisory. Customs laws have been modified on several occasions by this process. In the field of agriculture several laws have been passed. Of these the Law of 1964[12] conferred upon the Federal Government the power of legislating by decree in order to put into effect the regulations, decisions and directives of the Council and the Commission of the EEC governing the marketing of cereals, milk products and rice.

It is clear from this brief survey of the methods of implementing Community law that the member states have retained a measure of parliamentary control in this matter. The problem is by no means simple and in the interests of the smooth running of the Community as well as the efficacy of the Community law in the territory of the member states, it ought to be studied in depth with a view to formulating a common approach and a uniform procedure.

10 Law of 27 July 1957, BGBl II (1957), p. 753.
11 Law of 14 June 1961, BGBl I (1961), p. 758.
12 Law of 13 August 1964.

IV INCORPORATION THROUGH THE COMMUNITY COURT

(a) *The rôle of the ECJ*

We have already considered the meaning and effect of Community legislation as a source of Community law[13]; we should emphasise now the role of the Community Court in the process of the incorporation of Community legislation into the municipal laws. The Court has an indirect influence under EEC articles 173 and 177. Under article 173 the Court has the power of annulment and indeed, should the action for annulment be well founded, the Court will strike down the offending piece of Community legislation (article 174). On the other hand whatever is uncontested or declared valid by the Court has the force of law in the territory of the Member States. It is important to note that the decisions of the Court in respect of the validity of the Community legislation have a universal application; they are enforceable erga omnes (article 174 (1)).

However perhaps more significant, from a practical point of view, is the Court's impact through its interpretation of Community law. Where the national court requests interpretation the impact is direct and instructive. It is equally instructive in other cases, though the impact has to be measured through the doctrine of judicial precedent. Here the British and Irish judges are out of step with their continental brethren as they lavishly cite the decisions of the Community Court as well as the judgments of national courts[14]. However a rigid application of the doctrine of *stare decisis* must be discounted simply because the Community Court is not bound by its own decisions and a slavish adherence to a precedent no longer honoured on the continent would lead to serious anomalies and distortions of Community law by British or Irish judges.

In spite of the merely persuasive authority of precedents in continental jurisprudence the decisions of the Community Court are gaining prestige in national jurisdiction. They are being cited[15] and some courts occasionally cite decisions of national courts[16]. They do so not in principle or out of habit but because they

13 See pp. 96 et seq., ante.
14 See e.g. *Bulmer v Bollinger* op. cit., p. 53, ante.
15 *Fiorini v Société Nationale des Chemin De Fer Français* [1975] CMLR 459, CA; *Re Dry Shavers* [1975] CMLR 550; *Administration des Douanes v Société Cafés Jacques Vabres* [1975] CMLR 336, Paris Court of Appeal.
16 *Francesco Cinzano & Cie GmbH v Java Kaffeegeschäfte GmbH;* [1974] CMLR 21. Bundesgerichtshof.

appreciate the authoritative exposition of Community law by the Community Court and of the relevant national law by national courts. As for the authority of the Community precedents there is as yet no uniform approach to this matter. Reports indicate that the French *Cour de Cassation*[17] considered that French courts are generally bound by the rulings of the Community Court; the German Federal Supreme Court[18] felt that the decisions of the Community Court are binding 'beyond the instant case', whilst the Milan Court of Appeal applied[19] the Community Court's ruling in one case and considered it binding only inter partes, in another[20]. No doubt a trend towards recognition of Community precedents is gaining momentum.

Article 177[1] gives the Community Court the power of interpretation of the Treaty, of the acts of the Community organs and of the statutes of bodies established by the Council in the form of a preliminary ruling. This means that non-Community Treaties of the Member States even though noted in EEC regulations are not included in the interpretative competence of the Court[2]. The Treaty is silent as to the scope of this ruling: is it valid erga omnes or only quoad casum? Some writers[3] doubt the erga omnes effect, others[4] argue that it has this effect. Whether one can go that far, bearing in mind that a national court may repeatedly request a preliminary ruling in similar circumstances and the Community Court, not being bound by its previous decisions, may change its mind, is debatable. However, whatever the effect of the judgment,

**17** *Garoche v Striker Boats (Nederland)*, *Cour de Cassation* [1974] CMLR 469 but not so the Conseil d'Etat, see *Cohn-Bendit*, op. cit.

**18** Case KZR 7/69: *Re Brewery Solus Agreement* [1975] 1 CMLR 611. Same the Bundesverwaltungsgericht: *Rewe-Zentralfinanz GmbH v Landeswirtschaftskammer für das Saarland* [1978] 2 CMLR 594 and the Bundesverfassungsgericht: Case IZR 114/73: *Terrapin (Overseas) Ltd v Terranova Industrie* [1978] 3 CMLR 102.

**19** *Sirena SRL v EDA SRL* [1975] CMLR 409.

**20** *SAFA v Amministrazione delle Finanze* [1973] CMLR 152.

**1** ECSC, art. 41; EAEC, art. 150.

**2** Case 28/68: *Caisse Regionale de Sécurite Sociale du Nord v Torrekens* [1969] CMLR 377.

**3** E.g. Catalano, N., *Manuel de droit des Communautés Européennes* (1965) (French Translation), p. 88.

**4** E.g. Zuccala, 'Di una forma d'intepretazione guirisprudenziale autentica delle leggi', Guirisprudenzia Italiana (1959), IV, Coll. 139-144; quoted by Constantinidès-Mégret, op. cit., pp. 39-40. Trabucchi, 'L'éffet "erga omnes" des décisions préjudicielles rendues par la Cour de Justice des Communautés Européennes' (1974) RTDE 56 quot. with approval by A. G. Warner in Case 112/76: *Manzoni v Fonds National de Retraite des Ouvriers Mineurs* [1977] ECR 1647 at 1661-1663, [1978] 2 CMLR 416 at 429-430.

it is an instrument of integration of Community law with municipal law and of uniformity throughout the Community. Therefore preliminary rulings should have a universally binding effect despite the warning against the spectre of the 'government by judges'[5]. This effect can be inferred not only from the function of the Court but also from the procedure on reference which provides for the intervention of the member states and the Commission as well as the recent amendment of the rules which allows issues on which there is an established body of law to be decided by a chamber of three judges instead of the whole Court[6].

Article 177 should be read together with article 20 of the Protocol on the Statute of the Community Court which provides for the procedure to be applied when a preliminary ruling is sought. Accordingly when any Court or tribunal of a member state decides that it cannot proceed to judgment without the elucidation of a point of Community law relevant to the case the proceedings are suspended and the Court or tribunal refers the matter to the Community Court. The decision to seek a ruling is notified by the Registrar of the Community Court to the parties, the member states and to the Commission, and also to the Council if the act, the validity or interpretation of which is in dispute, originates from the Council. Within two months of this notification, the parties, the member states, the Commission and, where appropriate, the Council, are entitled to make their submissions or observations to the Court. In this way the matter ceases to be of sole concern to the parties and the adjudicating court; it becomes of common concern to the whole Community. By giving the national judge access to the Community Court, whilst enabling all the member states and the Community organs to make representations, the Treaty sets the stage for an understanding between the municipal courts and the Community Court and for a development towards a common law of the Community. At the same time the Treaty asserts the superiority of the Community Court.

## (b) *The reference*

Many cases have been submitted for a preliminary ruling and the Court has developed a certain practice in this field. In the first case[7]

5 Lecourt, R., *Le juge devant le Marché Commun*, (1970), p. 57.
6 Rules of Procedure, art. 95; cf. Case 120/75: *Riemer v Hauptzollamt Lübeck-West* [1976] ECR 1003.
7 Case 13/61 *Kledingverkoopbedrijf de Geus en Uitdenbogerd v Boschen Van Rijn* [1962] ECR 45, [1962] CMLR 1.

under article 177 the Court advised that the referring court is free to adopt a direct and simple form of reference which will enable the Community Court to rule strictly within the limits of its jurisdiction. Thus formalism was dispensed with but at the same time the Court implied that it would not be politic to decide the issue otherwise than in the terms of interpretation of Community law. Furthermore the Court stressed that whilst two different legal orders are involved (national and Community) the national court is about to administer Community law albeit under the guidance of the Community Court.

In the *Van Gend* case[8] the Court observed that the considerations which may guide the national court in the choice of its questions and their pertinence to the issue to be decided are outside the jurisdiction of the Community Court. In this case a Dutch Administrative Tribunal enquired whether article 12 of the EEC Treaty 'entailed internal legal effects, that is whether or not an individual may directly derive rights which have to be protected by his national courts'. Article 12 provides that member states shall refrain from introducing between themselves any new customs duties on imports or exports, or any charges having equivalent effect, and from increasing those which they already apply in their trade with each other. The question raised a constitutional issue, that is whether the Community Court was really interpreting Community law or whether it usurped the power to interpret the Dutch Constitution (i.e. the power to levy taxes). The Dutch Government was of the opinion that the Community Court had no jurisdiction in matters involving Dutch customs duties. However the Community Court firmly asserted its jurisdiction and the power to rule in the matter, as it pointed out that article 12 came for interpretation not for application according to Dutch law. In this delicate situation the Court refrained from ruling upon the conflict between Dutch and Community law but firmly declared that article 12 had a direct effect though the mode of application was left to the internal process of the Netherlands.

In *Costa v ENEL* the Court held that it had power to select what was relevant from the list of questions imperfectly formulated by the referring court and in this way refused to be drawn into an internal conflict. 'Consequently,' held the Court, 'the decision should be given not upon the validity of an Italian law in relating

---

8 Case 26/62: op. cit.; see also Case 56/65: *Société Technique Minière v Machinenbau Ulm GmbH* [1966] ECR 235, [1966] CMLR 357.

to the Treaty but upon the interpretation of the above mentioned articles in the context of the points of law stated by the *Guidice Conciliatore*[9].'

In *Schwarze v Einfuhr-und Vorratstelle für Getreide und Futtermittel*[10] the Court had to decide whether a badly drafted reference should be sent back whence it came as suggested by the French government. The ECJ refused to do this and held that 'when it appears that questions asked by a municipal court for the purpose of interpretation in reality concern the validity of a Community act, it is for the Court of Justice to enlighten the national court immediately without insisting upon a formalism which would be purely dilatory and which would be incompatible with the true nature of the machinery established by article 177.' Thus the ECJ will, in a helpful manner, assist the referring court in focussing its attention upon the relevant aspects of Community law and will, if necessary, re-formulate the reference[11]. This does not mean that the ECJ will decide[12] the issue for the referring court or become involved in a national controversy[13].

However, no matter how helpful the Community Court is in the process of the elucidation of the points before it, there is a limit to its competence for the object of the reference is limited to answering questions on issues raised by the referring court[14]. Therefore it cannot be used to apply the Treaty to a particular situation or determine the validity of an internal measure[15], and thus do the work of the referring court.

Nevertheless the ECJ may be able to extract points of Community law from the reference and deal with these as if properly presented[16]. The ECJ sees itself as having a duty to accept the reference without questioning the reasons for it or criticising the referring court[17]. However it is incumbent upon the referring court

9 [1964] CMLR 425 at 455.
10 Case 16/65: [1965] 2 ECR 877 at 886, 887, [1966] CMLR 172 at 186–187.
11 E.g. Case 78/70: *Deutsche Grammophon GmbH v Metro-SB Grössmärkte GmbH* [1971] 2 ECR 487, [1971] CMLR 631.
12 *Van Gend*, op. cit.
13 *Costa v ENEL*, op. cit.
14 Case 51/72: *Fratelli Grassi v Amministrazione delle Finanze* [1973] CMLR 332.
15 Case 20/64: *SARL Albatros v SOPECO (Société de Pétroles et des Combustibles liquides)* [1965] ECR 29, [1965] CMLR 159; Case 100/63: *Kalsbeek v Sociale Verzekeringsbank* [1964] ECR 565 at 572.
16 Case 82/71: *Pubblico Ministero della Repubblica Italiana v SPA Società Agricola Industria Latte* [1972] ECR 119, [1972] CMLR 723.
17 Case 10/69: *Portelange SA v SA Smith Corona Marchant International* [1969] ECR 309, [1974] 1 CMLR 397; Case 155/73: *Italian State v Sacchi* [1974] ECR 409, [1974] 2 CMLR 177; Case 126/80: *Salonia v Poidomani and Baglieri* [1982] 1 CMLR 64.

to determine the facts of the case[18] and therefore reference will be rejected if the issue is merely 'academic' in the sense that it does not reveal any real dispute between the parties[19]. Presumably the national court of its own motion will refuse to refer if facts have not been ascertained to its satisfaction[20] or if, despite the arguments to the contrary, it is clear that no point of Community law is involved[1].

## (c)  *The timing*

The question arises as to when the reference should be made[2]. It goes without saying that a question of Community law must be raised before the national court and that the answer to it must be relevant to the issue, that is, necessary to enable the court to adjudicate. Community law does not determine either the timing or the degree of necessity. All this is left to national procedures. As far as references from the English High Court are concerned it is expressly provided[3] that such an order may be made at any stage of the proceedings. This is correct because the court controls the proceedings from the beginning to the end and the court alone is in the position of judging the timing and the necessity.

A subsidiary question regarding interlocutory proceedings has been raised and answered in the affirmative[4]. The position is covered by article 177 (2) because a problem of Community law may occur at the initial or interlocutory stage of the proceedings and has to be settled by the court before proceeding further. The court may have to make a ruling which will determine the subsequent course of the action or even dismiss it.

---

409, [1974] 2 CMLR 177; Case 126/80: *Salonia v Poidomani and Baglieri* [1982] 1 CMLR 64.

18 Case 222/78: *ICAP Distribution Srl v Beneventi* [1979] ECR 1163, [1979] 3 CMLR 475.

19 Case 104/79: *Foglia v Novello* [1980] ECR 745, [1981] 1 CMLR 45. Case 244/80 *Pasquale Foglia v Mariella Novello* (No. 2) [1982] 1 CMLR 585.

20 *Church of Scientology of California v Customs and Excise Comrs* [1980] 3 CMLR 114, CA; on appeal [1982] 1 CMLR 48.

1 *British Leyland Motor Corpn Ltd v TI Silencers Ltd* [1980] 1 CMLR 598; *Re Virdee* [1980] 1 CMLR 709, English High Court; *Re Budlong and Kember* [1980] 2 CMLR 125; *Surjit Kaur v Lord Advocate* [1980] 3 CMLR 79, Ct of Sess.; but see Case 175/78: *R v Saunders* [1979] ECR 1129, [1979] 2 CMLR 216 (which should not have been referred).

2 See Jacobs F., 'When to refer to the European Court' (1974) 90 LQR 486.

3 RSC Ord. 114, r. 2 (1).

4 Case 107/76: *Hoffman-La Roche v Centrafarm Vertriebsgesellschaft Pharmazeutischer Erzeugnisse mbH* [1977] ECR 957, [1977] 2 CMLR 334; see Jacobs, F. [1977] 2 ELRev 354.

(d) *Multiple references*

These are admissible[5] and even desirable to save time and expense. In the cited case such a multiple reference gave the ECJ an opportunity of ruling on turnover equalisation tax in relation to various groups of product. Perhaps a more interesting variant of multiple reference was the *EMI v CBS*[6] case which was concerned with a trade-mark dispute between an English and an American company, the matter being litigated simultaneously in England, Denmark and Germany. Since the questions raised in all three countries were basically the same, it was possible to bring these within one reference and dispose of accordingly.

(e) *Questions of criminal law*

The enforcement of Community law is in the hands of national authorities. They dispose of coercive rules and of the machinery to apply these. Even in the limited area of direct Community coercion the fines and periodic penalties imposed by the Commission to enforce the rules of competition are, under EEC article 192, executed by the competent national authorities in accordance with national law and procedures.

Where a Community rule has to be supported by a criminal sanction the relevant legislative Community act can merely provide that such sanction will be enacted by the member states. Failure to enact the sanction would not give rise to a reference to the Community Court so that it could be read into the national legislation in question but rather to an enforcement action as, e.g., in the *Tachograph* case[7]. Therefore references involving questions of criminal law are likely to occur in cases where the defendant seeks protection of Community law from the existence or severity of a national criminal sanction. Indeed such references are admissible[8]. In theory where the national law is manifestly incompatible with Community law the doctrine of supremacy should enable the court to disregard the offending national law but, in practice, it is more likely that a reference will be made. Indeed the position is not always clear. A few random samples illustrate the point:

5 Case 29/68: *Milch-Fett-und Eierkontor GmbH v Hauptzollamt Saarbrücken* [1969] ECR 165, [1969] CMLR 390.
6 Case 51/75: *EMI Records Ltd v CBS (United Kingdom) Ltd* [1976] ECR 811, [1976] 2 CMLR 235.
7 See p. 100, note 9, ante.
8 Case 82/71: *Pubblico Ministero v SPA Societa Agricola Industria Latte* [1972] CMLR 723.

A Dutch licensed victualler, prosecuted for selling liquor at prices below the minimum fixed by the national law, successfully pleaded article 30 of the EEC Treaty (movement of goods) in his defence[9]. Similarly, in the *Northern Irish Pigs* case[10] a conviction under the Movement of Pigs Regulations (Northern Ireland) 1972 and forfeiture of the pigs in question were held contrary to Regulation 2759/75 governing the market in pig meat.

However a German baker[11] was unable to persuade the Court that the German bakery law which prohibits baking and deliveries of the product during certain hours at night was contrary to the provisions of articles 7 and 30-34 of the EEC Treaty.

A migrant worker[12] was able to resist an expulsion order served by an administrative authority as an object lesson to other foreigners but not so a rapist[13]. Expulsion was held to be too severe a sanction for a breach of a minor offence against immigration rules[14]. Requirements for a driving licence irrelevant to road safety could not be enforced by criminal sanctions[15].

Importers of pornographic materials contrary to a national law had their convictions confirmed as falling within the exception of public policy or public morality notwithstanding the fact that such materials were a merchandise in free circulation in another member state[16]. Pleas based on the Community principle of the freedom of movement of capital and goods were of no avail to persons convicted according to national rules for the illegal importation of Krugerrands and attempted exportation of silver alloy coins no longer in circulation[17]. Forfeiture of both gold and silver coins followed[18].

Prosecutions arising from breaches of national sea fishery laws have led to references to the ECJ[19] and indeed to a head-on collision

9 Case 82/77: *Openbaar Ministerie of the Netherlands v van Tiggele* [1978] ECR 257, [1978] 2 CMLR 528.
10 Case 83/78: *Pigs Marketing Board (Northern Ireland) v Redmond* [1978] ECR 2347, [1979] 1 CMLR 177.
11 Case 155/80: *Re Sergius Oebel*, [1981] ECR 1993.
12 Case 67/74: *Bonsignore v Oberstadtsdirektor der Stadt Köln* [1975] ECR 297, [1975] 1 CMLR 472.
13 Case 131/79: *R v Secretary of State for Home Affairs, ex p Santillo* [1980] ECR 1585, [1980] 2 CMLR 308, [1980] 3 CMLR 212, [1981] 1 CMLR 569, [1981] 2 All ER 897.
14 Case 157/79: *R v Stanislaus Pieck* [1980] ECR 2171, [1980] 3 CMLR 220.
15 Case 16/78: *Public Prosecutor v Michael Choquet* [1978] ECR 2293, [1979] 1 CMLR 535.
16 Case 34/79: *R v Henn, R v Darby* [1979] ECR 3795, [1980] 1 CMLR 246.
17 Case 7/78: *R v Thompson* [1978] ECR 2247, [1979] 1 CMLR 47.
18 *Allgemeine Gold und Silberscheideanstalt v Customs and Excise Comrs* [1980] QB 390, [1980] 1 CMLR 488, CA.
19 E.g. Cases 3, 4, 6/76: *State v Kramer* [1976] ECR 1276, [1976] 2 CMLR 440;

between two member states, one of which suing the other on behalf of one of its citizens convicted of offences against the fishery law of the latter[20]. Whilst holding the defendant state guilty of a breach of the Community law the ECJ lost no time in stressing that: ... 'Where criminal proceedings are brought by virtue of a national measure which is contrary to Community law a conviction in those proceedings is also incompatible with that law.[1]'

These samples confirm that points of criminal law are referable to the Community Court for a preliminary ruling and illustrate the potential of further developments in this field.

### (f) *The ruling*

In a sense the rulings of the ECJ under article 177 may be regarded as abstract points of law because the Community Court, content with the definition of the law, leaves its application to the referring national court. This indeed is the message of the *Van Gend* case reflecting a division of functions between the Community and the national jurisdictions. It is, therefore, necessary to distinguish between 'interpretation' and 'application', the former being the task of the ECJ, the latter of the national court involved[2]. Indeed when concluding for example that the national measure which is the subject matter of the reference is contrary to Community law, the ECJ contents itself with saying that it is 'incompatible' with the relevant provision of the Treaty. The obvious inference that it ought not to be applied because it is 'invalid' is left to the referring court. The same, when the prosecution and conviction founded upon national law is declared to be 'incompatible' the inference is that the conviction ought to be quashed by the national court. Sometimes, having stated the principle to be applied, the ECJ refers matters of fact back to the referring court. E.g. the question whether a national trade agreement[3] which restricts the supply of national but not of foreign newspapers to retailers does have an effect on inter-state trade was referred back with the reminder that it is for the referring court to decide, as a matter of fact, whether or not it does so.

---

812/79: *A-G v Burgoa* [1980] ECR 2787, [1981] 2 CMLR 193; *R v Tymen* [1981] 2 CMLR 544; Case 269/80: *R v Tymen* [1982] 2 CMLR 111 OJ, 1982, C 13/8.

20 Case 141/78: *France v United Kingdom, Re Fishing Net Mesh Sizes* [1979] ECR 2923, [1980] 1 CMLR 6.

1 Ibid.

2 Case 183/73: *Osram GmbH v Oberfonanzdirektion Frankfurt* [1974] ECR 447 at 485, [1974] 2 CMLR 360 at 366.

3 Case 126/80: *Salonia v Poidomani and Baglieri* [1982] 1 CMLR 64.

It is instructive to follow case through to see how the preliminary ruling was applied but few records are available in this respect. In the British references there has been no reluctance in applying the rulings[4].

However in the *Santillo* case the Queen's Bench Divisional Court[5] appears to have misinterpreted the ruling but the apparent error was corrected by the Court of Appeal[6]. No difficulty arose in a social insurance case[7] where the National Insurance Commissioner, applying a ruling of the ECJ which he had requested, held that an Irishman claiming British benefits was not disqualified for the period of his imprisonment in Ireland although an Englishman imprisoned in the United Kingdom would be so disqualified.

## (g) *Courts and tribunals*

Article 177 is addressed to both the courts and tribunals 'against whose decision there is no judicial remedy under national law[8]' and 'any court or tribunal[9]'. The former include, prima facie, the Supreme Courts and the highest specialist courts of the member states, i.e. the *Cour de Cassation* and the *Conseil d'Etat* in Belgium and France; the *Corte di Cassazione*, the *Consiglio di Stato* and *Corte Costituzionale* in Italy; the *Bundesgerichtshof*, the *Bundessozialgericht*, the *Bundesverwaltungsgericht*, the *Bundesdisziplinarhof* and the *Bundesfinanzhof* in Germany; the *Hoge Raad*, the *Tariefcommissie* and the *College van Beroep* in the Netherlands; the Supreme Court in Eire; the *Højesteret* in Denmark; the House of Lords and in some cases the English Court of Appeal, the Scottish Court of Session and the Northern Irish Supreme Court in the United Kingdom. However, in *Costa v ENEL*[10] the Community Court accepted a reference from a *Guidice Conciliatore* of Milan on the ground that because of the small claim involved, the magistrate

---

4 See Case 129/79: *Macarthys Ltd v Smith* [1980] ECR 1275, [1980] 2 CMLR 205; ibid [1981] QB 180, [1980] 2 CMLR 217, CA. *R v Thompson*, op. cit. *R v Henn and Darby* [1979] 2 CMLR 495, HL; *DPP v Henn and Darby* [1981] AC 850, [1980] 2 CMLR 229, HL, *Pigs Marketing Board v Redmond* [1979] 3 CMLR 118.

5 *R v Secretary of State for Home Affairs, ex p Santillo* [1980] 3 CMLR 212.

6 Ibid [1981] QB 778, [1981] 1 CMLR 569.

7 *Kenny v Insurance Officer* [1978] 1 CMLR 181; Case 1/78: *Kenny v Insurance Officer* [1978] ECR 1489, [1978] 3 CMLR 651; *Kenny v Insurance Officer* [1979] 1 CMLR 433.

8 Dont les décisions ne sont pas susceptibles d'un recours juridictionnel de droit interne; dessen Entscheidungen selbst nicht mehr mit Rechtsmitteln des innerstaatlichen Rechs angefochten werden können; avverso le cui decisioni non possa proporsi un ricorso giurisdizionale di diritto interno.

9 Une juridiction, ein Gericht, una giurisdizione.

in question was a court of the first and last instance. The Court's *dictum* that reference can be made from any court whose decisions are final (*sans recours*) has broadened the basis of article 177 (3). The reference to 'any court or tribunal' (article 177 (2)) includes, presumably, apart from the inferior courts of law, any adjudicating body or institution which in the domestic jurisdiction exercise judicial functions[11], including, of course, the English magistrates' courts but not a professional[12] body like the Paris Bar or private arbitrators[12a].

The position of the National Insurance Commissioner in the British system has posed some questions[13] since his decisions are not subject to appeal though they may be quashed for error of law by the High Court. It seems that he has no obligation to refer[14] though this can be done by the High Court on an application for judicial review[15]. It can also be done by the Commissioner himself[15a].

Whilst reference from the 'final court' is obligatory[16] it is only discretionary from the other courts or tribunals[17] that is, if the court considers it necessary to enable it to give judgment. However, obligatory reference does not mean that the Supreme Court will in every case involving Community law seek a ruling from Luxembourg. Should it be so the Community Court would become a kind of court of appeal from the national jurisdiction which it was never meant to be, for its jurisdiction under article 177 is limited to interpretation of Community law in cases where such interpretation is requested by national courts. There is, therefore, no automatic

10 Case 6/64 [1964] ECR 585, [1964] CMLR 425.
11 See Case 61/65: *Vaassen-Göbbels v Beambtenfonds voor het Mijnbedrijf* [1966] ECR 261, [1966] CMLR 508 and Case 246/80: *Broekmeulen v Committee for Registration of Medical Practitioners* [1982] 1 CMLR 91.
12 Case 138/80: *Re Jules Borker* [1980] ECR 1975, [1980] 3 CMLR 638.
12a Case 102/81: *Nordsee Deutsche Hochseefischerei GmbH v Reederei Mond an Reederei Friedrich*, [1982] OJ, C 94/4.
13 Jacobs, F., 'Which Courts and Tribunals are bound to refer to the European Court?' (1977) 2 ELRev 119.
14 See *Re Holiday in Italy* [1975] 1 CMLR 184.
15 Case 41/77: *R v National Insurance Comr, ex p Warry* [1977] ECR 2085, [1977] 2 CMLR 783; Case 143/79: *Walsh v National Insurance Officer* [1980] ECR 1639, [1980] 3 CMLR 573.
15a *Kenny*, op. cit., p. 296, note 7; Case 110/79: *Und Coonan v Insurance Officer*, [1979 OJ. C 199/16.
16 'That court shall; cette juridiction est tenue; dieses Gericht ist verpflichtet; tale giurisdizione è tenuta.'
17 'That court of tribunal may; cette juridiction peut; so kann; tale giurisdizione può.'

reference but a judicial reference which implies uncertainty of the law in the opinion of the referring court and this, to use the expression of Advocate-General Lagrange[18], embodies *une règle de bon sens et de sagesse*. Presumably if both parties to the case oppose it the reference will not be made[19]. This does not mean, however, that parties can engineer a reference by inserting into their contract an 'article 177 clause[20]'.

### (h)  *Acte clair*

This rule of common sense will differ, no doubt, according to the style of the national judiciary, their sense of independence and their Community orientation. Since reference under article 177 involves interpretation, perhaps the most vital factor in the decision whether or not to refer is the confidence of the national court in the art of the interpretation of Community law. Indeed, if the court is certain of the position it need not, in accordance with the doctrine of *acte clair* or *sens clair*, seek the ruling of the Community Court. *Acte clair* implies that the legal rule in question is clear and, therefore, requires no interpretation in accordance with the maxim *clara non sunt interpretanda*. However, *certainty* may mean literally certainty in an objective and undisputed sense. It may also mean *certainty* as a form of subterfuge applied to avoid the cumbersome machinery of preliminary ruling as remarked bluntly by a French *Avocat Général*[1] '*bien entendu, la théorie de l'acte clair intervient essentiellement pour mettre un obstacle au renvoi pour interprétation*'. On the other hand courts, being well versed in the art of interpretation, need not be reminded that reference to Luxembourg should be an exception rather than a rule and that it should be resorted to out of necessity and not out of habit[2].

### (i)  *Appeals*

The principle of *acte clair* applies to the inferior as much as to the final courts but in this context a practical question of appeals against

---

**18** In Case 28/30/62: *Da Costa en Schaake v Nederlandse Administratie der Belastingen* [1963] ECR 31, [1963] CMLR 224 at 234; See also Lagrange, M., 'The Theory of the Acte Clair: A Bone of Contention or a Source of Unity?' (1971) 8 CMLRev 313.

**19** See *English-Speaking Union of the Commonwealth v Customs and Excise Comrs* [1981] 1 CMLR 581.

**20** Case 93/78: *Mattheus v Doego Fruchtimport und Tiefkühlkost eG* [1978] ECR 2203, [1979] 1 CMLR 551.

**1** Quoted by Pescatore, P., 'Interpretation of Community Law and the Doctrine of "Acte Clair"', *Legal Problems of an Enlarged European Community*, ed. by Bathurst, M. E., et al. (1972), p. 42.

**2** Cf. Graham, J., in *Löwenbrau München v Grünhalle Lager International Ltd* [1974] CMLR 1.

the reference from the inferior courts arises. This basically is a matter for each individual country and there is no uniform practice among the ten. In Germany, Denmark³ and the Netherlands the reference goes forward to the Community Court whilst in Belgium and France the appeal has first to be disposed of. In the United Kingdom⁴, and Eire⁵ appeal has precedence over reference. The Community Court, on the other hand, follows its own guidelines which are determined by its function in the Community. This was succinctly stated in the *Bosch* case⁶:

> 'In fact, just as the Treaty does not prohibit domestic supreme courts from receiving the appeal for annulment, but leaves the examination of its admissibility to domestic law and to the opinion of the domestic judge, the Treaty subjects the jurisdiction of the Court of Justice solely to the existence of a request within the meaning of article 177, without requiring the Community judge to examine whether the decision of the domestic judge is appealable under the provisions of its domestic law.'

However, the spirit of non-intervention has not solved the problem as in two cases involving the same parties the Court was in effect asked to make a ruling on a conflict of opinion between German courts⁷. This conflict was, in the terms of the reference from the *Bundesfinanzhof*, reduced to the question whether an inferior court had an unfettered right of reference to the Community Court or whether article 177 upheld the hierarchy of national courts with the effect that on points of law an inferior court is bound by the ruling of a superior court. The Community Court, addressing itself to the *Hessisches Finanzgericht*⁸, ruled that article 177 did not preclude an inferior court making its reference to the Community Court whilst the Community Court had no choice but to attend to the questions put before it. Addressing itself to the *Bundesfinanzhof*⁹ the Community Court ruled that the existence of a rule of domestic law whereby a court is bound on points of law by the rulings of the court superior to it cannot of itself take away the

3 *Firma Hans Just i/s v Ministeriet for Skatter OG Afgifter* [1980] 1 CMLR 4; (Danish Supreme Court) Decided by ECJ: Case 68/79: *Hans Just I/S v Danish Ministry for Fiscal Affairs* [1981] ECR 501, [1981] 2 CMLR 714.
4 Order 114 (5); see Chapter 12.
5 E.g. *Irish Creamery Milk Case*, op. cit. p. 278, note 17, ante.
6 Case 13/61: *Kledingverkoopbedrijf De Geus en Uitdenbogerd v Bosch en Van Rijn* [1962] ECR 45 at 50, [1962] CMLR 1 at 26.
7 *Rhein-Mühlen-Düsseldorf v Einfuhr- und Vorratstelle für Getreide und Füttermittel* [1974] ECR 33, [1974] 1 CMLR 523 and 146/73: [1974] ECR 139, [1974] 1 CMLR 523.
8 Case 146/73: [1974] ECR at 147.
9 Case 166/73: [1974] ECR at 38, 39.

power provided for in article 177 of referring cases to the Court. If inferior courts were bound without being able to refer matters to the Court, the jurisdiction of the latter to give preliminary rulings and the application of Community law at all levels of the judicial systems of the member states would be compromised. It seems that the problem is basically a domestic one though for the sake of uniformity and in the spirit of the integration of judicial remedies within the Community a common solution should be found.

The relationship between the Community Court and the Judiciary of the member states is delicately poised between the recognition of the independence of the courts of sovereign states and the need for a uniform application of Community law throughout the Community. It is a problem which, one hopes, will solve itself in the course of time and as a result of the consolidation of the Community, though nuances between the styles of the national judiciaries are bound to remain.

Chapter 11

# Enforcement of Community law

ENFORCEMENT OF TREATY OBLIGATIONS

The EEC Treaty is a self-executing treaty, a well designed instrument of international co-operation. The member states not only assume the duty of carrying out the measures prescribed by the Treaty and the Community organs but also submit to the judicial authority of the Community. In this way the state acts as an intermediary if not a subordinate instrument of the execution of the Treaty.

The enforcement of the Treaty is safeguarded by political, economic and legal means. The most important weapon, which in classic international law states may resort to in order to frustrate a treaty, is interpretation. This weapon has been taken away from the signatories of the EEC Treaty and so they cannot resort to legal subterfuge. Though they can defy the Treaty by breaking it they cannot get round it or, under the guise of sovereignty, flout their obligations with impunity. Moreover they cannot claim, as Italy[1] did, the benefit of an 'international agreement' when the Treaty obligations have been further specified by a decision, i.e. decision 66/532 urging Italy to accelerate the reduction of the import rates on the basis of the continued protection of the Italian lead and zinc industry.

The interpretation of the Treaty has been entrusted to the Community Court (article 164 and 177) but there is a double check because by article 219 'the Member States undertake not to submit any dispute concerning the interpretation or application of the Treaty to any method of settlement other than those provided in the Treaty'. This, in addition to administrative action, establishes a judicial system of settling disputes, the Community Court having a monopolist position.

1 Case 38/69: *Customs Duties on Lead and Zinc, EC Commission v Italy* [1970] ECR 47 at 56, 57, [1970] CMLR 77 at 89–90.

Restricted in their classic weaponry the member states may be tempted to flout the Treaty overtly but this too was provided for. The Treaty provides for repressive measures, should this occur. The procedure of repression is gentle and well suited to the type of the likely offender. The Commission must first inform itself of the alleged breaches and this the Commission can do under article 213 which provides that 'for the performance of the tasks entrusted to it, the Commission may collect any information and carry out any checks required within the limits and under the conditions laid down by the Council'. Several other articles compel the member states to furnish information to the Commission, but under article 213 the Council has approved Regulation 10[2] which gives the Commission authority to collect information on earnings and conditions of employment in some fourteen industries. The general power to seek information is limited by article 223 (1) which, safeguarding the sovereign status of the Member States, enables them to withhold information they consider contrary to the essential interests of their security. The states themselves determine what is essential in the interests of their security, but security is confined to military matters and should not provide a subterfuge to frustrate the objectives of the Treaty.

Having collected information which indicates a breach of the Treaty the Commission will take further steps to enforce the Treaty. In this connection article 93 provides a good illustration. If the Commission finds that subsidies granted by a state to producers are incompatible with the common market, the Commission will direct the state to abolish[3] or adjust these subsidies within a prescribed time. If the state fails to comply the Commission or any other interested state may refer the matter directly to the Community Court[4] as being in breach of the provisions of article 169 and 170.

If the Court finds the accused state guilty of failing to carry out its obligations such a state must, in accordance with article 171, 'take the measures required for the implementation of the judgment'. The Court has no power to impose sanctions but its judgment is a judicial declaration of fact and a reminder of the obligation to comply with the judgment[5].

2 JO, 31 August 1960.
3 E.g. Decision 64/65 addressed to Belgium; see *Re Subsidies to Ford Tractor (Belgium) Ltd* 64/651/EEC, 28 October 1964, [1965] CMLR 32.
4 Decision 556/EEC addressed to France, JO No. 181, 12 October 1966; referred to the Community Court, quoted by Campbell, op. cit., Vol. 2, 2115, p. 85.
5 Cf. Case 6/60: *Humblet v Belgian State* [1960] ECR 559.

Member states can sue one another before the Community Court but before doing so they must bring their complaint before the Commission (article 170 (2)). In practice the task of suing the defaulter is undertaken by the Commission in the light of its duty 'to ensure the proper functioning and development of the Common Market (article 155)'. The reluctance of states suing each other is understandable: such actions are invidious and the plaintiff state of today may well be the defendant tomorrow. Moreover a suit by the Commission tends to be technical rather than vindictive and, from a Community point of view, the Commission has the title to represent the Community's objective interests. Should, however, the Commission fail to act, the member state or the other institutions of the Community may bring the action against the Commission[6] (article 175 (1)). In the light of this procedure France[7] suing the United Kingdom directly over the arrest of a French trawler exhibits a deviation from the norm understandable perhaps in the atmosphere of the *guerre des moutons*[8].

Should a state fail to execute the judgment of the Community Court it may once more be sued this time for breach of article 171. This procedure has in fact been applied but the member state in question complied with the original judgment.[9] There is also a precedent that a Member State had refused to comply[10] with the judgment.

The efficacy of the enforcement procedure has inherent limitations because a recalcitrant state cannot really be forced to abide by the judgment of the Court. This indeed is the last vestige of sovereignty. In this respect the Community differs from a federal state which may have federal means at its disposal for the execution of the judgments of the federal court or the decisions of the federal executive. Therefore the ultimate sanction in the EEC is political and economic. The former consists of the pressure of public opinion within the Community and persuasion by the member states.

6 See Case 59/70: *Netherlands v Commission* [1971] ECR 639 brought under ECSC, art. 35.
7 Case 141/78: *France v United Kingdom (Re Fishing Net Mesh Sizes)* [1979] ECR 2923, [1980] 1 CMLR 6.
8 Case 232/78: *EC Commission v France, Re Restrictions on Imports of Lamb* [1979] ECR 2729, [1980] 1 CMLR 418.
9 Case 7/68: *EC Commission v Italy (first art treasures case)* [1968] ECR 423, [1969] CMLR 1, and Case 48/71: *EC Commission v Italy (second art treasures case)* [1972] ECR 527, [1972] CMLR 688.
10 Cases 24, 97/80 R: *EC Commission v France (Second Imports of Lamb case)* [1980] ECR 1319.

The economic sanction lies in the common interest inherent in the preservation and improvement of the Community quite apart from any counter-measures which may be taken by the member states individually or collectively. Though the machinery of enforcement is far from perfect there is no reason to believe that states would wantonly act contrary to the accepted obligations. They are only too well aware that the smooth working of the Community depends on their co-operation and that the economic intertwining cannot be disentangled without self-inflicted hardship.

ENFORCEMENT OF COMMUNITY LAW AT COMMUNITY LEVEL

Away from the lofty stage of inter-state conflicts or internal Community disputes, the enforcement of Community law (including the Treaty) occurs in the more usual setting of disputes in which individuals, corporations and states are involved. Such disputes are decided either at Community or state level bearing in mind that Community law is state law and, therefore, subject to the judicial notice of municipal courts.

The underlying philosophy of the Community and, indeed, the practical assurance of the Community development in accordance with the Treaty and the Community legislation is the doctrine of the supremacy of Community law. It is still a theory because in spite of the constitutional adjustments of the member states there is, generally, a certain amount of hesitation, if not reluctance, to accept the monist doctrine and by-pass national legislatures. At the root of this is not only distrust of the Brussels bureaucrats who are neither directly controlled by nor responsible to the member states but, more importantly, an instinctive aversion to external laws and authorities invading, as it were, the sacred preserve of sovereign states. These states have a long and proud history and a strong sense of national identity coupled with an individualistic notion of national interest. Therefore psychological barriers have to be removed in order to make the legal obligations enshrined in Treaties and subordinate legislation meaningful and acceptable. In the circumstances it is not surprising that the lead in the process of the enforcement of Community law had to come from the Community Court.

The main difficulty is that apart from article 189 the EEC Treaty contains no formal and unequivocal assertion of the supremacy of Community law. Yet, it is common ground that the edifice of the

Community would collapse if the Community were to degenerate into a legal Tower of Babel. Thus the Community Court in a number of cases formulated and re-affirmed the principle of supremacy. The Court, as the guardian of legality and instrument of cohesion within the Community has, from the start, been in a strong position to define the status of the Community law and to give it precedence when in conflict with the municipal law of the member states. Most of these cases were brought under article 177 and the Court did not hesitate to use its authority in furthering the aims of the Community.

Whilst the Community Court in its judicial capacity has no rival system of law to administer and is only remotely concerned with the political consequences of its decisions, the municipal courts have to face the juristic and practical problems arising from the conflict between domestic law and Community law forming part of their national system. The theory that Community law is part of national law does not solve these problems.

Indeed municipal courts often have to face the fact that the Legislature has not removed from the national statute book measures which have been declared by the ECJ 'incompatible with Community law'. Impliedly such measures are *invalid* but the ECJ has no power to strike them out. It can only expect that they will be either formally repealed by the Legislature or disregarded by the municipal courts. At a Community level this is a matter of state responsibility for its legislature and, therefore a state in default incurs the risk of enforcement action under article 169. At a national level the problem remains unresolved. Therefore, as the Tribunal de Grande Instance recently asked in Paris, 'Are these measures directly and immediately inapplicable[11]?'

The question arose from the prosecution of importers and advertisers of certain apéritifs for offences under the French 'Drinks Code'. Certain provisions of this Code, notwithstanding the health implications, were declared to have breached article 30 of the Treaty and the ECJ[12] condemned France in the stereotyped terms of its judgments in comparable cases, i.e. ... 'The Republic of France, regulating the advertising of alcoholic beverages in a discriminatory manner, thus maintaining obstacles to freedom of intra-Community trade, has neglected to fulfil the obligations

11 *Europe*, No. 3287; 14 January 1982, p. 12.
12 Case 152/78: *EC Commission v France Re Advertising of Alcoholic Beverages*
[1980] ECR 2299, [1981] 2 CMLR 743.

imposed on it under article 30 of the EEC Treaty' ... However the Republic took no notice of this dictum and the public prosecutor continued his work. The trial court put its problem thus at a knife point: '... It seems that Community law, although possessing authority which is superior to that of French internal law, does not necessarily have to be directly and immediately applicable to internal code of law. It must be determined then whether Community law such as it has been laid down ... by the Court of Justice, renders directly and immediately inapplicable the articles L1, L17, L18 and L21 of the Drinks Code and the measures against alcoholism in French national Law ...[13]'

However, the fact that municipal courts are not only prepared to follow the Community Court but also to assert independently the supremacy of Community law is quite significant. It shows that they are prepared to follow the rule of law established by the Community Court and in doing so do not hesitate to disregard the possible claim of municipal law or of their national government to confine disputes involving Community matters to domestic jurisdiction and municipal law. The judge sworn to administer the law of his country has to overcome the temptation to give precedence to the law in which he has been trained over the law derived from an external source.

### ENFORCEMENT OF COMMUNITY LAW AT NATIONAL LEVEL

The corollary to the incorporation of the Treaties and Community legislation into municipal law is the judicial notice of Community law in the member states. Community law, being part of the national legal structure, is applicable and enforceable by the municipal courts as the internal law of the states irrespective of its external origin. However, conflicts arise in practice and an analysis of the decisions of the municipal courts shows, at least during the first decade of the operation of the EEC Treaty, a great deal of confusion and erratic jurisprudence. National judges and lawyers had to settle down to the novel experience and assimilate the challenge of Community law. In this process, the doctrine of supremacy of Community law elaborated by the Community Court and the lessons drawn from preliminary rulings under article 177 had a steadying effect. The recognition by national courts of the direct effect of certain rules of Community law and of its supremacy, is therefore,

---

**13** Quot. from Europe, op. cit.

the most important factor in the process of enforcement of Community law at the Member State level.

We have already observed that, in some cases in which a preliminary ruling under article 177 was requested, the national courts were involved in conflicts between Community law and national law. Moreover, conflicts were often made more acute when the Constitution, the highest law of the land, was said to be infringed. The Community Court refrained from entering the lists, confined itself to interpretation of the relevant rule of Community law, but, nevertheless, albeit indirectly, indicated that Community law had to prevail, irrespective of whether the conflict was with the Constitution or the ordinary law of the land.

It seems, in the light of the experience of the founder members of the Community, that once the Treaties have been duly ratified and incorporated into their legal systems, allegations of unconstitutionality of these Treaties can hardly be made an issue of litigation. By the same token, the constitutionality of the Community legislation can ex hypothesi hardly be raised because, in order to be 'unconstitutional', the Community acts would have to be inconsistent with Community law and this is a matter for the Community Court. In theory, the Community Court could, by upholding the validity of Community legislation, contribute to a constitutional crisis in a member state, the outcome of which cannot be predicted. If the supremacy of Community law and the authority of the Community Court were to prevail, the state concerned would have to put its own house in order; if, on the other hand, the authority of the Community Court were to be questioned, the matter would develop into a political crisis within the Community which could be solved only by political means. Putting these highly conjectural questions aside, it seems that more typical is the conflict between Community law and the ordinary law of the member states. Indeed, as far as the United Kingdom is concerned, it is from this type of conflict that lessons can be learned simply because we do not have an hierarchy of legal norms as our Acts of Parliament have the same status whether they are concerned with the reform of the House of Lords or the reform of the law of illegitimacy.

Arising from Treaties the Community law, notwithstanding its incorporation into the legal systems of the member states, presents certain problems of enforcement by municipal courts when in conflict with municipal law. According to the prevailing doctrine, international law takes priority over municipal law in the jurisprudence of the International Court of Justice[14] but there is no uniformity in state practice. France, the Netherlands and Luxembourg admit supremacy of international law over municipal law, but the other countries treat the rules of international law on an equal footing with the rules of municipal law. In the British[15] system a distinction is made between customary and conventional rules of international law. The former are incorporated through the doctrine of precedent, the latter through legislation. The Greek[16] Constitution recognises supremacy of international conventional law over ordinary non-constitutional enactments but customary rules are on an equal footing with domestic law. However Community law, though generated by Treaties, is not, strictly speaking *international law* in the traditional sense of the term. Therefore the analogies with international law which are occasionally raised are not particularly helpful. Being a *sui generis* system it has to be treated as such and its enforcement has to be seen in the light of the practice evolving in the members states. One starts with international law as far as the Treaties are concerned but secondary Community law raises specific Community problems. At the basic practical level these problems can be reduced to the application of Community law (including the doctrine of supremacy) and the readiness to seek preliminary rulings from the ECJ.

## France

In the light of article 55 of the French Constitution of 1958, Parliament must refrain from passing legislation inconsistent with the international obligations of France since 'a treaty duly ratified has, from the moment of its publication, an authority superior to that of statutes[17].' Should such a bill be presented to Parliament it could be declared unconstitutional by the *Conseil Constitutionnel* (article 61)[18]. The Judiciary and public authorities have to conform. As confirmed by the *Conseil d'Etat* in the *Kirkwood* case[19] an indivi-

---

14   *The Free Zones Case* [1932] PCIJ Rep Ser A/B No 46; *The Wimbledon Case* [1923] PCIJ Rep Ser A No 1; *German Settlers Case* [1923] PCIJ Rep Ser B No 6.

15   Lasok, D., 'Les traités internationaux dans le système juridique anglais' (1966), *Rev Gén de Droit Int Public*, p. 1 (at 3).

16   Evrigenis, D., 'Legal and Constitutional Implications of Greek Accession to the European Communities' (1980), 17 CML Rev, p. 157 at 166.

17   *Per* Commissaire du guvernement Mme Questiaux in *Re Syndicat Général des Fabricants de Semoules Conseil d'Etat* [1970] CMLR 395 Dalloz 285.

18   E.g. *The Abortion Law* held constitutional (1975) II. JCP 180 30 (*Conseil Constitutionnel*).

19   Decided on 30 May 1952, quoted by Constantinidès-Mégret, op. cit., at p. 85.

dual may contest the validity of administrative acts of the state on the ground that they violate international obligations. Case law[20], even under the previous Constitution, conforms to the rule that international obligations have to be honoured by the courts, and judges, through the instrumentality of interpretation, endeavour to avoid conflicts on the assumption that Parliament did not intend to violate international law.

The existence of the Community Court with its inherent jurisdiction gave rise to the theory that since the Community Court solely administers Community law, whilst the national courts administer both the municipal law and Community law, the latter is called upon to resolve conflicts between the two systems without reference to the former[1]. In practice French courts have experienced some difficulty, probably because 'traditionally French tribunals, at least in the past, regarded foreign legislation and pronouncements of foreign courts with some mistrust'[2]. Consequently they were rather reluctant to administer Community law. Thus in *Re Shell-Berre*[3] the *Conseil d'Etat*, applying the doctrine of *acte clair*, refused to refer to the Community Court the question whether a law of 1928 which enabled the government to exercise control over the import and distribution of oil was incompatible with articles 3, 7, 30, 35, 37, 59, 62, 85, 92 and 96 of the EEC Treaty. A similar attitude was shown by the first subsection of the *Conseil d'Etat* in *Syndicat Général des Fabricants de Semoules*[4] which held that a French decree introducing an import levy on semolina inconsistent with Community regulations was to prevail. It could be said that the case was rather exceptional as it concerned imports from Algeria which, by virtue of French legislation, were to remain within the French customs frontiers but in fact the *Conseil d'Etat* preferred to apply French law to Community law. The breakthrough came in *Re Syndicat National du Commerce Extérieur*[5]. In that case a syndicate dealing in cereals requested the interpretation of the term 'any

20  Cited by Constantinidès-Mégret, ibid., at p. 86.
 1  See *Riff v Soc Grande Limonaderie Alsacienne*, decided by the Cour de Cassation (Chambre Criminelle), 19 February 1964, [1965] 1 Clunet 85-90; 2 CML Rev 448-449; *Etat Français v Nicolas and Société Brandt*, decided by the Cour d'Appel of Amiens, 9 May 1963; [1963] CMLR 239 at 245; [1964] Clunet 93; upheld on other grounds by the Cour de Cassation (Chambre Criminelle), 22 October 1964, [1965] Clunet 90; 2 CML Rev 449.
 2  Simon, M. 'Enforcement by French Courts of European Community Law' (1974) 90 LQR 467 at 471.
 3  [1964] CMLR 462, [1964] Clunet 794.
 4  [1970] CMLR 395, [1968] Dalloz 285, 6 CML Rev 419.
 5  [1971] Dalloz 576 and 645.

holder' (EEC regulation 1028/68) to be referred to the Community Court as it considered itself to be prejudiced by the narrow interpretation of this term by the ONIC (i.e. the National Cereals Board). The *Conseil* agreed that the Community Court gave a wide interpretation which, in turn, enabled the *Conseil* to annul the decision of the ONIC in this respect.

Dealing with the individuals the *Conseil* acted in a rather individualistic manner. It set aside a Prefect's order to deport aliens who applied for a residence permit in order to establish a production co-operative known as a 'Pioneer European Village[6],' but denied admission to a person who in his youth, a decade earlier, achieved notoriety during the student troubles[7]. The latter case is remarkable because the *Conseil* ignored the relevant Community precedents, refused to make a reference to the Community Court and ruled that directives (in particular directive 64/221) cannot be invoked by individuals in national proceedings in order to challenge an administrative act.

The Civil Courts appear to be more favourably disposed towards Community law but they too had their difficulties. In the *Consten*[8] saga involving the validity of an exclusive distribution contract, the Paris Court of Appeal quashed the judgment of a Commercial Court (which effectively denied the application of EEC regulation 17/1962 in this respect[9]) and stayed the action until the Commission had made its decision in the matter. Two years later a Court of First Instance dealing with the same problem[10] noted the Commission decision in the previous case and stayed the action to await the outcome of the proceedings before the Community Court. From that time on the French Civil Courts became quite prepared to resort to the proceedings under article 177, a notable early example being the *Ulm* case[11]. Thus, the Paris Court of Appeal, applying the judgment of the Community Court in the *Beguelin* case[12], held article 85 and regulations 10/1965 and 67/1967 directly applicable in France with the effect that a contract between a French and a Dutch firm, granting the former exclusive distribution rights,

---

6  *Re Hill and Holzappel* [1978] 2 CMLR 554.
7  *Minister of the Interior v Cohn Bendit* [1980] 1 CMLR 543, [1979] Dalloz 155.
8  Cases 56, 58/64: *Consten and Grundig v EC Commission* [1966] ECR 299, [1966] CMLR 418.
9  *Consten v UNEF* [1963] CMLR 176, [1963] Dalloz 189.
10  *Consten v Willy-Leissner, Rev. Trim. de Droit Européen* (1965) 487.
11  Case 56/65: *Société Technique Minière v Maschinenbau Ulm GmbH* [1966] ECR 235, [1966] CMLR 357.
12  Case 22/71 *Beguelin Import Co v SAGL Import-Export* [1971] ECR 949, [1972] CMLR 81.

was declared invalid. The decision was confirmed by the *Cour de Cassation*[13].

The Criminal Chamber of the *Cour de Cassation* also made its contribution. In *Administration des Contributions Indirectes, etc. v Ramel*[14] the *Cour de Cassation* dismissed an appeal against the acquittal of the respondent on the charge of offering for sale inferior wine imported from Italy. The wine was admitted to France under the EEC regulations although its quality did not comply with French law. In the *Republic v Von Saldern et al*[15] the *Cour de Cassation* dismissed an appeal against conviction for breach of exchange control regulations involved in the import of chemicals from the USA. The appeal was based on Community customs regulations concerning the valuation of imported goods which were issued after the alleged offence. Since these regulations were not retrospective the appeal had to fail and the question of conflict with national law did not arise. In the *Guerrini* case[16], concerning a conviction for an offence under a 1939 law laying down standards for the marketing of eggs, the Court of Appeal at Aix disregarded the relevant EEC regulations (122/67 and 1619/68) as it considered itself bound by the unrepealed statute. However the *Cour de Cassation* reversed that decision on the ground that the regulations had a direct effect repealing, as it were, the French legislation from the date on which the regulations came into force.

However, perhaps the most significant case is that of *Directeur Général des Douanes v Société des Cafés Jacques Vabre et Société Weigel Cie*[17]. The central point of that case was whether importers of instant coffee from Holland were legitimately charged with import duties which put them at a disadvantage as compared with French manufacturers of the product and thus suffered discrimination contrary to EEC article 95. The French customs authorities claimed that article 265 of the *Code de Douanes*, being enacted after the French accession to the Community, had to be applied and that article 55 of the Constitution notwithstanding, French courts had no jurisdiction in the matter of the constitutionality of the Code. In the Court of First Instance and the Paris Court of Appeal these arguments were rejected and finally the *Cour de Cassation* decided

13 *Entreprises Garoche v Société Striker Boats Nederland* [1974] CMLR 469.
14 [1971] CMLR 315, [1971] Dalloz 211.
15 (1971) 10 CML Rev 223.
16 *Guerrini Case*, 7 January 1972 (JCP 1972, II), 10 CML Rev 451.
17 Court of Appeal, Paris, 7 July 1973, Dalloz (1974) 159, Cour de Cassation, [1975] 2 CMLR 336. Also see Simon, M. (1976), 92 LQR 85.

that the EEC Treaty established a separate legal order which prevails in France even over subsequent legislation. The requirement of reciprocity under article 55 of the Constitution has been satisfied in the Treaty of Rome. It held

> '... the treaty which by virtue of the above-mentioned article of the Constitution has an authority superior to that of statutes, established its own juridical order integrated with that of member states, and by virtue of this special character the juridical system which it has created is directly applicable to the nationals of these states and is binding on their courts; and therefore ... article 95 of the Treaty has to be applied ... to the exclusion of article 265 of the Customs Code, despite the fact that the latter is of a later date.'

Recognising the supremacy of Community law (i.e. the right of establishment) the *Cour de Cassation* quashed the judgment of a court of appeal and ruled that a German was entitled to recover his farm from a French tenant on expiry of the lease despite the provision of the *Code Rural* which insists that aliens are not allowed to farm in France without a special permit to that effect. It held that ... 'the provisions of French internal law which imposed the requirement of an administrative permit on those who wanted to farm in France have ceased to be applicable[18] ...'

There seems to be a world of difference between the civil and the administrative jurisdictions in France.

### The Netherlands

Since the amendment of the Netherlands Constitution in 1953 and 1956, there seems to be no doubt that, in principle, Community law should be given precedence before Dutch law. We have already noted the *Van Gend en Loos* case[19] which, prior to coming before the Community Court for preliminary ruling, unfolded as a case involving a conflict between the Constitution and Community law. Similarly in *de Geus v Bosch*[20] the argument that only rules of international law of a 'universal application' take precedence over national law failed. These decisions had, undoubtedly, a profound effect upon the practice of Dutch courts.

Of more recent cases *Centrafarm*[1] calls for special mention. In

---

**18** *Von Kempis v Geldof* [1976] 2 CMLR 152, Cour de Cass. Civil Chamber, 15 December 1975.
**19** Case 26/62 [1963] ECR 1, [1963] CMLR 105.
**20** Case 13/61: [1962] ECR 45, [1962] CMLR 1.
 **1** Case No. 10. 712, *Centrafarm BV and De Peijper v Sterling Drug Inc* [1976] CMLR 1.

that case the *Hoge Raad*, applying the preliminary rulings of the Community Court, refused an injunction to a trade-mark holder and a patentee which would restrain the marketing in Holland of thus protected pharmaceutical products originating from the United Kingdom.

In *Officer Van Justitie v Adriaan de Peijper, Managing Director of Centrafarm BV*, the *Kantongerecht*[2] at Rotterdam pronounced upon the freedom of movement and parallel imports of pharmaceutical products but left a question open as to whether certain rules of national law regarding the authentication and certification of such products, imposed by another member state, were contrary to the EEC principles of the freedom of movement of goods. Applying the ruling of the ECJ[3] the *Kantongerecht* acquitted the importer of drugs therapeutically indistinguishable from approved national products from a charge arising under national drug control legislation which requires certain documentation which could not be procured because the drugs in question were imported[4].

In the *Ruigrok* case[5] the Supreme Court upheld the conviction for cultivating hyacinth bulbs commercially without a licence. Thus the convicted cultivator had to pay the fine notwithstanding the fact that the relevant Dutch law was inconsistent with Community law as previously decreed by the Community Court. Whilst accepting the ruling of the ECJ as binding (and resulting in the quashing of the conviction in the cited case) the Supreme Court distinguished the present case in so far as it concerned an application to set aside a judgment which had become absolute and this, according to Dutch law, was inadmissible. The conviction was a result of an error of law and not of fact unknown to the court at the time of the conviction and sentence and, therefore, could not be set aside.

Dealing with aliens, the *Raad van State*, without referring the matter to the ECJ, held that a British subject continuously wilfully unemployed was not entitled to have his residence permit renewed[6]. However another[7], though in irregular employment and guilty of petty offences was allowed to stay in Holland. More recently the question whether a British wife of a South African citizen[8] was

2 [1976] CMLR 19.
3 Case 104/75: *Re de Peijper* [1976] ECR 613, [1976] 2 CMLR 271.
4 *Officer Van Justitie v de Peijper* [1977] 1 CMLR 321.
5 [1977] 1 CMLR 306.
6 *Williams v Secretary of State for Justice* [1977] 1 CMLR 669.
7 *Simbula v Secretary of State for Justice* [1978] 2 CMLR 74.
8 Case 53/81: *Levin v Staatssecretaris van Justitie* (delivered on 20 January 1982); *Europe* 25 March 1982 (Reference [1981] 3 CMLR 663).

entitled to the status of 'favoured EEC citizen' for the purpose of residence despite the fact that her earnings were below the national subsistence level, was referred to the ECJ. At stake was her status as 'worker'. Advocate-General Sir Gordon Slynn thought that the principal test was not the number of hours worked but whether 'work was the genuine and substantial purpose of the application to reside.' The ECJ concurred.

The *Raad van State* held ·inadmissible the appeal against the refusal of the Government to bring before the ECJ an action for annulment of a Council regulation which imposed a levy for the production of the isoglucose. Such a Government decision was not subject to juridical review in accordance with Dutch administrative law and, therefore, a citizen could not force the Government to bring an action in this respect[9].

### Luxembourg

The Constitution of Luxembourg contains no provision regarding the relationship between international law and municipal law, but the judiciary, in the course of time, has evolved the principle of supremacy of international law[10]. In this process a judgment of the *Conseil d'Etat* of 1950 and a judgment of the Superior Court of 1954 have a special significance as they established the principle that a rule of international law will prevail over a rule of national law even if the latter is subsequent to the former[11].

### Belgium

The Belgian Constitution of 1831 has been revised, mainly to accommodate Belgian membership of the European Community. Since 1925 Belgian courts gave precedence over national law if inconsistent with a treaty[12]. This rule was broadened by the *Cour de Cassation* in 1964[13]. The court distinguished between treaties binding the state and treaties creating rights and obligations directly enforceable by individuals. Only the latter, by their very nature, can be in conflict with Belgian domestic law and if they are in conflict they must have precedence over municipal law. This

---

9  *Koninklijke Scholten-Honig NV v Minister of Agriculture and Fisheries* [1978] 3 CMLR 251.

10  Pescatore, P., 'Prééminence des traités sur la loi interne la jurisprudence luxembourgeoise', *Journal des Tribunaux*, 1953, p. 445; see also Constantinidès-Mégret, op. cit., p. 88, 89.

11  Cases cited in *Les Novelles: Droit des Communautés Européennes* (1969), p. 67.

12  Ibid., p. 63.

13  Ibid., p. 63.

ruling was complemented by a decision of the *Conseil d'Etat* made a month before the decision of the *Cour de Cassation*[14]. In a case brought against the Belgian Ministry of Agriculture, the Treaty of 1953 between Belgium and France concerning the protection of birds was construed as an obligation binding the state alone and having no direct effect upon the rights and obligations of citizens. It would appear, accordingly, that depending on their classification (i.e. whether binding the citizen or merely the state) some provisions of the EEC Treaty are directly enforceable by Belgian courts, whereas others are not so enforceable. Following this philosophy the *Tribunal de Commerce be Bruxelles* considered article 85 (1) of the EEC Treaty directly applicable[15]. Being directly applicable, the Treaty may render void a contract valid when made[16].

No doubt the process of accommodating Belgian traditions to the problem of Community law enforcement was influenced by the two famous cases *Costa v ENEL* and *Van Gend en Loos* which made a considerable impact within the Community. Their influence can be seen in the decision of the Magistrates' Court of Antwerp[17] which, having lavishly cited authorities and juristic opinion, concluded that, should there be a conflict between the EEC Treaty and subsequent Belgian legislation, the former would prevail[18]. The Belgian Government too agreed that the Treaty should be given precedence over any subsequent legislation inconsistent with the Treaty[19].

In the field of social legislation the District Court of Tongeren has held that article 12 of Community Regulation 3 prevailed over Belgian legislation on industrial accidents in accordance with the principle that *lex posterior derogat priori*[20].

In the *Corveleyn*[1] case the *Conseil d'Etat* applied the Community directive 64/221 of 25 February 1964 in order to quash a deportation order. But the high water mark of the evolution towards the

---

**14** Ibid., p. 64.
**15** *Van Heuvermeiren v Buitoni* [1967] CMLR 241 at 245, (1966) 1 *Cahiers de Droit Européen* 317.
**16** *Association Générale des Fabricants de Ciment Portland Artificiel v SA Carriére Dufour* [1965] CMLR 193 at 207-208.
**17** *Sociaal Fonds voor de Diamantoarbeiders v Chougol Diamond Co* [1969] CMLR 315 at 320-323.
**18** The Community Court in another context (effects of the introduction of the common external tariff) involving the same parties, implied the same result; cases 2-3/69: [1969] ECR 211 at 221-224, [1969] CMLR 335 at 349-353.
**19** *SPRL Corn and Food Trading Co v Etat Belge* (1968) *Cahiers de Droit Européen*, 550 at 554.
**20** *NV Essimex v J Jans* [1972] CMLR 48.
**1** See p. 102, ante.

recognition of the supremacy of Community law was reached in the decision of the *Cour de Cassation* in *Minister for Economic Affairs v SA Fromagerie Franco-Suisse 'Le Ski'*[2]. This case, concerning a claim for money paid by mistake on the ground that, by reason of article 12 of the EEC Treaty, the duties in question did not apply to the products imported from member states of the Community, gave the Procureur-Général Ganshof van der Meersch, an opportunity to discuss the nature of the self-executing provisions of the Treaty, the binding force of Community law, sovereignty and the relationship between Community law and the law of Belgium. In his erudite submissions, he reviewed a host of learned writings and 48 cases decided by the Community Court, the Belgian courts and the courts of Luxembourg and Germany[3]. Quoting *Van Gend en Loos* and *Costa v ENEL* he submitted that:

'... Community law is integrated in the law of member states. From its very nature, it follows that a subsequent measure of state legislation cannot be set against it ... As Professor Pescatore has said: "One is entitled to think that the fundamental argument is to be found in this last passage: the very existence of the Community is called in question if the Community legal system cannot be established with identical effects and with uniform effectiveness over the whole geographical areas of the Community ...[4]

... The primacy of the rules of Community law is doubly justified on legal grounds. First by their agreement on the transfer of their rights and obligations under the Treaty to the Community legal system, the states definitely limited their "sovereign rights", or to put it more accurately, "the exercise of their sovereign powers". The Community system implies some surrender of sovereignty and Community law is a specific law which gives effect to this surrender. The integration aim of the Treaties of Paris and of Rome is attained by handing over to the Community institutions powers having as their object and effect the determination of a corresponding limitation of the powers of Member States ...

... Thus was created for these states a duty to abstain from action in the fields regulated by the Treaty and a duty to take all complementary steps needed to enforce Community legislation.

... Secondly, Community law is a specific and autonomous law which is binding on the courts of the member states and makes it impossible to set against it any domestic law whatsoever. The very nature of the legal system instituted by the Treaties of Rome confers that primacy on its own foundation, independently of the constitutional provisions in

2 [1972] CMLR 330.
3 See, in particular, ibid., pp. 351–358.
4 Pescatore, P., *Droit communautaire et droit national* (1969), p. 183, quoting from *Costa v ENEL* [1964] CMLR 425 at 455, 456.

states[5]. The specific character of Community law stems from the objectives of the Treaty which are the establishment of a new legal system to which are subject not only states, but also the nationals of those states. It also stems from the fact that the Treaty has set up institutions having their own powers and especially that of creating new sources of law. From their very structures, these institutions reflect the will of the authors of the Treaty to go beyond the state framework and to impose obligations directly on individual persons and to confer rights directly on them[6]... If the Community system is not recognised as superior, rules would not be the same within each member state, and the consequences would be that such a situation would necessarily give rise to forms of discrimination proscribed by the treaties, that obligations would not bear equally on everybody and that not everyone would derive equal benefit from the rights derived from the treaties ...'

This long passage represents the quintessence of the Belgian and Community *doctrine* and reflects, it seems, the mood within the Community. The Court, on the other hand, in its terse judgment ruled:

'... Even if assent to a treaty as required by article 68 (2) of the Constitution, is given in the form of a statute, the legislative power, by giving this assent, is not carrying out a normative function. The conflict which exists between a legal norm established by an international treaty and a norm established by a subsequent statute, is not a conflict between two statutes.

The rule that a statute repeals a previous statute in so far as there is a conflict between the two, does not apply in the case of a conflict between a treaty and a statute.

In the event of a conflict between a norm of domestic law and a norm of international law which produces direct effects in the internal system, the rule established by the treaty shall prevail. The primacy of the treaty results from the very nature of international treaty law. This is a fortiori the case when a conflict exists, as in the present case, between a norm of internal law and a norm of Community law.

The reason is that the treaties which have created Community law have instituted a new legal system in whose favour the member states restricted the exercise of their sovereign powers in the areas determined by those treaties.

Article 12 of the Treaty ... is immediately effective and confers on individual persons rights which national courts are bound to uphold.

It follows from all these considerations that it was the duty of the judge to set aside the application of provisions of domestic law that are contrary to this Treaty provision ...'[7]

5 Quoting Tallon, D., *Le droit communautaire* (1966) I *Cahiers de Droit Européen* 571.
6 Quoting his own writings, 'Le droit communautaire et ses rapports avec les droits des Etats membres', in *Droit des Communautés européennes* (1969), Nos. 138-139.
7 [1972] CMLR at 372, 373.

*Federal German Republic*

Judging by the number of cases decided by various German courts and the Community Court, enforcement of Community law in Germany gave rise to specific problems in the absence of an express provision in the Federal Constitution governing the relationship between international and municipal law. Rules had to be evolved by the courts assisted by learned writers and, in this process, decisions of the Community Court played a significant part. The starting point is the strong dualist tradition of which Triepel[8] was perhaps the most influential exponent. According to this doctrine a rule of international law becomes enforceable only if expressly incorporated into the municipal law. Having been so incorporated, it ranks in the hierarchy of legal norms among the ordinary rules of internal law (statutes) and is subject to the principle *lex posterior derogat priori*. However, in this context, Community law was soon recognised as having a special status being a sui generis law though the courts have, for a while, followed an erratic course.

Learned writers, especially Ophüls[9], Ipsen[10] and Wohlfart[11], advocated a departure from the tradition arguing that Community law ought to have precedence over national law. The courts, on the other hand, had to deduce the rule of supremacy from the provisions of the Federal Constitution which, by article 24 (1), enables the Federal State to transfer sovereign powers to international institutions and, in article 25, proclaims that the general rules of international law form an integral part of the federal territory. Ipsen[12] called article 24 the *Integrationshebel* (lever of integration) and Vogel[13] argued that the legislature must contribute towards European integration. The judges must follow the legislature and give precedence to Community law inconsistent with internal

8 Triepel, H., *Völkerrecht und Landesrecht* (1899); *Rec. de Cours de l'Académie de la Haye*, 'Les rapports entre le droit interne et le droit international', 1923, Vol. 1, pp. 76 et seq.

9 Ophüls, C. F., 'Zwischen Völkerrecht und staatlichem Recht, Grundfragen des europäischen Rechts', *Juristen-Jahrbuch*, Vol. 4 (1963-64), pp. 137-162.

10 Ipsen, H. P., 'Rapport du droit des Communautés Européenes avec le droit national', *Le Droit et les Affaires* (1964), No. 47.

11 Wohlfart, E., 'Europäisches Recht, Von der Befugnis der Organe der europäischen Wirtschaftsgemeinschaft zur Rechtsetzung', *Jahrbuch für Internazionales Recht*, Vol. 9, pp. 12-32.

12 Ipsen, op. cit., p. 26.

13 Vogel, K., *Die Verfassungsentscheidung des Grundgesetzes für eine internationale Zusammenarbeit* (1964), p. 46.

law[14]. The prevailing juristic opinion favoured supremacy of Community law but courts were faced with arguments that Community law was 'unconstitutional' in so far as it contravenes 'fundamental rights'. Under a written constitution which guarantees 'fundamental rights' with little ingenuity any question can be raised to a constitutional issue.

The following are the landmarks on the road to the supremacy rule.

In *Re Tax on Malt Barley*[15] the Federal Constitutional Court (*Bundesverfassungsgericht*) clarified the position of the EEC Treaty Ratification Law and the Community agricultural regulations whose constitutionality was doubted by the *Finanzgericht* of Rheinland-Pfalz. It held[16]:

'... Section one of the EEC Treaty Act is based upon the power contained in article 24 (1) of the Constitution, and is within the limits imposed on the transfer of sovereign rights to international authorities by article 79 (3) of the Constitution. A balanced system for the co-operation of the Community's Council, Commission and Parliament guarantees a control of power which is institutionally preserved as effective as the traditional separation of powers. It satisfies the most stringent demands of "the rule of law" ...'

Turning to the Regulation issued under the EEC article 189, the Court declared:

'... Article 189 is of great importance in the framework of the whole Treaty. But it would be wrong to conclude from this that the whole Treaty would be purposeless if article 189 and the regulations passed thereunder were not immediately binding in the Federal Republic. In the Court's opinion, the nullity of one provision does not in principle entail the invalidity of the whole act or law. The whole law would only be void in such a case if on its true construction, the remaining provisions had no significance on their own or if the unconstitutional provisions are part of a self-contained set of regulations which would have no sense of effacacy if one of their constituent parts is taken away.
... These provisions apply to Treaty law too. The effect of their application to section one of the EEC Treaty Act is that, even if this provision were to be held unconstitutional in so far as it relates to article 189 of the Treaty, the EEC Treaty Act would still not become totally invalid; the effectiveness of the remaining provisions in the German Federal Republic would not be disturbed ...'

14  Fuss, E. W., 'Rechtsschutz gegen deutsche Hoheitsakte zur Ausführung des Europäischen Gemeinschaftsrechts', *Neue Juristische Wocheinschrift* (1966), p. 1782.
15  Case III 77/63 [1964] CMLR 130.
16  2 BvL 29/63: *Re Tax on Malt Barley* [1967] CMLR 302 at 311, 316.

As a result, a substantial body of case law has confirmed the view that article 189 and the Treaty are applicable in Germany[17].

On the question of Community law being inconsistent with previous German Law the *Finanzgericht* of Münster held ...[18]

'... the organs of the Community were given powers of legislation in matters pertaining to the Community and that legislation is binding on the Member States. If those powers are to mean anything Community legislation must have the effect, within its sphere of competence, of amending or repealing, by implication, national legislation which is repugnant to it ...'

The Courts went further because in a number of cases[19] they held that Community law superseded subsequent German legislation.

On the specific question of direct application of the EEC Treaty (article 95) two cases should be specially noted. In the *Mölkerei* case[20] the Court held that the rate of compensatory tax imposed on an imported agricultural product from another state violated the non-discrimination principle. The Court arrived at this conclusion because '... in so far as the court finds that there is a contravention of that rule of Community law it must take account of the *precedence* of Community law. That is the only way in which the immediate effectiveness accorded to article 95 by the European Court[1] can be interpreted and a corresponding juridical protection be given to the individual subjects of the member states of the Community ...' In *Re Imported Thai Sand Flower*[2] the *Finanzericht* of Bremen held that imported products had to be classified for the purpose of customs duties according to the EEC Regulations governing the common organisation of the market for cereals rather than German rules. The Court ruled that '... to the extent that the member states have assigned legislative powers in levying tariff matters to the Community in order to ensure the proper operation of the common market for cereals, they no longer have the power to make legislative provisions in this field'.

17  See cases listed by Campbell, op. cit., Vol. 1, 1.83 and Supplement No. 2, p. 15.
18  In Case IVc 20–21/63: *Re Import of Pork* [1966] CMLR 491 at 498–499.
19  See cases listed by Campbell, op. cit., Vol. 1, 1.103, and Supplement No. 2, p. 16, Suppl. 1975, p. 43.
20  VII 156/65 *Mölkerei-Zentrale Westfalen/Lippe GmbH v Hauptzollamt Paderborn* [1969] CMLR 300 at 312.
 1  In *Lütticke v EEC Commission* [1966] CMLR 378.
 2  [1971] CMLR 521 at 523.

However, in a case[3] involving the validity of export deposits said to be in violation of the German Constitution, the Administrative Court in Frankfurt am Main held that Community law enjoyed only a limited superiority over national law.

The Court reviewed a substantial body of juristic opinion representing inter alia the view that Community law can be scrutinised against the provisions of the Federal Constitution which the Federal legislature has no power to abrogate or restrict. The Court held that article 12 (3) of Regulation 120/67 of the EEC Council of 13 June 1967 and article 9 of Regulation 473/67 of the EEC Commission of 21 August 1967, which require export deposits, constituted an infringement of the Federal Constitution because they infringed the 'freedom of development, economic freedom and the principle of proportionality' and were, therefore, unconstitutional. The Court considered that 'these regulations are not German statutes but legal provisions of the European Economic Community which constitute neither public international law nor national law of the Member States' and concluded that like statutes (*Gesetze*) operating in Germany they are subject to scrutiny against the fundamental principles of the Constitution. However it referred the matter for a preliminary ruling to the Community Court which rejected its arguments holding that[4]:

'... The validity of acts of the Community institutions may be assessed only by reference to Community law since national legal provisions ... cannot have priority over the law created by the Treaty ... unless its character as Community law is to be denied and the legal basis of the Community itself questioned. The validity of a Community act and its applicability to a member state cannot therefore be affected by the claim that fundamental rights ... or the principles of its constitution have been infringed ...'

The Administrative Court, not satisfied with the ruling, submitted the case to the Federal Constitutional Court[5] which considered that the contested ruling on deposits did not offend the fundamental rights guaranteed by the German Constitution but affirmed its determination to scrutinise the secondary Community law in the light of the *Grundgesetz*. It also expressed the hope that complete integration of the Community and the development of a Community

---

3 *Internationale Handelsgesellschaft mbH v Einfuhr- und Vorratsstelle für Getreide und Futtermittel* [1970] CMLR 294.
4 Wording taken from a Note to European Parliament, P.E. 37.907 (Directorate for Research and Documentation) p. 5. Also see [1972] CMLR 255.
5 [1972] CMLR 177.

Parliament should bring about a Community Charter of Fundamental Rights. Until this has occurred conflicts between Community law and German Fundamental Rights are not excluded and in such conflicts the German law may claim priority[6].

The many references to the ECJ noted in the preceding pages demonstrate a liberal application of article 177 by the German courts. However the cases to be especially noted are those involving constitutional issues. Another interesting feature of the German case law is the willingness to acknowledge the persuasive authority of the judgments of the European Court.

Recently the Supreme Federal Administrative Court[7] citing several EEC precedents, saw no contravention of the constitutional guarantee of property rights in the refusal of the National Agricultural Intervention Agency to buy agricultural produce under the CAP system. It also ruled that a retrospective national regulation issued by virtue of a Commission direction restricting subsidies in respect of home produced wheat was not unconstitutional since the German Constitution does not prohibit legislation having a retrospective effect.

The same court held that a time-barred[8] action could not be revived after the ruling of the ECJ in favour of the appellant[9]. Thus an applicant, who waited until the ECJ had decided in his favour, was unable to obtain reimbursement of illegally levied phythosanitary inspection fees on apples imported from France. The national limitation statute was applied.

The Federal Supreme Court[10] expressly recognised the persuasive authority of a Community precedent[11] in so far as the existence of such a precedent absolved the Supreme Court from the obligation of making a reference under article 177.

Ruling in the matter of direct elections to the European Parliament the Federal Constitutional[12] Court held that the European

---

6 Note to European Parliament, PE 37.907, p. 7. Also see [1974] 2 CMLR 540.
7 *Re Intervention Buying* [1978] 2 CMLR 644.
8 *Rewe-Zentralfinanz v Landeswirtschaftskammer für das Saarland* [1978] 2 CMLR 594.
9 In Case 33/76: *Rewe-Zentralfinanz RG and Rewe Zentral AG v Landswirtschaftskammer für das Saarland* [1970] ECR 1989, [1977] 1 CMLR 533.
10 *Terrapin (Overseas) Ltd v Terranova Industrie CA Kapferer & Co* [1978] 3 CMLR 102.
11 Case 119/75: *Terrapin (Overseas) Ltd v Terranova Industrie CA Kapferer & Co* [1976] ECR 1039, [1976] CMLR 482.
12 *Re the European Elections Act* [1980] 1 CMLR 497.

Parliament had functions similar to national parliaments. In European elections the principles of the German electoral law were applicable.

The same court, upholding, no doubt, the principle of the separation of functions between the Community institutions and the national institutions, ruled that the validity of Community legislation applicable in the Member States cannot be reviewed by German courts[13].

## Italy

In Italy's practice, the dualist doctrine, represented by Judge Anzilotti[14], has left a deep imprint on the relationship between Community law and Italian law. The dualist tradition coupled with a rigid Constitution put the Italian judge in a position which is more difficult than that of the judge in any other country of the EEC. The relevant provisions of the Constitution (articles 10 and 11) state that the Italian legal order conforms to the generally recognised rules of international law and that Italy will agree, on equal terms with other states, to the limitation of sovereignty necessary to establish a lasting peace and justice among nations. This is hardly conducive to the courts being Community minded when confronted with the compelling challenge to obey the Constitution.

Italy's problem is well reflected in the *Costa v ENEL* case which, parallel to its career in the Community, had a full run at home. The Constitutional Court, as we have seen, was called upon to decide whether or not the decree nationalising the electricity industry and establishing a monopoly in the shape of the ENEL as well as certain provisions of the EEC Treaty were contrary to the Constitution. According to the Constitution, the constitutional court has the power to review legislation and declare 'illegitimate' Acts of Parliament and subordinate legislation which do not conform to the Constitution (article 136 (1)). Community law was brought into the contest as it was alleged that articles 37 (2), 53, 93 (2) and 102 of the EEC Treaty, which were relevant to this case, infringed article 11 of the Constitution. In terms of the conflict of legislations, the nationalisation decree of 1962 was said to have repealed an earlier (Community) law.

---

13 *Firma Steinike und Weinlig v Bundesamt für Ernährung und Forstwirtschaft* [1980] 2 CMLR 531.
14 Anzilotti, D., *Corso di Diritto Internazionale*, Vol. 1 (3rd edn 1928), pp. 51 et seq.

The Court dealt with the problem in a classic dualist fashion: infringement of the Treaty would entail international responsibility of the State of Italy, but would not necessarily affect the validity of the law enacted in contravention of treaty. In this way, the Court, in accordance with the dualist doctrine, accorded to the Treaty no higher rank than that of the ordinary legislation. The problem was reduced to a conflict between two 'internal' laws where the principle *lex posterior derogat priori* should apply. It appears that the position would have been different[15] if the Treaty had been promulgated as a *constitutional law* in accordance with article 138 of the Constitution in which case the nationalisation decree would have to be tested in the light of the Treaty. However, article 11 of the Constitution enabled the State of Italy to surrender by treaty some of its sovereign powers to an international institution and this indeed occurred when the EEC Treaty was ratified. The Court recognised this, but concluded that it did not have to discuss the nature of the EEC or the consequences of the ratification of the Treaty, or, indeed, decide whether or not the decree infringed the Treaty[16].

The decision of the Constitutional Court stimulated the jurists and the lively discussions which followed produced a trend in favour of the supremacy of Community law which was in conflict with Italian law. This has been deduced by Quadri[17] and others from article 10 of the Constitution. They reasoned in their dualist fashion that, transformed into Italian law, a rule of international law is binding: *pacta recepta sunt servanda.*

The second support of the Italian doctrine of supremacy is derived from article 11 of the Constitution. The most plausible is the argument of the former judge of the Community Court, Catalano[18] who sees two effects of article 11: a permissive effect which enables the Italian State to delegate its sovereignty and a dispositive effect which limits the powers of the constitutional organs of the State. He argues further that, although the measure which in effect limits sovereignty may take the form of an ordinary law, it differs nevertheless from ordinary law because it has a constitutional effect. If, therefore, a treaty limits the legislative power of the Italian lawmaking bodies within certain areas, the legislature, acting within

15  Neri, S., 'Le juge italien et le droit communautaire', *Le juge national et le droit communautaire* (1966), p. 81.
16  24 February–7 March 1964, *Foro Italiano* (1964), I, 465.
17  Quadri, R., *Diritto Internazionale Pubblico* (1963), pp. 59 et seq.
18  Catalano, N. 'La position du droit communautaire dans le droit des Etats membres', *Droit communautaire et droit national* (Bruges 1965), pp. 61 et seq.

the scope of its authority, can no longer exercise its power in these areas.

In *Société Acciaierie San Michele v High Authority of the ECSC*[19] the Constitutional Court recognised the 'permissive' effect of article 11. In this case the appellant, a steel company, contested the constitutionality of a fine imposed by the High Authority of the ECSC for failure to produce invoices relating to the consumption of electricity by the appellant. The Court, in dismissing the appeal, held: '. . . in recognising the Community order the state was endeavouring not so much to insert the same in its own system, but rather to make way within such system for the international co-operation which the state has as its aim . . . the organs of our internal jurisdiction are not qualified to criticise acts by organs of the ECSC because the latter are not subject to the sovereign power of the member states of the Community, and cannot be found within the framework of any such state. Therefore, their acts can only be subject to a legislative qualification on the part of individual member states albeit within the limits where there may exist an obligation not to refuse to acknowledge their effects . . .'

Recognising the 'right of the individual to his jurisdictional protection' the Court acknowledged the power of the Community Court to exercise its jurisdiction and of the Italian subject to plead Community law where appropriate.

The principle of supremacy of Community law was thus accepted, but it fell to a body of jurists assembled in Rome in February 1966 to affirm supremacy not only in respect of previous but also in respect of subsequent Italian legislation. An important exception to the rule *lex posterior derogat priori* was conceded in favour of Community law. But, at the same time, the jurists affirmed the power of the Italian Judiciary, especially the Constitutional Court, to scrutinise Community acts and determine whether or not they conform to the Italian Constitution[20].

Developments in the post *San Michele* period testify to general compliance with the principle. In *Salgoil SpA v Ministry for Foreign Trade*[1] the Rome Court of Appeal, following the ruling of the Community Court in the same case[2], held that article 31 of the EEC Treaty gave rise to individual rights which can be enforced by

19 Case 98/65: [1967] CMLR 160, 4 CML Rev 81, [1965] *I Foro Italiano* 569.
20 French text of the Jurists' Resolution, Neri, S., 'Le droit communautaire et l'ordre constitutionnel italien' (1966), *Cahiers de droit européen* 363 at 376, 377.
1 [1970] CMLR 314 at 335-336.
2 Case 13/68 [1968] ECR 453 at 462, 463, [1969] CMLR 181 at 196.

national courts, though such rights have to be regarded as rights within the national system of law. The Italian attitude is conveniently summarised in *Frontini v Ministero delle Finanze*[3]. On a reference from the *Tribunale* of Turin the *Corte Costituzionale* confirmed the constitutionality of the Italian EEC Treaty Ratification Act and upheld the supremacy of Community regulations. By the same token the supremacy of the EEC Treaty itself was implicitly recognised. The *Corte Costituzionale* made a significant reservation in connection with human rights. It recognised that the European Court was the guarantor of the rights and interests of individuals in fields of law concerned with economic relations. But, if ever the legislative power of the EEC were to be used to violate the fundamental principles of the Italian Constitution or the inalienable rights of man, then the *Corte Costituzionale* would reserve the right to control the continuing compatibility of the EEC Treaty with such principles and rights.

The question whether all Italian courts have to refuse to apply national law when inconsistent with Community law or whether this is a matter reserved exclusively for the Constitutional Court (left open in the *Frontini* case) was considered in the ICJC case[4]. Whilst the Italian and the Community texts concerning the application of the import licensing system for cereals were identical there was the technical question whether the Italian text, being the *lex posterior* to the relevant Community regulation, was the governing text to be applied by the courts. There was also a problem of divergent interpretation as between the ECJ and Italian courts. The *Corte Costituzionale* declared the national text unconstitutional saying that . . . 'There was no reason . . . to reproduce the regulations . . . in national laws. The adoption of the corresponding Italian law violates the principles of . . . the Treaty, whose constitutionality has been accepted . . .'. However on the practical point of direct application of the Community law the Court held that . . . 'the existing legal order does not attribute to the Italian judge any power to refuse the application of subsequent internal rules . . . on the ground of the general priority of Community law over national law. . . . Therefore the judge is bound to raise the question of the constitu-

---

3  [1974] 2 CMLR 372. Cf. the attitude of the German Constitutional Court discussed above.

4  *Industrie Chimiche della Italia v Minister of Foreign Trade*, Constitutional Court, 20, 30 October 1975, No 232 CC III., 1975, 319-327; (1976) RTDE 396-403. Quotations taken from Brinkhorst, L. J., and Schermers, H. G., *Judicial Remedies in the European Communities* (2nd. ed. 1977), pp. 217-220.

tionality of legislative rules which reproduce directly applicable Community regulations and transform them into internal law. ....'

This attitude was in strong terms condemned unequivocally by the Community Court in the *Simmenthal (No. 3)* case[5] where it held that:

> '... every national court must ... apply Community law in its entirety and protect rights which the latter confers on individuals and must accordingly set aside any provision of national law which may conflict with it, whether prior or subsequent to the Community rule.
>
> Accordingly any provision of a national legal system ... which might impair the effectiveness of Community law by withholding from the national court ... the power to do everything necessary at the moment of its application to set aside national legislative provisions which might prevent Community rules from having full force and effect are incompatible with those requirements which are the very essence of Community law ...'

In the ICJC case the *Corte Costituzionale* hinted at the need of legislation to solve the problem and this seems to be the only way out of the impasse.

### New Member States

We shall consider in the following chapter the attitude of the British courts to the challenge of Community law. In Denmark in an action for infringement of a trade-mark in which Community law was introduced at a late stage, the court decided to hear the arguments and give judgment on the points of Danish law first. Points of Community law were deferred with the possibility of reference to the Community Court[6].

We can say, in the light of this review of practice in the members of the Community, that Community law is enforced as 'Community law', or the 'internal law' and that, in the case of conflict with municipal law, whether previous or subsequent, the Community rule prevails. This situation has not come about without difficulty or heart-searching as the dualist tradition entrenched in the national systems of law had to succumb to the challenge of the Community. In this process, the Community Court acted as the pacemaker and, as we have noted, some of its decisions not only settled matters for the given member state, but also set a trend within the

---

5 Case 106/77: *Amministrazione delle Finanze dello Stato v Simmenthal SpA* [1978] IECR 629, [1978] 3 CMLR 263.
6 *EMI Records Ltd v CBS Grammofon A/S* [1975] 1 CMLR 572.

Community. The Community Court acted as an agent of cohesion and uniformity. However, without the stimulating contribution of jurists the message of Luxembourg would not have been as effective and successful as it was. Here the *doctrine* came into its own as an auxiliary source of law. Its power and authority on the Continent should not be underestimated.

## Chapter 12

# Community law in the United Kingdom[1]

RATIFICATION OF THE TREATIES

By the constitutional law of the United Kingdom treaty-making power is a prerogative power vested in the Sovereign and customarily exercised on her behalf either by her Ministers or by duly authorised plenipotentiaries. Ratification is the formal act whereby the Crown confirms and finally agrees to be bound by the terms of a Treaty. Under the terms of article 2 of the First Treaty of Accession the High Contracting Parties undertook to ratify the Treaty in accordance with their respective constitutional requirements and to deposit their instruments of ratification with the Italian Government by 31 December 1972 at the latest. In the event three of the four applicant states complied with that obligation and the Treaty entered into force on 1 January 1973[2]. By the act of ratification the United Kingdom acceded to the three European Communities. Article 2 of the Act annexed to the First Treaty of Accession thus provides that 'from the date of accession, the provisions of the original Treaties [as defined in article 1] and the acts adopted by the institutions of the Communities shall be binding on the new Member States and shall apply in those States under the conditions laid down in those Treaties and in this Act'.

In the United Kingdom, the Courts, and for that matter Parliament, have no role to play in the negotiation and ratification of treaties. In a case concerning a treaty of 1842 between the Crown and the Emperor of China Lord Coleridge CJ stated that the Queen had 'acted throughout the making of the treaty and in relation to each and every of its stipulations in her sovereign character, and by her own inherent authority; and, as in making the treaty,

---

1 For a more detailed treatment of this topic, see Collins, L., *European Community Law in the United Kingdom* (2nd edn, 1980).
2 As a result of Norway's decision not to ratify, the Council used its authority under the Treaty of Accession, art. 2, para. 3 to make the necessary adjustments; see Adaptation Decision of 1 January 1973, OJ 1973, L2.

so in performing the treaty, she is beyond the control of municipal law and her acts are not to be examined in her own Courts.[3]' Thus when in 1971 a Mr Blackburn applied for declarations to the effect that by signing the Treaty of Rome Her Majesty's Government would be irrevocably surrendering part of the sovereignty of the Queen in Parliament and by so doing would be acting contrary to law his statements of claim were struck out as disclosing no reasonable causes of action. The Court of Appeal unanimously upheld Eveleigh J's dismissal of the plaintiff's appeal against the Master's order. The court applied the dicta of Lord Coleridge CJ cited above. In the words of Lord Denning MR 'The treaty-making power of this country rests not in the courts, but in the Crown; that is, Her Majesty acting upon the advice of her Ministers. When her Ministers negotiate and sign a treaty, even a treaty of such paramount importance as this proposed one, they act on behalf of the country as a whole. They exercise the prerogative of the Crown. Their action in so doing cannot be challenged or questioned in these courts[4].'

## INCORPORATION OF THE TREATIES INTO THE LAW OF THE UNITED KINGDOM

Although, at least since the time of Blackstone, the customary rules of international law have been regarded as part and parcel of the common law and directly enforceable by English judges, the United Kingdom adopts a distinctly dualist approach to treaties. A treaty to which the United Kingdom is a party is, as we have seen, the result of an exercise of the prerogative and as such is not self-executing in the sense that the provisions of such a treaty do not automatically have the force of law in the United Kingdom. The intervention of Parliament is necessary in order to enable the provisions of such a treaty to be enforced in British courts. The classic statement of this doctrine is contained in an Opinion of the Judicial Committee of the Privy Council in 1937:

'It will be essential to keep in mind the distinction between (1) the formation, and (2) the performance, of the obligations constituted by a treaty, using that word as comprising any agreement between two or more sovereign States. Within the British Empire there is a well-

---

3 *Rustomjee v R* (1876) 2 QBD at 74.
4 *Blackburn v A-G* [1971] 1 WLR 1037 at 1040; Salmon and Stamp LJJ to the same effect at 1041.

established rule that the making of a treaty is an executive act, while the performance of its obligations, if they entail alteration of the existing domestic law, requires legislative action. Unlike some other countries, the stipulations of a treaty duly ratified do not within the Empire, by virtue of the treaty alone, have the force of law. If the national executive, the government of the day, decide to incur the obligations of a treaty which involve alteration of law they have to run the risk of obtaining the assent of Parliament to the necessary statute or statutes. To make themselves as secure as possible they will often in such cases before final ratification seek to obtain from Parliament an expression of approval. But it has never been suggested, and it is not the law, that such an expression of approval operates as law, or that in law it precludes the assenting Parliament, or any subsequent Parliament, from refusing to give its sanction to any legislative proposals that may subsequently be brought before it. Parliament, no doubt ... has a constitutional control over the executive: but it cannot be disputed that the creation of the obligations undertaken in treaties and the assent to their form and quality are the function of the executive alone. Once they are created, while they bind the State as against the other contracting parties, Parliament may refuse to perform them and so leave the State in default. In a unitary State whose Legislature possesses unlimited powers the problem is simple. Parliament will either fulfil or not treaty obligations imposed upon the State by its executive. The nature of the obligations does not affect the complete authority of the Legislature to make them law if it so chooses[5].'

This doctrine applies equally to the Community Treaties so that the mere accession of the United Kingdom to those Treaties did not give them the force of law within the United Kingdom. Legislation was necessary to achieve that result and in the absence of such legislation, as the Court of Appeal has pointed out, the Community Treaties would fall outside the cognisance of British Courts[6]. Thus one of the aims of the European Communities Act 1972 is to give the force of law to those provisions of the Treaties which are intended to take direct effect within the member states. Section 2 (1) of the Act provides that:

'All such rights, powers, liabilities, obligations and restrictions from time to time created or arising by or under the Treaties, and all such

5 *A-G for Canada v A-G of Ontario* [1937] AC 326 at 347, 348, per Lord Atkin. A similar statement was made in *Legal and Constitutional Implications of United Kingdom Membership of the European Communities* (1967) (Cmnd. 3301), at para. 22. Section 6 of the European Assembly Elections Act 1978 has introduced a constitutional innovation in that British ratification of any treaty which increases the powers of the European Parliament is subject to the prior approval of the United Kingdom Parliament.
6 *McWhirter v A-G* [1972] CMLR 882 at 886, per Lord Denning MR and at 887 Phillimore LJ.

remedies and procedures from time to time provided for by or under the Treaties, as in accordance with the Treaties are without further enactment to be given legal effect or used in the United Kingdom shall be recognised and available in law, and be enforced, allowed and followed accordingly; and the expression "enforceable Community right" and similar expressions shall be read as referring to one to which this subsection applies.'

Therefore, what the Act terms 'enforceable Community rights' are to be given direct effect in the United Kingdom. This provision is strengthened by section 3 (2) which provides inter alia that United Kingdom courts shall take judicial notice of Community Treaties, which term is defined by section 1.

IMPLEMENTATION OF COMMUNITY SECONDARY LEGISLATION IN THE UNITED KINGDOM

It has already been pointed out in earlier chapters that Community secondary legislation falls into two categories: that which is and that which is not directly applicable in the member states. As far as the former is concerned, viz. decisions in the ECSC and regulations in the EEC and Euratom, whilst within the Community legal system they will be binding on the United Kingdom as soon as they are made, they need statutory authority to give them the force of law within the United Kingdom, just as in the case of the provisions of the Treaties themselves. Section 2 (1) of the European Communities Act applies to them also and without further enactment they are to be given legal effect within our domestic legal systems. Thus the entire body of ECSC decisions and EEC and Euratom regulations in force at the commencement of British membership automatically became part of the law of the United Kingdom on 1 January 1973. Similarly all such decisions and regulations made after the commencement of British membership will also automatically become part of the law of the United Kingdom as soon as they are made. In addition those provisions of Community secondary legislation which have direct effect in the legal systems of the Member States constitute 'enforceable Community rights' under section 2 (1) of the European Communities Act and as such are enforceable in the courts of the United Kingdom.

An important issue in connection with directly applicable Community secondary legislation made after British entry is the role of the United Kingdom Parliament. Whilst the actual making of such secondary legislation will be in the hands of the Council or Commission and outside the direct control of Parliament, in the absence of effective democratic control within the Communities themselves it is vital that Parliament should have an opportunity to consider such legislation. By the time, say, an EEC regulation has been made it will be too late for comment for such a regulation will already be part of United Kingdom law. In order to enable Parliament to examine and comment upon proposed Community legislation and thus express views for the guidance of the British representatives on the Council of the Communities, each House has established a select committee to scrutinise Community secondary legislation: the House of Commons Committee on European Secondary Legislation and the House of Lords Committee on the European Communities. Both Committees are concerned with draft Community legislation which has been proposed by the Commission to the Council, but there are differences in approach and in terms of reference. The reports of the Commons Committee express opinions whether the proposed legislation raises questions of legal or political importance and how it may affect matters of principle or policy. The Lords Committee, which is organised into specialist sub-committees, not only reports on matters of policy and principle but also on the merits of the proposed legislation. The Committees are able to confer together. Each is assisted by a legal adviser. Debates are held in each House on the recommendation of its Committee. The procedure is a useful one but there are practical difficulties of timing and of a congested Parliamentary timetable[7].

In the case of Community secondary legislation which is not directly applicable, such as ECSC recommendations and EEC and Euratom directives, but leaves the choice of the means of their implementation to the individual Member States[8], there are two possible courses of action. Such Community legislation could be implemented in the United Kingdom either by statute or by subordinate legislation. Whilst the European Communities Act does not expressly rule out the use of statutes for such purposes its emphasis is on the use of delegated legislation. Thus section 2 (2)

7 See Erskine May's *Parliamentary Practice* (19th edn, 1976), at pp. 669, 671. For an account of the work of the Scrutiny Committees, see Bates T St JN, 'The Scrutiny of European Secondary Legislation at Westminster' (1975–76), 1 *European Law Review*, p. 195. Also see Niblock, M., *The EEC: National Parliaments in Community Decision-Making* (1971).
8 See Chapter 4 ante.

of the Act confers extensive authority upon Her Majesty in Council and upon Ministers and Government Departments to make subordinate legislation:

> '(a) for the purpose of implementing any Community obligation of the United Kingdom, or enabling any such obligation to be implemented, or of enabling any rights enjoyed or to be enjoyed by the United Kingdom under or by virtue of the Treaties to be exercised; or
>
> (b) for the purpose of dealing with matters arising out of or related to any such obligation or rights or the coming into force, or the operation from time to time, of subsection (1) above.'

The wide extent of these delegated law-making powers is confirmed by section 2 (3) which lays down that a provision made under sub-section (2) includes 'any such provision (of any such extent) as might be made by Act of Parliament'. In other words the subordinate legislation made under section 2 (2) to implement Community obligations can be used to repeal or amend any past or future Act of Parliament the provisions of which are incompatible with Community law.

But these powers of making subordinate legislation are not entirely without limitation and are subject to Schedule 2 to the Act. That Schedule provides that the powers conferred by section 2 (2) shall not include the power:

> '(a) to make any provision imposing or increasing taxation; or
>
> (b) to make any provision taking effect from a date earlier than that of the making of the instrument containing the provision; or
>
> (c) to confer any power to legislate by means of orders, rules, regulations or other subordinate instrument, other than rules of procedure for any court or tribunal; or
>
> (d) to create any new criminal offence punishable with imprisonment for more than two years or punishable on summary conviction with imprisonment for more than three months or with a fine of more than £400 (if not calculated on a daily basis) or with a fine of more than £5 a day.'

These limitations are also given a measure of entrenchment since section 2 (4) states that they shall remain in force unless and until amended or repealed by a subsequent statute. As far as the form and procedure of such subordinate legislation is concerned Schedule 2 states that the power to make regulations shall be exercisable by statutory instrument and that wherever the power is exercised without a draft having been approved by resolution of each House of Parliament, then it shall be subject to annulment in pursuance of a resolution of either House[9]. This gives the Government a choice as to the procedure to be adopted and that choice will no doubt be exercised in the light of the subject matter of the legislation[10].

Thus under the provisions of section 2 of the Act ample provision appears to have been made for the implementation of Community secondary legislation in the United Kingdom subject to the important constitutional safeguards in Schedule 2. Community law is having an immediate and a continuing impact on the law of the United Kingdom and whilst that impact should not be underestimated it also should not be exaggerated. In the words of the White Paper reporting on the negotiations 'the English and Scottish legal systems will remain intact. Certain provisions of the treaties and instruments made under them, concerned with economic, commercial and closely related matters, will be included in our law. The common law will remain the basis of our legal system and our courts will continue to operate as they do at present. ... All the essential features of our law will remain, including the safeguards for individual freedom such as trial by jury and habeas corpus and the principle that a man is innocent until proved guilty as well as the law of contract and tort (and its Scottish equivalent), the law of landlord and tenant, family law, nationality law[11] and land law[12].'

## ENFORCEMENT THROUGH THE COMMUNITY COURT

The enforcement of Community law through the agency of the European Court is achieved by direct and indirect means. The direct means takes the form of actions against Member States who fail to fulfil their obligations under the Treaties[13]. By means of such actions the Court can directly influence the enforcement of Community law in the national legal orders of the Member States. Thus if the United Kingdom either legislates contrary to Community law or fails to legislate as required by Community law that would amount to a failure to fulfil Treaty obligations and the Commission or another Member State would be able to bring proceedings

9 Statutory Instruments made to implement Community obligations are conveniently reproduced in Sweet & Maxwell's *Encyclopedia of European Community Law*, Vols. AI and II, Part A3.
10 Sch. 2, para. 2.
11 But on the question of immigration, see Lasok, D., *The Law of the Economy in the European Communities* (1980), pp. 95-115.
12 *The United Kingdom and the European Communities* (Cmnd 4715), para. 31.
13 See Chapter 9 ante.

against the United Kingdom in the European Court[14]. If judgment were given against the United Kingdom there would arise an obligation to take steps necessary to comply with the judgment[15]. Actions have been brought against the United Kingdom both by the Commission under the terms of article 169 of the EEC Treaty and by a fellow member state under the terms of article 170. Two cases decided in 1979 will serve as illustrations.

The first case concerned potatoes[16], which are included among the agricultural products which come within the common agricultural policy of the Community. The United Kingdom operated a system for regulating the market in potatoes which included controls on their import and export. In December 1977 the United Kingdom Government imposed a ban on the import of potatoes until further notice. In the view of the Commission such a ban was contrary to the United Kingdom's obligations under the EEC Treaty. An article 169 action resulted in which the Court gave judgment against the United Kingdom. It held that the import ban was contrary to the Community's freedom of movement of goods between the Member States[17]. The second case concerned measures to conserve fisheries[18]. The Community has authority over all questions relating to the protection of fishing grounds and the conservation of the resources of the sea. In pursuance of that authority the Community resolved that the member states should not take any unilateral conservation measures without first consulting and seeking the approval of the Commission. In April 1977 the United Kingdom Government, without referring to the Commission, made an order prohibiting the use in British waters of certain small mesh nets. The master of a French trawler was subsequently fined for infringing that order. France (supported by the Commission) complained that this United Kingdom order did not comply with Community policy. In the resulting article 170 action the Court gave judgment against the United Kingdom because of the failure to consult and seek the approval of the Commission.

14  E.g. under the terms of EEC Treaty, arts. 169, 170.
15  E.g. by virtue of EEC Treaty, art. 171.
16  Case 231/78: *EC Commission v United Kingdom* [1979] ECR 1447, [1979] 2 CMLR 427.
17  In particular art. 30 of the EEC Treaty which prohibits quantitative restrictions on imports between member states. For further art. 169 actions against the United Kingdom see Cases 128/78: [1979] ECR 419, [1979] 2 CMLR 45; 170/78: [1980] ECR 417, [1980] 3 CMLR 716 and 32/79: [1980] ECR 2403.
18  Case 141/78: *France v United Kingdom* [1979] ECR 2923, [1980] 1 CMLR 6.

The European Court also influences the enforcement of Community law indirectly by means of its competence to give preliminary rulings on points of Community law at the request of national courts and tribunals. The provisions of the Treaties which give the right, and in some cases impose the duty, to request preliminary rulings became part of the laws of the United Kingdom by virtue of section 2 (1) of the European Communities Act 1972 which specifically refers to 'remedies and procedures' provided for, by or under the Treaties. This right/duty applies not only to the ordinary courts, from lay magistrates up to the House of Lords, but also to tribunals. Thus all courts and tribunals in the United Kingdom have been able to request preliminary rulings in appropriate cases since 1 January 1973 when the European Communities Act came into force. The unfamiliarity of such a procedure in the United Kingdom prompted the drawing up of special rules of procedure for some, but not all, courts. As far as the English courts are concerned[19] rules have been made for the High Court and Court of Appeal, Civil Division[20]; the Court of Appeal, Criminal Division[1]; the County Court[2]; and the Crown Court[3]. No changes have been made to the Judicial Standing Orders of the House of Lords and it is believed that when requesting preliminary rulings the House makes use of the procedure adopted by the Supreme Court[4]. The rules of magistrates' courts have not been changed, but the attention of magistrates' clerks has been drawn to the possibility of seeking a preliminary ruling by a Home Office Circular[5]. In connection with tribunals, consultation with the responsible government departments led to the conclusion that adequate procedural machinery exists to deal with references to the European Court[6].

The Rules which have been made for English courts all follow a particular pattern. Orders referring questions to the European

---

**19** For Scottish Courts, see S.I. 1972 No. 1981, and S.I. 1973 Nos 450 and 543. For Northern Irish Courts, see SR & O 1972, Nos 317, 354 and 380.

**20** Rules for the Supreme Court (Amendment No. 3) 1972 (S.I. 1972 No. 1898 L27) which added Order 114 to the Rules of the Supreme Court.

**1** Criminal Appeal (References to the European Court) Rules 1972 (S.I. 1972 No. 1786 (L 25)).

**2** The County Court (Amendment No. 2) Rules 1973 (S.I. 1973 No. 847 (L.13)).

**3** Crown Court (References to the European Court) Rules 1972 (S.I. 1972 No. 1787 (L26)).

**4** This statement is based on information kindly supplied by the Judicial Office of the House of Lords.

**5** Circular No. 149/1973 (CS 18/1973), dated 4 September 1973.

**6** This statement is based on information kindly supplied by the Council on Tribunals and the Lord Chancellor's Office.

Court may be made before, or at any stage during, the trial or hearing of a cause or matter. Such Orders shall be made by the Court requesting the preliminary ruling and shall normally have the effect of staying proceedings pending the ruling. In all cases the transmission of an Order requesting a preliminary ruling to the Registrar of the European Court is undertaken by the Senior Master of the Supreme Court (Queen's Bench Division). Where such an Order is open to appeal the Senior Master must not forward it to the European Court until the time for appealing has expired, or, if an appeal is brought, until the appeal has been settled. It has been argued by some commentators that both the use of the Senior Master as an intermediary between English courts and tribunals and the European Court, and making Orders requesting a preliminary ruling subject to appeal are incompatible with Community law[7]. As far as the transmission of the request for a preliminary ruling is concerned it is the practice of continental courts to deal directly with the European Court, which does, for this purpose, form an integral part of the legal systems of the member states. On the question of a request for a preliminary ruling being subject to appeal it has already been pointed out that Continental practice is not uniform[8] nor has the question been decided conclusively by the European Court[9]. The English rules on appeals may certainly be questioned to the extent that they have the effect of interposing an obstacle between the English courts and the European Court. The use of the Senior Master and the possibility of appeal may also cause unjustifiable delays in the reference procedure[10].

It has already been pointed out that while courts and tribunals which are not of last instance have a discretion whether to seek a preliminary ruling, courts and tribunals of final instance are under an obligation to do so. Some doubts exist in the United Kingdom

---

7  See Jacobs, F. G. and Durand, A., *References to the European Court: Practice and Procedure* (1975), at pp. 164, 165, 171, 172 and Advocate-General Warner in case 166/73: *Rheinmühlen-Düsseldorf v Einfuhr-und Vorretsstelle für Getreide und Futtermittel* [1974] ECR 33 at 47. For a contrary opinion, see Collins, L., *European Community Law in the United Kingdom* (2nd edn, 1980), at p. 90.

8  See Chapter 10 ante.

9  See the case and literature cited in note 7, ante.

10  These factors may have contributed to the inordinate delay in transmitting to the European Court the first United Kingdom request for a preliminary ruling in *Van Duyn v Home Office*. The Order requesting a preliminary ruling was dated 1 March 1974 (see [1974] 1 WLR at 1118) and it was lodged at the European Court on 13 June 1974 (see [1975] 1 CMLR at 14).

concerning which courts and tribunals are those 'against whose decisions there is no judicial remedy under national law[11].' The position of the House of Lords is clear; subject to the relevant Treaty provisions it will be obliged to request preliminary rulings. But the position of the Court of Appeal is not so clear. The Court of Appeal may be a court of final instance in two situations. The Court of Appeal may be declared by statute to be the final court of appeal as in the case of bankruptcy proceedings initiated in a County Court[12]. If a question of the validity or interpretation of Community law came before the Court of Appeal in such proceedings then it would clearly be obliged to seek a preliminary ruling from the Community Court. But rather more problematic may be the commoner situation in which despite the possibility of an appeal to the House of Lords the Court of Appeal may be, and indeed usually is, the final court of appeal. Since appeal to the House of Lords is only by leave that leave may either not be sought or may be sought and refused. In such situations it is suggested that the Court of Appeal should be obliged to seek a preliminary ruling in an appropriate case since, although it is not the supreme appellate court, there is no judicial remedy against its decisions in those situations. A similar problem arises in connection with tribunals. Is a tribunal from whose decision there is no appeal but which is open to review by certiorari obliged to seek a preliminary ruling? Certiorari is a form of judicial remedy under national law. But, it is a discretionary and highly technical remedy and in most cases the decision of such a tribunal would be final. It is therefore suggested that, as in the case of the Court of Appeal, such a tribunal should regard itself as under the obligation to request a preliminary ruling[13]. Thus in terms of the dispute in Continental legal circles between the 'concrete' and 'abstract' theories of article 177, paragraph 3 of the EEC Treaty the 'concrete' theory is thought to be preferable[14].

---

11 This expression replaces 'from whose decisions there is no possibility of appeal under internal law' which was used in the earlier unofficial Foreign Office translation. The new translation certainly seems to be closer to the French 'dont les décisions ne sont pas susceptibles d'un recours juridictionnel de droit interne'.

12 See Bankruptcy Act 1914, s. 108 (2) (a).

13 Cf. Jacobs, F. G. and Durand, A., op. cit. at pp. 162, 163. Also see Freeman, Elizabeth, 'References to the Court of Justice under article 177' (1975) 28 *Current Legal Problems* 176 at 184–186.

14 See Donner, A. M., 'Les rapports entre la compétence de la Cour de Justice des Communautés Européennes et les tribunaux internes', 115 *Recueil des Cours de la Haye* (1965) at pp. 42 et seq. Also see case 6/64: *Costa v ENEL* [1964] ECR 585 at 592.

The initial reaction of English courts and tribunals to this question did not, however, reflect this attitude. In the Court of Appeal no general view has yet emerged. In *Bulmer v Bollinger* Lord Denning expressed the opinion that 'short of the House of Lords no other English Court is bound to refer a question to the European Court at Luxembourg[15]'. But in the same case Stamp and Stephenson LJJ refused to commit themselves on that point in the absence of further argument[16]. More recently, a member of the Court of Appeal has expressed his support for a variant of the 'concrete' theory in terms that the ultimate court of appeal in England is either the Court of Appeal if leave to appeal to the House of Lords is not obtainable, or the House of Lords[17]. Lord Denning's opinion is echoed in a judgment of the National Insurance Commissioner. He held that since his decisions may be set aside by certiorari, he did not 'constitute a tribunal against whose decision there is no judicial remedy under English law, even though an application for an order of certiorari cannot be made without the leave of the High Court[18]'. The House of Lords has recognised its obligation to refer issues concerning the applicability and interpretation of Community law to the European Court[19].

THE QUESTION OF SUPREMACY[20]

It has been repeatedly laid down by the Community Court and is in general accepted by the original six member states that the

15  [1974] Ch 401 at 420.
16  Ibid. at pp. 427, 430.
17  *Hagen v Fratelli D and G Moretti SNC* [1980] 3 CMLR 253 at 255 per Buckley, LJ. Such a compromise would clearly give rise to procedural difficulties for the English courts.
18  Decision R(S) 4/74 *Re a Holiday in Italy* [1975] 1 CMLR 184 at 188. One British commentator has referred to this as 'a sensible approach': Collins, L., op. cit. p. 123, n. 140.
19  See *Miliangos v George Frank (Textiles) Ltd* [1975] 2 CMLR 585 per Lord Wilberforce; *R. v Henn and Darby* [1979] 2 CMLR 495; *Garland v British Rail Engineering Ltd* [1981] 2 CMLR 542.
20  The literature on this topic from the British standpoint includes the following: Martin, A., 'The Accession of the United Kingdom to the European Communities: Jurisdictional Problems' (1968–69) 6 CML Rev 7; Hunnings, N. M., 'Constitutional Implications of joining the Common Market', ibid., 50; de Smith, S. A., 'The Constitution and the Common Market: a tentative appraisal' (1971) 34 MLR 597; Wade, H. W. R., 'Sovereignty and the European Communities' (1972) 88 LQR 1; Mitchell, J. D. B., et al., 'Constitutional aspects of the Treaty and Legislation relating to British membership' (1972) 9 CML Rev 134; Trinidade, F. A. 'Parliamentary Sovereignty and the Primacy of European Community Law' (1972) 35 MLR

Community Treaties have established a new and distinct system of law, the rules of which are inherently superior to the rules of the municipal laws of the member states. Thus from the commencement and for the duration of British membership the municipal law of the United Kingdom must yield in cases of conflict to the superior Community law. To the generations of British lawyers schooled in the Diceyan orthodoxy such a prospect is no doubt unthinkable if not impossible; but nevertheless it is one of the obligations of membership. The implications were clearly summarised in the 1967 White Paper:

'The Community law having direct internal effect is designed to take precedence over the domestic law of the Member States. From this it follows that the legislation of the Parliament of the United Kingdom giving effect to that law would have to do so in such a way as to override existing national law so far as inconsistent with it. This result need not be left to implication, and it would be open to Parliament to enact from time to time any necessary consequential amendments or repeals. It would also follow that within the fields occupied by the Community law Parliament would have to refrain from passing fresh legislation inconsistent with that law as for the time being in force. This would not however involve any constitutional innovation. Many of our treaty obligations already impose such restraints—for example, the Charter of the United Nations, the European Convention on Human Rights and GATT[1].'

As far as the body of Community law in force on the eve of British membership was concerned no difficulty was experienced. That law, as we have seen, was given legal force in the United Kingdom by section 2 (1) of the European Communities Act and will have precedence over prior British law by the simple operation of the rule *lex posterior derogat priori*[2]. Certain difficulties may arise, however, in avoiding and resolving conflicts between Community law and statutes passed after the commencement of United Kingdom membership. The 1967 White Paper stated that Parliament will have to refrain from passing fresh legislation inconsistent with Community law and remarked this was by no means an innovation because of existing restraints under other treaties. But the critical

375; and Winterton, G., 'The British Grundnorm: Parliamentary Supremacy Re-examined' (1976) 92 LQR 591.

1 *Legal and Constitutional Implications of United Kingdom Membership of the European Communities* (Cmnd 3301), para. 23.
2 Certain express amendments are in fact made by Part II of the European Communities Act.

question is whether our doctrine of Parliamentary sovereignty means that such restraints must always be voluntarily imposed by Parliament or whether they can be compulsorily guaranteed.

The application of the orthodox doctrine of the absolute sovereignty of Parliament to statutes designed to implement treaty provisions into United Kingdom law has meant that such statutes have been regarded as in no way different from ordinary statutes and may be either expressly or impliedly amended or repealed by subsequent inconsistent statutes. It is true that there is a legal presumption that Parliament does not intend to derogate from international law, but such a presumption cannot prevail in the face of an expressly inconsistent subsequent enactment[3]. If this doctrine were to be applied to Community law it would hardly satisfy the Communities since there would be no legal guarantee of Parliament's good behaviour.

There are a variety of possible solutions to this problem. Some are suggested in the writings of those contemporary constitutional lawyers who challenge the orthodoxy of Dicey and his followers. Professor Mitchell has argued that the Act of Union with Scotland 1707 is fundamental law which imposes legal restraints on the United Kingdom Parliament and just as a new legal order was established in 1707 so there is no reason why another new legal order in the context of the Communities should not be created in 1972[4]. Professor Heuston, whilst not denying that Parliament is sovereign in terms of the area of her power, maintains that limitations may be imposed on the manner and form by which that power is exercised[5]. Applied to the matter in hand that thesis would involve the imposition of procedural restrictions on Parliament's freedom to legislate inconsistently with Community law which would not absolutely prevent such legislation but would make it more difficult. But not all of the possible solutions are of such a fundamental nature. It has been suggested that a formal clause be inserted in all statutes[6], or that the enacting formula of all statutes should be amended[7], to include a statement that the statute is to be construed as not conflicting with Community law. Another com-

---

3  See *IRC v Collco Dealings Ltd* [1962] AC 1, [1961] 1 All ER 762.
4  See Mitchell, J. D. B., et al., loc. cit. in note 20, ante, and Mitchell, J. D. B., *Constitutional Law* (2nd edn), Chapter 4. For an even more drastic solution, see Hood Phillips, O., *Reform of the Constitution* (1970), Chapter 7.
5  See Heuston, R. F. V., *Essays in Constitutional Law* (2nd edn), Chapter 1.
6  See Hunnings, N. M., loc. cit. in note 20, ante.
7  See Wade, H. W. R., loc. cit. in note 20, ante, and Wade, H. W. R., *Constitutional Fundamentals* (1980), Chapter 3.

mentator has drawn on the experience of the Canadian Bill of Rights and has suggested that a strongly worded presumption against anything other than an express derogation from Community law should be written into the enabling act[8]. Yet others have suggested that reliance should be placed on the gradual emergence of a constitutional convention by which it would be recognised that Parliament could not legislate contrary to Community law[9].

In dealing with the problem of the supremacy of Community law the European Communities Act adopts a subtle approach which does not incorporate any of the fundamentalist or procedural solutions described above nor is it content to rely on the uncertain emergence of conventional limitations. The Act avoids any outright statement of the supremacy of Community law. It was probably thought that this was unnecessary in view of the practice of the original six member states. It would also be contrary to the main stream of British constitutional practice and it would in any event have been politically dangerous to have adopted such an approach. The supremacy of Community law in the United Kingdom is effectively guaranteed by the combined operation of provisions of sections 2 and 3 of the Act. As we have seen section 2 (1) gives present and future Community law legal force in the United Kingdom and creates the concept of enforceable Community rights. Thus since the doctrine of the supremacy of Community law is part of that law section 2 (1) makes that doctrine part of the law of the United Kingdom. The effectiveness of that doctrine is guaranteed by two further provisions. Firstly, section 2 (4) provides that, subject only to the limitations specified in Schedule 2, 'any enactment passed or to be passed, other than one contained in this Part of this Act, shall be construed and have effect subject to the foregoing provisions of this section', in other words, subject to the rule of the supremacy of Community law which is an enforceable Community right[10]. Secondly, section 3 (1) provides that:

'For the purposes of all legal proceedings any question as to the meaning or effect of any of the Treaties, or as to the validity, meaning or effect of any Community instrument, shall be treated as a question of

8  See de Smith, S. A., loc. cit. in note 20, ante, and *R v Drybones* (1970) 9 DLR (3d) 473.
9  See Martin, A., loc. cit. in note 20, ante, and cf. Lloyd, Lord, *The Idea of Law* (1966) at pp. 169, 170.
10 See the statement by the Lord Chancellor, Lord Hailsham, when introducing the Bill in the Lords, *Parliamentary Debates, House of Lords*, Vol. 333, No. 111, 25 July 1972, col. 1230.

law (and, if not referred to the European Court, be for determination as such in accordance with the principles laid down by and any relevant decision of the European Court).'

Thus in all matters of Community law the courts and tribunals[11] of the United Kingdom are to defer to the relevant decisions of the Community Court whether or not such matters have been actually referred to the Community Court. This is a very important factor since the doctrine of supremacy has been developed by the Community Court.

The European Communities Act does not therefore seek to guarantee the supremacy of Community law by forbidding Parliament to enact conflicting legislation. Instead the guarantee is provided by denying effectiveness to such legislation within the legal systems of the United Kingdom to the extent that it conflicts with Community law. Thus the ultimate sanction remains an extra-legal one. There is nothing to prevent a future Parliament from repealing the European Communities Act in its entirety. If it chose to do so it would indicate that the political will that the United Kingdom should remain a member of the Communities was lacking and in the last analysis there is nothing which any mere rule of law can do in such a situation. In other words it must be assumed that as long as the United Kingdom is a member of the Communities she will honour the legal and constitutional obligations of membership. The legal guarantees of good faith contained in the Act are adequate, subject to the political will of the member states that the Community system shall succeed[12].

The question of supremacy has received some attention from the judiciary. In the pre-accession case of *Blackburn v A-G* Lord Denning observed 'we have all been brought up to believe that, in legal theory, one Parliament cannot bind another and that no Act is irreversible. But legal theory does not always march alongside political reality[13].' After referring to the practical impossibility that Parliament would legislate contrary to the statutes emancipating the Dominions and Colonies he added, 'Legal theory must give way to practical politics[14].' He then went on to say that if and when

---

11  See *Shields v E Coomes (Holdings) Ltd* [1979] 1 All ER 456 per Lord Denning MR and *Worringham and Humphreys v Lloyds Bank Ltd* at 461, 462 [1980] 1 CMLR 293 at 300, per Kilner Brown J.

12  Cf Warner, J-P., 'The Relationship between European Community Law and the National Laws of the Member States' (1977), 93 LQR 349 at 364, 365.

13  [1971] 1 WLR 1037 at 1040.

14  Ibid.

Parliament legislated contrary to Community law 'we will then say whether Parliament can lawfully do it or not[15]'. Since the accession, the supremacy of Community law has not yet been a real issue before United Kingdom courts and tribunals; but there is clearly an awareness of the implications of that doctrine. In *Esso Petroleum v Kingswood Motors Ltd* Bridge J observed that where Community law 'is in conflict with our domestic law the effect of the [European Communities] Act of 1972 is to require that the Community law shall prevail[16].' Similarly in *Aero Zipp Fasteners v YKK Fasteners*, Graham J said that the European Communities Act 1972 'enacted that relevant Common Market law should be applied in this country and should, where there is a conflict, override English law[17]'. In *R v Secchi* a Metropolitan magistrate has remarked that the effect of making Community law part of English law 'is to make English law, both statute and common law, subject to Community law, in those fields in which Community laws have been passed[18]'. Obedience to Community law is clearly implicit in a recent unanimous judgment of the House of Lords[19].

In a number of cases the Court of Appeal, particularly in the judgments of Lord Denning, has commented on the response which English courts should make to incompatibilities between English law and Community law. Lord Denning's approach differentiates between mere inconsistencies on the one hand and deliberate derogations on the other. In the former case, where the incompatibility is inadvertent, it is suggested that English courts are under a duty to apply Community law. It is to be presumed in such a case that Parliament intends to fulfil the Treaty obligations of the United Kingdom: 'If on close investigation it should appear that our legislation is deficient—or is inconsistent with Community law—by some oversight of our draftsmen—then it is our bounden duty to give priority to Community law[20].' 'That priority is given by our own law. It is given by the European Communities Act 1972 itself. Community law is part of our law: and, whenever there is any inconsistency, Community law has priority. It is not supplanting English law. It is part of our law which overrides any other part

---

15 Ibid.
16 [1974] 1 QB 142 at 151.
17 [1973] CMLR 819 at 820.
18 [1975] 1 CMLR 383 at 386.
19 *DPP v Henn and Darby* [1980] 2 CMLR 229.
20 *Macarthys Ltd v Smith* [1979] 3 CMLR 44 at 47, *per* Lord Denning, MR. Also see *Shields v E Coomes (Holdings) Ltd* [1979] 1 All ER 456 at 460, per Denning MR.

which is inconsistent with it[1].' But where the incompatibility is deliberate and intended by Parliament, it is suggested that English courts are under a duty to apply English law: 'If the time should come when our Parliament deliberately passes an Act—with the intention of repudiating the Treaty or any provision in it—or intentionally of acting inconsistently with it—and says so in express terms—then I should have thought that it would be the duty of our courts to follow the statute of our Parliament ... Unless there is such an intentional and express repudiation of the Treaty, it is our duty to give priority to the Treaty[2].' Such a view is certainly consistent with both the European Communities Act and with British constitutional tradition.

COMMUNITY LAW BEFORE UNITED KINGDOM COURTS AND TRIBUNALS

Since the commencement of British membership the courts, tribunals and lawyers of the United Kingdom have been confronted with the 'incoming tide' of Community law[3]. They have been faced with the unprecedented challenge of participating in a novel and unique system of law based on unfamiliar Continental legal principles. During this time, points of Community law, of varying degrees of significance, have arisen in numerous reported British cases. All levels of the judicial hierarchy have been involved: Value Added Tax tribunals, industrial tribunals, the National Insurance Commissioner, the Employment Appeal Tribunal, magistrates, county courts, crown courts, judges of the High Court, the Queen's Bench Divisional Court, both Divisions of the Court of Appeal and the House of Lords[4]. Earlier in this chapter reference has been made to the light which these cases throw on the questions of the supremacy of Community law and the identity of those courts and tribunals which are under the obligation to request preliminary rulings from the European Court. In addition the cases reveal the nature and extent of judicial understanding

---

1 *Macarthys Ltd v Smith* [1980] 2 CMLR 217 at 218, per Lord Denning MR. This presumably is the basis of the decision of the National Insurance Commissioner in Case CS 7/76, *Re an absence in Ireland* [1977] 1 CMLR 5 in which a provision of the Social Security Act 1975 was held to be overridden by a 1971 Community regulation.

2 *Macarthys Ltd v Smith* [1979] 3 CMLR 44 at 47, per Lord Denning MR. Also see *Felixtowe Dock and Rly Co v British Transport Docks Board* [1976] 2 CMLR 655 at 664, 665, per Lord Denning MR.

3 Cf. Lord Denning in *H P Bulmer v J Bollinger SA* [1974] Ch 401 at 418.

4 For examples see the cases cited in Collins, op. cit., at 116, 117.

and assimilation of Community law in the United Kingdom at present.

The first and obvious question concerns the extent to which the rules of Community law have become part of the corpus of law which the courts and tribunals of the United Kingdom themselves apply. There is clearly a general acceptance that Community law can now form part of the law of the United Kingdom[5]. As far as the EEC Treaty is concerned there was until fairly recently a mistaken impression that every provision of the Treaty must now be given legal effect by United Kingdom courts and tribunals. Lord Denning was a proponent of that view[6]. His judgments contain such statements as 'the Treaty is part of our law. It is equal in force to any statute. It must be applied by our courts[7]' and the Treaty of Rome 'is by statute part of the law of England[8]'. But the heresy that all Treaty provisions are part of the law of England and enforceable by its courts has now been abandoned in favour of the established view that only those provisions which satisfy the conditions for direct effect have that status[9]. In the context of the secondary legislation of the Community there appears to be a general recognition that regulations are directly applicable in the United Kingdom. As far as the direct enforceability of the secondary legislation of the Community is concerned, after some initial wavering[10], there now seems to be a general appreciation of the circumstances in which this applies. For example, under the influence of Vice-Chancellor Pennycuick's judgment in *Van Duyn v Home Office*[11] and the European Court's ruling in that case[12], it is now accepted that

5 E.g. *Lerose Ltd v Hawick Jersey International Ltd* [1973] CMLR 83 at 95 per Whitford J; *Minnesota Mining Co v Geerpres Europe Ltd* at 95; [1973] CMLR 259, at 264, 265, per Graham J; *Dymond v G B Britton (Holdings) Ltd* [1976] 1 CMLR 133 at 135, per Oliver, J.

6 Also see *Esso Petroleum Co Ltd v Kingswood Motors Ltd* [1974] 1 QB 142 at 151, per Bridge J.

7 *Application des Gaz SA v Falks Veritas Ltd* [1974] Ch 381 at 393.

8 *Schorsch Meier GmbH v Hennin* [1974] 3 WLR 823 at 830. Also see *H P Bulmer Ltd v J Bollinger SA* [1974] Ch 401 at 418, 419 and *Re Westinghouse Electric Corpn Uranium Contract* [1978] AC 547 at 564. For an early case in which the significance of Treaty provisions was clearly appreciated see *Van Duyn v Home Office* [1974] 1 WLR 1107 at 1116, per Pennycuick VC.

9 See, for example, Lord Denning's exposition of the 'direct applicability' of Treaty provisions in *Shields v Coomes (Holdings) Ltd* [1979] 1 All ER 456 at 461.

10 Compare *H P Bulmer Ltd v Bollinger SA* [1974] Ch 401 at 418, 419 with *Processed Vegetable Growers Association Ltd v Customs and Excise Comrs* [1974] 1 CMLR 113 at 127, 128.

11 [1974] 1 WLR 1107 at 1037, 1040.

12 Case 41/74: [1974] ECR 1337 at 1348, 1349.

directives can confer rights on individuals which are enforceable by them in English courts and which those courts must protect[13]. Similarly, in recent request for a preliminary ruling the Court of Appeal was clearly motivated by the belief that certain directives which were in issue might be directly enforceable[14].

Another matter which emerges from the reported cases is the mode of interpretation of Community law. The unfamiliarity of the style and format of the EEC Treaty and Community secondary legislation have provoked judicial comment. The Treaty 'lays down general principles. It expresses its aims and purposes, all in sentences of moderate length and commendable style. But it lacks precision. It uses words and phrases without defining what they mean. An English lawyer would look for an interpretation clause, but he would look in vain. There is none. All the way through the Treaty there are gaps and lacunae.'[15] The ultimate authority of the European Court on the interpretation of Community law has been acknowledged[16] as also has the necessity of uniform interpretation of that law in all the member states.[17] As aids to interpretation the case law of the European Court and of the national courts of the member states has been invoked and some use has been made of the texts of Community instruments other than those in English[18]. But the generality and apparent incompleteness of the texts of Community law has led some English judges, notably the Master of the Rolls, to claim the right to play a creative role in interpreting Community law so as to fill gaps in its formal fabric. English courts have been exhorted to 'divine the spirit of the Treaty and gain inspiration from it. If they find a gap, they must fill it as best they can. They must do what the framers of the instrument would have done if they had thought about it[19]'. This is indeed what the European Court does and what national courts guided by the European Court may do. But if that approach is adopted without seeking guidance from the European Court then the integrity and uniform-

---

13 *Shields v E Coomes (Holdings) Ltd* [1979] 1 All ER 456 at 462, per Lord Denning MR.
14 *Worringham and Humphreys v Lloyds Bank Ltd* [1980] 1 CMLR 293 at 308, 309, per Lord Denning MR.
15 *H P Bulmer Ltd v J Bollinger SA* [1974] Ch 401 at 425, per Lord Denning. Also see *Application des Gaz SA v Falks Veritas Ltd* [1974] Ch 381 at 393, 394.
16 *H P Bulmer Ltd v J Bollinger SA* [1974] Ch 401 at 419, per Lord Denning.
17 Ibid., at 425. Also see *EMI Records v CBS Ltd* [1975] 1 CMLR 285 at 297, per Graham. J.
18 *Re a Holiday in Italy* [1974] 1 CMLR 184 at 190.
19 *H P Bulmer Ltd v J Bollinger SA* [1974] Ch 401 at 426, Lord Denning.

ity of Community law may be put at risk. This is particularly so in the case of a member state whose legal traditions differ in many ways from the Continental legal traditions upon which the Community legal order is founded.

At the time of British accession there was an influential body of judicial opinion in England that difficulties over the interpretation of Community law will not often arise; in the majority of cases lower courts and tribunals should have no difficulty in interpreting Community law; courts and tribunals should not be too ready to request preliminary rulings from the European Court because of the burden that would place on the Court and because of the increased cost and delay for the litigants[20]. The judgment of Lord Denning in *Bulmer v Bollinger* represents the high-water mark of this approach[1]. Stress was placed on the complete discretion of all courts other than the House of Lords to decide when a preliminary ruling is necessary. Drawing largely upon the national case law of the six original member states, the Master of the Rolls purported to lay down 'guidelines' to assist English courts in deciding whether a reference is necessary and in exercising their discretion. Quite apart from the fact that the practice of national courts on preliminary rulings is not necessarily an accurate representation of Community law on preliminary rulings, a number of questionable recommendations are contained in the 'guidelines', without qualification. These include recourse to the *acte clair* doctrine; that the facts of a case should always be decided before a decision is taken to request a preliminary ruling; that judges' discretion should be influenced by such factors as time, the burden on the European Court, the nature and importance of the question in issue, expense and the wishes of the parties. All of these 'guidelines' are subject to serious reservations[2]. Lord Denning's assumption that the importance of a question of Community law is directly related to the position in the national judicial hierarchy of the court in which the question arises[3] is not borne out by the experience of the European

---

20 See Lord Diplock, 'The Common Market and the Common Law' (1972), 6 JALT 3 at 13, 14; Lord Denning in *The Times, Forward into Europe*, Part 1, 2 January 1973 at 11; Lord Hailsham in an extract from a speech to magistrates appended to Home Office Circular No. 149/1973 (CS 18/1973).

1 [1974] Ch 401 at 420–425, particularly.

2 For critical comments, see Mitchell, J. B. D., 'Sed Quis Custodiet Ipsos Custodes?' (1974) 11 CML Rev. 351; Jacobs, F. G., 'When to Refer to the European Court' (1974) 90 LQR 486; Freeman, Elizabeth, 'References to the Court of Justice under Article 177' (1975) 28 *Current Legal Problems* 176.

3 [1974] Ch at p. 421.

Court. Questions of fundamental importance to Community law and its development have not infrequently come before the European Court in the form of references from lowly national courts and tribunals[4]. Whenever there is a risk of divergent views on Community law it is in everyone's interest, not least that of actual and potential litigants, to seek a ruling from the European Court at the earliest opportunity[5].

The threat to the uniformity of Community law posed by national courts and tribunals, when interpreting that law, going on voyages of discovery of their own without taking advantage of the navigational aids provided by the European Court is clearly illustrated by one of the early cases which came before the Court of Appeal. In *Schorsch Meier GmbH v Hennin*[6] the defendant was indebted to the plaintiffs in a sum of German Marks. The debt was not paid and as a result of a fall in the value of sterling the plaintiffs brought an action in the County Court claiming payment in German Marks. The judge rejected the plaintiffs' argument based on article 106 of the EEC Treaty on the ground that the article had no bearing on English law, and a request that the matter be referred to the European Court was refused. The plaintiffs appealed against both of those rulings. In connection with the first, on the assumption that the EEC Treaty has the status of an Act of Parliament, the Court of Appeal unanimously held article 106 to be a rule of law for English courts to apply. No consideration was given to the case law of the European Court concerning the direct effect of Treaty provisions. In the absence of any European or national case law on the direct effect of article 106, no reference was made to scholarly commentaries on the subject[7]. When interpreting article 106 the Court of Appeal took the lead of the Master of the Rolls who said 'There is no need to refer the interpretation to the court at Luxembourg. We can do it ourselves[8]'. The Court of Appeal then

---

4   E.g. Case 6/64: *Costa v ENEL* [1964] ECR 585; Case 61/65 *Voor Het Vaasen (née Göbbels) v Beambtenfonds Mijnbedrijf* [1966] ECR 261, [1966] CMLR 508; Case 33/70: *SpA SACE v Ministry for Finance of the Italian Republic* [1970] ECR 1213, [1971] CMLR 123.

5   Cf. Case 190/73: *Officer van Justitie v J W J van Haaster* [1974] ECR 1123, at 1136, per Advocate-General Mayras.

6   [1975] QB 416, [1975] 1 All ER 1520.

7   E.g. *Les Novelles: Droit des Communautés européennes*, chapter VI; Campbell, A., *Common Market Law*, Vol. 3, paras. 15.99 to 15.103; Kapteyn, P. J. G. and Verloren van Themaat, P., *Introduction to the Law of the European Communities* (1973) at p. 222.

8   [1975] QB 416 at 426.

attempted to divine the purpose and intent of the article. Since it is concerned, inter alia, with the obligation of member states to authorise payments connected with the movement of goods in the currency of the member state in which the creditor resides, the Court of Appeal held that the German plaintiffs were entitled to payment in German currency[9]. Beyond that no genuine attempt was made to interpret the article as a whole nor to place it properly in the context of the Treaty. The case raised entirely novel points of some importance and a preliminary ruling from the European Court was manifestly necessary.

Lord Denning's 'guidelines', as might be expected, have exercised some influence on judicial attitudes towards preliminary rulings, particularly in the case of tribunals and the lower courts. A Metropolitan Magistrate, for example, has observed that the Master of the Rolls has supplied 'the essential guidelines which English courts must follow[10]'. A Value Added Tax Tribunal[11], the Employment Appeal Tribunal[12] and a High Court Judge sitting in the crown court[13] have all recently accepted the authority of the 'guidelines'. Under their influence preliminary rulings have not been sought apparently on the simple ground that the parties believed that it would be contrary to their interests[14]. On the other hand, the reported cases also show that English judges and others exercising judicial powers acknowledge the significance and importance of preliminary rulings and demonstrate their willingness to seek the guidance of the European Court. There has been a steady and increasing flow of references on such diverse questions as: the scope of the Community's equal pay provisions[15]; the direct enforceability of directives[16]; uncertainty concerning Community rules on

---

9 Since art. 106 appears in the part of the Treaty concerned with economic policy and balance of payments it is probably of public law rather than private law significance, that is concerned with exchange control rather than the currency in which debts may be paid. The relevance of art. 106 to judgment debts has been questioned obiter in the House of Lords; *Miliangos v George Frank (Textiles) Ltd* [1975] 2 CMLR 585 at 596, per Lord Wilberforce.

10 *R v Secchi* [1975] 1 CMLR 383 at 386.

11 *English Speaking Union of the Commonwealth v Customs and Excise Comrs* [1971] 1 CMLR 581 at 599.

12 *Burton v British Railways Board* [1981] 3 CMLR 100 at 102.

13 *R v Tymen* [1980] 3 CMLR 101 at 107.

14 *Extrude Hone Corpn v Heathway Machine Sales Ltd* [1981] 3 CMLR 379 at 399 and *English Speaking Union of the Commonwealth v Customs and Excise Comrs* [1981] 1 CMLR 581 at 599.

15 *Macarthys Ltd v Smith* [1979] 3 All ER 325, [1979] 3 CMLR 44.

16 *Burton v British Railways Board* [1981] 3 CMLR 100.

intellectual property[17]; the authority of the United Kingdom to introduce fish conservation measures[18]; the meaning and effect of the free trade agreement with Portugal[19]; whether a self-employed person is a worker for the purpose of the social security provisions of the Community[20]; and the validity and meaning of a regulation concerned with the financial structure of the common agricultural policy[1]. The House of Lords has even obtained a preliminary ruling for the purpose of giving the Criminal Division of the Court of Appeal an elementary lesson in Community law[2].

After an understandably hesitant start United Kingdom cases reveal no reluctance to consider and apply Community law[3]. United Kingdom courts and tribunals are now, on the whole, adopting a positive and constructive approach to the challenge of this novel body of law. The reasons for this promising outcome lie partly in the clearly observable differences between English and Community law[4].

It is becoming acknowledged that Community law demands a different approach and this should help to promote a fruitful relationship between the law of the United Kingdom and the law of the Community.

**17** *EMI Records Ltd v CBS United Kingdom Ltd* [1975] 1 CMLR 285.
**18** *R v Tymen* [1981] 2 CMLR 544.
**19** *Polydor Ltd v Harlequin Records Shops Ltd* [1980] 2 CMLR 413.
**20** Case 21/5: *Re an illness in France* [1976] 1 CMLR 243.
  **1** Case 146/77: *British Beef Co Ltd v Intervention Board for Agricultural Produce* [1978] 2 CMLR 83.
  **2** *DPP v Henn and Darby* [1980] 2 CMLR 229 at 234, per Lord Diplock.
  **3** The Court of Appeal has even been restrained by the House of Lords for over-enthusiasm. See *James Buchanan & Co Ltd v Babco Forwarding and Shipping (UK) Ltd* [1978] 1 CMLR 156 at 164 per Viscount Dilhorne and *The Siskina* [1978] 1 CMLR 190 at 220 per Lord Diplock.
  **4** See Bridge, J., 'National Legal Tradition and Community Law: Legislative Drafting and Judicial Interpretation in England and the European Community' (1981), 19 *Journal of Common Market Studies* 351.

Part IV

# The law of the economy

Chapter 13

# The Community law of the economy: The Common Market

An analysis of the EEC Treaty will reveal that, like the Constitutions of modern Germany or Italy, it consists of a political and economic charter. The former comprises the 'Organisational' or the 'Constitutional' Law of the Community, the latter the law of the economy. We have discussed the former in the preceding pages but to complete the picture it seems apposite to summarise, albeit briefly, the rudiments of the Community law of the economy. A more detailed analysis will be found in a work[1] complementary to this volume.

## I The concept of the law of the economy

The economic structure of all the Member States reflects a 'mixed economy' i.e. a system based on private enterprise and state control of the 'basic' industries. Moreover the omnipresent state, through the instrumentality of the government, purports to direct the economic life of the nation in a variety of ways and in various degrees of intensity[2]. Thus the national systems subscribe to the theory of the *économie dirigée* but differ in the details of its application. This, in turn, is reflected in the lay-out of the Treaty which purports to create an 'Economic Community' out of the national varieties by defining common policies and designing the means and ways of their implementation. Structurally two objectives are envisaged: an economic integration within the Community and the projection of the Community as a single trading entity in the world market.

In a historico-political sense the West European Community is an answer to the challenge of our times[3] but there is also an eco-

1 Lasok, D., *The Law of the Economy in the European Communities* (with a Chapter on Agriculture by J. W. Bridge), 1980.
2 Ibid, p. 9 et seq.
3 Soldatos, P., *L'explication historico-politique des la genèse de Communautés européennes*, in Lasok, D. and Soldatos, P., *Les Communautés Européennes en Fonctionnement (1981)*, p. 41 et seq.

nomic explanation of its raison d'être[4]. In other words the creation and continued existence of the Community implies an interaction of politics and economics because the political integration of Western Europe reflects the progress of its economic integration. In this process the Law plays a significant part since it binds the Member States together by a system of reciprocal duties[5] and a duty of solidarity towards the collective they have created[6]; it provides the institutional framework of the 'new legal order'[7] and lays down policies as well as the rules for their implementation and enforcement. The dual rôle of the law as a force of integration is that of organising the Community and its economy. Therefore the Community law of the economy is the body of rules addressed to the Member States, individuals, and private and public corporations which in their entirety purport to govern the economic life both at a state and individual level. Since the Community can be built only by stages[8], starting from a broad base of 'European solidarity', the Community law of the economy purports to create first a Common Market and then bind the Member States into an Economic Union.

Whilst the Community legal order supports a unitary economic order in the making it displays certain federalist characteristics. Thus it proceeds from a division of functions between the Community and the Member States and a separation of competences between the Community and national institutions[9]. Its relationship with the national systems, on the other hand, is based on the triple quality of Community law: autonomy, direct applicability and supremacy[10].

In accordance with article 2 of the EEC Treaty[11] the principal task of the Community is to establish a Common Market and to approximate the economic policies of the Member States. To that end the Treaty lays down the elements of the Common Market and

---

4 Bourrinet, J., *L'explication economique de la genèse des Communautés Européennes*, ibid. p. 65 et seq.

5 Lasok, D. Duties of Member States in the European Communities, *Fundamental Duties* (ed by D. Lasok et al), 1980, p. 16 et seq.

6 Donner, A. M., 'The Constitutional Powers of the Court of Justice of the European Communities' (1974) 11 CML Rev 128.

7 Case 26/62: *Van Gend en Loos v Nederlandse Administratie der Belastingen* [1963] ECR 1, [1963] CMLR 105.

8 Schuman, R., Declaration, 9 May 1950, launching the idea of a Coal and Steel Community.

9 See Case 30/59: *De Gezamenlijke Steenkolenmijnen in Limburg v High Authority of the ECSC* [1961] ECR 1.

10 See p. 129 et seq., ante.

11 See also ECSC, art. 2 and EAEC, art. 2.

defines policies which, when implemented, will move the Community from the stage of the Common Market to the stage of the Economic Union. Taken together the elements of the Common Market and the common policies constitute the substantive contents of the Community law of the economy. The procedural contents i.e. the rules of the Community process of defining, implementing and enforcing the Treaty objectives, complement the Community corpus juris.

Whilst priority is given to the development of the Common Market the Treaty envisages a simultaneous development of policies. Therefore a rigid classification into these two segments of economic law would appear rather pedantic if not artificial. However it is made here deliberately in order to identify the legal problems and to mark the developments to date. The Common Market rules are in operation, most of the policies are still in the making.

## II The Common Market

In a technical sense we have three Common Markets, each conceived by a Treaty founding the Coal and Steel, Euratom and Economic Community, respectively. However the EEC, being the most prominent of the three and virtually all-embracing, is the subject matter of this study.

The Common Market is a single 'internal' market embracing several sovereign states i.e. autonomous economic territories. The Common Market territory[12] is marked out by the political frontiers of the Member States subject to special arrangements with regard to certain overseas and European territories for which the Member States are responsible. Within these frontiers the economic forces of supply and demand are allowed to operate freely in the context of 'directed economy'. The chief elements of the internal Common Market comprise the four freedoms, i.e. the freedom of movement of goods, persons, services and capital as well as the two principal policies i.e. the Common Agricultural Policy and the Competition Policy.

The single 'internal' market projects the Community on the world market as a single trading unit. This projection is to be achieved through the Common Customs Tariff and the Common

12 EEC, art. 227.

Commercial Policy. The former appears to be completed, the latter, facing world-wide problems and entrenched Member States' obligations, remains yet to be completed.

Though the internal and the external facets form two inseparable characteristics of the single Common Market they have not developed uniformly. This, in a sense, reflects what has been said earlier, that is, that elements of the Common Market and Economic Union do not develop in isolation but tend to overlap. Thus, whilst the 'internal' Common Market (subject to the transitory position of the youngest Member State, Greece) has been accomplished the 'external' Common Market has been slow on the uptake because of the nature of the Common Commercial Policy. Though affecting the internal market, it forms part of a wider issue and has to be seen both as an element of trade and external relations of the Community. It combines economics and politics.

# III  The Four Freedoms

(A)  MOVEMENT OF GOODS

(*i*) *Customs disarmament*
The Treaty provides for the elimination of customs duties[13] and quantitative restrictions[14] as well as charges having equivalent effect to customs duties and measures having equivalent effect to quantitative restrictions in trade between the Member States of the Community. Since none of the relevant concepts has been defined by the Treaty it fell upon the ECJ to determine in specific cases whether or not a breach of the Treaty has occurred. In the leading case[15] the Court held article 12 directly applicable and thus afforded an importer protection from national law imposing on a product coming from a fellow Member State a duty in excess of the Community rate. Because the obligation to eliminate customs duties is absolute any exception must be clear and unambiguous and has to be interpreted strictly[16].

Quotas to restrict imports or exports are also abolished. The classic example of this prohibited practice was the suspension of

13 EEC, arts. 9-17.
14 Ibid., arts. 30-35.
15 *Van Gend* op cit.
16 Cases 52 and 55/65: *Germany v EEC Commission* [1966] ECR 159, [1967] CMLR 22.

the import of pork products into Italy in which case Italy was held to be in breach of the Treaty[17]. More recent examples include the British restriction on the import of Dutch potatoes[18] and the French refusal to accept sheepmeat from Britain[19].

Charges having equivalent effect to customs duties have been defined by the ECJ as 'duties whatever their description or technique, imposed unilaterally, which apply specifically to a product imported by a Member State but not to a similar national product and which by altering the price, have the same effect upon the free movement of goods as a customs duty'[20].

In the *Scotch Whisky* case[1] the ECJ offered a rather broad description of measures having equivalent effect to quantitative restrictions saying that these include 'all trading rules enacted by Member States which are capable of hindering, directly or indirectly, actually or potentially, intra-Community trade'. However in the second whisky case[2] the Court modified its extreme stance holding that the prohibition on marketing the product without documentary proof that it was genuine did not per se constitute an infringement of the Treaty.

Examples of charges equivalent to customs duties and measures equivalent to quantitative restrictions are legion as if the Member States deliberately set out to avoid their Treaty obligations. The *Simmenthal* cases[3] contain both: sanitary inspection procedures of frozen meat and live cattle at the Italian frontier were held to be equivalent to quantitative restrictions and fees charged equivalent to customs duties.

Treaty provisions designed to remove trade barriers addressed to the Member States may also be applied to private parties if such parties relying upon rights, such as intellectual property rights,

**17** Case 7/61: *EEC Commission v Italy* [1961] ECR 317, [1962] CMLR 39.
**18** Case 231/78: *EC Commission v United Kingdom* [1979] ECR 1447, [1979] 2 CMLR 427.
**19** Case 232/78: *EC Commission v French Republic* [1979] ECR 2729, [1980] 1 CMLR 418.
**20** Cases 2 and 3/62: *EEC Commission v Luxembourg and Belgium* [1962] ECR 425 at 432, [1963] CMLR 199 (Gingerbread).
**1** Case 8/74: *Procureur du Roi v Dassonville* [1974] ECR 837, [1974] 2 CMLR 436.
**2** Case 2/78: *EC Commission v Belgium, Re Import of Spirituous Drinks* [1979] ECR 1761, [1980] 1 CMLR 216.
**3** Case 35/76: *Simmenthal SPA v Italian Minister for Finance* [1976] ECR 1871, [1977] 2 CMLR 1; Case 106/77: *Simmenthal (No 2)* [1978] ECR 629, [1978] 3 CMLR 263; Case 70/77: *Simmenthal (No 3)* [1978] ECR 1453, [1978] 3 CMLR 670.

created by national laws aim to divide markets or restrict the movement of goods in the Common Market[4].

## (ii) *Tax aspects*

Member States are often tempted to impose taxes upon foreign goods in order to protect their own products. Such discriminatory taxes are prohibited by article 95 of the EEC Treaty[5]. However it should be borne in mind that article 95 does not purport to regulate both fiscal policy and customs law. Yet it may correct a Member State's behaviour where it impinges upon customs by applying disparate and discriminate rates to similar domestic and imported products. In such a case a tax would be a charge having equivalent effect to a customs duty.

## (iii) *Derogations under article 36*

Article 36 allows the Member States to derogate from their obligations on several grounds provided such derogations do not constitute 'a means of arbitrary discrimination or a disguised restriction on trade'. These grounds include 'public morality[6], public policy[7], and public security[8]; the protection of health[9] and life of humans, animals or plants[10]; the protection of national treasures[11] possessing artistic, historic or archaeological value; or the protection of industrial and commercial property'. Being in the nature

---

4 E.g. Cases 56 and 58/64: *Consten SARL and Grundig Verakufs v EEC Commission* [1966] ECR 299, [1966] CMLR 418; Case 78/80: *Deutsche Grammophon GmbH v Metro-SB-Grossmärkte GmbH & Co KG* [1971] ECR 487, [1971] CMLR 631.

5 Case 28/67: *Mölkerei-Zentrale Westfalen-Lippe v Hauptzollamt Paderborn* [1968] ECR 143, [1968] CMLR 187 at 217; *Tax on Imported Spirits Cases* op cit.

6 *R v Henn, R v Darby* [1978] 3 All ER 1190 CA; affd. [1981] AC 850, [1979] 2 CMLR 495, HL; Case 34/79: [1979] ECR 3795, [1980] 1 CMLR 246.

7 Case 7/78: *R v Thompson* [1978] ECR 2247, [1979] 1 CMLR 47.

8 *McAfee v Smyth and Quigley (radios used by terrorists)* [1981] 1 CMLR 410, Belfast Magistrates' Court.

9 Case 29/72: *Marimex SpA v Ministero delle Finanze* [1972] ECR 1309, [1973] CMLR 486; *Simmenthal Cases* op. cit; Case 153/78: *EC Commission v Germany* [1979] ECR 2555, *Re Health Control on Imported Meat* [1980] 1 CMLR 198; Case 788/79: *Re Gilli and Andres* [1980] ECR 2071, [1981] 1 CMLR 146; Case 30/79: *Land of Berlin v Firma Wigei* [1980] ECR 151, [1981] 3 CMLR 746.

10 Case 39/73: *Rewe-Zentralfinanze GmbH v Direktor der Landwirtschaftskammer Westfalen-Lippe* [1973] ECR 1039; Cf. Case 89/76: *EC Commission v Netherlands* [1977] ECR 1355, [1978] 3 CMLR 630.

11 Case 7/68: *EC Commission v Italy* [1968] ECR 423, [1969] CMLR 1. Case 18/71: *Eunomia di Porro e C v Italian Ministry of Education* [1971] ECR 811, [1972] CMLR 4.

of an exception to the rule these grounds have to be construed restrictively.

In a number of cases the Community Court had to grapple with the problem of measures having equivalent effect to quantitative restriction arising from the claims to protection of intellectual property rights. Faced with the argument that these rights are protected under article 36 and article 222 of the Treaty the ECJ distinguished between the existence of such rights and their abuse in order either to impede the movement of goods[12] or frustrate the Community rules of competition[13]. In the ruling of the Court the protection of article 36 can be afforded only for the purpose of ... 'safeguarding rights which constitute the specific subject matter of that property ...'[14] which means that the use of intellectual property rights in contravention of a paramount principle of the Common Market such as the free movement of goods cannot be justified.

(iv) *State monopolies*
State monopolies of 'a commercial character' shall be progressively adjusted in order to eliminate discrimination in the conditions under which goods are procured and marketed between nationals of Member States (article 37). Thus not all the monopolies are incompatible with the Common Market[15]. If a State continues with a monopoly, e.g. for the manufacture, import and sale of tobacco[16] despite the resolution to abolish it, a party may raise article 37 in defence against prosecution for offences committed in breach of the national monopoly law. Similarly a charge upon imported alcoholic drink levied in order to support the state monopoly in spirits is incompatible with article 37[17].

---

12 E.g. Case 192/73: *Van Zulylen Frères SA v Hag AG* [1974] ECR 731, [1974] 2 CMLR 127; Case 15/74: *Centrafarm BV and De Peijper v Sterling Drug Inc* [1974] ECR 1147, [1974] 2 CMLR 480; Case 3/78: *Centrafarm BV v American Home Products Corpn* [1978] ECR 1823, [1979] 1 CMLR 326; Case 119/75: *Terrapin (Overseas) Ltd v Terranova Industrie CA Kapferer & Co* [1976] ECR 1039, [1976] 2 CMLR 482; Case 102/77: *Hoffmann-La Roche & Co AG v Centrafarm Vertriebsgesellschaft etc* [1978] ECR 1139, [1978] 3 CMLR 217.
13 Cases 56 and 58/64: *Consten and Grundig* op. cit; Case 24/67: *Parke, Davis & Co v Probel* [1968] ECR 55, [1968] CMLR 47; Case 40/70: *Sirena Srl v Eda Srl* [1971] ECR 69, [1971] CMLR 260; Case 78/70: *Deutsche Grammophon GmbH v Metro-SB-Grossmärkte GmbH & Co KG* [1971] ECR 487, [1971] CMLR 631.
14 In *Terrapin* op. cit. at 505.
15 See Case 6/64: *Costa v ENEL* [1964] ECR 585, [1964] CMLR 425.
16 Case 59/75: *Pubblico Ministero v Manghera* [1976] ECR 91, [1976] 1 CMLR 557.
17 Case 45/75: *Rewe-Zentrale des Lebensmittel-Grofshandels GmbH v Hauptzollamt Landau-Pfalz* [1976] ECR 181, [1976] 2 CMLR 1.

## (v) *Common Customs Tariff (CCT)*

The CCT, adopted in 1960, is at present governed by the up-dated version of 1979[18]. The CCT is the principal element of the uniform customs law applicable to trade with the world outside the EEC. It consists of a list of goods and products arranged in groups under headings and sub-headings and of quotas and duties applicable thereto. Subject to special provisions of different trade agreements between two member states, one of which suing the other on behalf of one of its citizens convicted of offences against the fishery law of the latter[20]. Whilst holding the defendant state guilty of a breach of the Community law the ECJ lost no time in stressing that: ... 'Where criminal proceedings are brought by virtue of a national measure which is contrary to Community law a conviction in those proceedings is also incompatible with that law.[1]'

Since the adoption of CCT the Member States can no longer 'enact autonomous rules in this field'[1]. Moreover they are bound by the CCT nomenclature and the explanatory notes and tariff notices issued by the Council[2].

Importers have to declare the country of origin of the goods or produce and to comply with the Customs formalities laid down by the Community. However national procedures may still interfere with the smooth working of the system.

Subject to certain exceptions[3] customs duties are computed on an ad valorem basis. Therefore the importer has to declare the true value of the goods concerned. As much as the description of goods their valuation, despite detailed Community regulations, has given rise to litigation.

## (vi) *Common Commercial Policy (CCP)*

In a narrow sense the CCP[4] complements the CCT, the two being the twin regulators of the Community external trade. However the

**18** OJ 1978, L.335; Bull 1978/11, point 2.1.19.
**19** EEC art. 10; Case 179/78: *Procureur de la République v Rivoira* [1979] ECR 1147, [1979] 3 CMLR 456.
**20** Case 34/78: *Yoshida Nederland BV v Kamer van Koophandel etc* [1979] ECR 115, [1979] 2 CMLR 747; Case 114/78: *Yoshida GmbH v Industrie-und Handelskammer Kassel* [1979] ECR 151, [1979] 2 CMLR 747.
**1** Case 74/69: *Hauptzollamt Bremen-Freihafen v Waren-Import-Gesellschaft Krohn & Co* [1970] ECR 451, [1970] CMLR 466.
**2** Case 14/70: *Deutsche Bakels GmbH v Oberfinanzdirektion München* [1970] ECR 1001, [1971] CMLR 188.
**3** See e.g. *The Angels Case* 248/80: *Firma Gebrüder Glunz v Hauptzollamt Hamburg-Wattershof* decided on 3 February 1982 (ceramic angel-like candlesticks dutiable according to weight).    **4** EEC arts. 110–116.

CCP has to be seen in the broader context of the Community external relations policy[5] dictated not only by economic but also by political considerations.

As part of the Common Market the CCP is concerned with international trading agreements. The EEC in its own right and on behalf of the Member States takes part now in the negotiations within GATT. However it pursues its own policy developing a network of association and trade agreements throughout the world. In this process, as we have observed earlier[6], the treaty-making power of the Community is used extensively thus replacing the traditional rôle of the Member States and projecting the Community as the sole trade unit. By virtue of article 234 of the EEC Treaty the existing trade agreements to which the Member States are parties remain valid but must be adjusted to their obligations within the Community. The period of adjustment has been extended to the end of 1981. New agreements negotiated by the Member States in their own right are subject to Community guidelines and regulations but the logic of the Common Market suggests that such activity will be possible only within the 'framework agreements' previously negotiated by the Community.

(B) MOVEMENT OF PERSONS

The economic object of the freedom of movement of persons is to create a Common Market in manpower. The political object is to create a greater cohesion of the peoples of the Community through the elimination of barriers to migration and the promotion of a 'Community citizenship'. In a technical sense the body of law can be divided into immigration and social security rules.

(i) *Immigration*
The Treaty makes a distinction between 'workers'[7] and 'self-employed persons'[8]. The former enjoy the 'freedom of movement' the latter the 'freedom of establishment'. However the right of establishment, necessary to exercise a profession or to render a service, is not confined to individuals. It is available to companies and bodies corporate which are treated like individuals[9]. However the distinction between the freedom of movement and the right of

5 Lasok, op cit. p. 342 et seq.
7 Arts. 48–51.
9 EEC art. 58 (1).

6 See p. 39 et seq., ante.
8 Arts. 52–58.

establishment remains essential to Community law at least because the Community continues to legislate separately in these fields.

Freedom of movement implies the right of entry[10], residence[11] and exit. It means in particular the right to accept offers of employment; move[12] freely within the territory of the host country for this purpose, reside in a host country for the purpose of employment; and remain there after the termination of employment in accordance with implementing regulations[13]. Expulsion is also governed by Community rules[14]. As a corollary the Member States are bound to abolish any discrimination based on nationality between workers as regards employment, remuneration and other conditions of work and employment[15].

In principle only the citizens of the Member States are entitled to move freely within the Community. However the privilege has been extended to certain categories of persons, i.e. families[16] of Community citizens, stateless persons and refugees as well as the inhabitants of certain dependent and associated territories.

The principal Community legislation now in force, that is Regulation 1612/68[17], is addressed to 'workers' in the sense of Community law[18] rather than national law. The term comprises persons in actual employment in the host country; persons looking for employment; unemployed who are capable of working and have previously been employed; persons incapable of working through illness or injury sustained during employment in the host country;

---

10 Case 41/74: *Van Duyn v Home Office* [1975] Ch 358, [1974] ECR 1337. Cf. *Minister of the Interior v Cohn-Bendit* [1980] 1 CMLR 543.

11 Case 118/75: *Re Watson and Belmann* [1976] ECR 1185, [1976] 2 CMLR 552; Case 48/75: *Re Royer* [1976] ECR 497, [1976] 2 CMLR 619; *R v Secchi* [1975] 1 CMLR 383. *Williams v Dutch Secretary of State for Justice* [1977] 1 CMLR 669, Queen of the Netherlands in Council. Case 8/77: *German Federal Republic v Sagulo* [1977] ECR 1495, [1977] 2 CMLR 585; Case 157/79: *R v Pieck* [1980] ECR 2171, [1980] 3 CMLR 220. Case 2A 72/72: *Re Residence Permit for an Egyptian National* [1975] 2 CMLR 402 (Admin. Court of Appeal, Rheinland).

12 Case 36/75: *Rutili v Minister for the Interior* [1975] ECR 1219, [1976] 1 CMLR 140.

13 EEC art. 48 (3).

14 See p. 365, post.

15 Ibid. 48 (2).

16 For the interpretation of 'spouse' see Case 9/79: *Wörsdörfer (née Koschniske) v Raad van Arbeid* [1979] ECR 2717, [1980] 1 CMLR 87.

17 JO 1968, L257/2.

18 Case 75/63: *Hoekstra (née Unger) v Bestuur der Bedrijfsvereniging voor Detailhandel en Ambachten* [1964] ECR 177, [1964] CMLR 319; *Levin v Secretary of State for Justice* [1981] 3 CMLR 663 (Reference from Supreme Admin Court, Netherlands, ECJ Case 53/81: op. cit., p. 313, note 8, ante).

as well as retired persons, i.e. persons who have reached the normal age of retirement whilst working in the host country.

Freedom of movement does not include 'employment in the public service[19]' though once so employed the worker is protected from discrimination on the ground of his nationality[20].

According to the Treaty[1] the Member States may restrict the movement of workers, self-employed persons and providers of services on the grounds of public policy, public security and public health. However, being in the nature of a derogation, this power of the Member States has to be interpreted strictly[2]. Several cases involving refusal of entry[3] and expulsion[4] have highlighted the problem of defining 'public policy', i.e. whether to allow the Member States to apply their own criteria or whether to formulate a Community concept of public policy. The matter is still to be settled though the Court has stressed on occasions that public policy, allowing a derogation from the principle of free movement, has to be interpreted strictly and that the Member States' discretion has to be applied within the limits of the Treaty. It means, in effect, that the use of derogation is reduced to cases of a particularly repulsive behaviour of the individual concerned[5], criminal convictions not being per se a ground of expulsion, and that it cannot serve an economic purpose[6] such as to protect the jobs of a Member State's citizens. There must be fair hearing, a right of appeal and the procedure ought not to be more onerous than the procedure in comparable and administrative cases of a domestic nature[7].

## (ii) *Social security*

Social security provisions are corollary to immigration rules[8] but

**19** Article 48 (4) on the meaning of 'public service' see Case 149/79: *Re Public Employees, EC Commission v Belgium* [1981] 2 CMLR 413.
**20** Case 152/73: *Sotgiu v Deutsche Bundespost* [1974] ECR 153.
**1** Article 48 (3), 56 (1), 66.
**2** *Van Duyn* op. cit.; *Rutili* op cit.
**3** E.g. *Van Duyn* op. cit., *Cohn-Bendit* op. cit.
**4** E.g. Case 67/74: *Bonsignore v Oberstadtdirektor der Stadt Köln* [1975] ECR 297, [1975] 1 CMLR 472; Case 30/77: *R v Bouchereau* [1977] ECR 1999, [1977] 2 CMLR 800.
**5** Cf. *Bouchereau* op. cit.
**6** Directive 64/221, OJ S. 1952–66, p. 117; art. 2 (2).
**7** Case 98/79: *Pecastaing v Belgian State* [1980] ECR 691, [1980] 3 CMLR 685.
**8** Case 10/78: *Belbouab v Bundesknappschaft* [1978] ECR 1915, [1979] 2 CMLR 23.

there is no Community social security system as such since the primary object of the basic Community legislation[9] is merely to co-ordinate national systems and thus provide protection to migrant workers and their families in the host countries. As with the immigration rules the status of worker[10] is essential to social security rights. However the term 'worker' does not necessarily include persons eligible for employment such as students[11]. Conversely a social benefit may be available to a handicapped person who was never a worker and is incapable of employment but is a child of a worker[12].

Since affiliation to an insurance scheme is the decisive criterion the distinction between 'workers' and self-employed (i.e. persons enjoying the right of establishment) is of little practical significance as far as social security benefits are concerned[13]. However essential to the system is the classification of benefits into 'social security' and 'social welfare' benefits since, in principle, only the former are covered by the Regulation. Social security benefits are available as of right in consequence of the affiliation to an insurance scheme (national or private) but social welfare benefits depend on the needs of the individual claimant and are awarded out of the public purse. Since there is no uniformity in the Community in this respect each Member State has to make a declaration explaining the nature of the benefits available under its system. However the ECJ held on several occasions that these declarations were inconclusive since the two categories of benefits overlapped and in such cases found for the claimants[14].

Under the Regulation 1408/71 certain benefits can be claimed in all the Member States as 'Community' benefits. These include:

---

9 At present reg. 1408/71; OJ 1971, L149/1, codified version: OJ 1980, C138/1 and reg. 574/72, OJ 1972 L74/1, codified version: OJ 1980, C138/65.

10 Case 44/65: *Hessische Knappschaft v Maison Singer et fils* [1965] ECR 965, [1966] CMLR 82; Case 75/63: *Hoekstra etc* op. cit.

11 Case 66/77: *Kuyken v Rijksdienst voor Arbeidsvoorziening* [1977] ECR 2311, [1978] 2 CMLR 304 but see Case 93/76: *Liègois v Office National de Pensions pour Travailleurs Salaries* [1977] ECR 543, [1977] 2 CMLR 757 ('post-student'); and Case 84/77: *Caisse Primaire d'Assurance Maladie d'Eure et-Loire v Tessier (née Recq) (au pair* girl) [1978] ECR 7, [1979] 1 CMLR 249.

12 Case 63/76: *Inzirillo v Caisse d'Allocations Familiales de l'Arrondissement de Lyon* [1976] ECR 2057, [1978] 3 CMLR 596.

13 Case 17/76: *Brack v Insurance Officer* [1976] ECR 1429, [1976] 2 CMLR 592.

14 E.g. Case 35/77: *Ermin (née Beerens) v Rijksdienst voor Arbeidsvoorziening* [1977] ECR 2249, [1978] 2 CMLR 320; Case 14/72: *Heinze v Landesversicherungsanstalt Rheinprovinz* [1975] 2 CMLR 96.

sickness[15] and maternity benefits; invalidity[16]; old age pension[17]; unemployment benefit[18]; accident at work and occupational diseases[19]; death grants[20] and family benefits[1] which include family allowances and supplementary or special allowances for orphans. The Regulation (article 4 (4)) expressly excludes benefits for victims of war[2]. However in certain grey areas the ECJ relying on the principle of non-discrimination extended the protection of national law to migrant workers and their families. These include widows' rights[3], handicapped persons' allowances[4]; educational[5] grants and

**15** Arts. 18-36; Case 23/71: *Janssen v Alliance Nationale des Mutualités Chrétiennes* [1971] ECR 859, [1972] CMLR 13; Case 117/77: *Bestuur van het Algemeen Ziekenfonds Bestuur van het Algemeen Ziekenfonds Drenthe-Platteland v Pierik (No 2)* [1979] ECR 1977, [1978] ECR 825, [1978] 3 CMLR 343; Case 182/78: *Bestuur van het Algemeen Ziekenfonds Drenthe-Platteland v Pierik (No 2)* [1979] ECR 1977, [1980] 2 CMLR 88; Case 75/63: *Hoekstra* op. cit; Case 17/76: *Brack v Insurance Officer* op. cit; Case 1/78: *Kenny v Insurance Officer* [1978] ECR 1489, [1978] 3 CMLR 651; Case 41/77: *R v National Insurance Comr, ex p Warry* [1977] ECR 2085, [1977] 2 CMLR 783; Case 69/79: *Jordens-Vosters v Bestuur van de Bedrijfsvereniging voor de Leder-en Leder-Verwerkende Industrie* [1980] ECR 75, [1980] 3 CMLR 412 (maternity).

**16** Case 7/76: *Re an Absence in Ireland* [1977] 1 CMLR 1; 2/72: *Murru v Caisse Régionale d'Assurance Maladie de Paris* [1972] ECR 333, [1972] CMLR 888.

**17** Art. 44-51, Case 2/67: *de Moor v Caisse de Pension des Employés Privés* [1967] ECR 197, [1967] CMLR 223; Case 1/72: *Frilli v Belgian State* [1972] ECR 457, [1973] CMLR 386.

**18** Arts. 67-71; Cases 126/77: *Frangiamore v Office National de l'Emploi* [1978] ECR 725, [1978] 3 CMLR 166; Case 76/76: *Di Paolo v Office National de l'Emploi* [1977] ECR 315, [1977] 2 CMLR 59.

**19** Reg. 1408/71, art. 51 (a) replaced by Reg. 2864/72, art. 1 (17); Case 173/78: *Villano v Nordwestliche Eisen-und Stahl-Berufsgenossenschaft* [1979] ECR 1851, [1980] 1 CMLR 613; Case 268/78: *Pennartz v Caisse Primaire d'Assurances Maladie des Alpes-Maritimes* [1979] ECR 2411, [1980] 1 CMLR 682.

**20** Reg. 1408/71 arts. 64-66.

**1** Ibid arts. 72-79; Case 106/76: *Gelders-Deboeck v EC Commission* [1977] ECR 1623, [1978] 2 CMLR 627; Case 134/77: *Ragazzoni v Caisse de Compensation pour Allocations Familiales Assubel* [1978] ECR 963, [1979] 3 CMLR 67; Case 32/76: *Saieva v Caisse de Compensations des Allocations Familiales for the Mining Industry of the Charleroi and Basse-Sambre Coalfields* [1976] ECR 1523, [1977] 2 CMLR 26; Case 115/77: *Laumann v Landesversicherungsanstalt Rheinprovinz* [1978] ECR 805, [1978] 3 CMLR 201.

**2** See Case 93/75: *Alderblum v Caisse Nationale d'Assurance Viellesse des Travailleurs Salaries de Paris* [1975] ECR 2147, [1976] 1 CMLR 236; Case 144/78: *Tinelli v Berufsgenossenschaft der Chemischen Industrie* [1979] ECR 757, [1979] 2 CMLR 735; Case 9/78: *Directeur Régional de la Securité Sociale de Nancy v Gilliard* [1978] ECR 1661, [1978] 3 CMLR 554.

**3** Case 130/73: *Vandeweghe v Berufsgenossenschaft für die Chemische Industrie* [1973] ECR 1329, [1974] 1 CMLR 449.

**4** Case 39/74: *Costa v Belgian State* [1974] ECR 1251; Case 7/75: *Fracas v Belgian State* [1975] ECR 679, [1975] 2 CMLR 442; Case 76/72: *Michel S v Fonds National de Reclassement Social des Handicapés* [1973] ECR 457; Case 63/

facilities (in reliance on article 7 of Regulation 1612/68) and special benefits to 'large families'[6].

Subject to certain exceptions the national law to be applied in order to determine the social rights in specific cases is the law of the workplace of the worker who claims directly or who provides the entitlement of his dependants[7]. However there is a problem of overlapping benefits[8] resulting in claims under different titles and being available in more than one country. Article 12 of Regulation 1408/71 which purports to solve this problem has not been entirely successful. Another problem arises from the principle of aggregation of insurance periods under different national systems for the purpose of the entitlement[9] and the apportionment of the liability between the Member States involved. Aggregation enables the claimant to qualify for the benefit by adding up periods of insurance credited to him in several Member States even if such periods credited in individual States were insufficient. However, because of the different levels of benefits in the Member States the actual calculation and apportionment may result in a lower benefit than that available under a single national law. In such a case, ruled the ECJ[10], the entitlement under national law may not be reduced by Community rules. A claimant may opt for a more advantageous entitlement[11] where benefits overlap.

---

76: *Inzirillo v Caisse d'Allocations Familiales de l'Arrondissement de Lyon* [1976] ECR 2057, [1978] 3 CMLR 596.

5 Case 9/74: *Casagrande v Landeshauptstadt München* [1974] ECR 773, [1974] 2 CMLR 423; Case 68/74: *Alaimo v Préfet du Rhone* [1975] ECR 109, [1975] 1 CMLR 262.

6 Case 32/75: *Cristini (or Fiorini) v Société Nationale des Chemins de Fer Français* [1975] ECR 1085, [1976] 1 CMLR 573—railfare concession; Case 237/78: *Caisse Régionale d'Assurance Maladie (Lille) v Palermo (née Toia)* [1979] ECR 2645, [1980] 2 CMLR 31—allowance to elderly mother of a large family.

7 Reg. 1408/71, art. 13 (2), but lex domicilii of orphans; Case 807/79: *Gravina v Landesversicherungsanstalt Schwaben* [1980] ECR 2205, [1981] 1 CMLR 529.

8 E.g. Case 83/77: *Naselli v Caisse Auxiliaire d'Assurance Maladie-invalidité* [1978] ECR 683, [1979] 1 CMLR 270; Case 105/77: *Bestuur van de Sociale Verzekeringsbank v Boerboom-Kersjes* [1978] ECR 717, [1979] 1 CMLR 270, widow's pension under Dutch law and survivor's benefit under German law.

9 Reg. 1408/71, art. 46, Case 176/78: *Schaap v Bestuur van de Bedrijfsvereniging voor Bank-en Verzekeringswezen, Groothandel en Vrije Beroepen* [1979] ECR 1673, [1980] 2 CMLR 13.

10 Case 26/78: *Institut National d'Assurance Maladie-Invalidité v Viola* [1978] ECR 1771, [1979] 1 CMLR 635; *Naselli* op. cit.

11 Case 180/78: *Brouwer-Kaune v Bestuur van de Bedrijfsvereniging voor het Kledingbedrijf* [1979] ECR 2111, [1980] 2 CMLR 145; see also Case 236/78: *Fonds National de Retraite des Ouvriers Mineurs v Mura* [1979] ECR 1819, [1980] 3 CMLR 27.

Having provided the benefit the paying State is entitled to a reimbursement from the other States involved pro rata the insurance periods credited in each of them[12]. Should the liability result from a wrongful act the paying State is, in accordance with the principle of insurance, subrogated to the rights of the beneficiary[13] and may pursue its right of recovery in accordance with the lex loci injuriae[14].

The rules summarised above form part of the emerging Community 'social law' which remains to be developed in conjunction with the Community social policy[15].

### (iii) *Freedom of establishment*

As mentioned earlier the freedom of movement of persons encompasses, next to 'workers' another group, i.e. self-employed or professional persons. Immigration rules, broadly the same as for workers, govern their mobility but the full enjoyment of their 'right of establishment' depends upon the recognition of their professional qualifications and this, in turn, depends upon the progress of the harmonisation of national laws in this field. Independently of harmonisation of the national rules governing the formation of professional and membership of professional bodies the ECJ was able to remove some of the restrictions in accordance with the principle of non-discrimination. Thus it was held[16] that a Dutch national resident in Belgium with the appropriate Belgian qualifications to practise law could not be debarred from his professional activity on the ground that, according to Belgian law, a lawyer must be a Belgian national. Similarly ruled the Court in the case of a Belgian lawyer[17] and a British architect[18] qualified to practise in France.

The principle of non-discrimination on the ground of nationality

---

12 Reg. 1408/71 art. 63 implemented by Reg. 574/72, arts. 93/98; Case 793/79: *Menzies v Bundesversicherungsanstalt für Angestellte* [1980] ECR 2085, [1981] 1 CMLR 190.

13 Reg. 1408/71 art. 93; Case 27/69: *Caisse de Maladie des CFL Entre'Aide Médicale v Compagnie Belge d'Assurances Générales sur la Vie* [1969] ECR 405, [1970] CMLR 243.

14 Case 72/76: *Landesversicherungsanstalt Rheinland-Pfalz v Töpfer* [1977] ECR 271, [1977] 2 CMLR 121.

15 See note 6, p. 414, post.

16 Case 2/74: *Reyners v Belgian State* [1974] ECR 631, [1974] 2 CMLR 305.

17 Case 71/76: *Thieffry v Conseil de l'Ordre des Avocats à la Cour de Paris* [1977] ECR 765, [1977] 2 CMLR 373.

18 Case 11/77: *Patrick v Ministrie des Affaires Culturelles* [1977] ECR 1199, [1977] 2 CMLR 523.

was extended further when the Court held that residential qualification of a properly qualified person, was not a legitimate condition of his exercising the profession[19].

However conviction for the illegal exercise of the veterinary profession was upheld in the case of a person qualified in Italy who, having become naturalised in France, attempted to practise on his own without first obtaining the requisite French qualifications[20]. Such bar is justified pending the implementation of the harmonising directives[1].

In the absence of a Treaty definition of the class of persons entitled to the right of establishment the ECJ was, and is likely to be, confronted with fringe 'professions' including sports activities. So far the Court held that such activities may come under the non-discrimination principle if they entail 'economic activities'[2]. Amateur activities seem unaffected by Community rules.

In order to make the right of establishment effective the Community has embarked on a harmonising process in which the rules governing the formation and exercise of the medical profession have become the example to follow[3]. So far Council directives have been issued in respect of the nursing[4], dental[5], and veterinary[6] professions. The harmonisation of the rules governing the legal profession has not progressed to date beyond the Council directive[7] merely to 'facilitate the effective exercise by lawyers of freedom to provide services'[8]. Thus lawyers desiring to become professionally

---

**19** Case 33/74: *Van Binsbergen v Bestuur van de Bedrijfsvereniging voor de Metaalnijverheid* [1974] ECR 1299, [1975] 1 CMLR 298—lawyer; Case 39/75: *Coenen v Sociaal-Economische Raad* [1975] ECR 1547, [1976] 1 CMLR 30— insurance agent.
**20** Case 136/78: *Ministère Public v Auer* [1979] ECR 437, [1979] 2 CMLR 373; and [1981] 1 CMLR 749 (conviction confirmed by the Court of Appeal at Colmar).
**1** See p. 407, et seq., post.
**2** See Case 36/74: *Walrave and Koch v Association Union Cycliste Internationale* [1974] ECR 1405, [1975] 1 CMLR 320; Case 13/76: *Dona v Mantero* [1976] ECR 1333, [1976] 2 CMLR 578.
**3** Council Directives 75/362, OJ 1975, L167/1 (recognition of qualifications); 75/363, OJ 1975, L169/148 (medical training); 75/364, OJ 1975, L167/17 (advisory committee on medical training); Council Decision 75/365, OJ 1975, L167/19 (advisory committee of senior public health officials).
**4** Dir. 77/452 and 77/453, OJ 1977, L176/1 and L176/8.
**5** Dir. 78/686 and 78/687, OJ 1978 L233/1 and L233/10.
**6** Dir. 78/1026; 78/1027 and 78/1028; OJ 1978, L362/1; L362/7 and L362/10.
**7** 77/249, OJ 1977, L78/17.
**8** See Case 138/80R: *Re Borker* [1980] ECR 1975, [1980] 3 CMLR 638; *Public Prosecutor of Cologne v Lischka, Hagen and Heinrichson* [1981] 2 CMLR 189 German Court of Appeal Cologne.

established abroad must obtain the requisite qualification in the country concerned.

## (C) FREEDOM TO PROVIDE SERVICES

According to article 60 services mean 'services[9] for remuneration' in particular activities of an industrial and commercial character, craftsmanship and exercise of a profession. However the provision of services is often connected with the exercise of a profession and in this respect inseparable from the right of establishment. Since 1962[10] the Community has embarked on a vast harmonisation programme in this field[11], but discrimination, mainly on the grounds of nationality, residence or even the incorrect transposition of directives into national law, continues[12].

## (D) FREEDOM OF MOVEMENT OF CAPITAL (EEC articles 67–73)

In the only case so far decided by the ECJ capital has been defined as 'means of payment' and thus includes foreign gold coins but not silver coins no longer legal tender[13].

The economic freedoms on which the Common Market is based would be largely illusory without the corresponding liberalisation of financial operations whether by a migrant worker, a capital investor or a multinational corporation. To ensure the flow of capital within the Common Market the Member States are committed to 'the abolition as between themselves of all restrictions on the movement of capital belonging to persons resident in Member States and any discrimination based on the nationality or on the

---

9 E.g. Case 15/78: *Société Générale Alsacienne de Banque SA v Koestler* [1978] ECR 1971, [1979] 1 CMLR 89 (banking); Case 110/78: *Ministère Public and ASBL v Van Wesemael and Poupaert* [1979] ECR 35, [1979] 3 CMLR 87 (agents). Case 155/73: *Re Sacchi* [1974] ECR 409, [1974] 2 CMLR 177 (television advertising); Case 52/79: *Procureur du Roi v Debauve* [1980] ECR 833, [1981] 2 CMLR 362 (television advertising); Case 62/79: *SA Compagnie Générale pour la Diffusion de la Television, Coditel v SA Cine Vog Films* [1980] ECR 881, [1981] 2 CMLR 362 (both cases); Case 279/80: *Re Alfred John Webb* [1982] 1 CMLR 719 (employment agency).

10 General Programme, JO 1962, 36/62 (Establishment); JO 1962/32/32/62 (Services).

11 Lasok, op. cit. p. 145 et seq.

12 Twelfth General Report, 1978 item 117.

13 *R v Johnson et al* (1978) 1 CMLR 226, Crown Court; id. on appeal [1978] 1 CMLR 390, CA; on referral Case 7/78: [1978] ECR 2247; [1979] 1 CMLR 47; see also *Allgemeine Gold und Silberscheideanstalt v Customs and Excise Comrs* [1978] 2 CMLR 292; affd. [1980] QB 390, [1980] 1 CMLR 488, CA; for currency offences still governed by national law see Case 203/80: *Re Guerrino Casati* [1982] 1 CMLR 365.

place of residence of the parties or on the place where such capital is invested' (article 67 (1)). To that end they must liberalise 'the domestic rules governing the capital market and the credit system' (article 68 (2)). However each Member State is responsible for the standing of its currency and its own balance of payments though the rates of exchange as well as the financial stability of each Member State are matters of common concern to all in so far as they affect the functioning of the Common Market. The Treaty[14] provides a machinery for the co-ordination of their economic policy as well as the management of crisis situations.

As early as 1958[15] a Monetary Committee to review the monetary and financial situation of the Member States had been established and in 1974[16] the Council set up an Economic Policy Committee to link up financial and economic matters. However the most significant development in this field has been the creation of the European Monetary System (EMS) in the late seventies[17].

The liberalisation of capital movement has been far from dramatic. The combined effect of the first and the second directive[18] in this field was the elimination of exchange controls in respect of current transactions, transfers of personal funds, investments in real estate and transfers in connection with the movement of goods and the provision of services. The third directive[19] standardised the measures to be taken by the Member States to rectify disturbances of the capital markets, control international capital flows and minimise the detrimental effect of these measures upon domestic liquidity. Coupled with the above are the efforts to harmonise the services of banks and other financial institutions[20] in order to remove restrictions imposed on their activities by national legislations.

It is clear that the freedom of the movement of capital has hardly kept pace with the movement of goods or persons. Though essential to the Common Market a single capital market with a common monetary policy and a common currency is not round the corner[1].

14 Arts. 104–109.
15 JO 1958, 390; OJ 1952–1958, 60.
16 Decision 74/122, OJ 1974, L63–21.
17 For details see Lasok, op. cit. p. 156 et seq.
18 JO 1960, 921; OJ (Sp. ed. 1959–62) p. 49; and JO 1963, 63; OJ (Sp. ed. 1963–64) p. 5.
19 72/156, JO 1972, L91/13; OJ 1972, 296.
20 Council Dir. 73/183, OJ 173, L194/1.
 1 For details see Valaskakis, K., 'La politique monétaire', Lasok and Soldatos, op. cit. p. 461 et seq.

Chapter 14

# The Community law of the economy: Community policies

The progress from the Common Market to the Economic Union of the EEC is marked by the degree of implementation of the various policies laid down in the Treaty. The Treaty provides the legal framework of Community legislation and of Member States' duties to the Community and each other.

Two types of policy can be distinguished, i.e. the policies laid down in the Treaty and the new policies created out of necessity within the framework of the Treaty.

## 1. Treaty policies

### (A) AGRICULTURE (ARTICLES 38–47)[1]

1. *General principles*
In his report to the Messina Conference which paved the way for the creation of the EEC the Belgian statesman, Henri Spaak, wrote:

> 'On ne peut concevoir l'établissement d'un marché commun général en Europe sans que l'agriculture s'y trouve incluse. C'est l'un des secteurs où le progrès de productivité qui résulteront du marché commun, c'est-à-dire de la spécialisation progressive des productions et de l'élargissement des débouchés, peuvent avoir les effets les plus importants sur le niveau de vie des producteurs aussi bien que des consommateurs. En outre, cette inclusion de l'agriculture dans le marché commun est une condition d'équilibre des échanges entre les différentes économies des États membres ...'[2]

Agriculture, as an absolutely essential sector of the economy, had to be included in the concept of the Common Market together with

---

1 For a fuller account see Lasok, D., *The Law of the Economy in the European Communities* (1980), chapter 12.
2 Quoted by Olmi, G., 'L'Agriculture', *Les Novelles*, op. cit., p. 680.

industry and commerce. Moreover, because of its nature and role in the economy of the member states, agriculture had to be singled out for a special regime. In view of the conflicting interests of the member states, the problem of agriculture in the Community has proved to be not only special, but also the most difficult to solve.

Having been recognised as 'a sector closely linked with the economy as a whole' (article 39 (2) (c)) and given its 'particular nature' (article 39 (2) (a))[3] the agricultural regime of the Community rests on its own philosophy. This philosophy can be reduced to two principles enshrined in article 38 of the Treaty, i.e. that the rules governing agriculture derogate from the rules which establish the Common Market (article 38 (2)) and that the operation and development of the Common Market for agricultural products[4] must be accompanied by a common agricultural policy (article 38 (4)).

It follows that there can be no common market for agricultural products without a common agricultural policy. Whilst there is no definition of the agricultural policy in the Treaty, article 39 enumerates the objectives of this policy and article 43 gives considerable powers to the organs of the Community, authorising them to devise and enforce the common agricultural policy. It follows that there is no question of the co-ordination at the Community level of the various national policies but of the one policy for the whole Community.

As for the basic principles of the Common Market in Agriculture, article 42 provides that 'the rules of competition shall only apply to the production of, and trade in, agricultural products, to the extent determined by the Council'. The relevant Common Agricultural Policy Regulation 26[5], article 2, issued in 1962, exempts agreements essential to an agricultural market organisation or the production and sale of agricultural products from the operation of article 85[6] (prohibition of agreements between undertakings which may affect trade between member states and are designed to stultify free

---

3 This particular nature 'results from agriculture's social structure and from structural and natural disparities between the various agricultural regions': art. 39 (2) (a).

4 Agricultural products comprise the products of the soil, of stock-farming, of fisheries and products of first-stage processing directly related to the foregoing (art. 38 (1)). For a list of these see EEC Treaty, Annexe II.

5 JO/993/62 (S. Edn. 1959–62).

6 See pp. 388 et seq., below; Case 71/74: *Frubo v EC Commission* [1975] ECR 563, [1975] 2 CMLR 123 and Cases 40–48/73, etc: *Co-operative Vereniging 'Suiker Unie' UA v EC Commission* [1975] ECR 1663, [1976] 1 CMLR 295.

competition) and article 86[7] of the Treaty (prohibition of the abuse of a dominant trade position by one or more undertakings). Furthermore article 92 and 93 (2) of the Treaty do not apply to agriculture. Article 92 declares state aids incompatible with the Common Market and article 93 governs the procedure to be followed by the Commission in cases involving alleged breaches of article 92. It follows that state aids to agriculture are not ruled out as a matter of principle, but, in practice, specific Regulations[8] expressly provide that articles 92–94 of the Treaty shall not be derogated from unless stipulated to the contrary.

2. *Common agricultural policy*

Article 39 (1) sets out the objectives of the common agricultural policy as follows:

'(a) to increase agricultural productivity by promoting technical progress and by ensuring the national development of agricultural production and the optimum utilisation of all factors of production, in particular labour;

(b) thus to ensure a fair standard of living for the agricultural community, in particular by increasing the individual earnings of persons engaged in agriculture;

(c) to stabilise markets;

(d) to provide certainty of supplies; and

(e) to ensure supplies to consumers at reasonable prices'.

The member states are committed to adopt the common agricultural policy gradually during the transitional period. The new members are equally committed[9]. In order to achieve the objectives of the policy the member states must adopt a common organisation of agricultural markets (article 40 (2)).

3. *Common Organisation of Agricultural Markets*

The Common Organisation of Agricultural Markets has not been defined in the Treaty, but article 40 (2) provides that it should take one of the following forms depending on the product concerned:

7 See pp. 394 et seq., below.
8 Regulation 2759/75, on the common organisation of the market in pigmeat, art. 21, OJ 1975, L282.
9 First Act of Accession 1972, art. 50 et seq.; Second Act of Accession 1979, art. 57 et seq.

(a) common rules as regards competition;

(b) compulsory co-ordination of the various national marketing organisations;

(c) a European organisation of the market.

In practice (c) the 'European market organisation' model has invariably been followed. This involves the replacement of individual national marketing arrangements for an agricultural product by a single, Community-wide marketing structure for that product. That task has been entrusted to the Community Institutions and in the terms of article 43 (2): 'The Council shall, on a proposal of the Commission and after consulting the Assembly acting unanimously during the first stages and by a qualified majority thereafter, make regulations, issue directives, or take decisions, without prejudice to any recommendations it may also make.' The Commission's proposals emerged from a conference held in July 1958 at Stresa, which defined the guidelines of the Common Agricultural Policy[10]. In June 1960, the Commission, after consulting the Economic and Social Committee, submitted its proposals to the Council in respect of four main policies: structural, market, commercial and social[11]. Having had the benefit of the views of the Special Committee for Agriculture created in 1960 the Council adopted certain guidelines which were to form the future Common Agricultural Policy, viz. free movement of agricultural products within the Community, a joint commercial and agricultural policy, a common price level for agricultural products within the Community and co-ordination of national structural reform. These guidelines added practically nothing to the existing provisions of the Treaty, but reaffirmed the resolve to tackle the Community agricultural problem and in some respects interpreted the Treaty provisions. The importance of the problem is well reflected in the machinery of Community legislation which involved the co-operation of the Commission, the European Parliament and the Council.

The first regulation issued by the Council concerned the market organisation in cereals[12] and applied during the transitional period to wheat, rye, barley, oats, maize, buckwheat, millet, hardwheat, meal and groats of wheat and rye and processed grain products.

---

10 See *First General Report*, 1958, ss. 97-101.
11 See *Third General Report*, 1960, s. 230 and *Fourth General Report*, 1961, s. 103.
12 Regulation of 14 January 1962, No. 19, JO 933/62.

The current basic rules concerning the market in cereals are now contained in a consolidating regulation made in 1975[13]. This sets up a single Community market based on a common price system within the Community and regulates trade with third countries. The price system comprises a target price, an intervention price and a threshold price.

The *target price* is determined annually before 1 August by the Council acting on a proposal of the Commission after consulting the Assembly (article 43 (2)). This is not a fixed price, but a price intended to enable the producers to plan their production for the following year; it provides an expectation of the price the product should fetch during the next marketing year (1 August to 31 July). The target price is also designed, *inter alia*, to encourage trade in cereals from Community surplus areas to Community deficit areas. The target price therefore reflects the transport costs involved in such trade.

The *intervention price*, determined according to the same procedure as the target price, is the price which the national authorities must pay to producers who are unable to sell their product on the market. It forms a guarantee to farmers. However, whilst the target price is uniform within the Community, the intervention price varies as from area to area according to the circumstances of the area. The intervention price is lower than the target price. The basic intervention price has been fixed by the Council in relation to the market conditions in the area of the Community having the greatest surplus for all cereals.

The *threshold price* is the price fixed by the Community for cereals imported from third countries. It is fixed in respect of the same standard quality as the target price. It is calculated in relation to cereals, notionally imported through Rotterdam to be sold in the area of the Community having the greatest deficit for all cereals. The aim is that cereals thus imported should eventually sell at or above the target price. In other words, the threshold price is the target price less the cost of transport from Rotterdam to the area of greatest deficit.

The threshold price is determined by the Council in accordance with the procedure outlined above every year before 15 March. It is fixed in relation to a system of levies imposed on imported cereals, these levies being equal to the difference between the threshold price and the c.i.f. price at Rotterdam. The levies are fixed by the

13 Regulation 2727/75, OJ 1975, L281.

Commission whilst the c.i.f. prices for Rotterdam are calculated on the basis of the most favourable purchasing possibilities on the world market. It follows that the threshold prices are lower than the Community prices.

Whilst the price system is designed to ensure production within the Community and to guarantee a fair return to Community producers, the system of levies on imports is designed to protect Community producers against competition from third countries. In a sense, this is a Community preference and an example of the economic barrier round the Community. However, the Regulation requires strict control of the quality of the product to preserve not only a high standard of the market, but also an equitable basis of competition.

Target prices, intervention prices and threshold prices are reviewed monthly to take into account the cost of interest and stockpiling. These reviews result in price increases spread out over the marketing year.

In order to encourage exports, the Regulation provides for refunds to exporters from the Community to third countries. These refunds constitute a form of subsidy which is the same for the whole Community, but varies according to the destination of the products and the use to which they are to be put. The refunds are calculated in relation to the difference between the world and Community prices for the given product. This is necessary since world prices are usually lower than Community prices and there is a policy against the accumulation of surpluses within the Community. Exports and imports are under control by means of appropriate certificates.

At the Community level, the system is supervised by a Management Committee set up under the Regulation and consisting of representatives of the member states presided over by a representative of the Commission. The Chairman refers matters to the Commission either on his own initiative or at the request of the representative of a member state. The decisions are implemented by the Commission. If there is a difference of opinion between the Committee and the Commission, the latter must submit the matter to the Council which may adopt a different decision from that proposed by the Commission[14].

In addition to the Regulation for Cereals, the Community has adopted Regulations in respect of other essential sectors of Agri-

**14** See Chapter 8, ante.

culture, notably Pigmeat[15], Eggs[16], Poultry Meat[17], Fruit and Vegetables[18], Wine and Vines[19], Milk and Dairy Products[20], Beef and Veal[1], Rice[2], Vegetable Oils, Fats, Oil Seeds and Olives[3], Sugar[4], Tobacco[5], Wine[6], certain horticultural products[7] and Fisheries[8].

As a result of these Regulations, several essential sectors of agriculture have become subject to Community Rules. The organisation of these markets differs as from sector to sector, but, broadly speaking, the pattern of the Regualtion for Cereals, which we have considered as an example of a Community Market Organisation, has been followed.

## 4. *Structural reorganisation*

Alongside the Market Organisation the Community postulates a structural reorganisation of agriculture. The problem is by no means simple and has, over the years, focused the attention of the Community. In order to solve it, the Commission in 1968 submitted to the Council a 'Memorandum on the Reform of Agriculture in the European Economic Community' (Agriculture 1980)[9] and, in 1971, the Council adopted a resolution[10] based on this Memorandum. The Commission analysed and made recommendations in respect of several aspects of the structural reform of agriculture. In particular it considered the problem of the manpower engaged in agriculture, the size of farms and production methods.

On the first problem, the Commission concluded that in view of high productivity and overproduction fewer people will be needed in the farming industry of the future. This creates a social problem which the Community must alleviate by helping those who wish to leave the land, by assisting farmers over fifty-five years of age who

**15** Regulation 2759/75, OJ 1975, L282.
**16** Regulation 2771/75, ibid.
**17** Regulation 2777/75, ibid.
**18** Regulation 1035/72, JO 1972, L118 (S. edn 1972 II).
**19** Regulation 816/70, JO 1970, L99 (S. edn 1970 I).
**20** Regulation 804/68, JO 1968, L148 (S. edn 1968 I).
**1** Regulation 805/68, ibid.
**2** Regulation 359/67, JO 1967, L174 (S. edn 1967).
**3** Regulation 136/66, JO 1966 (S. edn 1965–66).
**4** Regulation 3330/74, OJ 1974, L359.
**5** Regulation 727/70, JO 1970, L94 (S. edn 1970 I).
**6** Regulation 989/62, JO 1962 (S. edn 1959–62).
**7** Flax and Hemp, Regulation 1308/70, JO 1970, L146 (S. edn 1970 II); Flowers, Bulbs and Live Plants, Regulations 234/68, JO 1968, L55 (S. edn 1968 I).
**8** Regulation 100/76, OJ 1976, L20.
**9** See *Second General Report*, 1968.
**10** JO 1971, C52.

wish to give up their occupation and by providing schemes for re-training and placement of those who wish to find another occupation.

On the second problem, the Commission found that the average farm within the Community was too small to engage in profitable industrial farming and recommended a definite policy for the increase of the size of farms in accordance with the type of production.

On the third problem, the Commission felt that the production methods were not modern enough and that, coupled with the lack of flexibility, this contributed to the relatively low incomes of farmers in the Community. It proposed the modernisation of production methods, greater adaptability to market needs and better marketing.

The Commission costed its recommendation estimating the relative contribution of the Community and the member states to the cost of the reform programme.

The Memorandum and the ensuing discussions in the European Parliament and the Economic and Social Committee led to the above mentioned Council Resolution on the subject which, in turn, paved the way for a new set of proposals by the Commission[11]. These proposals resulted in the issuing of directives on 17 April 1972 on the modernisation[12] of the farming industry, assistance to farmers leaving the land[13], professional training and advice[14]. A further directive concerned with the special problems of farming in less favoured areas was issued in 1975[15]. Steps have also been taken to formulate co-ordinated national or regional programmes for the processing and marketing of groups of agricultural product as a further means of advancing the economic aims of the common agricultural policy[16]. Taken together, with the Council Resolution, the emerging picture of agriculture is one of a modernised industry, manned by well-qualified and efficient farmers, organised into a competitive market and catering for the social and human problems involved in the movements of the farming population. In this set-up, state aids and subsidies authorised under articles 92 and 93 of the Treaty will have to go as the principles of a Common Market in agriculture will be implemented. However implementation has been delayed and problems continue to arise. To deal with

11 [1971] JO C75.
12 72/159, JO 1972, L96 (S. edn 1972 II).
13 72/160, ibid.
14 72/161, ibid.
15 75/268, OJ 1975, L128.
16 Regulation 355/77, OJ 1977, L51.

these problems the Commission, in November 1973, submitted a Memorandum to the Council in which the future of the CAP to 1978 has been considered. The objectives include proposals to deal with disequilibria in certain agricultural markets, to simplify the common organisation of markets and to reduce costs.

The current package of structural proposals made in 1979 (OJ 1979, C124) is still under discussion. These include increased flexibility on modernisation, precautions against aggravation of market imbalances in certain products as well as measures to meet regional problems (Agricultural Report 1980, pp. 35 et seq).

### 5. *Finance and implementation*
In connection with agriculture, two further points have to be mentioned: finance and the machinery for implementing the Community Agricultural Policy.

The financing of the common agricultural policy, although germane to agricultural problems, is really part of the Community budget. Indeed, agriculture figures prominently in the budget, representing in 1980 some 68 per cent of the whole[17]. The underlying philosophy of the financing of the agricultural policy is the principle that since there is a common policy and a common price system, the financial responsibility must be undertaken by the Community. Accordingly, on the basis of article 40 (4) of the EEC Treaty, the European Agricultural Guidance and Guarantee Fund[18] was set up and an elaborate system of Community agricultural finance was established.

As for the machinery to implement the Community Agricultural Policy, we have already observed that, at the Community level, the crucial decisions have to be taken by the Council after consulting the Assembly, whilst the background work and the administrative actions stem from the Commission. Agriculture has the constant attention of the highest Community organs. At the national level, the execution of the decisions of the Council has been left to the machinery of the member states. In particular the member states assume responsibility for the purchase of the agricultural product at the intervention price determined by the Council. They also operate the system of import and export certificates, collect levies and pay out refunds. Their financial liability to the Community forms part of their contribution towards the Community budget.

17 See *14th General Report*, 1980, p. 51, Table 2.
18 By Regulation No. 25, JO 991/62; the present definitive scheme is laid down by Regulation 729/70, JO 1970 (S. edn 1970 I).

The states who became members of the Community in 1973 and 1981 had to accept the Common Agricultural Policy as a condition of their accession. They are, therefore, committed to a process of adaptation and integration during the five years' transition period as set out in the Act annexed to the Treaty of Accession[19]. For the United Kingdom, this meant a radical change in the system. To implement the Community Policy provisions have been made for the setting up of an Intervention Board for Agricultural Produce and such consequential changes as appeared necessary[20].

The implementation of the Common Agricultural Policy requires a uniform body of Community law, as contended on behalf of the Commission[1]:

> '... The integral and exclusive nature of the competence of Community institutions in the agricultural sectors formed into "European market organisations" derives from the consistent body of case law of the Court of Justice[2] according to which any lacunæ in a system of organising agriculture cannot be filled by Member States since the institution of a European market organisation has deprived Member States of their original legislative power'[3]...

(B) TRANSPORT POLICY (ARTICLES 74–84)

An integrated transport appears to be an indispensible element of the Common Market. Yet the Transport Policy heralded in article 3 (c) of the Treaty remains still relatively undeveloped. The fact is that the transport system developed in each Member State was designed to serve the national needs (often military) rather than a wider territorial unit. Hence the problem of integration.

According to article 74 (1) the Transport Policy includes:

(a) common rules applicable to international transport to or from the territory of a Member State or passing across the territory of one or more Member States:

(b) the conditions under which non-resident carriers may operate transport services within a Member State: and

(c) any other appropriate provisions.

Article 84 of the Treaty refers only to 'transport by rail, road and inland waterway' but the Council may extend the policy to trans-

---

19 See First Act of Accession, 1972, arts. 50 et seq. and Second Act of Accession 1979 arts. 57 et seq.
20 See European Communities Act 1972, s. 6 and the orders and regulations made thereunder.
1 In Case 31/74: *Filippo Galli* [1975] ECR 1 at 54.
2 Case 159/73: *Hannoversche Zucker AG Rethan-Weetzen v Hauptzollamt Hannover* [1974] ECR 121.
3 Case 131/73: *Re Grosoli* [1973] ECR 1555, [1974] CMLR 40.

port by air and sea. However irrespective of the implementation of the policy the ECJ held that job discrimination on board merchant vessels on the ground of nationality could not be maintained[4].

In an attempt to implement the policy the Commission proposed in 1961[5] to establish a 'Common Market in Transport organised according to Community rules, able to respond to the needs of transport in the Community and ensuring elimination of discrimination based on nationality'. This was to be achieved through a uniform approach to the modes of transport, carriers and users; financial independence of carriers; operational freedom; co-ordination of investments and the users' freedom of choice between the modes of transport and carriers. Furthermore[6] the policy was to embrace the principle of sound competition between the various modes of transport and between the carriers. More recently[7] further elements reflecting the anxieties of our technological age have been added; regional needs, problems of urbanisation, pollution and energy[8].

The somewhat incoherent implementation of the Transport Policy has resulted so far in attempts to regulate operational, technical and social aspects of transport.

The operational harmonisation consists of tariff and non-tariff measures. The former consists of bilaterally agreed between Member States maximum and minimum charges (hence 'bracket tariffs') applicable to transport by rail, road and inland waterways. It was introduced experimentally in 1967[9] for a three-year period and further extended until 31 December 1982[10].

Non-tariff measures comprise the rules of competition and the various conditions for the operation of the transport service. Above all it is intended to liberalise transport from the national control and to reorganise the service in response to market forces of supply and demand.

The operation of the service is linked with insurance against civil liability arising from the use of motor vehicles on the road. The

4 Case 167/73: *EC Commission v France* [1974] ECR 359, [1974] 2 CMLR 216.
5 Memorandum of 10 April 1961, see also *Ninth General Report*, 1966, item 207 et seq.
6 Council Decision 67/790, JO 1967, 322/4; OJ 1974 (2nd) IV, 23.
7 Commission Memorandum of 24 October 1973, COM (73) 1725 final.
8 See Bull 12/1978; *Twelfth Gen. Report* (1978), 199; *Thirteenth General Report* (1979), 177.
9 Reg. 1174/68, JO 1969, L194/1; OJ 1968, 411.
10 Reg. 2831/77, OJ 1977, L334/22; See Commission arbitration award OJ 1980, L4/14; [1980] 1 CMLR 699.

exercise of the profession of transport operator, on the other hand, is subject to the freedom of the provision of services and the right of establishment of the operator. Council directives[11] lay down rules regarding the professional formation of road haulage and road passenger transport operators as well as the recognition of professional qualifications. However a Member State may refuse the operator's licence to a person with a criminal record[12]. The directives purport to establish an integrated profession resulting from formal training but allow the Member States to grant licences to persons with adequate practical experience[13].

Technical harmonisation is concerned with the rules governing technical standards of equipment, safety and comfort as well as the control of pollution. Directive 70/156[14] on the approximation of national laws relating to the type-approval of motor vehicles and trailers and Directive 74/150[15] on agricultural and forestry tractors provide a model of legislation in this respect.

Social harmonisation consists of Council regulations[16] setting out to establish common standards for working conditions in internal and inter-state transport. These standards apply to drivers irrespective of whether or not they are employees or independent traders[17]; the resting periods laid down by the Regulation apply not only to drivers but also to employers when driving[18] and the penal sanctions cannot be flouted[19]. The Member States[20] are bound to see that the use of certain road transport vehicles both in domestic

---

11 Dir 74/561, OJ 1974, L308/18; see also Commission Recommendation 77/608, OJ 1977, L248/27, to the United Kingdom; Dir 74/562, OJ 1974, L308/23, see also Commission Recommendation 77/609, OJ 1977, L248/29; Dir 77/796, OJ 1977, L334/37.

12 Case 21/78: *Delkvist v Anklagemyndigheden* [1978] ECR 2327, [1979] 1 CMLR 372.

13 See Case 145/78: *Augustijn v Staatssecretaris van Verkeer en Waterstaat* [1979] ECR 1025, [1979] 3 CMLR 516; Case 146/78: *Wattenberg v Staatssecretaris van Verkeer en Waterstaat* [1979] ECR 1041, [1979] 3 CMLR 516.

14 JO 1970, L42/1; OJ 1970, 96 amend by dir 78/315, OJ 1978, L81/1.

15 OJ 1974, L84/10, implemented in the UK by the Agricultural or Forestry Tractors (Type Approval) Regulation 1975, S.I. 1975, No. 1475.

16 Reg. 543/69, JO 1969, L77/49; OJ 1969, 1970 subsequently amended and modified.

17 Case 65/76: *Re Deryke* [1977] ECR 29, [1977] 1 CMLR 449.

18 Case 76/77: *Auditeur du Travail v Dufour* [1977] ECR 2485, [1978] 1 CMLR 265.

19 Case 97/78: *Re Schumalla* [1978] ECR 2311, [1979] 2 CMLR 176.

20 Case 128/78: *EC Commission v United Kingdom (Tachograph)* [1979] ECR 419, [1979] 2 CMLR 45; see also *Concorde Express Transport Ltd v Traffic Examiner Metropolitan Area* [1980] 2 CMLR 221 (Crown Court, Kingston-upon-Thames).

and inter-state traffic is controlled by means of the recording equipment prescribed by Council Regulation 1463/70[1].

Despite its importance both economic and social the transport policy remains still a much neglected area of Community activity.

## (c) COMPETITION POLICY (ARTICLES 85–90)

In the Preamble to the Treaty, 'fair competition' is recognised as one of the tenets of the European Economic Community. However, although the Treaty purports to institute a 'system ensuring that competition in the Common Market is not distorted' (article 3 (*f*)), competition, fair or otherwise, has not been defined either by the Treaty or the Community Court[2]. It seems to be treated as a self-explanatory term.

The Treaty sets out to establish a system of sound competition based on three sets of rules: rules applying to undertakings, rules against dumping and rules governing state aids.

### 1. *Rules applying to undertakings*

In the first set of rules, articles 85 and 86 form the backbone of rules addressed to 'undertakings' in general; article 90 is specifically concerned with 'undertakings' of a public nature. Article 85 prohibits as 'incompatible with the Common Market all agreements between undertakings, decisions by associations of undertakings and concerted practices which may affect trade between member states and which have as their object or effect the prevention, restriction or distortion of competition within the Common Market'. This does not import prohibitions of *all* combinations or *cartels* but some of them. Article 86, on the other hand, prohibits 'any abuse by one or more undertakings of a dominant position within the Common Market or in a substantial part of it as incompatible with the common market in so far as it may affect trade between Member States'. Here again, the 'dominant position' *as such* is not condemned, but merely its *abuse*.

Since the Treaty contains merely the bare principles, article 87 charges the Council with the task of elaborating detailed Community rules by means of directives or regulations to be designed with

---

1 OJ 1970, L164/1; JO 1970, 482 amended by reg. 1787/73, OJ 1973, L181/1; amended by reg. 2828/77, OJ 1977, L334/5.
2 See the leading case, Cases 56 and 58/64: *Consten and Grundig v EEC Commission* [1966] CMLR 418.

the assistance of the Commission and the Assembly. Articles 88 and 89 contain transitory provisions to be in force until the measures envisaged in article 87 have been enacted. The Council has issued a number of Regulations of which Regulation No. 17[3] is the principal one.

The provisions of articles 85 and 86 are addressed to 'undertakings', both private and public. The term 'undertakings'[4] has not been defined in the Treaty, but article 58 (2) gives a definition of 'companies or firms' by enumeration earmarking these, however, as profit-making entities. We can say that by analogy, an 'undertaking' means a legal entity, whether a physical person or corporation or an association of legal entities engaged in a profit-making activity.

The exact legal status of the entity (which is a matter for the national law concerned) seems of secondary importance as long as there are certain characteristics corresponding to the concept of a natural or juristic person[5]. After all, the entity must have a certain standing under the Treaty which implies capacity to enter into legal agreements, to sue and be sued[6]; and to own property should a punitive sanction be imposed for contraventions of the rules of competition.

In the light of the Commission's decisions individuals may be involved when engaged in economic activity by themselves[7] or when in control of a firm[8]. Associations of firms acting through a chairman or delegates of the associates[9] and even associations without any formal constitution[10] may also be caught by the rules.

The Community Court on several occasions has had to determine the meaning of the term 'undertaking' and has stated that 'an enterprise is constituted by a unitary organisation combining personal, material and immaterial elements attached to an autonomous juristic subject and pursuing permanently a definite economic ob-

---

3 Of 6 February 1962, JO 204/62, amended by Regulations Nos. 59 (JO 1655/62), 118 (JO 2696/63) and 2822 [1971] (JO L285).

4 French: *entreprise*; German: *Unternehmen*; Italian: *impresa*.

5 Cf. Cases 42 and 49/59: *SNUPAT v High Authority of the ECSC* [1963] CMLR 78.

6 EEC, art. 173 (2): 'Any natural or legal person may ... institute proceedings ...'

7 Decision 76/29: *AOIP v Beyrard* [1976] 1 CMLR D14.

8 Decision 76/743: *Reuter v BASF A-G* [1976] 2 CMLR D44.

9 Decision 76/684: *Pabst and Richarz KG v Bureau National Interprofessionnel de l'Armagnac* [1976] 2 CMLR D63.

10 Decision 74/431: *Re Groupement des Fabricants de Papiers Peints de Belgique* [1974] 2 CMLR D102; See also Decision 80/234: *Re Rennet* (a co-operative) [1980] 2 CMLR 402; OJ 1980, L51/19.

jective'[11]. It follows that, for the purpose of articles 85 and 86, an undertaking has to be endowed with a juristic and economic *autonomy* and has to be engaged in the production or distribution of goods or services. It may include a liberal profession within the scope of article 60 of the Treaty[12], but not purely personal pursuits[13].

Unlike article 80 of the ECSC Treaty, articles 85 and 86 of the EEC Treaty are not concerned with the geographical situation of the undertakings. They will come, therefore, under the rules even if situated in, or controlled from, a third country[14].

Some problems have arisen in connection with subsidiaries which, though having a separate legal status from their parent company (*juristic autonomy*), need not be independent (*economic autonomy*). If they are not independent, they cannot be regarded as economic entities in competition with their mother-company. This, in fact, was the conclusion reached by the Commission in *Re Christiani and Nielsen*[15], where a Dutch subsidiary, wholly owned by its Danish mother-company, was held unable to engage in independent economic activity. Therefore, held the Commission, 'the sharing of markets provided for in the agreement is nothing else but a distribution of tasks within a single unit'. In *Re Kodak*[16] the Commission held that a European subsidiary of an American company, acting on instructions from the mother-company, could not behave independently. Therefore, the agreements in question (i.e. between the mother-company and its subsidiaries) could not restrict competition between the parties although they could do so between one of the parties and third parties. However the existence of a joint[17] subsidiary implies agreement between the parent companies and, consequently, the channelling of sales through such a subsidiary may constitute a concerted practice prohibited by the Treaty.

11 Case 19/61: *Mannesmann A-G v High Authority of the ECSC* (1961) 8 Rec 675 at 705.
12 Deringer, A., *Das Wett-Bewerbsrecht der Europäischen Wirtschafts-Gemeinschaft Wirtschaft and Wettbewerb* No. 11 (1962), p. 794.
13 *Id.*, *Les règles de la concurrence au sein de la C.E.E.* No. 12 (1963), p. 37.
14 *Re Grossfiles* (decision of the Commission) (1964) 3 CMLRev 257; *Re Kodak* (decision of the Commission) 70/332/EEC, [1970] CMLR D19.
15 69/195/EEC: [1969] CMLR D36. See also *Re Aniline Dyes Cartel* 69/243/EEC [1969] CMLR D23.
16 *Re Kodak*, op. cit.
17 Commission decision 80/182: *Re Floral Düngemittelverkaufsgesellschaft mbH* [1980] 2 CMLR 285.

## 2. *Practices contrary to article 85*

Article 85 (1), states what kind of agreements, decisions and concerted practices are prohibited. They must exhibit two characteristics, i.e. they must prevent, restrict or distort competition and they must affect trade between member states. A textual comparison with article 3 (*f*) which states the general principle reveals that only the word 'distort' occurs in both articles 85 (1) and 3 (*f*). This is the key word and the words 'prevent' and 'restrict' seem purely subsidiary or explanatory of the key word. Thinking in terms of the English terminology 'restrictive practices' may appear narrower than the inelegant phrase 'distortive practices'. As free competition is one of the underlying philosophies of the Common Market, anything affecting that freedom adversely would constitute 'distortion' within the general meaning of the word. However, article 85 enumerates agreements and practices which, *in particular*, are considered to have that effect, because they:

'(a)  directly or indirectly fix purchase or selling prices[18] or any other trading conditions[19];

(b)  limit or control production[20], markets, technical developments or investments;

(c)  share markets or sources of supply[1];

(d)  apply dissimilar conditions to equivalent transactions[2] with other trading parties, thereby placing them at a competitive disadvantage;

(e)  make the conclusion of contracts[3] subject to acceptance by the other parties of supplementary obligations which, by their nature or according to commercial usage, have no connection with the subject of such contracts.'

---

**18** Commission Decision 69/240: *Re Quinine Cartel* [1969] CMLR D41; Case 45/69: *Boehringer Mannheim GmbH v EC Commission* [1970] ECR 769; Case 48/69: *Imperial Chemical Industries Ltd v EC Commission* [1972] ECR 619, [1972] CMLR 557; Commission Decision 78/163: *A Bulloch & Co v Distillers Co Ltd* [1978] 1 CMLR 400; see also in *Re Agreements of the Distillers Co* [1980] 1 CMLR 541.

**19** Commission Decisions in: *Re WEA-Filipacchi Music SA* [1973] CMLR D43; *Re Dutch Book Publishers* [1977] 1 CMLR D2; *Re IFTRA Rules for Producers of Virgin Aluminium* 75/497 EEC [1975] 2 CMLR D20.

**20** *Quinine Cartel*, op. cit.; Case 41/69: *ACF Chemiefarma NV v EC Commission* [1970] ECR 661.

**1** *Quinine Cartel*, op. cit.; Case 63/75: *SA Fonderies Roubaix v Fonderies Roux* [1976] ECR 111, [1976] 1 CMLR 538; Commission Decision 74/292: *Re European Glass Manufacturers* [1974] 2 CMLR D50.

**2** Commission Decision in the *Distillers Co*, op. cit.; Commission Decision 74/433: *Govers and Zonen v FRUBO* [1974] 2 CMLR D89.

**3** *IFTRA*, op. cit.

The list is by no means exhaustive, it simply comprises the most usual types of agreement and practices likely to affect the freedom of competition.

Such agreements and practices have to 'affect' trade between member states. Some problems of the interpretation of this word[4] have arisen in practice and Advocate-General Lagrange is on record as saying that one has to approach articles 85 and 86 in their spirit rather than letter [5].

The word 'affect' has a wide meaning and, it seems, has to be interpreted extensively to give effect to the Community interest in free trade. Indeed, if the Community is to be seen in its federal concept, there is an analogy in this field to the 'interstate commerce' of the United States of America[6]. An allusion to this position can be seen in the decision of the Community Court in the *Ulm* case[7]. Several cases decided by the municipal courts and the Community Court explain the position, but the following two decisions of the Community Court provide a good illustration of the judicial practice.

In the *Ulm* case[8] there was an exclusive dealing agreement between the German company *Machinenbau Ulm GmbH* and the French company *Technique Minière*, whereby the latter became exclusive dealer for the sale of machinery in France and the French overseas territories. The agreement provided that the French company would buy a specified number of levellers at a fixed price, maintain a stock of spare parts, organise repairs, look after the interests of the sellers and refuse to sell competing products unless authorised by the sellers. A dispute arose in France and the French company argued that the agreement was void under article 85 (1) and (2) of the Treaty, the German company asserted the opposite. The Court of Appeal in Paris sought a preliminary ruling under article 177. In his submissions, Advocate-General Roemer suggested a middle way between the Commission's view that a perceptible interference with competition must take place in order to

---

4 French: *affecter*; German: *beeintrachtigen*; Italian: *prejudicare*; Dutch: *ongunstig beinvloeden*; Ellis, J.J.S., 'L'interprétation du mot "affecter" dans l'article 85, par. 1er, du traité de la C.E.E. par rapport aux mots "empêcher", "restreindre", ou "fausser le jeu de la concurrence"' *Recueil Dalloz* (1963), Ch. XXII, pp. 221 et seq.

5 Case 13/61: In *Société Kledingverkoopbedrijf de Geus en Uitdenbogerd v Société de Droit Allemand Robert Bosch GmbH* [1962] CMLR 1 at 23.

6 *Les Novelles*, op. cit., p. 825.

7 Case 56/65: *Technique Minière v Maschinenbau Ulm GmbH* [1966] CMLR 357 at 375.

8 [1966] CMLR 357.

bring the matter under the rubric of article 85 (1) whilst the German company argued that the application of article 85 (1) should be excluded 'whenever the competition remains in existence notwithstanding the existence of the agreement'. He submitted that 'it would be excessive to place under the rigorous prohibition of article 85 (1) the slightest interference with competition ... and only to grant exemption within the context of article 85 (3)[9]. He referred to a risk of divergence in the municipal jurisdiction and concluded that national judges 'must take account of the real or seriously likely repercussions of the agreement on the market and examine in the particular case whether it has interfered with competition to a noticeable extent and trade between member states been affected to a noticeable extent[10].'

In its judgment the Court examined the purpose of article 85 (1) and held that an agreement must be considered in its economic context. If the object of the agreement cannot have 'a sufficient degree of harmfulness with regard to competition' the Court should consider the possible effect of the agreement, i.e. whether it is likely to prevent, restrict or distort competition 'to a noticeable extent'. In order to determine the extent the court must take into consideration: (1) the nature and quantity of the product, which is the object of the agreement; (2) the position and size of the parties to the agreement in the particular market; (3) the isolated nature of the agreement or its position in a series of similar agreements; (4) the severity of the clauses which aim at the protection of the exclusive rights or on the possibilities left for other commercial currents upon the same products by means of re-exporting and parallel imports[11].

In *Consten SA and Grundig-Verkaufs-GmbH v EEC Commission*[12] the German firm, Grundig, concluded with Consten, a French firm, an agreement for an indefinite period whereby Consten became the sole representative of Grundig for France, the Saar and Corsica. Consten undertook to buy Grundig products, carry out publicity, set up repairs workshops with sufficient spare parts and to undertake the guarantee and after-sales service. Consten also undertook not to sell similar products or to compete with Grundig. Grundig, on the other hand, undertook to retain sale rights and not

9 Ibid. at pp. 367, 368.
10 Ibid. at p. 372.
11 Ibid. at p. 376.
12 Cases 56 and 58/64: [1966] CMLR 418.

to deliver, either directly or indirectly, to other persons within the area covered by the agreement. Grundig authorised Consten to use the name and emblem of Grundig as registered in Germany and other member states. Moreover Consten registered in France, in its own name the trade mark GINT (Grundig International).

Since April 1961, the company UNEF had bought Grundig products from German traders who delivered them in spite of the export prohibition imposed by Grundig, and UNEF resold these in France at more favourable prices than those charged by Consten. Consten brought two actions against UNEF, one for unfair competition and one for infringement of the GINT trade-mark. The litigation in France led to a decision by the Commission[13], which held the agreement contrary to article 85 (1) and concluded that Grundig and Consten 'are required to refrain from any measure tending to obstruct or impede the acquisition by third parties . . . of the products set out in the contract, with a view to their resale in the contract territory'.

Both firms brought an action in the Community Court for annulment of this decision and the Governments of Germany and Italy intervened.

The Advocate-General Roemer and the Court considered very fully the implication of the Consten-Grundig arrangement and the several points raised by it. The Advocate-General submitted inter alia that to judge the criterion of an agreement capable of affecting trade 'account must be taken of the possible repercussions which it is reasonable to expect *on the market* (and this is so even though the Commission must be held correct in declaring that proof of an *increase* in international trade is not enough in itself to show that trade has not been affected)'[14].

The Court, considering the effect of the arrangement on inter-state trade, held that:

'. . . it is necessary . . . to know whether the agreement is capable of endangering, either directly or indirectly, in fact or potentially, freedom of trade between member states in a direction, which could harm the attainment of the object of a single market between states. So the fact that an agreement favours an increase . . . in the volume of trade between states is not sufficient to exclude the ability of the agreement to "affect" the trade . . . In the present case the contract . . ., on the one hand by preventing undertakings other than Consten importing Grundig products into France, and on the other hand by prohibiting Consten from

13 *Re Grundig Agreement* 64/599 EEC [1964] CMLR 489; JO 2545/64.
14 [1966] CMLR 418 at 434.

re-exporting those products to other countries of the Common Market, indisputably affects trade between member states. These limitations on the freedom of trade, as well as those which might follow for third parties, from the registration in France ... of the GINT trade-mark, which Grundig places on all its products, suffice to satisfy the condition under discussion ...[15]'

We should observe that trade need not be *actually* affected. It is sufficient that it *may* be so affected. This was particularly stressed in *Re WEA-Filipacchi Music SA*[16] by the Commission saying that ... 'the violation is already complete when an agreement has the object of restricting competition, even if it had not yet had that effect' ...

However the effect, actual or potential must not be insignificant since *de minimis non curat lex*. The *de mimimis* doctrine can be traced to the *Machinenbau Ulm* case[17]. It was judicially acknowledged in *Völk v Vervaecke*[18] and affirmed in the Commission Notices[19] concerning Agreements, Decisions and Concerted Practices of Minor Importance. However the threat to free competition, real or potential, must be 'appreciable'[20].

### 3. *Negative clearance*

An undertaking engaged in a practice of a restrictive nature may apply to the Commission for 'negative clearance'[1], that is to say a statement that 'on the basis of the facts in its possession' the Commission sees no grounds for action to be taken under articles 85 (1) and 86 of the Treaty. Such a statement offers no foolproof protection but can be pleaded in mitigation should subsequently an infringement be established.

### 4. *Exemptions under article 85 (3)*

Even where negative clearance cannot be obtained the undertaking in question may be exempt from the rigour of article 85 (1) if certain conditions can be proved to the satisfaction of the Commission. The onus is on the applicant to show that the agreement or practice in

**15** Ibid. at p. 472.
**16** Op. cit. p. 388, note 19, ante; see also Commission Decision 74/432: *Re Advocaat Zwarte Kip* [1974] 2 CMLR D79.
**17** Op. cit. p. 389, note 8, ante.
**18** Case 5/69: *Völk v Vervaecke* [1969] ECR 295, [1969] CMLR 273.
**19** OJ 1970, C64/1 amended by OJ 1977, C313/3.
**20** Commission Decisions 68/318: *Re SOCEMAS* [1978] CMLR D28, 68/376: *Re Agreement Johs Rieckermann KG and AEG-Elotherm GmbH* [1968] CMLR D78.
 **1** Regulation 17, of 6 February 1962 as amended, op. cit. p. 386, note 3, ante.

question 'contributes to improving the production or distribution of goods or to promoting technical or economic progress, while allowing consumers a fair share of the resulting benefit, and which does not:

'(a) impose on the undertakings concerned restrictions which are not indispensable to the attainment of these objectives;

(b) afford such undertakings the possibility of eliminating competition in respect of a substantial part of the products in question'².

The system knows two types of exemption, i.e. *individual exemptions* granted by the Commission in specific cases and *bloc exemptions* arising from Community legislation.

Individual exemptions are granted or refused by Commission decisions reached in the appropriate process. They are subject to judicial review³. The process itself involves notification of the practice making a full disclosure to the Commission so much so that mere response to an enquiry will not satisfy the requirements⁴.

Bloc exemptions have been introduced in order to speed up the process of exemptions. The authority for these rests upon Council Regulations 19/65⁵ and 2821/71⁶ which enabled the Commission to legislate. The former covers (1) two-party exclusive distribution agreements and concerted practices, and (2) two party agreements and concerted practices relating to intellectual property rights. The latter covers agreements, decisions and concerted practices relating to (1) the application of standards or types, (2) research and development, (3) specialisation, co-operation and joint ventures⁷. Practices falling within the bloc exemption rules are exempted automatically without the need of notification⁸.

---

2 EEC, art. 85 (3); See Case 30/78: *Distillers Co Ltd v EC Commission* [1980] 3 CMLR 121; Commission Decision in *Re the Agreement of the Distillers Co Ltd* [1980] 3 CMLR 244, Commission Decision in *Re the Application of Robert Krups & Co* [1980] 3 CMLR 274; Commission Decision in Case 37/79: *Anne Marty SA v Estee Lauder SA* [1980] ECR 2481, [1981] 2 CMLR 143. *Re the Application by the National Sulphuric Acid Association Ltd* [1980] 3 CMLR 429.

3 See e.g. Cases 19 and 20/74: *Kali and Salz A-G and Kali-Chemie v EC Commission* [1975] ECR 499, [1975] 2 CMLR 154.

4 Decision 78/670: *GB-INNO-BM SA v Fedetab* [1978] 3 CMLR 524. *FEDETAB v EC Commission* [1981] 3 CMLR 134.

5 JO 1965, 533: OJ 1965-66, 35.

6 JO 1971, L285/46; OJ 1971, 1032 amended by reg. 2743/72, JO 1972, L291/144; OJ 1972, 28-30 December, 60.

7 For details of Commission regulations see Lasok, op. cit. p. 299 et seq.

8 Case 1/71: *SA Cadillon v Höss* [1971] ECR 351, [1971] CMLR 420.

## 5. *Practices contrary to article 86*

Whilst article 85 prohibits certain arrangements which may affect interstate trade and are likely to distort free competition within the Community, article 86 prohibits abuse of a 'dominant position' which has a similar effect.

The notion of the 'dominant position' is not alien to the Community, as it is well entrenched in the municipal laws of Germany, France, Belgium and the Netherlands[9]. However, it is not defined in the Treaty. A dominant position means, in effect, a monopoly within a sector of the economy. Like cartels, not all the monopolies are prohibited, for they may result from the lack of appreciable competition or from mergers which increase efficiency and do not eliminate competition. On the other hand, as suggested in the *Continental Can* case[10], market shares in the range of 50% to 55% may constitute a dominant position—a picture somewhat different from a layman's concept of monopoly. 'Abuse' is, therefore, the key word. Article 86 enumerates such abuses as consisting in:

'(a) directly or indirectly imposing unfair purchase or selling prices or other unfair trading conditions[11];

(b) limiting production, market or technical development to the prejudice of consumers[12];

(c) applying dissimilar conditions to equivalent transactions with other trading parties, thereby placing them at a competitive disadvantage[13];

(d) making the conclusion of contracts subject to acceptance by the other parties of supplementary obligations which, by their nature or according to commercial usage, have no connection with the subject of such contracts'[14].

---

9 *Les Novelles*, op. cit., p. 837; see also art. 66 of the ECSC Treaty.

10 *Re Continental Can Co Inc* [1972] CMLR D11; see also Commission Decision 81/969: *Bandengroothandel Frieschebrug BV v Nederlandsche Banden-Industrie Michelin NV* [1982] 1 CMLR 643 (60 per cent share of market for tyres considered 'dominant').

11 Case 78/70: *Deutsche Grammophon GmbH v Metro-SB-Grossmärkte GmbH & Co KG* [1971] ECR 487, [1971] CMLR 631; Case 127/73: *BRT v SABAM* [1974] ECR 51, [1974] 2 CMLR 238; Case 22/79: *Greenwich Film Production, Paris v SACEM* [1979] ECR 3275, [1980] 1 CMLR 629.

12 Commission Decision *Re European Sugar Cartel* [1973] CMLR D65; Cases 40–48, 50, 54–56, 111, 113, 114/73: *Co-operative Vereniging Suiker Unce UA v EC Commission* [1975] ECR 1663, [1976] 1 CMLR 295.

13 Commission Decision 71/224 in *Re GEMA* [1971] CMLR D35 and 72/268: *Re Gema (No 2)* [1972] CMLR D115.

14 Case 85/76: *Hoffmann-La Roche & Co AG v EC Commission* [1979] ECR 461, [1979] 3 CMLR 211.

This list of abuses is illustrative rather than exhaustive. Indeed, in its First Report on the Competition Policy of the Community, the Commission gave notice that it intends to apply article 86 to situations in which consumers are adversely affected as a result of the abuse of a dominant position[15]. In its Third[16] Report on Competition Policy the Commission addressed itself mainly to the problem of 'industrial concentration' as an obstacle to the open market and effective competition threatening the 'unity of the Common Market'. To combat this mischief the Commission drafted, in 1973[17], a proposal for a regulation to provide control of concentrations between undertakings. If adopted the regulation would give the Commission (subject to review by the Community Court) jurisdiction to prevent concentrations (mergers) which it lacks at present unless one of the undertakings is already in breach of article 86.

The judicial definition of 'dominant position' is of a rather recent vintage. The Community Court was urged by the Italian Government to apply article 86 in the *Grundig* case[18] and in *Italy v EEC Council and Commission*[19] but the Court refused the temptation, contending that 'the possible application of article 85 to a sole agency agreement should not be excluded merely because the grantor and the concessionaire are not competitors inter se and not on a footing of equality'[20].

An opportunity to define dominant position arose in the *Sirena* case[1], where the Community Court held that an undertaking does not enjoy a dominant position by the sole fact of being able to prevent 'third parties from selling in the territory of a Member State products bearing the same trade-mark; moreover, since article 86 requires that this position covers at least a "substantial part" of the Common Market, it is necessary that it has the power of preventing effective competition within an important part of the market, considering also the possible existence and the position of producers or distributors of similar or substitute products ...'

This passage was substantially repeated in the *DGG v Metro* case[2] where the Community Court held that a price maintenance

15 *Fifth General Report*, 1971, pp. 99 and 103.
16 Annexed to the *Seventh General Report*, 1974, pp. 28 et seq.
17 1973 OJ C92.
18 Cases 56 and 58/64: [1966] CMLR 418.
19 Case 32/65: [1969] CMLR 39.
20 [1966] CMLR 418 at 470.
1 Case 40/70: *Sirena Srl v Eda Srl* [1971] CMLR 260 at 275.
2 Case 78/70: *Deutsche Grammophon GmbH v Metro-SB-Grossmärkte GmbH & Co KG* [1971] CMLR 631 at 658.

scheme operating in Germany not only in respect of goods produced in Germany bearing the same trade-mark but also imported from another member state coupled with the control of supplies constituted an infringement of article 86.

In *Laboratorio Chimico*, etc.[3] the Community Court confirmed the finding of the Commission that a company incorporated in a third country but having a substantial presence in the EEC and enjoying a world monopoly in the supply of certain raw materials used in the production of a drug did abuse its dominant position by refusing to supply the necessary material to one of its users in order to eliminate that user from competition in the manufacture of the drug.

In *BRT v NV Fonior*, etc.[4] the Belgian Association of Authors, Composers and Publishers, entrusted with the exploitation, administration and management of all copyrights and kindred rights of its members and associates was held to have abused its dominant position by imposing on its members obligations which encroached unfairly upon the freedom of exercising their rights.

*The Continental Can* case[5], on the other hand, involved takeovers of companies specialising in various kinds of containers and metal lids for glass jars. As a result of the concentration competition in the field would have been practically eliminated. The Commission, in order to prevent this, initiated a procedure under article 3 (1) of Regulation 17/62 against Continental Can and its subsidiary Europemballage and ordered these companies to divest themselves of the newly acquired control over other companies. The companies applied for annulment of the Commission decision on the ground, inter alia, that the Commission was unable to show in which market or markets these companies were supposed to have abused their dominant position. However the Court clarified an important point saying that:

'... Article 86 is not only aimed at practices which may cause damage to consumers directly, but also at those which are detrimental to them through their impact on an effective competition structure, such as mentioned in article 3 (f) of the Treaty. Abuse may therefore occur if an undertaking in a dominant position strengthens such position in such a

3 Cases 6–7/73: *Istituto Chemioterapico Italiano SpA and Commercial Solvents Corpn v EC Commission* [1974] ECR 223, [1974] CMLR 309.
4 Case 127/73: *BRT v NV Fonior; SABAM v NV Fonior; BRT v SABAM and NV Fonior* [1974] ECR 51 and 313; [1974] 2 CMLR 238; see also Commission Decision 82/EEC: *Interpar v Gesellschaft zur Verwertung von Leistungsschutzrechten* [1982] 1 CMLR 221.
5 Case 6/72: *Europemballage Corpn and Continental Can Co Inc v EC Commission* [1973] ECR 215, [1973] CMLR 199.

way that the degree of dominance reached substantially fetters competition, i.e. that only undertakings remain in the market whose behaviour depends on the dominant one ...'6'

In the *Sugar Cartel* case[7] the dominant position consisted in the control of the greater part of sugar production in Belgium and Luxembourg and in the *United Brands* case[8] in the world-wide control of the banana business. *General Motors*[9], on the other hand, holds a legal monopoly to issue certificates of approval for vehicles in its group. A similar position was enjoyed by *Hugin*[10], a Swedish manufacturer, in the cash registers case as he controlled the market for spare parts which were not obtainable elsewhere and which were not interchangeable. They all were held to have abused their dominant position.

To constitute an abuse of a dominant position the exercise of the economic power must relate to the 'relevant market'. This relates to product[11]; product substitution[12] and territory[13]. Considering the 'relevant market' not only the volume of the business but also the territorial control has to be taken into account in order to determine whether or not a 'substantial part of the Common Market' has been affected[14].

## 6. *Determination of infringements of articles 85 and 86*
The Commission, whilst exercising an exclusive authority in respect of exemptions under article 85 (3) shares, in part, this power

6 Ibid. at 245 (para. 26).
7 Op. cit. 394, note 12, ante.
8 Commission Decision in *Re United Brands Co* [1976] 1 CMLR D28; Case 27/76: *United Brands Co v EC Commission* [1976] ECR 425, [1976] 2 CMLR 147.
9 Commission Decision 75/75: *Re General Motors Continental NV* [1975] 1 CMLR D20; Case 26/75: *General Motors Continental NV v EC Commission* [1975] ECR 1367, [1976] 1 CMLR 95.
10 Decision 78/68: *Liptons Cash Registers and Business Equipment Ltd v Hugin Kassaregister AB* [1978] 1 CMLR D19; Case 22/78: *Hugin Kassaregister AB v EC Commission* [1979] ECR 1869, [1979] 3 CMLR 345.
11 E.g. *United Brands* op. cit. (bananas); *General Motors*, op. cit. (motor cars); *Lipton and Hugin* op. cit. (cash registers).
12 E.g. Decision 73/457: *Zoja v Commercial Solvents Corpn* [1973] CMLR D50; Cases 6–7/73: *Commercial Solvents Corpn v EC Commission* [1974] ECR 223, [1974] 1 CMLR 309 (basic drug); *Hoffmann-La Roche* op. cit. (vitamins); *Continental Can* op. cit. (metal lids).
13 E.g. *United Brands* op. cit.; Decision 76/172: *Re Bayer and Gist Brocades (NV's) Agreement* [1976] 1 CMLR D98; Decision in *Sugar Cartel* [1973] CMLR D65; Cases 40–48, 50, 54–56, 111, 113, 114/73: *Suiker Unie UA etc* [1975] ECR 1663, [1976] 1 CMLR 295.
14 Case 77/77: *Benzine en Petroleum Handelsmaatschappij v EC Commission* [1978] ECR 1513, [1978] 3 CMLR 174.

with the member states when dealing with infringements of article 85 (1) and article 86. In other words, the states may deal with the latter as long as the Commission has not initiated proceedings under article 2, 3 or 6 of Regulation 17[15]. This has caused some difficulty in practice and there is no uniformity in this matter in the Community[16]. The disadvantages of concurrent jurisdiction are quite apparent.

The question of the overlap between municipal law and Community law was considered by the Community Court in *Wilhelm v Bundeskartellamt*[17] and it was held that, in principle, both could apply simultaneously subject to the underlying philosophy that Community law has to be implemented by the member states and that in the case of conflict, Community law prevails.

According to article 3 of Regulation 17, infringements of articles 85 and 86 are dealt with by Commission either ex officio or at the instance of interested parties. The former implies independent investigations of a case which comes to the notice of the Commission informally or in the course of the exercise of its duties as laid down by the Treaty (article 155) and Regulation 17 (article 11). The interested parties who put the Commission on enquiry can be either states or undertakings or individuals who are, but need not be[18], affected by the alleged infringement. The Commission will use its powers of investigation and follow the prescribed procedure in order to reach a decision.

The Commission has the discretion whether or not to pursue a complaint but must advise the complainant if no action is to be taken[19].

If an infringement has been proved the Commission will take appropriate steps to have the offending practice terminated, may make recommendations to the offending party and apply sanctions provided by the Treaty and the Regulation.

Before taking a decision, the Commission must give the parties concerned an opportunity to express their views, give them a hearing and, where it intends to issue negative clearance it must publish the essential content of the application or notification, inviting all interested third parties to submit their observations (Regulation

---

15 EEC art. 88 and Regulation 17, art. 9.
16 *Les Novelles*, op. cit., p. 844.
17 Case 14/68: [1969] ECR 1, [1969] CMLR 100, cf: 'new commercial torts': *Application des Gaz SA v Falks Veritas Ltd* [1974] 2 CMLR 75. See also Case 253/78: *Procurer de la Republique v Giry* [1981] 2 CMLR 99.
18 Cases 32/78 and 36-82/78: *BMW Belgium SA v EC Commission* [1979] ECR 2435, [1980] 1 CMLR 370.
19 Case 125/78: *GEMA v Commission* [1979] ECR 3173, [1980] 2 CMLR 177.

17, article 19). Finally, it must consult the Consultative Committee on Cartels and Monopolies (Regulation 17, article 10).

## 7. *Sanctions for infringements*

In the case of infringement of article 85 and article 86, the Treaty provides for three different sanctions: nullity of the offending practice, fines and penalties.

According to article 85 (2) any prohibited agreements or decisions are null and void by operation of law, that is void ab initio[20] and not from the date of determination. This being a sanction *de plein droit*, there is no discretion in its application. The only exception applies to certain existing agreements, decisions and practices (Regulation 17, article 7).

The question whether nullity taints all has been answered by the Community Court in the *Ulm*[1] *and Grundig*[2] cases in the negative. Only the bad elements are tainted with nullity and these can be severed from the sound body of the contract or decision. The sanction of nullity does not strike activities under article 86.

According to article 15 of Regulation 17, the Commission may inflict heavy fines upon undertakings guilty of an infringement of article 85 (1) and article 86, and also for the supply of false or misleading information, for submission in incomplete forms of the books or other documents required or for refusal to submit to an investigation[3]. These sanctions are said to have no criminal or punitive character (article 15 (4)).

The Commission has power to inflict penalties[4] under article 16 of Regulation 17 in order to oblige the offenders to:

(a) put an end to an infringement of article 85 or 86;

(b) discontinue any action prohibited under article 8 (3) (*c*) of Regulation 17[5];

(c) supply completely and truthfully any information requested under article 11 (5)[6];

---

**20** Case 48/72: *SA Brasserie de Haecht v Wilkin-Janssen* [1973] ECR 77, [1973] CMLR 287.
**1** [1966] CMLR 357 at 376.
**2** [1966] CMLR 418 at 475.
**3** Commission Decision 80/334: *EC Community v Fabbrica Pisani* [1980] 2 CMLR 354, OJ 1980, L75/30.
**4** See 72/457/EEC *Laboratorio Chimico Farmaceutico Giorgio Zoja SpA v Commercial Solvents Corpn* [1973] CMLR D50, [1972] JO L299/51.
**5** Reference to a decision obtained fraudulently or by false information.
**6** See Commission Decision in *The Community v Telos SA* [1982] 1 CMLR 267; Commission Decision in *Community v Comptoir Commercial d'Importation* [1982] 1 CMLR 440.

(d) submit to any investigation ordered under the investigative powers of the Commission.

The penalties, depending upon the severity of the infringement, range from fifty to one thousand EUA per day.

## 8. *Judicial control*

At the national level the Community rules are enforced by national authorities whose decisions are subject to judicial control either by ordinary courts (e.g. the United Kingdom) or specialist tribunals (e.g. Germany). The national authorities may, of course, take advantage of the proceedings for a preliminary ruling under article 177 of the Treaty.

The Court has unlimited jurisdiction in respect of Commission decisions which it can affirm or annul in entirety[7] or in part[8]. It may also cancel, reduce[9] or increase fines and penalties imposed by the Commission.

The decisions of the Commission do not rank as res judicata. Indeed, decisions made under article 85 (3) may be revoked or amended. However, decisions which impose a pecuniary obligation on persons other than states are enforceable by the authority of article 192 (1) of the Treaty. The procedure of enforcement is left to the municipal law of the member states.

Decisions of the Commission are subject to judicial review either under proceedings for annulment or the principle of plenary jurisdiction. The former is governed by article 173 (2) of the Treaty, the latter by article 172. We should add that there is also a possibility of a *recours en carence* under article 175 (3) which enables any aggrieved party to complain to the Community Court that the Commission has failed in its duty.

## 9. *Extra-territorial effect*

The long arm of Community law may reach offenders established outside but involved in economic operations having effect inside the Community[10]. Proceedings within the Community will not absolve the offender from proceedings outside the Community.

---

7 E.g. *Continental Can* op. cit., Case 17/74: *Transocean Marine Paints Association v Commission* [1974] ECR 1063, [1974] 2 CMLR 459.

8 E.g. *Consten and Grundig* op. cit.

9 E.g. *Re Sugar Cartel* op. cit.; *United Brands* op. cit.

10 Case 48/69: *Imperial Chemical Industries Ltd v EC Commission* [1972] CMLR 557; Cases 52 and 53/69: *Geigy and Sandoz v EC Commission* [1972] CMLR 637; Dec. 76/642: *Community v Hoffmann-La Roche* [1976] 2 CMLR D25.

This may lead to double jeopardy and double sanction[11]. The problem can be solved only by international agreements.

### 10. *Rules applying to public undertakings*

Modern states are involved in trade and industry through the instrumentality of public undertakings. The forms and the degree of government control of these bodies differ considerably as from country to country and so does the area of their operation. They have, however, a common tendency towards monopolies and in that sense enjoy a 'dominant position'—the very negation of the idea of the Common Market. The Treaty attacks the problem from two angles. By article 37 the member states are committed to a policy of progressive adjustment of state monopolies 'so as to ensure that ... no discrimination regarding the conditions under which goods are procured and marketed exists between nationals of member states'. Rather than 'adjusting' their monopolies the Commission recommended[12] that states should bring about their abolition. Indeed a certain amount of progress has already been made in that direction though the end of state monopolies is not in sight yet. In the same spirit, the first Act of Accession (article 44) urges the new members to deal with their monopolies and authorises the Commission to make specific recommendations as from the beginning of 1973.

The second angle of attack is expressed in article 90 of the Treaty, which is addressed specifically to two types of undertakings, viz. 'public undertakings' and 'undertakings to which member states grant special or exclusive rights'—a classification rather difficult to substantiate in the light of the law of the member states, but corresponding to article 17 of the GATT. Accordingly, member states are obliged to 'neither enact nor maintain in force any measure contrary to the Treaty, in particular article 7 and articles 85 to 94'. The gist of the provisions as far as the rules of competition are concerned, is that a state enterprise is, in principle, reduced to an equal status with a private[13] enterprise. This is not without significance in view of the role played by state enterprises in the national

---

11 Case 45/69: *Boehringer Mannheim GmbH v EC Commission* [1970] ECR 769; Case 7/72: *Boehringer Mannheim GmbH v EC Commission (No 2)* [1973] CMLR 864; see also Commission Decision 80/1283 in *Eurim Pharm GmbH v Johnson and Johnson Inc* [1981] 2 CMLR 287.
12 [1970] JO L6 and L31.
13 See Case 10/71: *Ministère Public Luxembourgeois v Müller* (dredging operations) [1971] ECR 723.

economy and the traditional (especially on the Continent) preference accorded to 'public' interest. The privilege had to be sacrificed
on the altar of the Common Market.

However, not all was sacrificed because article 90 (2) provides an
exception in the case of 'undertakings entrusted with the operation
of services of general economic interest or having the character of
a revenue-producing monopoly'. In the first category one can place
undertakings procuring public utility services such as water, gas,
electricity[14] or transport where the elements of manufacture and
trade are, in a sense, in the background and 'service' to the public
at large[15] (having incidentally an economic value) is the primary
function of the undertaking. In the second category fall the
revenue-raising undertakings engaged in the manufacture and marketing of certain products of everyday use (e.g. salt in Italy, matches
in France and Italy) or luxuries (e.g. alcohol in France and Germany, tobacco in France and Italy). However, even these exempted
undertakings are subject to the Treaty, notably the rules of competition, in so far as the application of these rules does not obstruct
the performance of their specific tasks. And for good measure the
Treaty adds: 'The development of trade must not be affected to
such an extent as would be contrary to the interests of the Community' (article 90 (2)).

### (D)  DUMPING (ARTICLE 91)

There is no definition of 'dumping' in the Treaty. Dumping practices consist of exporting goods unsaleable at high prices in home
markets to foreign markets for sale at low prices in order to capture
a new market or maintain high prices in the home market. The
Commission is authorised to send recommendations to perpetrators
of dumping practices, but, if such practices continue, the 'injured
member state' may be authorised by the Commission to take protective measures under the control of the Commission.

'Boomerang' dumping, whereby products dumped from one
member state to another shall be re-admitted to the country of

---

14 E.g. Case 6/64: *Costa v ENEL* [1964] ECR 585, [1964] CMLR 425.
15 E.g. Case 155/73: *Re Sacchi* (television advertising) [1974] ECR 409 at 431,
    [1974] 2 CMLR 177 at 204; see also Case 52/79: *Procureur du Roi v Debauve*
    [1980] ECR 833, [1981] 2 CMLR 362 and Case 62/79: *SA Compagnie Générale
    pour la Diffusion de la Télévision, Coditel v Ciné Vog Films SA* [1980] ECR 881,
    [1981] 2 CMLR 362.

origin free of duties and quantitative restrictions, is provided for in article 91 (2).

In pursuance of their duties the Commission and the Council have issued regulations to control dumping[16] in general terms as well as in respect of individual products, e.g. poultry[17]. Dumping is regarded primarily as an 'injury' to Member States but they cannot act unilaterally for any allegation of dumping has to be investigated by the Commission. Whilst the Commission will make recommendation to combat dumping the Council will decide upon the application of anti-dumping duties where appropriate. Recently, perhaps in the climate of the world recession in trade, several complaints of dumping have been considered. These involved not only the notorious Japanese interests but also Scandinavian, East European and American, products[18]. Whilst anti-dumping measures can be enacted in the context of customs law and commercial policy of the Community the actual dumping practices undermine sound competition. Hence the linking of dumping with competition rules in the outlay of the EEC Treaty.

## (E) AIDS GRANTED BY STATES (ARTICLES 92–94)

Article 92 (1), in general terms, declares incompatible with the Common Market 'any aid granted by a member state or through state resources in any form whatsoever which distorts or threatens to distort competition by favouring certain undertakings or the production of certain goods'. We should note that not *all* the aids are prohibited and that the prohibition, applying to selected undertakings and goods, starts from the premise that such aids would affect trade between member states.

As an exception to the rule article 92 (2) regards certain state aids compatible with the Common Market, viz. those which:

(a) have a social character granted to individual consumers without discrimination as to the origin of the products concerned;

(b) are intended to alleviate hardship resulting from natural disasters or other extraordinary events;

16 Com. Reg. JO 1960, 21 amended by Reg. JO, 1961, 23 and Reg. JO, 1961, 25; Council Reg. 459/68, OJ 1968, L93/1 amended by Reg. 2011/73, OJ 1973, L206/3; Reg. 1025/70, [1970] JO, L124/6.

17 Reg. 123/67 and 565/68. See also Case 9/72: *Brunner KG Munich v Hauptzollamt Hof* [1972] ECR 961, [1972] CMLR 931.

18 See especially cases reported in [1979] 2 CMLR 257, [1981] 1 CMLR 98 et seq, [1981] 1 CMLR 490 et seq.

(c) are provided for certain regions of Germany to relieve the hardship resulting from the division of Germany.

A further exception to the rule may, in appropriate circumstances, be considered in respect of:

(a) aids intended to promote the development of regions afflicted by a low standard of living or serious unemployment;

(b) aids intended to promote an important European project or remedy a serious disturbance in the economy of a member state;

(c) aids intended to facilitate the development of certain economic activities or regions;

(d) aids specified by the Council on a proposal from the Commission.

In the spirit of article 92 (3) the Commission saw no objection to various measures for the promotion of artisanship in Sicily[19], or the development of the machine-tools sector in the United Kingdom[20] (subject to reservation regarding stockpiling), but objected to a Belgian project in aid of the production of tractors by the Ford Company[1]; French aids to textile industry[2]; a preferential rediscount rate for export credits introduced by France to support her exporters[3]; *A subsidy to Dutch Cigarette Manufacturers*[4]; and a subsidy to British pig producers[5].

To examine the aid system and bring about the elimination of aids incompatible with the Common Market, articles 93 and 94 define the powers of the Commission and the Council and determine the procedure to be followed in such cases. However, it should be borne in mind that these provisions are addressed to the member states and create no rights enforceable by individuals[6].

As a by-product of the problem arising from state aids, certain

19 *Les Novelles*, op. cit., p. 865.
20 *Europe*, No. 1946 (22–23 March 1976), p. 7.
 1 Case 64/651/EEC: *Re Subsidies to Ford Tractor (Belgium) Ltd* [1965] CMLR 32, JO 3257/64.
 2 Case 47/69: *Re Aids to Textile Industry France v EC Commission* [1970] CMLR 351.
 3 Cases 6/69 and 11/69: *EC Commission v France* [1969] ECR 523, [1970] CMLR 43.
 4 Decision 79/743 [1980] 1 CMLR 453, OJ 1979, L217/17.
 5 Cases 31/77 and 53/77: *EC Commission v United Kingdom* [1977] ECR 921, [1977] 2 CMLR 359.
 6 Case 6/64: *Costa v ENEL* [1964] ECR 515, [1964] CMLR 425.

Community policies begin to emerge. These are the regional policy[7] and industrial policy[8]. Irrespective of these, as a result of practice, a Community State Aids regime has developed[9]. However, whilst pertinent to State duties inter se, aids to industry tend to distort the competiveness between undertakings involved in the internal trade of the Community. This, no doubt, is the reason why the provisions to control state aids form part of the Community competition policy.

### (F) TAX PROVISIONS (ARTICLES 95–99)

It should be stated from the outset that uniform taxation throughout the Community is not the object of the Treaty, but a Common Market. Therefore the tax provisions of the Treaty should be seen in that perspective, that is, as relative to the free movement of goods, persons, services and capital. In so far as taxation is relevant to these objectives, it is a proper concern of the Community. Thus, with the abolition of customs duties and charges having equivalent effect, it is necessary to ensure that internal taxation will not replace the abolished customs duties.

Article 95 (1), which the Community Court has held to be directly enforceable in the Member States[10], prohibits the imposition on the products of other Member States of internal taxation of any kind in excess of the tax imposed upon similar domestic products. Article 95 (2) prohibits any internal taxation intended to afford protection to domestic products. Thus article 95 imports the principle of non-discrimination into the field of taxation of imported goods. Taxes on such goods can be levied, but only in the same measure as the internal taxes on similar goods.

Article 95 is complemented by article 96, which provides that

---

7 *Third General Report*, 1969, p. 277. Draft regulations regarding regional developments: 1971, JO C90; 1973, Report on Regional Problems in the Enlarged Community, *Bulletin of the European Communities*, Supp. 8/73; Regional Development Fund, 1973, OJ C86; *Bulletin of the European Communities*, 12/74; Council adoption of regulation to set up the Regional Fund on 18 March 1975. See *Eighth General Report* 1975, pp. 105 et seq.

8 *Fourth General Report*, 1970, p. 167. Commission memorandum, 1970, *Fourth General Report*, para. 205; Commission communication to Council, 1973, *Bulletin of the European Communities*, 5/73, para. 1101 and Supp. 7/73; *Eighth General Report*, 1975, pp. 169 et seq.

9 See Lasok, op. cit. p. 200 et seq. See also Case 730/79: *Holland BV v EC Commission* [1980] ECR 2671, [1981] 2 CMLR 321.

10 Case 57/65: *Lütticke GmbH v Hauptzollamt Saarlouis* [1966] ECR 205, [1971] CMLR 674.

'any refund of internal tax in respect of exported goods shall not exceed the internal tax imposed upon such goods whether directly or indirectly'. 'Direct' taxes are taxes charged upon finished products; 'indirect' taxes are charges upon the product at the various stages of production. Article 96 covers, therefore, both eventualities. However, from a practical point of view, a line has to be drawn between taxes affecting the undertaking and those which fall upon the product. The Community Court has held that a refund of taxes which are charged to the undertaking as a taxable entity to encourage exports was inconsistent with article 96[11]. Should this not be so, the undertaking would enjoy an advantage over another exporter and this, in turn, would affect free competition and trade between member states. This case is also important in so far as it provided an opportunity for an examination of tax refunds. The Community Court found the Italian system incompatible with the Treaty, especially that customs duties were included in the computation of the refunds[12].

Article 97, which is not directly enforceable[13], purports to bring about a simplification of the multi-stage turnover tax by introducing a single tax on imports according to products or groups of products. By the same token, tax refunds on exports should be subject to uniform average rates. In order to ensure that there is no infringement of articles 95 and 96, the Commission is authorised to issue directives or decisions to the state concerned (article 97). In pursuance of this provision, the Council issued a directive to provide a uniform system of calculating the average rates[14].

Article 98 purports to control charges 'other than turnover taxes, excise duties and other forms of indirect taxation'. More specifically, it prohibits exemptions and repayments in respect of exports and the imposition of countervailing duties in respect of imports from member states, unless approved by the Council.

Taking articles 95–98 together, we can see the overall concern with the complexities of the national tax systems and the desire to remove the obstacles to free movement of goods concealed in the technicalities of fiscal policies designed to promote export of national products and restrict import of foreign goods on a competitive basis of equality. Rationalisation of the tax provisions

11 Case 45/64: *EEC Commission v Italy* [1965] ECR 857, [1966] CMLR 97.
12 Case 45/64: *EC Commission v Italy* [1969] ECR 433.
13 Case 28/67: *Molkerei-Zentrale Westfalen-Lippe GmbH v Hauptzollamt Paderborn* [1968] ECR 143, [1968] CMLR 187 at 221.
14 Directive 68/221, 30 April 1968; OJ (Sp edn), 1968 (I) 114; JO L115.

necessitates a Community policy in this respect. Since, at this stage, a uniform tax system appears unattainable, a modicum of order appears possible through harmonisation of national tax systems.

A general scheme for the harmonisation of tax systems is provided in article 99, which enjoins the Commission to study the problem and, in the interests of the Community, find ways and means of harmonising the national legislation governing 'turnover taxes, excise duties and other forms of indirect taxation'. Harmonisation does not mean uniformity, but a tolerable state of affairs which permits diversity within the ideal of the Common Market.

In this sense, the Council, on the proposals of the Commission, issued a number of directives. The most important are the two directives of 1967 intended to introduce a common value added tax system (VAT)[15]. The first directive consists of a general outline of the principles, definition of the value added tax and the time-table according to which it should become part of a reformed tax system of the member states. The second directive elaborates the details and the guidelines of its application. Whilst members are committed to apply the principles, they are free to determine the rates of tax and exceptions.

The system was to be implemented by 1 January 1970 but certain countries were unable to do so. The third directive extended the limit to 1 January 1972. The fourth and fifth directives were addressed specifically to Italy since Italy was in default. By the Act of Accession the system came into force on 1 July 1973 whilst Italy, under the fifth directive was to have complied by 1 January 1973. The sixth directive, replacing the second directive, made the VAT system uniform but allowed the Member States to fix the rates of tax. This measure is particularly important since one per cent of this source of revenue constitutes a direct contribution to the Community's 'own resources'. The effort to harmonise taxes continues[16].

## (G) APPROXIMATION OF LAWS (ARTICLES 100–102)

### 1. *General principles*
It is considered that the approximation of laws of the member states is necessary for the proper functioning of the Common Market (EEC Treaty, article 3 (*h*)). This we have already observed since

15 67/227, JO 1967, 1301; OJ 1967, 14 and 67/228, JO 1967, 1303; OJ 1967, 16.
16 See Lasok, op. cit. p. 416 et seq.

the implementation of the economic freedoms of the Community depends on the degree of harmonisation of national laws affecting trade and the movement of persons and goods. Approximation (*rapprochement, Angleichung*) represents, by definition, a more intensive process of integration than harmonisation. The problem was well understood from the inception of the Community and the difficulties of changing laws, like changing the ways of life or forsaking the national heritage, were never underestimated. In spite of the lack of spectacular progress, there is a Community policy in this field and there is no lack of ideas or projects. The aims were thus summarised by the Commission[17]:

> 'the object is not the creation of a vast European law of a unique character, but of a system of a federal type which would draw its force and authority of the conviction of history and at the same time of the plurality of the living nature of the laws of the member states, of the common juristic heritage and of the necessity of an economic concentration'.

Community law, because of its nature and origin, should reflect the legal philosophy of the member states and their experience. It should, at the same time, contribute towards political and economic integration by building up a federal system of law. In this respect, the objectives are limited for they are centred, at this stage, on the concept of the Common Market. In other words the mechanism of harmonisation must be used for the removal of obstacles to the establishment of the Common Market. Whilst there is a challenge to comparative lawyers at the national and Community level, the Community organs, especially the Commission being entrusted with the task, must adopt a functional approach.

The guidelines can be found in articles 100–102 of the Treaty. Article 100 refers to 'such provisions laid down by law, regulation or administrative action ... as directly affect the establishment or functioning of the Common Market'. This is both a programme and its limitation. Moreover, laws are to be enacted by the member states on the basis of directives[18] issued according to the Community procedures. The power of the Council to issue such directives under article 100 is limited because unanimity is required and so a member state can veto the proposals of the Commission. Where,

---

**17** *Eighth General Report of the EEC*, 1965, para. 83.
**18** See Case 32/74: *Firma Friedrich Haaga GmbH v Rechtspfleger* [1974] ECR 1201, [1975] CMLR 32, in which for the first time the Court had to interpret an article in a directive (i.e. 68/151 of 9 March 1968 (OJ L65)) on harmonisation of company law.

however, the Commission finds a distortion of the conditions of competition arising from the laws of the offending state, the Commission shall, through consultation, eliminate such distortion, but should this effort fail, the Council may be called in (article 101). The Council must be unanimous during the first stage but thereafter may issue appropriate directives by a qualified majority. Where there is reason to fear that a state will create distortions through taking certain legislative or administrative measures, the Commission alone is empowered to act and shall issue appropriate recommendations (article 102). The sanction for ignoring the recommendation is that the other member states may disregard article 101 in relation to the offending state.

It appears that the above provisions proceed from the principle of the sovereign law-making power of the member states modified by the Treaty obligation. Nevertheless there is implied coercion and sanction since failure to enact a directive into national law correctly would, as in the case of a regulation, expose the member states to enforcement proceedings[19]. In fact several such actions have been initiated and withdrawn when the state in default decided to implement the measure.

## 2. *The area of approximation*

At first sight, articles 100–102 may appear rather narrow in scope, but, if one considers that they are concerned not only with the 'establishment' but also with the 'functioning' of the Common Market, the scope widens considerably and is as wide as the concept of the Common Market itself. The same applies to the mechanism of approximation. Although these articles are framed to emphasise the sovereign law-making power of the member states and, if interpreted narrowly, articles 101 and 102 would suggest that the Community organs will intervene only in a remedial capacity, there is

---

19 E.g. Case 95/77: *EC Commission v Netherlands (Re Directive on Meteorology)*, [1978] ECR 863; Case 100/77: *EC Commission v Italy (Re Directive on Meteorology)* [1978] ECR 879, [1979] 2 CMLR 655; Case 147/77: *EC Commission v Italy (Re Slaughter of animals)* [1978] ECR 1307, [1978] 3 CMLR 428; Case 69/77: *EC Commission v Italy (Re Agricultural tractors)* [1978] ECR 1749; Case 93/79: *EC Commission v Italy (Re Weighing Machines for Conveyor Belts)* [1979] ECR 3837, [1980] 2 CMLR 647; Case 42/80: *EC Commission v Italy (Re Wire-Ropes, Chains and Hooks)* [1980] ECR 3635, [1981] 2 CMLR 532; Case 133/80: *EC Commission v Italy (Re Public Supply Contracts Directive)* [1981] ECR 457, [1981] 3 CMLR 456; Case 163/78: *EC Commission v Italy (Re aersol dispensers)* [1979] ECR 771, [1979] 2 CMLR 394; Case 43/80: *EC Commission v Italy (Re non-automatic weighing machines)* [1980] ECR 3643, [1981] 2 CMLR 532.

ample authority for positive initiatives. These initiatives have resulted in general programmes of legislation[20] concerning the freedom of movement of persons, establishment, services and recognition of professional qualifications, as well as many directives ranging from industrial production, agriculture, trade, insurance, banking, transport and food, to motor vehicles, measuring instruments, pipe-lines and crystal glass.

So far harmonisation has served mainly to eliminate technical barriers to trade and to impose Community standards of goods and marketing. Such directives are usually drafted in considerable detail leaving no discretion to Member States. Certain proposals have been criticised, e.g. by the House of Lords Select Committee on the European Communities[1] as being ultra vires articles 100 and 235 but also strongly defended as perfectly justifiable[2]. However, the most challenging is the problem of approximation of company law, which has been lingering for years and which has inspired a great deal of learned writing[3].

It is apposite to mention in this connection the approximation of laws through international conventions under article 220. This article enumerates areas in which the law ought to be regulated by multilateral conventions, viz. protection of nationals of the member states in the territory of another state, abolition of double taxation, recognition of firms or companies and the reciprocal recognition and enforcement of judgments and arbitral awards. So far, two conventions have materialised: the Convention on the Mutual Recognition of Companies and Bodies Corporate, signed on 29 February 1969, and the Convention on Jurisdiction and the Enforcement of Civil and Commercial Judgments, signed on 27 September 1969. The latter came into force in the original six member states on 1 February 1973.

In addition there are two Conventions relative to patent[4] law,

---

20 18 December 1961, [1962] JO 36 et seq.; for progress see annual *General Reports*.

1 HL 131 Session 1977–78, 2nd Report, Approximation of Laws under article 100 of the EEC Treaty.

2 Close, G., 'Harmonisation of Laws: Use or Abuse of the Powers?' (1978) EL Rev 461.

3 *L'harmonisation dans les communautés*, Editions de l'Institut d'Etudes Européennes Bruxelles (1968); Bärmann, J., *Europäische Integration im Gesellschaftsrecht* (1970); Stein, E., *Harmonisation of European Company Laws* (1971); Lasok, op. cit. p. 401 et seq.

4 The Munich Convention for the Grant of European Patents 1973, International Legal Materials, vol. xiii; 1974, p. 270 et seq. The Luxembourg

and a *Draft Directive on Trade Marks*[5] (which was originally proposed as a Convention). In the field of the conflict of laws there is a Draft Convention on the Law applicable to Contractual Obligations[6]. The progress has been far from spectacular, the convention being an inefficient instrument of harmonisation.

### (H) ECONOMIC POLICY (ARTICLES 103-109)

Generally speaking the Community economic policy ought to embrace all matters economic but in the terms of the Treaty it consists of three elements; i.e. conjunctural policy, balance of payments and commercial policy.

### 1. *Conjunctural policy*

As the economy of a country or a group of countries (e.g. the European Community) is subject to fluctuations resulting in booms and depressions, it was thought necessary to deal with the problem on a Community basis. In other words, there ought to be a Community 'conjunctural policy' (*politique de conjoncture, Konjungturpolitik*).

Accordingly, article 103 is addressed to the member states who should consult with each other and the Commission in matters affecting economic trends and should regard these problems as Community problems.

In order to assist the member states and the Community, a Committee on Policy relating to Economic Trends was set up in 1960. Two other Committees, i.e. Medium Term and Budgetary, were added in 1964. All three were replaced by the Economic Policy Committee in 1974[7].

### 2. *Balance of payments*

The realisation that balance of payments problems have a chain reaction and may endanger the working of the Common Market is behind the provisions of the Treaty. Article 104 proceeds from the principle that the member states are responsible for their own balance of payments, whilst maintaining a high level of employment

---

Convention for the European Patent for the Common Market, 1975, OJ 1975, L17/1. For details see Lasok, op. cit. p. 269 et seq.
5 For the text see [1981] 1 CMLR 357.
6 For the text see [1979] 2 CMLR 776.
7 By Council decision 74/122, OJ 1974, L63/21.

and the stability of prices. In order to achieve these objectives, article 105 counsels co-ordination of the economic policies of the member states and sets up the appropriate machinery. Accordingly, an advisory and co-ordinating body has been established. This is the Monetary Committee[8] consisting of representatives of the governments and central banks of the Member States. Its function is 'to keep under review the monetary and financial situation of the member states and of the Community and the general payments system of the Member States and to report regularly thereon to the Council and the Commission' (article 105 (2)). It can also deliver opinions at the request of the Council or the Commission or on its own initiative.

Article 106 gives effect to the basic policies of the Common Market as it obliges the member states to remove restrictions on the outflow of currency in connection with the movement of goods, persons, services and capital. Moreover, the member states undertake to refrain from introducing as between themselves any new restrictions on transfers of currency in respect of the invisible transactions listed in Annexe III to the Treaty[9].

Article 107 refers to the rates of exchange which each member state is free to determine for its own currency bearing in mind the interest of the Community and the objectives of article 104. Should an alteration of its rate of exchange result in distortion of the conditions of competition, the Commission may step in and, after consulting the Monetary Committee, authorise other member states to take appropriate measures.

Article 108 purports to deal with balance of payments difficulties which may endanger the economy of a member state. The underlying philosophy is that no member of the Community should suffer and, in order to alleviate the resulting hardship, the Commission ought to assist the member facing such difficulties. In particular, the Commission is bound to investigate the problem and recommend appropriate measures. If necessary, the Council may authorise mutual assistance recommended by the Commission but, should this prove insufficient, the state concerned may be author-

---

8 Set up in 1958, JO 1958, 390; OJ 1952–1958, 60.
9 The list comprises some 60 items including earnings from transport, warehousing, repairs, technical assistance relating to the production and distribution of goods, commissions, travel and tourism, films, repair and maintenance of property, customs duties and taxes, fines, salaries and wages, dividends, interest, rents, royalties, pensions, maintenance, inheritances and dowries.

ised to take protective measures. Such measures may, in accordance with article 226, derogate from the Treaty obligations, but should cease when no longer necessary.

The French crisis of 1968 provides an illustration of the practical application of article 108. The Commission investigated the difficulties facing the French economy at that time and recommended that mutual assistance be granted. The Council issued a directive to that effect[10] and the Commission decided that France may adopt emergency measures including exchange controls of certain capital transactions, restrictions of certain imports and aid to exports[11].

Finally, article 109 authorises the member states to take provisional emergency measures when faced with a sudden crisis in the balance of payments. These measures must take into consideration possible repercussions within the Community, they should be appropriate to the emergency and the least harmful to the Common Market. The Commission and the other member states must be informed. The Commission may then recommend action under article 108 and the Council may decide, by a qualified majority, that the protective measures be amended, suspended or terminated.

These procedures were in 1974 applied in respect of Italy in order to assist that country to solve its financial difficulties. The Commission authorised[12] Italy to take protective measures, including restrictions on the supply of moneys and agreed that aid should be provided for but the Council opposed the latter.

### 3. *Commercial policy (articles 110–116)*

A common commercial policy, as one of the basic principles of the Common Market (article 3 (*b*)) is the necessary corollary to the establishment of a common customs tariff[13]. It means, in effect, a common attitude to the outside world, the Community acting virtually as one commercial unit. Article 111 regulates the position during the period of transition providing for a co-ordination of the commercial relations of the member states with third countries. Article 112 is concerned with export aids to third countries and article 113 regulates the position after the expiry of the period of transition. Article 114 connects article 111 (2) and article 113, providing that customs agreements and commercial treaties with

---

10 On 20 July 1968, [1968] JO L189.
11 See *Second General Report*, 1968, p. 110.
12 (1974) OJ L152.
13 See p. 362, ante.

third countries shall be concluded by the Council on behalf of the Community, acting unanimously during the first two stages and thereafter by qualified majority. Article 115 deals with the difficulties individual states may experience as a result of the common commercial policy and authorises such states to take protective measures under the guidance of the Commission. During the period of transition, in emergency situations, states may take unilateral measures but have to notify these to the other member states and the Commission. In choosing these measures, they must cause least disturbance to the operation of the Common Market. Finally, article 116, with reference to the end of the transitional period, brings the principle of co-ordination and common commercial policy into operation with regard to the participation of the states in international organisations of an economic character. At present transitional provisions apply only to Greece but they shall remain in operation as long as the Community continues to expand.

In the seventies there began a process of *convergence of policies* leading to a concept of a unified Community Economic Policy[14].

## (I) SOCIAL POLICY (ARTICLES 117–128)

### I. *Social provisions*

In the blueprint of the Community one can see a close connection between economics and social problems expressed in the general principles of the Treaty (articles 2 and 3 (i)) and the specific 'social provisions'. In this way, the Community law of the economy has been linked with social policy.

It seems, at this stage, premature to speak of a 'social law'[15] of the Community, as article 117 merely expresses an agreement between the member states 'upon the need to promote improved working conditions and an improved standard of living for workers' and their belief that 'such a development will ensue not only from the functioning of the Common Market, which will favour the harmonisation of social systems, but also from the procedures provided for in this Treaty and from the approximation of provisions laid down by law, regulation or administrative action'. A great deal of effort, both domestically and at the Community level, will be required to implement this programme.

14 For further details see Lasok, op. cit. p. 339 et seq.
15 But see Lyon-Caen, G., *Droit Social Européen* (1969); Ribas, J. J. *Droit Social Européen* (1973); Leaper, R. A. B., 'Social Policy' in Lasok and Soldatos, op. cit. p. 273 et seq.

Whilst social services and welfare state benefits are essentially a matter for the domestic concern of the member states, the Community is also interested not only because of its professed aim of a 'better Europe', but more practically because of the social problems consequent upon the movement of labour[16]. Hence the special concern with 'workers'. As the scope and standards of the social security systems differ as from country to country, it is essential to improve some and harmonise all into a system where the migrant worker and his family would find an adequate level of protection whether at home or in another member state. The long term policy of the Community seems to have this object in mind.

It follows that, in accordance with the general pattern of the Treaty, the Commission, assisted by the Economic and Social Committee, must address itself to certain specific tasks enumerated in article 118, viz. employment, labour law and working conditions, basic and vocational training, social security, prevention of occupational accidents and diseases, occupational hygiene, the right of association and collective bargaining between employers and workers. This may be the broad outline of the European social law.

Whilst it may be taken for granted that the member states are, within the general terms of the Treaty, committed to work towards an improvement of their social security system article 119 specifically enjoins the member states to 'ensure and maintain the application of the principle that men and women shall receive equal pay for equal work'[17]. This reflects the trend towards the equality of the sexes and the specific recommendations of the Convention of 24 June 1951 sponsored by the International Labour Organisation.

Article 120 is concerned with the maintenance of the existing equivalence between paid holiday schemes. Articles 121 and 122 are concerned with the function of the Council and Commission, and with studies and reports on social developments within the Community.

## 2. *The European Social Fund*
The Treaty sets up a European Social Fund to be administered by a Committee under the supervision of the Commission and

**16** See pp. 365 et seq. ante.

**17** Council directive 75/117 of 10 February 1975 OJ 1976, L39; Case 80/70: *Defrenne v Belgian State* [1971] ECR 445, [1974] CMLR 494 at 509; Cases 43/75: *Defrenne v SABENA* [1976] ECR 455, [1976] 2 CMLR 98; Case 149/77: *Defrenne v SABENA* [1978] ECR 1365, [1978] 3 CMLR 312; See also British cases, p. 000, ante.

governed by its own statute[18]. The title is rather misleading because the scope of the Fund is limited to 'the task of rendering the employment of workers easier and of increasing the geographical and occupational mobility within the Community' (article 123). The real purpose is to provide financial assistance, that is, to provide fifty per cent of the expenditure incurred by a state or a body governed by public law for the purpose of re-employment of workers or relief of temporary unemployment resulting from the conversion of an undertaking to another type of production (article 125 (1)).

The Fund has been reformed in 1971[19] in accordance with article 126 to undertake two different functions, i.e. to implement the Community policies and to deal with difficulties which impede the smooth working of the Common Market.

Article 128 gives the Council authority to lay down general principles for implementing a common vocational training policy capable of contributing to the harmonious development both of the national economies and the Common Market[20].

Clearly, the rudiments of social policy and its implementation are too fragmentary to provide more than a modest beginning of what may become in the future a body of rules complementary to the economic and commercial policies of the Community.

# II. Consequential policies

As the Community develops and the programme of action laid down in the Treaty is being implemented new policies emerge either in consequence of the developments or in response to necessity.

## 1. *Energy*

A continuous supply to meet the ever growing demand of energy is one of the imperatives to sustain the industrial economy and the standard of living of the peoples of the Community. This was well understood during the 1958 crisis in the coal industry. Some initial steps to develop a Community energy policy have been taken at

---

18 For the Statute, see JO 1201/60, 31 August 1960.
19 JO [1971] L28.
20 Cf. 'General Guidelines for a Community-level Programme on Vocational Training', JO C81, 12 August 1971.

that time[1] and efforts continue but, so far, apart from a statement of policy objectives[2] and exhortations at the highest level[3] little has been achieved. The 1973–74 energy crisis caused by the quadrupling of oil prices by the OPEC countries[4] found the Community in disarray each member state endeavouring to further its own interest. Though the adverse economic consequences continue to plague the Community and, it seems, a lesson has been learned by the industrial countries, the Community energy policy remains yet to materialise.

## 2. *Environment*

Industrial countries have paid a heavy price for their prosperity in the damage suffered by their physical environment. Technological development in the area of nuclear energy has added a further hazard to the present and the future generations. Thus concern for the conservation and protection of the environment, apart from the preamble to the EEC Treaty, has become the prime mover of the Community environmental policy. This reflects not only the world-wide interest in the protection of natural resources and amenities but also purely Community interests. International nuisance affects relations between the Member States[5] and leads to litigation[6]. Moreover disregard of the environment has wider repercussions in the areas of energy, consumer protection, industrial and regional policies as well as competition since manufacturing costs can be reduced at the expense of the environment.

The first action programme was adopted in 1973[7] and the second in 1977[8]. A number of decisions, recommendations, resolutions and directives followed suit[9]. The emerging environmental policy rests on the principle that 'the polluter pays for the prevention and elimination of environmental nuisance[10]' and the Community

---

1 Agreement of the Council of Ministers and the High Authority of the ECSC, JO 7 December 1958, 574.
2 EEC Bull Supp 4/74.
3 Dublin communiqué of the meetings of the Heads of State or Government, *The Times*, 1 December 1979.
4 Organisation of Petroleum Exporting Countries.
5 E.g. the Franco-Dutch dispute over the discharge of sulphur into the Rhine, Europe, 6 December 1979, p. 5.
6 Cf. Case 21/76: *Handelskwekerij GJ Bier BV and Stitchting Reinwater (Reinwater Foundation) v Mines de Potasse d'Alsace* [1976] ECR 1735, [1977] 1 CMLR 284.
7 JO 1973, C112/1.
8 JO 1977, C139/1.
9 See Lasok, op. cit. p. 378 et seq.
10 OJ 1975, L194.

measures range from the protection of natural amenities to the reduction of health hazards.

## 3. *Consumerism*

European consumerism owes a great deal to the developments in the USA but has taken a different turn from the legal confrontation between the manufacturers and the public which seems to dominate the American scene. So far two programmes have been adopted[11] but the progress to date has been far from spectacular. Perhaps the most significant achievement can be seen in the directives concerned with foodstuffs and cosmetics, product liability and consumer credit but the challenge still remains to be met.

## 4. *Industry*

The Community, because of its nature and objectives, seems unthinkable without an industrial policy linked to economic policy and State involvement in the economy. Yet, perhaps because of the industrial nature of West European societies, the formulation and implementation of such a policy has been fraught with difficulties. An Industrial Policy implies a change of entrenched attitudes in the face of technological advancement and a Community approach to sectoral interests. It means, in effect, an adaptation and sometimes a drastic revision of national capacity (e.g. in steel, textiles, shipbuilding) to accommodate the European and world markets. Social consequences inevitably call for reflection and prudence.

There is at present a framework of industrial policy proposed in 1970[12] and further elaborated in 1973[13] with the object of establishing ... 'a single industrial base for the Community as a whole'[14].

## 5. *Regionalism*

There is much in the EEC Treaty, beginning with article 2, to promote a regional policy not only to eliminate disparities between regions but also to promote a harmonious development of the Community as a whole.

The policy was initiated in 1969[15] but got off the ground as late as 1975 with the setting up by the relevant Regulations of the

11 JO 1975, C92/1 and OJ 1976, C241.
12 Commission Memorandum to the Council, Fourth General Report, 1970, item 205 et seq.
13 OJ 1973, C117/1.
14 Sixth General Report, 1972, p. 12.

Regional Policy Committee and the Regional Development Fund. Much has been done to establish a comprehensive system of analysis of the problems to be remedied and policy formulation to carry out the remedy. This process has to take into account not only the situation as presented but also the evaluation of the policy decisions on future developments and co-ordination at a national and international level. Though concerned primarily with economic and social problems the regional policy has far-reaching political implications. Operating on a geographical rather than strictly national basis the policy, when fully implemented, would tend to ignore political frontiers and territorial divisions and thus promote the unity of the Community at the expense of the concept of national state.

## 6. *Science and technology*

The roots of a Community policy for science and technology are in the ECSC and EAEC Treaties[16]. The EEC Treaty refers somewhat obliquely to 'technical progress' and research in agriculture[17]. However overall Community policy began emerging only from the exhortations of the Summer Conferences culminating in the four guidelines adopted in 1974[18]. These four guidelines include the co-ordination of national policies, the participation in the European Science Foundation, elaboration of a Community programme of research in science and technology and a programme of research for forecasting, assessment and methodology. The resulting Policy should, in particular, focus attention on the supply of resources (i.e. raw materials, energy, food and water), the competitiveness of the Community as a whole, the improvement of the standards of living within the Community and the protection and conservation of the environment.

## 7. *Education and culture*

A policy for education appears necessary not only to carry out certain Treaty provisions but also to promote the general well-being of the population of the Community. The EAEC[19] envisages specifically the setting up of an institution of nuclear science and technology whilst the other treaties refer to the vocational training

**15** Commission Communication to the Council, JO 1969, C152.
**16** Art. 55 and 4–11 respectively.
**17** Arts. 39 (1) and 41 (a).
**18** JO 1974, C7/4.
**19** Art. 9.

for workers[20] and farmers[1] as well as the recognition of diplomas[2]. Despite these desiderata progress towards a coherent policy has been slow and uninspiring. At last in 1976 the Council of Ministers adopted an action programme[3] comprising the following: cultural and vocational training for migrant workers and education of their children; vocational training of the young; education at a higher level (including the creation of the European University Institute at Florence); language teaching, teachers' and students' mobility; and dissemination of information and co-operation between the national educational systems. Since education affects all aspects of life a great deal remains yet to be done to establish a Community policy for education.

The movement towards West European unity, apart from its political and economic aspects, remains largely an act of faith in the future of the Continent sustained by common cultural heritage. Logic suggests that materialistic aspirations of the Community ought to be matched by cultural activities. This no doubt was behind the Commission's memorandum[4] to the Council on 'Community action in the cultural sector'. In the Commission's view this sector comprised 'the socio-economic whole formed by persons and undertakings dedicated to the production and distribution of cultural goods and services'. This curious definition can be understood perhaps in the light of what the Commission considered appropriate for Community action, i.e. freedom of trade in cultural goods, eliminating theft of cultural goods, movement of cultural workers, training of cultural workers, harmonisation of laws on copyright and related intellectual rights, preservation of the architectural heritage, development of cultural exchanges, co-operation between the cultural institutes of the Member States and promotion of socio-cultural activities at European level. The difficulties in moulding such an enterprise into a programme of action and, indeed, a legally enforceable policy are more than apparent. However the desire of complementing the 'European Economic' Community with a 'Cultural' Community provides a promising starting point.

20 ECSC Art. 56; EEC Art. 118.
 1 EEC Art. 41.
 2 EEC Art. 57.
 3 JO 1976, C38/1.
 4 EC Bull Supp 6/77, p. 5.

# The EEC law of the economy—a summary

The brief analysis of the relevant provisions of the Treaty projects a concept of the law of economy of the Community. In accordance with the legislative techniques developed in the civil law countries, the Treaty codifies the basic principles (i.e. the economic freedoms) of the Common Market, outlines the essential policies, sets up institutions and provides machinery for the implementation of the design. The law is used as an instrument of definition and enforcement.

As blueprints go, the design is clear but not as comprehensive as it could be, whilst the social aspects of this *Economic Community* are traced in rather pale colours. This is understandable in view of the responsibilities of the member states for their social services and it seems sufficient, at this stage, to emphasise the link between the economy and social and human problems.

Being only a reflection of a federal concept, the Community law of the economy has to be accommodated to the role of the sovereign state in the Community. Therefore, within the *dirigist* concept of the economy, the Treaty grants the bureaucratic organs of the Community only as much authority as is necessary to organise and harmonise the national economic systems by advice and persuasion rather than by the exercise of power. Where a decision is thought necessary, the Community organs are equipped with the requisite power backed by the corresponding treaty obligation undertaken by the member states.

The strengthening of the Community institutions would, it seems, bring a greater cohesion of the national economic systems and a more intensive degree of uniformity at the expense of the member states. Such a development is undoubtedly linked with the future evolution of the Community.

Appendix

# Lists of further reading

## Chapter 1

ANDERSON, S. V., *The Nordic Council. A Study of Scandinavian Regionalism* (1967)

AUBREY, H. G., *Atlantic Economic Cooperation. The Case of the OECD* (1967)

BRUGMANS, H., *L'idée européenne 1920–1970* (1970)

CAMPS, M., *Britain and the European Communities, 1955–63* (1964)

COONEY, J., *EEC in Crisis* (1979)

ESMAN, J., & CHEEVER, D. S., *The Common Aid Effort. The development assistance activities of the Organisation for Economic Cooperation and Development* (1967)

FORSYTH, M., *Unions of States: The Theory and Practice of Confederation* (1981)

GALTUNG, J., *The European Community: A Superpower in the Making* (1973)

GLADWYN, LORD, *The European Idea* (1966)

GROSSER, A., *Les Occidentaux, les pays d'Europe et les Etats-Unis depuis la guerre* (1978)

GRZYBOWSKI, K., *The Socialist Commonwealth of Nations* (1964)

JACOBS, F. G., *The European Convention on Human Rights* (1975)

JANSEN, M., *History of European Integration* (1975)

JOHN, I. G. (Editor), *EEC Policy towards Eastern Europe* (1975)

KITZINGER, U., *Diplomacy and Persuasion* (1973)

KITZINGER, U., *The European Common Market and Community* (1967)

KITZINGER, U., *The Second Try* (1968)

LORETTE, L. DE S., *Le Marché Commun* (1961)

*Manual of the Council of Europe, Structures, Functions and Achievements* (1970)

PALMER, M., & LAMBERT, J., et al., *European Unity, A Survey of the European Organisations* (1968)

PATIJN, S. (Editor), *Landmarks in European Unity* (1970)
POLLARD, S., *The Integration of the European Economy Since 1815* (1981)
PRYCE, R., *The Politics of the European Community* (1973)
RANSOM, C., *The European Community and Eastern Europe* (1973)
ROBERTSON, A. H., *European Institutions, Co-operation, Integration, Unification* (Third edn 1973)
SPINELLI, A., *The European Adventure* (1972)
*The European Free Trade Association and the Crisis of European Integration. An aspect of the Atlantic crisis?* (1965)
TORELLI, M., *Great Britain and the Europe of the Six: the Failure of Negotiations* (1969)
URWIN, D. W., *Western Europe Since 1945* (1968)
VAUGHAN, R., *Twentieth Century Europe* (1979)
WALLACE, W. (Editor), *Britain in Europe* (1980)

## Chapter 2

ALTING VON GEUSAU, F. A. M., *European Organisations and Foreign Relations of States* (2nd edn 1964)
AXLINE, A. W., *European Community Law and Organisational Development* (1968)
BATHURST, M., et al. (Editors), *Legal Problems of an Enlarged European Community* (1972), Part IV
BOURRINET, J., *et* TORRELLI, M., *Les relations extérieure de la Communauté économique européenne* (1980)
BRUGMANS, H., et al., *The External Economic Policy of the Enlarged Community* (1973)
CARDIS, F., *Fédéralisme et intégration européene* (1963)
COFFEY, P., *The External Relations of the EEC* (1976)
HALLSTEIN, W., *Europe in the Making* (1972)
HARTLEY, T. C., *The Foundations of European Community Law* (1981), Chapters 5, 6.
HAY, P., *Federalism and Supranational Organisations* (1965)
HENIG, S., *External Relations of the European Community* (1971)
*L'association à la Communauté économique européene. Aspects juridiques*, Bruxelles, Institut d'études européennes (1970)
*Les Communautés européennes et les relations Est-Ouest*, Colloque des 31 mars-1er avril, 1966 (1967)
NERI, S., *De la nature juridique des Communautés européennes* (1965)
PUISSOCHET, J.-P., *The Enlargement of the European Communities:*

*A Commentary on the Accession of Denmark, Ireland and the United Kingdom* (1975)

RAUX, J., *Les relations extérieures de la CEE* (1966)

SCHONFIELD, A., *Europe: Journey to an Unknown Destination* (1973)

SJÖSTEDT, G., *The External Role of the European Community* (1977)

WALL, E., *Europe: Unification and Law* (1969)

WEIL, G. L., *A Foreign Policy for Europe?* (1970)


ALTING VON GEUSAU, F. A. M., 'The External Representation of Plural Interests', (1967), *Journal of Common Market Studies*, 426

COSTONIS, J. J., 'Treaty making power of the EEC', [1967] *European Yearbook*, 31

LEOPOLD, P., 'External Relations power of the EEC in theory and in practice', (1977) 26 ICLQ 54.

RAUX, J. and FLAESCH-MOUGIN, C., 'Les accords externes de la CEE', (1975) *Rev. Trim. de Droit Européen*, 227.

SCHERMERS, H., 'Community Law and International Law', (1975) 12 CML Rev. 77.

USHER, J., 'The influence of national concepts on decisions of the European Court', (1976) 1 EL Rev 359.

WAELBROECK, M., *Traités internationaux et juridictions internes dans les pays du marché commun* (1969)

## Chapter 3

AKEHURST, M., 'Preparing the authentic text of the EEC Treaty', in Wortley, B. (Editor), *An Introduction to the Law of the EEC* (1972), at p. 20

*L'Avocat à l'heure du Marché Commun*, Rouen, Colloque International (1972)

BRINKHORST, L. J., & MITCHELL, J. D. B., *European Law and Institutions* (1969)

CAPELLETI, M. (Editor), *New Perspectives for a Common Law of Europe* (1978)

DAGTOGLOU, P. D. (Editor), *Basic Problems of the European Community* (1975)

DONNER, A. M., *The Role of the Lawyer in the European Community* (1968)

HÉRAUD, G., 'La Communauté Européenne et la Question Linguistique', (1981) 5 *Rev d'Integration Européenne*, 5

LECOURT, R., *Le juge devant le Marché Commun* (1970)

USHER, J., *European Law and National Law: The Irreversible Transfer?* (1981)

MITCHELL, J. D. B., 'Lawyers and the European Communities', (1971) 22 NILQ 149

PESCATORE, P., *The Law of Integration* (1974)

BROWN, L. N., 'Two legal traditions', (1980) 18 *Journal of Common Market Studies*, 246

BROWN, L. N., 'The linguistic regime of the European Communities', (1981) 15 *Valparaiso University L Rev*, 319

POLACH, J. G., 'Harmonization of Laws in Western Europe', [1959] *American Journal of Comparative Law*, 148

SIEDL-HOHENVELDERN, I., 'Harmonization of Legislation in the Common Market', [1962] *Journal of Business Law*, 247 and 363

SCHNEIDER, H. H., 'Towards a European Lawyer', (1971) 8 CML Rev 44

STEINE, E., 'Assimilation of National Laws as a Function of European Integration', (1964), 58 *American Journal of International Law*, 1

THOMPSON, D., 'Harmonization of Laws', (1965), 3 *Journal of Common Market Studies*, 302

## Chapter 4

BLECKMANN, A., *Europarecht* (1976)

CONSTANTINESCO, L.-J., *Das Recht der europäischen Gemeinschaften* (1977)

DETTER, L., *Law Making by International Organisations* (1965)

ECONOMIDES, C. E., *Le pouvoir de décision des organisations internationales européenes* (1964)

EHLERMANN, C.-D., *The Role of the Legal Service of the Commission in the Creation of Community Law* (University of Exeter, 1981)

HARTLEY, T. C., *The Foundations of European Community Law* (1981), Chapters 3, 4

EDESON, W. R. & WOOLDRIDGE, F., 'European Community Law and Fundamental Human Rights', LIEI 1976/1, 1

*Institut d'études européenes, La Décision dans les Communautés européenes* (1969)

KUTSCHER, K., *Methods of Interpretation as seen by a Judge at the Court of Justice* (1976)

LAUWAARS, R. H., *Lawfulness and Legal Force of Community Decisions* (1973)

*Les Novelles: Droit des Communautés européenes* (1969), Nos. 483–806, 1134–1172

LOUIS, J.-V., *Les réglements de la Communauté économique européenne* (1969)

MACKENZIE STUART, A. J., *The European Communities and the Rule of Law* (1977)

MITCHELL, J. D. B., 'Community Legislation' in Bathurst, M. E., et al., *Legal Problems of an Enlarged Community* (1972), 100

MORAND, C.-A., *La législation dans les Communautés européenes* (1968)

PESCATORE, P., *L'Ordre juridique des Communautés européenes* (2nd edn 1973)

RIDEAU, J., et al. *Droit Institutionnel des Communautés européennes* (1974)

SCHMITTHOFF, C. M., 'The Doctrines of Proportionality and Non-Discrimination' (1977) 2 EL Rev 329

ZULEEG, 'Fundamental Rights and the Law of the European Communities' (1971) 3 CML Rev 446


BEBR, G., 'Acts of representatives of governments of the member states', [1966] *Sociaal-economische Wetgeving*, 529

RASMUSSEN, H., 'A new generation of Community law?' (1978) 15 CML Rev 249

SCHWARTZ, I. E., 'Article 235 and law-making powers in the European Community', (1978) 27 ICLQ 614

## Chapter 5

BRAUN, N. C., *Commissaires et juges dans les Communautés européennes* (1972)

*La Commission des Communautés Européennes et l'Elargissement de l'Europe*, Bruxelles, Institut d'études européennes (1974)

COOMBES, D., *Politics and Bureaucracy in the European Community* (1970)

HENIG, S., *Power and Decision in Europe* (1980), Chapter 4

LINDBERG, L., *Political Dynamics of European Economic Integration* (1963)

MAYNE, R., *The Institutions of the European Community* (1968)

SASSE, C. et al., *Decision Making in the European Community* (1977), Part 2

SPINELLI, A., *The Eurocrats* (1966)
VON DER GROEBEN, H., et al., *Die Europäische Union als Prozess* (1980)
HALLSTEIN, W., 'The EEC Commission: a new factor in international life', (1965) 14 ICLQ 727
NOEL, N., 'The Commission's Power of Initiative', (1973) 10 CML Rev 123

## Chapter 6

CAMPS, M., *European Unification in the Sixties* (1967)
CONSTANTINESCO, V., *Compétences et pouvoirs dans les Communautés européennes* (1974)
ECONOMIDES, C. P., *Le pouvoir de décision des organisations internationales européenes* (1964)
HENIG, S., *Power and Decision in Europe* (1980), Chapter 3
HOUBEN, P. H. J. M., *Les Conseils de Ministres des Communautés européenes* (1964)
*Institut d'études européennes, La décision dans les Communautés européenes* (1969)
*Institut d'études juridiques européenes, La fusion des Communautés Européennes au lendemain des Accords de Luxembourg* (1967)
JAUMIN-PONSAR, A., *Essai d'interprétation d'une crise* (1970)
LOUIS, J.-V., *Les règlements de la Communauté économique européene* (1969)
NEWHOUSE, J., *Collision in Brussels* (1968)
SASSE, C., et al., *Decision Making in the European Community* (1977), Part I
SASSE, C., 'Kommission und Rat' (1972) EuR, 341
TORELLI, M., *L'Individu et le Droit de la CEE* (1970)
VON LINDEINER-WILDAU, K., *La Supranationalité en tant que Principe de Droit* (1970)
WALLACE, H., *National Governments and the European Communities* (1973)

ESCH, B. VAN DER, 'Legal policy in an enlarged European Community', (1973) 10 CML Rev 56
LAUWAARS, R. H., 'The European Council', (1977) 14 CML Rev 25
MORTELMANS, K. J., 'The Extramural Meetings of the Ministers of the Member States of the Community', (1974) 11 CML Rev 62

## Chapter 7

ALLOTT, P., 'The Democratic Basis of the European Communities,' (1974) 11 CML Rev 298

COCKS, SIR B., *The European Parliament* (1973)

COOMBES, D., *The Power of the Purse in the European Communities* (1972)

EUROPEAN PARLIAMENT, *The Case for elections to the European Parliament by direct Universal Suffrage* (1969)

FITZMAURICE, J., *The European Parliament* (1978)

FORSYTH, M., *The Parliament of the European Communities* (1964)

HENIG, S. (Editor), *European Political Parties* (1969)

HENIG, S., *Power and Decision in Europe* (1980) Chapter 5

HERMAN, U. & HAGGER, M., *The Legislation of Direct Elections to the European Parliament* (1980)

HERMAN, V. & LODGE, J., *The European Parliament and the European Community* (1978)

HOUBDINE, A. M., & VERGES, R., *Le Parlement Européen dans la Construction de l'Europe des Six* (1966)

HOVEY, J. A., *The Super-parliaments* (1967)

JACKSON, R. & FITZMAURICE, J., *The European Parliament: A Guide to Direct Elections* (1979)

LASALLE, C., *Les rapports institutionnels entre le Parlement européen et les Conseils de Ministres des Communautés* (1964)

LINDSAY, K., *European Assemblies* (1960)

MARQUAND, D., *Parliament for Europe* (1979)

NIBLOCK, M., *National Parliaments in Community Decision Making* (1971)

SASSE, C. et al., *Decision Making in the European Community* (1977), Part 3

SCALINGI, P., *The European Parliament* (1980)

TUGENDHAT, C., *European Community Budgetary Issues* (University of Exeter, 1980)

VINCI, E., *Il Parlamento Europeo* (1980)

WALLACE, H., *Budgetary Politics* (1980)

DRUNKER, I. E., 'Strengthening democracy in the EEC', (1964) 2 CML Rev 168

EHLERMANN, C.-D., 'Applying the new budgetary procedure for the first time', (1975) 12 CML Rev 325

## Chapter 8

BECKER, M., *La Banque européenne d'investissement* (1973)

BERNARD, N., et al., *Le Comité Economique et Social* (1972)

CEREXHE, E., *Le Droit Européen, Les Institutions* (1979)

ECONOMIC & SOCIAL COMMITTEE, *The Right of Initiative of the Economic and Social Committee* (1977)

*Institut d'études européennes, La Décision dans les Communautés européennes* (1969), 127–132

MENAIS, G. P., *La Banque européenne d'investissement* (1968)


BERTRAM, C., 'Decision making in the EEC: The Management Committee Procedure', (1967–68) 5 CML Rev 246

GENTON, J., 'La représentation et l'influence des opérateurs économiques dans la Communauté européenne', [1968] *Institutions Communautaires et Institutions Nationales* 75

SCHINDLER, P., 'Problems of decision making by way of the Management Committee Procedure in the EEC', (1971) 8 CML Rev 184

ZELLENTIN, G., 'The Economic and Social Committee', (1962), 1 *Journal of Common Market Studies*, 22

## Chapter 9

AUDRETSCH, H. A. H., *Supervision in European Community Law* (1978)

BEBR, G., *Judicial Control of the European Communities* (1962)

BEBR, G., *Rule of Law within the European Communities* (1965)

BRAUN, N. C., *Commissaires et juges dans les Communautés européennes* (1972)

BREDIMAS, A., *Methods of Interpretation and Community Law* (1978)

BROWN, L. N., & JACOBS, F. G., *The Court of Justice of the European Communities* (1977)

COLIN, J. P., *Le Gouvernement des Juges dans les Communautés européennes* (1966)

DONNER, A. M., *The Role of the Lawyer in the European Communities* (1968)

DONNER, A. M., *The Court of Justice as a Constitutional Court of the Communities* (University of Exeter, 1978)

FELD, W., *The Court of the European Communities: new dimension in international adjudication* (1964)

FERRIERE, G., *Le controle des actes étatiques par la Cour de Justice des Communautés européennes* (1968)

GREEN, A. W., *Political Integration by Jurisprudence* (1969)

HARTLEY, T. C., *The Foundations of European Community Law* (1981), Chapters 2, 10, 11, 12, 13, 14, 15, 16, 19 and 20

LAUWAARS, R. H., *Lawfulness and Legal Force of Community Decisions* (1973)

MANN, C. J., *Function of Judicial Decision in European Economic Integration* (1972)

MACKENZIE STUART, A. J., *The European Communities and the Rule of Law* (1977)

REEPINGHEN, C. VAN & ORIANNE, P., *La Procédure devant la Cour de Justice des Communautés Européennes* (1961)

*Reports presented to a Judicial and Academic Conference, Court of Justice, Luxembourg* (1976)

SCHEINGOLD, A., *The Rule of Law in European Integration* (1965)

SCHERMERS, H. G., *Judicial Protection in the European Communities* (2nd edn 1979)

TOTH, A. G., *The Protection of Individuals in the European Communities* (1978)

WALL, E., *The Court of Justice of the European Communities, Jurisdiction and Procedure* (1966)

WARNER, J.-P., *The Evolution of the Work of the Court of Justice* (1976)

## Chapter 10

BARAV, A., 'Some Aspects of the Preliminary Rulings Procedure in EEC Law', (1977) 2 EL Rev 3

BATHURST, M. (Editor), *Legal Problems of an Enlarged European Community* (1972), Parts II and IV

BEBR, G., 'Article 177 of the EEC Treaty in the Practice of National Courts', (1977) 1 CLQ 241

CONSTANTINESCO, L. J., *L'Applicabilité directe dans le droit de la CEE* (1970)

CONSTANTINIDES-MEGRET, C., *Le droit de la Communauté économique européenne et l'ordre juridique des Etats membres* (1967)

DE RICHEMONT, J., *Integration of Community Law within the Legal Systems of the Member States* (1978)

DONNER, A. M., *Le juge national et le droit communautaire* (1966)

*Droit communautaire et droit national*, Semaine de Bruges, Colloque
8–10 avril 1965, Bruges (1965)
HARTLEY, T. C., *The Foundations of European Community Law*
(1981), Chapters 7, 9
JACOBS, F. G., & DURAND, A., *References to the European Court* (1975)
PESCATORE, P., *L'ordre juridique des Communautés européennes* (1971)
RIDEAU, J., et al. *La France et les Communautés Européennes* (1975)
SAINT-ESTEBEN, R., *Droit communautaire et droits nationaux* (1967)

BEBR, G., 'How Supreme is Community Law in the National
Courts?' (1974) 11 CML Rev 3
DASHWOOD, A., 'The principle of direct effect in European Com-
munity law', (1978) 16 *Journal of Common Market Studies*, 229
IPSEN, H. P., 'Relationship between the law of the European Com-
munities and National Law', (1965) 2 CMLR Rev 379
WINTER, J., 'Direct applicability and direct effect: two distinct and
different concepts in Community law', (1972) 9 CML Rev 425

## Chapter 11

ADAMS, J. C., & BARILE, P., *The Government of Republican Italy* (1972)
BERGSTEN, E. E., *Community Law in French Courts* (1973)
CONSTANTINIDES-MEGRET, C., *Le droit de la Communauté économique
européenne et l'ordre juridique des Etats-membres* (1967)
DONNER, A. M., et al., *Le juge national et le droit communautaire*
(1966)
DONNER, A. M., *Le rôle de la Cour de Justice dans l'élaboration du droit
européen* (1964)
FINER, S. E., *Five Constitutions* (1979)
FORRESTER, I. S., & ILGEN, H. M., *The German Legal System* (1972)
GAUDET, M., *Conflits du droit communautaire avec les droits nationaux*
(1967)
HARTLEY, T. C., *The Foundations of European Community Law*
(1981), chapter 8
HAURIOU, A., *Droit Constitutionnel* (1970)
HERLITZ, N., *Elements of Nordic Public Law* (1969)
HOLBORN, L. W., et al., *German Constitutional Documents since 1871*
(1970)
HOLT, S., *Six European States. The Countries of the European Com-
munity* (1970)
*Institutions communautaires et institutions nationales dans le
développement des Communautés* (1968)

WARNER, J.-P., 'The Relationship between European Community Law and the National Laws of the Member States', (1977) LQR 349

MAJERUS, P., *L'Etat Luxembourgeois* (1970)

PEASELEE, A., *Constitutions of Nations*, 3rd edn, Vol. III Europe (1963)

SENELLE, R., *Revision of the Constitution 1967–1971* (1972)

WAELBROECK, M., *Traités internationaux et juridictions internes dans les pays du Marché commun* (1969)


BOULOUIS, J., 'L'applicabilité directe des directives. A propos d'un arrêt Cohn-Bendit du Conseil d'Etat', (1979) RMC 104

DAGTOGLOU, P. D., 'European Communities and Constitutional Law', [1973] C.L.J. 256

DONNER, A. M., 'Les rapports entre la compétence de la Cour de Justice des Communautés et les tribunaux internes', (1965) 115 *Recueil des Cours de l'Académie de la Haye*, 5

HAY, P., 'Supremacy of Community Law in National Courts', (1968) 16 AJ Comp L 524

SIMON, M., 'Enforcement by French Courts of European Community law', (1974) 90 LQR 467 and (1976) LQR 85 and 357

SIMON, M., & DOWRICK, F. E., 'Effect of EEC Directives in France', (1979) 95 LQR 376

## Chapter 12

BATHURST, M., et al., *Europe and the Law* (1968)

COLLINS, L., *European Community Law in the United Kingdom* (2nd edn 1980)

DE SMITH, S. A., *Constitutional and Administrative Law* (4th edn 1981), chapters 4, 5

HOOD PHILLIPS, O., *Constitutional and Administrative Law* (6th edn 1978), chapters 3, 4, 5

KEETON, G. W., & SCHWARZENBERGER, G., *English Law and the Common Market* (1963 Current Legal Problems)

LANG, J. T., *The Common Market and Common Law: Legal Aspects of Foreign Investment and Economic Integration in the European Community, with Ireland as a Prototype* (1966)

*Legal and Constitutional Implications of United Kingdom Membership of the European Communities*, Cmnd 3301 (1967)

PISANI, E., et al., *Problems of British Entry into the EEC* (1969)

*The United Kingdom and the European Communities*, Cmnd 4715 (1971)

WALL, E. A., *European Communities Act 1972* (1973)

WATSON, G., *The British Constitution and Europe* (1959)

BRIDGE, J. W., 'Community Law and English Courts and Tribunals: General Principles and Preliminary Rulings', (1975–1976) 1 *European Law Review*, 13

DE SMITH, S. A., 'The Constitution and the Common Market: a tentative appraisal', (1971) 34 MLR 597

FORMAN, J., 'The European Communities Act 1972', (1973) 10 C.M.L. Rev 39

GREMENTIERI, V., & GOLDEN, C. J., 'The United Kingdom and the European Court of Justice: an Encounter between Common and Civil Law Traditions', (1973) 21 AJCL 464

HUNNINGS, N. M., 'Constitutional Implications of Joining the Common Market', (1968–69) 6 CML Rev 50

MARTIN, A., 'The Accession of the United Kingdom to the European Communities: Jurisdictional Problems', (1968–69) 6 CML Rev 7

MITCHELL, J. D. B., 'What do you want to be inscrutable *for* Marcia?' (1967–68) 5 CML Rev 112

MITCHELL, J. D. B., et al., 'Constitutional aspects of the Treaty and Legislation relating to British membership', (1972) 9 CMLR Rev 134

SIMMONDS, K. R., '*Van Duyn v Home Office*: the Direct Effectiveness of Directives', (1975) 24 ICLQ 419

THOMPSON, D., & MARSH, N. S., 'The United Kingdom and the Treaty of Rome: some preliminary observations', (1962) 2 ICLQ 73

TRINIDADE, F. A., 'Parliamentary Sovereignty and the Primacy of the Community Law', (1972) 35 MLR 375

WADE, H. W. R., 'Sovereignty and the European Communities', (1972) 88 LQR 1

## Chapter 13

BERR, C. L., ET TREMEAU, H., *Le Droit Douanier* (1975)

BERTHAUD, C., *Le Marché Commun* (1975)

DAINTITH, T., *Report on the Economic Law of the United Kingdom* (1974)

FROMONT, M., *Rapport sur le droit économique français* (1973)

HARTLEY, T. C., *EEC Immigration Law* (1978)

HUBER, H., *Wirtschaftsverwaltungsrecht* (1953)

JAQUEMIN, A., & SCHRANS, G., *Le droit économique* (1970)

JEANNENCY, J. M., & PERROT, M., *Textes de droit économique et social français* (1957)

LASOK, D., *The Law of the Economy in the European Communities* (1980) chapters 1, 3

MAESTRIPIERI, C., 'Freedom of Establishment and Freedom to Supply Services', (1973) CML Rev 150

MORSIANI, G. S., *Rapport sur le droit économique italien* (1973)

PIEPENBROCK, R., *Der Gedanke eines Wirtschaftsrechts in der neuzeitlichen Literatur bis zum ersten Weltkrieg* (1964)

PROUDHON, P. J., *De la capacité politique des classes ouvrières* (1865)

RINCK, G., *Wirtschaftsrecht* (3rd edn 1972)

SALIN, P., *L'unification monétaire européene* (1974)

SLOT, P. J., *Technical and Administrative Obstacles to Trade in the EEC* (1975)

SVOBODA, K., *La Notion de Droit Economique* (1966)

VERLOREN VAN THEMAAT, P., *Le droit économique des Etats membres des Communautés européennes dans le cadre d'une Union économique et monétaire* (1973)

VERLOREN VAN THEMAAT, P., *Rapport sur le droit économique néerlandais* (1973)

ZACHER, H. F., *Rapport sur le droit économique en république fédérale d'Allemagne* (1973)

CHAMPEAUD, C., 'Contribution à la définition du droit économique', [1967] *Dalloz Chron.* 215

DAINTITH, T., 'Public Law and Economic Policy', [1974] JBL 9

KIRALY, F. DE, 'Le droit économique, branche indépendente de la science juridique', *Recueil d'études sur les sources du droit en honneur de F. Geny*, (1935) Vol. 3

LIMPENS, J., 'Contribution à l'étude de la notion de droit économique', (1966) *Il Diritto dell' Economia*, No. 6

SCHMITTHOFF, C. M., 'The Concept of Economic Law in England', [1966] *Journal of Business Law*, 309

WILBERFORCE, LORD, 'Law and Economics', [1966] *Journal of Business Law*, 301

## Chapter 14

ANDREWS, S., *Agriculture and the Common Market* (1973)

BALEKJIAN, W. H., *Legal Aspects of foreign investment in the European Economic Community* (1967)

BAROUNOS, D., et al., *EEC Anti trust Law* (1975)

BATHURST, M., et al. (Editors), *Legal Problems of our Enlarged European Community* (1972), Parts V, VI and VII

BAYLISS, B. T., *European Transport* (1965)

BELLAMY, C., & CHILD, D. G., *Common Market Law of Competition* (2nd edn, 1978)

BLAKE, H. M., *Business Regulations in the Common Market Nations*, Vols 1, 2 and 3 (1969), Vol. 4 (with J. A. RAHL), *Common Market and American Antitrust: Overlap and Conflict* (1970)

BONTEMPS, J., *Liberté d'etablissement et libre prestation des services dans le Marché Commun* (1968)

CAWTHRA, B. T., *Industrial Property Rights in the EEC* (1973)

CLOSE, G., 'Harmonization of Laws: Use or Abuse of the Powers under the EEC Treaty?' (1978) EL Rev 461

DERINGER, A., *The Competition Law of the European Economic Community* (1968)

DE RIPAINSEL-LANDY, D., et al., *Les instruments du rapprochement des législations dans la Communauté économique européenne* (1976)

DESPICHT, N., *The Transport Policy of the European Communities* (1969)

EASSON, A. J., *Tax Law and Policy in the EEC* (1980)

*European Competition Policy*, European Aspects Law Series No. 12 (1973)

FENNELL, R., *The Common Agricultural Policy of the European Communities* (1979)

GOLDMAN, B., *European Commercial Law* (1973)

JACQUEMART, C., *La Novelle Douane Européenne* (1971)

JOLIET, R., *Monopolization and Abuse of Dominant Position* (1970)

JOLIET, R., *The Rule of Reason in Antitrust Law* (1967)

KORAH, V., *Competition Law of Britain and the Common Market* (1975)

LASOK, D., *The Law of the Economy in the European Communities* (1980)

LASOK, D. & SOLDATOS, P., *The European Communities in Action* (1981) Part 3

LIPSTEIN, K., *The Law of the European Economic Community* (1974)

LYON-CAEN, G., *Droit social européen* (1969)

MARSH, J. S. & SWANNEY, P. J., *Agriculture and the European Community* (1980)

MAZZIOTTI, M., et al., *La Libre Circulation des travailleurs dans les Pays de la CEE* (1974)

MCLACHLAN, D. L., & SWANN, D., *Competition policy in the European Community* (1967)

PARRY, A. & HARDY, S., *EEC Law* (2nd edn 1981)

PENNINGTON, R. R., *Companies in the Common Market* (2nd edn 1970)

PERRET, F., *Coordination du droit des sociétés en Europe* (1970)

RENAULD, J., *Le droit européen des sociétés* (1969)

RIBAS, J. J., *La politique sociale des Communautés Européennes* (1969)

RIES, A., *L'ABC du Marché Commun Agricole* (1978)

SCHMITTHOFF, C. M., *The Harmonisation of European Company Law* (1973)

SEMINI, A., *La CEE Harmonisation des législations* (1971)

SHOUP, C. (editor), *Fiscal Harmonization in the Common Market*, 2 Vols (1967)

STEIN, E., *Harmonization of European Company Laws* (1971)

SUNDBERG-WEITMAN, B., *Discrimination on Grounds of Nationality* (1977)

THOMPSON, D., *The Proposal for a European Company* (1969)

VENTURA, S., *Principes de droit agraire communautaire* (1967)

WALLACE, H., et al. (Editors), *Policy Making in the European Communities* (1977)

WATSON, P., *Social Security Law of the European Communities* (1980)

WYATT, D. & DASHWOOD, A., *The Substantive Law of the EEC* (1980)

# Index